Corporate Personnel Management

Corporate Personnel Management

Coordinating Author:
Bryan Livy

Contributory Authors:
Greville Janner, QC, MP
Len Peach
Paul Roots
The Baroness Seear, PC

PITMAN PUBLISHING
128 Long Acre London WC2E 9AN

A Division of Longman Group UK Limited

© Bryan Livy, Greville Janner, Len Peach, Paul Roots, The Baroness, Seear 1988

First published in Great Britain 1988
Reprinted 1989

British Library Cataloguing in Publication Data
Livy, Bryan
    Corporate personnel management
    1. Personnel management.
    I. Title
    658.3   HF5549

ISBN 0–273–01950–3

Typeset by Wyvern Typesetting Ltd, Bristol

Printed and bound in Singapore

Contents

Preface and acknowledgements

Until the 1970s most contributions to the study of personnel management had been of American origin. Few British texts had appeared. Then a spate ensued. So why now another one?

The story goes back several years, to one summer's afternoon in the garden of Professor Paul Pigors (then retired from MIT) in Framingham, USA. Over tea of delicious waffles we discussed the emergent British literary scene. Leaving aside the obvious cultural differences across the Atlantic we both agreed, as it seemed to us, that line management bore a prime responsibility in spite of the existence of specialist personnel functions and thriving professional associations. Policies for planning the management of people should be linked closely to corporate strategy. Personnel management is a corporate responsibility – at both strategic and operational levels.

Any book is a personal statement by the author; it is a reflection of his or her own interpretation. For that reason I would have liked to adopt Pigors and Myers own sub-title: 'a point of view and a method' because that is what my own book would be if ever it took form and flesh.

My own teaching experience spans some eighteen years – mostly at City University, but including a spell at Ealing College. I shudder to realize that my occupational experience now spans nearly three decades. If this my fifth book were going to be written, it could not be deferred much longer.

Encouraged to embark on this formidable task, I considered a number of other issues. First, the constantly changing scenario in which personnel management operates could render any book obsolete quickly. On the other hand, there is a permanency of many human resourcing functions, although refinements to methodology are continuous. Any book would have to strike a balance between key issues and other circumstantial issues transient within a fluctuating environment.

To me, so many management books seemed dull, turgid and difficult to read. I set out with twin ambitions: clarity and readability. I hope these pages are 'user-friendly'.

To me, it seemed some books had attempted to encompass too much. My own efforts narrow to a finer focus. Important as the historical development of personnel management in any one country has been on the influence of the function – important as the organizational, role problems and social context of a specialist personnel function remain – of more utility to the present or potential practitioner would be a handbook elaborating on the 'what?', 'how?' and 'why?' of the subject-matter. No book can be prescriptive, but at least some normative base must be offered which seeks to generate understanding in the mind of the reader, so that principles and exemplary applications can be sensibly modified in approaches to novel situations.

This book takes a 'professional' model and discusses the functions of personnel management and the principles behind policies and procedures. It is aimed at line managers as well as personnel specialists, either practitioners or students. It should provide useful material for courses leading to IPM, BA Business Studies, DMS, MSc, MBA qualifications and management programmes generally, whenever the planning and control of human resources is considered. Discussion questions have been included at the end of each chapter to facilitate a participative approach in classroom teaching.

Deliberately, this book is not specifically about industrial relations or organizational behaviour. These subjects are well and fully documented elsewhere. It is a book about personnel management itself. Contextually, of course, behavioural science and industrial relations enrich the pastiche. Within the canvas of this book the warp and weft of their threads are interwoven. But the montage itself is a personnel one.

The book is a corporate effort. If it was to be a substantial volume it seemed prudent to seek the contributions of eminent persons, particularly in the areas where I felt I would have needed most support. To this end, Greville Janner, Len Peach, Paul Roots and Nancy Seear were invited to join in. It is with immeasurable thanks to them – for their efforts, patience and expertise – that this book was ever born. Both Nancy and myself would like to express our thanks to the late John Brock of the Runnymede Trust who contributed much of the material on ethnic minorities. All the co-authors were involved in the planning stage. As coordinating author I allowed free rein to my colleagues with regard to presentation and format. Their chapters are distinctively their own. Responsibility for continuity, coordination and overall content is mine. Inevitably there are differences in style between the contributors – less so than would occur in an edited book of readings – but enough perhaps to add variety.

A host of people have proffered advice and guidance at various stages, among them Professor Sid Kessler, Valerie Hammond, Dr James Vant and my own students, who fed back constructively. Thanks are also due to the Engineering Industry Training Board, Ford Motor Company, IBM (UK), and the Petroleum Industry Training Board for kind permission to reproduce illustrative examples. A heavy load fell to Professor Keith Thurley and Baroness Seear who both read the first draft of the manuscript in full – heavy, because it was far too long. The painful decision was taken to reduce. Inevitably, sacrifices were made. Even so, I hope the final compendium is not too daunting, nor the sacrificial omissions too deleterious.

Several stalwarts merit special gratitude. Throughout the preparation my editors at Pitmans were steadfastly encouraging. Anne Stewart at City

University was constantly typing with accuracy and dexterity. Professor Brian Griffiths, then Dean of the Business School (now Head of the Prime Minister's Policy Unit) kindly made financial assistance available.

Needless to say, all matters of analysis, interpretation, judgement, opinion, error or omission are entirely my responsibility. Finally, I would wish all readers happy and successful careers in personnel management.

Bryan L. Livy

CITY UNIVERSITY 1987

Biographical notes on the contributors

Bryan Livy (coordinating author) read economics at Exeter University and manpower studies at Birkbeck College, London, obtaining a master's degree with distinction. He is a Fellow of the Institute of Personnel Management.

In 1959 he took a Short Service Commission in the Royal Army Educational Corps, serving in Germany. Thereafter he worked mainly in industry, with Ford, British Steel (and after a spell of teaching at Ealing College) with Glaxo.

Since 1971 he has taught personnel management on MBA programmes at City University Business School where he is IPM course tutor. From there he has also undertaken a number of research and consultancy assignments – as External Specialist, Petroleum Industry Training Board, involving three Manpower Services Commission sponsored projects for the development of personnel selection criteria in off-shore North Sea oil drilling and gas operations, and assessment centres for rig management; as External Collaborator, International Labour Organization, Geneva, reviewing international practices in job evaluation; a DHSS project for the recruitment and retention of ancillary staff in NHS hospitals; a Nuffield project on the 'hidden economy'; management training for Barclays Bank; job evaluation for the National Joint Council for Local Authorities Services; and *ad hoc* assignments for the Equal Opportunities Commission and the National Economic Development Office.

He is Chief Examiner in Human Aspects of Management for the Chartered Institute of Bankers; and has been external examiner to Middlesex Polytechnic, North East London Polytechnic, the Polytechnic of Central London, and the London School of Economics.

He is the author of *Job Evaluation: a Critical Review* (Allen and Unwin, 1975); also published in American and Spanish editions; *L'Évaluation des Emplois* (ILO, 1984); *Management and People in Banking* (Institute of Bankers, 2nd edition 1985) the ILO book (1986) *Job Evaluation*, and various articles and research papers.

Greville Janner, QC, is MP for Leicester West. He was an Exhibitioner at Trinity Hall, Cambridge; President of the Cambridge Union 1962; Fullbright Scholar at Harvard Post Graduate Law School; Harmsworth Scholar, Middle Temple; and holds an honorary PhD from Haifa University.

A distinguished lecturer and broadcaster, Mr Janner is Chairman of the All-Party Parliamentary Industrial Safety Group; a member of the House of Commons Select Committee on Employment; a Fellow of the Institute of Personnel Management; a member of the National Union of Journalists; and has had many years of boardroom experience.

He is the author of over 50 books on employment and industrial relations law, and on public speaking. These include *Janner's Compendium of Health and Safety*, *Janner's Compendium of Employment Law*, *Janner's Employment Letters* and *Data Protection – the New Rules*.

Other activities include President, Board of Deputies of British Jews since 1979; President, Commonwealth Jewish Council, 1982; European Vice-President, World Jewish Congress; Founder Member, International Committee for Human Rights in the USSR.

Len Peach is Past-President of the Institute of Personnel Management. He read modern history at Oxford University and personnel management at the London School of Economics. For a while he was research assistant to Randolph Churchill, and in 1962 joined his parent company IBM (UK) Ltd, becoming Director of Personnel in 1971, Group Director of Personnel, IBM (Europe) in Paris in 1972, returning to the UK in 1975 as Director of Personnel and Corporate Affairs.

In November 1985, he was seconded by IBM for three years to the National Health Service Management Board, first as Director of Personnel, then as Acting Chairman, and since October 1986 as Chief Executive and Director of Personnel. He has now completed 30 years in personnel management, marked by high office in the IPM as Vice-President, International Committee, and later (1983–5) as President.

Other activities include Council Member, Institute of Manpower Studies; Governor, Portsmouth Grammar School; Trustee, Devonshire House Management Club; Trustee, Institute of Public Relations; Vice Chairman of the Court of Governors, Polytechnic of Central London; Fellow of the Institute of Directors.

He is a Visiting Professor at the University of Surrey, was Loudon Lecturer at Glasgow University 1975; and is the author of numerous publications.

Paul Roots was until recently Director of Industrial Relations, Ford Motor Company Ltd. After leaving school and a period in industry, he spent seven years in the Royal Navy. Thereafter, he studied personnel management at the London School of Economics and re-emerged into industry, including a period with the UK Atomic Energy Authority.

Mr Roots joined Ford in 1961 during the setting up of its Halewood plant and has spent nearly twenty-five years in various positions within the Company's Industrial Relations Staff. He was the Company's chief negotiator for over 12 years and was appointed Director of Industrial Relations in March 1981, and a Board Director in June 1981, and retired in 1986.

He has been Chairman of the CBI Health and Safety Policy Committee, and the CBI Health and Safety Consultative Committee; and a member of: CBI Council; Council of Management; the CBI Education Foundation; the CBI Working Party on the Employment of Disabled People; the CBI Employment Policy Committee; the IPM National Committee on Employee Relations; the IPM Joint Standing Committee on Discrimination. He has been a member of the NEDO Committee on the Supply and Utilization of Skilled Engineering Manpower, was a Vice-President (Employee Relations) of the Institute of Personnel Management 1981/83, and has served on the Subcommittee for Social Affairs of the CBI.

He is author of *Financial Incentives for Employees*, co-author of the IPM's book on practical employee involvement and participation, and chaired the group which produced the Institute's book on introducing new technology. He is a companion of the BIM and IPM, and is a member of the Engineering Industry Training Board, The Civil Service Final Selection Board and industrial tribunals.

The Baroness Seear is a Privy Counsellor and Leader of the Liberal Peers in the House of Lords since 1984. She has been Spokesman on Employment and Treasury matters. She became a Life Peer in 1971.

After reading History at Newnham College, Cambridge, and studying Social Science at the LSE Nancy Seear spent ten years in personnel management in industry. She later became Reader in Personnel Management at the LSE and was responsible for the Graduate Course in Personnel Management.

She has sat on numerous government and national committees including the Top Salaries Review Body, British Standards Institution and the Council of the Industrial Society. She is a past President of the Institute of Personnel Management. She is a Honorary Fellow of Newnham College, an Honorary LLD of Leeds University, an Honorary DLitt of Bath University, and Visiting Professor in Personnel Management at the City University.

Her various publications include *Married Women Working, A Career for Women in Industry, The Position of Women in Industry* and *The Re-entry of Women into Employment*.

Introduction

by Bryan Livy

Personnel management is part of the process of management in general. It is a constituent element in the complex business of running an enterprise. Personnel management is both a function (something which is done) and a discipline (a body of knowledge). Its contribution is specifically related to the 'people' side of things. Personnel management is the practice of managing people at work.

For most of this century, researchers, consultants, and managers themselves have investigated all manner of human problems at work. The core issue is always the quality of human organization in pursuit of common goals.

Whilst our knowledge has increased, we still cannot be prescriptive in novel situations, although we can offer systematic approaches in many instances. 'People' problems at work are dynamic. This makes the study of human relations more, not less, imperative.

Designing, producing and marketing a product or service has obvious technical, cost and profit constraints. Pure engineering is not enough. People have got to work the enterprise and make it grow. People must respond positively. At the heart of management lies a neat balancing act – reconciling the 'needs' of individuals with the 'needs' of the organization.

The employer seeks an optimum deployment of manpower. His prime concerns are costs and productivity. The personnel manager knows this. The personnel manager is at the fulcrum in balancing employers' and employees' interests.

A pertinent question is: who is the client of the personnel manager? Personnel managers occupy mediative positions in the middle ground of the employer–employee relationship. But personnel managers are part of the management team, paid for as such. Personnel management is a cost centre. The personnel manager is a manager first. His clients are other managers and the workforce. For the workforce he has a shared responsibility, but he is not their 'representative' nor is he directly responsible for the management of the organization. Personnel managers act reciprocally as representatives of management and as their advisers. Any attempt to develop the personnel function independent of business considerations is unlikely to succeed. Personnel managers are expected to find acceptable solutions and develop mutual strategies. Primary allegiance may be to management but the 'clientele' has duality. There are two sets of clients: employers and employees. There is often a dilemma in the diplomatic role.

Personnel managers work not only with the workforce whether in office, factory, plant, bank, hospital or local authority – but also with other managers. The management of people is interactive and cuts across formal functions. The personnel manager needs to 'talk turkey' with his managerial colleagues. He must first know the business: the nuts and bolts of the industry he is working in. Without this grasp he will be in a wilderness.

The personnel manager contributes to the team effort. His daily work will not just include interviewing prospective candidates or handling grievances or redundancies. He will sit on planning committees and steering committees, bringing in new products or services. He will be involved in feasibility studies. He will be concerned with staffing and manpower implications, productivity, work methods, manpower ratios, organization planning and design. He will be concerned with earnings settlements and trends, with manpower costing, with negotiations. He will give presentations and hold discussions with line management. He will be *expected* to contribute. Not least he must be an expert in his own field, a competent 'professional'.

To the casual observer, personnel management may appear as an uncoordinated array of activities. Often it is. Coherence is called for. It helps to have some classification of activities in accordance with their natural relationships – a systematic approach, which identifies the threads in the fabric, sets objectives, determines methods for attaining them, monitors events, validates and evaluates the outcomes. Validation is 'quality control'. Evaluation is 'cost control'. In personnel work many of these systems interrelate, whether for selection, payment, training or whatever. What an organization is paying for, hiring for, training for is a unit of work. Personnel policies are interactive. To that extent they should be based on clearly defined, and possibly common, *criteria*. The determination of criteria against which results and performance can be measured is a recurrent theme of this book.

Personnel management cannot take place in a vacuum. It is a complementary constituent of corporate strategy. Policies must be *planned* and specifically tailored to present and future needs. To use the vogue term 'human resource planning' is the development of forward-looking personnel policies which help to ensure that organizations have taken positive steps to recruit, retain and develop their staff in the light of changes likely to affect the survival and well-being of the enterprise. 'The "business manager" model of personnel management has started to emerge in the last decade. Personnel specialists within this model integrate their activities closely with top management and ensure that these are serving long-term strategic objectives.' (Tyson, 1985)

Reference

Tyson, S. (1985), 'Is this the very model of a modern personnel manager?', *Personnel Management*, May.

Planning Functions

CHAPTER I

Corporate strategy and personnel policies

by Len Peach

Chief Executive and Director of Personnel, National Health Service Management
  Board
Formerly Director of Personnel and Corporate Affairs, IBM (UK)
Immediate Past President, Institute of Personnel Management

Introduction

It is over three decades since Peter Drucker in his seminal work *The Practice of Management*, described the personnel manager's conception of his own role as 'partly a file clerk's job, partly a housekeeping job, partly a social worker's job and partly "fire fighting" to head off union trouble or to settle it'. He argued that line management tends to see 'personnel' as concerned with problems and 'headaches that threaten the otherwise smooth and unruffled course of production' (Drucker, 1955). Indeed the status and contribution of a personnel manager is often judged by his 'fire brigade' activities – his ability to handle the unions, conduct the daily or annual negotiations, to keep the track running. Yet the real requirement is proactive and constructive rather than defensive and reactive. To discharge their true role personnel managers must anticipate the needs of the organization in the short and the long term. They must develop the policies to produce solutions to anticipated problems resulting from the external and internal environment, whilst influencing and creating the attitudes amongst employees needed for the enterprise's survival and success.

But policy should not be developed independently of the strategy of the business. Personnel managers exist to forward the aims of the enterprise not to regard their companies as sociological laboratories.

All bodies, public or private, have objectives in common. They exist to satisfy a demand, whether for service or for products and they should seek to satisfy that demand in the most efficient, productive and low cost manner. Central and local government provide services which are paid for by the taxpayer and the ratepayer. Nationalized industries provide services and products supported by the consumer and the State with taxpayer's money. The private sector is concerned with the customer. Bob Ramsey writing in the *Financial Times* made the point that 'Morality in business must start with morality towards the customer. It is the satisfaction of customers' needs that provides employment. The whole gambit of progressive industrial relations policies and the like is only the means to that end, not an end in itself. The self-interest of the producer cannot be indulged at the expense of the customer'.

If the shareholders in any enterprise are the Government, the customers, the employees, the contractors and the community in general, then they all have an interest in the efficiency of the bodies which serve or use them and the quality of the product, since ultimately they must foot the bill.

Whilst there is a common need for customer orientation amongst all enterprises there will be different emphasis on the key areas of measurement in the various businesses, depending upon their marketplace, size or stage of growth. Drucker argued that there are eight areas in which objectives of performance and results have to be set: 'market standing; innovation; productivity; physical and financial resources; profitability; manager performance and development; worker performance and attitude; public responsibility'.

Industry and commerce may use as their prime objectives and measures the level of profitability, market share, production volumes and costs, returns on investment, amount of research and development. The public sector may have similar measurements though government borrowings may be an alternative or additional financial measure. Local government may have different measures for the public services it provides, though it too must return to the level of service provided in relationship to costs and customer satisfaction, in the form of the acceptance and reaction of the local inhabitants to those services and level of the rates which pay for them.

Thus personnel managers of all organizations are concerned with common problems of enabling line management to obtain improvements in productivity through changes in working methods and the implementation of new technology, and in improving the output of the organization in qualitative and quantitative terms, whether in services or goods. At the same time they must encourage that same line management to provide the maximum degree of satisfaction to employees in their assigned tasks.

The scope of the personnel strategist will vary according to the task he has been allocated within the organization and the nature of the organization itself. Some personnel directors are asked to limit themselves to the 'personnel management of management' and policies are formulated for this purpose. This is a feature of the headquarters function of a company which is a conglomerate and which judges its subsidiary businesses by their financial success, but recognizing that they are in disparate industries does not wish to have any coordination of their personnel activities other than that relating to the management. Another company may decide that it wishes to pursue common personnel policies and practices and since it is operating in one industry is well aware that different conditions in different locations will provoke unrest. So it pursues a centralized policy with controls over local action held firmly at headquarters. One company decides that to achieve growth it must proceed by acquisition with all the problems of different company cultures and conditions of employment which that brings. Another decides that its expansion will be organic. These strategic assumptions may initially determine the role or guidelines for Personnel which will enable the organization to evolve with a cooperative and productive workforce. Yet the organizational assumptions themselves are open to challenge and in its evaluation of the changes needed to accomplish business objectives the personnel function may find itself recommending modifications to or changes in direction.

All organizations, public or private, require a corporate strategy to determine the nature and level of the objectives they are seeking to attain, the problems they are likely to encounter and the methods and resources which they must employ in providing remedies and achieving targets. In smaller companies such a plan may be on the back of an envelope. In large companies it may run to many pages. The need however is common. The existence of the plan enables the functional dialogues to take place and the result of those discussions in the form of the amended plan is more likely to produce consistency in direction and purpose in achieving corporate objectives.

In a recent article, L. Alexander (1985) identified the six most frequently encountered problems frustrating the implementation of business strategies as follows:

		Percentage of companies which have encountered this problem
1	Implementation took more time than originally allocated.	76
2	Major problems surfaced during implementation that had not been identified beforehand.	74
3	Coordination of implementation activities not effective enough.	66
4	Competing activities and crises distracted management from implementing this decision.	64
5	Capabilities of employees involved were not sufficient.	63
6	Training and instructions given to lower level employees were not adequate.	62

The contribution of the personnel department through effective personnel planning, training and policy implementation should serve to alleviate all of these.

Sir Peter Parker (1983) summarized this strategic role and its relationship with the other duties of the personnel department in an article in *Personnel Management*. 'It is hard to get any movement if there is no vision of the future. It is hard to deal day to day with what's wrong if there is no clear idea of what's right long term. Change is hard to achieve in any individual organization in isolation of the social changes going on outside it.' 'The need to operate on two distinct time-scales means Personnel must develop long-term policies and strategies and it must also be in there pitching when day to day problems arise.'

The approach: a demonstration of the interaction of corporate strategy and personnel policy

Unless one is fortunate enough to begin with a new company and a 'green field' site, one inherits certain values in an organization. Often these are the ideals of the chief executive, and the history of organizations is rich with men who have left their personal impact on companies for decades after they have disappeared. Sometimes the values are unwritten and part of the culture, sometimes they have been carefully formulated in tablets of stone, which may or may not be relevant to the current business climate. Nor is the imposition of values restricted to the imprint of the founder or chairman. Even where a company is newly created it may inherit certain economic and social values from its employees. Many a business established in an area of persistent high unemployment, has had to cope with the attitudes and values of its work force, committed to low levels of attendance and productivity in the belief that the longer the current job lasts, the longer they will be employed. The dedication to the welfare of the group rather than that of the individual is a characteristic of such societies and so, for example, the same pay for similar grades of work, irrespective of individual contribution, may become an imposed requirement upon an employer.

It is therefore important for the personnel policy planner to ask the question: 'what are the current values of my organization?'. They may or may not be ideas relevant to the business plan, but unless the question is asked then the personnel policies which are needed to achieve the business objectives and success of the enterprise may be built upon false assumptions so that they have little chance of being implemented.

If security of employment is seen as important to the success of an enterprise (and it is clear in high technology companies that security is an important factor in determining the acceptance of change, and therefore the pace of change in a company), and if the history of an enterprise is one of frequent layoffs, then it is quite certain that the company will require a change of practice as well as policy and a communication programme of some depth. It will need rather more than the chairman's oft repeated statement that 'the human resources of the enterprise are the company's most valuable assets', – to be followed next week by yet another major redundancy – to provide the attitude in the workforce which not only accepts but welcomes the challenge of change.

The importance of deciding and listing current values and the interaction between personnel policies and business plans can be illustrated by one example. A number of organizations including British Telecom are committed to a practice of employment security – in other words guaranteeing lifetime employment with the organization subject to an overriding 'small print' limitation of an economic cataclysm. The commitment is not to job security. No organization can guarantee that a person will be employed in the same job for life. A policy of employment security has implications for both business and personnel plans. By definition, management is required to provide adequate retraining facilities to ensure that as old skills disappear and new skills are created, then resources are committed to that creation. The requisite union agreements have to be negotiated. In order to preserve its flexibility and to maintain its competitiveness management must ensure that its manpower plans ensure a productivity improvement of a high level on an annual basis. As a result, if unexpected business conditions are met and the economy declines, the company will be manned at the lowest possible level commensurate with achieving its business results. It will not then have to remove two layers of fat; the first that of overmanning; the second produced by the deteriorating business climate.

In addition, the management will have to make decisions about the relative size of the permanent labour force and that of the temporary group. All businesses employ temporary labour in some form. Trainees, Government scheme trainees, temporaries including students, agency temporaries and subcontract workers are the categories which generally supplement the permanent full-time and part-time workforce. In order to provide a buffer and to honour its security of employment 'contract' the decision may be taken to use temporary workers for a number of positions and to use subcontractors and their capital as suppliers. If the subcontracting decision is partly based on personnel considerations then the company using that solution will probably ask itself the question of the morality of passing on redundancies to its subcontractors. It may then decide to salve its conscience and in recognizing the social consequences of its actions it will limit the amount of work it places with any subcontractor. Unlike some companies which seek to dominate their suppliers by requiring their total or the greater part of their capacity to be devoted to their needs, the company which is concerned with the social impact of its changing requirements may determine that not more than a limited percentage of that contractor's total business should be dedicated to its requirements, so forcing the contractor to expand his business with other companies.

Thus, if a corporation has decided that it wishes to provide security of employment, its management finds itself committed to a set of decisions which may involve retraining, skills deployment agreements, high productivity to minimize manpower, the use of temporaries as a buffer and firm decisions on its policy of the loading of subcontractors. All these are derived from a single decision to provide as much security of tenure as possible, but the results of that decision flow through management plans and style across the company.

Another consequence of security of employment might be a 'single status' policy or the intention to provide common salary systems, benefits programmes and, as far as possible, similar working conditions for all employees. There is no doubt that the redeployment process is facilitated by this. If employees are divided by a variety of salary systems, different scales of benefits and, for example, different levels of cafeteria, then the process of introducing widespread reorganization and change is made so much more difficult. The visible signs of status, the level of dining room, the size of company car and so on, limit the changes which should provide managers with varied levels of experience and prevent the relegation of unsuccessful managers to the level at which they have previously performed well. So single status may be a policy which arises from management's recognition that the need of a business for rapid change within an organization may be inhibited by artificial barriers. Distinctions not based upon defensible business reasons should be swept away. In the pursuit of encouraging job mobility and managing change, the result is not only greater security and transferability of skills and labour, but also commitment to the enterprise, since individuals identify themselves with the well-being of the company as a whole and not with a particular, sectional group. Thus the desire for business reasons to achieve rapid change within an enterprise leads management to provide employees with security of employment, and to review many personnel policies and practices, some of which have been mentioned, but which probably will also include standards of recruitment and internal promotion systems.

With the process of defining current values and policies complete, the strategic planner in personnel management must now identify the current and future business objectives. The question he or she is beginning to ask is: 'what are the intentions for the business formulated by the operational strategists and what impact will these have on the existing personnel policies and principles of the company?'. Most companies choose a period of one to two years for operating plans and a period of between five and seven years for strategic plans, and although it might be argued that a longer period might be more suitable for high technology industries, the speed of change is such that five years or so is probably a reasonable time horizon. In addition most companies fall into the error of making strategic plans too detailed; they frequently read like seven-year operations plans. The result is that large amounts of the information and material are rapidly outdated. A strategic plan is best formulated with outline objectives and the minimum of supporting detail. The operating plan on the other hand is highly detailed since it provides the targets in production, sales and services, costs and profit margins for individual units which together constitute the measurement of the success or otherwise of the business in the succeeding period. The planner should ensure a correlation between the operating plan and the strategic plan. It is surprising how often one has only a limited relationship to the other!

The same need for planning exists in the public services. Here the level of resource available in finance and manpower and the level of service required are the main elements to be reconciled within the plan, and recognizing the different views of various political parties on public services, it is almost certainly necessary to have two plans, one a contingency allowing for a change of government. The same argument can be made for the private sector at times when elections are impending, such is the diversity of economic policies between the major political parties.

The corporate strategist is highly dependent on the quality of data available; data on the present state of the company and its marketplace and data to provide the basis for forecasting, whatever technique may be used. The personnel planner and policy maker has the same dependence. Other chapters in this book will deal in more detail with computerization of personnel data, including educational qualifications, skills, salary and records with the company. The ready availability of this information and its speedy access through computerization have revolutionized personnel planning. The painful search through individual records to determine the levels of skills, knowledge and aptitudes to meet future demands, should now for most medium and large organizations be a thing of the past. In addition, the ability to model age, career and salary profiles should be invaluable in enabling the planner to ascertain future salary and benefit costs and management and manpower stocks. The opportunity to analyse labour turnover by operating unit and to analyse the reasons for that turnover; to forecast management succession; and, for those companies which use opinion surveys, to identify morale problems, are additional benefits which computerization has made available more readily to the planner, and which in themselves may lead to modifications in personnel policy.

A typical personnel plan with indications of its impact on personnel policies

In setting out the plan, the personnel manager should be fully aware of the business targets for the enterprise over the planning period since he or she will clearly have to use these as yardsticks for current and future personnel policies. It may also be necessary to moderate the business objectives as a consequence of Personnel's view of the practicability of such targets. The ability to recruit the number of professional engineers, to reach agreement with the trade unions on the desired levels of productivity, to reduce the labour force to the desired level without serious consequences in efficiency or producing industrial unrest, the need to increase pay above the level which the profit targets will sustain could all be reasons why business objectives are not feasible. So Personnel does not only accept targets and produce the plans to attain them. As a function it must call out to line management its own ability to fulfil its part of the plan, as well as the ability or inability of line management to make apparent commitments happen.

In a large company the personnel director will construct his plan on a comprehensive and detailed base, according to a predetermined format. Experience leads one to follow a design which, after reviewing the business objectives, sets out the external environment against which the company will be operating during the plan period, then the internal personnel environment, and from the comparison of the three will emerge the modifications to personnel policies and practices of the company or decisions to resist changes for hopefully good reasons. To help the reader, the process of outlining the environment will now be reviewed in detail. This approach may seem somewhat cumbersome, since a written document on this will run to a substantial number of pages but it is necessary to emphasize that whilst in a smaller company it may not be a requirement to enter into so much detail the discipline of following the process gives structure to the personnel analysis. This enables the personnel manager to set out his or her own role in fulfilling the company's plans whilst setting out for line colleagues the impact which he or she believes external and internal factors will have on the company's operations. Only with such plans will Personnel's actions in an organization move from reactive to proactive.

The external environment

The first part of the external environment is devoted to a political forecast. The complaints which businessmen have made about the 'see-saw' nature of politics in the United Kingdom as the Conservative Party succeeds the Labour Party or vice versa, privatization follows nationalization, and one economic policy contrasts with another, find echoes in the personnel planner's mind. With a government's period in office restricted to a term of five years, business and personnel plans become difficult to project beyond that time-scale which is shortened as the next general election draws nearer. Indeed the shorter the period before an election the more need there is for a contingency plan to set out alternative business and personnel strategies if the other party rather than the one whose policies form the basis of the plan, is elected. With the two major parties at present demonstrating widely different perspectives on membership of the European Economic Community, trade union reform, the nature and measures of industrial democracy, the methods of management of the economy, particularly the level of public spending, the approach to unemployment and to planning at national, sector and company level, and in addition with the uncertainties about the electoral influence of the Social Democratic or Liberal Parties, the need for contingency plans is clear. Still the main plan has to be based upon a forecast of the political policies of the government in power and the planner must hazard a calculated guess at the timing and the outcome of a general election.

The second main section of the external environment statement is the economic forecast. The accuracy of this will have significant implications for the achievement of business targets and in volumes of sales, costs of manufacturing, costs of imports, and profit margins. For the personnel manager the impact will be on the cost of labour, both in wages and benefits, and he will be particularly interested in the forecast rate of inflation, knowing the influence this will have on union bargaining attitudes and indeed on the views of all employees including the management group, towards pay negotiations or pay increases. Here he is beginning to balance the costs of labour, numbers of employees, going rate, benefits and State costs against the productivity targets of the business. Against the background of the inflation forecast and that of unemployment, he must now begin to calculate the added or reduced cost of labour in the plan period which means assessing the likely outcome of bargaining in both pay and benefits, the cost of promotions, incremental or merit pay, and the impact of increased or decreased manpower by skill group.

The third element is that of social change. What events are taking place in society which may impact the business particularly in its internal, industrial or personnel relations? One major happening which has been taking place over the past few years has been the changing nature of and shortening in working hours. Under the general heading of the 'quality of life' in the 1970s, and with the stated objective of sharing work during the 1980s, there has been a trend towards providing more flexibility in working time and reducing the number of working hours required during a year either by shortening the working week or by increasing vacation time. Variable working hours or flexitime has spread rapidly from company to company, providing the individual employee with limited choice on starting and stopping times and, in some cases, changing substantially the management style of an organization. The reduction in the working year is a current phenomenon producing a management need for higher productivity to compensate for the loss of working time and complications in the arrangements for shift workers who in many cases already work a much shortened week.

A plan written some years ago would have commented on the social change by which unions were rapidly increasing their numbers amongst managers and senior professionals. Today it will be reflecting the diminishing numbers in the trade union movement with falling rolls largely produced by the unemployment situation, though it may be argued also impacted by the demonstrated inability of the unions to protect their membership at the time when that protection is most needed. Since no company is an island unto itself, this section should reflect the general industrial relations climate within the country, both within the public sector and the company's own industrial group. In recent years sometimes the threat of and sometimes strike action itself by public sector workers, notably the coal miners, railway workers and water workers has been of considerable concern to the private sector of the economy.

A section of the plan which might be considered separately or as part of the political analysis is the impact of recent or promised legislation. The requirements of appropriate acts such as the clauses of the Employment Acts 1980 and 1982, and the Trade Union Act of 1984, should be reviewed and their impact extrapolated. For example, the clause which requires companies employing more than 250 workers to include a statement in their annual reports to introduce, maintain or develop arrangements aimed at furthering 'involvement' has implications for management. Discussion papers such as

Green Papers on Trade Union Reform should be outlined so that the company can establish its position and decide whether to make a contribution to the public debate. The consequences of equal opportunity legislation, the Data Protection Act, the Youth Training Scheme and the Social Security and Housing Benefits Act 1982, for example, which required the transfer of responsibility from the Department of Health and Social Security to employers for paying statutory sick pay for the first eight weeks of sickness in any tax year, would fall into this section.

International developments should also take their place in this environmental description. The European Common Market has had under discussion a number of significant measures in the personnel field which would have an impact on management in both national and international companies if they are approved. For a number of years the most notable of these were the Fifth Directive and the Vredeling Initiative, the first aimed at harmonization of industrial democracy institutions amongst member states, the second at improving the flow of information from management to employees of companies operating within the EEC. Both have proved controversial, and both required companies to have clear views on the proposals and contingency plans to meet their enforcement. Both these measures have receded somewhat but others have taken their place.

The final part of this external environment should be the identification of public issues which will affect the company and its business results and on which the company should have a prepared position which it is willing to communicate to the public at large but particularly to its employees. Much has been written and said about the need for members of a company, private or public, to identify with the objectives of an organization, but it is difficult for them to do so if they are unaware of the company's views on a particular topic of importance to the success of the business. The employees of an enterprise are also its best ambassadors and the planning of proactive communications to them on important topics strengthens identification, enables them to play the ambassadorial role, and improves morale. For example, in the computing industry, public sector procurement policy, telecommunications liberalization and attitudes towards the acceptance of new technology are issues which affect the business substantially and on which employees should fully understand the company position. 'Communication' is not only concerned with what is happening within a company, but also with events and policies outside which have implications for the enterprise and its supporters.

The internal business environment

The perception and acceptance by employees of the key business changes planned over the next few years will be vital to the ability of the enterprise, whether public or private, to meet its business objectives. So part of the plan should address the likely changes and the impact on employee morale, whether potentially positive or negative. Forecasts of increased productivity and workload; the movement and margins of profits downwards or upwards; the methods by which the business is managed including perceptions of participation, centralization, bureaucracy and unnecessary work; major organizational upheavals required by new or revised business strategies; changes which affect employment of regular employees, temporaries, subcontractors or vendors in communities where the company has a substantial presence; the impact of special programmes such as those focusing on quality improvement; all of these and many other plans may affect the population serving the company. Foreseen, appropriate measures can be taken to minimize the negative elements of such changes and to maximize the positive aspects.

Whether centralized or decentralized, each operating unit should have its own personnel and communications plan to review and agree between line and personnel the approach to the problems of resource management, employee development, reward systems, industrial and personnel relations and communications which are required by the changes.

The internal personnel environment

This should probably begin with a general review of the morale of the company. Known and suspected problems in personnel relations should be set out since these will affect the new strategies and policies being addressed in the succeeding narrative. In the few companies in the United Kingdom which use attitude or opinion surveys on a regular basis, the problems should not be difficult to identify and morale can be easily quantified. In those which have a less systematic approach, the accumulation of data will be more subjective but it should not be shirked. One doubts the wisdom of addressing new problems without taking into account the presence of old, unresolved situations! It is also in this section that one must address the principles or values which are inherent or which have been created in the organization.

The opening section should be concerned with manpower resources with an indication drawn from the business plans of the numbers and changes in skills of employees needed during the plan period. Is the company increasing or decreasing in manpower? Does it seek to provide security of employment or does it regard labour as a dispensable asset? Is it prepared to retrain some of its existing employees in new skills or does it wish to hire those skills from the outside? The answers to those questions will produce very different strategies in companies engaged in the same industry. A commitment to security of employment means a willingness to relocate on the part of the employee and acceptance of the acquisition of skills, sometimes superior sometimes inferior to those already possessed. To the employer it means the formulation of personnel policies which support redeployment which may include the protection of earnings during retraining, the protection of job levels for a stipulated period, the willingness to meet relocation costs and the provision of expensive retraining. It also means communicating to the employee that what is being offered is employment protection and not job security. An employer who dispenses with his obsolescent labour and hires new skills from the market place will meet some of these problems but will have an entirely different environment within his company in terms of identification, productivity and acceptance of change. The businessman who is offering or seeking to maintain lifetime employment will seek to set rigorous selection standards which ensure flexibility and ease of retraining in recruits. He needs accurate forecasts of manpower needs, a knowledge of available skills, data on age distribution and retirement patterns and clear indications of the labour turnover which provides him with some flexibility, however limited. Above all he needs tight central control of hiring and redeployment against a background of management commitment at all levels to making the policy/ practice work. The personnel department becomes the guardian of the policy and authorizes hiring only when vacancies cannot be filled from within.

The impact of changing technology upon a skill group and the need to establish long-term plans to meet such problems can be illustrated from my own experience. In 1962 a management development workshop of customer engineering managers expressed concern about the problems which would result for their workforce because of anticipated changes in computer fault diagnosis and repair. The customer engineers are a group of highly trained service engineers, and it was believed that future software trends would enable the computer to diagnose its own problems and the task of the customer engineer would be reduced to replacing the faulty part on the instructions of the computer, with resulting minimal job satisfaction. As a consequence of that meeting the strategic plan required new recruits into customer engineering to meet not only the technical standards previously appropriate but also to reach appropriate levels on the programming aptitude test so that new skills could be acquired at a later date. The result over the next twenty years was a remarkable success. Not only did this group become the most redeployable group within the company in terms of skills flexibility but the company was able to broaden many of the jobs of the customer engineer to include a high degree of software competence. So a threat became an opportunity.

The importance of having a strategic approach to manpower and to interrelated policies is perhaps additionally illustrated by demonstrating the interdependence of manpower flexibility and the pension plan. In these uncertain economic times it is wise to have a pension plan which offers a generous, if expensive, approach to early retirement and a wide span of years during which retirement may be taken. Many companies now allow early retirement at 50. Then, if the manpower situation deteriorates, by use of additional lump sum redundancy payments the company can influence its older population in the age group above 50 to choose to retire earlier. Funding early retirement is expensive, but done over a number of years the costs can be kept under control. The strategic personnel manager is one who is solving the manpower problems of his successor!

Compensation constitutes a major segment of the plan, and the external political and economic environment will determine the nature of the strategic thinking. Of the three major political groups in the United Kingdom, one is committed to free enterprise in the private sector with companies deciding their own salary programmes and seeks a tight budgetary control over the public sector; another believes in an incomes policy; and a third a 'national consensus' method. Faced with these possibilities one company may decide that its compensation strategy must be to stay flexible with a reward system which is responsive to substantial changes in the environment. Another may determine that it is willing to allow government to make its compensation decisions for it. One may choose a sophisticated measurement system by which it compares its salaries with other leading companies, ensures that it pays on a par or compares favourably with them expressed in terms of deciles or quartiles and will choose a merit pay system. Another will seek to minimize its payments by negotiation with the trade unions on an operating unit basis with a decentralized pay system, if such an approach can be dignified by the word 'system'. Whatever method is chosen, however, it is important to recognize that it is a choice and that the decision has been consciously weighed and concluded, with the advantages and disadvantages fully acknowledged. A company system will provide greater equality and ready transferability of labour; a decentralized, subsidiary or local system will lead to comparisons which management will find difficult to justify and certainly will impede ready transferability, yet it may produce lower labour costs.

Salary is only part of the reward and expense system of a company. Other sections of the plan need to be devoted to benefits and perquisites – in other words to compensation in kind other than in the pay packet. Most employees receive an additional 30 per cent paid by those methods which has to be taken into consideration as part of the expenses of employment. Pension plans are the most costly element of the benefits package with funding rates varying from 10 to 40 per cent of base pay, depending upon the promised benefits, age structure and manpower dynamics. Two subjects, the 'index linking' of increases to pensions in payment, and the improving of deferred pension entitlements for those leaving service before retirement are major subjects of debate in the United Kingdom, and improvements in either or both are likely to be expensive for employers unless the existing pension fund is in a very healthy state and can support such payments without additional increases. The costs of private medical treatment for employees which some companies provide are also escalating, whilst, in the perquisites sector the demand for company cars continues to grow. The adequacy of the company's existing programmes should be considered in relation to national and local labour markets, with possible improvements evaluated in financial and employee perception and motivation terms.

Other sections should be devoted to personnel recognition and suggestion programmes, data security and privacy of personal information, employee development including equality of opportunity, occupational health and safety, and job development or enrichment.

There is a need for a corporate communications plan which may well be integrated with the personnel plan. This should address the timely, consistent and rational explanation of the enterprise's business direction, strategy and performance both at the overall company level and for its individual business units. It may well address corporate credibility, the gaps between plans and achievements, between promises and actions. It should explain competitiveness, in particular the need for change and improvements in productivity, innovation, use of technology, quality and information security (where the latter is vital for business success). It should be concerned with organizational requirements and changes, marketing and manufacturing missions. The personnel elements of the communications plan will probably contain job security, employee flexibility and mobility, career development, hiring programmes, reorganization and the impact of technology. The focus, however, should be on a number of key messages which become the theme of internal communications activities, with the objective of enabling the employee to identify with the enterprise in its business goals. The various communications channels available to act as vehicles for those messages should be reviewed, and clearly the need for increased disclosure of information whether resulting from changing managerial style, employee requirements or stipulated by legislation should be taken into consideration. The plan should not neglect methods of ensuring that feedback is obtained from employees on all relevant issues whether through formal or informal channels.

Recognizing the importance of obtaining the total commitment of managers to the objectives of the business, it may be appropriate to include a special section of the plan addressed to this group. It may be helpful to address top, middle and first line management or supervision separately. The major part of this section should be devoted to management development and should be an assessment of the effectiveness of the present promotion and training systems in the light of present and future business needs. Resources should be provided or requested to provide an appropriate amount of management training both off and on the job for experienced and new managers, and the curricula of both external and internal management training courses should be examined for their relevance to the needs of the business. The management development department should be staffed with an appropriate mixture of line management and personnel management. Management communications should also be covered in this section in order to fulfil the oft stated policy that management is the prime mechanism by which employees receive information about the company and its activities, as well as providing systems which supply important feedback to top management. The extent to which first line management feels integrated into the management team by methods such as all-managers meetings, roundtable meetings and management representation should be assessed and thought given to improving both mechanisms and processes.

No personnel plan would be complete without an examination of the trends in labour relations within both the country and the enterprise, and a consideration of what policies need to be modified as a result of that environment. Here the value judgements or management principles of the enterprise will determine the changes that need to be made or the practices which need to be reinforced. If the company believes that the maintenance of the direct employee/manager relationship is the cornerstone of its policy then its approach to communications through representative or unrepresentative bodies will be very different from that of companies which have decided that the union representatives are the only channel to employees – which was a common situation in Britain in the 1960s, but is less frequently encountered today. On the other hand, where representation exists, clearly a company should seek to develop constructive relationships, whilst preserving management flexibility and ensuring that it does not prejudice its contacts with the total workforce. The company should also be concerned to protect itself – or develop contingency plans – in the event of disruptive activities internally or externally. The review should also consider the nature of the Employers' Association, if the company is a member, whilst reflecting on any present or foreseeable changes in the mission of that Association which may impact the policy or strategy of its member companies.

The company should monitor trends in employee interest in representation and in the policies which the representative bodies are pursuing. Patterns of membership, participation in elections, composition of representative bodies, attendance at meetings, help to evaluate events and changes which are taking place in structure, policies and power distribution within the enterprise.

Summary

In summary, the personnel plan which takes into consideration the business strategies of the enterprise and which assesses the needs for changes in or the reinforcing of personnel policies should have the following format:

1 *External environment*
   (a) Political
   (b) Economic
   (c) Social
   (d) Legislative
   (e) Innovative employee practices
   (f) International developments
   (g) Public issues impacting the company
2 *Internal business environment*
   (a) Functional or unit business strategies
   (b) Forecasts of personnel impacts of business objectives
3 *Internal Personnel environment*
   (a) Employee morale
   (b) Manpower resources
   (c) Working time

    (d) Compensation and benefits
    (e) Personnel information
    (f) Employee communications
    (g) Personnel recognition programmes including suggestions
    (h) Job development/enrichment
    (i) Employee development
    (j) Equal opportunity
    (k) Occupational health and safety
    (l) Space and accommodation
    (m) New developments and innovations

4 *Internal management environment*
    (a) Management development
    (b) Management communications

5 *Labour relations trends*
    (a) Employers association
    (b) Employee representation
    (c) Legal cases of significance
    (d) Employee relations strategy, including industrial relations organization

Carried out efficiently the personnel plan should provide a short-term assessment which predicts the problems and policy reactions of the succeeding two years with a more general outlook covering a period of five to seven years. It should afford an analysis of trends and events in both the external and internal environments which may impact the operations of the enterprise. It acts as a vehicle for dialogue between line management and Personnel to focus on the Personnel implications of both old and new business directions and indicates early identification of personnel programmes and actions to support them. It gives preliminary indications of necessary reallocation of resources and it also identifies obsolete or low priority personnel programmes or practices which should be modified or removed. In ensuring that good employee relations and satisfactory labour relations are being planned the very existence of the personnel plan indicates that management is prepared to devote the time, energy and forethought to ensuring that its business strategies and personnel policies are correlated and that management does recognize the importance of the 'human assets' in the conduct of the business.

One final point needs to be stressed. The personnel plan must be 'owned' by the line management of the company or of the operating unit. It cannot be a document which is preserved in the files of the personnel director and which is not recognized by those who have the senior responsibility for the success of the business, whether public or private. The personnel function should use the mechanisms within the company to ensure line management approval and backing for the contents of the document which eventually emerges.

To be useful a plan has to be a source of reference. Circumstances change and business objectives are modified. In the same way it will be necessary to adapt and change personnel policy and practice. The existence however of a base plan enables such changes to take place with minimum delay and in the full context of their impact on other segments of the plan and the organization. To quote Kingsley Manning, 'To be successful, even a brilliant strategy has to be implemented, and that largely depends on the effective management of the human resource'. Without the involvement and input of the personnel department into the business plan, the chances of that brilliant strategy succeeding are much reduced.

Discussion questions

1   Describe the personnel values of an organization with which you are familiar.
2   Outline the business objectives of that organization.
3   What policies need to be introduced to change the current values to bring them more in keeping with the present and future objectives of the enterprise?
4   What obstacles and incentives exist which will impair or aid the introduction of these policies?
5   Draw up an external environmental statement for a personnel strategic plan.
6   Draw up an internal environmental statement for a personnel strategic plan.
7   Outline the factors which you believe should be covered in a personnel plan.
8   Describe a communications plan, indicating the advantages and disadvantages of the various mechanisms which exist to put over the key messages of the enterprise.

References

ALEXANDER, L. (1985), 'Successfully implementing strategic decisions', *Long Range Planning*.
DRUCKER, P. F. (1955), *The Practice of Management*, Heinemann.
PARKER, P. (1983), 'How I see the personnel function', *Personnel Management*, January.

CHAPTER 2

Manpower planning and information

by Bryan Livy

Manpower planning has maintained its imperatives for several reasons: (i) a growing awareness of the need to look into the future, (ii) a desire to exercise control over as many variables as possible which influence business success or failure, (iii) the development of techniques which make such planning possible.

In the 1960s persistent and acute shortages of labour in many occupations caused disruptions in production. Labour costs, then as now, made up a substantial proportion of operating costs. Priority was devoted to improving labour utilization. It became increasingly clear that labour supply was of critical importance and that such supply was not totally flexible. Manpower planning was seen as a means by which under (or over) supply of labour could be avoided. Planning techniques at this time tended to be fastidious; there was a bonanza in manpower planning. Planned targets were often not met, because primarily, plans were too complicated, 'fuelled by a tendency to collect masses of information and not use it; by the use of complex, sophisticated planning techniques which were insufficiently understood by senior managements; and by the divorce of planning from operational issues and concerns' (Bramham, 1983).

With the 1970s came chronic disturbances in the economic environment. Business organizations entered a period of uncertainty, suggesting the futility of detailed plans. Lessons were learned. Chief amongst these was that whilst organizations cannot expect to forecast future demand for people accurately, they should more clearly relate manpower requirements to business objectives. In an uncertain world, the approach has to limit itself to an examination of possible scenarios of the future: what happens if? what will the effects be?

The *need* to create some vision beyond the short term was not diminished; quite the contrary. A clear conception of contingencies remained the order of the day. Also, new pressures were coming into play. By the 1980s several identifiable factors obliged organizations to evaluate longer-term approaches to the management of manpower. The main influences can be summarized:

1   Increasing organizational complexity which requires a wider range of specialist skills. The provision of highly skilled, specialist or technical personnel has a long lead-time. Development programmes to counter obsolescence require time, training and experience. Their effects place curbs on the possible speed of employee replacement.

2   Protective employment legislation in the UK firmed up concurrently with the loss of full employment from 1974 onwards, placing further brakes on the possible speed by which employee establishments or organizational size could be reduced cheaply or quickly. Employees were becoming 'fixed assets'.

3   Pressures to survive the recession constrained manning levels to their most economic, and brought under the microscope questions of pro-ductivity and manpower costs. Reductions in manhours available (e.g. through worksharing, a shorter working week, overtime restrictions, longer holidays) plus a 'fixed assets' approach to existing employees, signalled clearly the need to control costs and resources to meet longer-term, rather than shorter-term, objectives. (See Chapter 21.)

4   At best, most organizations did not expect to expand with the vigour displayed in the past (with few exceptions). This raised serious internal implications for career prospects and job security. The organization's competition and profit drive was often countered by countervailing pressures from employees to avoid redundancies, meet promotional expectations and seek compensatory measures (e.g. worksharing) to redistribute available employment opportunities.

5   Technological advancement, particularly the advent of the micropro-cessor, raised hopes for productivity gains in large areas of white-collar employment in the service industries and in manufacturing; robotics similarly transformed the shop floor. Computerization of communica-tions and control systems began to erode the traditional structure of management, administrative, clerical and manual jobs, reducing demand for less skilled, routine employees, inflating the upward mobility of skill demands elsewhere. Technology inevitably boded displacement of labour and changes in work practices, often meeting resistance to the rate of change, but focusing attentions again on skill requirements, the phasing of new technology and associated manpower implications.

6   When organizations move from a state of growth to one of contraction, they often become unbalanced in the proportion of people employed in different corporate activities. Usually the first impact of redundancy bears on 'direct' labour – the workforce in office, factory or public service directly concerned with the provision of goods and services. 'Indirect' labour – administrative, managerial and support staff – still constitutes manpower overheads, but downward revision of estimates

to reduce headcount levels commensurate with changed trading conditions is much more difficult and imprecise. Slices of fat may be trimmed from the organization, often on spurious criteria. Proportionately, organizations tend to become increasingly overweighted with indirect staff. Some have used 'zero-budgeting' and 'base-rate' techniques, but the process is still inherently complicated.

7   Hasty, yet seemingly expedient early retirement policies, can lead to imbalances in the age distribution within an organization.

8   There is still a propensity for younger people, together with those employees with least years service, to leave an organization first, and to do so voluntarily. Recent research (Forbes and McGill, 1985) confirms the resilience of this traditional pattern of wastage.

9   Attempts to run an organization down by 'natural' wastage are often disappointing. A freeze on recruitment means that short-service employees are not replaced. Because there is a lower propensity to leave among longer serving employees who remain in the organization, future gross wastage falls below what might have been expected. Projected gross turnover rates do not materialize, leading to stagnation, and undermining the long-term trends on which manpower decisions might have been based.

10 Despite high aggregate unemployment levels, specific skill shortages persist nationally, with wide variations locally.

11 Wastage patterns, even for the same occupations, are not consistent (Rajan, 1984). Considerable variations can be exhibited between time periods and between geographical areas in response to external labour markets.

12 With volatility and uncertainty in manning requirements, there is a growing tendency to build in 'buffers' in the manpower stock, to cope with fluctuations, e.g. by contracting out spasmodic or ancillary functions to 'peripheral' workers in support of the permanent 'core' workers, and by the use of temporary and part-time employment.

13 Wider usage of computerized techniques for processing personnel information, trends in manpower distribution and costs, and other personnel 'profiles' make manpower monitoring possible.

14 Survival-adaptation policies in a recessionary climate have drawn all personnel management activities into the strategic management of the organization's business affairs. Personnel managers have been exhorted to raise performance and contribute positively to corporate objectives. The resource of the personnel manager is manpower, which if not planned, controlled and husbanded wisely, will surely cause the organization to wither. Manpower planning is a clear starting point for the development of employment practices.

Many of the economic problems, and thereby manpower problems, which have beset the UK in recent years are of external origin (e.g. exchange rates, the commodity boom, oil prices) and are *uncontrollable* factors. But there are also a number of internal shifts which are discernible, and therefore *controllable* in the sense that thought and action can be given to them now. The first of these is the recurrent stimulus to productivity, through new work methods and machines. Whilst automation may proffer advantages, it brings inevitable consequences of shorter working, earlier retirement and increased leisure. The die is cast for permanent unemployment; what has yet to be devised is an appropriate strategy for dealing with it.

In earlier years, it seemed to observers of British manpower, that low productivity was largely due to overmanning. The seriously inadequate economic growth of the post-war period was seen to stem in part from malpractices (whether the fault of management or unions is another matter) in the effective utilization of manpower. Such shortages of labour as occurred, e.g. during the 1960s, were the result of '"on-the-job" leisure', and employers were accused of hoarding labour for fear that they would be unable to re-recruit in times of (hoped for) expansion. With the shake-out which in fact occurred during the 1970s, and with business contraction leading to large-scale redundancies, the indictment must by now surely be less valid than hitherto. Although productivity increases are still low by international comparison, there are one or two signs of optimism.

Manpower is a generic term for people at work; and people are not all the same. Several broad trends in the national manpower stock can be discerned. It is getting older. The average age of the working population is rising; an increasing proportion (now over one-third) of the labour force is over 45 years of age. This has serious implications in times of rapid change for retraining and redeployment. 'Older' workers present particular problems when it comes to learning new skills. And the sex ratio is changing. Now over 40 per cent of the workforce are women. With the backing of protective legislation, maybe more part-time working, and the re-employment of married women after childbirth, their numbers may increase. Young people (under 25) are still presenting a persistent stumbling-block to effective manpower utilization, in that they now constitute a significantly larger proportion of longer-term unemployed (a phenomenon not uniquely British).

Any organization operates within a broader economic and social environment. Its activities, especially its demand for labour, will be influenced by its own internal situation *and* by the external environment. Thus an organization must consider:

1   its own internal situation (the demand for labour now and in the future; the way in which manpower is deployed and its associated productivity; its internal labour supply; relevant industrial relations policies; and expectations);

2   the external environment (competition from other employers in product

and labour markets; the external supply of labour; wage trends; and government policies affecting employment).

The degree of influence exerted by these various pressures is not constant. At any point one may be more compelling than another. It is with the interface between the internal and external environment, as well as the adequacy of the firm's own internal situation, that manpower planning is concerned.

Within organizations, comprehensive planning for all types and levels of manpower is now fairly well established, especially in large enterprises – oil companies, clearing banks, nationalized industries, the Civil Service. Most large organizations now have specialist manpower planning units, where planning is not a once-off operation nor necessarily a single strategy. In small organizations the situation tends to be rather more piecemeal, where perhaps unintegrated 'splinters' of planning are undertaken in respect of certain segments of the workforce, such as apprentice training and management succession.

There is also a difference between short- and long-run planning. Short-term forecasts and tactical plans for action still tend to be detailed, set in the broader picture of long-term forecasts and strategies related to the general direction of the organization. Degrees of accuracy tend to fall as one looks further into the future.

The necessity of attempting manpower planning is clear enough. But it is only during the last twenty years that it has assumed a central role, either as a personnel function or as a corporate planning function. Whatever the range of manpower planning, it must always be based on minimum hard data about people and jobs. Data unavailability is frequently an impediment to successful planning. Key elements in the planning process are:

1　the manpower stock
2　manpower information and records
3　manpower demand forecasts
4　manpower supply forecasts
5　manpower flows
6　the reconciliation of demand and supply
7　manpower maps.

The manpower stock

Any organization consists of a number of people performing various jobs and exercising a variety of skills at different levels in the hierarchy. Many of these jobs will be the same, performed several times over by a collection of people. Where there is this degree of similarity, we may think in terms of a 'trade' or 'occupational group'. Some jobs, however, will be quite specific; there may be only one or two of them. In any event there will be a *manpower mix* in the organization as a whole – i.e. a combination of abilities and responsibilities.

The manpower mix is further variegated by the age distribution and sex ratio. Moreover, people will be retiring at points in time which can normally be accurately predicted. People also leave for reasons other than retirement, due to death, changing job, pregnancy, redundancy, dismissal. There is a continuous *fall-out* constituting wastage or labour turnover. All these *outflows* affect total manning levels and such *manpower gaps* as arise must be dealt with, preferably in advance of their occurrence. *Manpower surpluses* might also arise – either temporarily or permanently – since the total number of people employed by an organization is never absolute, but will rise and fall as the organization, or any particular part of it, expands or contracts. The dynamism requires predictions of aggregate wastages, calculation of manpower demands and planned action to ensure commensurate manpower supply.

Outflows and inflows change the characteristics of the population employed by the organization. The population is also internally mobile. People rise (or otherwise) in the hierarchy. The first task of manpower planning is to match supply with demand, both quantitatively and qualitatively. If the size of organizations were static and all jobs the same, and if people were interchangeable units, then the process would be simple enough: one of succession and replacement. Complications arise since: people differ in their talents, abilities and aspirations; the age distribution of the manpower stock may be irregular; jobs are not uniform; job content is not static; skill requirements change or become obsolete; new skills emerge; productivity and work loads vary; job groupings and responsibilities change. The whole organizational pattern has a plasticity of form in response to the pressures upon it, both internal and external, and in response to its primary objectives: survival and growth.

Manpower information

Planning requires a good deal of information about the current manpower stock. This is the *manpower audit* and includes biographical details of all employees (up to the most senior level), skills, qualifications, occupational experience and training, performance appraisals and estimates of potential, special talents, career/job aspirations, leaving rates, levels of absenteeism, the age and sex distribution, etc. Most of this information should be available from personnel records, and most large, modern organizations will have computer facilities for its storage and retrieval.

PERSONNEL RECORDS AND INFORMATION SYSTEMS

Employers must keep at least some records about their employees, if only for wage and tax purposes. Although there is a minimum level of recording to be maintained, the needs of the individual firm dictate whatever additional information may be required. Figure 2.1 lists some basic items of personnel information and some of the main forms, documents and returns in common use.

Even small firms need to record the following information on each employee:

- Name, sex, date of birth, address, next of kin
- Date of joining, job, clock number, work location
- Pay code, tax code, national insurance number, hours of work, holiday entitlement
- Sickness, absence, overtime
- Accidents, disciplinary and training records
- Any disability

ACAS (1981) recommended that records should also show the following:

- The numbers and occupations of employees required for efficient production, including future production plans
- How well the age balance of the work force is being maintained
- The rate of labour turnover and retention of key workers
- How many and which employees have the potential for promotion within the organization.

There is no standardization of personnel record systems. Many have gradually evolved. In large corporate enterprises the recording of information and the uses to which it is put are sophisticated. The amount and type of information recorded, stored and analysed will depend on the extent to which it needs to be utilized for manpower or corporate decision-making. Personnel records can provide basic information for manpower plans, policies and procedures. If management knows more about its workforce, it has potential to improve performance and productivity within the business.

Headcounts (by department, division, plant, etc.)
Current vacancies
Staff/employee requisition request forms
Job descriptions
Job specifications
Application forms
Recruitment response rates and cost/effectiveness analyses
Company recruitment literature
Attendance for interview instructions/maps/expense claims
Interview assessment decisions and reasons (especially for race and sex
    discrimination)
Standard letters – acceptance/rejection/consideration
Letters of appointment and engagement notices
Contracts of employment
National Insurance, tax and pensions documentation
Work permits
Register of disabled persons
Clock numbers/ID cards

Employee biographical details
Employer's change of particulars forms
Employee work histories
Performance appraisal and assessment reports
Employee transfer requests
Training records
ITB and YTS returns, records and assessments
Training inspection reports
Labour turnover analyses
Absenteeism and sick pay
Holiday entitlements and hours of work
Health records
Accident statistics
Safety committees – minutes and actions
Health and safety inspection reports and notices
Union agreements
Collective bargains – procedural and substantive agreements
Joint consultation committees – minutes and progress reports
Redundancy agreements
Disciplinary procedures, actions and records
Grievance procedures, actions and records
Pay rates/job grades
Pay changes – dates and rates
Job evaluation reports
Salary progressions
Wage trends (by industry/local area)
Salary surveys
Incentive/bonus schemes
Benefit entitlements – cars, BUPA, etc.
Time-keeping/flexitime arrangements
Suggestion schemes
Organization charts
Succession planning charts
Forward manpower projections
Employment legislation and codes of practice
Termination of employment forms
Exit interview forms
Dismissals – procedures and reasons

Fig. 2.1 *Basic personnel information: forms, documents and returns in common use*

Apart from basic facts – names, addresses, job titles – there are also legal restraints on personnel systems. The introduction of laws or regulations on employment, unfair dismissal, discipline, health and safety, equal pay, sex and race discrimination, have all placed demands on the record system. Certain statistical returns are required for governmental use, for example, levels of earnings, labour turnover, and possibly industrial training.

Large organizations require detailed analyses of their entire workforce, including total wage/salary costs, individual salary progressions, absenteeism, labour turnover, age/sex/grade service profiles, training/development/ performance appraisal data, promotions/career prospects and pensions. For multi-site organizations, information requirements are almost endless – and constantly changing. As the nature of demands on the system and the pattern of enquiries evolves, so too should the record system itself. Systems must be continually monitored and amended where necessary. Otherwise the system will not be responsive, unable to provide current and accurate strategic manpower information. It could also house a museum of redundant data.

'Item' information on every employee is always needed, and such items may include biographical details, training and educational qualifications, and work histories, but users must first specify exactly what items are required.

'Profile' information may also be needed, such as the age distribution of employees, either by grade, position or organization as a whole, the sex distribution, and possibly also distributions of other categories, e.g. graduate trainees, ex-apprentices, or profiles of promotion, career earnings progressions, etc.

Other statistical information must be gathered for decision-making, e.g. labour turnover, absence monitoring and control, manhours lost through strikes and stoppages, etc., and this information must conform with legal requirements recording disciplinary action, accidents, etc.

Some of the information will be utilized regularly. Other enquiries (e.g. demands made on the system) will be *ad hoc*, or to investigate special features.

In the words of Barbara Dwyer (1983) existing systems 'will rarely have been consciously spelled out by any one person or group but will usually have emerged over a period as a result of individual perceptions of gaps or shortcomings in the system'.

Therefore, Dwyer advocates a three step approach:

- Define the general aim of a personnel record system
- Set the objectives for a particular system for the organization
- Specify the records, paperwork and procedures necessary to achieve the objectives.

The larger the organization, the more comprehensive the information required. A central or divisional personnel department has become increasingly concerned with the maintenance of the information data base.

Traditional manual record systems are a clerical chore. Such systems usually require various cards or forms to be completed and kept in filing cabinets. Items have to be recorded and kept up to date. Facts have to be copied from one file to another for different purposes. If the personnel department is fairly large and subdivided into different functional sections, the record system can become extremely complex with greater duplication and a greater chance of incorrect entry and recording. These old systems are extremely inflexible and can become self-perpetuating, although the main problems are poor enquiry facilities. Requests for information usually consume innumerable manhours spent flicking through well-thumbed dockets only to find out-of-date entries, or omissions. The associated delay and possibly inaccuracy in reporting to the original enquirer has often resulted in Personnel developing 'Drucker's syndrome', and quite rightly.

Without information a positive role for personnel management becomes almost untenable, for today's problems, let alone tomorrow's. Information must exist, be accessible and understandable. A good information input can highlight trends and facilitate Personnel's contribution. Manual record systems, except in very small firms, cannot cope.

Personnel managers are looking for automated facilities in a number of areas. Word processing is a regular requirement, especially for standardized letters. Much of recruitment administration and contracts of employment can be routinely dealt with, as can medical and accident records. There is now a growing emphasis (according to the IMS/IPM 1983 Survey 'Towards the Personnel Office of the Future', IMS Report 69) on the administration of performance appraisal and potential appraisal, job evaluation, skill search, salary planning and computer-based training packages. It is in the field of manpower information systems and manpower budgeting that perhaps the greatest scope lies, with regard to both white-collar and blue-collar employers. Manpower costs can be related to various business activities. Whereas retrieval from a conventional filing system relies on either alphabetic or numerical indexation, computers allow data to be retrieved according to a range of factors, either individually or simultaneously. Calculations and comparisons can be quickly produced, regarding, for example, branch workloads, cost information in relation to wages and salaries, the effect of remuneration policies on individual employees' or groups' over time, the costs and effects of different pay negotiation strategies, the costing of domestic awards, the effect of redundancy schemes, etc. These types of analyses facilitate expenditure control and can provide deeper insight into manpower deployment and productivity. Computer modelling enables complex relationships to be examined. Models can be set up for testing the effects of changed circumstances, for example the effects on manpower of a range of specified changes in work methods, or the effect of grade restructuring on career development. Various 'what if?' questions can be answered about the future.

The main reasons given for needing a system, according to a UK survey (Richards-Carpenter, C., 1985) are:

Routine personnel reports 90 per cent
Manpower planning 80 per cent
Salary administration 72 per cent
Ad hoc reports 38 per cent
Industrial relations negotiations 38 per cent

According to a following IMS survey (1983) Personnel are increasingly looking for labour saving programmes. Word processing and absence control mechanisms feature prominently. Growing interest is being shown in administration programmes for the contract of employment (67 per cent by 1984), performance appraisal (52 per cent by 1984), job evaluation (49 per cent by 1984). Of the current applications, the most common is some form of a payroll and pension administration system with, according to the survey, 96 per cent of respondents using one.

Some organizations maintain a totally integrated computerized administrative system. Others simply add on sets of computer tools and techniques as additions to existing systems and procedures in order to solve specific problems. The basic needs are for an administrative system which will replace manual recording and inter-link employee activities, provide key information on a regular basis and offer a system for the analysis of current problems.

The content of the database needs to be considered carefully. What information is *needed*? There is also a need for flexibility and the personnel information system may need to be linked with other items of company information. Speed of information retrieval is obviously essential, but this may vary according to the type of enquiry. Information on individual employees may be accessible immediately; information on selected groups may take some 24 hours. There are also requirements of confidentiality and cost considerations.

One of the initial questions is: who should set up the system? It is possible either to purchase an existing software 'package' or develop a tailor-made one. The organization's own data processing staff will doubtlessly be able to design a system, or use may be made of external bureaux or suppliers. In some instances, personnel staff may wish to design it themselves to be freed from conventional DP constraints. Many personnel managers use an on-line system with VDUs (visual display units), and many personnel departments are responsible for their own data inputs. In recent years there has been an increase in the use of mini- and micro-size systems, at the expense of mainframe use. 'The small microcomputer and an associated set of software packages on the personnel man's desk really do pay off' (Bennison, 1982). It allows him to explore and solve problems.

AN EXAMPLE OF A PERSONNEL COMPUTER SYSTEM IN OPERATION: IBM (UK) — A CENTRALIZED MAIN-LINE SYSTEM

When an employee is first recruited, the line manager responsible completes a starter's voucher with the basic details of the new employee and the job/salary the individual will start at (see Fig. 2.2). One copy is kept for the manager's own file while duplicates are sent to the divisional personnel unit to check the pay and forward the voucher to the central personnel unit for entry into the computer. The basic personnel record for each individual is initiated by this starter voucher. (Sensitive information such as confidential aptitude test results or reference letters are kept in an ordinary paper file.)

Whenever employment is terminated a 'termination' voucher is completed by the line manager and forwarded through the normal channels (see Fig. 2.3).

Additional information on qualifications, experience and other useful

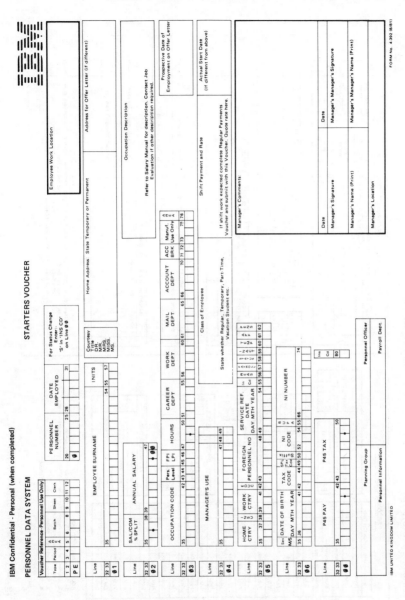

Fig. 2.2   *A starter voucher*

IBM

IBM CONFIDENTIAL – PERSONAL (when completed)
PERSONNEL DATA SYSTEM

TERMINATION VOUCHER

PERSONNEL USE ONLY

Personnel Information Use Only

| Payroll diary |
| Loan |
| DP/OP Salesman |
| Mortgage Guarantee |
| Bank Guarantee |
| C.A.P. |
| Personnel No Register |
| Address Card |
| Term. Report Received |
| T.E.D. sent |
| T.E.D. received |
| Leaver's book |
| Prof. Assoc. |
| 10 year Leaver |
| Medical |
| Reg. disabled |
| I.D. Card Received |

Voucher Reference

Type	Period	Amt	Batch	Sheet	Clerk
	1	2	3	4	5	6		8	9	10	11	12
P	C

Payroll Use Only
EC CT   Trans Country
34 35   36   38
P C   L

Batch Correction
Entry Code
New – Leave Blank
Change – Enter 'C'
Delete – Enter 'D'

Personnel Information Use Only

Payroll Use Only
Accrued Vacation – No. of days
Overtaken vacation – No. of days

PAYROLL ACTION
| Stock Purchase |
| Mortgage |
| Salary Advance |
| NHI Benefit |
| Commission |
| C.A.P. |
| BUPA. |
| V. & V.E. Plan |
| Car Loan |
| Shift |

OP Salesman
10 year leaver
Retirement
Death

ROUTING INSTRUCTIONS
1. Send top two copies (Pink and Blue) to Personnel Information
2. Send Salesman Section Report (Form No. 4-525-1), letter of resignation and Leave Card with these two copies.
3. Retain third copy (White).
4. Send bottom copy to Location Security (Yellow)

IBM United Kingdom Limited

THIS SECTION FOR MANAGER'S COMPLETION
INSTRUCTIONS – Always complete Sections A, B, C, D. Enter Sections E & F as required

MANAGER ALWAYS TO COMPLETE

A
Employee Surname   Inits.   Personnel Number   Date To Be Taken Off Company Payroll
Day Mth Yr
13   18   20   ∅   25 26   31

MANAGER ALWAYS TO COMPLETE

B
Leaving Code
62 63
x

C
No. of Days Taken this year's Vacation Entitlement (include IBM day)
Outstanding Days from Previous Year Vacation Entitlement
Division/Location

MGR. TO COMPLETE AS APPLICABLE
AFTER CONSULTATION WITH DIV.PERS.

D
Period of Payment in Lieu of Notice
Other Payments

DIVISIONAL PERSONNEL SIGNATURE

E
MANAGER TO COMPLETE IF LEAVING CODE = 3, 8
IBM Transfer Country

Manager's Signature   Date

Manager's name (print)

F
MANAGER ALWAYS TO COMPLETE
Address for sending P 45 cards

Manager's Manager's Signature   Date

Manager's Manager's name (print)

IMPORTANT
1. It is the Manager's responsibility to ensure that the employee returns the following to the company prior to leaving:
   (a) Identity Card   (c) Sales and SE Manuals
   (b) Meter Keys   (d) Any other IBM material, publications etc.
2. Employee must sign 'Termination of Employment Declaration on the day of leaving.

Form No. 2 - 706 (8/81)

Fig. 2.3 *A termination voucher*

career information is recorded straight from the original application form. Throughout an employee's subsequent career, each move or promotion or additional skill will be added to those on file. This information is checked every two years by sending a copy of the 'Personnel Information Survey' to each individual employee. The appraisal system is also monitored using the computer data base to 'prompt' overdue reports.

The Payroll utilizes a batch processing system based at Central Office. The system is updated every other day, and all employees are paid monthly in advance. The computer also produces the payslip and organizes the transfer of funds to employees' bank accounts. Changes to an individual employee's salary are made by the line manager using an 'employee profile – current information' computer-printed voucher (Fig. 2.4). The amount of any salary change is entirely under the control of the local line manager. This voucher is then forwarded to the divisional personnel unit for checking before the Central Payroll Group input the changes into the computer. After the computer's files have been amended, a copy of the 'employee profile' voucher with suitable amendment is returned to the line manager. On the back of this sheet is a summary of the career and payroll information for that employee over the previous three years, 'an employee profile – history' (Fig. 2.5). These forms are kept by the line manager to form a basic staff record.

With regard to salary planning, a computer programme has also been developed to assist the company in evaluating the likely cost of any given set of pay rises. Although the line managers control the pay increases for the individual, these are strictly within the guidelines established annually at national level. In this company the current cost of employees' salaries, national insurance and pensions is in excess of £300m per annum and the salary planning model is relied upon to forecast the additional cost of any salary increase to an accuracy of £30 000.

A complex system of security limits access to sections of the personnel unit where the computer terminals are kept. This physical security measure is reinforced by a password procedure which can restrict the user's access to certain predetermined areas of information. There is also a facility for various ad hoc inquiries to be made. These can take the form of a simple enquiry about a specific individual's details which can be dealt with immediately. More complex reports can be generated by the system in 'batch mode' while the operators continue their normal work. With large amounts of information stored on each individual employee, these requests for information can become extremely complicated.

COSTS AND BENEFITS

Any organization which keeps some form of a personnel record system can consider moving to a new computerized one. The additional expenditure and possible benefits from such a development should be closely examined. Costs are a major consideration in the harsh reality of the business world in which the personnel function exists. It is difficult to give actual figures for the likely

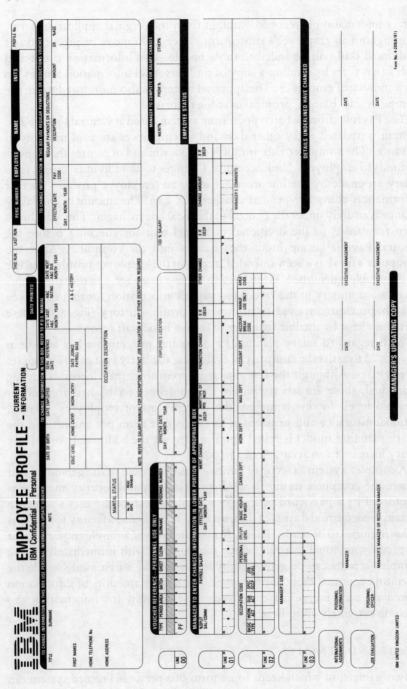

Fig. 2.4 *Employee profile – current information*

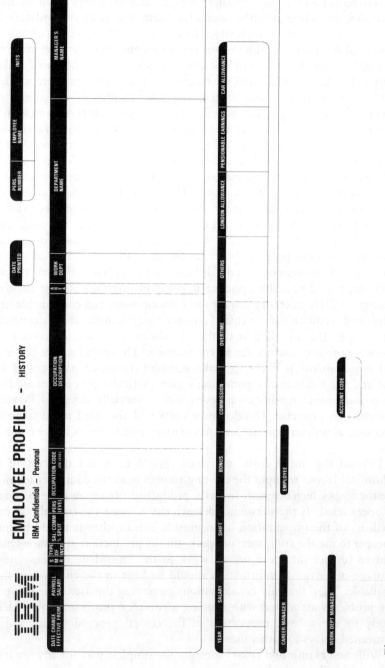

Fig. 2.5 *Employee profile – history*

overall costs involved in computerization because they depend on too many variables, including inflation, size of system; and costs of hardware and software vary with complexity. Two very basic questions should be answered whenever a computerized system is contemplated: how much will it cost? how much is it worth? These two questions should be considered not only before the installation of the system but also when it is operational.

Costs involved in a new system are easier to identify and evaluate in financial terms than possible benefits. The first set of costs consists of direct computer costs. These costs are important even if the organization has a computer already and Personnel are to be one of the many users, for the computer department will have to establish priorities and develop some form of costing policy. These direct costs are normally based on the size of the 'core' used and the time it is occupied. This in turn is dependent on the size of the information data bank and the amount of processing necessary to answer any inquiry. Further to this will be the cost of the hardware used, either within the Personnel department in the number of VDUs used for example, and the amount of peripheral data storage occupied in the computer centre. However, if the computer used is dedicated only to personnel work, the costs will simply be the purchase price of the computer itself and also the associated printers, VDUs, memory storage discs, maintenance and consumable costs. The steady reduction in the cost of microcomputers makes them an attractive alternative. But in addition to their hardware costs are the costs of the software programs which can be considerable. The special nature of Personnel requirements is likely to make standard databased packages of little use and the individual organization's own particular procedures are likely to require some modification, even with a specially designed Personnel information program. Development costs will also need to be taken into account, as will any special accommodation modifications to the computer itself.

Beyond the initial costs, to which should be added the cost of any additional labour to input the existing records onto the computer memory, are the costs which originate from the production of outputs once the system is operational. If the personnel department is using the central computer facilities of the organization or an outside bureau, then it would be much cheaper to use the computer 'off-peak' for the production of routine returns and to restrict the more urgent work to the immediate response mode. Storage of marginal information should be kept to the cheapest medium available. Then the only considerations governing the use of the computer are problems associated with running a complex processing job which is likely to use a large proportion of the central processing unit and the associated delays for other users.

Wille and Hammond (1981) consider the simplest way for any organization to calculate whether computerization is economical is to answer the following four questions:

1   How many people are required to run a manual system?

2 How many would be needed to maintain the desirable extra records a computer system would easily include?

3 How many people would be needed if a computer system were adopted?

4 What are the additional costs involved in using a computer system?

If the cost of $(1)+(2)$ is greater than $(3)+(4)$ then the organization should use a computer system. However, the equation should be more complex than stated, for it should also include some estimation of the benefits due to the computer.

Once the personnel function is freed from routine burdens, personnel specialists can be used more effectively. The introduction of an electronic machine into the personnel system will not *necessarily* make that unit any more effective or *automatically* benefit the organization. There is no guarantee. Information needs to be properly utilized. The organization should look for, and expect, a better service and greater personal attention. High quality information can improve the fair operation of promotion, transfer, training, welfare procedures, and help spot problem areas. The database can be interrogated quickly, but outputs from the system need to be in the format which can answer the questions asked by management within a desired time-scale. A computerized system presents the organization with tremendous opportunity to change its method of working. Tedious chores can disappear for ever. It may also be possible to simplify 'reporting' functions in so far as certain statistical returns will not only be printed by the system, but with all the necessary calculations already done. Decisions and actions can become proactive rather than delayed and reactive.

If the opportunities offered to the personnel function are used to full advantage, then both the organization and the individual should benefit. But little has so far been said of some of the wider implications. Trade unions are apprehensive of computers on a number of counts. At first, unions were concerned for the health and safety of computer operators (although no firm guidelines have been published as to the length of time an employee should use a VDU). But later, more important considerations emerged: security and confidentiality. These aspects have important implications for all the organization's employees. The 'Big Brother' phobia is not unsurprisingly of major concern. The Home Office suggested three areas of potential danger to privacy:

1 Inaccurate, incomplete or irrelevant information

2 The possibility of access to information by people who should not need to have it

3 The use of information in a context or purpose other than that for which it was obtained.

Unions have quite rightly made representations to employers about the inherent dangers in computerized record systems. Some organizations have even made part of the personnel department, a 'restricted area' to prevent access to confidential print-outs. Often organizations have attempted to preempt resistance by consulting unions on the content and purpose of the computer system before it is introduced. So great is the concern over computerized information storage systems that the Government has been forced to act.

The Data Protection Act 1984 represents the Government's response to pressures for legislation to protect the individual from the ever-growing computer data banks. Though the origins of the Bill were with the Younger Committee (established in 1970) and the later Lindop Committee (1975), the precise details owe their origin more to the Council of Europe Convention for the 'protection of individuals with regard to automatic processing of personal data', which the UK signed in 1981. The Act was really introduced not to extend individual freedom, but to protect those business interests which would have been prevented from obtaining information from Europe if Britain had not signed.

Although the legislation does not follow the European Convention entirely, because of religious beliefs, political opinions, racial origins and sexual life, the Act does seek to establish a Registrar with a Register of an estimated 80 000 data users. Data users will have to conform to the eight basic data principles outlined thus (in summary):

1   Data shall be obtained and processed fairly and lawfully.
2   Data shall be held only for one or more specified and lawful purposes.
3   Data held should not be used or disclosed in any manner incompatible with that purpose.
4   Data held shall be adequate, relevant and not excessive in relation to that purpose.
5   Data shall be accurate and up to date.
6   Data held for any purpose shall not be kept for longer than necessary.
7   An individual shall be entitled at reasonable intervals and without undue delay or expense, to be informed by any data user whether he/she holds personal data; and to access data of which he/she is the subject and where appropriate to have such data corrected or erased.
8   Appropriate security measures must be taken to prevent unauthorized access to, or alteration, disclosure or destruction.

If the data user does not meet the required standard, the user will be de-registered, although there is a right of appeal. The implications for the personnel function are that information kept should be readily circulated to the individual employee on a regular basis. Furthermore, the more confidential information on references, appraisal and medical input are not protected at all, provided they are kept in manual form and not on the computer. Further elaboration of the Data Protection Act is given by Greville Janner in Chapter 12.

But some of the impact of computerization on personnel management itself is intangible. Personnel teams will need to undertake a relearning exercise. New procedures are likely to be adopted. People need to become familiar with the various codes and languages. 'It may still be necessary for the personnel director from time to time to use intuitive judgement and to argue unquantified opinion, but the evidence available to him to present his case could now have a hard factual basis and need no longer be entirely founded on his opinion or that of his senior line colleagues. If "information is power", then the balance between Personnel and other functions is in the process of being redressed' (Peach, 1983).

Demand forecasting

A look at any organization shows that it is immediately obvious that people are employed according to the work that needs to be done. There is a direct relationship between work-load and manpower in any given category; this ratio may be constant or changing. If (an assumption) the work-load is properly divided out, if levels of productivity and work methods are appropriate, if the product is constant, if there is no change in the market or in sales volume, if nobody leaves, if everybody is properly trained, if no new developments come along, then manpower planning is unnecessary. Any deviation from the static assumptions listed above requires rational steps to be taken to achieve adjustment once more between jobs and people. There are two ways of doing this. One is to wait until change has occurred. This is what has been termed 'instant planning', reacting to a crisis; it is appropriate only when skill differentials are unpronounced, making job mobility easier, and when untrained people can perform unskilled jobs. Really it is 'zero planning', no longer adequate when one considers the lead-time necessary for training and development, career planning and management succession, potential shortages of skilled personnel, and the long-term budgeting necessary for controlling wage and salary costs as a proportion of overheads. The second way of doing it is to plan in advance, to anticipate changes and initiate remedial action before crises occur.

Manpower is taken on by a firm in response to existing business conditions, tempered by its expectations and confidence in the future. At other times, the workforce may be reduced. There is a direct relationship, albeit delayed, between levels of production and consequent levels of employment. In the upswing of a boom, a firm is likely to experience manpower shortages, especially with regard to 'direct labour'. Initial response to this shortage will be to increase (or initiate) overtime working; this tactic provides for an extra manpower input without extra hiring. As the boom develops, the degree of slack in existing manpower resources becomes stretched; excessive overtime may be unacceptable to workers and also raises employers' costs per unit of output. If hopes run high for the future, expansion necessarily means more recruiting. In the following typical downswing of the trade cycle, a firm is faced with a falling demand for its product and has a manpower strength surplus to requirements. The firm will respond first by a ban on overtime and freeze on recruitment, and as the recession deepens, by varying degrees of curtailment of the workforce, by short-time working, by temporary layoffs, in the expectation that normal levels of natural wastage will help bring the relationship more into equilibrium. Persistent recession and a gloomy outlook will cause a firm to reduce manpower further, this time by redundancies.

Employment follows production and a firm will seek to balance the two. Lessons for manpower planning which may be drawn are first, that controlled variations in the manpower stock *can* be manipulated by *ad hoc* adjustments, but secondly, that expediency only provides short-term solutions. What is really needed is a clear idea of where the firm is going, or likely to go, so that total manpower and the mix of human inputs, can be planned properly and carefully in advance. Fundamentally, the *demand for manpower is a derived demand*. This is the first concept on which company manpower planning is based.

We need to discover how many people need to be working in the organization at successive future periods (say the next 2–4 years) and what jobs will need to be done. As we have seen, the demand for manpower is a derived demand. The second main concept to be considered is that manpower is also an interdependent variable. It is affected by technology, productivity, automation and capitalization, aggregate consumer demand, markets and competition, and industrial rationalization. It is the interaction of so many variables that makes forecasting difficult.

To start with, we must know where the firm is going, or is likely to go. Market research can show whether the market for a particular product or service is growing or contracting, and what percentage share of the market the firm is likely to obtain. In the light of financial and capitalization requirements, profitability and costs, strategic plans can be drawn up for the enterprise as a whole. These fundamental starting points are not personnel activities as such, but part of corporate planning. Long-range planning involves the setting up of organizational objectives in the widest sense and particularly, from our point of view, determining their effects on manpower utilization and development. A Personnel input at the planning stage will be to provide information on the likely availability or otherwise of manpower according to the skills and capabilities needed and the locations where they will be required, estimates of the costs of such manpower for budgeting purposes, and the lead-times which might be necessary to develop people with appropriate levels of expertise. These issues will be more fully discussed when we consider the supply side of the equation. For the moment, the demand side derives directly from long-term corporate objectives. It is advisable that personnel departments be intimately involved in the overall planning process. Before they can get to grips with the essential task of ensuring that the right people are in the right place at the right time, they should be involved with, or at least acquainted with, some of the main methods used to determine the demand forecast.

The simplest way, particularly in smaller firms lacking a sophisticated corporate planning department, when looking to the future and assessing manpower requirements, is to collect the subjective estimates of individual operational managers. One would ask them what effects planned changes in product, output or methods of working would have on their manning requirements. For 'direct' workers, the answers may be more easily arrived at than for 'indirect' workers. Such an approach is inexact, but probably better than doing nothing.

Apart from these subjective possibilities, the application of *work study techniques* can give a more accurate picture of manning standards in situations when there is a standard relationship between manpower and production or services provided. Proposed increases in output, according to standard manning levels and standard labour times, as agreed between management and workforce, can provide more precise quantitative indications of manpower requirements. This is certainly true for direct workers. For indirect workers, one could examine the ratio of direct workers to indirect at various points in the past and extrapolate a trend into the future in relation to planned changes in the numbers of direct workers. This method, known as ratio–trend analysis, although more accurate than relying on guesswork, is of necessity still rather crude and is based on certain assumptions, namely that the past ratios were correct in the first place, and that no other organizational changes need to be made.

More complicated *statistical procedures* are possible, particularly in large-scale organizations where corporate planning is well established and where operations research facilities are available. Basically they consist of relating manpower needs to some other statistical series or indicator. Manpower statistics themselves form a time series. It is therefore possible for any organization or department to plot a histogram of changing manpower levels over time (Fig. 2.6).

From such an exercise it is possible to obtain estimates of likely manpower levels in the future. The approach is of course simplistic. What we really need to do is gain a better understanding of *why* there have been changes in manpower *in the past*. To gain a more accurate assessment of likely changes *in*

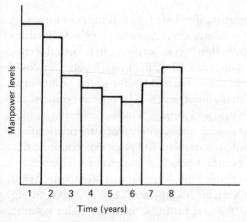

Fig. 2.6 *Histogram of manpower levels*

the future we need to relate manpower to some other measurable factor in which changes have occurred with direct repercussions on manning levels. We have noted already that manpower is interdependently tied up with many other aspects of organizational activities. The third concept we need to consider is *manpower as a dependent variable*, in relation to a *predictor variable*. We could take sales volume as an example and look at past patterns. In order to produce given units of sales, an appropriate level of manpower has been required. We could look at this graphically and plot the two dimensions as in Fig. 2.7. This is known as simple regression. At a time when the volume of sales was OS_1, the level of manpower involved was OM_1. At subsequent points in time, different levels of sales volume were associated with different levels of manpower; there would appear to be a link between them. By visual inspection or by 'least squares' we could draw in a line of best fit between these two variables. We would not expect the relationship between them to be constant, but by continuing the line of best fit (based on past data) into the future, i.e. for anticipated increases in sales volumes, we would have a fairly good indication of total manning levels necessary. What we have plotted is a vector of scores indicating the relationship between the dependent variables (manpower) and the predictor variables (sales).

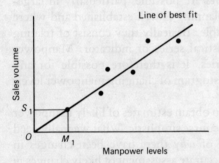

Fig. 2.7 *Relation between manpower (dependent variable) and sales (predictor variable)*

Now we have to realize that organizational life is in fact more complex. A number of factors, not only sales volume, affect manning levels. Capitalization and investment, levels of production, gross turnover in financial terms, profitability, are all dimensions which can affect manning levels. We could obtain a vector of scores on any of these dimensions for given points in an organization's history in relation to manning levels. The relevant dimensions need to be brought together and evaluated jointly. This is known as *multiple regression*. The result is a statistical model embodying structural relationships between manpower levels (dependent variable), and relevant economic data (the predictor variables). It then becomes possible to observe variations in a bank of predictor data (i.e. several relevant dimensions taken collectively) and relate them to the dependent variable 'manpower'. For example, in Fig. 2.8, the relevant dimensions selected are: profit, £ turnover, sales volume, capitalization, technology, and market share. These dimensions are predic-

	1983	1984	1985	1986	1990
Profit	p_1	p_2	p_3	p_4	$\rightarrow p_8$
£ Turnover	t_1	t_2	t_3	t_4	$\rightarrow t_8$
Sales volume	s_1	s_2	s_3	s_4	$\rightarrow s_8$
Capitalization	n_1	n_2	n_3	n_4	$\rightarrow n_8$
Technology	y_1	y_2	y_3	y_4	$\rightarrow y_8$
Market share	m_1	m_2	m_3	m_4	$\rightarrow m_8$
Manpower	M_1	M_2	M_3	M_4	$\rightarrow M_8$

Fig. 2.8   *Time series of predictor variables and dependent variable manpower (M)*

tors on which manpower is assumed to have some degree of dependence. We would plot a time series for each of the predictor variables (p_1, p_2, p_3, p_4 is a vector of scores on profit; and so on for the other variables). We would then look for relationships between the level of manpower in any time period (M_1, M_2, M_3, etc.) and the predictor variables collectively. Thus:

$$M_1 = ap_1 + bt_1 + cs_1 + dn_1 + ey_1 + fm_1 + \Sigma$$
$$M_2 = ap_2 + bt_2 + cs_2 + dn_2 + ey_2 + fm_2 + \Sigma$$

The model assumes that the year 1986 is the present time, and that data is available for the previous four years. Moving into the future, forecasts must be made of the predictors, say until the period M_8, and their combined effects on manpower calculated. On the face of it, a powerful forecasting tool can be built up in this way. There can, of course, be problems. The predictor variables themselves need to be accurately forecast, which is not always easy, since they are themselves dependent on fluctuations in the external environment. There are the underlying assumptions that the basic pattern of manpower utilization has remained stable and will continue to do so, and that the relative power of each predictor will remain constant. The results are quantitative, providing information on gross numbers of people required, but not giving qualitative information on levels of proficiency which may be called for. Furthermore, they make no allowance for the fact that the behaviour of individuals and groups varies. Some organizations have developed statistical measures for relating manpower to other business parameters, e.g. added value per employee, or wages and salaries as a percentage of gross sales revenue. In all, such methods do offer a more systematic and scientific way of estimating manpower needs.

Supply forecasting

The supply of manpower within an organization must be geared to expected demand. The most important role of the personnel department in manpower planning is to take action to meet the demand requirements. Apart from information of the existing manpower situation (the manpower audit, as emphasized earlier), there are three main inputs into the supply forecasting activity:

1　Forecasts of likely wastage (labour turnover).
2　Knowledge of external labour supply.
3　Forecasts of manpower flows through hierarchical levels in the organization according to promotion and development policies (including assessments of qualitative changes in the manpower stock).

FORECASTS OF LIKELY WASTAGE (LABOUR TURNOVER)

People may leave an organization for a variety of reasons at any time. Labour turnover can be categorized in different ways. 'Voluntary' turnover is self-explanatory – people decide to leave for their own personal reasons. 'Involuntary' turnover refers to people leaving due to death, retirement, redundancy, dismissal – circumstances over which they have little individual influence. The term 'natural wastage' is sometimes used to refer to voluntary turnover plus unavoidable involuntary leaving due to death or retirement (but excluding redundancy and dismissal).

MEASUREMENT OF LABOUR TURNOVER

Various measures can be used to quantify turnover rates:

I.　*Actual gross numbers* of people leaving provide a basis for recruitment and give direct indications of variations (and shortages) in manpower establishments. Gross numbers indicate overall changes in headcount. However, for purposes of comparison (e.g. between different organizations or departments, or between different points in time) an index is needed thus:

II.　*Crude Labour Turnover Rate* expresses turnover as a percentage of the number of people employed.

$$\frac{\text{No. of leavers (in 1 year)}}{\substack{\text{Average no. of people employed} \\ \text{(in the same year)}}} \times 100 = \% \text{ labour turnover}$$

This is the standard measurement for labour turnover (the BIM index). It is normally quoted as an annual rate, but can be used for other periods (e.g. quarterly or monthly). The main weakness of the measure is that it provides no information about the length of service of people leaving – for instance, they may have been employed for a long time or they may have recently joined and quit quickly. A rapid movement of short-term employees (fringe turnover) can seriously inflate the turnover figure (e.g. 400 per cent) when in reality there may be a hard core of stable, long-term employees.

Labour turnover is a measure of 'wastage' and is therefore a variable (which may or may not be constant) in the internal manpower supply of the organization. The term 'labour turnover' itself and the crude labour turnover index only give a partial indication of what is really going on in the labour force – they refer to the process of 'leaving' but give no indication of 'joining' or 'staying'. More widely defined labour turnover is a 'process of change in the composition of the labour force' (Bryant, 1972). It is therefore useful also to measure labour stability.

III. *Labour stability.* Assuming there has been no change in standard manning, the stability of the labour force over a period of time (usually 1 year) can be measured by the use of another simple formula:

$$\frac{\text{No. of employees with 1 or more years' service}}{\text{No. of people employed at the beginning of the year}} \times 100 = \% \text{ stability}$$

A reading over a period of at least one year is necessary to provide a fair representation of the true state of affairs, but longer periods can be taken if the data are available and it is felt that there has been a series of temporary short-term fluctuations in these rates during the year under review which tend to give a distorted picture.

A crude labour turnover figure of 5–10 per cent in any occupation would normally be regarded as good. The lower the labour turnover figure is, the better. The converse is true of the stability index; a higher figure indicates a highly stable workforce (e.g. 85 per cent).

In addition to these standard measures, there are a few others which can be useful for more detailed analysis or for research purposes.

IV. *Fringe turnover rate.* Whereas the labour stability index effectively provides a measure of the staying power of the workforce, the fringe turnover rate can calculate the percentage turnover of short-term workers; it can be used to distinguish the number of people who join and quit quickly from the overall turnover figure provided by the Crude Labour Turnover Index:

$$\frac{\text{No. of employees who joined and left within 1 year}}{\text{Average number employed during the year}} \times 100$$
$$= \% \text{ fringe turnover}$$

V. *Half-life survival rate.* Strictly speaking, the Labour Stability Index shows the number of people surviving as a percentage of the total workforce. The half-life survival rate can be ascertained by taking that point at which half of a group of entrants (i.e. a cohort) who joined at the same time had left; in other words, it is the median length of service. We could then compare the half-life survival rate of different cohorts. This kind of analysis has particular utility if we are considering the staying power of a group of newly joined trainees or cohorts of recruits. The half-life survival rate (whether shorter or longer) provides a better basis for comparison between different groups.

VI. *Angela Bowey's Stability Index*. Angela Bowey has developed several measures of stability. Her best-known stability index can help a company decide at what level it is desirable for wastage to occur.

Too high a stability rate (as conventionally measured) may be an indication that the manpower establishment is becoming top heavy, e.g. the average age may be rising, and within the manpower staff there may be an incipient 'retirement cohort'. Angela Bowey's index is a measure of 'over stability':

$$\frac{Ln}{\frac{1}{2}NK}$$

where: Ln = total length of service of all present employees in years

N = total numbers of employees at present

K = the number of years between average recruitment age and average retirement age.

Optimum stability is thought to be achieved when the entire labour force is just replaced within the normal working life span. When the result of the application of the above formula is less than 1, the work force, according to Angela Bowey, is unstable, because it cannot achieve an optimum rate for labour replacement. If the result is greater than 1, an over-stable workforce is indicated. In other words, there is an inadequate infusion of new blood to sustain the organization in the future. This specific kind of analysis has particular utility for considerations of management succession.

SURVIVAL AND WASTAGE CURVES

Various aspects of labour turnover can be depicted graphically as survival and wastage curves.

The relationship of labour turnover to length of service may be represented by a survival curve which plots the rate of leaving over a given period (say 3 months) as a proportion of an original group of entrants (or cohort), as in Fig. 2.9. Typically such a graph shows more rapid turnover in the first few months than it does later on. Such a curve could also highlight for us the half-life survival rate. We can see at a glance how long it takes for half of an original cohort to have left.

Survival curves can be drawn for any large group of employees. It can measure how successful any section or department is in retaining new intakes. A survival curve, however, may not accurately reflect the general or continuing pattern of turnover because it focuses on a single cohort. An alternative trend may be obtained from a *wastage curve*. This measures the *crude wastage index* against the age of employees. For each age group, the

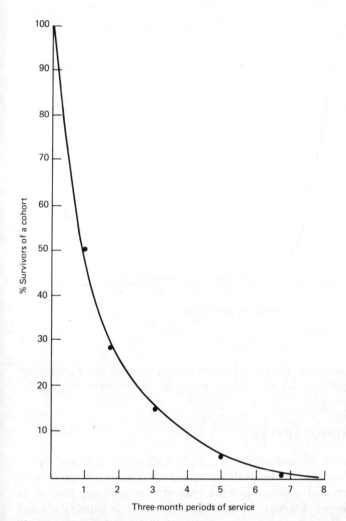

Fig. 2.9 *Survival curve*

Crude Wastage Index is calculated and plotted as a percentage on the graph. Typically, wastage curves peak in the first years of employment, fall to a fairly steady low between the 30–50 year age groups and rise again approaching normal retirement age, as in Fig. 2.10. Similarly crude wastage could be plotted against length of service.

From measuring labour turnover we are provided with a monitor of current wastage which can be compared with past patterns of leaving, but more particularly can form the basis for predicting the trend in the future (by extrapolation), and to which we can further add subjective estimates about the effect on turnover of any planned changes in working practices, or effects of movements in external wage rates or alternative employment opportunities. We are then provided with indications for recruitment targets to

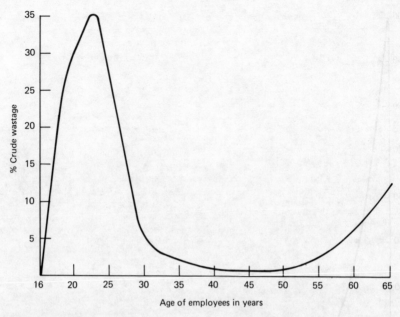

Fig. 2.10 *Wastage curve*

compensate for wastage. The rate of turnover is a pertinent factor governing the internal supply of labour; indeed it is one of the main engines of manpower planning.

EXTERNAL LABOUR SUPPLY

Apart from wastage, the internal labour supply is ultimately governed by the external labour market. Qualitatively and quantitatively, people can only be recruited and retained if the employing organization is competitive in its terms and conditions of service. So much is well known, as indeed is the fact that it must remain in this competitive position. But to do so requires (a) a knowledge of existing affairs in the labour market, be it local or national, and (b) an assessment of how things are likely to develop in the future. One needs to know where competition for labour will come from, when, its likely effect on one's own recruitment and wastage, the likely movement in wage rates, changes in alternative employment opportunities and possible skill shortages. The future availability of labour can prove a vital factor to the success or failure of a business.

Manpower flows

People in any organization are part of a dynamic system which is constantly changing in shape, size and direction. The structure of the organization defines the aggregate number of people employed and the way in which they are deployed. The total stock of people consists of a series of sub-stocks (people employed in various grades and classifications). There is a 'flow' of people moving through the organization overall (by joining and leaving) and through the various grades or sub-classifications (by promotion). The manpower system is characterized by a series of flows which may be measured by the length of service in any given grade (rate of promotion) or by other methods (e.g. salary progressions or job evaluation points). For the purposes of manpower planning it is therefore necessary to construct models of aggregate flows of manpower through the organization and within it. The techniques for attempting this are of a statistical nature, but we should consider some of the main principles, particularly deterministic and stochastic methods.

DETERMINISTIC METHODS

The most commonly used deterministic method is the construction of a stationary population model which examines the approximate relationship between the rates of promotion and wastage by grade and employee strength. The method itself is derived from actuarial techniques (e.g. the use of life tables) and is based on a census system, looking at a cross-section of the organization at a particular point in time. Although there are weaknesses in this approach since it does not take account of possible changes in the overall or internal shape or size of the organization, it is nevertheless worthy of examination because it highlights some of the problems involved. Such a model is, however, more useful when one is considering what is sometimes known as a 'closed system', in which recruitment only takes place at one level (at the bottom) or at very few other fixed points, where there are clearly defined internal grades which largely coincide with age or length of service, and where there is a consistent policy of promotion from within – for example, organizations such as the armed services, police force, Civil Service, or the clearing banks.

STOCHASTIC METHODS

The organization constantly seeks to renew itself, since it is faced with the problem of loss (of manpower). Stochastic methods are statistical techniques which explore various possibilities, predict outcomes, and therefore serve as an aid to optimal decision-making. They tend to become highly complicated and are the province of persons trained in operations research. The stochastic method is to construct a renewal model for the whole organization including its grading system, sometimes using Markov chain theory and sometimes renewal theory. Renewal theory which considers the replacement of items subject to loss, looks at the organization from the top downwards; it is a 'pull' system which commences with the higher levels. Unlike Markovian chain theory, it assumes that grade sizes are fixed. The essential thinking behind Markovian chain theory is that the stock of manpower changes over time and that there are fixed probabilities of the flows between grades; it commences at the lower levels and is a 'push' system. These flows, as we have seen, emanate from the processes of recruitment, wastage and promotion. All these processes are to an extent controllable, recruitment more so than the other two. Manipulation of the grading system can be used to control rates of promotion. The Markov chain theory describes the effects of changes in a graded manpower system where the flows between grades are governed by 'transition probabilities', and where the composition of each grade is regarded as homogeneous, i.e. each member has the same probability of making any particular transition. The movements between the grades (or states) are expressed as probabilities. It is therefore possible to explore the potential outcome of various manpower strategies coupled with variations in the grading structure over time. Such models are based on probabilities, not averages (as in deterministic models) and include an element of uncertainty. Stochastic models are more sophisticated, and are particularly useful in fast-changing environments. Since in most organizations there tends to be a combination of 'push' and 'pull' flows, computer models have been developed which incorporate both sorts of movement. Such models are known as 'push-pull' models (Bramham, 1983).

MANPOWER SYSTEMS

An organization is very similar to a 'population pyramid'. For any society of people, such as a nation, a population pyramid can be constructed to show the number of people in existence in relation to age (from birth to death). Figure 2.11 depicts such a pyramid showing as it would normally total numbers divided between the two sexes. Indeed, the two curves bounding each side of this diagram could also in fact be taken to represent wastage – they depict

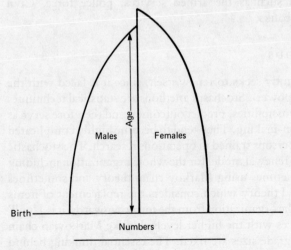

Fig. 2.11   *Population pyramid*

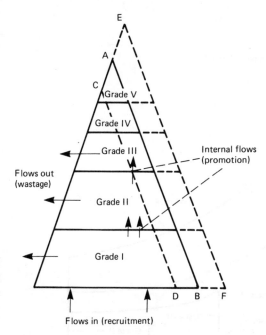

Fig. 2.12   *Flows in a manpower system*

decreasing numbers in the total population over time. An aspect of a 'population pyramid' is that wastage is slow at first and increases as age advances. It is not quite the same in organizational life where the rate of leaving is usually higher in the early stages and gradually diminishes until the point of retirement. However, the principle of continuing wastage and outflow persists.

Another difference between a population pyramid and an organization is that in an organization wastage rates may not follow a smooth trend, but fluctuate; and an organization, or any part of it, may move rapidly from the status quo into expansion or contraction.

Figure 2.12 represents flows in a manpower system. Here, the rate of recruitment or replacement will depend on three main variables:

1   the overall rate of wastage, which in turn influences
2   the overall rate of promotion, and
3   changes in the overall size of the organization (by expansion or contraction) as indicated by a move in the diagrammatic perimeter of the organization from the line AB to CD (contraction) or to EF (expansion).

We can now relate this kind of thinking to manpower planning. The manpower system depicted in Fig. 2.12 (i.e. in effect an organizational population pyramid) could be represented in a different way. It could be redrawn as a conventional 'survival curve' (of the type considered earlier in Fig. 2.9) as shown in Fig. 2.13.

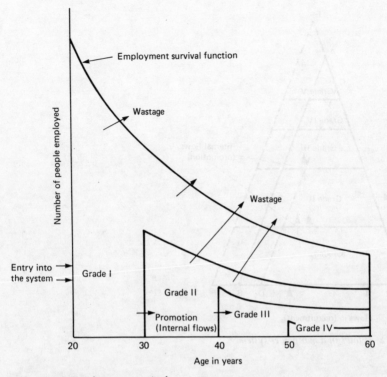

Fig. 2.13 *Employment survival*

The survival function is again downward sloping and the area under the curve represents the number of people employed (i.e. the manpower stock). The manpower stock will be divided into a number of grades, with fewer people employed in the more senior grades than in the junior ones. For simplicity the diagram depicts an organization containing only four grades, and assumes that people are recruited at the age of 20 years and retire at 65 years. The immediately observable facts illustrated by this diagram are:

1   All people enter the system into Grade I (at age 20);
2   Some people (according to subsequent performance) will be promoted to Grade II;
3   There are more people employed in Grade I than any other grade; the manpower stock of each successive grade becomes smaller.

The immediate manpower problems which arise are:

1   How many people need to be recruited *now* to maintain the establishment strength of Grade I, allowing for wastage of the existing stock, and how many will need to have potential for promotion to Grade II? The same line of thinking must be applied to a consideration of each successive grade.

2   On the assumption of a predictable rate of labour turnover (wastage) appropriate numbers can be recruited, but it may not quite work out so

smoothly in practice. At various times over the next few years wastage might fluctuate; at times there might also be recruitment difficulties. Either of these contingencies could be triggered by changes in the external environment over which the firm has no control.

3 The whole model rests on the assumption that the organization will not change in gross size and the relationships between internal grades will remain constant (i.e. effectively over a 45 year period) – it is a stationary population model.

Let us consider the effects induced by changes in the level of wastage *and* difficulties in recruitment. If for a period of years the external labour market tightens and new recruits are hard to find because of better alternative earnings and opportunities elsewhere, the organization's intake of manpower is reduced and its activities must contract (to the extent that the shortfall cannot be made up by the use of overtime, part-time working, or revision of work practices). The smooth survival function in Fig. 2.13 becomes distorted. After the period mentioned there will be considerably fewer young people in the organization than before and the shape of our curve will look rather more as in Fig. 2.14, where the area D represents the deficiency in the originally planned intake.

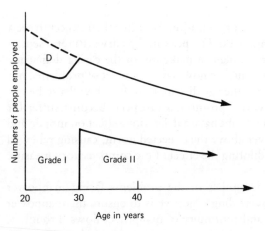

Fig. 2.14

This situation creates serious problems for the future and for the present. The deficiency will be an on-going problem and must be rectified as soon as possible. Whilst there will be better promotion prospects for younger employees, it may not be a good thing for the organization if the criteria for entry into Grade II are not met by a sufficiently large proportion of younger people, and decisions will then have to be made whether to reduce standards or cut back on the number of Grade II jobs.

Assuming that rectification takes the form of expanding the intake as soon as the labour market permits (or by offering increased rewards), in order to

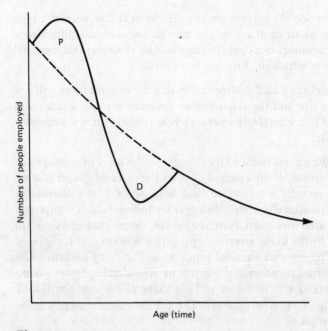

Fig. 2.15

re-establish the overall size of the organization, we must then expect to see a bulge in our schedule as in Fig. 2.15. The peak in the curve (P) represents a compensatory increase in recruitment to make up for the earlier deficiency (D). Having made this adjustment, we now have a new set of problems, not least of which is an imbalance in the age distribution, which will also be ongoing. In the short run, however, promotion prospects become stiffer for newer entrants, which will no doubt have a deleterious effect on morale and possibly inflate labour turnover above the expected norm, causing renewed pressure on recruitment and diluting the effect of the compensatory measure in the first place.

From this simple model a number of the problems facing manpower planners can be seen; their overriding objective is to ensure the manpower survival of the organization and continuity of manpower flows through it. Monitoring flows and wastage is clearly important, to highlight movements in the supply side of the manpower equation.

Reconciliation of demand and supply

An essential part of manpower planning is the reconciliation of demand forecasts with supply. The process of reconciliation should first throw up discrepancies between manpower demand and supply projections, and secondly point to *action plans* to optimize the best demand/supply fit. Figure 2.16 represents diagrammatically the 'marriage' of both projections.

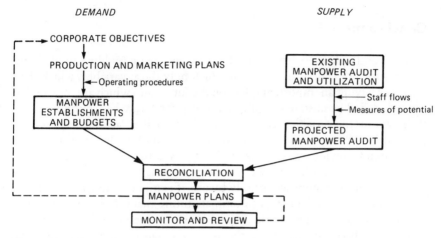

Fig. 2.16   *The manpower planning process: reconciliation of demand and supply*

Action plans should be formulated for recruitment targets or limits, promotion policies, estimates of wastage or redundancy, training and development needs. As these plans are subsequently put into effect, progress should be continuously monitored to ensure targets are being met, and to make any adjustments to revised targets as necessary. In effect, the whole operation becomes an on-going rolling plan.

Manpower maps

How far ahead can one look? Accuracy obviously decreases the further one probes into the future. No one can predict the precise rate and direction of economic, political, social and technological change, all of which impinge on the organization. Short-range plans are easier to formulate than long-range plans. But the resourcing side of personnel management must rest on as firm a foundation as possible. Recruitment, selection, training, promotion must all be geared to the needs of the organization.

It should be clear that manpower models can be used to project manpower supply given assumptions about grade sizes, patterns of wastage, promotion, transfers and recruitment policies. A weakness is that the more sophisticated methods have tended to underemphasize non-quantifiable factors. The Institute of Manpower Studies sees the process as one of drawing 'maps' for manpower decisions (Bennison, 1985, Bennison and Casson, 1984).

Single forecasts of the number of jobs needed are not enough. It is essential to find trends which have a practical meaning – i.e. the repercussions of changes in business activity on staffing – in order to clarify manpower decisions. A manpower map may then be constructed by running a suitable model on any combination of factors to assess their combined effect on the decision.

Conclusions

Until recently planners have tended to concentrate on building models and systems for predicting the future in which only those variables which they regard as having an important effect on the future and which are measurable are included. The unstated assumption is that the future has continuity with the past; thus the variables selected are those which the *planner* considers have previously influenced the system and the relationships between them are those found previously. One example of this is the use of the current or extrapolated relationships between wastage and length of service and grade in predicting future manpower supply by use of computer models. Another is the use of ratio-trend analysis to estimate future manpower numbers. The really important changes in the future, however, are the events and trends which are discontinuous with the past and which therefore cannot be predicted by planners' models (Holroyd, 1980).

It may well be that manpower planning will demonstrate that corporate manpower objectives are *not* achievable. In that case, the exercise was most certainly worth while.

'. . . Mismatches of people and jobs, redundancy programmes unrelated to future manpower requirements, and the inability of many managers to determine accurately manpower requirements in times of recession and expansion are some of the failures which underlie the need for manpower planning to be considered by personnel managers in the recessionary conditions of the 1980s' (Smith, 1982).

Summary

Manpower planning is a branch of corporate planning. An organization consists of a stock of manpower and a variable manpower mix. The planning process begins with establishing forecasts for the anticipated demand for various types of labour, skills, roles and positions required throughout the organization over a given period of time. The approach is systematic. Changes in manpower requirements emanate from changes in corporate size and scope according to anticipated expansion or contraction in response to the markets for which goods or services are provided by the firm.

The demand for manpower is a derived demand. Manning levels are interrelated with other organizational activities. Estimates of manpower can be calculated in various ways, often by assessing it as a dependent variable in relation to a predictor variable or a bank of predictor variables. If the predictor variables can be accurately forecast and the relationship between the predictor and manpower is known, manpower projections can be devised.

An essential part of the process is matching or reconciling supply and demand. Fundamentally, manpower planning seeks to measure and make this adjustment. An assessment must therefore be made of the supply side of the equation. The internal supply of manpower is affected by various flows of people within the organization and by wastage. Supply can be modified through planned recruitment, training, development, career progression. Within the organizational hierarchy, the grading structure and rates of progression need to be established.

The start-up, administration and monitoring of a manpower planning system requires a good database of personnel employed and on manpower flows. It is difficult to establish a perfect system. Forecasts have to be made on shifting bases even in a relatively stable situation and there are therefore differences in accuracy between short-term and long-term planning. Statistical techniques can help but these can become complicated and are really the province of operations research management. Manpower planning is ongoing and leads to the creation of adjustable rolling plans.

Manpower planning is about evolution, about organizational adaptation. Its purpose is to make effective use of manpower over time. Its procedures are scientific, but it is in the end an exercise in the art of the possible. Paucity of basic information, shifts in managerial priorities, errors in corporate planning data, procrastination in tackling potential problems, inadequate or piecemeal setting of targets, failure to update and respond, all reduce the effective power of the techniques. It is not something which can be done once and forgotten about. It requires constant attention, commitment and vigilance.

Discussion questions

1 In what ways do you think manpower planning techniques might develop?
2 Without manpower planning, on what other bases could personnel resourcing policies be geared?
3 How would you set up and develop a manpower planning system in your own organization?
4 Devise a personnel record system relevant to your own organization.
5 Consider the various personnel activities which might in the long term be computerized.

References

ACAS (1981), *Personnel Records*, Advisory Booklet No. 3, Advisory, Conciliation and Arbitration Service, London.
BENNISON, M. (1980), *The IMS Approach to Manpower Planning*, Institute of Manpower Studies, Report No. 8.
BENNISON, M. (1982), 'The new opportunities for personnel', in *Computers in Personnel*, Institute of Personnel Management and Institute of Manpower Studies.
BENNISON, M. (1985), 'Manpower planning' in Livy, B. *Management and People in Banking*, 2 edn, Chartered Institute of Bankers, London.

BENNISON, M. and CASSON, R. J. (1984), *The Manpower Planning Handbook*, McGraw-Hill, London.

BRAMHAM, J. (1983), 'Manpower planning', in Guest, D. & Kenny, J. (eds), *A Textbook of Techniques and Strategies in Personnel Management*, Institute of Personnel Management.

BRYANT, D. (1972), 'Recent Developments in Manpower Research', *Personnel Review*, 1, 3.

DWYER, B. (1983), 'Developing and maintaining personnel records', in Guest, D. and Kenny, J. (eds), *A Textbook of Techniques and Strategies in Personnel Management*, Institute of Personnel Management.

FORBES, A. F. and McGILL, D. (1985), *Understanding Wastage*, Institute of Manpower Studies, Report CN426.

HOLROYD, P. (1980), 'Future research: new directives', *Long-Range Planning*, Vol. 13.

IPM/IMS (1983), *Computers in Personnel: Towards the Personnel Office of the Future*, IMS Report 69, Institute of Personnel Management and Institute of Manpower Studies.

PEACH, L. (1983), 'Computers in personnel', Chairman's Address, in IMS Report 69, *Towards the Personnel Office of the Future*, Institute of Personnel Management and Institute of Manpower Studies.

RAJAN, S. (1984), *New Technology and Employment in Insurance, Banking and Building Societies*, Institute of Manpower Studies Series, Gower Press, London.

RICHARDS-CARPENTER, C. (1985), 'The changing state of computers in personnel', in *Computers in Personnel*, Institute of Personnel Management and Institute of Management Studies.

SMITH, R. A. (1982), *Corporate Manpower Planning*, Gower.

WILLE, E. & HAMMOND, V. (1981), *The Computer in Personnel Work*, Institute of Personnel Management.

PART TWO

Recruitment and Selection

CHAPTER 3

Job analysis, description and specification

by Bryan Livy

According to the British Standards Institution, job analysis is 'the determination of the essential characteristics of a job' (BSI, 1979). Since 'an organization structure consists of the work necessary to achieve the organization's objectives, divided into job-sized pieces, held together by a network of contacts and procedures between jobs and sub-units' (Fowler, 1985), job analysis is a fundamental activity and a basic requisite for a range of personnel activities, for example:

Organization planning and role definition
Manpower planning
Manpower utilization and deployment
Recruitment, selection and placement
Criterion development
Performance appraisal and assessment
Training and development
Career planning, promotion and transfers
Pay determination, job evaluation, grading and classification
Job design, work restructuring, methods of work
Industrial relations
Job descriptions
Job specifications
Personnel research

Recent developments in job analysis techniques have tried to get away from the traditional narrative descriptions of what gets done, and to describe jobs more in behavioural terms. Most of these approaches are American in origin.

One of the most important contributions has come from the US Department of Labor (1974) which defines job analysis 'as any process of collecting, ordering and evaluating work, or worker-related information. The information may reflect job content, expressed in terms of specific work activities and procedures, or it may consist of the worker characteristics (skills, knowledge, aptitudes, tolerances, etc.) required for adequate job performance'.

The distinction between job-oriented and worker-oriented aspects is quite clear. The former are 'descriptions of job content that have a dominant association with, and typically characterize, the *technological* aspects of jobs and commonly reflect what is achieved by the worker. On the other hand, worker-oriented elements are those that tend more to characterize the generalized human behaviors involved'.

In short, job analysis is a process of investigation to identify a job's core components. The investigation has two aspects:

1 Task-oriented analysis   – to identify duties, responsibilities, work methods, etc.
2 Worker-oriented analysis – to   identify   behavioural   characteristics required of the worker for successful performance.

In different parts of the world there are correspondingly different approaches to job analysis, work measurement and job or occupational nomenclature. The British Standards Institution acknowledges that 'some ambiguities exist in the meanings conveyed by such terms as "job", "task", "operation" and "element" and their relationship to one another'. The Institution defines the term as follows:

'Job:
1 All the tasks carried out by a worker or group of workers in the completion of their prescribed duties and grouped together under one title (or definition).
2 A defined area of accountability within an organization.

Task:
An identifiable part of a job, comprising a combination of operations.

Operation:
1 The smallest unit of work used for a planning or control purpose.
2 A combination of elements.

Element:
A distinct part of an operation selected for convenience of observation, measurement and analysis.'

The semantics used by various organizations and authorities differ, but should not be allowed to obscure the crux of the matter which is basically this: to define the scope of the job and its ingredients.

Reasons for undertaking job analysis are manifold, and there are various ways of carrying out the investigation. It should be apparent, therefore, that the end purpose for which the information is to be used, must be borne in mind from the very beginning. For example, the sort of information which is necessary for job evaluation may differ from the sort of information which may be useful for personnel selection, or for the identification of training needs, or for work restructuring. The point of any investigation is to find answers to the things about which questions will be asked (i.e., values and judgements about work content, skills, etc.) in the context of any particular personnel management activity (Gael, 1983). Since there can be such a wide variety of applications for the findings of job analysis, the depth, extent and degree of detail will be dependent upon the requisites of the end purpose. Nevertheless, the basic process of eliciting information is common.

Sifting the important from the trivial aspects of a job during and after the analysis is really what the whole exercise is about. Attention finally should be directed at the significant attributes of the jobs, having first collected all the relevant information necessary to form a complete picture of any particular unit of work. A common danger is to collect too much information, making it difficult to see the wood for the trees. On the whole this is a more common pitfall than making just a cursory examination and ending up with a sketchy, incomplete picture. In making the analysis, if a fact is unimportant, it should immediately be discarded. To this end, the scaling procedures (as outlined in point 7 below) are useful.

Before beginning a job analysis exercise, it is desirable to clarify the relationship of one job to another, the number of *discrete* jobs which actually exist, and the exact *boundaries* of responsibilities, tasks, and duties involved in a job. If a work unit, or an office, employs say, 100 people doing *exactly the same job*, then the analysis need not be done 100 times, but basically only once, supported by a small number of corroborative analyses to ensure the accuracy and validity of the findings. A composite job analysis programme is therefore not geared to the total number of employees, but to the total number of discrete and identical jobs. Having delineated a particular 'job' (i.e., what one person actually *does*, either as an individual or as part of a team) the main analysis is to identify and assess its various parts. Procedurally, the process can be broken down into a number of main steps (charted in Fig. 3.1) thus:

The Main Steps in the Process of Job Analysis
A: *Task-oriented aspects*
1   *Who* does the job? What is the job title?
2   *What* does the job entail? What is the nature of the work? Identify and isolate, for the purposes of study:
  (i) *the component tasks*
      Some of these tasks may consist of a number of sub-tasks (operations or elements in BSI terminology)
  (ii) *the duties performed*
      some of these duties may be *regular* and others *occasional*
  (iii) *the responsibilities*
      responsibility for assignments of work, for the work of others;
      responsibilities for money, plant and equipment, materials;
      the exercise of discretion and judgement;
      planning, decision making, communications
3   *How* is the job carried out? How are the tasks and duties performed? What methods are used to accomplish the job? Are tasks performed in

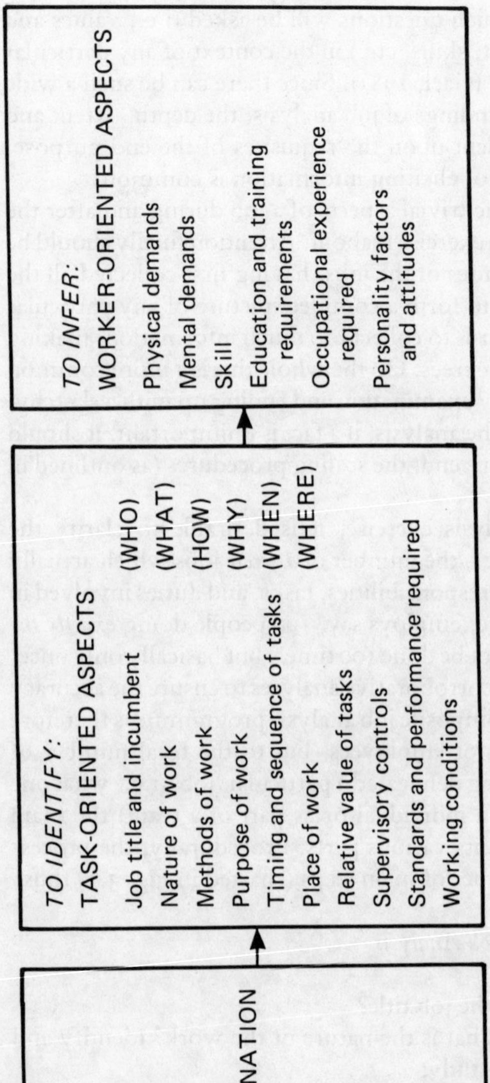

JOB ANALYSIS
is the
SYSTEMATIC EXAMINATION
of
WORK

TO IDENTIFY:
TASK-ORIENTED ASPECTS

Job title and incumbent   (WHO)
Nature of work   (WHAT)
Methods of work   (HOW)
Purpose of work   (WHY)
Timing and sequence of tasks   (WHEN)
Place of work   (WHERE)
Relative value of tasks
Supervisory controls
Standards and performance required
Working conditions

TO INFER:
WORKER-ORIENTED ASPECTS

Physical demands

Mental demands

Skill

Education and training
requirements

Occupational experience
required

Personality factors
and attitudes

Fig. 3.1   The job analysis process

isolation, or as part of a team effort? What machines, materials and instruments are used? In what order are the various operations executed?

4 *Why* are tasks and duties performed as they are? What is the purpose of each? What is the relationship of each task to other tasks and to the whole job? How does each part fit into the total operation?

5 *When* are tasks and duties performed? What is the sequence of events? How often are tasks and duties performed? How is their incidence related to the work system, machine pacing, procedures, etc.? When are various responsibilities exercised?

6 *Where* are tasks and duties performed? In what locations or work stations?

7 The *relative* values of tasks, duties and responsibilities one to another, by *scaling* each of them according to their
  (i) difficulty
  (ii) frequency
  (iii) importance

8 To whom is the worker responsible? What are the supervisory/managerial controls, policies, procedures, instructions, reporting systems? What are the limits of the individual jobholder's discretion?

9 To what standards of performance? What are the standards of accuracy, tolerance, proficiency or competence required? Are there any on-the-job training arrangements?

10 *The prevailing working conditions* should be noted, in respect of the physical, social and financial aspects of the job.
  (i) *Physical environment* (temperature, noise, dirt, danger, work in restricted spaces, awkward working positions, comfortable office facilities etc.)
  (ii) *Social environment* (whether the work is isolated or in the company of others, in teams or shifts, whether affecting domestic or family life, etc.)
  (iii) *Financial conditions* (basic wage rate or salary, any bonus, incentive schemes, fringe benefits, etc.)

Basic analysis can be provided by answers to the who? what? how? why? when? where? questions posed in items 1–6. A more detailed interpretation can be gained by making assessments of the relative values of the main job components, the supervisory controls, and standards of performance required, as in items 7–10. It will be noted that all these items are task-oriented. Answers to them provide a bald statement of the bare bones of the job (in fact, a job description).

The second part of the analysis, items 11–16, moves on to determine the behavioural or worker-oriented requirements of a job – i.e. personal qualities necessary (in fact, a job specification).

B: *Worker-oriented aspects*

11 *Physical demands*

(e.g. muscular energy, stamina, sedentary work, travel, hours of work, appearance, bearing, speech, any basic medical requirements, etc.)

12 *Mental demands*

(e.g. (i) intellectual demands of the job, and (ii) knowledge required.)

(i) Intelligence. It may be observed that a job requires intellectual demands appropriate, say, to holders of a university degree, or more generally that the job requires 'average', 'below average' or 'above average' intelligence. Any specific intellectual demand (e.g. verbal or numerical ability, proficiency in foreign languages, problem-solving abilities, should also be noted).

(ii) The knowledge component of a job should also be assessed at this stage (i.e. know-how, as distinct from intelligence) at least in general terms, although further elaborated under the heading of 'education and training', itemized below.

13 *Skills*

(i) Psychomotor skills, if relevant, especially in regard to speed and accuracy.

(ii) Social skills which form an important part of many jobs, e.g. contact with others, leadership, supervision, communications.

14 *Education and training*

Formal education and training necessary to perform the job should be specified explicitly wherever possible, together with any formal qualifications required.

15 *Occupational experience*

Some jobs call for considerable occupational experience, previously held levels of responsibility, control or decision-making, others not. Sometimes it is possible to quantify this factor in terms of a given number of years, but an assessment of the levels and depth of experience (i.e. types of job and previous background) may be adequate.

16 *Personality factors and attitudes*

(e.g. such things called for in the job as the ability to work through other people, to provide leadership, to initiate, to work without close supervision, to possess a degree of extroversion, or the kind of temperament to cope with dull, routine procedures, etc.)

This approach to job analysis has been in two parts, first a factual summary of the job content, and secondly an appraisal of worker-oriented inputs. The second part identifies many of the attributes which should be included in a job specification; the first part identifies the basic data for a job description.

A *job description* is a written statement of the main duties and responsibilities which a job entails, i.e. a 'job profile', or according to the BSI 'a written outline of the main tasks of a job'. Job descriptions are used fundamentally in organization planning, job grading and evaluation, job design, and form the basis for personnel selection procedures. The British Institute of Management (1979) states, 'their chief function is to describe the purpose of a job', and for that reason the description is task-oriented. A *job specification*, which reflects the worker traits brought to bear on the job, is sometimes referred to as a 'person specification' – a list of criteria in terms of the personal capacities and inclinations deemed necessary for successful job performance – i.e. a 'person profile'. A job specification is therefore a key instrument in personnel selection and recruitment, and in the identification of training needs.

Frequently the personal demands which a job makes on an individual incumbent must be inferred – they are not easily measurable. It should be re-emphasized that the term 'personal demands' is not a description of the attributes which the present incumbent happens to possess, but the identification and assembly of those essential attributes (or qualifications) which are *deemed necessary for successful performance*, and without which it would not be possible to do the job properly.

Methods of conducting job analyses

There are three basic methods, either singly or in combination, which may be adopted for the fact finding process: (i) observation, (ii) interviews, (iii) questionnaires.

OBSERVATION

Where work activity is overt, direct observation of what the jobholder actually does can yield most of the information required to answer questions about the work itself and make judgements about personal demands made on the worker. Some jobs lend themselves particularly to direct observation, e.g. routine jobs with a high manual content, where much of the job activity is there for the eye to see, and where not too much is hidden in the form of mental processes or in the exercise of individual discretion, and where standardized, short-cycle activities are the norm. More senior jobs, in the management and administrative areas, are therefore less suitable for analysis by observation.

Activity sampling is a more sophisticated development than simple observation. In activity sampling, a large number of observations are taken at random intervals during the complete working cycle. The purpose of each observation is to snapshot what the jobholder is actually doing, and at the end of the period – which may be extended over several days or weeks – to express the number of times an activity occurs as a percentage of the total number of observations made in order to arrive at the relevant importance or frequency of various visible worker operations. However, observation by any method is unlikely of itself to provide all the information required without the addition of interviews and discussion. The cycle of operations over which the analysis extends may vary from a matter of minutes to several years. It is imperative that what is viewed by the analyst be further elaborated and amplified. Since the best method of learning is by doing, is there any reason why the analyst himself should not perform the work to be studied for a short period of time 'to get the feel of the job'?

INTERVIEWS

As with any form of investigation, it is profitable to begin by knowing what to look for. The schemata presented for conducting the job analysis provide a good starting point for a discussion of the job which can be worked through systematically. Properly structured and patterned in this kind of way, the interview can elicit information about all aspects of the job, the nature and sequence of the various component parts, the whys and wherefores. The approach must be systematic.

Some appraisal can be made of the skills and personal attributes required to do the job. It is useful to cross-check the information obtained with incumbents of identical or similar jobs, to highlight any discrepancies in reporting, and to consult with the immediate supervisor on the final outcome with a view to validating the accuracy of the details obtained. Most interviews are of the 'individual interview' type – a direct dialogue between the analyst and the employee, and/or his supervisor. Where there are an appreciable number of identical positions, one can apply 'group interviews' – discussions with groups of employees doing the same work. All interviews, however, are notoriously unreliable with regard to the accuracy of the information obtained and the judgements made about it. Bias and distortion creep into interviewee accounts and different pictures emerge (and are recorded) according to the perceptions of the interviewer. A team of interviewers, comparing notes with each other from analyses of an adequate sample of jobs will go some way towards achieving a balance. Even better, interviews should be combined with other methods of investigation.

QUESTIONNAIRES

Questionnaires have the immediate and apparent advantage that they are structured and can be pre-planned to cover the whole area of work activity. Interviews may be similarly structured, but there is a greater tendency to digress. Moreover, questionnaires provide an economical method (in terms of time) of collecting information from a larger number of people. It is obvious that the information could vary widely. The questionnaire *must* be tailor-made to elicit the right sort of responses. A preliminary feel of the job must be first obtained in order to start asking pertinent questions. In general, it is useful if the questionnaire follows the what? how? why? when? where? format suggested earlier.

At least one trade union has debated the respective merits of interviews versus questionnaires. 'Both techniques have their merits and deserve consideration. An important factor in deciding which technique to use will be the number of jobs. . . . The main difficulty with interviewing, however, lies not so much with the technique itself but with the quality of the interviews. Very few union representatives or members of management have received training in the techniques of interviewing. Too many imagine interviewing to be relatively simple, whereas nothing could be further from the truth. . . . The interviewer must be able to win the confidence of, and establish rapport with, the jobholder. Very few possess this skill . . .' (Edwards and Paul, 1978).

Not that questionnaires are without their problems. The questionnaire having been prepared, it must be test-run, and if necessary revised. Although the questions asked may be completely clear to the analyst, they may in fact be interpreted in many different ways by the respondents. It is difficult for a respondent to elaborate on a questionnaire, and the rather impersonal approach of paper shunting may leave the analyst with a rather superficial view, and certainly without any 'gut feeling' for the job. But data obtained by this method can easily be quantified and computerized.

The best solution is to seek information by a combination of as many ways as possible. As well as the methods listed, other techniques include the use of checklists, diaries, the 'critical incident' approach which attempts to highlight critical aspects of the job (but without providing an integrated picture), and by the method of factor analysis.

THE JOB ANALYST

Preferably the analysis and writing-up of job descriptions should be done by a trained job analyst. In large organizations, with many jobs constantly changing and coming under review, personnel specialists are to be found who devote most of their time to this kind of work. Small organizations do not normally justify the employment of such individuals. The process of job analysis therefore falls to a personnel officer as part of his general duties, or to an outside consultant. If the guidelines for a systematic procedure are followed, and if the findings are discussed fully with jobholders and with line management, then lack of a specialist may not be too detrimental.

There are a number of general considerations which also deserve attention. The job analyst is nearly always regarded with suspicion. People ask: 'Why is he doing this? What is the purpose behind the questioning?' The analysis can well be seen as an intrusion into the privacy of the individual at work. And if it is thought that changes may result from the investigation, natural feelings of anxiety and insecurity may well cause concealment of pertinent facts. And many people may well inflate their answers in the hope of upgrading their jobs. In all honesty, job analysis may be used as the basis for the recruitment of future employees, but even this seemingly innocuous and sensible method of data collection can cause alarm. People know very well that job analysis often results in change – in recruitment and selection criteria, which can have repercussions on manning levels, work practices, training programmes, promotion avenues, levels of supervision, and on the emotive issue of pay. The job analyst is sometimes thought to be interfering in work matters which are outside his jurisdiction. It is therefore of utmost importance to gain the trust, confidence and cooperation of those whose jobs are being placed under scrutiny. Five pieces of advice can be offered to any job analyst:

1   State specifically the purpose of the exercise
2   Obtain union agreement and support
3   Maintain detachment and objectivity
4   Be tactful and diplomatic in dealing with people
5   Listen, watch and think – rather than do all the talking.

In short, job analysis is an exercise in communication. After the analysis has been completed, people should be allowed to comment on their job descriptions and seek a revised analysis if there seems to be just cause for disagreement. Constraints imposed by the sheer size of the organization and volume of work to be done severely limit the degree of discussion and participation which is possible, but every effort should be made to see that all contentions are aired, suspicions dispelled, and uncertainties answered. It is clearly only within an atmosphere of trust and cooperation that truthful and constructive relations between job incumbent and job analyst can be achieved. With anything less, the results would be contaminated, distorted and most probably, quite invalid.

OTHER APPROACHES TO JOB ANALYSIS

Other approaches have been put forward at various times. The US Department of Labor (1974) has developed a widely used method. Adopting the US Employment Services definition of job analysis at what the worker does in relation to data, people, things; the methodologies and the techniques employed; the materials, products, subject-matter, and services involved; machines, tools, equipment, and work aids used; and the behavioural traits required of the worker for satisfactory performance – the US Department of Labor has categorized five sets of information that must be obtained in order to meet the requirements of a complete analysis of a job:

1   Worker functions
2   Work fields
3   Machines, tools, equipment, and word aids (MTEWA)
4   Materials, products, subject-matter, and services (MPSMS)
5   Worker traits.

A technique has been devised to assist the job analyst to describe a job–worker situation in standard concise form, using a particular sentence construction in order to form a brief, declarative statement. The framework for the sentence analysis is constant: an implied subject, a verb, object, and modifying infinitive phrases. A job–worker situation may then be described as in Fig. 3.2.

In addition to the work actually performed, personal demands are made on the worker, who requires to bring to the job certain worker traits, and these

US Dept. of Labor	Analysis		
		Infinitive Phrase	
			Object of
Verb	Immediate Object	Infinitive	Infinitive
Worker Function	**MTEWA, Data, People**	**Work Field**	**MPSMS**
Compares	gas thermometer, fan controls, equipment action with specifications	to dry	coal
Takes instruction from	supervisor	to dry	coal
Operates and controls	coal drier, auxiliary equipment	to dry	coal

Fig. 3.2

are reflected in the following components (i) training times (ii) aptitudes (iii) temperaments (iv) interests (v) physical demands. This body of job information provides a sharper focus on the type of work involved and the trait demands made on the individual worker concerned. It is claimed to be helpful in counselling, job development, training, and other manpower activities.

Functional Job Analysis (FJA) is a technique developed by Dr Sidney Fine of the W. E. Upjohn Institute for Employment Research (Fine and Wretha, 1972). Key aspects of the approach are derived from the US Department of Labor methodology, but with some additions and a few significant changes. The most important change is the inclusion of job analysis with systems analysis, by examining first the main purpose of the organization in which the jobs occur. There are also modifications to the worker function scales and the addition of new scales.

According to FJA, the systems approach begins by examining the purposes and goals of the organization. Once the goals are known, the analyst determines what must be done to achieve them. This process includes setting specific objectives (defined as 'a restatement of a purpose or a goal in relation to the realities of a specific local situation, taking into consideration the constraints of time, money, manpower geography, and consumer response'); identifying subsystems ('a general grouping of procedures or technologies required to implement a specific objective'); and identifying tasks which need to be done to accomplish the objectives of each subsystem.

FJA is concerned with identifying both the way in which work is currently performed in an organization and the tasks which serve to advance the organization's objectives, regardless of whether they are currently being performed in the organization or not. Thus, a database is established which not only reflects present realities but may also indicate new tasks.

The Position Analysis Questionnaire (PAQ) from Purdue University dichotomizes job-oriented and worker-oriented aspects, concentrating particularly on worker-oriented elements, 'since they offer some possibility of serving as bridges or common denominations between jobs of very different technologies'. The PAQ consists of 189 'job elements'. These elements are not tasks, since they do not refer to specific worker activities in a given technological context. Instead they represent 'generalized human behaviors involved in work'. Each job element is rated on an appropriate scale such as 'importance', 'extent of use', or 'time'. Extensive statistical research with the PAQ has resulted in the identification of 32 basic job dimensions. The principal uses of the data are in the areas of test validation, developing job families, and in wage and salary classification.

The United Nations takes an even broader view and considers not only 'positions' (i.e. specific jobs or posts), but also 'classes' (or classifications) into which jobs may be grouped and the wider issues of grouping allied job families into occupational structures and classes. The UN approach resulted from a study in the 1970s aimed at assisting governments of developing countries and 'designed to demonstrate how a focus on the "post" can be achieved and how it can contribute to all aspects of personnel administration'.

Job description

A job description is the accurate and complete description of a position or job as it is currently constituted, resulting from the process of job analysis. It is a written statement of those facts which are important regarding the duties, responsibilities, and their organizational and operational interrelationships. As such, the statement itself is behaviourally sterile. It is a statement of facts. Seldom – if ever – does a description of anything require the reporting of each and every detail of a subject. The best descriptions are those which present a good overall picture, but concentrate on the most important aspects. A good description will present all pertinent facts about the job on a couple of pages.

The Institute of Administrative Management (Scott, 1976) has summarized the basic information which a job description should include as 'identifying information so that the job can be quickly placed within the organization and checked at later dates. This will cover details of the department and section in which the job is found; a job code number if jobs are classified; the person to whom the jobholder is responsible; the job title; the names of the jobholder, analyst or manager responsible for preparing the description; the date of preparation; and possibly the grading subsequently allocated to the job . . . a brief general description of the purpose of the job, usually consisting of one or two sentences, and possibly a small organization chart showing how the job relates to other jobs immediately above, below, and around it in the departmental structure . . . a concise summary of all the main duties of the job'.

The need for a written job description as the basis for personnel administration is widespread in Western cultures – although it should not be seen as something simply bureaucratic. It is in fact a frame of reference, around which employee-centred personnel policies can be developed.

And of course jobs change. Job descriptions should not be seen as rigid lines of job demarcation, inexorable and inflexible. Jobs themselves are a dynamic constellation of work activities. People themselves influence their jobs and change them. Job situations and the working environment change; so too do work methods and procedures. Over time, job descriptions become out of date. An out-of-date job description is useless. The need for updating is therefore self-evident. Current and accurate information is essential. It is also more useful if the information contained in a job description is presented in a standard format. This makes for ease of reference and facilitates comparisons between jobs.

There are no hard and fast rules as to the best format for a job description. Most job descriptions take the form of a narrative essay broken down under various subheadings. Others are more analytically described and scaled. Several examples of job descriptions are given below. The first (Fig. 3.3) is for a semi-skilled oil-rig worker, which outlines the work performed, responsibilities, education and skills, supervision and environmental conditions. As an example, it is typical of the descriptive précis found commonly in use.

A more elaborate example, a 'job profile' of a toolmaker (Fig. 3.4) reveals the degree of information which can be obtained by a more analytical approach. In this example, the key factors of responsibility, working conditions, physical demands and mental demands are identified and presented in a standard format used for a range of jobs. The factors are then scaled: low/moderate/high/exceptional. In the case of the toolmaker, the relevant job aspects are then scored (judgementally by the analyst) and recorded. Skill requirements and the effects of sub-standard performance and errors are also noted. As such, this particular example contains both task-oriented and worker-oriented information.

A managerial job description cannot be so precise. An example is given (Fig. 3.5) for a plant manager in Belgium. It will be seen that the description is broader and more expansive than the detailed, prescribed aspects of the much more routine toolmaker's job. Similarly, the example of the salesman's job description (Fig. 3.6) is equally broad, although examples do exist of more quantitative approaches to sales positions.

Job specification

Job specification is sometimes tied in with a job description, but not always. Unfortunately, in the literature and in practice generally, the various terminologies are sometimes used interchangeably. This creates confusion. Strictly speaking, the job specification is concerned with the behavioural or worker-oriented aspects of the job; it specifies the physical and mental

PETROLEUM INDUSTRY TRAINING BOARD

JOB DESCRIPTION

1.	JOB TITLE	Rig Floorman (Offshore).
2.	FUNCTION	Drilling
3.	CATEGORY	Semi-skilled worker
4.	LOCATION	Offshore
5.	SHIFT TIMES & BREAKS	12 hour day - 2 weeks on 2 weeks off.
6.	JOB SUMMARY	Assists all operations on the drilling floor, which will cover the following functions.

    1 Tripping-in and tripping-out of hole
    2 Checking mud and mud levels
    3 Maintenance and minor repairs to equipment
    4 Assisting specialist service companies in
       performance of their work. (Running casing,
       cementation, wireline operations)

7.   WORK PERFORMED AND RESPONSIBILITIES

1 Steady the piping/casing and to transfer single
   pipes between the ramp, mousehole and drilling
   string. Manually swings all piping into the
   required positions, stack them in threes when
   tripping. Uses power spanner to connect pipes,
   positions tongs and places stopper in rotary
   table.

2 Works on spider deck beams when lifting/lowering
   the Blowout Preventer (BOP) stack, fixing guide
   wires, hoses, etc. Also helps overhaul the stack
   on the spider deck. Renews constant tension
   winch wires and Rucker wires when required.

3 Operates air hoists to transfer joints of marine
   riser from the drill floor, to main deck and
   works closely with the crane operators.

4 Under the supervision of the Derrickman checks
   crown block at top of derrick. Cleans and checks
   sheaves, winches and travelling block. Greases
   track of travelling block.

5 Assists the Derrickman in greasing and maintaining
   all valves in standpipe manifold, back pressure
   manifold and all mud lines. (This can necessitate
   the tripping out of worn or leaking valves repairing
   and replacing where required so they can withstand
   the appropriate pressure test).

6 The Rig Floorman is also required to adjust and
   replace drawworks brake bands under supervision
   of driller and assist the rig mechanic in all
   other drawworks repairs, e.g. adjusting or
   renewing drive chains, removal of catheads to
   replace clutch plates, etc.

7 During the normal course of duties the rig floorman
   is required to clean, grease, inspect and repair
   all drill floor equipment such as slips, elevators,

safety clamps and rotary tongs. He must also clean, grease and measure drill pipe subs, etc. before adding to drill string.

8   Assist with the slipping and cutting of the drawworks cable when it has completed sufficient services.

9   Assist in rigging up equipment for the specialist service companies.

10 During testing the rig floorman works with production team assisting with rigging up and breaking down of their tools and equipment. He is required to connect and disconnect chicksan swings to Christmas tree while heaving and works on a platform while connecting and disconnecting lubrictors). This operation also requires the rig floorman to attach and detach guide ropes to four corners of the derrick).

11 Assists in mud mixing and mud maintenance while drilling is in progress.

12 The floorman is required to dig out and hose clean the mud ditch, the mud tanks, and when the occasion arises the mud suction and transfer lines.

13 Assists the derrickman in adjusting and replacing shaker screens, and when necessary adjusts or replaces gland packings on centrifugal pumps.

14 Wash down rig floors, substructures, stairways, machinery etc. Paint parts of these structures and equipment from time to time.

8. EDUCATION & SKILLS

Minimum: secondary education up to the age of 15. Should be conversant with the use of hand tools.

9. SUPERVISION

Responsible to the Driller and, at times, Derrickman (required to be completely integrated with driller, derrickman and other rig floormen – will work occasionally with pump man, chargehand, mechanic, etc). Degree of supervision – continuous on rig floor, light elsewhere.

10. OPPORTUNITIES FOR ADVANCEMENT

Line of promotion – Derrickman.

11. ENVIRONMENTAL CONDITIONS

It is stressed that in these duties time is at a premium both because of the high daily operating cost of a rig and because when extra pipe is added during drilling, mud circulation stops and control of downhole conditions severely reduced. The flow of mud should therefore be restored as soon as possible and speed and team work can save time significantly. e.g. tasks performed during running in and pulling out may be separated up to 100 times each trip. Thus any time saved in each will be significant as a cumulative total. The physical effort required in performing these duties (100 times separated by 1–2 minutes) is also exceptional.

Furthermore, rig crews must be able to respond to other people's actions under stress conditions as a member of a team. In turn they must be aware of and put into practice all safety precautions necessary on or around the rig floor.

Fig. 3.3 *Job description for an oil-rig worker*

FORD MOTOR COMPANY LIMITED

JOB PROFILE HISTORY SHEET

١٦٥١١

Job Title	Division	Plant	Dept	Loc.	Ref. No.
Toolmaker	M S & B	River Dag.	Toolroom		5/5

Date received by Review Committee

Date considered by Review Committee

Date profile referred back to Assessing Team

Reason profile referred back to Assessing Team

(a) To check degree under Characteristic No.......
(b) To clarify note under Characteristic No.......
(c) To check facts under Characteristic No.........
(d) To amplify job precis
(e) Other reason

See detailed query list overleaf

Date profile agreed and passed to Central Review Committee

Date considered by Central Review Committee

Date profile referred back to Division/Operations Review Committee

Date agreed by Central Review Committee

Reason profile referred back to Division/Operations Review Committee

(a) To check degree under Characteristic No.......
(b) To clarify note under Characteristic No.......
(c) To check facts under Characteristic No.........
(d) To amplify job precis
(e) Other reason

P.T.O.

LAB. REL. 30732
8/69

Fig. 3.4 *Job profile of a toolmaker*

FORD MOTOR COMPANY LTD - JOB PROFILE

Page 1

Job Title	Division	Plant	Dept	Loc.	Ref No.	
Toolmaker		River Dagenham	M S & B Toolroom		5/5	

Passed by .... Div. Review Committee		Agreed by Central Rev.Comm.		Profiled by	Date
Signature	Date	Signature	Date	(a)	22.11.6
				(b) ✓	

RESPONSIBILITY. What is the level of responsibility (capable of occuring due to operator carelessness) for ?

	LOW	MODERATE	HIGH	EXCEPTIONAL
1. Damage to expensive machinery or equipment	6 Helper B/F 35 Headliner 32 Torch Solderer	42 Fitter - Vehicle Maintenance 2 Sand Muller Op. 55 Carpenter & Joiner	54 Machine Repairman 3 Machinist Auto Block line (Boring & Honing) 5 Construction Millwright	25 Diemaker - Tryout 49 H.P. Boiler Operator ✓

Notes: Uses Holbrook 18 centre lathe, Huron KU 6 miller, Cincinnati and Butler 36", Churchill Redman universal shaper, Mass VRM 50A universal drill, Asquith vertical drill, Lumsden grinder, small surface grinder and all hand tools.

	LOW	MODERATE	HIGH	EXCEPTIONAL
2. Damage to materials or products	50 Labourer - Swarf Handler 18 Assembler - Gearbox 15 Fettler	19 Storekeeper - Tool Stores 12 Assembler - Engines	10 Dynamometer Tester 13 Rigger 11 Welder - Grade 1 ✓	44 Experimental Mechanic 28 Crane Driver

Notes: Incorrect assembly or manufacture of dies could cause extensive damaged, i.e. incorrect timing of cams

	LOW	MODERATE	HIGH	EXCEPTIONAL
3. Effect of poor work on subsequent operations	6 Helper B/F 15 Fettler	20 Setter Operator Bar Autos 22 Metal Finisher 32 Torch Solderer	40 KD Packer 8 Floor Moulder 26 Electrician-Resistance Welder ✓	9 Bricklayer 45 Experimental Electrician 17 Quality Inspector - Grade I

Notes: Poor work would result in delays to try out, press schedule programme, delays to production and sub standard panels, also new model launching

	LOW	MODERATE	HIGH	EXCEPTIONAL
4. Safety of other people	31 Inspector Grade II 38 Assembler - Elect. 16 Con-Rod Machinist	30 Metal Assembler 34 Wet Deck Operator 29 Production Welder Grade II	54 Machine Repairman 56 Pipe Fitter 42 Vehicle Maintenance Fitter	13 Rigger 47 Shunter 51 Fork Truck Driver ✓

Notes: Uses various machines, grinders and air chisels and handling heavy steel levers and bars in proximity of other operators. His product, the dies, will be used by other operators

Fig. 3·4 – cont.

RESPONSIBILITY (contd)

	LOW	MODERATE	HIGH	EXCEPTIONAL
5. Co-operation with other operators in team work	41 Cutter Grinder 55 Carpenter and Joiner.	21 Crankshaft Grinder 24 Toolmaker - Bench Fitter 27 Lead Discer	4 Power Hammer Man 2 Sand Muller Operator 12 Engine Assembler	47 Shunter 28 Crane Driver 44 Experimental Mechanic

Notes: Must co-operate with other toolmakers when constructing dies of same set, i.e. 11, 14, 29, 30 etc. and machine operators when required

	HOURLY	MORE THAN DAILY	DAILY	LESS THAN DAILY
6. Is the job supervised ?	38 Electrical Assembler 22 Metal Finisher 12 Engine Assembler	46 Parts Recall Op. 26 Electrician Resistance Welder 36 Sewing Machinist	43 Sheet Metal Worker 7 Pattern Maker 39 Cycle Checker	4 Power Hammer Man 9 Bricklayer

Notes: Supervision check on progress rather than standard of work

I. WORKING CONDITIONS - DISAGREEABLENESS. How does this job compare with other jobs in the Company's factories in respect of :

	LOW	MODERATE	HIGH	EXCEPTIONAL
1. Fumes or odours	40 Production Packer KD 38 Electrical Assembler 53 Clerk (Preventive Maintenance)	23 Heavy Press Operator 34 Wet Deck Operator 42 Fitter - Vehicle Maintenance	32 Torch Solderer 56 Pipe Fitter 47 Shunter	1 Coke Oven Operator 33 Final Enamel Sprayer 52 Oiler - Mystic Pit

Notes: Uses cleaning spirit, marking ink, dope and oil.

	LOW	MODERATE	HIGH	EXCEPTIONAL
2. Temperature or humidity	37 Cushion Builder 48 Assembler (Rear Wheels) 39 Cycle Checker	55 Carpenter & Joiner 51 Fork Truck Driver 28 Crane Driver	5 Construction Millwright 2 Sand Muller Operator 34 Wet Deck Operator	1 Coke Oven Operator 9 Bricklayer 14 Metal Pourer

Notes: Moderate shop temperature occasionally comes in contact with hardening and welding processes.

Fig. 3.4 – *cont.*

II. WORKING CONDITIONS (Contd)

	LOW	MODERATE	HIGH	EXCEPTIONAL
3. Noise and/or vibration	40 Production Packer KD 35 Headliner - Assembly 39 Cycle Checker	42 Vehicle Maintenance Fitter 45 Experimental Electrician 48 Assembler - Rear Wheels	47 Shunter 56 Pipe Fitter 4 Power Hammer Man	43 Sheet Metal Worker 10 Dynamometer Tester 15 Fettler

Notes : Constant noise from machines, hammering and air chisels etc

	LOW	MODERATE	HIGH	EXCEPTIONAL
4. Chips of engineering material, dust, dirt, oil, petrol, water, paraffin, paint	12 Engine Assembler 38 Electrical Assembler	28 Crank Driver 24 Toolmaker - Bench Fitter 18 Gearbox Assembler	21 Crankshaft Grinder 11 Maintenance Welder Grade I 3 Honer & Borer Auto Block Line	13 Rigger 20 Setter-Operator Bar Autos 33 Final Enamel Sprayer

Notes : Comes in contact grinding dust, dirt, oil grease, dope, cleaning spirits, etc (

	LOW	MODERATE	HIGH	EXCEPTIONAL
5. Working in unusual posture	17 Quality Inspector Grade I 51 Fork Truck Driver 49 H.P. Boiler Op.	41 Cutter Grinder 22 Metal Finisher 19 Storekeeper (Tool Stores)	5 Millwright Construction 29 Production Welder Grade II 4 Power Hammer Man	9 Bricklayer 25 Diemaker/Tryout

Notes : Required at times to lay under dies, inside dies, bend stoop, stretch and crouch

	LOW	MODERATE	HIGH	EXCEPTIONAL
6. To what extent is there a possibility of industrial disease or accident ?	39 Cycle Checker 40 Production Packer 53 Clerk - Preventive Maintenance	16 Machinist - Con Rod Line 28 Driver Crane 30 Metal Assembler	26 Electrician Resistance Welder 32 Torch Solderer	14 Metal Pourer 27 Lead Discer 44 Experimental Mechanic

Notes : Working on engineering machinery carrying heavy steels, using heavy die bars, working inside spotting presses, also required to stand on top of work on some drilling operations

Fig. 3.4 – cont.

III. PHYSICAL DEMANDS. What is the level required and compared with other jobs in the Company's factories for :

	LOW	MODERATE	HIGH	EXCEPTIONAL
1. Physical Effort	53 Clerk - Preventive Maintenance 31 Inspector Grade II	20 Setter - Bar Autos 14 Metal Pourer 36 Sewing Machinist	23 Heavy Press Operator 50 Labourer - Swarf Handler 13 Rigger	15 Fettler

Notes: Needs to lift fair number of die steels, approx 56lbs and moving heavy steels with assistance from other operators. Uses heavy die bars and levers approx. 90lbs weight

	LOW	MODERATE	HIGH	EXCEPTIONAL
2. Paced Muscular Effort	43 Sheet Metal Worker 9 Bricklayer 4 Power Hammer Man	21 Crankshaft Grinder 32 Torch Solderer 36 Sewing Machinist	22 Metal Finisher 2 Sand Muller Operator 48 Assembler - Rear Wheels	14 Metal Pourer 23 Heavy Press Operator

Notes: Not required

	LOW	MODERATE	HIGH	EXCEPTIONAL
3. Manual Dexterity	6 Helper B/F 16 Machinist Con-Rod 19 Storekeeper - Tool Stores	42 Fitter Vehicle Maintenance 27 Lead Discer 5 Millwright Construction	29 Welder Production Grade II 12 Engine Assembler 8 Floor Moulder	32 Torch Solderer 25 Die Maker/Tryout 45 Experimental Electrician

Notes: Required to do large amount of fine finger and wrist movements when filing, using machinery, pencil grinders checking media etc.

	LOW	MODERATE	HIGH	EXCEPTIONAL
4. Sensory Accuracy (keeness of sight, hearing, touch, smell)	19 Storekeeper - Tool Stores 52 Oiler Mystic Pit 53 Clerk - Preventive Maintenance	9 Bricklayer 35 Headliner-Assembly 30 Metal Assembler	22 Metal Finisher 43 Sheet Metal Worker 4 Power Hammer Man	25 Diemaker/Tryout 17 Inspector Grade I 7 Pattern Maker

Notes: Required to use sight, - touch and hearing when using hand and machine tools, surfacing steels, and sounding out for cracked dies etc.

Fig. 3.4 - *cont.*

III. PHYSICAL DEMANDS (contd)

	LOW	MODERATE	HIGH	EXCEPTIONAL
5. Hand/Eye Co-ordination	52 Oiler Mystic Pit 1 Coke Oven Operator 50 Labourer Swarf Handler	18 Gear Box Assember 3 Machinist - Auto Head Line (Boring & Honing) 37 Cushion Builder	29 Production Welder Gde.2 13 Rigger 10 Dynamometer Tester	36 Sewing Machinist 33 Final Enamel Sprayer 28 Crane Driver

Notes: Required to co-ordinate hand and eye movements when using hand and machine tools

IV. MENTAL DEMANDS. Need for:

	LOW	MODERATE	HIGH	EXCEPTIONAL
1. Knowledge of machinery, tools and equipment	40 Packer Production 35 Headliner-Assembly 15 Fettler	56 Pipe Fitter 30 Metal Assembler 14 Metal Pourer	26 Electrician-Resistance Welder 3 Honer & Blocks - Auto Block Line 43 Sheet Metal Worker	49 Boiler Op. (H.P.) 24 Toolmaker - Bench Fitter 44 Experimental Mechanic

Notes: Knowledge to operate machines listed in characteristic 1, plus precision instruments and hand tools

	LOW	MODERATE	HIGH	EXCEPTIONAL
2. Knowledge of process	15 Fettler 16 Con-Rod Machinist	12 Engine Assembler 6 Helper (B/F) 23 Heavy Press Op.	41 Cutter Grinder 31 Inspector Grade II 20 Setter-Operator Bar Autos	54 Machine Repairman 46 Parts Recall Op. 7 Pattern Maker

Notes: See page 8

	LOW	MODERATE	HIGH	EXCEPTIONAL
3. Ability to carry out shop mathematical calculations, formulae	35 Headliner-Assembly 19 Storekeeper - Tool Stores 31 Inspector Grade 2	4 Power Hammer Man 10 Dynamometer Tester 8 Floor Moulder	44 Experimental Mechanic 49 H.P. Boiler Operator 41 Cutter Grinder	45 Experimental Electrician 7 Pattern Maker 11 Inspector Grade I

Notes: Required to use trigonometry, decimals, conversion from metric to British Standard measurement

Fig. 3.4 – cont.

IV. MENTAL DEMANDS (contd)	LOW	MODERATE	HIGH	EXCEPTIONAL
4. Ability to visualise shapes and spatial relations in three dimensions	16 Machinist Con-Rod Line 18 Gear Box Assembler 29 Production Welder	51 Fork Truck Driver 1 Coke Oven Operator 20 Setter - Bar Autos	45 Experimental Electrician 8 Floor Moulder 55 Carpenter & Joiner	4 Power Hammer Man 43 Sheet Metal Worker 7 Pattern Maker

Notes: Works mainly from drawings when constructing dies also makes engineering changes without drawings from which drawings are made at later date

	LOW	MODERATE	HIGH	EXCEPTIONAL
5. Short term memory	37 Cushion Builder 16 Machinist Con-Rod Line 27 Lead Discer	28 Crane Driver 56 Pipe Fitter 53 Clerk - Preventive Maint.	21 Crankshaft Grinder 47 Shunter 10 Dynamometer Tester	49 Boiler Operator (H.P.) 25 Diemaker Tryout 26 Electrician - Resistance Welder

Notes: Required when working from drawings spotting in steels, making specific calculations

	LOW	MODERATE	HIGH	EXCEPTIONAL
6. Appreciation of Detail	50 Labourer - Swarf Handler 6 Helper B/F 52 Oiler - Mystic Pit	55 Carpenter & Joiner 48 Assembler (Rear Wheels) 36 Sewing Machinist	2 Sand Muller Operator 22 Metal Finisher 39 Cycle Checker	46 Parts Recall Operator 49 H.P. Boiler Operator 26 Electrician - Resistance Welder

Notes: Needs to appreciate differences between drawings and die build up, also surface condition attained against requirements

	LOW	MODERATE	HIGH	EXCEPTIONAL
7. Speed of decision making	53 Clerk - Preventive Maintenance 17 Inspector Grade I 37 Cushion Builder	54 Machine Repairman 33 Final Enamel Sprayer 15 Fettler	6 Helper B/F 32 Torch Solderer 47 Shunter	1 Coke Ovens Operator 51 Fork Truck Driver 49 H.P. Boiler Operator

Notes: Required when using all machines etc.

Fig. 3-4 – cont.

IV. MENTAL DEMANDS (contd)

	LOW	COMPLETING PREPARED FORMS IN TERMS OF SIMPLE READINGS	COMPLETING PREPARED FORMS IN TERMS OF COMPLEX READINGS	FULL REPORTS
8. Ability to communicate in speech and writing	27 Lead Discer 21 Crankshaft Grinder 34 Wet Deck Operator	11 Welder - Maintenance Grade I 53 Clerk - Preventive Maintenance 51 Fork Truck Driver	31 Inspector Grade II 10 Dynamometer Tester 8 Floor Moulder	44 Experimental Mechanic 46 Parts Recall Operator 17 Quality Inspector Grade I

Notes :   Makes out complex written, also verbal reports to toolmakers on following shift and supervision

	SIMPLE JOB REPETITIVE OPERATIONS	ROUTINE JOB REPETITIVE WITH VARIATIONS	VARIABLE JOB VARIATION IN METHOD	COMPLEX JOB CONSIDERABLE VARIATIONS NOT PREVIOUSLY WORKED OUT
9. Judgment and Logical thought in planning work	6 Helper B/F 16 Con-Rod Machinist	12 Engine Assembler 38 Electrical Assembler 40 Production Packer	9 Bricklayer 13 Rigger 46 Parts Recall Operator	11 Welder - Maintenance Grade I 43 Sheet Metal Worker 24 Toolmaker - Bench Fitter

Notes :   Pakns work according to priority constructing dies (prototype) new models

	APPROXIMATE	MODERATE	HIGH	EXCEPTIONAL
10. Degree of accuracy required on job	15 Fettler 48 Assembler (Rear Wheels) 50 Labourer - Swarf Handler	38 Electrical Assembler 5 Construction Millwright 30 Metal Assembler	42 Fitter Vehicle Maintenance 33 Final Enamel Sprayer 21 Crankshaft Grinder	24 Toolmaker - Bench Fitter 17 Inspector Grade I 7 Patternmaker (Metal)

Notes :   Large degree of finished and dimensional accuracy required

Fig. 3·4 – *cont.*

IV.   MENTAL DEMANDS (contd)

	SLIGHT ATTENTION	AVERAGE/INTERMITTENT ATTENTION	HIGH SEMI CONTINUOUS ATTENTION	HIGH CONTINUOUS ATTENTION
11. Concentration	50 Labourer - Swarf Handler 52 Oiler - Mystic Pit	9 Bricklayer 34 Wet Deck Operator 18 Gearbox Assembler	36 Sewing Machinist 25 Diemaker/Tryout 14 Metal Pourer	51 Fork Truck Driver 2 Sand Muller Operator 1 Coke Oven Operator

Notes: High degree of concentration required during certain periods

BRIEF JOB DESCRIPTION

The job consists of 2 parts - 1. The repair or alteration of existing dies 2. Manufacture of new dies.
To carry out both these operations he must have sound engineering knowledge, both practical and theoretical. Be able to read tooling drawings and work to fine limits with both machine and hand tools. On die repair, working from information received he will decide best method of repair, considering the construction of the die and the time allocated for job (Period die can be out of service with regard to production). For the construction of new dies he will commence with the rough casting. He will mark off casting for machining which he will either hand over to a full time machine operator or complete himself. (Depends on machine and · labour availability at the time). Working from drawings he will proceed to make and fit steels, guide pins stop blocks, lifters, etc. to meet engineering specifications. He may be required to follow the job through to home line tryout. Toolmaker occasionally would be expected to carry out .   heat treat and hardening operation.   The operator is responsible for training of company apprentices in all aspects of toolmaking. He also makes out detailed machining instructions for machine operators carrying out work on his behalf. From time to time he is required to make complex verbal reports on the action taken or progress made concerning tools being repaired or manufactured. Uses full range of machine tools listed under characteristic 1.1.

Operator leaves complex written line up for following shift.

Fig. 3.4 – *cont.*

STATEMENT OF FUNCTIONS

Ford of Europe Incorporated

18-J-E

MANUFACTURING
BODY AND ASSEMBLY OPERATIONS
GENK OPERATIONS

Position Title: PLANT MANAGER, ASSEMBLY PLANT

RESPONSIBILITIES:

The Plant Manager is responsible for the development and implementation of a detailed operating plan aimed at the optimal utilization of the facilities material and labor resources of the plant, and ensuring that production schedules, engineering specifications, quality standards, good labor relations, cost levels and general operational efficiency are achieved in accordance with overall manufacturing policies and objectives.

FUNCTIONS:

1. Planning, development and implementation of a detailed operating plan aimed at the optimal utilization of the capital, labor and material resources of the plant in manufacturing finished passenger and light commercial cars, including paint, trim and final assembly operations, in accordance with established production program requirements, quality standards and cost levels.

2. Development of detailed daily production schedules for all manufactured parts, components, sub-assemblies and finished passenger and light commercial cars, in accordance with established production programs; maintenance of inventory records for externally sourced production and non-production material and manufactured parts, components, assemblies and finished vehicles; ensurance of availability of necessary production material by issuing the necessary material control releases and by receiving, recording, storing and distributing all production and non-production material.

3. Direction of the implementation of established testing and inspection methods and techniques to ensure that materials, parts, assemblies and finished vehicles, requisitioned, produced and processed by the plant conform to established quality standards; recommendation of changes to testing equipment, methods and techniques to improve quality objectives; evaluation of the quality performance of the plant; investigation of quality problems associated with production, identification of sources of faults, and initiation of corrective action; preparation of periodical reports on quality performance.

Continued...

- 2 -

4.   Implementation of established manufacturing processes, techniques
     and methods, and recommendation and implementation of process,
     equipment, layout, material handling and work standard changes
     to achieve a more economic utilization of labor, material and
     facilities;   review and maintenance of labor and material usage
     standards;   direction of the design and engineering of specific
     tools, equipment, gauges and fixtures as required by the plant;
     direction of the investigation and resolution of all manufacturing
     engineering problems resulting in a reduction of quality or
     quantity of production.

5.   Direction of the maintenance and repair of all production and
     non-production machinery and equipment, facilities, transportation
     equipment, buildings and roads and utilities distribution systems
     within the plant;   scheduling and implementation of a preventive
     maintenance program;   direction of the manufacturing and design
     of specific tools, gauges and fixtures required by the plant;
     preparation and implementation of specific facilities projects
     required by the plant.

6.   Development of annual budgets for the plant, and ensurance of
     adherence by the various plant activities to budget forecasts;
     continuous review of the financial performance of the plant;
     analysis of off standard conditions and recommendation of corr-
     ective action as necessary;   review of cost trends and develop-
     ment, recommendation and implementation of action to improve
     plant financial performance.

7.   Ensuring the availability of the necessary labor resources
     required to meet plant objectives;   implementation of industrial
     relations programs and plans in accordance with established
     industrial relations policies and procedures, and aimed at
     achieving and maintaining optimal labor relations;   initiation,
     review and implementation of organization change proposals
     within the plant;   development and implementation of personnel
     development and training programs.

Fig. 3.5   *Managerial job description*

demands, skills, education and training, occupational experience, personality
factors and attitudes needed by an incumbent for successful performance.
There is no reason in logic why the job specification should not be regarded as
a *part* of a job description. Sometimes it is difficult to distinguish between the
two – particularly in higher level managerial and administrative jobs where
the work actually done may be much more a reflection of a person's qualities,
than in lower level jobs where so much of the work activity is prescribed. A
job specification teases out the differences between jobs in terms of human
capabilities; it can be regarded as the dimension along which jobs differ in
human terms. The main purpose of a job specification is to assist in personnel
selection. In this area we need to know what attributes a person needs to bring
to the job, both those which are *essential* and those which are *desirable*.

JOB SPECIFICATION FOR PERSONNEL SELECTION

Personnel selection is a process designed to achieve an appropriate 'fit' or
'match' between the demands of a job and the people who are to perform
them. Job-matching therefore requires:

DESCRIPTION: Salesman

POSITION CONCEPT:

To attain sales objectives as defined by management. Continue giving
existing accounts high level of service and satisfaction, to develop these
accounts and ensure that they have effective support. To continually
review territory area, identifying new prospects and develop business
forecasts.

RESPONSIBILITIES:

1.   Accountable for retention and development of existing accounts, and
      achievement of quota objectives as defined at annual review.

2.   Continually review territory area to identify new prospects and
      appropriate sales forecasts. Develop plans to secure these accounts
      identifying support needs including information, demonstrations, or
      other assistance needed to obtain this business.

3.   Develop on an annual basis realistic sales forecasts identifying
      current or new business and support needed. Prepare cost estimates
      covering all operating costs - except salary - to meet sales objectives.

4.   To accept total account responsibility and be the sole interface -
      unless otherwise delegated - with the customers. Provide satisfactory
      administration, follow defined Company contractual procedures, monitor
      order and delivery schedules, and manage rendering and clearance of
      accounts. To give the customer a proper level of service and maintain
      an overall level of satisfaction.

5.   Maintain an awareness of competitor activity and highlight potential
      exposures to the Company's continued operations.

6.   Understand and keep updated on the Company's product range attending
      training courses as required. To identify short falls in product range
      and where improvements might be effected to maintain to grow current
      sales forecasts.

7.   To observe at all times Company policies on marketing activities.

Fig. 3.6 *Salesman's job description*

1   a description of the jobs to be done
2   some idea of the personal qualities necessary.

These are the first steps. Later (as described in Chapter 4) the selection process
also includes:

3   assessment of individual candidates in terms of the qualities specified
4   predictions of how candidates are likely to perform on the job.

These are in fact a series of interlinked systematic studies.

One of the pioneers of a systematic approach to personnel selection
methods in Britain was the late Professor Alec Rodger. His ideas laid the
foundation for many large-scale recruitment and selection programmes, and
over the years these ideas have been further elaborated and developed. One of
his well-quoted tenets is worth repeating: 'If matching is to be done
satisfactorily, the requirements of an occupation (or job) must be described in

the same terms as the aptitudes of the people who are being considered for it'. In other words, the descriptions and assessments of both people and of jobs must be reduced to a common format based on a common set of dimensions. Clearly, only ambiguity and confusion will arise if we start measuring people and jobs in different ways, and then start to compare different sets of measurements based on different dimensions and different scales of assessment. If we are not to place square pegs in round holes, we must at least begin by developing methods of assessment which are complementary. However, whilst theoretically it would be desirable to have a common yardstick, in practice it is much more difficult to achieve. The stark fact remains that people are not uniform creatures, nor are their particular qualities and attributes easily measurable, nor sometimes even definable. Jobs, on the other hand, are but units of work grouped together for some technical or administrative expediency. There is no logical reason to suppose that jobs necessarily have common elements which fit neatly in comparison with people's attributes. Nevertheless, without any attempt at identifying and qualifying 'job characteristics' in order to compare against 'people characteristics', the result will be very messy personnel selection decisions.

We have already seen that a *'profile' of a job* can be drawn up, and so can a *'profile' of personal attributes*. The purpose of personnel selection is to match people to jobs based on comparative sets of data.

The purpose of measurement, of course, is to reduce areas of speculation and uncertainty, and to force us to make more exact definitions and observations. Ideally (and theoretically) we need a 'uni-dimensional measure' – i.e. a scale of measurement describing variations in one dimension along a straightforward numerical sequence *without being influenced by any other characteristics*. To take a simple example, people's weight, height, hair colour, can be measured independently. But this kind of independent measurement is likely to be elusive when we are looking at specific job requirements or behavioural characteristics. For example, it is well known that general intelligence influences most other forms of ability, even the performance of psycho-motor skills. If we measure how well someone plays the piano, we are also to some extent measuring their general intelligence; there is a degree of contamination from one measure to the other. Likewise, in the performance of industrial or commercial jobs, we are not always able to tease out each specific behavioural characteristic and measure it in isolation from all the others.

Moreover, one of the most common criticisms levelled at personnel selection procedures, both in the UK and the USA, is that the main psychological principles on which they are based, either explicitly or implicitly, is still rooted in the 'psychometric tradition' (Herriot, 1984). The assumption is that people can be described in terms of various characteristics or psychological constructs which explain their behaviour. A further assumption is that jobs can likewise be described in terms of their task content, and by implication, of the human characteristics involved. The dynamics of job variation and human adaptation tend to be ignored.

We ought to take a more pragmatic approach and ask the question: what *are* the main capacities and inclinations which need to be brought to bear on any given job at any time? To set up a personnel selection procedure we still need to know the job requirements, but also:

1 candidates' capacities (what they CAN do), and
2 candidates' inclinations (what they WILL do).

Broadly speaking, *capacities* refer to people's mental and physical attributes; and *inclinations* refer to their prevailing attitudes, wishes, and occupational choices. The various capacities and inclinations which people possess, and may be prepared to exercise, are the dimensions along which people differ in ways relevant to job demands. Whilst the approach does not entirely get out of the psychometric trap, it does take cognizance of behavioural versatility.

As a starting point, from a modification of the famous 'Seven Point Plan' (Rodger, 1971) a checklist of the main relevant capacities and inclinations can be set out as follows:

Capacities
Physical: physical build, speech, manner, appearance, visual acuity, manual
dexterity, etc.
Mental: general intelligence, verbal ability, numerical ability, other (e.g.
spatial) ability.
Attainments and Experience: educational, vocational training, occupational
achievements.

Inclinations
Attitudes: to work, to life.
Motivation: consistent, realistic goals and objectives.
Drive and Determination: particularly its strength.
Social Abilities: acceptability, influence over others (leadership), teamwork/
solitary preferences, and aptitudes.
Personality Factors: maturity, emotional stability.

If this checklist is accepted as a suitable framework for identifying what are likely to be the key characteristics, the next question to be asked is: *how can we determine the relevant capacities and inclinations in any given work situation?*

The answer is again largely based on Rodger's work – by a diagnosis of the most commonly experienced *difficulties* and *distastes* – particularly where these are of marked generality and persistence as manifested (or expressed) by those people currently employed in the jobs or occupations in question. This technique is a celebrated approach which is practically useful, and which has stood the test of time. One of the latest applications has been in the successful development of selection and labour retention criteria for drilling personnel in the North Sea oilfields (Livy and Vant, 1979, 1980).

Difficulties in a work situation, as experienced, are the main factors which give rise to mistakes or failure and/or are the most demanding aspects of a job in terms of physical or mental skills, abilities, judgement or experience. These are the 'critical' job requirements. From them can be inferred the individual *capacities* needed to tackle them.

Distastes most commonly expressed, or experienced, in a work situation by people on the job are the factors which give rise to indifferent motivation, slackness, omission, absenteeism, decisions to quit, withdrawal and other symptomatic signs of occupational maladjustment or disturbance. Whatever the overt symptom, it is of itself likely to be less important than the underlying root cause. One must then pinpoint the elements in a job giving rise to these problems and find out what *kind* of people are best able to cope with them, particularly if there is a pattern of marked generality and persistence. From this data can be inferred the individual *inclinations* which people need to possess in order to cope with the work satisfactorily.

Exit interviews and attitude surveys, properly constructed, are extremely useful in identifying those aspects of a job amongst any group of employees which people find distasteful – and if we can then relate this data by cross-referencing to the kinds of people who are making which kinds of response – then we have a potent indicator of the kinds of people who should be recruited and those who should be avoided.

The assessment of a job (or occupation) in terms of both capacities or inclinations can provide an outline of the most 'suitable' kind of candidate – i.e. a person profile in relation to a job profile.

Another way is to look at the differential behaviour between groups of employees who are regarded as either 'successful' or 'unsuccessful', and compare these findings with biographical variables. Successful or unsuccessful groups of people may have certain things in common which show up in their backgrounds (i.e. education, trade, skill or other occupations, experience, job history, goals and aspirations, interests, or other biographical variables, e.g. age, domestic circumstances). If a picture of marked generality and persistence does in fact emerge in a discrimination between successful and unsuccessful people on the job, we have additional clues to add to the job specification and to criteria for personnel selection. In fact 'biodata' (historic and verifiable information about an individual) is 'in principle a source of the most valid predictors of job success yet discovered' (Herriot, 1984).

Personnel selection is one of several techniques aimed at the efficient use of manpower. This aim can be viewed from two separate positions – from the point of view of the employer and from the point of view of the employee. What the employer seeks is a satisfactory level of performance – as measured by levels of productivity, output, tenure on the job, 'good' behaviour, etc. What the employee seeks is a measure of job satisfaction – as measured by his/her suitability for the work, the way in which it is organized, opportunity for growth and advancement. These twin considerations really constitute a notion of 'occupational adjustment'.

No personnel selection process or procedure ever provides complete and accurate answers (i.e. the prediction of performance on the job) for three main reasons:

(i) jobs change over time – moreover the concept of a 'job' may in fact imply a 'series of jobs', career ladder, or simply *ad hoc* changes due to revised organizational requirements;
(ii) people develop, and change in other ways over time;
(iii) techniques of assessment (measurement) are imperfect.

These are issues to which we shall turn in the next chapter.

Summary and conclusions

Job analysis helps to create a clear picture of what is meant by a 'job'. It therefore can make a fundamental contribution to organizational planning. It is a fundamental technique in the organization of work, manpower utilization, and manpower planning. It makes an obvious and direct contribution to personnel recruitment, selection and placement. It provides hard data about job requirements and is therefore an indicator of the kinds of people who should be employed. Job analysis also forms the foundation of an equitable pay structure, and it provides a starting point for the redesign of jobs. One of the organizational requirements of today is at the same time both to provide form and structure and create units of work which are meaningful and challenging to the people actually doing them. Job analysis also has a role to play in the design and development of training programmes, and provides a partial solution to the identification of training needs.

Methods of job analysis may be 'task-oriented' or 'worker-oriented' or a combination of the two. A useful checklist of task-oriented aspects is provided by the basic questions who? what? how? why? when? where?, by scaling tasks according to their difficulty, frequency and importance, by identifying the areas and levels of responsibility, supervisory controls, standards of performance required, and working conditions.

Worker-oriented aspects can also be determined by a checklist approach covering the areas of physical demands, mental demands, skills, education and training required, occupational experience, and personality factors and attitudes.

Job analysis information is obtained primarily by observation, interviews and questionnaires. In this process the job analyst has both an investigatory and diplomatic role to play. The findings of a job analysis exercise are normally reported in the twin form of a job description and a job specification. A job description is a written statement of job content, and tends to be task-oriented. A job specification is a checklist of the personal attributes required, and tends to be worker or behaviourally oriented.

In the United States attempts have been made to produce universal models – generalized schemata for the classifications of positions or occupations. Whilst these may be interesting in theory, and may have utility for national manpower research and planning, the fact remains that since job analysis focuses on individual jobs and incumbents, an individual tailor-made approach might be more acceptable and directly relevant. However, by whatever method, job analysis is a fundamental tool in personnel management. 'From one perspective an organization may be viewed as a pattern of roles and a blueprint for their coordination. Job analysis represents such a blueprint, for individual jobs are the basic building blocks necessary to achieve broader organisational goals . . . Job Analysis is to the personnel specialist what the wrench is to the plumber' (Cascio, 1982).

Discussion questions

1   As a personnel specialist, how would you seek to gain the support and cooperation of line management, and of trade unions, in setting up a job analysis exercise?
2   What training do you think a job analyst should receive?
3   In what work situations, and under what circumstances, do you think job analysis would be unnecessary?
4   Your company will soon be branching out into new commercial activities. New jobs will be created. Management requires information *now* about job content and job specification, with a view to gearing up recruitment and training plans. How would you analyse as yet non-existent jobs?
5   What similarities and differences in approach would you expect to be adopted in drawing up a job specification for a shopfloor operative, a computer operator, and a senior manager?

References

BRITISH INSTITUTE OF MANAGEMENT (1979), *Job Evaluation*, IBM, London.
BRITISH STANDARDS INSTITUTION (1979), *Glossary of Terms Used in Work Study and Organisation Methods*, BS3138, London.
CASCIO, W. P. (1982), *Applied Psychology in Personnel Management*, 2nd edn, Reston Pub. Co., Reston, Virginia.
EDWARDS, R. and PAUL, D. (1978), *Job Evaluation: a Guide for Trade Unionists*, APEX, London.
FINE, S. A. and WRETHA, A. (1972), *An Introduction to Functional Job Analysis: a Scaling of Selected Tasks from the Social Welfare Field*, Wiley, New York.
FOWLER, A. (1985), 'Getting in on organisation restructuring', *Personnel Management*, February.
GAEL, S. (1983), *Job Analysis: A Guide to Assessing Work Activities*, Jossey-Bass, London.
HERRIOT, P. (1984), *Down from the Ivory Tower: Graduates and their Jobs*, Wiley, Chichester.
LIVY, B. and VANT, J. H. B. (1979), 'Formula for selecting roughnecks and roustabouts', *Personnel Management*, February.
LIVY, B. L. and VANT, J. H. B. (1980), 'Oil rig workers in the North Sea: their selection and retention', Working Paper 18, The City University Business School, London.
RODGER, A. (1971), *The Seven Point Plan*, National Institute of Industrial Psychology, London.
SCOTT, K. (1976), *Office Job Evaluation*, The Institute of Administrative Management, Beckenham, Kent.

UNITED NATIONS (1976), *Introduction to Administration of Position Classification and Pay Plan*, New York.

UNITED STATES DEPARTMENT OF LABOR (1974), *Job Analysis for Human Resources Management: a Review of Selected Research and Development*, Manpower Research Monograph No. 35.

CHAPTER 4

Personnel recruitment and selection methods

by Bryan Livy

Recruitment

Recruitment is the first part of a personnel selection procedure; it is a resourcing activity. Recruitment should be distinguished from selection. Selection is that part of the procedure which is concerned with making choices between applicants. Recruitment is concerned with finding those applicants. The purpose of recruitment is to locate appropriate sources of supply of labour; to communicate job opportunities and information through various media; and to generate an interest in vacancies. To be effective, the recruiter needs to be equipped with two broad sets of information: (i) job specifications as determined by job analysis, and (ii) a knowledge of the labour market.

The 'labour market' is a nebulous concept, defined in various ways by economists. For our purposes we need to think of the national or local supply of labour as may be relevant to particular types of trade, skill or occupation that we predominantly employ. Today the recruiter operates in a 'buyer's market'. The recession, redundancy, and unemployment mean that the recruiter can potentially draw on a large pool. As well as the unemployed, the labour market in a wider sense contains a large, latent reserve of ability. Many people currently in gainful occupation are seeking to change jobs and employers. Employment is still a matter of exchange between employer and employee. At any time many people are seeking job advancement, wider experience, or higher monetary rewards. A degree of voluntary labour turnover persists at quite high levels. Therefore there is a degree of mobility in the labour market. The recruiter needs labour market 'intelligence' – he needs to follow national manpower statistics, levels of earnings, skill shortages and excesses, and he needs to maintain active liaison with agencies (particularly government agencies set up specifically for the purpose of channelling people into jobs, e.g. Job Centres) and also with educational institutions in the local community who annually supply the labour market with an influx of new blood. The supply of labour available at any one time will depend partly on economic circumstances, partly on the degree of competition between employers in bidding for and securing people for work, partly on the attractiveness of the job, partly on travel problems, and partly on the 'image' which any organization has as an employer. Since so much of the recruiter's job is to build a favourable image of his company as part of the general process of generating interest in the organization, much of his time must be spent on career talks in local youth centres, schools, etc. and on a wider net with exhibitions and presentations of the company's line of business, prospects and employment opportunities. A recruiter operates at the interface between an organization's demand for manpower and the supply of people as may be available on the open market.

Recruitment is concerned partly with the present and partly with the future. Its primary purpose is to fill existing job vacancies, but it must also be concerned with the long-term needs of the company. The level and phasing of recruitment must therefore be geared to manpower plans – to both current and anticipated requirements. Projections of changing job requirements influence recruitment decisions.

Every vacancy presents management with both an opportunity and a choice. Management has the opportunity to consider whether the job is in fact necessary, or whether the same job could be accomplished by some reorganization of work schedules. The choices with which it is confronted are mainly whether to recruit, whether to promote internally, or whether by means of training, existing employees could be redeployed. In many organizations there is an agreement with trade unions that all posts falling vacant should be advertised internally, and wherever possible promotion from within should be the norm. This is also largely true of the public sector.

The main aim of any recruitment campaign is to attract a good field of candidates from which to make selection decisions in order to fill required vacancies at required levels. Recruitment can be expensive and time-consuming. It behoves the recruiter to minimize expense, effort and delay, to develop the most efficient procedures, and to home-in on the target population.

METHODS OF RECRUITMENT AND MEDIA

If external recruitment is to be followed, the recruiter needs to consider which of the various media would be most appropriate. The most common medium is the press – either national or local, depending on costs and the extent of coverage required. Managerial jobs may frequently merit national advertisements, whereas the local press may be more suitable for clerical and operative jobs, depending on the nature of the local labour market. For specific skills (e.g. accountants, engineers, computer personnel), various trade, technical and professional publications may be more appropriate, although there is some time lag with these kinds of periodical. The important points to consider are the readership and circulation of any particular publication, and whether the choice of any of them would seem better in terms of relevance or urgency.

Commercial radio, television and cinemas are becoming increasingly popular media, particularly where large-scale recruitment campaigns are being mounted. Where job information and career opportunities can be presented in the form of video tapes, the stimulation of prospective job hunters and their response rates to such advertisements may be superior to either the written or spoken word.

Private employment agencies may help a recruiter to fill a position quickly, for a fee. A range of such agencies exists, specializing in clerical, technical or professional and managerial staff. They act as middlemen in the labour market. They may have already on their books people seeking re-employment or a job change, and will frequently undertake an initial pre-screening of candidates to feed the company recruiter with those most suitable. The degree to which such agencies have been given accurate job information will affect the efficiency of the outcome. But remember, an agency's desire is also to secure business.

The Department of Employment's Job Centres maintains inventories of job vacancies in their local areas and steer people towards appropriate job openings and/or government schemes of training. All agencies, whether public or private, are by nature removed from an employer's scene of operations. It therefore behoves the recruiter to maintain close liaison with such agencies as he chooses, in order to familiarize them closely and on an up-to-date basis with the needs of the jobs he is trying to fill and the particular personal qualities and attributes he is seeking.

Traditionally, one of the oldest forms of recruitment was via a company noticeboard prominently displayed in the factory forecourt. This can still be an effective method of recruitment, especially for manual or clerical jobs, but in these hard times one sees fewer such hoardings.

Other methods of recruitment are more informal. Many applicants make unsolicited approaches to companies, often because they have heard of impending vacancies through the grapevine, or from members of their family. Indeed, in some occupations, new entrants have to be 'spoken for' by established workers; this applies especially to those industries where there has been a tradition of sons following in fathers' footsteps, e.g. in the docks and the coalmines. Elsewhere particular occupations demand recruits who are 'acceptable', so that common attitudes and work practices can be maintained. In some developing countries, *only* members of families currently employed have any chance of getting a job. In some cases, trade unions have an influential role to play in the recruitment and selection of newcomers, e.g. the printing industry. Headhunting – whereby unofficial and informal approaches are made to successful executives – is a form of recruitment which seems to have grown in recent years in most European countries as an extension of transatlantic practice. The choice of the most appropriate recruitment methods or media requires knowledge of the coverage, pulling power, cost and timing of publications, of advertisements, of what services can be provided by specialist agencies, and an understanding of the cultural background.

THE MESSAGE

An advertisement will only succeed if it conveys the right information to the right people. Careful job analysis must be the foundation of the advert. Candidates will only be attracted if they can recognize from the facts as given the suitability of the post for them and the prospect of greater satisfaction. The advertisement must contain enough information about the work itself, the attributes, experience and attainments required, location, prospects, and an earnings indicator. Part of the recruitment procedure must be to generate a degree of 'self-selection' in the target population: it must begin to narrow down the field of candidates as well as encourage potential applicants. Careful copywriting is therefore critical. In the words of one authority, it must: 'Claim Attention – Convey a Story – Arouse a Desire – Stimulate Action' (Ray, 1980).

NON-DISCRIMINATION IN RECRUITMENT

Recruiters should guard against discrimination. Recruitment advertisers, like everyone else, are subject to the laws of the land; and to the Code of Advertising Practice, the advertising industry's self-regulating arrangements to ensure that advertisements are legal, decent, honest and truthful.

Perhaps the most sensitive areas are non-discriminative on grounds of race or sex. The legal requirements are set out in detail by Greville Janner in Chapter 12, and the principal implications are explored by Baroness Seear in Chapters 15–18. In summary, at this stage it is unlawful to advertise in places where women are unlikely to be aware of vacancies. The Sex Discrimination Act (1975) is quite specific about the form and content of the advertisement. An advertisement must not indicate any 'intention to discriminate' nor must it be implied. Nor must it specify sex (apart from genuine occupational qualifications). Recruitment literature should state that the company is an equal opportunity employer – applicants of either sex can apply.

The Sex Discrimination Act applies to all stages of the selection procedure – to job specification, conditions of employment, and arrangements for interviews. Similar precautions should be observed in the case of racial non-discrimination, under the Race Relations Act 1976. In both cases, discrimination is illegal either *directly* (by treating one person or group less favourably than others), or *indirectly* (by applying a requirement or condition which, whether intentionally or not, adversely affects one group more than another, and which cannot be justified under the terms of the Acts).

In relation to employment the term 'disabled person' has a statutory definition as set out in the Disabled Persons (Employment) Act 1944: 'A person who, on account of injury, disease, or congenital deformity is substantially handicapped in obtaining or keeping employment, or in undertaking work on his own account, of a kind which apart from the injury, disease, deformity would be suited to his age, qualifications and experience.'

The Secretary of State for Employment maintains a register of disabled persons who are issued with a certificate of registration. Registration indicates that such persons are capable of undertaking paid employment.

In employment, the main protection offered to disabled people is the original 1944 Act which established the *Quota Scheme*. Under this scheme any employer of 20 or more people who employs fewer than 3 per cent of registered disabled people (the 'standard percentage') must obtain a permit in order to engage someone other than a registered disabled person. Employers who are obliged to employ a quota of disabled persons must keep appropriate records. In theory, if an employer fails to satisfy the quota he must offer every fresh vacancy to a registered disabled person, normally through the Disablement Resettlement Officer. Certain jobs, e.g. lift or car park attendants, have become traditionally designated for disabled persons. Only if a registered disabled applicant is not available can the employer be issued with a permit to employ a non-disabled worker.

Despite a moral obligation, commentators have pointed to a widespread failure of nationalized industries, local authorities and central government departments as well as private companies to meet their quota requirements. Often, bulk exemption permits to employers which free them from their obligation has meant that few need to reach the quota. Disabled persons, like ethnic minorities and other disadvantaged groups, are adversely affected in the increasingly competitive world of employment.

The nature of disability is also changing. The Act was originally brought in to help those injured in the two wars; but now there are more suffering from degenerative or chronic illnesses and more children disabled at birth are now surviving – like those with spina bifida (i.e. a congenital malformation of the spine). Above all, there has been an increase in those with mental handicaps: organic nervous diseases and psychiatric histories.

Although the Quota Scheme gives priority to a disabled person with equal qualifications, it does not give any positive incentive to employers to employ disabled people and to re-examine their job specifications in order to fit the skills which a person can offer. There is, as yet, no legal requirement for new premises to provide access and facilities for disabled people, since places of employment are not covered by the Chronic Sick and Disabled Persons Act 1970. The Quota Scheme applies to registered disabled workers, and many employers say that if all disabled people were compelled to register, their quota levels would be much higher. The reasons for failure to register are understandable. If disabled persons are in a job already, there is no point in registering, for being registered is no help if they are dismissed and the Act has no power to reinstate or compensate them. Disabled people themselves may not accept that they have a disability which prevents them from getting or keeping the job. To some registration is a handicap. They feel it stamps them in an employer's mind as being difficult to employ, or needing special treatment.

Anti-discrimination laws regarding disabled people were proposed by a government-appointed committee in a report published 26th May 1982. The Committee on Restrictions Against Disabled People (CORADP) wants the

Government to set up a new Commission to champion the disabled along the lines of the Equal Opportunities Commission and the Commission for Racial Equality. Essentially, the Report calls for changes in the law to make it illegal to discriminate against disabled people in jobs, education, pension schemes, insurance, transport, the provision of goods, facilities, and services and membership of clubs. What is really needed is a positive approach.

It may be tempting or deemed prudent for an employer to discriminate against people with previous criminal convictions especially at the time of recruitment or selection. But there is some protection for the transgressor.

The Rehabilitation of Offenders Act 1974 lays down that people who have been convicted of criminal offences and have completed their sentences are, with some exceptions, not obliged to disclose those convictions. A conviction becomes '*spent*' after a period of time, depending on the severity of the sentence (ranging from 1 year for a conditional discharge, 5 years for a fine, 10 years for imprisonment of 6–30 months). The main exceptions are life imprisonment, prison sentences exceeding 30 months, or detention at Her Majesty's pleasure.

After a conviction becomes spent, an offender is known as a '*rehabilitated person*'. Such a person is not obliged in law to disclose the nature of the offence or the conviction, although he may be asked. In employment, failing to admit to a past conviction in the terms laid out are not justifiable grounds for non-engagement, dismissal or refusal to promote. Exceptions arise under the Rehabilitation of Offenders Act 1974 (Exceptions) Order 1975 whereby certain people in the medical profession, lawyers, teachers, accountants and police offenders are in fact required to disclose spent convictions. Anti-discrimination in this case is quite discriminatory!

THE IPM RECRUITMENT CODE

In 1985 the Institute of Personnel Management issued a Recruitment Code. In summary, a recruiter's obligations are stated as:

'1   Job advertisements should state clearly the form of reply desired, in particular whether this should be a formal application form or by curriculum vitae. Preferences should also be stated if handwritten replies are required.

2   An acknowledgement or reply should be made promptly to each applicant by the employing organization or its agent. If it is likely to take some time before acknowledgements are made, this should be made clear in the advertisement.

3   Applicants should be informed of the progress of the selection procedures, what there will be (e.g. group selection, aptitude tests, etc.), the steps and time involved and the policy regarding expenses.

4   Detailed personal information (e.g. religion, medical history, place of birth, family background, etc.) should not be called for unless it is relevant to the selection process.

5   Before applying for references, potential employers must secure permission of the applicant.
6   Applications must be treated as confidential.'
7   The Code also recommends certain courtesies and obligations on the part of applicants.

Finally, the advertisement must give instructions to the candidate as to what to do either to obtain more information or to pursue an application. Those who do pursue the matter further can usefully be sent a 'job preview' – a synopsis of the main aspects of the job in rather more detail than was possible in the space of an advertisement.

ADMINISTRATION

The administrative steps to be followed in recruitment are:

1   Obtain approval for engagement in accordance with manpower budgets and manning levels.
2   Update and confirm job description and specification.
3   Select media.
4   Prepare advertising copy.
5   Place advertisements.
6   Allow time for replies (maybe indicating a closing date).
7   Screen replies.
8   Shortlist candidates for initial interview.
9   Devise and programme the selection procedure to be followed.
10 Advise all applicants accordingly.

ANALYSIS OF RESPONSES

Any particular medium attracts an 'audience' whether by radio, television or press. Little published research has been made available into the effectiveness of any recruitment medium. As far as publications are concerned, the recruiter needs to know the scope of their readership and circulation. Various media sometimes conduct surveys upon readership and publish them, but few categorize their readership into occupational groups of direct relevance to the recruiter – such surveys are more likely to be conducted on a socio-economic basis. More important, not all readers are job hunters; many are casual readers. And of those who respond, many may be merely curious.

The 'pulling power' of an advertisement will depend partly on having aimed the shot accurately, and partly on timing. 'Traffic' varies, i.e. the number of readers on any given day. Response rates fluctuate according to the time of the year or week. For example, all statutory holidays and the summer months are relatively quieter for most levels of employment; although July, August and September bring a new harvest of school leavers and graduates.

Responses to an advertisement can be measured by number and quality. No amount of refinement or sophistication of the subsequent selection procedure, however skilful, can compensate for a poor shortlist of candidates.

Recruitment must also be cost effective. This requires a careful analysis of recruitment campaigns. A simple formula:

$$\frac{\text{recruitment costs}}{\text{number starting work}}$$

provides an index which can be applied to successive recruitment campaigns. A falling index shows an improvement in cost terms. An organization needs to build up an 'intelligence' of its own recruitment performance. The main variables to be listed are given in Table 4.1.

Although recruitment display advertisements fell in volume during the recent years of recession, costs continued to escalate. Some of the largest firms in the UK now have annual recruitment advertising budgets of over £1m. Improvements in recruitment efficiency come from improvements in the way in which an organization taps the labour market.

Recruitment is a 'positive' act of management, of going out into the

Table 4.1   Recruitment information

Job reference number
Media used
Was advertisement for one job, two jobs, or 'general opportunities'?
Were the number of vacancies to be filled stated?
Were full job specifications given?
Was the company named?

Style of advertisement: line/semi-display/display
Size of advertisement (area of space)
Number of insertions
Day of week and month appearing
Was a box number used?

Numerical response – number of replies per medium/per insertion
Number of application forms and further details sent
Number of applications returned
Number of 'suitable' applications
Numbers invited for initial interview
Number of job offers made
Number of job offers accepted
Advertising costs
Recruitment expenses (e.g. travel)
Hidden costs (e.g. postage, literature)
Costs per reply
Costs per hire
Total recruitment costs.

marketplace, communicating and attracting. Selection is largely a 'negative' act – it is the process of 'rejection', since more candidates are likely to be turned away than hired.

The criterion problem

The purpose of personnel selection is to *predict* the future success of applicants on the job. This leads to several fundamental theoretical and practical questions which personnel selectors must ask, and try to answer.

First: What are we aiming at? (i.e. what are the 'criteria' of actual job behaviour and specified levels of performance?)

Second: What are the precise constituents of *successful* performance? What are their dimensions? How do we recognize them? How do we measure them?

Third: What are the relevant indicators (i.e. 'predictors') which will tell us how various candidates are likely to perform?

Predictors are techniques of measurement or assessment which, when applied to a field of as yet unselected candidates, enable us to discriminate between them in a way which will reflect their probability of success in the job. Interview ratings, test scores, etc. are 'predictor scores'. Clearly the starting point must be the job itself. Careful definition of the criterion must precede the setting-up of a selection procedure, the choice of predictors, and the determination of a scale of predictor assessments (scores) and appropriate 'cut-off' points below which we would not accept candidates for the jobs to be filled.

There are two sets of assessments which need to be reconciled:
 (i) performance at the criterion.
(ii) performance on the predictor.

As a theoretical ideal, the performance of any individual on both sets of assessments should be identical (i.e. both on the predictor used in selection and subsequent performance on the job). If not, there is something deficient with the predictors, or with an accurate determination of the criterion.

Conceptually and diagrammatically, the two complementary sets of assessments (predictor and criterion) can be represented as in Fig. 4.1 (developing the models of Blum and Naylor, 1968; Guion, 1976; Cascio, 1982).

If personnel selection is perfect and if predictors totally reflect job requirements, performance of an individual on both sets of assessment should be identical. There would then be a perfect correlation between predictor and criterion. Diagrammatically, in Fig. 4.1, the two circles would overlap completely. In practice, this rarely obtains; imperfections arise from deficiencies in the predictors, contamination in the criteria adopted because of the difficulties of identifying them and isolating them, and various forms of bias and error which creep into the ratings and assessments used. More usually, the correlation between predictor and criterion measures, i.e. the degree to

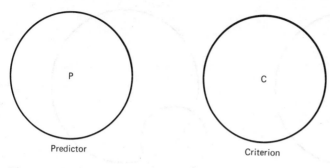

Fig. 4.1 *Predictor and criterion*

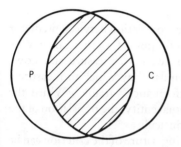

Fig. 4.2 *Predictor/criterion correlation*

which they co-vary in a systematic fashion, is relatively low. Using our circles again (correctly called Venn diagrams) the amount of bivariate predictor – criterion association – may be illustrated as in Fig. 4.2. The degree of relationship between these two sets of measurements or between any two variables, is simply the extent to which they vary together in a systematic way. The degree to which they are linearly related can be indicated by a measure of correlation, such as the Pearson product moment correlation coefficient, r. If both sets of scores are perfectly and systematically related to each other, then r is said to be 1.00. As a tentative guide to the interpretation of validity coefficients, we can say that anything over 0.70 is a very high correlation, between 0.40 and 0.70 is a medium correlation, between 0.20 and 0.40 is a low correlation, and 0.00 to 0.20 is a negligible relationship. Low scores are not meaningless, since correlations are often computed on only a sample of possible data, and predictors developed on pilot groups are not always completely generalizable.

The main reason for lack of perfect correlation is due to the fact that most predictor assessments in practice can only be based on simulated or partial samples of job behaviour, and not on the totality of the job. Simple, straightforward jobs can be replicated in selection situations fairly easily, e.g. a typing test for a typist. With more complex jobs, the selection procedure can only incorporate certain parts of the actual job. Diagrammatically this point can be illustrated in Fig. 4.3.

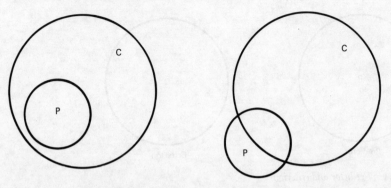

Fig. 4.3   *Predictors can only correlate with parts of a job*

Part of the explanation for the lack of perfect correlation between predictor and criterion also lies in the fact that the definition of a criterion may be elusive. Basically the 'criterion problem' is: what to measure and how? Effectively, the criterion is an 'evaluative standard' by which to measure a person's performance; it is therefore a 'performance variable'. Whilst the criterion can easily be understood as a conceptual entity, the translation of the criterion into practical terms is much more difficult.

Diagrammatically, the dynamic and changing nature of the criterion can be illustrated as in Fig. 4.4.

Successive criterion measures (C_1, C_2, C_3, C_4, C_5) represent successive jobs in a career of promotions. Job dimensions are likely to get bigger. Although there are links between them, the ultimate criterion (C_5) may have totally different job demands from the immediate or intermediate criteria.

There exists then, in theory and in practice, a series of successive criterion measures. In formulating a selection procedure, we are forced to choose one particular criterion – knowing full well that we are excluding certain aspects of the work situation. However, we must come to a decision. Obviously,

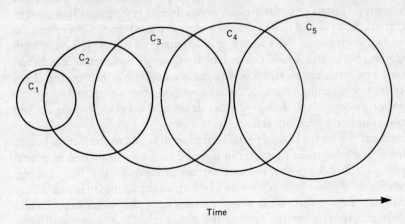

Time

Fig. 4.4   *Changing nature of criteria over time*

any criterion adopted must be measurable, realistic and acceptable (to personnel selectors, management, and trade unions if they are involved).

The first practical problem is that the criterion is not independent of time. Criteria change as jobs change; or as an individual moves up a hierarchy of jobs. It is conventional and convenient to distinguish between the *immediate*, *intermediate* and *ultimate* criteria. The immediate criterion is that which obtains immediately after the point of selection and when an employee first begins work. This is a fairly short-run view and we may have very clear ideas about what the immediate job requirements are. However, the job may modulate after a short period of time, perhaps after the employee completes a probationary period, or is promoted up the next rung of the ladder. We may still at this stage have a fairly clear idea of the intermediate criterion, but it is likely to have altered. The real question is: what have we appointed this employee for? To do a basic low-level job? Or to make progress? Finally, if we look much further into the future, we may have only a very vague idea of what later, ultimate criteria will be.

The point is well illustrated in a company which recruits people into the bottom levels of the organization and then by promotion from within moves them successively through a series of posts, each having greater responsibility. The Clearing Banks provide an example. Bank clerks begin their careers doing routine, fairly closely supervised work, and later progress to more demanding work, e.g. securities or foreign exchange. Some of them will eventually move into managerial appointments. Quite clearly the criterion of performance for a bank clerk is quite different from that of a branch manager. The later criterion incorporates business, leadership, judgemental and administrative skills.

For guidance, it is helpful to focus on three critical criterion issues:

1 time: We must come to a decision as to which point in time the criterion shall in fact be applied (and ignore any other point in time, since not to do so would become practicably unworkable);
2 type of performance measure to be adopted: Since there are a number of ways in which one could legitimately assess performance on the job (e.g. results-oriented performance, ratings by supervisors, or length of stay in the job), the type of performance measure adopted must be specified precisely;
3 level of performance: According to the type of performance measure adopted, what is regarded as an acceptable level or standard must also be specified.

We might further add that, of all the possible criterion measures available, it is unlikely that any one single criterion will adequately reflect the whole job. An individual can be a good worker for any number of diverse reasons. So a combination of various criteria should be chosen – to provide a 'multidimensional' set of criteria – and combined using a statistical weighting scheme according to the relative importance of the various aspects. However, in any kind of multiple criterion, it may well be that the various components are not independent of each other; in which case they should be used singly, perhaps measuring and using each to validate a different selection instrument (predictor).

PREDICTORS

Predictors are techniques of assessment used in personnel selection which provide a means of discrimination between candidates, and offer predictions regarding subsequent performance (at the criterion).

Obviously, predictors must be *relevant* to the needs of the job (there is no point in measuring candidates' hair colour or ability to climb over a brick wall if the job does not call for this; there is no point measuring candidates' intelligence precisely if we are not able, with equally accurate precision, to recommend a specific intellectual level for the job, etc.).

Predictors must possess two basic qualities:

1   Reliability, i.e. consistency, repeatability (producing the same results on successive applications) and freedom from contamination and random error variance. The key point here is that any predictor, if it is reliable, can be used with certainty; it is a standard yardstick of measurement.

2   Validity, i.e. accuracy. Does the predictor measure what it purports to measure? Or does it measure something else (perhaps as well as its main purpose)? Is it contaminated? Does it give us a *true* indication of what we are looking for?

The term *validation* refers to the degree to which predictor scores or other measures predict criterion measures.

There are in general use four kinds or interpretations of validity:

1   *Face validity*: Apparent relevance, acceptability and credibility of a predictor.

2   *Content validity*: the predictor must be representative of job content, and be composed of the right kind of subject-matter.

3   *Concurrent validity*: this is the extent to which a predictor will discriminate between *present* employees, e.g. good/bad in accordance with the results obtained from another independent measure, e.g. the subjective ratings of their supervisors. In other words, this is one of the ways of testing a test. Since we have information about our present employees in terms of how well they perform (which may have been acquired by means of another test, or by their measurable performance on the job, or what their boss already thinks of them) we can see whether a predictor produces the same kind of results as those which we already have. To the extent that it does so it is said to be concurrently valid.

4   *Predictive validity*: this is the extent to which a predictor is capable of predicting subsequent performance, and discriminating between future employees, e.g. good/bad. Technically, predictive validity is the extent to which variance in a predictor score is associated with variance in

subsequent criterion measures. In practice, predictive validity is the most important element.

There is a further type of validity: 'construct' validity which psychologists would argue is important, and relates to whether the predictor gives an answer to an established psychological construct, e.g. anxiety, neurosis, intelligence.

The concepts of reliability and validity are extremely important. Only if selection techniques have high reliability and validity can we have any confidence in them.

Predictor techniques fall into two main categories: *objective* and *subjective*. The main objective techniques are those which can be derived from overt behaviour and can be quantifiable; psychological tests fall into this category, and are probably the best example. Subjective techniques are based on people's opinions and ratings, often recorded with the use of rating scales. Subjective techniques are essentially those which are based on human judgements, i.e. those made by assessors, interviewers, supervisors, etc. The main subjective techniques commonly in use are interviews of various kinds, group selection methods, and assessment centres. The main problem with subjective measures is that they are particularly susceptible to errors of judgement, halo and bias.

Predictive decisions are usually made on the basis of multiple sources of information. Since jobs consist of so many component parts, we may wish to measure a person's aptitude for each part separately. It is therefore important to recognize that an applicant who scores satisfactorily on any one particular selection device may not, *ipso facto*, be the right person for the job. He or she may be found wanting in some other characteristics, which we must assess by other selection devices – by a 'battery' of assessments. A number of different predictor devices may then each probe at a certain element of job require-ment. Each predictor might separately measure a proportion of the criterion, or some of the predictors might overlap.

The criterion itself may change over time, and there are many different ways of defining it. The objective of the exercise is to pin-point the key elements on which success or failure will depend. Having identified these key elements, appropriate predictors (or techniques of assessment) can be used or developed provided that they are relevant to the requirements of the job and really tell us something useful about how the candidate may perform or behave in the real world. In other words, an attempt must be made to predict future performance from a sample of present performance.

Preselection

Personnel selection is a process of job-matching, and must begin with a description of the jobs to be done and the identification of personal qualities necessary for their successful execution. We must, therefore, in a sense, work backwards from the job itself and try to identify crucial, performance criteria and the capacities and inclinations necessary – by highlighting the main things which cause mistakes, failure or indifferent motivation – and define our jobs in such a way that they make sense when we are trying to compare them against people's attributes. Profiles of jobs and people must be couched in the same language and presented in the same format (as discussed in Chapter 3).

Personnel selection procedures attempt to predict the future. The basic methodology of the selection process is to compare each individual candidate against the job specification, and against each other candidate. Both in the real world and in the literature, the importance of job analysis is constantly stressed to identify the intellectual and social skills as well as personality traits required of candidates. Job analysis is a key component in the preparation of a candidate profile which is then used to formulate the preselection system and interview schedule.

The aim of a selection procedure is to narrow the field of candidates by progressively eliminating those who do not measure up to the specification. Depending on the degree of accuracy required and the complexity of the job requirements, a selection procedure may consist of a number of steps. At each step a decision must be made as to whether a candidate should be considered further – and progress to the next step – or be rejected. The main steps which are normally included in a selection procedure are: an application form, an initial interview, a second interview perhaps with line management, the application of psychological or situational tests, group selection methods, references and medical examination. Not every procedure needs to include all these items nor need they necessarily be in the order given. The more information one needs to have about a candidate the more extended the procedure needs to be. In any case, the first 'sift' is the application form.

APPLICATION FORMS

An application form is a tool for summarizing basic information about a candidate; it is designed to capture biodata predictive of job performance. The application form must therefore be structured to elicit the kind of information required. Ideally, each application form should be tailored to the job, setting out questions in accordance with the format of the job specification. However, this is uneconomical for most companies and standardized application forms must normally suffice, but they ought to be more elaborate and searching for managerial and professional jobs than for clerical or manual jobs. The basic areas which any application form should cover are:

1 basic biographical facts (e.g. age, education, training, qualifications, domicile)

2 work or occupational experience, job histories, previous employers, duties undertaken and levels of responsibility

Table 4.2

IBM

IBM UNITED KINGDOM LIMITED
IBM UNITED KINGDOM LABORATORIES LIMITED
IBM INFORMATION SERVICES LIMITED

APPLICATION FOR EMPLOYMENT

The information contained in this form will be treated as strictly confidential and no reference will be taken up without your permission.

SURNAME

FIRST NAMES

HOME ADDRESS

TELEPHONE No.

TEMPORARY ADDRESS
(if different from above)

TELEPHONE No.

PRESENT BUSINESS TEL No.
(if convenient)

DO YOU HOLD A CURRENT FULL UK
DRIVING LICENCE?

WILL YOU NEED TO OBTAIN A WORK PERMIT?

(if you are in any doubt about the need for a work permit you should contact the Home Office on 01-686-0688 for advice before returning this form)

POSITION APPLIED FOR

AT WHICH IBM LOCATIONS WOULD YOU
PREFER TO WORK?

SOURCE OF APPLICATION (eg newspaper name, date and advertisement reference, name of person, educational establishment, professional association, etc.)

DATE AVAILABLE FOR EMPLOYMENT OR PERIOD
OF NOTICE YOU HAVE OR WISH TO GIVE

PLEASE INDICATE WHETHER YOU HAVE MADE
AN APPLICATION TO IBM PREVIOUSLY

Date
Location
Position Sought
Have you ever been employed
by IBM?
If so, when

HAVE YOU ANY RELATIVES EMPLOYED BY
THIS COMPANY. IF SO, PLEASE STATE

NAME

RELATIONSHIP

DEPARTMENT

IF REQUIRED, WOULD YOU BE WILLING TO
WORK SHIFT WORK?

UK FORM 5-935 (7/77)

Table 4.2 – *cont.*

Education (Secondary Onwards)

Dates (month & year) From	To	Type	Full name and address of establishment	Courses taken and subjects studied (please state whether full-time, part-time or sandwich)	Qualifications gained/Examinations passed		
					Examination	Subjects	Grade/class

Any additional training or development courses attended

Please state any school, college, university, professional or other societies/bodies to which you belong(ed), indicating any position held.

Do you have knowledge of any foreign languages? If so, please state:

Language(s)

Degree of fluency

Table 4.2 – *cont.*

STATE WHAT TYPE OF WORK INTERESTS YOU, WHY YOU ARE APPLYING FOR THIS POSITION
AND ALSO ANY LONG TERM CAREER AIMS YOU MAY HAVE

PLEASE GIVE BELOW ANY ADDITIONAL INFORMATION YOU THINK MAY SUPPORT YOUR APPLICATION
OR ANY INFORMATION OF WHICH YOU THINK WE SHOULD BE AWARE, WHEN CONSIDERING YOU
FOR EMPLOYMENT

TO THE BEST OF MY KNOWLEDGE AND BELIEF THE ABOVE STATEMENTS ARE TRUE AND I UNDERSTAND
THAT WITHHOLDING OR MIS–STATING FACTS CALLED FOR ABOVE MAY BE THE CAUSE FOR REFUSAL
OR TERMINATION OF EMPLOYMENT WITH THE COMPANY

SIGNATURE   DATE

Registration Nos: 741598, 618957, 791289

Table 4.2 – *cont.*

Past and present employment

Former employers will not be approached without your permission. Record your positions in chronological order, ending with your present job.
Please account for any intervals of non-employment and include temporary jobs and full-time service in H.M. Forces.

Dates (month & year) From To	Name and full address of company/employer	Type of business	Position(s) or rank(s) held (with dates)	Duties and responsibilities	Salary or earnings (on starting and on leaving)	Reason for leaving

DO YOU HAVE ANY COMMITMENT TO ANOTHER EMPLOYER WHICH MIGHT AFFECT YOUR EMPLOYMENT WITH IBM?

3 work interest patterns of the candidate in general, but particularly career aspirations and the expectations which the candidate has about the job applied for.

An example of an application form is given in Table 4.2.

Sometimes a 'weighted' application form can be used to facilitate preliminary screening, an approach more prevalent in the United States. Weights applied to any of the factors have to be carefully devised according to the key criteria for success in the job. 'Knock-out' items may be included where certain factors are deemed detrimental to job performance. It might also be possible to place candidates in a preliminary rank order.

To use an application form actuarially would require collecting data from a large number of recruits and relating this statistically in the manner of a conventional credit-scoring system to their subsequent job performances appropriately measured. If the weights established are relatively constant over time, then the resulting linear additive model can be used to sift later application forms on a routine basis. However, it would seem that very few organizations in the UK use application forms in this way, with most rated subjectively and with different assessors, even within the same organization, using different decision-making strategies.

Most selectors use the application form to build up a preliminary picture – albeit subjectively and impressionistically, constructing 'a coherent picture of the applicant in accordance with the recruiter's implicit personality theories and their views of the types of applicant required for jobs in their organization' (Herriot and Wingrove, 1984).

The interview

The interview is the most commonly used selection technique. During the interview two people are seeking understanding through an interactive social process. The most obvious feature about the interview is its dual nature; it forms a human link between applicant and organization. It is a process of two-way communication and therefore of two-way decision-making. At the end of the procedure a decision is only made by mutual consent, and a contract of employment voluntarily entered into.

The interview as a technique can have a variety of uses and purposes, e.g. counselling, discipline, performance appraisal and personnel selection. In all cases it provides for an exchange of information, judgements and opinions. 'A selection interview is an extension and development of the inevitable meeting which takes place between an employer and a prospective employee' (Graham, 1980).

Commonly, writers have defined the interview as 'a conversation with a purpose', but it is not only conversational (using language) but also observational (using non-verbal behaviour and the senses) to explore a candidate's ability, acceptability and surface personality. The interview is a dynamic and interpersonal experience, influenced by a host of motivational and perceptive variables. It is also an exercise in public relations. The interviewer is a front man portraying favourable images as an employer. The candidate seeks to sell himself.

Given the universality of the selection interview as a technique for making employment decisions, it is not surprising that it has spawned both antagonists and protagonists. It has been the subject of considerable research. From the evidence, a number of indications emerge as to how the interview can be improved.

There are probably as many types of interviewing as there are interviewers. Attempts have been made to classify interview methods (Siegel and Lane, 1974) according to the degree of structure and depth and number of interviewers involved. One particular categorization (Fear, 1973) defined interviews as 'direct, indirect and patterned'. In a *direct* interview, the interviewer asks specific questions, keeping control of the proceedings much as a doctor might use a diagnostic checklist. This method can produce a lot of factual information quickly but is not likely to encourage generalized opinions, feelings or detailed accounts.

The *indirect* interview is unstructured (i.e. non-directed). In this case, the interviewer takes a passive role and follows no clear direction or pursuit of a particular goal. The onus rests on the interviewee to focus the exercise. Whilst the candidate might speak more candidly, the shape, format and content of interviews will therefore vary so much between interviewees that any assessments made are likely to be highly subjective and probably of low reliability. The discursive nature of the indirect interview is likely to have more relevance where jobs are ill-defined as may be the case in senior managerial appointments, but the technique itself was originally developed in psychiatric circles as a means of encouraging people to speak freely.

A *patterned* interview is one which is both structured and standardized, based upon a comprehensive questionnaire. The purpose of an interviewer's guide is to achieve uniformity between various interviewers and consistency.

A further type of interview is known as *planned* interview (or depth interview). If the interview is not to be haphazard, it must be based on a carefully constructed plan and worked through systematically. The plan of the interview should largely be dictated by the job specification, indicating necessary areas of investigation and highlighting key requirements about which assessment must be made regarding performance criteria. In the UK a variety of interview plans are widely used. One of these is the seven-point plan developed by the National Institute of Industrial Psychology (Rodger, 1971), originally evolved for vocational guidance. The seven points are:

1   physical make-up
2   attainments
3   general intelligence
4   special aptitudes
5   interests

6   disposition
7   circumstances.

A caveat is called for. Neither this nor any other plan has utility for personnel selection if interviewers are unable to categorize the job specification under the same subheadings or facts. It may well be that many jobs do not lend themselves to this precise format.

> 'We must not let the apparent tidiness of the plan tempt us into imagining that the device of splitting a person's attributes and circumstances into seven "segments" is anything better than a rather regrettable necessity. The divisions we make are for convenience.' (Rodger, 1971)

A similar plan developed by J. Munro Fraser (1970) identifies five main points:

1   impact on others (the kind of reaction the applicant draws out from other people)
2   qualifications or acquired knowledge
3   innate abilities or brains
4   motivation (those aspects of personality which concern the setting of targets, working consistently towards their achievement, displaying initiative in overcoming difficulties)
5   adjustment (the ability to stand up to stress).

There are obvious dangers in adopting a ready-made plan which may not fit perfectly. The purpose of any plan is to facilitate job matching. Most authorities would argue that we definitely need some kind of framework (Higham, 1979a). It may be better to draw up a specific plan in accordance with our own clear identification of job requirements, from job analysis. Clearly, the better versed an interviewer is in the actual job requirements, the better will be both the interrogatory content of the interview and the decision-making process. It follows that a planned procedure is necessary to ensure that the key points are covered in each interview, and that candidates are consistently treated. Absence of an interview guide leads to lower intra-interviewer consistency and superficiality in topic coverage (Keenan and Wedderburn, 1980). Interviewers' whims or idiosyncratic styles should be avoided if equity is to prevail.

RAPPORT AND EMPATHY

Interviews are delicate, sometimes stressful experiences – candidates should be made to feel comfortable in a relaxed, supportive atmosphere. Even the way in which a candidate is invited to interview is important. Precise directions and (if possible) convenient timings are basic courtesies. The interview room should be private and free from interruption. The welcome and initial overtures should be open and friendly, for the interviewer is 'host'.

His or her first job is to establish confidence and trust. The interviewer holds a position of power – a 'gatekeeper' controlling access to employment resources. As the custodian of opportunities he or she is likely to be viewed with some trepidation. Many applicants may be tense and ill at ease. The interviewer must dispel anxiety and show understanding. He or she must develop rapport, 'the development of sensitivity to a candidate's attitudes and feelings' (Anstey, 1977a).

The interviewer should begin on a neutral conversational topic but get down to business fairly quickly, outlining the objectives of the meeting and the agenda. The interviewer might explain how he or she will conduct proceedings, saying for example: 'First, I will tell you something about the job and the company. Then we will go through your own background to date. But most of the time we will talk about the job, its problems, and challenges, in more detail.' The interviewer is responsible for setting the tone and conduct of the interview and for making sure that the ground is covered adequately. His or her overt behaviour must be one of politeness and respect, making the interviewee feel that the interview is important. Interviewer and interviewee must try to identify with each other.

> 'Once rapport has been established, the actual questions matter less and less. The candidate senses what one is getting at without worrying about the form of words, and becomes increasingly at ease and responds more spontaneously.'
> (Anstey, 1977b)

How the interview goes depends much on the interaction of personalities – on *empathy*. Empathy, the 'power of projecting one's personality into (and so fully comprehending) the object of contemplation' (according to the *Concise Oxford Dictionary*) can be communicated through choice of phrase, emphasis, manner and facial expression. Effort must be directed at trying to understand a candidate, and to refrain from criticism.

CONDUCTING THE INTERVIEW

The interview is an exercise in communication, in social and verbal skills. This is also one of its weaknesses, for a conversational approach has to be adopted for an analysis of what may well be non-conversational skills as far as the requirements of the job are concerned. The interview covers a brief time span; therefore it must be highly condensed. For this reason a structure is essential and enough time must be allocated. The procedure must be organized systematically but conducted flexibly. It is often useful to begin by going through a candidate's biographical background, for this is an area with which the candidate is obviously familiar, and it helps to generate confidence before going into the more tricky business of seeing how a candidate might actually cope with the job. The main biographical areas to be covered are education, work experience and present activities and interests. From this the interviewer should begin to build up a picture of a candidate's strengths and weaknesses and from then on probe these more deeply in accordance with the job specification.

The role of the interviewer is to listen, probe, facilitate and interpret. The questions should be *open-ended*, inviting applicants to talk. *Closed* questions (e.g. 'Do you like working with figures?', as opposed to 'What attracts you most to working with figures?') only invite monosyllabic yes/no answers. The interviewer must be probing all the time. *Probe questions* can be prefaced by what? how? why? etc., with a view to uncovering a deeper significance of a candidate's background, achievements and work experience. 'At times the interviewer is sharp and in focus, specific and rational; at other times, intuitive, picking up nuances and rationalizations' (Bayne, 1977). Depending on the job in question, the interviewer may be looking for the responsiveness of a candidate, self-expression, the relevance of past experience to the job in hand, questions of adaptability and motivation, interpersonal relationships, leadership skills, and consistency in a candidate's growth and development. An interrogatory style is called for, and the interviewer must be particularly on the lookout for inconsistencies and omissions. Rather as in a cross-examination, the interviewer should first build on incontrovertible facts, then probe and seek fuller information on areas of omission where these are of relevance to the job in question; it is important to watch for inconsistencies in motivation, attitude and achievements at various times in the past and try to elicit a candidate's reconciliation of these inconsistencies or further explanations as to why they may have come about.

At all times the candidate must be encouraged. The close attention of the interviewer is paramount. To help the flow and direction of the interview, the interviewer can ask *facilitating questions*. For example, repeating or rewording a question is useful if a candidate strays from the point or does not comprehend. Paraphrasing an applicant's responses can help to consolidate the ground covered and give further encouragement. The interviewer can also ask neutral questions or make general comments, to 'punctuate' the interview, and provide the candidate with a breathing space or time to collect his or her thoughts.

Finally, the interviewer has to establish whether the candidate has the level of ability to manage the immediate (or long-term) criterion requirements. This can be achieved from inference of an ability to cope with the requirements of a job by hypothesizing various problems and seeing whether the candidate adopts a logical and knowledgeable approach to the solution. For example, an interviewer might ask, 'A problem which this company is faced with is . . . how would you go about it?' This kind of problem-solving approach may well lead into technical matters, and for this reason it might be better to have a technical expert or line manager present. Alternatively, this part of the interview assessment can be left to a subsequent occasion. The first interview may simply be used as an initial screening process. In any case, the clues which the interviewer obtains must be cross-examined and checked to look for patterns of consistency. Ideally, information and impressions collected at interviews should be complemented by other sources and methods whenever possible. Corroborative evidence may be obtained by other selection devices, from other assessors, or by the use of references (although these should be treated with care).

The key elements in an interview are knowing *what* to look for and *how* to find it. When the purpose of the interview has been accomplished, the interviewer should bring it to a satisfactory conclusion by summing up and advising the candidate of what the next step in the procedure will be. At the end of the meeting the candidate must leave feeling he has had a full and fair hearing.

ANALYSIS AND INTERPRETATION

Thereafter, the interviewer must be in a position to make a decision whether to take the matter further with regard to any particular candidate, or to reject. This means that after the interview he or she must reflect on a candidate's strengths and weaknesses, possession of desirable/essential qualities, experience, etc. Those candidates who pass this particular hurdle then need to be compared with each other. To help an interviewer crystallize his or her observations, an Interview Rating Form is helpful. An example is given in Table 4.3. The rating form will consist of a number of factors (relevant to the job specification) and against each factor the interviewer can make his assessments, maybe on a five-point scale. The use of a rating form forces an interviewer to concentrate his or her thoughts and to record them (before they are eroded by distortions of memory or the confusions which arise from seeing a succession of candidates).

CRITICAL APPRAISAL OF THE INTERVIEW

No selection procedure can dispense with the interview. It provides a personal touch, a face-to-face exchange. The interviewer is in the unique position of being able to integrate all the information obtained. He or she is able to see the 'whole' person. In personnel selection, the interview is utterly conventional; it is both accepted and expected. It is also economical of time and effort when compared with many other methods. It is not perfect, nor does it embrace every facet. It is impressionistic rather than analytical. But there is often a business imperative to make decisions quickly (even if only 90 per cent accurate) rather than devote resources to protracted procedures aiming at scientific objectivity.

The interview clearly has limitations and problems. Stern critics have renounced it as unreliable and invalid. It is not really possible to say whether the fault lies with the interview itself as a technique, or the method by which it was conducted. Many of the interviews which have been used in experimental research and form the basis of this condemnation have been unplanned and the interviewers unskilled, relying on off-the-cuff questions, playing it by ear. It is argued that the interview is not a valid predictor of an applicant's ability to do a job. This may well be true in those interviews

Table 4.3 Interview Rating Form

JOB TITLE:				CANDIDATE:	
Factor	A	B	C	D	E
First impressions and impact					
Physical aspects					
Intelligence					
Commonsense					
Qualifications					
Occupational experience					
Technical competence					
Special aptitudes					
Powers of reasoning/Problem-solving					
Oral expression					
Social skills					
Maturity					
Stability/Adjustment					
Attitude to work					
Drive and motivation					
Career goals					
Interests					
Domestic circumstances					
(Any other relevant factors)					
—					
—					
—					
Impression gained at interview					
Overall assessment of suitability					

NB: The criterion standard to be taken is that required for successful performance on the job. In the 5-point scale adopted C=average.

which do not have a clear objective. Indisputably, interviews are not as rigorously standardized as tests, and different interviewers use different structures and methods. The interview's greatest failing is its subjectivity. Interviewers are part of a situation and cannot detach themselves to make a purely clinical observation. Their own behaviour affects the outcome. The situation is artificial. 'Interviewers use the interview to make personality attributions on the basis of interview behaviour rather than to discover more about the applicant's past history and future aspirations' (Herriot and Rothwell, 1983).

And there are perceptual difficulties – people see what they want to see. Bias, prejudice and cultural influence can all contaminate the judgemental process. Unconscious biases of interviewers seeking to recruit in their own image may be compounded by deliberate and conscious bias of candidates projecting a calculated presentation. Interview bias, the 'fundamental attribution error' (Ross, 1977) seriously clouds judgement. Stereotyped convictions about people stem from entrenched personal prejudices.

Bias may enter fairly early into an interviewer's decision. First impressions make most impact. In the famous McGill University studies (Webster, 1964), interviewers not only jumped to quick conclusions, but were also most influenced by 'negative' aspects (pointers for rejection). Since the 1920s, it has often been found that interviewers are more influenced by outstanding characteristics than by an overall assessment. The well-known 'halo' effect suggests that overall assessments are inflated by one or two strong attributes. Conversely, this can also work negatively – the 'horn' or 'cloven hoof' effect, whereby a few bad points can undermine evaluations. Contradicting the McGill studies, however, occasion has also been demonstrated when interviewers avoided premature judgement and made up their minds in the last half of the interview (Huegli and Tschirgi, 1975).

In summary, biases take several forms (Arvey and Campion, 1982), particularly (i) *primary* effects – where initial information carries disproportionate influence; (ii) *halo* effects – where distinct attributes are not assessed independently; (iii) *contrast* effects – where candidates are not assessed independently from previous or subsequent inteviewees; and (iv) various degrees of leniency or severity of assessors not applying common standards.

In the United Kingdom, H. J. Eysenck has for years been in the forefront of those who disparage the interview (Eysenck, 1966). He noted that interviewers were convinced of their own correct judgement, and drew attention to the lack of follow-up studies by which interview assessments could have been validated. He argued (and rightly so) that if the interview is to be of any use, it must produce consistent results whenever it is repeated (either by the same interviewer or by another interviewer) and drew attention to the fact that interviews are notoriously 'unreliable'. Eysenck feels that the interview should be used *to supplement other information* and should concern itself with things which cannot be better measured by other means. He concludes that 'interviewing is an extremely inefficient method which cannot be rationally defended'.

The selection interview is the focal point of any recruitment process. But it is invariably treated by rigorous theoreticians as another psychometric tool and subject to the same tests of *validity* (i.e. that it can predict job behaviour) and *reliability* (i.e. consistency).

'Judged by the acid test of psychometric efficiency – that is, its validity – the selection interview is a miserable failure. Review after review of the literature has indicated that the degree of validity is lower than that obtainable by means of appropriate psychological tests, and much lower than for biodata' (Herriot, 1984).

Other psychologists have been more constructive (e.g. Mayfield, 1964; Heneman, 1975) showing that interview ratings may be consistent where structured interviews are used. Predictors of job success are improved by a team approach; and higher reliabilities can be achieved with the use of job specifications than without them (Langsdale and Weitz, 1973). It has been further shown (Webster, 1964) that more agreement can be obtained between experienced rather than inexperienced interviewers.

However, the interview must also be viewed in its social context with the recognition that the reciprocal behaviour of both parties is role-determined and subject to certain ambiguous and unwritten rules of the game. 'In the selection interview is a rule-governed social interaction with clearly defined reciprocal roles allocated to both parties' (Herriot, 1981). Expectations of the parties may in fact differ. For example, the interviewer expects the applicant to talk more about his or her experiences and ambitions, who in turn expects the interviewer to discuss the job (Herriot and Rothwell, 1983). The behaviour of the interviewer and interviewee and their respective likes and dislikes play a major role in job offer/acceptance rates (Keenan, 1977), suggesting that both affective and cognitive components are present in an interview situation. It is also frequently argued that the interview may assess extraneous attributes irrelevant to job performance (e.g. mannerisms, clothes, speech). People do not always present themselves in true character. Not surprisingly, interviewers' judgements may be emotional rather than rational.

Why does the interview persist, in the face of its relatively low validity, reliability and susceptibility to bias and distortion? The key issue is that whilst the interview may adequately measure sociability, self-expression and verbal fluency, it does not necessarily form the basis for a prediction of job behaviour. So much depends on influence. Some interviewers may be better than others, but this may be mitigated by pooling interviewers in a research context. Part of the justification for the continued acceptance of the interview lies in the deficiencies of other areas of psychometric technology, e.g. the prediction of work motivation. Partly, too, many job characteristics do not lend themselves to precise scientific analysis, e.g. the ability to cope with the unexpected. And in part, convention and convenience, perpetuate the technique. Moreover, the interview fulfils functions broader than purely picking a candidate in terms of measurable attributes. It is also concerned to inform and develop realistic job expectations. Finally, personnel selection is not concerned with absolutes; it is concerned with making relative judgements between one candidate and another, each of whom is quite free to accept or reject any offer made. And that offer may be bargained.

No one really seems to know how interviewers reach their decisions, or what makes a good interviewer. The desirable goals are inter-rater reliability (agreement between two or more interviewers), intra-rater reliability (consistent assessment by the same interviewer at different points in time), and high validity. The question of validity is really whether interview decisions are the right ones. There is no doubt, however, in the light of some contradictory findings, that there is room for improvement.

Clearly, better interviewers will be thoroughly familiar with the needs of the job and organizational climate. A flair for interviewing, rather than repugnance, is obvious. Better interviewers are aware of their own biases and prejudices and guard against them. According to Anstey (1977a), good interviewers are naturally interested in other people, sensitive towards their feelings, but reasonably detached – although there are 'no born interviewers'. An interviewer does not need to be a psychologist, but does need to be trained in interview techniques, skills in information-getting and counselling. Various approaches to the training of interviewers are in existence (e.g. Hackett, 1981) using role play exercises. Research suggests (Arvey and Campion, 1982; Dipboye, Stramler and Fontenelle, 1984) that interviewers should concentrate on assessing social skills, motivation and personality, follow a structured interview format and base their investigations systematically on job characteristics. Whatever the demerits of the interview, it remains the prime selection instrument in terms of its universal application. Interviewing is one of the major skills in the personnel manager's armoury. It is so important that some hints on interviewing are summarized in the Appendix.

OTHER TYPES OF INTERVIEW

Multiple interviews combine or pool the judgements of various assessors. A series of individual interviews with different interviewers may be conducted in succession. Alternatively, interviewers may assemble jointly to conduct group interviews such as panels or boards. Such combined assessments are likely to provide for a better balance of opinion, but the problem with panels and boards is that a formidable array of assessors may be inhibiting to a candidate. Rapport is in any case better achieved in a one-to-one situation.

Technical interviews are those kinds of assessments where specialist expertise is examined. Technical interviews have advantages where professional or specific skills are required in a job. It would be foolish to expect a layman to make judgements about technical competence.

Stress interviews, which had their origins in selection for German officers in World War II, and later by the US Government for selecting undercover agents, are a totally different exercise. The purpose of a stress interview is to see how people control themselves and cope in stressful situations. The style of the interview is an exacting interrogation. Interviewers may be aggressive or insolent. Hostility is directed towards the candidate, seeking to annoy, harass and frustrate. The interview is contrived as an unnerving and heavily booby-trapped obstacle course, rather than a face-to-face conversation. It is more of a confrontation. There are some jobs where these kinds of skills may be called for (e.g. aggressive sales jobs) and some success in this area has been claimed in the United States. On the whole, unless the content of this kind of interview is criterion-related, it offends most of the principles of interviewing.

By whatever method, the interviewer must reach a conclusion about each applicant, having systematically gathered, sifted and analysed data from various sources. The task is to develop an understanding of the candidate and make a prediction about subsequent performance.

The use of tests

'Tests, when properly used and well constructed are a reliable source of information which is obtainable relatively quickly. Test results are used objectively to supplement the information obtained from other sources such as interviews, references, and application forms.' (NFER, 1981)

A test is an example of scientific method applied to human behaviour; it is a means of sampling a person's performance or behaviour from which generalized statements can be made about *total* performance and behaviour. Like many technical devices, the use of tests is confined to those people who are qualified to administer and interpret them. The British Psychological Society divides tests into three main categories: attainment tests, psychological tests, and clinical instruments. For practical purposes it might be more useful to distinguish between (i) tests of ability (present or potential), (ii) tests of attainment or achievement, and (iii) measures of attitudes, interest and personality (where there may be no right or wrong answers, and where the answers paint a picture of how a person usually reacts in a given situation). We might also distinguish between individual tests and group tests. Individual tests can be given to one person at a time; group tests may be given to many testees simultaneously. There are also pencil and paper tests (in which answers are to be written) and performance tests in which some skill has to be overtly demonstrated (e.g. manual dexterity).

As an aid to objective and fair appraisal of an individual's suitability for employment in a given job, tests may be used as an adjunct to the selection procedure. Their aim is to determine how closely an applicant matches the criteria and they may be used to discriminate more finely between candidates' capacities and inclinations. For some positions, academic achievement may be sufficient evidence, making further testing unnecessary. But where there is an excess of applicants, some further objective measure of suitability based on specifically job-related criteria may facilitate differentiation between otherwise seemingly well-qualified people. Similarly, when academic standard is not directly related to job performance, further appropriate testing might be helpful, or in a case where a candidate has no relevant previous experience or qualifications. Tests may measure existing qualities, learning potential or special aptitude more thoroughly than is possible by interview alone. Tests may measure most faculties as a whole, or in the form of their constituent parts. Tests show up samples of an individual's behaviour along certain dimensions (e.g. intelligence, or specific verbal, numerical, mechanical, spatial, motor, social abilities and aptitudes). Tests present an artificially organized and controlled situation; they are short-cut methods. Further, they may be a valid predictor of one index of success, but not of another. Job behaviour itself is not widely studied in the available test material. Measures of success are mainly in terms of *potential ability* to do the job, rather than an analysis of actual job performance. For this reason, tests probably have greater utility in the areas of educational psychology and occupational guidance, than personnel selection.

A test is a *standardized* instrument – in terms of the questions or *test items* and in terms of *scoring*. Any test results must be scaled against the performance of representative and relevant groups of people, i.e. interpreted against a *norm group*. In other words, all test results must be expressed in meaningful terms in the context in which they are given. A score of seventy-five out of one hundred and fifty is less meaningful than (say) seventy-five is equal to that given to the top 20 per cent of all candidates. The 'population' against which an individual's scores are compared is important. *Norm lists* giving such comparisons are available whenever tests are administered. Several different norm lists may be available for any one test (e.g. for particular age groups, for an occupation, for the industry/organization, or nationally). In *test manuals*, norms are expressed in different ways and their interpretation requires familiarity with certain statistical concepts in order to understand the diverse ways in which norms can be produced.

Norms are really a set of data which inform us how *other* people have performed on the tests (either a random sample of the whole population or certain groups). If a certain group has taken the test, we need to know the *mean* or *average* mark – by adding up all the scores obtained and dividing this figure by the total number in the group. The mean is but one of a number of measures of central tendency; another is the *median* (the figure below which and above which 50 per cent of the group comes); and yet another is the *mode* (the score obtained by more people than any other score). In addition to measures of central tendency we need to know how *scattered* the scores are. To do this we can produce percentile scores. A *percentile score* is a score below which a certain percentage of people who have taken the test come. For example, the nintieth percentile is the point below which 90 per cent of such people fall. From percentiles we can see how any individual ranks in comparison with others, although they still do not tell us how the scores were distributed. To answer this we can look at the *frequency distribution* showing how many of the people in the group obtained each score. The amount of variability or scatter in a number of scores can be measured statistically by the *standard deviation* (the positive square root of the variance). We need further to look at the relationships between standard deviation and the so-called normal distribution (the way in which a particular characteristic such as height, intelligence or a particular aptitude is distributed throughout a population). If we took a large random sample of people we would most likely find that the majority were of average height or intelligence and that far fewer people were actually extremes. This kind of distribution can be represented graphically in the form of a bell-shaped curve. What matters is the relationship between the normal distribution and standard deviation. In a distribution of scores which are normally distributed, 68.26 per cent of the scores lie within one span of deviation of the mean score, 95.44 per cent of the scores lie between two standard deviations of the mean and 99.73 per cent of the scores lie within three standard deviations of the mean (Fig. 4.5). The mean and standard

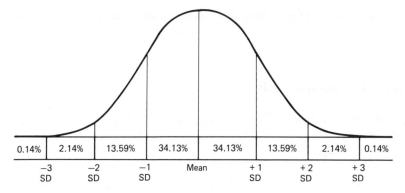

| 0.14% | 2.14% | 13.59% | 34.13% | 34.13% | 13.59% | 2.14% | 0.14% |

| −3 SD | −2 SD | −1 SD | Mean | + 1 SD | + 2 SD | + 3 SD |

Fig. 4.5 *The normal distribution*

deviation of the score obtained by members of a particular group provide us with useful background information so that when we test somebody else, we can see how he or she stands in relation to the appropriate reference group. (For further explanation, see e.g. Ashford, 1977.)

Tests must be *reliable*, i.e. show consistency of performance on a number of trials of equivalent tests, expressed in terms of a reliability coefficient (the correlation between two or more measurements obtained in the same manner, or the standard error of measurement on different occasions). Each test gives a sample of a person's performance but the ultimate true score would be the figure obtained from averaging all the scores available from a long series of trials (which perhaps would be impractical). The error is the variation of fluctuation of scores within such a series. If a test is subjected to such a scrutiny, and the error is below an acceptable level, the test may be regarded as a reliable measure, and confidence may be placed in it.

A test must also be valid, and predict what it claims. Particularly, *concurrent validity* (discriminating between the present employees) and *predictive validity* (predicting subsequent performance, or the extent to which variance in a test is associated with variance in subsequent criterion measures).

An element of error occurs in any kind of measurement, 'constant error' (appearing consistently in repeated measurements) and 'random error' (which influences different measures to different degrees).

Within the particular area for which tests are available, they are likely to be better predictors of behaviour than interviews. Tests are usually more useful when there is a greater range of attributes to be measured, and they tend to predict training success better than actual job performance or length of stay on the job. Ability tests are probably the most efficient, personality question-naires and interest inventories may be useful research tools but there is little direct evidence of their valid use in selection. A further criticism of tests is that they are not demonstrably fair, but neither for that matter are interviews. The main merit of a test is that it is of short duration. Tests are objective and standardized behaviour samples which lend themselves to statistical evalua-tion; they are less subject to bias than interview assessment; but their acceptability varies. They cannot stand alone as selection devices. Properly administered and interpreted they may aid certain kinds of selection decisions.

Group selection methods

One problem with the use of interviews for selection purposes is that they do not allow the candidate to display a full range of interpersonal skills. By employing an expanded – or 'extended' – selection procedure in which several candidates tackle simulated problems at the same time, employers are able to observe a wider range of behaviours, and also achieve some measure of comparability between candidates.

Group selection has a specific role to play in choosing people for jobs where evidence of leadership qualities or group working ability is needed. The procedures were first developed during the 1939–45 war for selecting officers for the Armed Services (British, Commonwealth, German and American), when traditional recruitment methods had proved ineffective. As a result War Office Selection Boards (WOSBs) were set up and great care was taken in devising various physical, mental and social group exercises, incorporating them as part of an overall selection procedure (including interviews and tests) and in validating them. Since the war, group methods have continued to be used extensively for officer selection in H.M. Forces and also in the Civil Service Commission for recruitment into the Administrative class via Civil Service Selection Boards (CSSBs). The approach has been taken up widely by private industrial firms and by the nationalized industries.

Group selection procedures tend to be suitable for (i) choosing between promotion candidates within a company where the higher-graded job is of management level; and (ii) selection of university graduates or 'A' level school leavers for training schemes with a defined progression towards management. The aim is to acquire information about the candidate both as an individual and as a member of a group.

Group selection methods are appropriate for assessing:

1   *Social skills* – which might include tactfulness, sensitivity to the views and opinions of others, aggressiveness, hostility, cooperation, friendliness, reaction to disagreement and criticism, the handling of conflict and contradiction, the ability to influence and persuade others, and the kind of leadership or passive role adopted.
2   *Intellectual skills* – which might include signs of ability to think clearly (particularly at short notice), clarity of expression, the deployment of forceful argument, the application of knowledge or experience, consideration of the merits and demerits of other arguments put forward, and general flexibility in discussion.
3   *Attitudes* – particularly where these may be of relevance to a person's efficiency at work (e.g. political, racial, religious views and attitudes to authority).

Since it would seem from research that surface personality is a key variable affecting selection decisions, and that 'at least as far as graduate recruitment is concerned, personality ranks highly in the majority of recruiters' lists of desirable attributes' (Keenan, 1982), group selection methods provide a valuable source of information, and procedures and methodology are well documented in the literature.

Obviously group selection methods should only be used when criteria included in the job specification include the kinds of attributes listed above and when the principles of an extended systematic selection are justified. Such jobs are most likely to be of a 'managerial' nature. This is a complex area where there are unduly difficult criterion problems. Many elements – intellectual, social, motivational and experiential – contribute to effective managerial performance.

FORMAT

Typically, a group of five to eight applicants will assemble in an off-the-job, maybe 'country house', setting for a period of (say) two days. They will be required to perform a series of tasks, either as a group or individually, under observation. Group selection is a multiple assessment technique. Ideally, the applicants should be of similar age, education and experience. Assessments should be made using a defined measurement system related to the qualities demanded in the job specification.

There are variations which can be contrived, but basically the exercises may be conducted as 'leaderless' or with a 'designated leader'. Leaderless group discussions involve presenting the group of applicants with a topic for discussion, and normally advising them that they are expected to reach a conclusion within a defined period of time. The topic may be related to the job in question, i.e. of a problem-solving nature (say, 'consider the costs and benefits of developing a new product – in the light of given production, financial and marketing information') or maybe of a more general nature (say, 'should Britain maintain a nuclear deterrent?'). Individual contributions are scored on an appropriate scale which might include such factors as: assertiveness, quality of thought and expression, analysis of important variables, synthesis of group's opinions, leading group towards a decision, etc.

Apart from leaderless situations, some tasks may be set up with a designated leader by rotating the role of chairman, each candidate taking over in turn. The use of a chairman changes the situation from an informal to a formal one.

Occasionally a more protracted method of assessment may be employed in which applicants are given a typical job problem to solve individually in a set time. At the end, each person is required to explain his solution to the other members of the group and to defend his views against the group's criticisms.

ASSESSORS

Assessors are usually drawn from members of line and personnel management, with maybe a psychologist present. Members of an assessment panel bring different but complementary approaches to the decision-making process. The final judgement is not made by a single assessor but by pooled judgements. Assessors rate participants' performances on each exercise and an overall assessment rating (OAR) is finally derived by discussion. The interpretations that assessors make may vary considerably. Clearly, where several assessors are scoring the behaviour of people involved in a group discussion, it is important that they all employ the same criteria and standards of assessment if their pooled judgements are to have any value. To overcome the more obvious difficulties, assessors should be trained in methods of observation and scoring, and correlation between their scores should be checked. This goes some way towards establishing the reliability of assessors' judgements.

During these exercises the assessors should be inconspicuous, sitting at irregularly spaced intervals around the group and some distance away from it. Efforts should be made to avoid a focal gallery to which candidates may be tempted to play, and to avoid distracting candidates' attention.

ADVANTAGES AND DISADVANTAGES

Group selection can only be used in conjunction with other methods of obtaining data about the job applicants. It acts in support of and not as a substitute for those methods. Application forms, psychological tests, references and individual and panel interviews will all provide some information that could not be obtained by using group processes. However, the group process will be better at establishing how a person behaves in the company of others. Administratively, it may be convenient to include some formal tests on the same day as the group procedures. Advisably, individual interviews should be conducted after the group procedures in order to examine further a candidate's attitudes as exhibited and allow a candidate to justify his views and behaviour in confidence.

Group methods can provide information about a candidate's potential performance as a member of a group which it is virtually impossible to obtain by other techniques. This is particularly so when the exercises simulate the real job, and the collective observation of assessors takes place over a sufficient period of time. The method also provides a means for confirming or rejecting information which may have been gained from other techniques and sources. The methods are particularly useful when little historical information is known about the candidate in relation to the qualities to be assessed, e.g. when the candidates are undergraduates, school leavers, management trainees. The methods can include various situations and provide a better opportunity for assessing the individual as a 'whole' person. If every candidate is treated in the same way, the method is likely to be seen to be fair, and if the discussion topics are relevant and well-structured, they seem to have face validity and 'synthetic validity'.

Groups would normally be preselected, having filtered through some form of interview. The method, therefore, tries to make very fine discriminations between similar people. Moreover, they are acting in competition. Conflicts of interest may obscure the process. The success of group selection depends on the cooperation of the individual applicants involved. Uncooperative applicants, although possessing all the skills required for the job, will not display these unless they are convinced that there is some merit in using the group process. On the other hand, some participants will recognize quickly what is required, and this will lead to role-playing and attention-getting behaviour. Moreover, group members will be feeling insecure, looking for acceptance, judging their fellows. Luck may be involved, and performance may differ from overall ability.

When the process is established as part of the selection procedure, there should be careful monitoring of the performance of candidates selected by that method if they are subsequently employed on the job. Large-scale studies in this area, backed by long-term follow-up, have shown that when properly constructed, and when assessors are properly trained, high degrees of success can be obtained. This finding was true in the 25-year follow-up of officer entrants to the Royal Navy (Gardiner and Williams, 1973) and more particularly in the Civil Service in the 30-year follow-up of an extended interview procedure. This follow-up showed a high validity correlation coefficient between the selection board assessment and subsequent rank attained (Civil Service Department: Behavioural Sciences Research Division, 1976).

Group selection procedures are likely to be somewhat superior to the conventional interview method of assessing people, because they provide a more prolonged and varied set of situations in which to observe and interpret. But they are just as dependent as the interview on the skill, experience and impartiality of the observer. Provided that the inter-test reliability of an interviewer's judgement is confirmed, that there is a high degree of inter-rater reliability and the validity of the exercise has been established, then group methods are *likely* to provide better predictors, because there is a better database and because, on the whole, pooled judgements are likely to have a higher degree of accuracy than the judgement of a single interviewer.

Does the success rate justify the extra time and cost involved? In the vast majority of employment settings the procedures have not been sufficiently uniform nor the field of candidates sufficiently numerous for adequate analysis. In many areas the application of the technique has outstripped research into it. Universal validity is lacking; frequently the value of such approaches is unproven. The main exceptions are the various long-term follow-up studies which have been conducted, although group selection methods bear close similarity to internal assessment centres (see Chapter 6) for which there is additional evidence.

The whole picture is further complicated by the fact that group selection methods are always used in conjunction with other methods. Establishing the contribution of group methods without cross-contamination is not easy.

Group selection is time-consuming and expensive to operate – it means training assessors, devising tasks, testing them. To some extent, control of the exercise is determined by the structure and nature of tasks given; areas of discussion are predetermined.

More interesting, though, is the question of the criterion variable: i.e. what are such methods actually measuring? Research suggests that they may be predictive of long-term potential – as measured by promotion and salary – but not necessarily of performance on the job (Turnage and Muchinsky, 1984). They may simply reflect assessors' ideas of the 'right type' of person who is likely to get on. The result is a field marshal's baton in the haversack of new recruits selected by this method. The prophecy is self-fulfilling.

Summary and conclusions

Selection begins with job analysis and job specification, and the determination of performance criteria. Appropriate techniques of prediction must be derived. The application form, if it is properly constructed, can provide an initial screening mechanism. Interviews are the most common and acceptable means of making individual assessments. Although they have certain weaknesses, particularly with regard to reliability and validity, their efficiency can be improved by careful planning. Group selection methods may sometimes be used to provide better insights into social and leadership skills if they are called in for the job. Most selection methods are subjective. Tests are more objective, but may have limited use in selection procedures. Interviews are still the main selection technique, but the use of 'assessment centres' (see Chapter 6) and biodata are increasing (Makin and Robertson, 1986). Interviewing is by far the most important skill to be acquired by personnel managers and other selectors.

Appendix: Some hints on personnel selection interviewing

A   Be quite clear what it is you are trying to achieve at the interview. Clarify your objectives and methods of 'interview search' to be adopted. Prepare the groundwork. Collect as much information as possible in advance – from job specification, application form, references.

B   Clarification of selection criteria can only come from a careful study of the duties, responsibilities and requirements of the job to be filled and an assessment of relevant personal characteristics (general education, specific training, type and depth of experience, analytical ability, social skills, psychomotor skills, written and verbal powers of communication, numerical ability, powers of comprehension and judgement, personality factors relating to adaptability and acceptability, attitudes to responsibility and authority, etc.) deemed necessary for successful performance.

C Do not simply accept the job specification at face value (it may be out of date and inaccurate). Check it. Get a feel for the job. Chat to other job incumbents and line manager or supervisor. Verify the job specification.

D Guidance in formulating key criteria can be obtained from an analysis of the most commonly reported 'difficulties' and 'distastes' occurring in this or closely similar jobs. What are the main 'trouble spots'; the most attractive and unattractive aspects? A study of these two critical variables will give clues as to the main capacities needed for successful performance on the job and the personal inclinations that have a bearing both on performance and on job satisfaction.

E Precise details of the duties and responsibilities should be written up in a job description, and the qualities necessary specified in a job specification. Both documents should lack ambiguity, be concise statements of crucial elements in a job, and be the subject of consensual agreement between line management, the personnel department or job analyst, and where possible other similar job holders.

F Recruitment advertisements should contain as much information as space and cost permit so that a certain amount of self-selection can take place in the target population. Care should be taken judiciously to place advertising copy in the most appropriate media for the type and level of the job concerned and the nature of the labour market.

G An application form properly structured can form a useful step in the selection process. Forms should be designed to elicit pertinent, non-trivial information about an applicant's attributes and autobiographical details. Standard forms make cross-comparison between candidates easier than open letters of application. Preselection decisions can be made on the basis of this written evidence.

H Study all the data available. Interviewers should be thoroughly conversant with all relevant aspects of the job and general organizational environment.

I Letters of notice giving times and place of interview and reporting instructions should be sent out well in advance.

J Make sure the interview is conducted in comfort, free from interruptions, noise or other diversions. Allow enough time for adequate discussion.

K   Prepare a flexible plan on which to conduct the interview. Popular models (e.g. Rodger, Fraser) may have utility, but there is no substitute for a tailor-made criterion-related check-list of substantive elements of the job.

L   Think in advance about the form, phrasing, and sequence of questions relating to the main areas of exploration that will most effectively penetrate and probe the key areas. There are no scientific formulae for this. Each job situation and each candidate will be different. Each interview is an unique social interaction – but the interviewer should have some idea of the way in which he or she wishes to direct and control it.

M   General points to bear in mind at interview are:

(1)   Begin on an easily conversable topic, maybe some achievement reported on the application form, to establish a measure of confidence.

(2)   Do not ask leading questions.

(3)   Ask open-ended questions which require more than monosyllabic answers.

(4)   Follow the interviewees' lead wherever possible.

(5)   Check the accuracy of candidates' responses by an interrogatory style, probing in depth the relevant areas of experience, looking for traits of marked generality, consistency and persistence.

(6)   Examine the successes reported by a candidate in detail. Try to assess the factors which were conducive to that success, and look for corroborative evidence elsewhere in a candidate's background or history. Similarly, failures and omissions should be examined. The point here is to ascertain a candidate's strengths and weaknesses. Cross-examination on a matter-of-fact, non-threatening basis should help to highlight discrepancies or bring forward supporting evidence. Questions may be of a probing or facilitative nature.

(7)   Avoid trick questions designed to reveal inconsistencies. Trick questions foster antagonism.

(8)   Be flexible, and maybe circuitous in your approach.

(9)   Hold back difficult questions (i.e. of a problem-solving nature) until later in the interview, when rapport has been established.

(10)   Do not reveal too specifically what it is you are looking for. Candidates have a habit of slanting their replies and distorting their experiences accordingly.

(11) Control the interview – but do not appear to be rushed or distracted.

(12) Do not make moral judgements. Realize your own biases and prejudices, and try not to let them affect your judgement.

(13) Do not interrupt a candidate in full flow, but try to create a supportive atmosphere as a prompter or catalyst of the exposition, perhaps summarizing a candidate's remarks to show that you have understood, paraphrasing his comments as a lead into the next question or to generate further spontaneous information.

(14) Do not be loquacious.

(15) Listen very carefully (attentively, not marginally) to everything that is said. Give your undivided attention to the proceedings.

(16) Observe, and try to interpret, facial expressions and body language for signs of frustration, conflict, dissonance.

(17) Give the candidate a full and fair hearing. The candidate must leave the interview feeling that he or she was honourably treated. The interview is also a public relations exercise; the candidate will leave with an impression of your company.

(18) Make sure the interview plan is fully covered.

(19) Ensure that you have enough information about a candidate on which to make comparative decisions *vis-à-vis* the other candidates; and on which to come to a decision.

(20) Pay particular attention to a candidate's revealed or underlying 'difficulties' and 'distastes', and the capacities and inclinations which his or her record and general impression indicate to be the relative strengths and weaknesses for overcoming them.

(21) Never terminate an interview without inviting the candidate to ask any further questions, or mentioning any factors which he or she might consider relevant. And try to answer them.

(22) The assessment of technical or professional knowledge may require the assistance of a technically competent second interviewer.

(23) End on a cheerful, agreeable note; and indicate the next step in the procedure.

(24) Record your observations and ratings whilst they are still fresh in your memory.

N Note-taking can be a useful aide-mémoire but it is probably better left until after the interview has been terminated.

O   Beware of halo effects and stereotyped judgements. A forced distribution of ratings against predetermined criteria may help. Collect corroborative evidence (references, test results, etc.) where appropriate.

P   Arriving at sound judgements and discriminating fairly between individuals is probably the most difficult task of all. Inferences must be drawn from the evidence as presented. Expertise in this area is partly intuitive, partly due to training, practice, and experience, but in all cases considerably enhanced by careful preparation and a systematic approach.

Q   Inform candidates of the outcome as soon as possible.

R   The interview is a technique for collecting information and forming subjective impressions and judgements in a limited space of time. It may have deficiencies on the grounds of reliability and validity, but there is also an important consideration to bear in mind: objective predictor tests are only applicable where criterion dimensions themselves can be accurately defined or quantified.

Discussion questions

1   By what various criteria could the efficiency of recruitment be measured?

2   Should the members of the management team who are going to be responsible for selection also be responsible for the recruitment process? Or is it desirable to treat the two activities separately?

3   What advantages and disadvantages would you expect to accrue from the more widespread use of allowing groups of employees to be themselves responsible for the recruitment and selection of the new entrants who will subsequently join them?

4   Do you think it would be useful to involve line managers in the determination of selection criteria?

5   How useful are formal academic qualifications as predictors of success at work?

6   What are the main problems confronting the determination and clarification of good work-based performance 'criteria'?

7   Is the 'criterion problem' only of interest to psychologists?

8   In what ways can an understanding of the theoretical issues underlying

personnel selection decisions raise the level of expertise and efficiency of a personnel manager responsible for selection procedures?

9 What selection methods would you advocate for selecting:
(a) gas fitters installing domestic central heating systems,
(b) insurance salesmen,
(c) head teachers of schools,
(d) shop assistants,
(e) personnel officers?

10 How would you train line managers to become more effective interviewers?

11 Should the use and development of tests for personnel selection purposes be more widely encouraged?

12 Is personnel selection really so important, when so much can be done in the way of facilitating occupational adjustment by means of training and job redesign?

13 Should jobs be made to fit people, rather than people be made to fit jobs?

References

ANSTEY, E. (1977a), *An Introduction to Selection Interviewing*, Civil Service Commission, London.
ANSTEY, E. (1977b), 'A 30-year follow-up of the CSSB procedure, with lessons for the future', *Journal of Occupational Psychology*, **50.**
ARVEY, R. D. and CAMPION, J. E. (1982), 'The employment interview: a summary and review of recent research', *Personnel Psychology*, **35,** pp. 281–322.
ASHFORD, J. (1977), *Statistics for Management*, Institute of Personnel Management, London.
BAYNE, R. (1977), 'Can selection interviewing be improved?' *Journal of Occupational Psychology*, **50.**
BLUM, M. C. and NAYLOR, J. C. (1968), *Industrial Psychology: Its Theoretical and Social Foundations*, Harper, New York.
CASCIO, W. F. (1982), *Applied Psychology in Personnel Management*, 2nd edn, Reston Publishing Co., Reston, Virginia.
CIVIL SERVICE DEPARTMENT: Behavioural Sciences Research Division (1976), *Civil Service Administrators: a Long-Term Follow-up*, BSRD Report 31.
DIPBOYE, R. L., STRAMLER, C. S. and FONTENELLE, G. A. (1984), 'The effects of the application on recall of information from the interview', *Academy of Management Journal*, **27,** No. 3, pp. 561–575.
EYSENCK, H. J. (1966), *Uses and Abuses of Psychology*, Penguin, London.
FEAR, R. A. (1973), *The Evaluation Interview*, 2nd edn, McGraw. Hill, New York.
FRASER, J. M. (1970), *Employment Interviewing*, Macdonald and Evans.
GARDINER, K. E. and WILLIAMS, A. P. O. (1973), 'A 25-year follow-up of an extended interview selection procedure in the Royal Navy – Part I', *Occupational Psychology*, 47.
GRAHAM, H. T. (1980), *Human Resource Management*, 3rd edn, Macdonald and Evans.
GUION, R. M. (1976), 'Recruiting, selection and job placement', in: Dunette, M. D. (ed.), *Handbook of Industrial-Organizational Psychology*, Rand McNally, Chicago.

HACKETT, P. (1981), *Interview Skills Training*, Institute of Personnel Management, London.

HENEMAN, G. (1975), 'The impact of interview training and interview structure on the reliability and validity of the selection interview', *Proceedings: Academy of Management*, New Orleans.

HERRIOT, P. (1981), 'Towards an attributional theory of the selection interview', *Journal of Occupational Psychology*, **51.**

HERRIOT, P. (1984), *Down from the Ivory Tower: Graduates and their Jobs*, Wiley, Chichester.

HERRIOT, P. and ROTHWELL, C. (1983), 'Expectations and impressions in the graduate selection interview', *Journal of Occupational Psychology*, **56**, pp. 303–314.

HERRIOT, P. and WINGROVE, J. (1984), 'Decision processes in graduate pre-selection', *Journal of Occupational Psychology*, **57**, pp. 269–275.

HIGHAM, T. H. (1979a), 'Choosing the method of recruitment', in Ungerson, B. (ed.), *Recruitment Handbook*, 2nd edn, Gower.

HIGHAM, T. H. (1979b), *The ABC of Interviewing*, Institute of Personnel Management, London.

HUEGLI, J. M. and TSCHIRGI, H. (1975), 'An investigation of the relationship of time to recruitment interview decision making', *Proceedings: Academy of Management*, New Orleans.

KEENAN, A. (1977), 'Some relationships between interviewers' personal feelings about candidates and their general evaluation of them', *Journal of Occupational Psychology*, **50**, pp. 275–283.

KEENAN, A. (1982), 'Candidate personality and performance in selection interviews', *Personnel Review*, **11**, 1.

KEENAN, A. and WEDDERBURN, A. A. I. (1980), 'Putting the boot on the other foot: candidates' descriptions of interviewers', *Journal of Occupational Psychology*, **53**, pp. 81–89.

LANGSDALE, J. A. and WEITZ, J. (1973), 'Estimating the influence of job information on interviewer agreement', *Journal of Applied Psychology*, **57**, 1.

MAKIN, P. and ROBERTSON, I. (1986), 'Selecting the best selection techniques', *Personnel Management*, November.

MAYFIELD, E. C. (1964), 'The selection interview: a re-evaluation of published research', *Personnel Psychology*, **17.**

RAY, M. E. (1980), *Recruitment Advertising – A Means of Communication*, Institute of Personnel Management, London.

RODGER, A. (1971), *The Seven Point Plan*, National Institute of Industrial Psychology, London.

ROSS, L. (1977), 'The intuitive psychologist and his shortcomings: distortions in the attribution process', *Advances in Experimental Psychology*, **10.**

SIEGEL, L. and LANE, M. (1974), *Psychology in Industrial Organizations*, 3rd edn, Irwin, Homewood.

TURNAGE, J. J. and MUCHINSKY, P. M. (1984), 'A comparison of the predictive validity of assessment centre evaluations versus traditional measures in forecasting supervisory job performance: interpretative implications of criterion distortion for the assessment of paradigm', *Journal of Applied Psychology*, **69**, No. 4, pp. 595–602.

WEBSTER, E. C. (1964), *Decision-making in the Employment Interview*, Eagle, Montreal.

PART THREE

Training and Development

Training and Development

CHAPTER 5

Principles and practice of training and learning

by Bryan Livy

The selection process takes place before people take up employment. The training process may take place prior to employment or at various times throughout an individual's employment history. Most training is directed at people who are currently employed and focuses on the requirements of their present job and their future jobs. Training within the work situation is commonly referred to as 'industrial training'. This broad term includes commercial training, management development, the training of apprentices, technicians, office workers, supervisors, in any sector of employment whether industrial or non-industrial.

There is a clear link between selection and training: both are concerned with adapting and fitting people to job requirements; both are concerned with securing better occupational adjustment.

A further link between training and selection can be seen in the underlying methodology. Both processes are concerned with achieving targets. Objectives are set and planned interventions instigated to achieve them. The definition and measurement of criteria of performance are just as important in training as they are in selection. It is against predetermined criteria that the success of various interventions and strategies (e.g. training programmes) can be monitored. From results obtained, lessons can be learned about the efficacy of programmes and improvements made. Training is not an act of blind faith.

The prime purpose of training is to raise performance. But there are also other reasons why training is in the forefront of personnel management. Training is also concerned with developing people's potential, helping them to 'grow'. Social and educational change in the wider world has repercussions on the training function.

Training is to some extent a management reaction to change, e.g. changes in equipment and design, methods of work, new tools and machines, control systems, or in response to changes dictated by new products, services, or markets. On the other hand, training also induces change. A capable workforce will bring about new initiatives, developments and improvements – in an organic way, and of its own accord. Training is both a cause and effect of change. Employing organizations are obliged to take cognizance of more demanding, assertive employees. Higher expectations force the training function into an ongoing proactive role.

There is inevitably some intermingling of ideas about training with those of education. The distinction is not an academic nicety nor simply a matter of semantics. Responsibilities in the United Kingdom for education and training in the real world are sometimes diffuse and ill-coordinated. For the International Labour Organization (Clerc, 1982) training is considered 'in its widest sense, meaning every possible form of educational activity – information, creating awareness, and the actual imparting of skills – wherever such activities may be conducted'. Further 'the technological society which casts its net even over rural life, transforming social relationships, makes formal training which is geared to man, and especially man at work, more than ever essential as a balancing factor'. Education and training are both concerned with learning and effecting permanent changes, but there is a fundamental difference in the *raison d'être* of the two activities. The term 'education' has an academic flavour and is more concerned with 'why' certain things happen, or should happen, and their interrelationships. The term 'training' is much more concerned with 'how' things happen and is essentially practical. Management, therefore, has a vested interest in training. Research in training methods, setting criteria, validating training outcomes, has led to the establishment of an approach on which good training should be based – a 'technology' of training.

There may be incongruity or conflict in the identification of training needs and establishment of priorities. This can arise from the two sets of needs which need to be reconciled: organizational needs and the needs which people themselves perceive to be pertinent. An organization may wish to move in a certain direction, and an individual may wish to develop his expertise in another. Fundamentally, the organization wishes to survive and its own needs tend to predominate. This means taking a long-term view in training and development activities. They must be geared explicitly to manpower planning requirements. An organization also needs a systematic body of knowledge on which to make projections about the development of people, and this kind of knowledge is normally drawn from regular performance reviews of people in their jobs and assessments of potential specifically set up for the purpose.

Training is normally regarded as a specialist function of personnel management. But it is not only a personnel management responsibility. Line managers, who have a responsibility for getting work done, and motivating their employees, have an intimate role to play in training. Line managers more than anyone else, being more conversant with the actual job, as well as the people who are in their charge, have a direct role to play in training-need identification and in the follow-up of performance after training has been completed.

It is well known in training circles that participation in a learning exercise facilitates the achievement of its given objectives. Training participation is usually viewed narrowly – as between trainer and trainees. The real wealth of experience lies with accomplished practitioners, supervisors, line managers, men and women in touch with jobs as they are organized on the ground, in the office, or out in the field. Who does the training? Often a remote instructor. Who should train? Ideally, training should be a combined and integrated exercise involving experienced line personnel, the individual trainee, and the trainer acting as catalyst. The trainee should be included in a participative approach, but repeatedly people are trained *without really identifying their individual needs* and expectations. Indeed, the purpose of training may be vague. What *are* we training for? To do the job well? To stay with the company? To fit in? To fill a manpower gap? To feel part of the organization? To find new and better ways of doing things? To grow and develop?

If these questions are ignored, we should not be surprised at inefficient outcomes. It is so much easier to 'satisfy' the training needs of individuals by re-running old programmes – in fact identifying learning objectives based on the needs of past trainees, or on aspects of a job which lend themselves most conveniently to a classroom or off-the-job setting. Homogeneity of needs across an entire group of trainees may be wrongly assumed, and a standardized training package produced less than effectively.

One of the misconceptions about training is that it is often seen as a tool for modifying people's performance. So often managers assume that where performance of the subordinates is below par, the answer must lie in some form of training course when this is not necessarily so. Substandard performance may arise from poor motivation, inappropriate pay scales, inappropriate supervision, faulty working methods, etc. The crunch question to ask (Jones, 1980) is 'Could they do it if their lives depended on it?' If the answer is 'yes', then there is no training problem; remedies (and causes) lie elsewhere. Not all areas of a problem will yield to a training solution.

Line managers may expect too much from training if they do not themselves take an active part. It is an abdication of line management responsibility to appoint training officers to act in a surrogate capacity. Learning takes place interactively. Managers and supervisors often do not realize that they themselves will change as their own subordinates learn, develop and become more proficient. Moreover, roles, norms and social pressures affect performance as much as knowledge, skills and attitudes. It is therefore quite impossible to single out a segment of the job from its social and physical environment and present it as a 'training package'. Learning, to be effective, can only be accomplished *by training people together with those with whom they actually work*. Not only does this make learning experiences more relevant, it also enables such experiences to be transferred and integrated into the work and social context more easily. Members of a group learn from each other. In this way they also influence each other, as perceptions, expectations and attitudes mutually intermingle. A common defect of training programmes is that they ignore feelings, values and emotions. Training is seen as a means of maintaining a system (e.g. fitting the person to the job). Performance on-the-job is a manifestation of behaviour – and underpinning this behaviour are not just skills, techniques and know-how but a whole range of emotive issues.

A systematic approach to training

In an effort to make more efficient use of manpower via the most relevant form of instruction, traditional training processes have in recent years been subjected to thorough analysis. A new technology – training systems – emerged, sometimes also described as 'instructional technology' or 'performance oriented training'. The systems approach to training has found wide acceptance in the USA and UK and other Western countries.

A training system may be defined as the application of scientific methods to the process of learning and the design of training. It embraces job analysis and job specification, the determination of relevant job training objectives, the design of courses, the selection and use of appropriate training methods and media, the design and conduct of tests of performance, and the validation and evaluation of training. Like any management activity, training is a planned process, 'the systematic development of the attitude/knowledge/skill/ behaviour pattern required by an individual in order to perform adequately a given task or job' (Department of Employment, 1981).

The identification of *training needs* is fundamental to all systematic training. Training 'needs' reflect differences between operational requirements of jobs and what performers can currently do; subtracting the present level of competence from the required level of competence. The differential is the 'learning gap' which it is the purpose of training to fill. Training needs are not therefore necessarily uniform between trainees.

Previous levels of ability and skill competence of prospective trainees (prior to training) are known as *entry behaviour*. This can be determined by an appropriate *pre-test*, whether of skills, knowledge or whatever.

The next step is to determine job performance requirements by job analysis (see Chapter 3), particularly the task-oriented and worker-oriented aspects. For highly or semi-skilled jobs a deeper skills analysis would be required (see later in this chapter), and for managerial or administrative jobs some kind of role analysis. From these investigations we can determine the goals of proficiency which we will expect trainees to reach at the end of a training exercise – *terminal behaviour* – the criteria of performance on the job. Diagrammatically, these links can be shown as in Fig. 5.1. Furthermore, training 'needs' must be translated into a training programme, or learning experience, which will lead to the desired results, as in Fig. 5.2.

Performance targets must be specified. The concept of ultimate desirability in an employee may consist of a number of different aspects each having different lead times to develop. Therefore this ultimate goal must be broken down into various sub-targets.

In training terminology there is sometimes confusion between 'aims' and

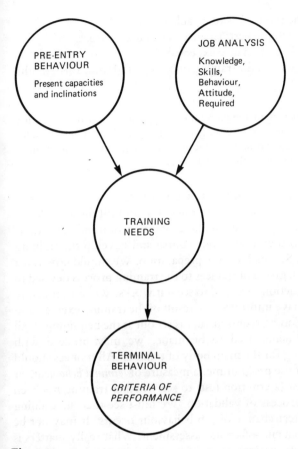

Fig. 5.1

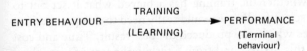

Fig. 5.2

'objectives'. The aim is the ultimate goal and the objectives are the sub-goals or targets which have to be fulfilled before the aim can be obtained. Objectives may be of varying priority and corresponding difficulty. In a well-defined aim, a hierarchy of objectives must be established.

It is not adequate to describe *training objectives* in broad, umbrella terms, for example 'to understand how a radio works' or 'to understand an electrical system'. Such statements are vague and ambiguous. What are required are clear and specific details, preferably formalized as a written statement and spelt out in precise behavioural, observable and measurable actions described by an action verb. This means that desired terminal behaviour should be specified by name or kind, thus:

– Performance – what the trainee has to be able to do.
– Conditions – under which the performance has to take place.
– Standards – the level of performance expected.

A simple example taken from the training of bank staff (Jones, 1980) might be:

> 'Given a list of products with a maximum of 8 digits and a rate of interest for each, be able to convert to a sterling amount using bank interest tables provided. All answers to be rounded to the nearest penny, and performed under normal working conditions within half an hour'.

Having established training objectives, we must then decide upon our *training strategy* – the ways in which we attempt to impart skill and knowledge – through the selection of appropriate methods of instruction and opportunities for practice. We can then design our course and develop the training material to be used in it. So much for the preparation. We should now run a *pilot test*, exposing a small group of trainees to the training process devised to ascertain their general reaction to it, and to see if it works. We must measure to what extent trainees have improved as a result of the training exercise and compare this with the training requirements as set out at the beginning. If all is well, and no adjustments need to be made, we may proceed with implementing the training for the main body of trainees. All trainees should be assessed at the end of the programme, a measure of *terminal behaviour*, or given a post-training test (a criterion test) to see whether training has been successful. This is the process of validation. We must see that the training works and that the correct change of job behaviour occurs. It may not be enough simply to have an end-of-course assessment. What really matters is improved or appropriate performance *back on the job*, and to this end superiors' reports may later be called for. The validation of training is really an assessment to see whether the training has achieved what it set out to achieve. To validate it scientifically we would really need to compare various training methods to see which one produced the best result. Time and cost constraints may limit this luxury, and from a technical point of view there may also be problems with experimental design.

Finally, we need to *evaluate* the training – that is to assess the results in cost-benefit terms. Was the investment worthwhile? Can we show that the costs of the training exercise were justified in terms of contribution to performance and organizational objectives?

Diagrammatically, the main steps in a systematic approach to training are set out in Fig. 5.3, and summarized in tabular form in Table 5.1.

Problems of validation, for anything other than very simple tasks, can be difficult. Many effects cannot be measured, especially those relating to attitudes and interpersonal skills. The effect of training can often only be assessed intuitively, i.e. subjectively, and is not open to impartial judgement. There is also the difficulty of measuring the effectiveness of a training programme when, say, a manager goes back to work. A newly learned or

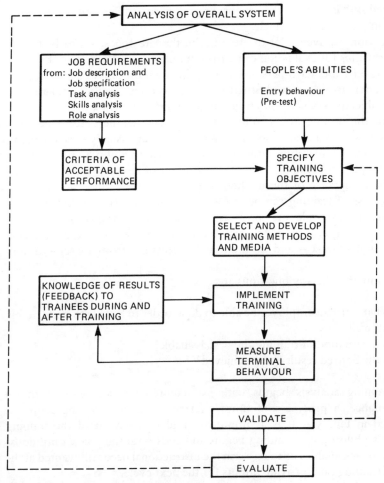

Fig. 5.3 *Systematic approach to training*

Table 5.1

A SYSTEMATIC APPROACH TO TRAINING

1 Identify areas of a problem which yield to a training solution.
2 By appropriate methods of analysis, define training requirements.
3 Determine acceptable standards and prepare criterion tests of required behaviour.
4 Define training objectives in behavioural terms.
5 Determine training strategy and select appropriate methods.
6 Design the course and training material.
7 Pilot test the training (and possibly revise).
8 Implement the training.
9 Measure terminal behaviour.
10 Validate the training.
11 Evaluate the training.

improved skill is only part of a manager's token equipment and the 'transfer of learning' may meet obstacles.

Evaluation received a lot of attention in the late 1960s and early 1970s. Most pressures for evaluation came from trainers themselves. The choice of criteria is difficult. Each person will have his own objectives and hence his own criteria. Burgoyne and Stuart (1977) concentrate on the evaluation of *learning* objectives, since it has been found so difficult to link training to any change in the organization. Hamblyn (1978) argues that there are no methods to measure such a link anyway. Training methods are usually selected on the basis of their acceptability, rather than on any proven ability to respond to a particular need for training. Often, the amount of research varies inversely with the acceptance of the method. Cascio (1982) has suggested that the effectiveness of training can be assessed according to various criteria. Performance, for example, may be measured qualitatively or quantitatively. As well as learning criteria which may be merit-worthy *per se*, there are also behavioural criteria – and in addition (but distinct from these) – results criteria.

In summary, the key questions are:

(1)　What must an employee be able to do in order to be able to perform his job well?
(2)　Is the method of training the best available?
(3)　Is the desired result being achieved?

A training analysis begins with *job* requirements and ends with *job* performance, a process sometimes referred to as the 'training loop', as depicted in Fig. 5.4. It is a simplified graphic statement of the training system's philosophy. Training begins and ends with the job. Continuous-loop feedback enables us to research the instructional need still wanted at the end of training, and provide imputs for the next cycle.

Factors which facilitate learning and training

A distinction is to be drawn between learning (the internal process within an individual) and performance (the external results). Performance is the observed effect of learning on behaviour. Interest in industrial training derives from two sources – the needs of organizations which are predominantly concerned with performance, and the concern of trainers in methods of learning. It is the emphasis on *learning* (i.e. what the learner does) as opposed to *teaching* (i.e. what the teacher does) which most marks the changes in education and training in recent years.

Learning is a 'black box'. The ways in which skill, knowledge and attitudes are absorbed by an individual are not easily seen, although we do know something about how to facilitate the process. Performance is a demonstration of the fact that learning has taken place; it is the measurable behaviour

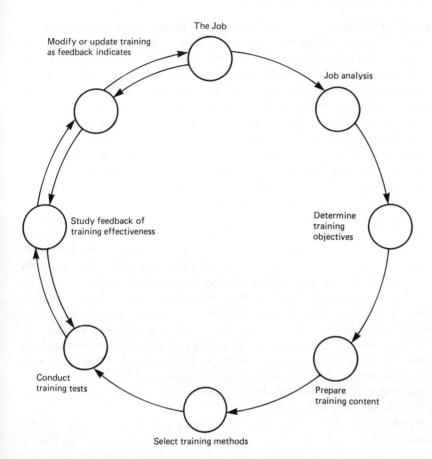

Fig. 5.4 *The training loop*

from which underlying learning can be inferred. The aim of a technology of training is to expedite the process by arranging conditions so that learning is much more rapid and effective.

There is not one separate theory of learning, but a number which overlap, and which underpin industrial training. Learning is a common activity and occurs naturally; it is an abstract process. To an extent, past learning brings considerable influence on new learning situations, but not entirely. Learning is change resulting partly from experience and partly from responding to a situation. For the 'behaviourist' school at least, learning is treated as a link between stimulus and response (and this is of vital importance for skills training). The four basic concepts are: Drive, Stimulus, Response, Reinforcement (feedback).

Drive can result from motivation or deprivation. There are primary drives (which are innate, i.e. unlearned) such as hunger, thirst, etc. There are also secondary drives (which are learned), e.g. for achievement, accomplishment, status, money. It is the basic drive or motivation which is necessary for all activity or behaviour, and without which human organisms would be inactive. Coupled with drive, and as a trigger for its direction, there is also the concept of Stimulus. A stimulus may be any object, event, cue, or signal which causes something to happen; it is an occasion for a Response. A response, then, is the behavioural result of stimulation. In this way responses become connected with stimuli. Some responses may be obvious, others may be difficult to observe. A 'reinforcer' is any object or event which serves to increase or maintain the strength of the response, e.g. rewards, money, compliments. If a stimulus produces a response and is *immediately* reinforced, then that response is likely to occur again (Thorndike's 'Law of Effect'). By observing things which are reinforcing to an individual it is possible to affect behaviour. The learner however may be unaware of what is going on, as is the case with the formation of attitudes, some of which may become so entrenched (as prejudices) they are difficult to unlearn or change. Just as there are primary and secondary drives, so are there primary and secondary reinforcers. Primary reinforcers are those things which reduce drives directly (e.g. food satisfies hunger). These primary reinforcers are innate. Secondary reinforcers are usually based on past associations (e.g. money, reward, praise, promotion, job security, independence, better work) and are not innate, but are found to be satisfying due to prior learning experiences.

The relationships between a stimulus and response tend to emphasize habit formation (associative learning). As far as industrial training is concerned, trainers have to concentrate on secondary reinforcers. The whole issue of the stimulus/response relationship has been both a cornerstone and a controversy in the development of learning theory.

Pavlov's dogs are well known. In the early part of this century Pavlov noticed that dogs salivated at the sight of food – an unconditioned, unlearned, innate response. By pairing stimuli, by shining a light into the dog's eyes at the same time as displaying food, Pavlov was able to generate a conditioned response. Dogs salivated at the sight of light only. This relationship between stimulus and response became known as 'classical conditioning'. The dog was induced to behave in a given way, although the organism was still basically passive. However, Pavlov introduced tangibility and objectivity (which replaced the previous philosophical and intuitive approaches to psychology) and his explanation for behaviour was the stimulus/response relationship. Others, such as Clark Hull suggested that the process was not so simple. There may be intervening variables in learning, e.g. inhibitions or the degree of habit strength attaching to any given stimulus which may well affect the outcome. Then came B. F. Skinner of Harvard who demonstrated that a response could be strengthened by following it with reinforcement. Skinner introduced the concepts of 'operant behaviour' and 'operant conditioning'. In experiments with pigeons and rats he was able to persuade the organism actively to do something (e.g. pressing bars to produce pellets of food). Behaviour was sustained so long as the reward was kept up. Learned behaviours could be induced.

Both operant conditioning and classical conditioning have many things in common. The essential element of operant conditioning is that rewards are given after the correct behaviour has been executed in order to encourage its active and purposeful repetition. In experiments, various regimes of reward produced various responding rates (in fact demonstrating Thorndike's Law of Effect). Skinner's approach has had considerable influence on many aspects of industrial training – notably on programmed instruction. The principle is to maximize reward during learning by arranging for the learner to make numerous correct responses to numerous small-step frames in a learning programme in which the content of instruction is so paced as to give the learner the near certainty of making correct answers – although the principles of programming do not show how to organize material into steps if it has a cognitive structure more complex than a list. Satisfaction wanes if rewards are continuous, but may be regenerated by rewarding at irregular intervals. Similar recent lessons in the use of praise by managers have been demonstrated (Blanchard and Johnson, 1982).

Inevitably, there were rival theories against the S–R school. the 'cognitivist' school argued that a learner did not require response habits but rather information maps on which to plan and act. Tolman, particularly, argued that all activity, based on cues and past experience, has a purpose leading to a particular goal. After the preoccupation with conditioning and learning came the cybernetic movement, which with computer machinery enabled information to be processed and transformed into an answer. This is just what psychologists had been trying to model. At last ideas of simulation broke free from the simple S–R unit. Later came a movement towards 'educational technology' which looked at ways in which people utilize and seek information in building up concepts, for example the learning loop (Kolb and Fry, 1975) as in Fig. 5.5. Kolb showed by practical experiments that some people are more adept at one particular part of the cycle. Following from this, Mumford and Honey (1982) developed a Learning Styles Questionnaire enabling an individual to develop his own particular style of learning as:

Activists – who enjoy the here and now, dominated by current experiences.

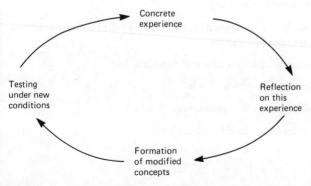

Fig. 5.5 *Kolb's learning loop*

Pragmatists – interested in experimenting with new techniques.

Reflectors – who like to stand back, observe and think.

Theorists – who like to analyse and synthesize new models and systems.

While the theorists are still learning about learning, there are some particular considerations which are useful for the industrial trainer (summarized in Table 5.2).

Table 5.2 Summary: Applications of learning theory to industrial training

1 *Capacities* of learners are important. Individuals differ in ability.

2 Learning is best achieved at the trainee's own *pace*.

3 *Motivated* learner learns quicker.

4 Motivation under stress (pain, fear) creates emotional distraction and is less effective than 'no motivation'.

5 Learning under a *positive incentive* (reward is better than punishment).

6 Learning is facilitated by 'meaningful' material – an integration of learning experiences which the trainee can transfer from training to the job.

7 Active *participation* is better than passive reception.

8 *Knowledge of results* (feedback) is vital.

9 *Reinforce* – frequently and immediately.

10 Space and distribute presentation and practice as appropriate.

11 Provide ample opportunity for practice and repetition.

12 Learning rate may be influenced by personality interactions of instructor/learner.

13 Role of teacher is to assist trainee in his willingness to change.

14 Some *guidance* is necessary.

15 There may be some *transfer* of training.

16 A *systematic* approach should be adopted to the identification of training needs and to the planning of training programmes.

17 *Validation*: comparison of criterion tests and pre-entry tests.

18 *Evaluation* of training in cost-benefit terms.

19 Training is not a solution to every problem.

20 Alternative ways of learning should be considered.

INDUCTION

Induction is the name given to the process by which new entrants are introduced into an organization and familiarized with the way things are done, the main personalities – including co-workers, the nature of the organization's business and employee services. It is a process by which newcomers are made to feel welcome and at home. Frequently such people feel at a loss when confronted with a strange environment. This is particularly true of school-leavers, and to some extent, also of graduate trainees and immigrants. The purpose of an induction programme is to help newcomers understand their new environment and find their feet.

A company showing particular concern for induction is not 'featherbedding'. Research shows that a peak in labour turnover occurs almost universally during the first few weeks or months of employment in a new job – the so-called 'induction crisis'. This is commonly attributed to the fact that whatever the prospects of advancement or job security may be, initial anxieties and uncertainties held by new employees – if not dispelled – cause them to quit before the necessary adjustments have taken place. A high quit rate in the early stages of employment is detrimental to an employer's interests and exacerbates recruitment and training costs. Typically, an induction programme can be phased over the first few weeks of employment on a part-time basis, occupying perhaps just a few hours at a time, including short talks, company films, conducted tours, and meeting people with whom the new employee will most frequently have contact. The administration of induction programmes is made easier when new employees join as a group (or as 'cohorts'). It is easier to neglect the new employee who joins individually, but it is for them particularly that the induction crisis can be most severe, since group support and morale may be lacking.

The aim of an induction programme should be to bring new employees into their working groups as effectively as possible – a process of integration and socialization. The new employee needs to know where to turn for advice, guidance and counselling. It behoves the line manager as much as a personnel officer to take on the role of 'moral tutor' with regard to every new employee. To shun this responsibility is to retard the integration process and foster alienation. 'Effective induction focuses first on the anxieties of the new employee and only later on what the employee should be told' (Torrington and Chapman, 1983).

KNOWLEDGE OF RESULTS

Knowledge of results can have a strong motivational edge. A learner who knows when a response is right or wrong, or whether he is improving or not, can set goals for himself. This not only makes the learning process more interesting, but self-development, itself a powerful motivator, implies the involvement of employees in setting their own training objectives. According to some authorities (Kolb, Rubin and McIntyre, 1980) good 'feedback' should be specific, well-timed (immediate) and checked to ensure good communication.

MOTIVATION

For effective learning, trainees must *want* to learn. They must perceive the learning process as the means of achieving certain desired goals. *Intrinsic* motivation is inspired by the need to fulfil personal, deeply felt needs. Industrial training programmes may not always appear to the trainee to be of relevance to his or her innermost needs. However, there are some helpful ways of utilizing intrinsic rewards: to stress the future utility of the learning activity (e.g. using problems of a kind that the trainee is likely to face in a future job), provide feedback during the learning experience (showing the extent to which trainees are progressing towards the final training objectives), relate the learning activity to interesting and meaningful material, and try to maintain suspense during the learning programme.

The training programme may only partially be able to rely on intrinsic motivation. To compensate, use must be made of *extrinsic* motivational rewards which may be artificially related to the task and therefore reinforcing it. A learner may be encouraged to learn because certain desired rewards are contingent upon certain forms of behaviour – such as praise, promotion, financial incentives, opportunities for development. The trainer will usually find it useful to emphasize long-term benefits. In any case, it is generally more effective to reward – and to maximize the probability that the learner will experience success – than it is to punish errors, mistakes and failures. Punishment is a poor motivational technique because its consequences are not so predictable. Although punishment may deter wrongdoing, it gives no indication of the correct response. Punishment may be counter-productive in that it tends to fixate behaviour rather than eliminate it. It tends unduly to focus the attention of a trainee on the wrong responses. Punishment may also be emotionally disturbing and create negative attitudes towards the instructor or the task. And the effects of punishment on behaviour are relatively less permanent than those of reward.

ANXIETY

Training situations can give rise to anxiety for obvious reasons. It is the responsibility of the trainer to remove anxiety from a learning situation by building a non-threatening environment. Emotional disturbances arising from anxiety can interfere with the learning process. Apart from the common fears of failure and embarrassment, too high a level of motivation can lead to stress. There is some evidence to suggest that there may be an optimum level of motivation or 'arousal' for any given learning situation; a *small* degree of anxiety may be necessary for stimulation.

GUIDANCE

At extremes, there may be maximum or minimum guidance. Skinner favoured maximum guidance. But with too much guidance the learner may become dependent upon it and find it difficult to adjust to the post-learning situation when support is removed. With minimum or zero guidance, a learner proceeds on a trial-and-error basis uninformed of his correct responses and not prevented from making errors. Total lack of guidance prolongs the learning period and may lead to the formation of bad habits which are difficult to eradicate. Most experts agree that both extremes are undesirable; it is a question of balance.

DISCOVERY LEARNING

In training programmes designed to teach complex skills, guidance should be limited to provide an opportunity for trainees to discover common elements, principles and relationships for themselves – by 'insight'. The so-called 'discovery method' has been used successfully in 'conversion training' for older workers who have to learn new skills, and also in the initial training of young people with little formal educational background. Active participation in the quest for understanding tends to result in more effective learning and retention (Belbin and Belbin, 1972).

FORGETTING

That which has been learned can so easily be forgotten. Practice is necessary for the maintenance of a skill or the retention of knowledge. Unless practice is continued, forgetting takes place very rapidly, although the rate of forgetting varies between individuals and according to the subjects or skills learned. There is evidence to suggest that perceptual-motor skills can be retained for a fairly long period of time. This is not true of most forms of learning which fall into passive decay through disuse. In general, something which needs to be retained for a long period of time needs to be *'overlearned'*. Forgetting can occur for a number of reasons, e.g. inhibitions (retroactive inhibition, where the learning of new material interferes with things learned in the past), and proactive inhibition (where old learning may inhibit or interfere with learning new things). What is more, we may actually be motivated to forget something (i.e. repression) which we found distasteful. One consolation is that relearning something takes less time than the original learning.

TRANSFER OF TRAINING

The term 'transfer of training' refers to the 'carry-over' effects or the extent to which proficiencies and abilities acquired during a training session or learning programme may be applied to actual work on the job or the learning of some new, but related, skill. It may be that in some situations *negative transfer* occurs because the learning experience may have created inhibitions which impede the acquisition of new skills. Occasionally there may be no observable effect. *Positive transfer*, however, refers to cases where learning in one situation actually enhances learning in another (Gagne, 1977). Positive transfer may be due to a number of causes. One of these is through the '*transfer through principles theory*' which states that once a general principle has been learned, all the problems of a given class may be solved as soon as they are presented. However, it is still necessary for the learner to recognize common properties in the two 'stimulus' situations (say, the learning one and the job one). This principle underlies much off-the-job training, particularly training for transferable skills. Another technique is the '*identical elements theory*' which draws attention to the relationship between the degree of similarity between 'stimuli' and 'responses' in one situation (e.g. learning) and another (e.g. on the job). A problem here is that it may be difficult to measure the degree of similarity between stimuli or responses, although the technique is applicable to situations where specific stimuli and corresponding responses can be clearly identified (e.g. learning to drive a car). In more complex tasks, learners progress from making simple stimulus-response connections through trains of thought and verbal associations, to the ability to discriminate between situations and develop rules and concepts so that they finally develop the ability to solve problems for themselves. The implication is that there is a learning hierarchy and that *training should proceed from lower to higher levels*.

Skills analysis

What is a skill? The question has been asked for many years. The late Sir Frederick Bartlett, one of the great researchers in this area, defined skill as 'a smooth, well-timed performance'. It has also been defined as 'ability acquired through practice' (Crossman, 1964). Others (Annett and Kay, 1957) have noted that 'one of the primary features of skilled performance is the perceptual ability of the operator in receiving incoming signals and an important problem is how we assess this ability'. Welford (1968) suggested that all skills, industrial and psychological, motor and mental, possessed three characteristics:

1 Building up an organized and coordinated activity – involving a chain of sensory, central and motor mechanisms

2 They are learned behaviours

3 They are serial, i.e. coordinated in a temporal sequence.

Skilled performance is a coordinated and unitary process, but according to Welford involves three distinct sub-processes – (i) the receptor processes (the use of various human senses by which cues and stimuli are recognized); (ii) the central processes occurring in the cortex of the brain which organize incoming information and provide the neural impulses, and (iii) the effector processes (the contraction of muscles from our bodily movements and use of limbs, etc. needed to perform the task).

The performance of any physical operation involves skills. When performing a task of a physical nature a person is involved in a continuous control function which adjusts and controls the body. There are several links in this chain. First comes the recognition, collection and interpretation of cues and information about the task. These are stimuli. The information is picked up by the senses and processed by the brain into messages which are passed to the fingers, hands, arms, etc. This is the sensory process. Responses are made by those parts of the body receiving the messages from the brain. These movements are referred to in medical jargon as the motor response. Motor responses have to be selected, timed and coordinated. Skilled performance always requires some action to be taken in response to stimuli which trigger the timing, force and direction of movements, temporarily and spatially adjusted in anticipation of later stages of activity. In complex skill, these processes take place simultaneously.

The two links – receiving signals and taking appropriate actions – comprise the sensory motor activity. The sensory motor activity is known as skill. Two of its components, the transfer of information and the internal transmission of decisions from the brain are carried out within the individual, and cannot be readily appreciated. Thus, when an instructor demonstrates a skill he is only showing the physical components. The main problem confronting the study of overt skilled performance is that we cannot see what is actually going on *inside* the performer – yet this is the most important aspect – and we really fudge the issue by measuring skills according to the difficulty of a task or operation, the speed of performance, accuracy, etc.

One of the key elements in the processing of information is feedback and knowledge of results. Skilled performance requires knowledge of the success or quality of past and immediate reactions so that counterbalancing compensations can be made, both with regard to present performance and anticipated future performance. The trainee must be able to identify sensory feedback. There is abundant research evidence to demonstrate the necessity of (preferably instantaneous) feedback in order to improve skilled performance. When for example, an operator taps a thread in a hole, he will feel resistance to the cutting edge of the tap. This tells him about his current performance, and his brain will use this information in deciding whether to proceed or stop. If he proceeds and breaks the tap, he has immediate feedback of his performance. Thus in this operation key elements cannot be analysed by observation because this is an internalized process. The trainee must be made aware of the sensory feedback in order to carry out an efficient job. This feedback comprises two parts – the knowledge of performance and the knowledge of the success/failure of that performance.

The difference between skills is not so much one of kind as one of extent; the semi-skilled worker usually concentrates on a single task or small group of tasks, whereas the craftsman has the ability to accomplish a whole range of tasks and determine the means for achieving them. It is generally agreed that the basic factors contributing to skilled performance are the same and cannot be distinguished in their nature, and that skilled performance shows a certain kind of refinement which is not shown by the inexpert worker. Experienced, or skilled workers, usually employ smoother and more consistent movements, make better use of sensory data, operate more rhythmically, react in an integrated way to sensory signals, and make organized responses to them. Of course, not all skills can be explained completely on a stimulus and response basis. Psychological factors such as perception also enter the process, and so does the question of motivation. The whole process is in effect a communication process carrying information which is used for control or cybernetics. The skills employed in industry exhibit the same features as those employed in other activities and are performed with the same human resources, but the goals and environment are different. Industrial workers are increasingly required to handle mechanical and electrical forces, exercising control skills which involve less physical effort, resulting however in an increase of the importance of small delicate movements and especially of fine fingerwork. A large brain area is devoted to finger movements, but speed and accuracy of repetitive movements appear to depend on the consistency of repeated muscular contractions. It is this consistency of operation which produces the consistency of quality standards required for modern batch or flow production. However, individuals do differ in their ability to maintain the desired constituency of response and in their ability to attain it.

In devising training programmes, we need to supply the right amount of information in the right way at the right time. We need to determine exactly what the trainee has to learn, which should be based on an analysis of the task, not only in terms of *what* the trainee must know and do, but also *how* he or she has to carry out the mental and physical activities involved. The best methods of helping a trainee to learn these activities will be based on our understanding of the nature of the task, together with a knowledge of how people learn. We must always provide ample opportunities for practice and feedback of knowledge and results. The whole question of skill training has much to do with the design of machines, and man–machine interactions (the study of ergonomics taken up in Chapter 20). In view of the continually changing demands for training due to technological innovation, it is imperative to keep constantly under review the demands of any particular job and to relate them to the training programme.

Skills need to be analysed, and in summary, can be carried out under the following headings.

1   What cues or stimuli need to be recognized?
2   What senses are involved? (a) Vision, (b) touch, (c) other?
3   What left-hand operations are required?
4   What right-hand operations are required?
5   What foot operations are required?

6   Are any counterbalancing operations required?
7   Are there any interactions with other operatives?

A fuller example, 'Extract from a skills analysis' from the Engineering Industry Training Board is shown in Table 5.3.

Operators

Operators are 'work people directly concerned with production or service in a wide range of industries and occupations, possessing varying degrees of a skill and knowledge which is usually of a narrower range and capable of a lesser degree of adaptation than that of a craftsman' (Kenney, Donnelly, and Reid, 1979). But as Singer (1977) has said: 'The term "semi-skilled" is often a misnomer in that the skills possessed by some workers in this category are of a high order, though over a restricted range of tasks'.

Operator jobs usually have the following characteristics:

(1)   Short learning time
(2)   Standard training programmes
(3)   Limited knowledge content
(4)   Significant manual skill content
(5)   Minimal educational requirements
(6)   Off-the-job training facilities.

Operator training courses may be necessary not only for new recruits, but also for holders of an existing job, or for those transferred on to a new machine or process.

So the operator needs to be trained for the actual job he or she has to do, and acquire some level of skill. This training should be based on a systematic analysis of the skill required and an identification of the actual training needs. The purpose is to forge the best link between the worker and the job. Skills analysis training was pioneered in the early 1940s by Dr A. H. Seymour who combined principles of industrial psychology and work study. Tasks are trained to work measurement standards and broken down into steps, based on the performance of experienced operators (experienced worker standard, or EWS). Later, Industrial Training Boards made formidable progress and achieved a revolution in training for the skilled trades. By using modern approaches, productivity can be raised quickly, the learning curve accelerated, and time saved.

Older methods of operator training are now discredited. By the age-old semi-exposure technique of 'sitting next to Nelly' trainees were placed alongside experienced operators and remained there until capable of some productive work of their own. Throughout, the experienced workers were responsible for supervising the productive effort of their protégé, supervision tailing off as the novices became more efficient. During the Second World War, the Training Within Industry (TWI) scheme emerged. Now sponsored

Table 5.3 Extract from a skills analysis (EITB, 1981a)

Job: Manufacture Plate for Support Bracket

Element: Drill three 12mm ($\frac{1}{2}$") diameter holes in plate

Equipment: Twin spindle pillar drill with Fixture No. 1789Q and Bush Plate No. 2217F

Left Hand	Right Hand	Vision	Other Senses	Comments
Component assembled to bush plate and loaded in fixture vice. Machine running. Vice in RH position				
Reach to vice	Reach to vice	To vice		
Grasp LH side of vice, F1234 on side, Th. on front face	Grasp RH side of vice at base. F1234 on side. Th. on front face.	Checks position of RH		Vice will bind in fixture grooves if RH grasp is too high
Assist RH to position vice	Move vice to left to position LH hole in bush plate under No. 1 spindle drill	Controls positioning by judging alignment of drill and bush plate hole	Kinaesthetic control of sideways movement. Feels for any binding of vice in fixture grooves	Direction of push must be parallel to grooves. Eye/hand co-ordination important. Drill point approx. $\frac{1}{2}$" above bush plate

Hold vice	Release vice. Reach to RH drill handle	To drill point	Kinaesthetic for position of handle	
	Grasp drill handle F1234 around. Th. over end			End grasp important to give maximum sensitivity
Makes fine adjustment to vice position as required	Pull handle down to position drill in bush plate hole	Checks alignment of drill and hole	Kinaesthetic controls rate of drill descent. Touch checks drill clears bush plate	Coordination of eye and LH
Holds vice	Pulls handle down to drill component	Checks condition of swarf	Kinaesthetic controls rate of cutting. Listens for sound of correct cutting	Swarf to be continuous with no heat discolouration

by the Department of Employment and encompassing a series of 3-day instructional courses for chargehands, foremen, and experienced workers, the objective is to train one or more experienced hands in how to teach others. Elementary job breakdowns are prepared as an aid to instruction. The approach is an improvement on simple exposure, but often not critical enough to produce optimum results. Nevertheless, it was a forerunner to the current more detailed systematic analysis.

The objectives of modern systematic approaches to operator training are:

(1) To reduce time taken to learn a new job or task and thus reduce costs.
(2) To achieve, maintain or improve quality standards.
(3) To introduce or standardize correct methods.
(4) To enable new entrants to reach average performance and average wage levels as soon as possible.
(5) To minimize accidents caused by ignorance or carelessness.
(6) To increase the versatility and flexibility of the worker.
(7) To ensure better care of machines and tools by the operator.
(8) To improve job satisfaction.

Basic training needs will be revealed by job analysis, but a full-blown skills analysis will go three stages further:

1 Sequencing of operations
2 Perceptual and motor components
3 Difficulty, frequency, importance analysis.

By *sequential analysis*, a job is divided into its sequential parts according to the logical and orderly way in which the various job elements are developed to form the total operation. We identify the temporal sequence, beginning with initial activities and moving through the series of operations step by step. Simple tasks may lend themselves to this approach. We may be able to identify training needs which are in a sense progressive as the total job is built up. Training is given to each part in isolation and then linked up by the so-called 'progressive' part method or 'cumulative' method (see later).

More complicated tasks, which do not necessarily always follow a fixed sequence or cycle of operations, may be better viewed according to their various *perceptual or motor components*. In such cases we need to identify the signals that the operator picks up to respond in a particular way, and what are the training requirements of each of these responses.

Once an outline of the job, in whatever degree of detail, has been established, we can further weight the various job components according to their *difficulty, frequency, and importance*. Obviously more difficult, important and frequent elements command attention – but there may sometimes be conflict between the competing claims of these three criteria. The point is that it is not always necessary to train for every single detail or occurrence. We must establish an order of priorities according to this scaling procedure.

In any operator job there are two basic areas which need to be analysed (as in Fig. 5.6) and these are knowledge and physical requirements.

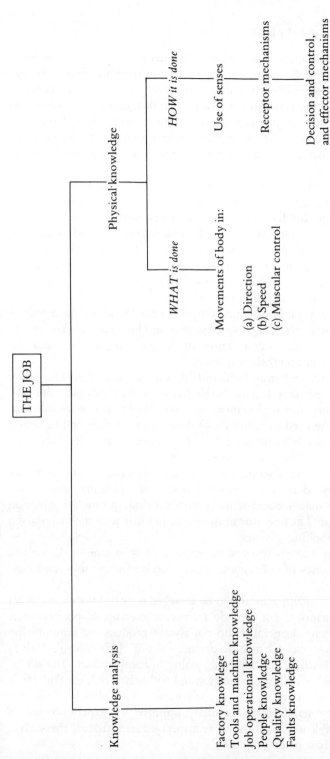

Fig. 5.6 *What is being analysed: knowledge and physical requirements*

ANALYSIS OF KNOWLEDGE

Knowledge is information. It is *what* an individual needs to know in order to do something. In practice it may sometimes be difficult to separate knowledge from skills and split the job into two halves. But for the purposes of analysis the distinction is useful – it ensures that the analyst does not ignore aspects external to overt job performance. These twin aspects have been developed in traditional learning methods over a long period. The presentation of job knowledge in a systematic way is an important factor in reducing training time.

Analysis of knowledge depends to a large extent on purely verbal communication, unlike the analysis of manual skills. Good communication between analyst, jobholder and supervisor are essential. The analyst must find answers to basic questions. Items of knowledge need to be identified and facts need to be verified. A distinction should be made between that which is 'desirable' and that which is 'essential' and again, we may wish to scale these.

Some of the particulars which comprise the area of knowledge analysis (as indicated in Fig. 5.6) are as follows.

Factory knowledge is fairly obvious. Operators need to know the layout of machinery and equipment, the respective uses and how each contributes to the overall process. They need to know the broad layout of the factory or plant so that they can find their way around.

The range of *correct tools* must be identified, using the names by which they are known to the operators. It may also be necessary to identify parts of tools. Storage, availability and replacement of tools should also be established. Operators certainly need to know about the equipment they will be using, how it works, how it is maintained, how it is operated safely, and the basic design and function of jigs, lathes, fixtures, etc.

Job knowledge consists of seeing how various operations fit into an overall cycle, the interdependence of the various parts, broad operating instructions, and the effects of machine and work methods including time standards on quality and output. The operator must also be familiar with the materials to be used and the booking of work.

The operator also needs to *know the people* with whom he or she will be working – the names of colleagues, supervisors and inspectors, and their responsibilities.

The *knowledge of quality standards* to be achieved is vital. Quality, together with time and quantity, can provide a criterion measure of performance. Even fully experienced operators do not always produce the same quality standard in every cycle. Chance occurrences within their control, such as unintentional activation, may alter the quality of their product. The skilled operator knows what will pass inspection and will only rectify the fault if it is serious enough to attract the inspector's notice. This ability to identify acceptable quality standards is normally acquired by experience and is particularly valuable in situations where inspection standards are themselves wholly or partially subjective.

The *analysis of faults* has gained increasing prominence in recent years. 'Operators working in process industries or in the monitoring of automated equipment need training that brings out the role of the worker as part of a complex person–machine system within which mistakes can result in great loss. Training is therefore required not only in routine procedures, but also in the recognition of systems out of control, together with the steps necessary to restore system equilibrium' (Baron, 1981). Faults analysis is a means of identifying any malfunction which can occur in an operation, its cause, remedies and prevention. It is an extension of job analysis and helps to identify the quality of standards which can be set for any task. Perhaps the most useful approach is the development by the Engineering Industry Training Board (The Training of Adult Operators, Booklet No. 3, EITB, 2nd edition, 1981).

Faults analysis involves answering the following questions:

1   Name – identify the fault by name.
2   Appearance – how is the fault recognized?
3   Cause – what are the causes of the fault in order of most probable appearance.
4   Effect – what is the effect of the fault on the component, following operations, and/or end product?
5   Responsibility – who is responsible for the fault having occurred?
6   Action – what action should be taken on detecting the fault?
7   Prevention – how can similar faults be prevented?

An example is given in Table 5.4 'Extract from faults analysis – manufacture plate for support bracket' (reproduced by kind permission of EITB).

CONDUCTING THE TRAINING

Should the training be on or off-the-job? On-the-job training may not be feasible due to the use of costly machinery and potential damage. Off-the-job training must be properly reinforced at the workplace to aid transfer of skills. Vestibule training, slightly removed from the workplace, is normally used for one-man operations. A combination might be adopted, according to the skills required, the number of trainees, ability levels, individual differences, relative costs.

THE SPACING OF TRAINING SESSIONS

Training may be presented as a whole (massed) or parts (distributed) and there is some debate as to the relative merits of whole or part learning. Generally, the spacing out of training sessions is desirable. This is especially true where motor skills are concerned. Evidence is equivocal regarding verbal learning or other complex learning situations. Rest periods throughout the training programme allow for the dissipation of response fatigue which if allowed to build up interferes with learning in long sessions.

Table 5.4 Extract from faults analysis – manufacture plate for support bracket (EITB, 1981b)

Name	Appearance	Cause	Effect	Responsibility	Action	Prevention
Undersize Hole	Diameter of hole too small. 'Go' end of gauge will not enter	1. Incorrect drill selected 2. Worn drill	Component cannot be assembled	Operator	Change drill. Re-drill to correct size	Check size and condition of drill before fitting
Oversize Hole	Diameter of hole too big. 'No go' end of gauge enters hole	1. Incorrect drill selected 2. Blunt drill 3. Build up of swarf on drill point. 4. Drill ground off centre 5. Worn bush plate 6. Worn drill spindle	Component scrapped	1. Operator 2. Operator 3. Operator 4. Cutter Grinder 5. Fitter 6. Fitter	Inform foreman and complete scrap record 1. Change drill 2. Change drill 3. Change drill 4. Change drill	Check size and condition of drill before fitting. Operator cannot prevent 5, 6

Drill Run	Hole not vertical. Detected by Inspection Fixture No. 6723/4/F	1. Feed rate of drilling too high 2. Drill too long for job 3. Swarf between component and vice 4. Component not hard down on bottom of vice 5. Worn bush plate	Component scrapped	1. Operator 2. Operator 3. Operator 4. Operator 5. Fitter	Inform foreman and complete scrap record 1. Change drill 2. Change drill 3. Change drill 4. Change drill	1. Ensure swarf is not discolouring whilst drilling 2. Drill not to be longer than 6" 3. Clean fixture before loading 4. Press down on component whilst clamping Operator cannot prevent 5
Tapered Hole	Diameter of hole larger at one end than other	1. Worn drill 2. Blunt drill 3. Worn drill spindle 4. Worn bush plate	Component scrapped	1. Operator 2. Operator 3. Operator 4. Fitter	Inform foreman and complete scrap record 1. Change drill 2. Change drill	Check size and condition of drill before fitting. Operator cannot prevent 3, 4

Rest periods also allow for the consolidation of the learned material in the memory store. Massed learning can adversely affect motivation by increasing boredom. In massed learning situations there may arise some cross-interference of responses from trainees who have experienced a highly concentrated series of inputs or stimuli. As a rule, learning is facilitated where rest periods are shorter in the early stages of training and become longer later on.

Where the material to be learned is not particularly meaningful, or where it is difficult and there is a lot of it, distributed practice should be favoured. Conversely, if the subject-matter is very simple, short and meaningful massing is likely to produce better results more quickly. The 'whole' method may be better for highly intelligent learners, and where the material is coherent and unified. Less capable and less experienced trainees are likely to derive more benefit from 'distributed' practice. Also, material learned by distributed practice is likely to be retained for a longer period, although the whole method may be better for learning a psycho–motor skill (such as riding a bicycle).

There is of course a difference between practice and presentation. Presentation is the art of exposition, explanation, generating understanding, whereas practice is the application of a skill. Not all conceptual aspects (as presented) need to be *practised* separately, although isolated treatment in presentation may add clarity. The nature of the material or task to be learned and the characteristics of the trainee will indicate whether it is better to be presented and practised as a whole or in parts.

The 'part' method is widely used in training for semi-skilled work, such as the training of operatives. In such cases, the part method may be organized either by dividing a task into its *sequential* parts or into *perceptual* and *motor* components so that the more difficult components are practised in isolation before tackling the task as a whole. The main disadvantage of the part method (and its variations) is the problem of combining the learned parts into the whole operation (see Fig. 5.7).

Research suggests that the part method is still superior where tasks involve a complex sequence of interdependent operations and where a mistake in any one part can upset the whole cycle (e.g. shoe machining) or where perceptual (as opposed to motor) components of a task present learners with the greatest difficulty (e.g. understanding electrical circuits in the repair of an electric machine). In complex operations, whatever method of presentation and practice is employed, considerable time at the end of the training programme must be devoted to practising the whole (e.g. playing musical instruments).

ASSESSMENTS OF LEARNING

People learn at different rates, and some forms of training may be more effective than others. It is therefore desirable to trace the progress which a trainee is making. Where changes in performance are overt and can be measured, the rate of progress can be plotted as a *learning curve*. A learning

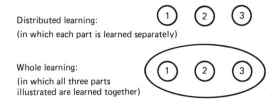

Distributed learning:
(in which each part is learned separately)

Whole learning:
(in which all three parts
illustrated are learned together)

Progressive part learning:

(showing two variations by which units of learning may be grouped
together. The numbers show the numerical sequence of groupings)

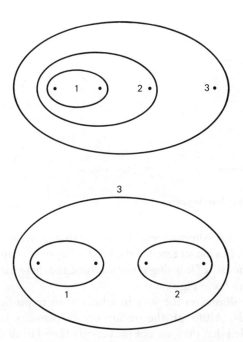

Fig. 5.7 *Diagrammatic representation of distributed, whole and progressive part learning
(after Seymour)*

curve shows the relationship between proficiency at a task or skill (a
dependent variable) with practice or experience or successive trials (an
independent variable). Such a relationship could be depicted as in Fig. 5.8).
Unfortunately people do not continue to improve forever, and most
frequently after a period of time there is likely to be a levelling off in the rate of
progress (as in Fig. 5.9). This levelling off is commonly known as a '*plateau*'.
Plateaux occur in the learning of any task or skill, although they only really
show that no *new* learning is evident. It may be that certain unseen, abstract

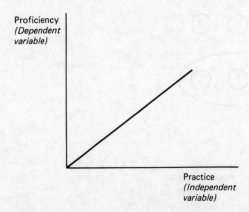

Fig. 5.8 *Representation of proficiency (learning) increasing with practice*

Fig. 5.9 *Negatively accelerating learning curve*

processes are still progressing. Alternatively, it may be that motivation has declined, or that the trainee has in fact reached the limit of his or her capacity, or that (as is quite likely) the rate of learning is not uniform and there may be a series of plateaux over time (as in Fig. 5.10).

The shape of the curve illustrates the way in which gains in proficiency vary with successive trials. Although the occurrence of plateaux is very common, it should be added that they are not universally found in all skilled learning. The most common shape of a learning curve is as depicted in Fig. 5.9, which is negatively accelerating. The learning progression shown here is most typical in tasks that are easy or where the trainee already possesses relevant skills and experience.

Learning seems to be most rapid in the early stages and slows down later. There are occasions when the learning curve may be positively accelerating (Fig. 5.11). This may simply occur because of lower motivation at first, but it is more likely to be found where the learning material is difficult and complex, and which with gradual absorption and practice later gives rise to a cumulative rate of progress.

Learning curves were developed many years ago (for work in telegraphy).

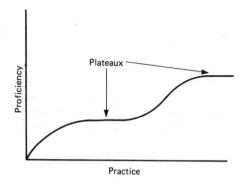

Fig. 5.10 *Learning curve showing early plateau and subsequent gains leading to another plateau*

Fig. 5.11 *Positively accelerating learning curve*

The shape of the curve, of course, is not only a reflection of the rate of learning, but also a direct result of the *type of measure* used. For example, one could plot progress by measuring quantity or quality or the time taken. Having adopted a convenient measure, one must then be consistent and apply the same measure successively. Learning curves can be used to assess the rate of learning between one trainee and another. They can also be used to compare the effectiveness of one training method against another.

In truth, what is in effect going on in the learning process is much more complicated than is depicted by a simple curve. The curve indicates *overall behavioural change*, but that change may have come about for a variety of reasons. What is actually being learnt changes during the training programme, and different attributes may be brought to bear on the task at different times. Learning curves are most useful in the measurement of 'skilled' performance – and this was their original use. Although we may get a picture of overall behavioural change, we still do not know *which* specific attributes or factors account for skilled performance at any point in time.

Apprentices

Historically, apprenticeships in the UK were really only for boys who wanted to learn a craft. A boy was 'bound apprentice' to an established member of an appropriate guild. A document was drawn up – an 'indenture' – signed by the apprentice master, the apprentice and his parent or guardian. The consent of all parties was required to terminate the agreement, but at the end of serving his time, usually 5 years, the boy became a man, a 'skilled craftsman'. Once, a premium had to be paid to take up an apprenticeship, a requirement later relaxed, and eventually even wages were paid. Today arrangements and training programmes are quite different, but most of the advances have only occurred in the last 20 years or so.

A definition of apprentice or craftsman is again offered by Kenney, Donnelly and Reid (1979): 'A skilled worker in a particular occupation, trade or craft who is able to apply a wide range of skills and a high degree of knowledge to basically non-repetitive work with a minimum of direction and supervision'. Singer (1977) adds 'The essential skill of a craftsman is that he is able to diagnose a situation and then call upon the required knowledge and physical skills he has learnt to achieve what is required. Apprentices should at first acquire proficiency in the basic skills of their trade and these should be mastered so that they can be performed at experienced worker's standard'.

The Industrial Training Act of 1964, influenced by the 1958 Carr Committee, did much to improve craft apprentice training and so did the ITBs. Previously it had been carried out in a rather haphazard way, even up to the late 1950s, when indifferent on-the-job training was given with no trade testing and with little opportunity for day-release to colleges of further education. Traditionally, craftsmen and those in the skilled trades have been the product of the apprenticeship system. Today, modular systems of training, with regular trade testing, are now well developed. Cumulative advances in public thinking and policy tried to bring about more comprehensive and unified approach to the whole panoply of skills training.

For apprentice training, the main components of a recognized course would nowadays include the following:

1   Careful selection, to ensure that young people have the right aptitudes, and to cut down wastage from apprenticeship schemes
2   Induction training
3   Formal and simulated training in workshops
4   Practical training on the job
5   Technical education
6   General education and related studies
7   Skill and educational attainment testing.

The learning process is therefore more complicated (and lengthy) than that for semi-skilled operators.

For an example of apprentice training, we can probably do no better than look at the Engineering Industry Training Board scheme ('The training of engineering craftsmen', EITB, 1981b). The EITB uses a 'modular' system suitable for both school leavers and experienced craftsmen changing or broadening their skills. It has eight basic principles:

1   Flexibility – to provide a wide range of skill and allow for changes to other occupations.
2   The length of training depends on the individual's rate of learning, so that there is an incentive to qualify quickly.
3   Standards of craftsmanship are set and recognized by certification.
4   Assessments are made of progress using a system of tests and training records.
5   Further development is encouraged by offering the chance to acquire further knowledge by returning to the training system and by linking up qualifications.
6   Instruction has a formal element under the guidance of trained specialists.
7   Further education is not ignored – day release is given to attend a college of further education.
8   The status of craftsmen is enhanced by requiring approved programmes of training, standards of performance, certification and registration.

During the first-year training programme a choice is made of modules to be pursued subsequently, offering different skill specialities. Choice depends on the needs of the firm and the aptitudes of the trainees. The Board provides a *Skill Training Specification* for each module, an *Instruction Manual* and a *Log Book*. Training in the chosen module proceeds in accordance with the appropriate training specification and to the standards prescribed by the skill specification. In support of each module of training completed, a period of controlled experience is necessary in a production environment to practise the skills acquired. The main purpose of the time spent on experience is to gain maturity and dexterity under the industrial pressures of cost and time. Day or block release is given for a suitable course of study throughout the year, such as those of the City and Guilds Institute. Successful completion of modules leads to a Certificate of Craftsmanship. Many craft trainees are able to reach the minimum satisfactory standards of skill by the end of their third year of training.

The EITB scheme is a notable example of craftsman training. Most of the craft trades are to be found in engineering and related industries, shipbuilding, construction, motor repairers and distributors, and in paper, printing and publishing, but a general trend in all industries in recent years has been one of falling numbers of new entrants.

The Youth Training Scheme

The Youth Training Scheme officially began operating in late 1983. After £2m spent on press and TV advertisements, many people in education and industry still only had a hazy idea how it would work. Politicians, educationists, trade unionists and youth workers were deeply divided. Norman Tebbit, then Employment Secretary, declared it 'the most far-reaching and ambitious proposal for industrial training ever put before Parliament'.

One year later, many key issues were still being fought out between officials and representatives of the various groups involved (*Training for Jobs*, Cmnd 9135, 1984).

The Youth Training Scheme purported to be a new and permanent training system for school leavers. Its purpose was to provide a bridge between school and work, to widen opportunities for youngsters, and to create a better-equipped workforce. It was aimed at young people under 17 (mainly) who had left school or further education. At first, priority was given to 16-year-olds. The scheme offered all trainees a year of experience of work integrated with high quality training, and a period of off-the-job training and education. Most trainees were placed with employers, encouraged to start their training. Some trainees were treated as normal employees and paid ordinary wages, but the majority received an allowance fixed by the Government. A smaller number were sponsored by colleges or local authorities and voluntary organizations and trained through courses or special workshops and community projects. It was planned for an estimated 452 000 youngsters to undergo YTS training in 1983/4, two-thirds with employers. But in that year only 400 000 places were sought and not all youngsters completed a full year. In 1983/4 some 42 per cent remained on the scheme for 48 weeks or more. Some 60 per cent of trainees secured jobs. More optimistically, many employers began to regard their in-house YTS schemes as the exclusive source of company recruitment (Atkinson, 1985). Over a million youngsters had entered the scheme by the close of 1985.

The YTS replaced the Youth Opportunities Programme although it did not, at least to begin with, have room for all the unemployed youngsters who would have been eligible for YOP. It also replaced the Unified Vocational Preparation Scheme under which young workers in jobs without formal training got some foundation training on day or block release. It does not, however, replace apprenticeship and similar established systems for training recruits for skilled jobs, but a lot of apprenticeships, and maybe nearly all of them, will eventually be brought in. The aim is to try to include in the YTS scheme everyone in the eligible age group who starts work. This does not mean that all will have the same training, the same conditions, the same prospects, or the same pay and status (although many will receive the same pay).

From April 1986, YTS was extended to give *all* 16- and 17-year-olds entering the labour market the opportunity to achieve:

1   competence and knowledge of a job;
2   competence in a range of 'core skills' – in numeracy, literacy, communication, problem-solving, computers and information technology – 'transferable' to various occupations;

3   inter-personal skills and self-reliance;
4   a recognized qualification based on standards of competence rather than
    time-served criteria.

YTS provides two years of training for 16-year-olds and one year for 17-
year-olds. Programmes must now include at least 20 weeks off-the-job
training or further education. Initial broad-based training will occupy the
first (foundation) year; the second year will be devoted to more occupation-
ally-based skills.

Overall responsibility for the scheme is vested in the Manpower Services
Commission (MSC). Bringing all existing training into the scheme makes
one thing inevitable – that neither the content of the foundation year nor the
way it is provided can be dictated directly by the MSC although it has overall
responsibility and foots the bill.

Almost everyone with a stake in the future of young people agrees that the
kinds of learning proposed for YTS trainees sound good. But not even the
most enthusiastic supporters believed that all employers could be trusted to
provide training and learning opportunities to the standards the MSC
prescribed. Few can ignore the experience of the Youth Opportunities
Scheme which showed that, left to their own devices without effective check-
ups, many employers simply used the youngsters as cheap labour. So the
MSC entrusted matters to the Youth Training Board, Area Manpower
Boards and a host of 'managing agents'.

Under the YTS, to moderate the 'hands off' policy which leaves so much
to the managing agents, there are 54 Area Manpower Boards, local watch-
dog bodies set up to oversee YTS and other MSC schemes. Their membership is drawn from the CBI, Unions, Local Authorities, Education and the
Voluntary Sector – but not the Youth Service or the youth organizations –
plus any extra people who are co-opted. The Boards approve schemes and
discuss problems which arise. The TUC wanted its members to have a right
of veto over the schemes, but after long discussions at national level, it agreed
to compromise that AMBs would not approve schemes where appropriate
officials of recognized trade unions had clearly indicated that they did not
support the proposals.

Each area office is run by an area manager responsible to one of nine
regional directors, themselves answerable to the MSC's Training Services
Division Headquarters at Sheffield. At headquarters, the Training Division's
YTS programme branch has been negotiating schemes with major national
organizations; the YTS development branch is deeply involved in curriculum
development and the YTS implementation branch is concerned with funding, eligibility, etc. None of the policies developed can go ahead without the
approval of the Youth Training Board. This body, set up on similar lines to
the Area Boards (with the addition of a youth representative) meets regularly
and is responsible for approving nationwide YTS projects.

Every trainee has a sponsor responsible for arranging his or her programme. At first this was under *Mode A* or *Mode B*. Mode A sponsors were

employers or groups of employers funded by a block grant plus a managing agent's fee. Mode B were the rest. (Briefly, there were three types of provisions under Mode B1 – community projects, training workshops, information technology centres. Mode B2 provided various linked schemes.) The two kinds of sponsorship were funded quite differently; there were different arrangements for supervising and monitoring, a different basis for the pattern of training and education; and a different relationship between sponsor and trainee. But the MSC and Ministers were soon making it increasingly plain that they regarded Mode A as by far the most desirable kind of sponsorship.

The original idea, as put forward by the YTS task group, was that managing agents would be large employers, industrial training bodies, chambers of commerce and similar organizations, voluntary organizations and local authorities who have the experience to recruit youngsters, design programmes for them, and place them with the employers who will act as sponsors. The managing agents were to be given responsibility for the maintenance of quality and standards 'within a particular locality'.

But since then, the MSC's scramble to reach its target of Mode A places has altered the picture a good deal. First, it has been telling local education authorities that it would rather not have them as managing agents, while encouraging big firms to act simply as agents for their own schemes. Companies with branches spread out over the country, furthermore, were being made national managing agents which certainly does not limit their operations to one locality. In effect, big employers were being given responsibility for policing themselves.

Mode A and Mode B were therefore unified in the revisions coming into force in April 1986. Administration was simplified, although the basic structure of arrangements remained. Exchequer contributions comprise a basic grant of £160 a month for each filled training place, and in certain cases additional 'premium grants'. Weekly allowances paid to trainees were set for £27.30 for the first year and £35 for the second (free of tax and national insurance).

In the future (scheduled for April 1987) only 'approved training organizations' will be able to take part in the scheme; 'training agreements' will be drawn up between trainees and their sponsors; and a Training Standards Advisory Service will be set up within the MSC to maintain training standards. One of the MSC's 1987 priorities is the interface of YTS with other programmes, especially pre-vocational education, by developing links with initiatives introduced into schools, such as the certificate of Pre-Vocational Education (CPVE) and the Training and Vocational Educational Initiative (TVEI). By 1990, all trainees are to receive 'enterprise training' as an integral part of the programme.

Summary

Learning should be directed to the needs of individuals or groups but individuals should be the focus of attention since their capacities and abilities vary widely and they learn best when allowed to learn at their own pace.

The motivated learner learns quicker; motivation under stress creates emotional disturbance and should be avoided. Learning under a positive incentive (reward) is better than under a negative incentive (punishment).

Learning is facilitated by 'meaningful' material; by active participation rather than passive reception; where knowledge of results is given and reinforcement is frequent and immediate. The spacing of presentation and practice are important matters and ample opportunity should be provided for practice and repetition. Learning rates, particularly for skilled operations, can be plotted graphically as learning curves.

Skills are coordinated, unitary processes involving the perception of cues and selection of appropriate motor expenses. One can only really measure the overt effects of skilled performance, yet training for skilled tasks involves an analysis of underlying activities.

All training can be treated systematically, relating the needs of the job to the abilities of the learner. The most important aspect is to establish objectives in behavioural terms, and to check on the efficiency of the training (validation).

Alternative ways of learning should always be considered. Training is not a solution to every kind of performance problem.

Discussion questions

1 Design a training programme for any job with which you are familiar.
2 By what methods would you compare the efficiency of one training programme against another?
3 Discuss ways in which training could be more integrated into normal work practices.
4 How would you select and train training officers?
5 Who should be responsible for training in an organization?
6 Outline ways in which learning theory could be applied to improve your own current course of study.
7 By what means would you try to facilitate the 'transfer of training'?
8 What is your opinion of the Youth Training Scheme? How far is it likely to achieve transferable skills?

References

ANNETT, J. and KAY, H. (1957), 'Knowledge of results and skilled performance', *Occupational Psychology*, **31**.

ATKINSON, K. (1985), 'Developing youth training', *Industrial and Commercial Training*, Nov.

BARON, B. (1981), 'Systematic training', in: Cowling, A. G. and Mailer, C. J. B., *Managing Human Resources*, Arnold, London.

BELBIN, E. and BELBIN R. M. (1972), *Problems in Adult Re-training*, Heinemann, London.

BLANCHARD, K. and JOHNSON, F. (1982), *The One Minute Manager*, Fontana/Collins, London.

BURGOYNE, J. and STUART, R. (1977), *Management Development Content and Strategies*, Gower, London.

CASCIO, W. G. (1982), *Applied Psychology in Personnel Management*, 2nd edn, Reston Publishing Company Inc., Reston, Virginia.

CLERC, J. (1982), 'Training as an instrument of a strategy for the improvement of working conditions and environment', *International Labour Review*, Vol. 121, No. 5, Sept–Oct.

CROSSMAN, E. R. F. W. (1964), 'Information processes in human skill', *British Medical Bulletin*, 20, 1.

DEPARTMENT OF EMPLOYMENT (1981), *Glossary of Training Terms*, HMSO.

ENGINEERING INDUSTRY TRAINING BOARD (1981a), *The Training of Adult Operators*, EITB Booklet, No. 3 (2nd edn).

ENGINEERING INDUSTRY TRAINING BOARD (1981b), *The Training of Engineering Craftsmen*, EITB Booklet.

GAGNE, R. M. (1977), *Conditions of Learning*, 3rd edn, Holt Rinehart Winston, New York.

HAMBLYN, A. C. (1978), *Evaluation and Control of Learning*, McGraw-Hill, Maidenhead.

HMSO. (1984), *Training for Jobs*, Cmnd: 9135.

JONES, G. F. (1980), 'The technical training of bank staff', in Livy, B., *Management and People in Banking*, Institute of Bankers, London.

KENNEY, J., DONNELLY, E. and REID, M. (1979), *Manpower Training and Development*, 2nd edn, Institute of Personnel Management, London.

KOLB, D. A. and FRY, R. (1975), 'Towards an applied theory of experiential learning of group processes', in Cooper, C. L., *Theories of Group Processes*, Wiley, New York.

KOLB, D. A., RUBIN, I. M., MCINTYRE, J. M. (1980), *Organisational Psychology: An Experiential Approach*, 3rd edn, Prentice-Hall, Englewood Cliffs.

MUMFORD, A. and HONEY, P. (1982), *The Manual of Learning Styles*, McGraw-Hill, Maidenhead.

SINGER, E. J. (1977), *Training in Industry and Commerce*, Institute of Personnel Management, London.

TORRINGTON, D. and CHAPMAN, J. (1983), *Personnel Management*, Prentice-Hall, Englewood Cliffs.

WELFORD, A. T. (1968), *Fundamentals of Skill*, Methuen, London.

CHAPTER 6

Performance appraisal, assessment centres and management development

by Bryan Livy

Performance appraisal

Performance appraisal is the name given to procedures which make regular assessments of employee performance. Normally, they are conducted annually. Conventionally, superiors assess, record and discuss performance levels with their subordinates. Performance appraisal enables employees to receive feedback on their performance, identify training needs and make further plans for development. It is a systematic review of progress.

Performance appraisal can achieve multiple objectives:

1. performance review
2. salary review
3. goal setting and action plans
4. counselling and career guidance
5. feedback
6. identification of training needs
7. identification of potential.

The process attempts to satisfy the various and combined needs of individual subordinates, the boss or superior, and an organization's qualitative manpower audit. With several clients, the question arises as to whether it is possible to satisfy all needs in *one* systematic operation. 'The different aims of appraisal frequently clash' (Fletcher, 1983).

Initial consideration should be given to:

1. clarification of objectives
2. establishing performance criteria
3. performance planning.

The link-pin in the whole operation is the line manager: it is he who makes appraisals, it is he who discusses progress with subordinates. The success of the system rests with the line manager. Personnel may devise and implement the scheme (in conjunction with others), but it is the line manager who (a) has a direct responsibility for employee performance, and (b) relates between employees and an organization's central personnel department. The line manager feeds back information to both parties. He lets the subordinate know how he/she is getting on. He also supplies the central organization with qualitative manpower information to be used for career and succession planning.

A performance appraisal system normally incorporates a manager's report, together with opportunities for discussion between the parties involved. It thereby supplies the platform to provide reassurance to the employee, to resolve problems, highlight areas where guidance is necessary, identify training needs and provide opportunities for the parties to have a frank discussion about future career progression.

The boss can use this system to develop a greater understanding of subordinates' problems, improve communication and performance, clarify and set targets. The boss needs first of all to be convinced of the utility of the performance appraisal system. He needs to be committed to it, devote time to it, and regard it as an important function. It could be argued that performance appraisal as conventionally instigated is unnecessary for the good manager who is constantly in touch with his subordinates and keeping an open door for a frank exchange of views and problems. However, there is a further need in a large-scale organization, where recommendations may be made for promotion or salary review, etc. that *uniform criteria be adopted and uniform standards of recommendation be made*. An attempt should be made to introduce fairness and equity across the board, and performance appraisal can be a means to that end. It therefore means that no manager acts in isolation but in accordance with an agreed company policy.

The aims of appraisal govern the type and scope of the scheme adopted, as well as the use made of the information derived. For administrative convenience, most appraisal schemes seek to achieve a multiplicity of aims at one and the same time. The advantages of separate reviews of performance, salary, and potential have been persuasively argued by Randell *et al.* (1984) on the grounds that the different elements require different treatment and that to combine them may make each less than satisfactory, although a contrary view is expressed elsewhere (Lawler *et al.*, 1984). Despite the possible theoretical advantages deriving from separation, a unified scheme has administrative simplicity and is clearly less time-consuming.

To encourage commitment and involvement in performance appraisal, it is essential that the basic purposes of the system are communicated to managers, supervisors and staff. Where unions are involved, they should be consulted about the operation of the scheme and the purposes to which it is to be put – although British trade unions do not seem to show much interest in performance appraisal. However, there is no doubt that performance appraisal is most likely to be resented when it is imposed from above and conducted bureaucratically.

CRITERIA

What should be appraised? For a true evaluation of performance, criteria should be tied to evidence – evidence of what actually happened during the period under review, described in meaningful and measurable terms. Assessing performance on the job means identifying critical job variables. This link is illustrated in Fig. 6.1.

Fig. 6.1 *Performance appraisal derives from job requirements*

Herein lies a methodological problem. Jobs differ; therefore criteria of performance differ. But the organization as a whole needs to establish *common*, relevant criteria. How else is one to make *comparative* judgements between people? Most of the early performance appraisal systems adopted a common set of criteria by which all employees were assessed. This obviously led to difficulties and currently some organizations are moving away from this blanket approach.

A leading expert from the Civil Service (Anstey, 1974) has suggested several desirable features of any staff assessment scheme:

1 the basic information must be reliable
2 assessments must be related to a common standard
3 people must know what is expected of them
4 jobs must be described in terms of what has to be achieved
5 the information should be easy to use
6 management, supervisors and staff must all be clear about the purposes of the scheme and convinced of the need for it
7 the scheme must be a 'human' one.

We might wish to add to that list:
1 the boss must have opportunity to observe and gain information about a subordinate's performance
2 the boss must review the overall work situation
3 the procedure should help to identify an individual's strength and areas for improvement
4 the boss must make judgements
5 the boss must give feedback to the subordinate
6 the scheme should form an integral part of a well-developed personnel

policy and also provide a means for the evaluation of other personnel management techniques such as selection and training.

PERFORMANCE OR PERSONALITY?

One aspect which has received considerable attention from academics is the relative merits of rating behavioural incidents as against personality traits. In other words, should performance or personality be assessed? Personal qualities have questionable validity as a measure of performance, and may introduce unreliability since they are prone to ambiguity and have moral connotations. Most authorities now agree that reliability is enhanced by assessing persons *on the basis of what they do* rather than what they are. In practical terms, this philosophy has encouraged the use of results-based appraisals (such as Management By Objectives) and the development of job-related performance criteria. Performance is generally more amenable to the development of objective standards.

PAST PERFORMANCE OR FUTURE POTENTIAL?

There is some debate in discussions about performance appraisal as to whether it should be geared to a review of *past* performance or to *future* potential. The assessment of potential in both the short and long term is particularly liable to subjective judgement. There is in fact quite a difference between assessing somebody for immediate promotion and making a long-term projection. Many schemes simply require a broad overall 'guess' as to how far the appraisee might progress and when. If assessment of potential is to be meaningful, it must be related to the higher level duties rather than to performance on the present grade, yet the responsibilities and skills might be quite different. To this end, Assessment Centres have been developed (see later).

The trend in performance appraisal systems appears to be away from making forecasts of future potential. An IPM survey (Gill, 1977), showed that the most important purposes of appraisal at that time were firstly to assess training and development needs, and secondly to help improve current performance. This represented some shift of emphasis over previous years. The current view is to have *separate* appraisals for performance and for promotability.

TECHNIQUES

Formal reporting systems provide systematic information, not only for planning, postings, promotion and training – but they also reduce the risk of favouritism and ensure that everybody is considered. The approach compels reviewers to make a comprehensive survey of each individual and makes employees feel they are not overlooked.

Underlying performance appraisal, at least as classically viewed, is the need to discriminate between individuals. In reality, the need to discriminate is only of use when making recommendations for promotion, or in determining differential salary awards. The process of discrimination is not essential to the main purpose of providing feedback and encouraging development. An array of techniques for performance appraisal systems are to be found in the textbooks, many of them of American origin.

Rating Scales

These require first the determination of relevant factors in the job, e.g.: (i) job knowledge, (ii) performance against targets, (iii) judgements and decisions, (iv) staff motivation, (v) customer relationships. Secondly, each factor must be rated according to agreed standards of assessment. For example:

A. Performance is outstanding overall and superior to that expected in every major area.
B. Performance is superior to that expected in some major areas.
C. Performance matches that expected from a good employee in every area.
D. Performance does not fully match that expected. Some improvements needed in one or more major areas.
E. Performance just acceptable overall, but employee needs training in several major areas and/or motivation is lacking.
F. Performance not satisfactory in any way.

A pro-forma is usually devised for this purpose as in Fig. 6.2. Managers are required to make assessments and discuss their deliberations with subordinates. This type of format forms the basis of the Ford Personnel Appraisal Form in Fig. 6.3 (which, it will be noted, includes both performance factors *and* personal characteristics).

Rating scales are the oldest and most widely used form of performance appraisal. The approach is analytical. It is a form of points rating.

Factor	A	B	C	D	E	F
Job knowledge						
Performance against targets						
Judgement and decision						
Staff motivation						
Customer relations						

Fig. 6.2 *Typical performance appraisal rating scale*

Ford Personnel Appraisal: Employees in Salary Grades 5-8

Date of Review	Time on Position		S.G.	Age	Name
	Yrs.	Mths.		Yrs.	
Period of Review	Position Title				Area

Important: Read guide notes carefully before proceeding with the following sections

Section One	Performance Factors						Section Two	Personal Characteristics				
	N/A	U	M	SP	E	O		1	2	3	4	5
Administrative Skills							Initiative					
Communications – Written							Persistence					
Communications – Oral							Ability to work with others					
Problem Analysis							Adaptability					
Decision Making							Persuasiveness					
Delegation							Self-Confidence					
Quantity of Work							Judgement					
Development of Personnel							Leadership					
Development of Quality Improvements							Creativity					

Section Three Highlight Performance Factors and particular strengths/weaknesses of employee which significantly affect Job Performance

Overall Performance Rating (Taking into account ratings given)

Prepared by: Signature .... Date .... Position Title ....

Section Four Comments by Reviewing Authority

	I.R. Review Initial
Signature .... Date .... Position Title	Date

Section Five Supervisor's Notes on Counselling Interview

Signature .... Date .... Position Title ....

Section Six Employees Reactions and Comment

Signature .... Date ....

P. & O.
October 1982 4168B/1

Performance Classification

Outstanding performance is characterised by high ability which leaves little or nothing to be desired.

Personnel rated as such are those who regularly make significant contributions to the organisation which are above the requirements of their position. Unusual and challenging assignments are consistently well handled.

Excellent performance is marked by above-average ability, with little supervision required.

These employees may display some of the attributes present in '**outstanding**' performance, but not on a sufficiently consistent basis to warrant that rating. Unusual and challenging assignments are normally well handled.

Satisfactory Plus performance indicates fully adequate ability, without the need for excessive supervision.

Personnel with this rating are able to give proper consideration to normal assignments, which are generally well handled. They will meet the requirements of the position. '**Satisfactory plus**' performers may include those who lack the experience at their current level to demonstrate above-average ability.

Marginal performance is in instances where the ability demonstrated does not fully meet the requirements of the position, with excessive supervision and direction normally required.

Employees rated as such will show specific deficiencies in their performance which prevent them from performing at an acceptable level.

Unsatisfactory performance indicates an ability which falls clearly below the minimum requirements of the position.

'**Unsatisfactory**' performers will demonstrate marked deficiencies in most of the major aspects of their responsibilities, and considerable improvement is required to permit retention of the employee in his current position.

Personal Characteristics Ratings

1. – Needs considerable improvement – substantial improvement required to meet acceptable standards.
2. – Needs improvement – some improvement required to meet acceptable standards.
3. – Normal – meets acceptable standards.
4. – Above normal – exceeds normally acceptable standards in most instances.
5. – Exceptional – displays rare and unusual personal characteristics.

P. & O
October 1982   **4168B/1** Reverse

Fig. 6.3   *Ford Personnel Appraisal Form*

Graphic scales

These are similar in intent, but dispense with formal internal points (usually indicating a midpoint to force an overall plus or minus rating) as in Fig. 6.4.

Factor: Customer Relations

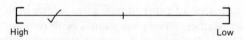

High   Low

Fig. 6.4   *Graphic scale*

Ranking

Subordinates are placed one above the other in overall rank order.

Forced distribution

Managers are obliged to assume a normal distribution in their subordinates which constitute their 'population' and to produce a distribution of assessments which conforms to that pattern, i.e. to allocate 10 per cent employees to the top end of the scale, 20 per cent to the next category, 40 per cent in the middle bracket, 20 per cent in the next lowest category, 10 per cent in the bottom grade.

Behaviourally Anchored Ranking Scales (BARS)

The appraiser has to rate the employee against factors previously identified as crucial to successful performance. Scales are prescribed precisely in relation to behaviour/performance variables. BARS have attracted considerable attention amongst researchers. They form a rigorous, scientific approach, but are difficult to develop and have statistical problems.

THE APPRAISAL INTERVIEW AND COUNSELLING

'The appraisal interview which is the most important part of the process may be considered in three phases: namely the preparation, the interview itself and the subsequent action' (Walker, 1983). Appraisal interviewing is a highly skilled affair in which the manager's recorded assessments and observations form the basis for discussion. The interviews provide for a review of progress, feedback to the employee, and an opportunity for participation as an aid to motivation. The manager's role includes 'assessing, counselling, persuading, listening' (Anstey, Fletcher and Walker, 1976).

A boss should start the *appraisal interview* with a summary of the period under review – an appraisal of performance on the various tasks and assignments which have been completed. This feedback should be frank but tactful. The good points should first of all be brought out in due praise and recognition, followed by a selection of just a few areas for improvement, inviting the subordinate to comment on why things did not go quite so well and what support the manager could give to improve things. The purpose of performance appraisal is not to punish the wrongdoer, but rather to adopt a problem-solving approach with the main emphasis, as the name of the system implies, to improve performance. The performance appraisal interview does not constitute the termination of proceedings, after which both parties may breathe a sigh of relief. Rather, *action plans* should be drawn up, outlining new tasks and assignments to be attempted, mutual objectives and focusing particularly on the ways in which strengths can be further developed and weaknesses supported or improved. The action plan then provides a meaningful frame of reference against which subsequent performance can be monitored, and without necessarily having to wait until the next formal performance appraisal session.

Performance appraisal cannot possibly be contemplated or completed unless *performance standards are both determined and understood* by all parties. Without performance standards, performance appraisal becomes virtually meaningless – it can only be an appraisal against some vague notion of relative 'goodness' or 'satisfactoriness' assessed subjectively for an individual in the context of his peer group or against some set of standards held (arbitrarily, and maybe uncommunicated) by a manager. Many writers have concentrated on the technical aspects of getting the criteria right, developing consistent norms of judgement, training of managers as assessors, and generally trying to develop a sounder methodology – whilst rather fewer have noted that performance appraisal is a highly inter-personal exchange with many emotional and political barriers. However, the essence of the exercise must be to set performance standards as unequivocally as possible. A manager requires opportunity to observe and view performance, and form judgements about standards. And managers can be trained to do this (Thornton and Zorich, 1980).

EXAMPLE OF A PERFORMANCE APPRAISAL SCHEME

A good performance appraisal scheme has to satisfy a coalition of interests. It must not be too bureaucratic and must somehow relate directly to the needs of individual employees.

Key items which a system should include are:

1 employee's current career interest
2 a manager's evaluation of these interests
3 the identification of development needs and plans to achieve them.

A *performance plan* should clarify (on an individual participative basis) the broad *objectives*, the *performance criteria* by which achievements are to be assessed, their *rank order* of priority, and a mechanism for *rating*.

Preparation for the review interview is equally important. Prior to the interview, the manager should quietly recollect the events of the past year and record his thoughts – particularly his subordinate's strengths and perceived areas for improvement. During the interview itself, constructive dialogue should be encouraged, and the employee's views, opinions and aspirations should not only be heard but also recorded as part of the total record.

In many organizations, it is not only the manager who reviews. A review of the manager's comments is often made by the next senior manager – the 'grandfather' approach – as a means of achieving consistency.

An example of this kind of performance planning and appraisal (from IBM) and related documentation is given in Fig. 6.5.

SETTING UP A PERFORMANCE APPRAISAL SCHEME

The starting point for setting up a performance appraisal scheme is first of all to crystallize the purpose for which it is intended. Secondly, to devise a system appropriate to that end. Since it requires fundamentally the coopera-

APPRAISAL & COUNSELLING PROGRAMME

PERFORMANCE PLANNING & APPRAISAL RECORD

| Employee name & initials | Personnel number | Pay location (name & number) |

| Present job title | Date this position/level | Date this appraisal | Date last appraisal |

How to complete this form

1 At the beginning of the appraisal period, the manager and the employee jointly agree on objectives for the coming period. These objectives are entered on pages 1 and 2 together with performance criteria and the rank (indicating the relative importance of the objectives to the achievement of overall success in the job. Page 2 is signed by the employee, the manager and the manager's manager, to indicate their agreement to the objectives.

2 During the appraisal period, the form is retained for reference and review by the manager and a copy given to the employee. This performance plan may be updated at any time by using continuation sheets if necessary.

3 At the end of the appraisal period, the manager completes the 'Notes on Attainment' column on pages 1 and 2 and rates each objective. The manager then enters an overall rating on page 2 based on the ratings allocated to the individual objectives. The manager also completes the comments sections on page 3.

4 Before the appraisal interview is conducted with the employee, the manager's manager reviews and signs off the manager's 'Notes on Attainment' and ratings on pages 1 and 2; the overall rating on page 2; and the two comments sections which the manager has also completed on page 3. The manager's manager's signature, with any comments, should be at the bottom of page 3.

5 Following the interview, the manager completes the 'Summary of Interview' section of page 4, and invites the employee to add his or her comments and signature on page 4.

6 To complete the form, the manager's manager adds any comments and signs on page 4 to confirm that the appraisal programme has been correctly conducted and documented.

7 The completed form is sent to the Personnel department for retention in the employee's personnel file.

Fig. 6.5 *IBM Performance, Planning and Appraisal Form*

Page 1

PERFORMANCE PLAN

OBJECTIVE	PERFORMANCE CRITERIA	RANK	NOTES ON ATTAINMENT	RATING

Fig. 6.5 – *cont.*

OBJECTIVE	PERFORMANCE CRITERIA	RANK	NOTES ON ATTAINMENT	RATING

Page

We agree that the above objectives are a fair basis on which this work will be planned and appraised

Review of performance plan by manager's manager

Employee   Manager   date

Manager's manager   date

Overall rating

Rating descriptions:

1 Results far exceeded the requirements of the job in all areas

2 Results achieved consistently exceeded the requirements of the job in most areas

3 Results achieved met the requirements of the job and exceeded them in some areas

4 Results achieved met the requirements of the job

5 Results achieved did not meet the requirements of the job

Fig. 6.5 – *cont.*

BEFORE INTERVIEW

Manager's comments on employee's attainment of objectives

Strengths

Areas for improvement

Manager's comments before appraisal interview

Signature   date

Manager's manager review of comments and ratings before interview

Fig. 6.5 – *cont.*

AFTER INTERVIEW   Page 4

Manager's summary of appraisal interview

Signature   print   date

Employee's comments

In signing this section the employee is not necessarily indicating agreement with the interview,
only that he or she has seen this form and has discussed it with the manager.

Signature   print   date

Manager's manager review of completed form

Signature   print   date

(If more space is required please use back of this form)

Fig. 6.5 – *cont.*

Signature   date

APPRAISAL & COUNSELLING PROGRAMME

EMPLOYEE DEVELOPMENT PLAN

This plan should focus primarily on the next two to three years ahead. It supersedes any previous development plan.

Employee's name & initials	Personnel number	
Present job title	Division/Location	

Employee's current career interests - Based on employee's views and comments.

Manager's evaluation of above

Jobs for which employee could be considered - Include other work areas and locations as appropriate.
An entry below means that this employee's name may be put forward as a candidate if a suitable vacancy occurs.

Type of position and/or function	Date (Q/Yr)	Geographic mobility

Form No. 7-048
IBM United Kingdom Limited
IBM Confidential — Personal (when completed)   **FORM B**

Fig. 6.5 – *cont.*

IBM Confidential — Personal (when completed)

CAREER INVENTORY VOUCHER

THIS SECTION SHOULD BE COMPLETED BY THE MANAGER ON THE BASIS OF THE
INFORMATION PROVIDED ON THE PREVIOUS TWO PAGES

FOR COMPLETION INSTRUCTIONS, REFER TO THE CAREERS MANUAL

EMPLOYEE
NAME & INITIALS (PRINT)

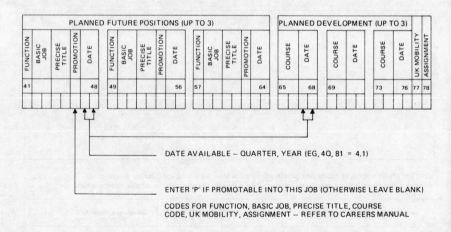

C = Change to an existing Record
N = To insert a **completely new** Record. If used to update
only one field it will reset the others to blank

DATE AVAILABLE — QUARTER, YEAR (EG, 4Q, 81 = 4.1)

ENTER 'P' IF PROMOTABLE INTO THIS JOB (OTHERWISE LEAVE BLANK)

CODES FOR FUNCTION, BASIC JOB, PRECISE TITLE, COURSE
CODE, UK MOBILITY, ASSIGNMENT — REFER TO CAREERS MANUAL

PERSONNEL OFFICER SIGNATURE _____

IBM United Kingdom Limited   Form No. 7-048 (8/81)

Fig. 6.5 – *cont.*

Development needs - Which work experience, special assignments, personal improvement, education and training, or further information would be helpful to the employee?

___

Development plans - What have you agreed to do to meet these development needs?
- Which of you will be responsible? When will they occur?

___

Any formal training planned - Include technical and developmental training.

Course title and subject	Date planned (Q/Yr)

Employee's comments

Signature   date

Prepared by manager

Signature   print   date

Reviewed by manager's manager

Signature   print   date

Fig. 6.5 – *cont.*

tion of the line managers, and since largely it is for their particular use and purpose, they should be involved from the outset in determining what they would like to see the system achieve, the criteria which should be adopted, and the standards of performance which should apply. If the scheme is not to be too paternalistic, then the interests of subordinates are equally important. Tackled properly, performance appraisal can be a powerful technique in successful human resource management. Improperly applied, it can have negative effects. Bad handling of the system has evoked considerable criticism over the years. Weaknesses in performance appraisal systems normally arise from the confusion which ensues from an ill-defined purpose, and a lack of commitment on the part of line managers. So often the ritual of an annualized 'paper-chase' with poor credibility inevitably falls into disuse. There is no doubt there are a number of potential problems which need to be avoided.

PERSONNEL COORDINATION

It is normally the role of the central personnel department to initiate the scheme, to coordinate performance assessments, to gather the information and take action, to set in motion training and development programmes for people considered worthy of promotion, in accordance with manpower planning requirements, to redeploy people in order to build in the extra experience that managers may have recommended, and possibly to see that merit or salary reviews are executed in accordance with company policy.

Whether the scheme works well or badly, Personnel will take the praise or blame. Performance appraisal permeates the whole organization; its tentacles of repercussion are quite extraordinary.

POTENTIAL PROBLEMS

Structurally, a performance appraisal system centres on the criteria or factors which are to be rated. One of the main inadequacies of performance appraisal systems is that the criteria are often irrelevant. So often factors are selected on the basis of convenience: e.g. knowledge, drive, initiative, decisiveness, judgement, social quality, ability to communicate, cooperation and disposition, adaptability, final results. If the appraisal is to be meaningful, as the Stewarts (1977, 1981) well argue, *criteria must be related to success or failure in the job, and be amenable to objective rather than subjective judgement.* Criteria cannot be pulled out of thin air. There is a 'need to base performance criteria on empirical research into the real needs for success in the job'.

It is from the selection of inappropriate criteria that the main sources of contamination and deficiency in performance appraisal systems arise. The criteria must be relevant and must discriminate between good and bad performers, and the factors selected for the appraisal scheme must be appropriately weighted. Frequently, scores on various factors are summated to provide an overall discrimination between one employee and another, but the assumption is that the various attributes form a simple additive list. This is not always so. Scoring well on factors A and B may be multiplicative rather than additive in relation to the overall assessment; simple addition implies that the qualities are mutually exclusive and independent. Aggregate ratings may be misleading. As an analogy, if we looked at a student who in every examination came 10th out of 100, we would be likely to find that his overall position would be better than 10th. And not all factors in every performance appraisal scheme are of equal value – they are not equally weighted even if they have the same maximum numerical value. This is because to combine scores produces a result in which the scores weight themselves in proportion to their respective variability (i.e. standard deviations).

Rating scales are themselves tricky items. Most commonly they are of a uniform five points; but there are examples in practice which vary from nine points to three points. Different point lengths imply that the appraiser should be able to discriminate precisely to the degree required by the scale. This is of course not always so. And if some factors are more important than others, this means that scales could be used as a weighting mechanism to arrive at a total point score. In fact, varying length scales provide a relative weighting rather than an indication of the degree of discrimination sought. It may be better to have a constant length scale with a weighting multiplier applied to each rating.

A high degree of *reliability* is necessary if the scheme is to be both acceptable to the staff concerned and capable of providing meaningful data, i.e. showing consistency in the ratings, either by different raters or by the same rater at different times. Performance appraisal schemes are particularly sensitive to the fallibility of human judgement, requiring as they do the critical evaluation of one human being by another on the basis of factors that may be imperfectly understood. Errors can arise from a variety of sources, e.g. differences in raters' personality, the design of rating forms, a lack of familiarity of the job in question, or failure properly to observe performance, notwithstanding the problems of subjectivity and the fact that one's opinion is always strongly influenced by the most recent past.

Halo effect occurs in the judgemental process here as elsewhere. So too does central tendency, i.e. a clustering of ratings around the average. In large modern organizations, the evaluation of assessments by computer can identify and modify problems of inter- and intra-rater uniformity and uniformity between departments and divisions (Sale, 1980. Where ratings are generous or lenient, compared to the average, reviews might be called for. The general tendency to cluster ratings around the central point of the scale, avoiding extreme measures, may simply reflect the fact that the majority of employees are average performers, or a rater's dislike of having to justify unfavourable markings. Central tendency may be avoided, and greater discrimination encouraged (where this is called for) by forced distribution, ranking or prepared comparisons.

There is also the psychological quirk of an appraiser's causal attributions to the success or failure of a subordinate, i.e. how an appraiser explains the causes of good or poor performance. To what extent can the outcome be attributed to circumstances or events rather than to the individual's own efforts or abilities? By the *fundamental attribution error* there is a tendency to take account of circumstances in explaining one's own behaviour, but less so in explaining the behaviour of others. Other people's errors are their own fault!

There is still a need for devising procedures which make for common inter-rater reference points and standards of marking. One way of tackling this is for the raters, as a committee, to select one or more average subordinate with whom all are familiar and compare the remaining employees with him/them. The theoretical attraction of this may, however, be outweighed by administrative complications, and with detrimental effect on staff relations if individuals are deliberately identified.

Where job rotation arrangements result in subordinates working for more than one superior during the year, a *multi-rater approach* may counteract the reduction in familiarity and improve reliability. As an extension of the multi-rater approach, advantages might be gained by seeking assessments from people's subordinates and peers (buddy ratings) as well as their superiors.

Performance appraisal forces managers into a judgemental – even 'policing' role. Quite often they are reluctant to appraise. Researchers have noted that managers find it difficult to discuss personal weaknesses, that performance appraisal may be a violation of the integrity of the individual, that schemes are mechanistic and manipulative; and can lead to the duplication of the same kind of people.

The traditional concept of the superior knowing best may now be both culturally irrelevant and less than satisfactory. At least the days when 'secret' reports were written seem to have gone. Nowadays there are contemporary arguments in favour of *self-appraisal*, though these are less concerned with reliability than with promoting the participation and involvement of the individual (Germain and Burgoyne, 1984). There is evidence to suggest that employees are capable of self-evaluation (Mabe and West, 1982; Fletcher, 1984). Self-appraisal forms part of an inductive learning process and is more likely to lead to improvement. Self-appraisal can offset the bias of the boss and replace it with a higher (but fairly consistent) degree of leniency or harshness.

For an organization as a whole there is the need to establish common, relevant criteria by which to assess the performance of a wide range of subordinates. Is it possible to obtain an all-embracing set of criteria? Are all criteria of equal value? Should they be weighted? Should the criteria which are used in a performance appraisal system conform with those which are used in a personnel selection system? If not, does it not suggest that there has been some fudge in the development of the two systems? Surely, performance appraisal systems and personnel selection systems are attempts to measure the same thing – except one takes place before employment and the other takes place during employment? Yet rarely in practice do the two systems seem to coincide. It would seem that both systems are normally developed separately, with one imposed upon the other. These questions are fundamental to the methodology of assessing staff performance. Theoretically, one might wish to carry the argument further – into the field of job evaluation, and argue that the criteria for the evaluation of jobs – which is what a company is paying for – incorporate the same set of criteria by which to evaluate performance, and by which people were selected in the first place. Performance appraisal *should* be a means by which to validate selection criteria and training criteria. An integrated approach seems to be lacking. In mitigation, it might be argued that whilst performance appraisal does have *some* elements in common with other personnel activities concerned with *assessment*, it also incorporates rather more than this, which is why it has probably devolved separately.

Despite the significance of performance appraisal as a key managerial tool, there is not enough evidence of any attempt to develop a comprehensive framework for analysing and determining the effectiveness of different schemes. The majority of authors tend to concentrate on the purpose of appraisal and the potential difficulties inherent in any scheme – but this is not sufficient basis for the evaluation of a particular system. It is certainly not possible to posit a prescriptive model since every organization has unique environmental and resource means.

Performance appraisal schemes are fraught with problems. Researchers have been fascinated by the subject. The deeper one goes, the more complicated it becomes. Most practitioners simply want a worksheet which identifies the strengths and weaknesses and provides a basis for counselling and action plans, even if it does only provide an approximation of discriminatory performance. As a diagnostic device, a means for analysing past performance, performance appraisal schemes have much to offer. As a basis for prediction, they are much more limited. For this reason, other techniques such as Assessment Centres have become more popular.

Assessment centres

An Assessment Centre Programme is a method of identifying a person's potential to do a job (normally of higher level) and incorporates the simultaneous assessment of several individuals by a group of trained observers using a variety of group and individual exercises. The exercises can help to reveal training needs, or people's present (untrained) abilities, or potential for development. An Assessment Centre is not normally the sole instrument used – but the findings revealed may be considered together with the other facts and opinions held about an employee (and perhaps derived from a conventional performance appraisal scheme).

Assessment Programmes had wartime military origins. After the war the methods were adopted by civilian organizations on both sides of the Atlantic. Although used at first for the selection of new high-calibre recruits, Assessment Centre techniques are now used to identify potential amongst existing employees where the traditional policy is 'promotion from within'. Much of the modern impetus has come from the USA.

By the 1970s British firms became interested in developing similar management programmes. In a major survey of existing UK practice (Gill, Ungerson and Thakur, 1973), the researchers thought they were witnessing the beginning of a large increase in the use of Assessment Programmes, but within four years had to report that they had not made such enormous impact (Gill, 1977). Still, a large number of industrial organizations have made use of these techniques, including Standard Oil, BP, Shell, Seers Roebuck, IBM, Ford, Bell, ITT, British Leyland, General Electric. Recently they have been used to identify and develop rig managers in the North Sea oil-fields (Vant and Livy, 1982).

SELECTION OF PARTICIPANTS

Participants to come forward to an Assessment Centre are usually nominated by their own manager. Nominations must usually be consistent with performance appraisal reviews over the previous few years. In some companies, nominations are reviewed by a panel of senior managers who make the final selection. This preliminary sifting is important. All intending candidates should at some time have exhibited potential. An Assessment Centre is not designed to be a lottery in which any applicant can chance his hand.

TYPICAL LEADERSHIP QUALITIES

The qualities most commonly assessed include: assertiveness, persuasive or selling ability, oral communications, written communications, organizing ability, self-confidence, resistance to stress, energy level, decision-making abilities, administrative ability, and interpersonal skills.

TYPICAL EXERCISES FOR DETERMINING LEADERSHIP QUALITIES

A battery of varied exercises can provide observers (assessors) opportunities for insight and evaluation of the desired qualities. The exercises most commonly used include the following: *individual presentations*, an *in-basket exercise* (in which candidates have to deal with a mass of information in a limited space of times), a *business exercise* (which might seek to bring out such matters as the profitability of operations, problems of stock control, maintenance procedures, customer relations, contracts, payment systems, budgeting and costing, etc.). A business exercise is normally designed to test a candidate's broader awareness of commercial problems. Preparation may take up to an hour and candidates may be required to present their case either in writing or discuss it within the group. Sometimes a *personnel case study* will be included involving a 'problem employee'. Candidates would be required to assess the problem and make recommendations which were both practical and humane. There may be a *Leaderless Group Exercise* and an *Assigned Leadership Exercise* (as discussed in Chapter 4). Normally *management interviews* are also included to assess candidates' reaction to the procedures and to provide feedback from the assessors. In this kind of 'debriefing' session candidates may review their performance and may sometimes be invited to complete a 'self-appraisal'.

THE ASSESSORS

The normal practice is for assessors to be line managers who are preferred because of their thorough knowledge of the job for which participants are being assessed. Line management involvement encourages management commitment, sense of ownership of the scheme, and therefore acceptability. In some cases outside professional assessors are also used to monitor the programme.

The ratio of assessors to participants is variable but 1:3 would seem to be a workable average. The demands on a line manager's time are therefore quite high.

The training of assessors is a major 'start-up' consideration. They should gain practice, and have tuition in, observation methods. The main practical problem which needs to be overcome is the achievement of consistency in the standards of assessment being used, both as between assessors and over a period of time (inter- and intra-rater reliability). One solution is to develop a team of assessors drawn from the industry concerned who are prepared to repeat the Assessment Centres at given periods. A second solution is to develop a 'panel' of assessors who would rotate, but still keep to common standards.

Scoring of assessments

Normally a scale is used (e.g. a five-point scale) for each of the qualities being assessed as demonstrated in the various exercises. Each assessor makes his own rating per candidate and the results are pooled and averaged. Less attention is usually paid to absolute score values than to the relative dispersion of scores on an overall basis (i.e. each quality or factor is usually assumed to be additive). The results reveal the combined judgement of the assessors regarding the relative merits/demerits of the candidates under scrutiny. Only after a prolonged period of research (i.e. the follow-up in performance of successful candidates) and the correlation with Assessment Centre score values would it be possible to make any recommendation regarding an absolute cut-off score (i.e. below which a person would not be promoted). Theoretically, there is the further possible refinement of 'weighting' the particular qualities assessed according to their importance in overall job performance. In practice, 'buddy ratings' are sometimes also used by the participants themselves and incorporated into the overall evaluation.

ADVANTAGES AND DISADVANTAGES OF ASSESSMENT CENTRES

The preceding paragraphs have drawn attention to some of the more typical qualities, and are examples only. Centres differ in the qualities which they assess. Mostly these qualities are determined by subjective judgement (rather than factor analysis). Clearly there will be qualities or personal attributes which may be specific for a given job in a particular industry. The key requirement is that the qualities be demonstrably relevant to the jobs in question. The determination of these relevant qualities can only be decided by a careful study of the jobs, the skills which people bring to them, the capacities and personal attributes required, an appraisal of what are regarded (by existing incumbents) as the most difficult and demanding aspects. The methodology here is no different from the determination of criteria for successful performance in any other selection process (see Chapters 3 and 4). Assessment Centres are concerned to develop predictive assessments for internal candidates moving to higher level jobs. The current emphasis is to provide a more effective database for making observations, judgements and decisions. Without an appraisal system of one kind or other, 'it would be only accidental that development efforts would be aimed in the right direction' (Anderson, 1980).

Although the main purpose of multiple assessment methods is to help in the selection and promotion of future supervisors and managers, they can also have wider uses – not only the identification of training and development needs – but also provide opportunities to discuss supervisory and industry-wide problems, develop participation, and provide self-learning opportunities for candidates. A key purpose of any appraisal system is to create a learning experience (Cameron, 1982).

There are of course time and cost constraints. Costs are variable according to the length and number of programmes. But there may be human problems. There is certainly the need for delicate handling of feedback. All participants experience some stress and occasionally, withdrawal.

Assessment Centres attempt to simulate typical supervisory and management problems. Because the assessments which are made are 'multiple', they are *likely* to be fairer and more accurate. If the emphasis of the Centre is on development, then the experience can be motivating. In short, Centres provide more information about people than can be gained from conventional appraisal systems, and facilitate the diagnosis of training and development needs. Psychologists have frequently reported high face validity and group predictive validity for Assessment Centres. Moreover, they appear to be particularly practical and realistic (Stewart and Stewart, 1981; Dulewicz, 1982). 'The practical integration of the Assessment Centre techniques into the company's activities has moved naturally from criterion-based interviews into the area of feedback. More and more this has been welcomed as a basis for employees' personal development plans' (Stevens, 1985).

Management development

Management development constitutes a series of processes, activities and events within and/or outside the organization designed to improve performance of both the organization as a whole and the individuals within it. Its direct aim is to aid organizational survival in the supply of trained and experienced managers. Its indirect aim is to improve financial performance and long-term growth.

With the large input of resources, both capital and labour, that are incurred in the training of management, it is appropriate to re-emphasize the conventional importance of manpower planning as the starting point for any discussion of management training and development. There is a certain 'lead-time' necessary for the development of successful managers. Programmes which are set up for this purpose must be geared to organizational requirements generated by the corporate plan.

Coupled with organizational needs are the needs of individuals – the skills and qualities they may require in order to perform their jobs competently both now and in the future. Stemming directly from manpower planning, therefore, is the need for succession planning, and a review of individuals' abilities and potentialities (obtained from performance appraisal systems). As manpower must be planned, so must the training and development of managers on a systematic basis to ensure the continuity of management within the organization.

All good management development programmes are tied in with *succession planning*. Succession planning *does not* simply mean shortlisting potential successors for any given post. More importantly, it first means planning a succession of experiences for an individual, either by cross-fertilization or promotion, to form a pattern of linked and progressive moves designed to develop a manager's breadth to reach a more advanced state of accomplishment – 'grooming' in short – and only then considering his or her redeployment to a more senior position on a permanent basis. Lateral movements can form part of a planned career structure to gain experience of other functions – particularly for managers who may attain general management levels and above. Clearly such programmes cannot be haphazard. They must be carefully coordinated, integrated into the overall succession plan, and directly related to the needs of the individual's planned career growth. Such moves are not appropriate for everybody; the process must be selective.

High fliers may be treated as crown princes and accede to their respective thrones. But for organizations wanting a proficient stock of managers at all levels, the approach must encompass a wider catchment. The main reasons for across-the-board management development programmes are:

1 To improve the performance of individual managers in their current jobs
2 To supply future management manpower needs
3 To plan managers' careers to match their capabilities with the future needs of the organization

4   To provide a bank of varied management experience
5   To develop a results oriented performance review system (Such as MBO)
6   To establish an appropriate climate within the organization which enables and encourages managers to grow and to perform at a high level
7   To develop the effectiveness of the entire management team.

These objectives can obtain at various levels – corporate, individual and group. A number of contributory activities are needed. At corporate level there should be a personnel audit of managerial resources, an audit of the organization structure, a forecast of management/manpower needs, a succession plan, a performance review system for assessing potential and identifying training needs, and an overall training and development plan. At individual level there may well be an agreed job description, goal setting, a performance review interview, a career counselling interview, and an assessment of potential and development needs.

In large organizations, some kind of structure and master-plan is essential. This has often led to the accusation that management development is mechanistic and manipulative. To some extent this is true. From a commercial point of view, the organization is seeking to satisfy its own ends. These may conflict with the natural growth and development of any one individual. However, the same criticisms could be levelled at any other form of 'systematic' training which is a process designed to achieve predetermined goals. Another common criticism is that management development programmes often adopt a 'blanket' approach – a broad programme or package for all managers. For obvious reasons, such approaches have had limited success. Management development, properly administered, aims to identify the training and development needs of individual managers in terms of the changes in knowledge, skills or attitudes needed to improve performance in their current job, or in preparation for possible future jobs. No particular theory, technique or approach should be universally advocated for improving managerial performance (Lorsch, 1979). We should use whatever techniques or strategies most appropriately satisfy the individually identified need – a custom-built approach.

Many companies support management development in the quite firm belief that it provides for the needs of management succession and leads to an improvement in organizational performance. Not all would agree. Some authorities (e.g. Handy, 1982) argue that *the organization should be developed at the same time as the individual*. Attempts by organizations to improve the effectiveness by simply changing individuals have often resulted in (i) little or no change in behaviour; (ii) perception by the individual that the organization is seeking to control his/her life; (iii) loss of investment when that individual leaves the company.

A different, or complementary approach, comes from Organization Development (OD) – processes of planned change in an organization's total environment – helping teams of managers and organizations to develop simultaneously, concentrating not only on objectives, but also on interpersonal behaviour, attitudes, values, and innovations (Williams, 1983).

Management development can be a confusing subject because it is possible to develop different perceptions, e.g.:

1 Management Development as an organizational support function
2 Management Development as a philosophy or style of management
3 Management Development as an agent for change – bringing about changes in managers' behaviour to achieve organizational goals
4 Management Development as the continuing education of individual managers at all stages in their careers.

Definitions of Management Development are correspondingly variable. To choose one concise definition, it is a 'conscious and systematic decision-action process to control the development of managerial resources in the organization . . . for the achievement of organizational goals and strategies' (Ashton, Easterby-Smith and Irvine, 1975). Further, 'Management Development must be treated as part of any organization – it is not an appendage or a growth and it must be part of the job of every manager' (Ashton and Easterby-Smith, 1979).

Difficulties of definition stem from the highly variegated nature of managers' jobs. Managerial work is kaleidoscopic, which varies within and between organizations and cultures. Success is influenced by personality, acceptability, and the real power and authority exercised. Generalization on the subject of management development is not meaningful. The logical conclusion is that management development programmes should be tailor-made – the cloth cut to suit both individual and employer. Management development takes on a double orientation – a 'needs' orientation and a 'job' orientation. For the management trainer there are two clients – the manager *and* the organization.

The dual nature of the 'market' means inevitably that management development must operate in several directions. Ashton and Easterby-Smith (1979) crystallized the possible conflict by contrasting both 'top down' and 'bottom up' approaches to management development. The 'top down' approach starts with the goals and plans of the organization. The 'bottom up' approach starts with individual needs in developing potential as a manager. The two approaches should be complementary and brought into alignment as far as possible.

TRAINING NEEDS

Present training needs are easier to identify than future ones. This brings us to the important distinction between management 'training' and management 'development'.

Management *training* is concerned with present task requirements, to equip a manager to meet current performance criteria. Much of management training is *remedial*, and may concern:

1   knowledge and skills needed to do the job, especially updating
2   inadequacies revealed by performance.

Management *development* is much broader, helping people to grow, to meet their ambitions, to build on their strengths, and to fulfil the increasing demands made on them. Development is part of the broader area of motivation. Management development then is more than management training. It is an assessment of a company's human strengths and weaknesses.

The accepted sequence for defining training needs begins with the job description, and an appraisal of how a manager is doing. This is compared with the stated objectives. Quite simply, the gap between the two supposedly represents training needs. Whilst this procedure can identify current management training needs, developmental considerations are less tangible. Potential appraisal is usually tackled by additional questions on the performance appraisal form, which relate to qualities considered important at higher levels – judgement, decisiveness, willingness to delegate, acceptance as leader. Many commentators (e.g. Hague, 1974) consider this to be the weakest link in the chain. The assumption that training needs become self-evident if job descriptions and appraisals are available is sometimes false. Much depends on the accuracy, thoroughness and commitment of the superior reporting manager. Development needs can be blurred, disguised or non-reported. The management trainer's task is to articulate the value of the appraisal system and gain support.

The diagnosis of training needs has been fully explored by Stewart (1979) and includes many other methods such as structured interviews, self-reporting, questionnaires, psychological tests and behavioural analysis.

Most management training needs fall in the following areas:

1   Technical (i.e. knowledge)
2   Administrative (planning, procedures, etc.)
3   Social and behavioural (working with other people)
4   Intellectual (interpretation and judgement)
5   Mathematical (quantitative and logical analyses)
6   Problem-solving
7   Decision-taking
8   Attitudes and values
9   Leadership style.

Many of these aspects *are* general in the sense that they relate to most managerial jobs. Some will be more specific to some jobs than others. There is no universal criterion of an effective manager; effectiveness depends on the demands of the situation.

Once training needs have been established, a programme can be developed to enable the manager to learn. A wide range of techniques and planned experiences for management training and development are available. Most programmes are spread over several years – maybe a career – comprising selected combinations of interspersed 'exposures'. 'Management training is based on the assumption that managers should at least be willing to consider changing their behaviour and that a change will often be desirable' (Stewart and Marshall, 1982).

There must be carefully planned matching between individual expectations and organizational reality. Neither the human nor the organization will remain static. Both will be subject to the changing needs of the environment. It is the matching processes of selection, training and development which should ensure a richly rewarding relationship between organization and individual. However, people's needs vary as to the things they require from an organization. Activities related to self-development, career development and family development are interrelated. How well or badly a person performs within an organization will depend to a large extent on factors outside the immediate work setting. This is particularly important when considering career pathways extending over a long period of time, during which all sorts of individual maturation processes are taking place. Work, family, and outside interests, interact. Inter-role conflict can arise when pressures and demands of role membership within one organization (e.g. the organization) conflict with pressures and demands arising from membership within another group (e.g. the family). Interestingly, a recent study (Davidson and Cooper, 1983) found that women managers reported significantly higher pressure in respect of career and spouse/partner conflicts, career/home conflicts and marriage/childbearing conflicts than men. Schein (1978) approaches adult development 'as a continuous series of new developmental tasks which require constructive coping and which enhance the person's total repertory of responses'. Whilst attempts to harness career development and personal development may be educationally or psychologically desirable, in practice organizational life may preclude it. Organizations are interested in personal growth only in so far as it relates to economic goals – maybe at variance with individual needs. This is the paradox.

At the end of the day, Management Development is still essentially 'self' development. It is the pro-active person, the initiator, the independent learner who will develop most rapidly and, as a result, receive the support of his organization (Pedlar et al., 1978).

CAREERS

One aspect of contemporary management development is the underlying concept of career. Management as an 'occupation' has a degree of independence from particular employers. Managers are relatively mobile. They look ahead for opportunities, and if they cannot find them in their present organization, they look elsewhere. Whereas once managers were prepared to trust the company and allow it to arrange their careers, views have changed. Now participative approaches extend to joint cooperation in planning managerial careers. 'The concept of career is central, it being the concept of role given a time dimension. A manager's career is that pattern of evolving work activity that constitutes his work history, and which will extend into the future' (Burgoyne, 1983).

For Burgoyne, there are two issues which surround every manager's career:

1   *Structural* – the mechanisms by which the career is advanced, e.g. manpower and succession planning, appraisal systems.
2   *Developmental* – educational and training arrangements to acquire relevant knowledge, skills, etc. which enhance action and performance at each career stage.

To quote: 'both the structural and developmental aspects of managerial careers takes place at a meeting point between individuals and organizational processes. Structural changes in individual careers take place at the point of coincidence, negotiation or compromise between individual aspirations' (Burgoyne, 1983).

COACHING

Coaching is an on-the-job technique conducted by a superior. 'Senior managers frequently claim that they made the greatest strides in their own development when working for an outstandingly good boss earlier in their careers. Coaching implies more, however, than merely working for a good boss. It represents an active process in which the boss provides feedback on performance to the subordinate and gives advice and encouragement that fosters development' (Cowling, 1981).

Coaching may be informal, but it has to be planned within the general framework of staff development. Hague (1974) considers it the best method of management teaching. The good manager/coach:

1   Delegates and uses whatever situations arise as teaching opportunities
2   Sets individual projects and assignments
3   Helps his staff to succeed.

A good coach acts as a catalyst in helping a subordinate to diagnose and solve problems (through observation, listening, open-mindedness, and reviewing the learning that has taken place).

SENSITIVITY TRAINING AND T-GROUPS

We all have various ego drives, defences, and emotional baggage to carry around. Our behaviour, our postures, are geared to project our images and protect our sensibilities. Appearances are superficial. Expressed sentiments may be misinterpreted. We may not understand the values or attitudes of others. We are not aware of each other. We are strangers. No progress can be made in any social relationship until there is a degree of confidence, understanding, trust and mutual respect. Thus, most people fail to communicate effectively.

To develop 'awareness' and interpersonal skills, T-groups were developed (T=training). They comprise small groups of some 8–12 members who gather together to study their own behaviour with the aid of one or two staff trainers, although the trainers do not take on a conventional leadership role. The group may meet for a few days, or for up to a fortnight, usually in an informal setting away from interruptions of everyday life.

The group is 'unstructured' with regard to the rank of its members and to the programme itself. Discussion within the group is devoted to patterns of leadership, participation in the group, and a comparison of members' feelings to each other.

The trainer will usually open proceedings by explaining the purpose of the T-group. His later role will be to help the group learn from its experiences. At first there may be complete lack of agreement on how to proceed. The trainer may intervene by asking members to focus their attention on behaviour within the group. He may pose the questions 'What is happening? Who is behaving in what way? What feelings are being generated as a result?'

The group usually finds this self-analysis hard to accept. The group receives no guidance as to what its behaviour patterns *should* be, nor on how to proceed when traditional forms of behaviour prove ineffective. Bolder members may experiment with new patterns of behaviour. Some may find the experience frustrating and become aggressive or withdraw. As time passes, a degree of group unity develops.

A T-group can be characterized by three distinct phases:

1   Uncertainty
2   Aggression
3   Unity – or 'psychological safety'.

The T-group member gradually builds up a picture of how others respond to his/her customary behaviour. Individual members learn to give and receive feedback of a constructive kind. The effect of the T-group method is to heighten the impact of interaction at the personal level.

A recurring problem in the early stages of any T-group is the apparent need of members to appoint a leader or chairman. Problems of leadership and influence have to be resolved through 'power struggles'.

The aim of a T-group – 'sensitivity training' – is to change attitudes and behaviour. Such changes are difficult to achieve by conventional methods (such as a lecture which may create an awareness of the problem but is unlikely to modify attitudes). T-groups permit more direct learning through a shared experience of the 'here and now' situation. The T-group recognizes that the findings of social psychology are more acceptable if they are rediscovered anew by each individual participant. In their later stages, T-groups provide a supportive atmosphere of trust in which individuals can experiment with different kinds of behaviour in different situations. T-groups are processes of social influence and re-education. They encourage change, or at least favourable attitudes towards change, and have wider use than developing managerial sensitivity. They can also be instruments for organizational change and organizational development.

T-groups originate from experimental work in group dynamics by Kurt

Lewin, working at the National Training Laboratory at Bethel-in-Maine, USA, from about 1947 onwards. Originally a deficiency-oriented training technique, their use has since expanded into community leadership, youth work, and cross-cultural studies, as well as to supervisors and managers. In some areas, they are beginning to take on deeper therapeutic dimensions than Lewin imagined.

T-groups assume specific training needs and a generic learning experience comes to all kinds of clients, and that members having reached a state of psychological safety will articulate and produce constructive feedback. There is also an assumption that group members can in fact agree on another's behaviour.

T-groups can be stressful for anyone, an ordeal for neurotic or hypersensitive people. Total withdrawal from the situation is not uncommon. But the main problem is 're-entry' back into the work situation, and the transfer of any learning which may have occurred.

In summary, T-groups aim to encourage:

1   Understanding oneself, increased self-insight and awareness
2   The ability to listen
3   Sensitivity to others
4   Diagnosis of group problems and processes which inhibit or facilitate group functions
5   The ability to communicate
6   Interpersonal skills
7   The ability to relate one's behaviour to a specific situation.

T-groups can make an important contribution. They have been criticized on the grounds that their lack of structure may cause ambiguity (although it is possible to have 'structured' T-groups) and they may not always be seen as relevant to participants (Smith, 1980).

There have also been objections on personal or moral grounds. However, they were a landmark in the study of group dynamics. Attention later turned to broader team-building approaches around some kind of structured framework.

TEAM-BUILDING

Various approaches, or 'packages' have achieved popularity, and we will examine just three of them (Coverdale, Adair and Blake). These training packages are sometimes known as 'active' courses. Trainees participate in off-the-job activities by taking part in live exercises. Courses vary in content, degree of structure, participant mix and length of time. They can be organized internally or run outside the company for mixed groups.

COVERDALE

Coverdale learning is a system for the self-development of individual managers and effective teams. It fosters an understanding of how to work with others and learn the skills of productive team work. Named after its originator, the late Ralph Coverdale, in conjunction with Bernard Bab-bington-Smith, both psychologists, it was developed from about 1958 onwards.

A central precept is that people working in groups will behave differently than when working alone, and that the behaviour of group members is influenced by their personal interactions and the social processes operating around them.

Although Coverdale uses group methods of training, the group is largely a means to the end of individual learning and not an end in itself. Coverdale training does not encourage cosy 'groupiness'. An individual has the oppor-tunity to practise and tone up his or her leadership skills within the group. Coverdale does not subscribe to a particular leadership theory. Leadership is seen as the intelligent and sensitive control of group activity in respect of:

1 Setting aims and objectives
2 Using a systematic approach to getting things done
3 Gaining cooperation and commitment (see Fig. 6.6).

Listening is a vital skill. Every individual, because of his or her uniqueness, has something to offer. It is therefore worth while to listen. An effective team multiplies its strengths by using the skills of *all* its members and does not assume that the leaders should be omnipotent. Similarly, the leader exploits, in the best sense of the word, the skills and strengths of members.

Putting time and effort into observation is an important skill which enables people to improve individual and interactive behaviour in the light of feedback received. It involves an awareness and appreciation of: (a) people, thinking, acting, feeling and evaluating and (b) the effect one is having on others and vice versa.

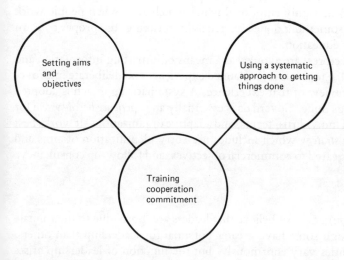

Fig. 6.6 *Leadership (Coverdale)*

In groups on Coverdale preparatory courses there are one or two observing members for each task, briefed to look for ways in which people help the group to make progress and for difficulties which the group needs to overcome. In giving feedback, the emphasis is on *positive success feedback*, rather than on negative error feedback since, it is argued, in organic systems one should build on strength in order to make weakness irrelevant.

Communication is seen as a two-way process involving the use and continual improvement of specific interpersonal skills, such as listening for meaning, thinking before speaking, timing one's contribution carefully, giving and seeking clarification, observing effects on others.

Just as one can plan to improve task performance, so one can plan to improve the use of these 'process skills'. Delegates on Coverdale courses are encouraged to do this by deliberate process planning to improve human interaction.

Learning by doing is a principle which underlies the development of process skills. Coverdale is not primarily concerned with *teaching* anybody anything, but providing *planned experience* through various tasks of increasing complexity designed for their learning values. This enables people to begin to discover certain lessons for themselves – and then go on to learn from subsequent experience. An important corollary of learning-by-doing is that the Coverdale coach is not a teacher or group leader, but a promoter and enabler. One implication of the word 'coach' is that skill and strength are already there in the group and need to be cultivated.

Practical tasks are carried out by group members and are used as vehicles for learning. Since they always involve an action stage, they enable people to discover a realistic balance between thought and action and prevent them from prolonging futile discussion and endlessly postponing the risk of action. Tasks provide a safety valve for releasing tension when the group is frustrated and bogged down. They reflect the principle (which distinguishes Coverdale from T-groups) that only emotional issues which arise when people work together to get something done are, generally speaking, the proper concern of management education.

Words (i.e. lectures) are avoided as a means of imparting information and developing skill. Emphasis is on planned experience and deliberate improvement through review of that experience. A systematic approach is adopted for getting things done. Coverdale is essentially an *experience based system* for development of individuals, teams, and adaptive organizations. It works best as a *regenerative strategy* which includes pre-entry identification of aims and success criteria geared to commercial objectives, and follow-up consultancy.

ADAIR

John Adair (1979) does not believe that leaders are 'born' due to their innate qualities, although some have greater potential for leadership than others. Leadership abilities vary enormously, but the function of leadership arises out of a 'situation', a combination of 'task needs' (what has to be done),

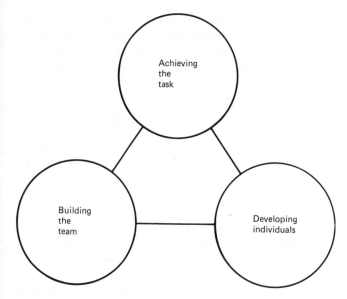

Fig. 6.7   *Leadership (Adair)*

'group maintenance needs' (if the group is to achieve its objectives its members must cooperate effectively), and 'individual needs'. Diagrammatically, the three sets of needs are shown in Fig. 6.7. Failure to meet any one of these needs will adversely affect the other two. The important thing, therefore, is what the leader *does*, not what he *is*. Adair's Task Actuated Leadership was developed largely at the Royal Military Academy, Sandhurst, from the late 1960s onwards. Courses include role-playing, and case studies. A rotating leadership role enables members to observe and practise leadership.

BLAKE'S MANAGERIAL GRID

Robert Blake and Jane Mouton devised the 'managerial grid' as a means of classifying managerial styles, based on a manager's twin concern for 'production' and 'people' (Blake and Mouton, 1979). A grid can be constructed with a nine-point scale on each axis (both scaled from 1 to 9) showing concern for production on the horizontal axis and concern for people on the vertical axis. A high concern for people and production is called the 9.9 style which is regarded as the optimum management style. In round terms, five main managerial styles can be discerned. Managers learn to recognize the gap between their own style and the optimum style, and through standard exercises are encouraged to acquire new behaviours to bridge the gap. The aim of the course is a systematic attempt to induce a change in management behaviour towards the optimum style. There are six phases in training programmes using the managerial grid. The total programme takes a minimum of four years to complete and aims to bring about a change in management behaviour throughout the company (an organizational change programme). More often, individual phases are used to change management styles within a team; or interdependent teams are brought together so the technique can be applied to resolve problems preventing cooperation between departments or functions.

MANAGEMENT EDUCATION AND FORMAL COURSES

Since the 1960s fuelled by fears of international uncompetitiveness, management education in Britain has experienced fairly continuous expansion, not peaking until the late 1970s, and retracting only marginally in the recessionary years of the early 1980s. 'Management education' (as opposed to training and development as such) has an academic flavour and can begin at an early age. Universities and polytechnics offer a range of courses leading to degrees and professional qualifications. Undergraduate courses in business studies are commonplace – often providing the first rung of the ladder for a managerial career.

At a more advanced level, and at a later career stage, the Diploma in Management Studies (DMS) for junior managers is run by polytechnics and colleges of education. More aspirant and academic pursuants may follow Master of Business Administration degrees (MBA).

A proliferation of universities and polytechnics provides management education in some shape or form. Many of the newer technological universities created 'business schools' for first degrees and postgraduate studies. Also, in some of the older seats of learning, management-related research and teaching is to be found. Chiefly, the universities which offer management educational facilities include Aston, Bath, Bradford, Brunel, Cardiff, City, Cranfield, Durham, Leeds, Liverpool, London School of Economics, Loughborough, Warwick, Strathclyde, amongst others. Apart from full-time courses, provision is often made for part-time or evening attendance. The London and Manchester Business Schools were specifically set up as centres of excellence following the Franks Report of 1963. Together with other centres, e.g. Henley, – The Management College, Ashridge Management College and Templeton College, Oxford which put on a variety of programmes, seminars and conferences, the UK is well endowed with facilities for formal, undergraduate, postexperience and specialist management education.

Companies themselves may run their own management education training centres, often in 'country house' settings, and conduct a series of 'in-company' courses or 'workshops'. Use may also be made of various external courses run by professional bodies (e.g. The Institute of Personnel Management, and The British Institute of Management), or the major business schools in Europe or America.

There are obvious economic advantages in gathering people together for imparting knowledge, and educational advantages for the development of interpersonal and participatory skills. But courses have serious limitations with regard to the *transfer of learning* back to the workplace, and sometimes with regard to their relevance. Management development should not simply be thought of as attending courses.

ACTION LEARNING

Managers learn by doing. There may be certain principles which can be taught formally, but the application of knowledge and the ability to solve problems for which there is no absolute solution are the real challenges. 'Real' problems are unique. There are no prescriptions. The emotional and political tangles, stress and risk which beset managerial work, can be better tackled by exposure – particularly if this can be planned in a constructive and supportive way. Most learning occurs through experience. The management teacher needs to develop learning situations to realize this.

Growing scepticism of the value of management training and development – especially in classroom settings – has been evident for some years. Various team-building exercises as described were attempts to overcome this. But one person in particular, Reg Revans (1983) has been a leading iconoclast. The only way that managers can learn how to manage is through practice in situations which they actually manage. Managers must make their own decisions and act on them, observing results and judging their own perform-ance. Academic subjects may be useful – but are rather remote and perhaps pretentious. Managers learn when faced by real challenge.

Revans has identified two types of learning – P and Q. P learning is the acquisition of existing programmed knowledge. Q learning is the ability to ask new questions and adapt. When faced with a problem, the manager uses his existing stock of understanding in general, and of the situation in particular, to decide a strategy and decide how to implement it. He then acts, and later reflects upon the outcome. For Revans, the learning experience is enhanced if acquired in a group situation. There must also be a willingness to keep probing with quite basic questions. Opportunities must be given to managers to work on real problems.

As part of the Revans philosophy, much of it pioneered in Belgium, exchanges are made between managers in cooperating organizations. They literally change places. Managers undergoing such a project take up real jobs in their host organization for a year or so, and from time to time reassemble as a training group to monitor their progress, exchange experiences and ideas.

Revans' approach has evoked a lot of interest. The light has dawned in the newest British business school – The Management Centre at the University of Buckingham – which breaks away from the traditional business school approach. 'The schools themselves have been conscious that it is not enough to teach theory in isolation, and some have devised limited experiments in live management programmes, otherwise known as action learning. The operative word, unfortunately, is "limited". Action learning and partnership with business enterprises, have been peripheral features of the established management education scene, whereas for us they will be central. This implies moving away from the relatively easy, safe, well-trodden paths of classroom teaching towards an altogether more challenging, less well-mapped terrain' (Wills, 1983).

A common cry is that the business schools have been too far removed from the needs of businessmen, over-emphasizing knowledge and flirting with various vogues and gimmicks. Many businessmen have been disappointed with the fruits of formal management development programmes. Some academies have sought to shift the schools into the business arena (Griffiths and Murray, 1985) via privatization.

'As in so much of British education, the approach was elitist; these institutions focused on excellence, elegance and sophistication. Perhaps some of us were seduced by the combination of academic brilliance (sometimes) and elegant surroundings. No doubt, this appealed to the "snobbishness" within the English national character. The truth is that the knowledge and sophisticated skills taught in these institutions were largely irrelevant to the needs of business managers. Furthermore, the means for helping participants link what they could learn to their own and their organization's goals and needs were inadequate. Hence, any tangible benefit to the organization was extremely rare. How could we have expected the unique and complex needs of individual managers to be met by standardised courses attended by 30 or 40 people?' (Nixon, 1982).

Summary

The objectives and purposes of a performance appraisal scheme must be clearly determined. The predominant purpose is usually to improve current performance. Appropriate performance criteria must be established, derived from the needs of the job. People must know what is expected of them, for their performance is reviewed in relation to these criteria. Assessments of performance during the review period – usually one year – can be measured and recorded in various ways, often by use of a rating scale. The first parts of the procedure are mechanical. The interview and counselling are the more important organic aspects of the process. Feedback must be given to subordinates and action plans drawn up to support areas which need improvement. There are technical problems of administration – the most crucial is determining common standards throughout the organization in order to ensure equity. Longer-term predictions of potential are more difficult to formulate. To this end, Assessment Centres are more appropriate. A central personnel department is provided with qualitative information which can be related to forward manpower plans.

Management Development seeks to match the growth needs of individuals to the adaptive needs of organizations. It is primarily a long-term activity. There is a difference between management training and management development. Contributions to management training and development can come from formal management education and training programmes, job

rotation and planned experience, coaching, MBO schemes, sensitivity training and various team-building exercises. Contemporarily there is growing
emphasis on the practical aspects of developing managers for the real world,
and on self-development.

Discussion questions

1 What steps would you take to set up a performance appraisal system in
   an organization which had not previously had one?
2 By what means would you attempt to identify relevant criteria or factors
   for assessment?
3 How would you seek to obtain inter-rater reliability and thereby fairness
   in the scheme?
4 How would you try to secure the commitment of line managers?
5 What recommendations would you make for the training of line
   managers in matters relating to performance appraisal?
6 What role could a grievance procedure play for employees who felt they
   had not been appropriately assessed? How would you prevent the abuse
   of such a procedure?
7 Why have performance appraisal?
8 How could Assessment Centres be improved?
9 What contribution do you think formal education can make to management development?
10 Are professional qualifications really necessary for managers?
11 What makes a good management coach?
12 Should management development be available for all staff employees or
   for persons selected as having potential?
13 Why do sensitivity training and social skills training form such important parts of management development?
14 What are the advantages of trying to develop managers and organizations together? What are the difficulties?
15 Can individual and organizational goals ever really be reconciled?
16 How far ahead is it really possible to plan a career?
17 How would you like to see management development develop?

References

ADAIR, J. (1979), *Action-Centred Leadership*, Gower Press, London.
ANDERSON, G. C. (1980), *Performance Appraisal in Theory and Practice*, Working Paper 8002,
   Strathclyde Business School, Glasgow.
ANSTEY, E. (1974), 'People matter – people differ', *Management Services in Government*, Paper 29.
ANSTEY, E., FLETCHER, C. and WALKER, J. (1976), *Staff Appraisal and Development*, Allen &
   Unwin, London.
ASHTON, D., EASTERBY-SMITH, M. and IRVINE, C. (1975), 'Management Development: Theory
   and Practice', MCB Monographs, Bradford.

ASHTON, D. and EASTERBY-SMITH, M. (1979), *Management Development in the Organisation*, Macmillan, London.

BLAKE, R. R. and MOUTON, J. S. (1979), *The New Managerial Grid*, Gulf Publishing Co., Houston.

BURGOYNE, J. (1983), 'Management development', in Williams A. P. O., *Using Personnel Research*, Gower, London.

BURGOYNE, J. and STUART, R. (1977), *Management Development: Content and Strategies*, Gower, London.

CAMERON, D. (1982), 'Performance appraisal and review', in Bowey, A. M., *Handbook of Salary and Wage Systems*, Gower, London.

COWLING, A. G. (1981), *Managing Human Resources*, Edward Arnold, London.

DAVIDSON, M. J. and COOPER, C. L. (1983), 'Women managers: their problems and what can be done to help them', University of Manchester Institute of Science and Technology/Manpower Services Commission.

DULEWICZ, S. V. (1982), 'The application of Assessment Centres', *Personnel Management*, Sept.

FLETCHER, C. (1983), 'Performance appraisal', in Guest, D., and Kenny, T., *A Textbook of Techniques and Strategies in Personnel Management*, Institute of Personnel Management, London.

FLETCHER, C. (1984) 'What's new in performance appraisal?', *Personnel Management*, Feb.

GERMAIN, C. and BURGOYNE, J. (1984), 'Self-development and career planning: an exercise in mutual benefit', *Personnel Management*, April.

GILL, D., UNGERSON, B. and THAKUR, M. (1973), *Performance Appraisal in Perspective*, Institute of Personnel Management, London.

GILL, D. (1977), *Appraising Performance*, Institute of Personnel Management, London.

GRIFFITHS, B and MURRAY, H. (1985), 'Whose business? A radical proposal to privatise British business schools', Hobart Paper 102, Institute of Economic Affairs, London.

HAGUE, H. (1974), *Executive Self-Development*, Macmillan, London.

HANDY, C. (1982), *Understanding Organisations*, Penguin, London.

LAWLER, E. E., MOHRMAN, A. M. and RESNICK, S. M. (1984), 'Performance appraisal revisited', *Organizational Dynamics*, **20**.

LORSCH, J. W. (1979), 'Making behavioural sciences more effective', *Harvard Business Review*, Mar/April.

MABE, P. A. and WEST, S. G. (1982), 'Validity of self-evaluation of ability', *Journal of Applied Psychology*, **67**.

NIXON, N. (1982), 'Last Chance for Management Development', *Industrial and Commercial Training*, Sept.

PEDLAR, M., BURGOYNE, J. and BOYDELL, T. (1978), *A Manager's Guide to Self-Development*, McGraw-Hill, New York.

RANDELL, G. A., PACKARD, P. M. A., SHAW, R. L. and SLATER, A. J. (1984), *Staff Appraisal*, Institute of Personnel Management, London.

REVANS, R. W. (1983), *The ABC of Action Learning*, Chartwell-Bratt, Bromley.

SALE, R. (1980), 'Personnel recruitment, selection and appraisal', in Livy, B. L., *Management of People in Banking*, Institute of Bankers, London.

SCHEIN, E. H. (1978), *Career Dynamics*, Addison-Wesley, Reading, Mass.

SMITH, P. B. (1980), *Group Processes and Personal Change*, Harper & Row.

STEVENS, C. (1985), 'Assessment Centres: the British experience', *Personnel Management*, July.

STEWART, A. and STEWART, V. (1981), *Tomorrow's Men Today*, Institute of Personnel Management, London.

STEWART, R. and MARSHALL, J. (1982), 'Managerial beliefs about managing: implications for management training', *Personnel Review*, **11**, 2.

STEWART, V. and STEWART, A. (1977), *Practical Performance Appraisal*, Gower, London.

STEWART, V. (1979), *Managing the Manager's Growth*, Gower, London.

TAYLOR, M. (1979), *Coverdale on Management*, Heinemann, London.

THORNTON, G. C. and ZORICH, S. (1980), 'Training to improve observer accuracy', *Journal of Applied Psychology*, **65**.

VANT, J. H. B. and LIVY, B. L. (1982), 'Management development programme for identifying leadership qualities and possible training needs in potential drillers and toolpushers', *Petroleum Industry Training Board*.

WALKER, J. (1983), 'Performance appraisal', in Williams, A. P. O., *Using Personnel Research*, Gower, London.

WILLIAMS, A. P. O. (1983), *Using Personnel Research*, Gower, London.

WILLS, G. (1983), 'The Buckingham Business School: a base for transferring theory into practice', *Personnel Management*, April.

Payment Systems

Payment Systems

CHAPTER 7

Job evaluation

by Bryan Livy

Job evaluation is about the value of work. How much is a job worth? What are the relative differences between jobs? How should these differences be reflected in remuneration? How far can job evaluation help to answer these questions?

There are many ways of determining pay scales (see Chapter 8). Job evaluation is but one. It is consistent with a performance-based remuneration policy, which implies that jobs contributing most to corporate objectives should receive the highest level of remuneration, and that relative worth is a sound basis on which to achieve fairness (Smith, 1983). Job evaluation tackles internal consistency in pay differentials. External consistency falls into the realm of collective bargaining and/or market mechanisms.

Job evaluation is itself a generic term and comprises a range of techniques. By the application of judgement and analysis their essential characteristic is to appraise the salient features of a job according to the range and degree of the human demands which it makes upon incumbents, and according to the relative contribution of the job to the organization as a whole, to provide yardsticks for assessment, and to provide basic data on which to come to conclusions and agreement about the rate for the job in monetary terms. This philosophy rests on the fundamental principles of logic, equity and justice. The methodology of job evaluation is systematic and comparative. It can make good economic, social and political sense if properly administered. However, it can also be open to criticism on both theoretical and practical grounds. It focuses on the job, not the person doing it. It identifies differences between jobs, their relative values, not absolute values. It is more concerned with internal relationships within the employing organization and less with external relationships. It frequently attempts the seemingly impossible, to compare unlike jobs. It always contains a subjective element. Some of the newer techniques are highly sophisticated, but perfection is elusive. Basically, there is no *right* answer to the question: how much is a job worth?

Job evaluation provides a framework on which, by discussion and negotiation, it is possible to reach acceptable and workable approximations. Its objectives are to produce a rational, coherent pay structure with a consequent reduction in anomalies and grievances, to help ensure equal pay for equal work, and to provide a basis for fixing differentials where a case for these can be demonstrated. It works best when founded on consensus. Success is not automatic. So much depends not simply on the mechanics of a particular system, but on the way in which it is introduced and implemented. Views differ widely about whether job evaluation should be used at all, although schemes of various kinds have been in existence for many years. Controversy still exists, but resistance seems to be waning. Certainly job evaluation is not a panacea. It requires considerable investment of time and effort. It does not offer a quick solution to a crisis situation, but does offer the twin prospects of system and stability, if planned for and developed on the bases of consensus, cooperation and concord.

Strictly speaking, job evaluation is concerned with determining the relative position of one job to another. It is a preliminary exercise for the establishment of grades and associated wage or salary levels.

> 'Job evaluation seeks to determine the value of a job relative to other jobs within the same organisation. The importance of that job to the organisation as a whole can thereby be established, and it can be placed in the appropriate position within an overall job-grade structure.' (BIM, 1979)

Larger numbers of people are increasingly employed in the same workplace as the result of organizational growth, amalgamations, takeovers, and the expansion of bureaucracies. Such people are inevitably provided with opportunities for direct comparisons of relative pay. Remuneration is an emotive issue. The crux of the pay determination problem is in assessing and agreeing the fairness of differential pay.

The problems of defining and fixing suitable wage/salary relationships between groups of jobs and workers are of considerable importance in both theory and in practice. In theory the issues are mostly economic, related to the laws of supply and demand for labour, skill shortages, labour markets, the levels of alternative earnings, company profitability and the size of the payroll as a proportion of overheads. In practice, too, the bargaining power of various groups of workers, whether manual or white collar, exerts pressure on the price of manpower. These external factors complicate the environment. Job evaluation groups 'like jobs' together which may then be treated collectively for pay purposes. In collective bargaining, the system can be advantageous for employers and employees in that it is possible to negotiate groups of jobs at a time, rather than each one individually. Such bargaining may concern itself with the establishment of a minimum rate of pay for each grade (or group of jobs) on top of which other matters (e.g. overtime, shift work premia) may be separately bargained. In other cases, bargaining may concern itself with the scale of payment for any given grade. Most of these matters are concerned with internal pay structures and relationships. But sometimes in the process of collective bargaining, employers and trade unions base their position on comparisons with wages or wage changes in other firms and industries, and it has not been uncommon internationally for arbitration awards and decisions of minimum wage-fixing authorities to refer to wage adjustments in other parts of the economy as an important factor in determining a proper or fair wage adjustment for the workers concerned. Sometimes such comparisons are made in order to ensure equal pay for roughly equal or, by some standard, equivalent work. Sometimes they may be made in order to maintain or create wage differentials that are regarded as justified, either on traditional grounds, or for newer substantive reasons, such as the introduction of new technology and changes in work practices. Legislation in some countries, particularly Britain, Europe and America, has been brought to bear on issues of discrimination in employment, and internal yardsticks of comparison are necessary, through job evaluation, to help establish parity in payment for persons doing work of a similar nature and value. Internal consistency and fairness in pay rates within a firm are generally considered to be matters not only of morality, but also sound business acumen. At the same time, all job evaluation systems recognize the need for a suitable relationship between internal and external rates. Issues of comparability are therefore wide and far-reaching.

The principles of job evaluation

Job evaluation begins with a factual study of work content. This means that jobs must be analysed and subjected to the process of job analysis, which systematically reviews duties and activities undertaken by a job incumbent, the degrees of responsibility and discretion exercised, and the skills brought to bear in the execution of the job. Since comparisons are to be made, it is essential that information obtained by the process of job analysis be recorded in a standard format – the job description. Moreover, the type of job analysis required will depend on the job evaluation scheme to be adopted (see Chapter 3).

The success of a job evaluation exercise depends in the long run upon its acceptability to the population it serves – employers and employees. Job analysis and the writing up of job descriptions should be conducted under the guidance of persons expert in this area, but even at this initial stage, involvement of the parties concerned (unions and management representatives *and* job holders) should take priority. A *job evaluation committee* will need to be constituted, representative of the parties concerned, which will subsequently have the task of evaluating jobs and hearing grievances. Participation in job evaluation usually takes the form of such a committee, which may have either advisory or executive functions.

The choice of a particular job evaluation scheme is a matter to be influenced by the range and types of jobs to be evaluated, the numbers concerned, the time and cost involvement which would be necessary and the degree of accuracy required. Processes of evaluation essentially compare jobs against each other as 'whole jobs', or break them down into constituent parts (or 'factors'), weighting, comparing and scoring these factors in order to arrive at a summated value for the job as a whole.

The outcome of the evaluation exercise is to produce a *rank order* of jobs. This hierarchy will reveal the perceived differences in job values. Depending upon the scheme adopted, these values may or may not be quantitatively expressed. In any event, the differences revealed will reflect values placed on the jobs internally by the organization; they do not of themselves indicate monetary differentials; they do not necessarily at this stage bear any relation to external market rates or values.

After the comparisons have been made, in order to reduce the miscellany of jobs arrayed in rank order to manageable proportions, jobs are normally grouped into grades in which either (i) jobs of broadly similar value are grouped together, or (ii) job grades are formed representing natural divisions in the existing organizational structure. The translation of job grades into levels of payment is a separate exercise requiring either negotiation or settlement unilaterally by management after a consideration of market rates and the type of remuneration policy they would like to see emerge consistent with the rankings produced (see Chapter 8).

Questions of *communication* and *training* are pertinent in any matter affecting change in personnel policy. Job evaluation is no exception. Job holders should be kept fully informed of the procedures at all stages. Representatives on the job evaluation committee should receive appropriate training in the basic principles of job evaluation and in the details of the particular scheme to be applied. *Manuals or handbooks* should be produced to explain the mechanics to employees. *Grievance and appeal procedures* should be set up through which individuals (or groups) may seek redress if they feel aggrieved by their relative position or if they misunderstand the system.

Where job evaluation results are to form the subject of negotiation between unions and management, once the evaluation exercise *per se* has been completed (and agreed) it would be normal for union and management representatives to discontinue their joint, collaborative deliberations in committee, and for each side to take up *negotiating postures* to determine rates of pay for respective grades of work.

For the purposes of collective bargaining, or for wage and salary administration where such matters are not bargained, job evaluation serves as a tool for (i) the analysis of job content, (ii) comparability and (iii) as an administrative device for grouping jobs into a framework.

Finally, work relationships are never static, and therefore any job evaluation scheme, once installed, must be kept constantly under review – monitoring changes in job content and assessing the value of new jobs.

The basic job evaluation schemes

There are four main types of job evaluation schemes based on four different methods, namely;

1   The ranking method
2   The grade or classification method

3   The points rating method
4   The factor comparison method.

The first two are usually referred to as 'non-analytical' (and sometimes as 'non-quantitative' or 'summary' methods) while the latter are known as 'analytical' (or 'quantitative' methods). It is common nowadays for hybrid schemes to be developed from a composite use of one or more of these approaches. Underlying particular systems there are, however, certain broad principles. It is necessary to be quite clear as to the criteria for evaluation which are to be applied. Normally at some stage it is necessary to define either *grades* in which jobs will be placed and *factors* in terms of which they will be evaluated. These criteria must be defined in clear and unambiguous terms. Definitions of grades and factors have to be drawn up very carefully. Grade definition will relate strongly to organizational structure, but the *predetermination* of grades is pertinent only to the classification method, elsewhere it is a *post-evaluation* exercise. *Factor definition* is directly and unequivocally related to job content, to the identification of essential, common job elements. These preliminary exercises are normally undertaken after the job analyses have been conducted and after consultation between members of the job evaluation committee. Usually, after some provisional definitions have been prepared, these are pilot tested by applying them to certain key jobs to see whether the definitions can form a basis for meaningful comparison and acceptable wage relations between them. In the light of such experiments the definitions may be revised. Once they have been established in final form, the various definitions provide the basis for evaluation.

JOB RANKING

Each job is considered as a 'whole' – an overall view is taken of the demands of the job and its contribution to the organization. There is no detailed analysis or examination of the individual parts of the job. As always, a job description is a necessary prerequisite, and assessors should have sufficient familiarity with the range of jobs in question to come to an informed opinion. Each job is placed, as the name of the scheme implies, into a rank order.

To facilitate the process, it is usual to begin by selecting a number of 'key' jobs or '*benchmark*' jobs. These form the cornerstone against which other jobs are compared. Benchmark jobs must therefore be representative of the general range of jobs in question and they must also be well known and understood by the assessors in order to serve as adequate points of reference. Indeed, the choice of benchmark jobs is critical.

The main attraction of the ranking method is its simplicity, and therefore the speed and ease with which it can be set up. Its simplicity is also its main source of weakness. There are wide margins for error or misjudgement, and precisely because the scheme lacks detail, there is no formal means of providing substantive evidence for the decisions reached. However, the scheme is popular in small organizations, where assessors are probably more closely in touch with the jobs being evaluated than might be the case in large, diffuse, complex organizations. It is also useful where the jobs under scrutiny are of a similar type or occupation.

The ranking procedure compares each job against the nearest, most appropriate benchmark job, and ranks it above or below, according to the considered evaluation. In this way, taking each job in turn, the rank order is gradually built up. If there are too many jobs to be evaluated, the ranking method is unlikely to be appropriate; a more finely discriminating technique would be better. Ranking is also more suitable for low-level jobs, and where a detailed examination of factor components would be regarded as superfluous.

A refinement of the ranking scheme is *paired comparison*, in which assessments are not simply made against benchmark jobs or against one or two 'proximal' jobs, but under which each job is compared with all the others in turn. In each case the assessor is faced with a pair of jobs and must make a decision as to which is the more important (or whether they are equal). The use of modern computer facilities makes this kind of approach feasible and can provide a more accurate overview of the general level of consensus when applied not only to all jobs in the survey but also to each of the assessors.

Jobs having been ranked, the next step is grading. The rank sequence must be subdivided into a convenient number of grades. This process could be almost arbitrary but the considerations to be borne in mind are that jobs within any one grade should have cognate similarities and that *between grades there should be significant differences in job content*.

From grading to pricing. Grades derived from the ranking exercise must be awarded monetary values. This can take the form of a *spread of range* (difference between maximal and minimal remuneration limits) within which occupants of a grade will be paid. Alternatively, the results of the grading exercise may enter the field of negotiation, usually by bargaining the minimum level for the pay of each grade, i.e. a minimum rate for the job.

CLASSIFICATION

This approach is alternatively known as the grade or classification method; sometimes it is called 'predetermined grading', and in the United States, the 'grade description system'. The method is both similar to ranking, and at the same time, in another sense, diametrically opposite. It is basically a ranking operation in the sense that the job infrastructure is marshalled into grades, but the procedure is reversed. The structure and pattern of grades, and the relationship between them, are determined first. Jobs are then evaluated and allocated to a particular grade. Each successive grade reflects a higher level of skill and responsibility, with less supervision. The approach is more centralized, mechanistic, and closely related to organizational design. Indeed, the grading system reflects the organization chart showing formal relationships between hierarchical levels. In this method it is not necessary to develop an individual rank order of jobs, but it *is* necessary to have a clearly defined grade hierarchy. This hierarchy, divided into a fixed number of grades, with written definitions developed for each grade, provides a scale or canon against which jobs can be compared, assessed and slotted in.

Like ranking, the method assesses the job as a 'whole'; there is no subdivision and comparison of component factors. It is a broad, generalized approach, requiring as much clarity in job description as it does in grade definition.

Unlike ranking, it is in fact possible to agree or determine pay levels for each grade before the evaluation exercise even begins, although this order of events is unusual. The classification system, with a pre-determined number of grades, does provide a method for tighter budgetary control, which can be further enhanced (if somewhat autocratically) by additionally specifying in advance the *ratio* between grades (i.e. the number of jobs in any particular grade in relation to any other grade). In effect this is what happens in the armed services, where the number of lieutenant-colonels bears a relationship to the number of officers and other ranks. As part of the establishment of a grading structure, an organization may decide not only the number of grades and differences between them, but also the size of each grade in terms of the number of jobs incorporated within it.

Normally, awarding rates of pay for grades takes place after the evaluation exercise by unilateral action or by collective bargaining. The classification method is most commonly applied in white-collar employment in the public sector (i.e. where public monies are allocated and accountable). Although this is not universally true, instances can be found in manufacturing industry, including manual jobs. There are a number of long-established and successful schemes in operation, in government service and in office administration, notably the UK Civil Service and the position classification system in the United States Civil Service Commission.

The classification method is relatively simple, inexpensive and easy to apply, if perhaps rigid. It could be argued that manipulating jobs to fit a predetermined structure could lead to distorted job interrelationships and a less than equitable pay structure, since the criterion of comparability between jobs within a grade is an assumption, made for administrative convenience.

Speed and administrative simplicity, although clearly advantageous, may not of themselves guarantee success. Dissent is sometimes provoked by the use of non-analytical methods. It can sometimes be more difficult to justify and uphold decisions based on purely subjective criteria. Where jobs are more complex, and justify greater accuracy, or where an organization wishes to adopt a more rigorous approach, analytical methods may be employed.

POINTS RATING

Points rating has become one of the most popular methods in recent years; it has also been father to a number of offspring. Many of the schemes developed by management consultancy firms embody and modify the principles of points rating to include new thinking on the subject, or to fit the needs of a client. Either in its basic form or as a hybrid, points rating is the most extensively used method of job evaluation. It has a number of particular merits: its methodology insists upon detailed job analysis, and by virtue of the structure of the scheme, the format of job analysis is prescribed and related directly to the job criteria. The degree of fit between the method of analysis and evaluation can be tailored to the constructs used. The technique can distinguish between common and specific attributes in a constellation of jobs (and combine them); and it can cater for wide variations in jobs selected for comparative study. It is possible for points rating schemes to encompass a greater degree of participation, an evaluation can be re-run on an iterative basis until consensus is achieved. Where differences of opinion occur, the roots of dissent can be more easily identified. The approach is systematic. Practitioners can be trained in its methodology and application. Details of the outcome of the evaluation and successive steps in the operation can readily and easily be explained.

The first step in establishing a points rating system is to identify a number of factors (or constituent elements) which are found to be common in the range of jobs to be evaluated. Such factors may include qualities necessary for the successful performance of the job (e.g. education or training required), the responsibilities entailed (e.g. for people, assets, resources) or such factors as judgement or authority for decisions, leadership, communications and contacts with others. Other factors may lend themselves to direct quantification, such as volume of business or sales turnover. Essentially, *factor identification* revolves around basic job ingredients such as skill, effort, responsibility and working conditions.

The British Standards Institution (1979) defines the points rating method as:

'The method of numerically evaluating jobs by the detailed analysis of component job factors. Each factor is defined and given a range of point values, so that every job can be assessed numerically within the established range.'

Benchmark jobs help to crystallize out those factors that are most important. A benchmark job should be one which is fairly typical of the group to be evaluated, and one in which the constituent elements are common, general and persistent throughout the group of jobs. In practice, the number of factors employed in points rating job evaluation schemes varies widely. More complex jobs usually require more factors than simpler routine jobs – although it should be stated that complex jobs do not, *ipso facto*, necessarily need a complex factor structure. The important point is that the choice of factors identifies the critical variables and enables assessors to tease out the essential differences between jobs. From a study of the literature, it can be seen that many possible factors exist (Elizur, 1980). According to the International Labour Organization (1986), the most frequently used job factors comprise the following:

Accountability
Analysis and judgement
Accuracy
Complexity
Contact and diplomacy
Creativity
Decision-making
Dexterity
Education
Effect of errors
Effort
Initiative
Judgement
Know-how
Knowledge
Knowledge and skills
Mental fatigue
Mental effort
Mental skills
Physical demands
Physical effort
Physical skills
Planning and coordination requirements
Problem-solving
Resources control
Responsibility for cash and materials
Responsibility for confidential data
Responsibility for equipment or process
Responsibility for records and reports
Social skills
Supervision given
Supervision received
Task completion
Training and experience
Work conditions
Work pressure

It is obvious that many of these factors overlap (co-variance between factors). The inclusion of all of them, even if relevant, in any given scheme would probably create confusion. On the other hand, there should be no important areas of work which are not covered by an appropriate factor.

Weighting of job factors

It is unlikely that all factors will be of equal value or that they will each make an identical contribution to the performance of the job. Some factors will be more important than others, and should be weighted accordingly. The starting point for determining the weighting of factors is the proposition that the value of all the factors combined constitutes 100 per cent of the total job. The next step is to place the factors in rank order on the basis of the pooled judgement of the job evaluation committee and to try to agree percentage shares for each factor, e.g.

Factor A	30%
Factor B	25%
Factor C	20%
Factor D	15%
Factor E	5%
Factor F	5%
	100%

The ranking of factors and their interrelationships in percentage terms still only indicates their relative importance, not their absolute values, so a range of points scores (maximum and minimum) must then be assigned to each factor.

Rather than have a host of individual factors, it may sometimes be more convenient to divide them into broad groups of 'generic' factors with each group composed of sub-factors. Here is a British Institute of Management (1970) example:

Generic Factor	Specific Sub-factor
Acquired skill and knowledge	Training and previous experience
	General reasoning ability
	Complexity of process
	Dexterity and motor accuracy
Responsibilities and mental requirements	Responsibility for material equipment
	Effect on other operations
	Attention needed to orders
	Alertness to details
	Monotony
Physical requirements	Abormal position
	Abnormal effort
Conditions of work	Disagreeableness
	Danger

Where sub-factors are used to facilitate the factor analysis (as a way of avoiding covariance and making it easier to adjudicate on the relative position of each item, they must be similarly weighted). Sub-factors taken together must account for 100 per cent of the generic factor to which they subsume.

For example:

Generic Factor A: consists of sub-factor x 50%
sub-factor y 30%
sub-factor z 20%

Since generic factors are themselves weighted (e.g. A 30%, B 25%, C 20%, D 15%, E 5%, F 5%) it means that sub-factors will assume varying importance within the total scheme according to the relative size of the generic factor and the number of sub-factors within it.

Division of job factors into degrees

The purpose of the factor weightings is to compensate for their differential contribution and importance within the range of jobs under consideration. This merely provides part of the framework. It should be borne in mind that the long-run objective of the exercise is to tease out differences *between* jobs within the range. Therefore, it should be recognized that each factor will be manifest in jobs to a varying extent. The division of job factors into 'degrees' helps to achieve more discriminating ratings between the jobs.

Generic factors are accorded a percentage share of the total value to achieve an appropriate balance between them, but it is against the sub-factors that ratings are actually going to be made, and it is these which are broken down into degrees. Each degree represents a progressive increment in the demands of that sub-factor.

For illustration, the sub-factor 'experience' as required to perform a given job could be broken down thus:

First degree	Up to 3 months
Second degree	Over 3 months and up to 1 year
Third degree	Over 1 year and up to 3 years
Fourth degree	Over 3 years and up to 5 years
Fifth degree	Over 5 years.

Degrees are simply indications of the amount by which a sub-factor may be present in a given job. Using five degrees to form a five-point scale, as is commonly done, is largely a matter of administrative convenience. In fact, any number of degrees could be used. Furthermore, it is not necessary to utilize a uniform number of degrees for each factor – some may require six or seven degrees, others only four. The important consideration is that the structure of the degree classification should wherever possible be representative of convenient, natural, or easily measurable variations in job content.

As a general guideline, it is useful to consider the range of jobs to which the system is to be applied from the point of view of the criterion variables which are likely to result in successful performance. So that, in deciding the number of degrees to be allocated to the factor of 'education', one should determine and specify the minimum amount of that factor likely to be called for in a given range of jobs. That level of education then assumes the degree of 1. Similarly, one then looks at the maximum amount of the education factor which is likely to be called for in that range, and if one is employing a five-point scale, it assumes the degree of 5. The number of degrees must be wide enough to create a meaningful dispersion, but there is danger of allocating too many degrees. Too few, however, will cramp the system by inhibiting its powers of discrimination.

The allocation of points values to degrees

Degrees having been established, numerical values must then be assigned to each particular degree. To do this, an initial decision must be made as to the maximum number of points to be awarded under the scheme. In round figures say 100, or whatever. The total number of points available under the scheme is allocated in proportion to the factor weightings. If a factor is awarded 20 per cent of the total, it would receive 20 points (in a scheme with a maximum score of 100). The function of degrees is to distribute the factor awards across the spectrum of the factor range.

The actual points values ascribed to these may be determined by any one of three formulae:

1 Arithmetic progression
2 Geometric progression
3 Variable percentage differentials.

Arithmetic progression is the most common – whereby an equal points difference occurs between each degree, thus:

Generic Factor	Subfactors	Degrees					
		1st	2nd	3rd	4th	5th	
Qualifications	Education	15	30	45	60	75 ⎫	points
	Experience	20	40	60	80	100 ⎭	

Arithmetic progression is in fact increasing the degree value to the extent of 100 per cent of the *first degree value* each time, the numerical difference between the degrees is therefore constant.

Geometric progression, however, increases the degree value by 100 per cent of the *preceding* degree value each time. A constant multiple is applied. The point value is doubled at each successive stage, and would obtain as follows:

Subfactors	Degrees				
	1st	2nd	3rd	4th	5th
Education	15	30	60	120	240 ⎫ points
Experience	25	50	100	200	400 ⎭

Geometric progression clearly results in a wider points range, and therefore is more suited to schemes which embrace a high number of total points.

A *variable percentage progression*, alternatively, could be used either to produce a narrower points range, or to overcome the fallacy built into both arithmetic and geometric progressions, that degree values (i.e. the work demands made on job incumbents) do in fact increase by a constant percentage each time. With varying differentials, the evaluation committee may allocate the maximum number of points available to each degree on what is judged to be a fair basis, thus:

Subfactors	Degrees					
	1st	2nd	3rd	4th	5th	
Education	15	20	30	45	75	points
Experience	20	30	45	65	100	

In this case the differential increases progressively between each degree. The results tend to favour higher scoring jobs, and may cause unwanted loadings in the higher degree range. It also makes the scheme administratively more complicated than it need be and produces a result which is probably less defensible.

By whichever method, degrees assume points values. This mechanical part of the exercise facilitates the scoring and evaluation that is to come later. It is also absolutely essential that the framework produced is supported by some measure of consensus from the job evaluation committee.

All jobs, of course, contain a minimal level of demand, and sometimes this may not show up in the allocation of factor weightings and degree values. A way of acknowledging this is by the use of a *datum*. A datum is a flat-rate addition, e.g. so many points to the total points score of each job. The preference of many job evaluators is to ignore the datum altogether. Its inclusion as an arbitrary flat rate tends to skew distribution.

The scoring of jobs

Once the factor plan has been prepared, the process of evaluation by the committee can begin. First, apply the factor plan to the benchmark jobs which were selected to provide guidance on the choice of job factors. Score each factor at the appropriate degree level. These points scores can be totalled to produce an aggregate score for each benchmark job. Then take each other job in turn, score it factor by factor, add up the points scored. For each job under review it is possible to arrive at a total score, factor by factor. The summation for each job as a whole indicates its relative position in the hierarchy, and more precisely, the numerical relationship between one job and another, as in the following example (which has a total possible points score of 1000):

Rank Order of Jobs	Total Points Scored
Job A	180
Job B	183
Job C	188
Job D	190

Job E	195
Job F	205
Job G	214
Job H	222
Job I	238
Job K	270
Job L	275
Job M	290
Job N	315
Job O	350
Job P	375
Job Q	410
Job R	500
Job S	580
Job T	675
Job U	760
Job V	840
Job X	850
Job Y	950
Job Z	997

The task now is to convert the scores into monetary values. Jobs are not simply paid off pro rata against points scored. Points scores are no more than a guide to the relative dispersion of jobs. Various ways of translating points scores into monetary scales exist. These are discussed in detail in Chapter 8.

Whilst the points system may appeal to the analytical mind, and have greater content and validity than the non-quantitative methods described earlier, it has a number of inherent weaknesses. These stem from the exercise of judgement, from the need for approximation, and possibly from prejudice or preconceived attitudes regarding the relative importance of different factors in the first place. The choice of factors may not necessarily have been 'right' ones. There could have been areas of deficiency in the factor plan. One of the problems is to find a factor plan which will fit a wide range of jobs – this must necessarily make it broad. To make factor plans specifically relevant, it may be necessary to confine them to particular job families, e.g. marketing, finance, production. To the extent that they are made relevant to the family in question, they cannot be used for cross-comparison between job families. To make the plans more versatile, factor plans are often extended. Too many factors create confusion, and possible covariance. Within the plan, too wide a points range encourages assessors to seek an illusory degree of precision. In any case the conversion of jobs into numerical scores does not render the process any the more objective. Although analytical methods are less prone to drift and distortion over time, they still deteriorate (original factor scores and weightings may become irrelevant as a job tends to creep up the points scale) and need to be regularly reviewed.

FACTOR COMPARISON

The factor comparison method, though less refined than points rating, is rather more complicated in practice. It is also unpopular.

As originally developed, the method involves the ranking of different jobs in respect of certain factors and usually also involves assigning money wages to the jobs. The fact that the method leads *directly* to the determination of wages is regarded as an undesirable feature by those who consider that the only task of job evaluation is the comparison of job contents.

The first task in applying the method is to select the factors to be used. These may be, for example: skill, mental and educational requirements; physical requirements; responsibility; working conditions.

The ranking of jobs in respect of each of the factors and subsequent wage fixing are first carried out for a number of benchmark jobs which serve as points of reference for the evaluation and ranking of other jobs. For this purpose, the benchmark jobs should satisfy a number of conditions. They should be capable of clear description and analysis in terms of the factors used, and adequately reflect them. When the rates for the benchmark jobs are to be used as a standard for determining wages for other jobs, these rates should be regarded as 'appropriate', and not differ too much from the rate paid for these or similar jobs in the local labour market. Finally, benchmark jobs should include jobs covering a sufficiently wide range of grades from lowest to highest. The number of benchmark jobs thus required for the factor comparison method depends on the number and variety of jobs in the organization. First, the key jobs are ranked successively by reference to each of the factors chosen. When the ranking is done by a committee the usual practice is for each member to make his or her own ranking and for the results to be averaged. After such agreement has been reached, the jobs are ranked again but according to a different procedure. The wage rate for each key job is broken down and apportioned to each of the factors according to the value which each is thought to have in its contribution to the totality of the job itself. When the rates for all key jobs have been divided in this way, the jobs have been ranked implicitly again (evaluated) with respect to each of the factors.

Two separate assessments have been carried out: *factor ranking* and *factor evaluation*. The two sets may not necessarily coincide and will need to be reconciled by increasing or decreasing the money values of the different factors of the jobs concerned or by examining the job content again to see if a suitable adjustment can be made in the factor rating. *Reconciliation* is essential if the job is to act as a benchmark job against which other jobs in the organization, on the basis of job descriptions, are themselves to be evaluated.

Evaluations are done directly in cash terms; there is no conversion process of assessments into monetary values (with rare exception). A Factor Comparison Schedule (or matrix) needs to be constructed, with pay rates on one axis and factors on the other. With benchmark jobs acting as yardsticks, each non-benchmark job is slotted into position on a comparative basis *vis-à-vis* the other jobs. It sounds very simple. In fact it is notoriously difficult and frustrating. The reconciliation of ratings and evaluations presents a persistent stumbling-block. Theoretically, the method can be seen to have certain attractions: each factor is worth a certain proportion of the rate for the job and some factors are worth more than others. An analytical approach of this kind should be a fairly scientific way of identifying and rewarding compensable job factors on a comparative basis, and of obtaining a high degree of congruence and internal consistency in the pay structure. Resistance in practice is largely derived from the (hidden) complexities and the assumption on which it is based: that the rates of pay for benchmark jobs are incontrovertible axioms.

Validity

The acceptability in practice of job evaluation as a determinant of income, and no less its acceptability in theory, must depend on its reliability and validity. Reliability is a measure of consistency – the extent to which results are reproducible. Validity is concerned with the accuracy of job evaluation as an instrument of measure. Does it in fact measure differentials in a balanced series of jobs? To what extent, if at all, does it measure something else, either hidden or observable? To what extent may it fail to measure certain parts? Where degrees of contamination or deficiency exist, the instrument is less than perfectly valid.

To answer the question: is job evaluation a valid instrument? one must first specify what it is one is trying to measure. There could in reality be several answers, e.g. the relative worth of jobs? a socially equitable distribution of income? a fair rate of pay? equal pay for work of equal value on sexually non-discriminating criteria? Precisely because job evaluation can mean different things in different situations, the question cannot be answered in general terms. Answers get caught up in circular arguments. The criterion we are aiming at must be specified.

One of the easiest ways to validate a technique of job evaluation is to compare its outcome with that of another technique. If the results are compatible, this may demonstrate validity, but conversely it may not; it may simply replicate the faults of the first technique and demonstrate no more than tautology. Another method would be to compare the results of a job evaluation exercise with existing rates. A near-perfect correlation might suggest a high degree of validity, but again not necessarily, for the criterion of existing rates might not be the right one. In fact, if the criterion of existing or market rates is adopted, one is bound to end up by underwriting the status quo. Every technique, except that of Jaques falls into this trap (see later). Conventional assessments of job worth and the distribution of income are replicated and perpetuated.

One measure of validity is whether the system achieves the sort of pay structure people are prepared to accept as just and fair. But there is no doubt

that the validation of job evaluation plans as wholes, or the various supposedly correlated factors included in them, is a tricky exercise.

Yet this issue is absolutely crucial in the latest test to which job evaluation is
now put: equal pay for work of equal value (see later). For this purpose a job
evaluation study must be a *valid* one. 'By "valid" is meant that it must
"objectively" determine the differential rates of pay on the basis of job
demands' (Equal Pay Act, s. 1 (5)). The use of the term 'objective' in this
context is unhelpful. Few job evaluation experts would be happy with this
adjective, and would prefer "systematic" on the ground that it is possible to
control subjective judgement in job evaluation, but not eliminate it (see Livy,
1975). Lawyers may have to accept that it is this element of systematic control
over the exercise of judgement which is important in establishing validity,
not some "pure" objectivity which is impossible of realization' (Thomason,
1985).

Trends in job evaluation

Since the industrial revolution, workers have been increasingly grouped
together. Rapid technological advances and the collective aspirations of
working people have increasingly caused a focus of attention on the pay
problem, which has basically two aspects: absolute earnings level and
questions of relativity. Feelings about pay are deep-seated. Greek philo-
sophers long before the classical European economists, mulled over disparities in wealth. Ideas about equitable payment are Aristotelian in origin.
Conceptually, these notions are important to job evaluation, but no serious
application of them to pay determination took place until the advent of
'scientific management'.

Real interest developed with the birth of work study. The origins of
analytical study work may be traced back (partly to Babbage in the
nineteenth century) but more clearly to pioneers such as Taylor, the Gil-
breths, and Bedeaux in the early part of the twentieth century. From their
studies the three management techniques of method study (motion study),
work measurement and job evaluation have emerged. Job evaluation is the
youngest of the trilogy, and is in many ways quite distinct and separate,
although it stems from a common root – the careful analysis of jobs.

Armed with new thinking about the principles of scientific management
and work study, and equipped with emerging techniques, industrialists
generally, but especially in the United States, began early in the twentieth
century to consider problems of productivity and the related problems of
remuneration, particularly for manual workers. Interest was not confined to
industrialists. Growth in the public sector also brought with it new problems
regarding employee remuneration. By 1909 both the Civil Service Commission in Chicago and the Commonwealth Eddison Company were evaluating
jobs by the ranking method. The Bureau of Personnel Research at the
Carnegie Institute of Technology was developing non-analytical methods

and in 1926 Lott developed a points system. The first 'scientific' plans were being drawn up. In the same year, Benge installed the first factor comparison method in the Philadelphia Transit Company. In the United States, wage rate inequities in the 1930s gave rise to intensive union pressures for formalization of remuneration plans. Lott's original 13-factor points scheme was utilized primarily for metal workers. Two prominent American associations, the Electrical Manufacturers' Association and the National Metal Trades Association developed plans for rating hourly paid jobs in factories. Michael and Fisher both of the Western Electric Company had devised both of these schemes and reduced the Lott factor complex to four generic factors: skill, effort, responsibility and working conditions (Langsner and Zollitsch, 1967). The principle for determining them was by reference to those characteristics most commonly appearing across the job family. Reference to any contemporary job evaluation scheme is likely to reveal that these factors are still regarded as fundamental job components. Kress (1939), himself a pioneer of points rating, was responsible for the factor installation in Western Electric. Modifications were made for the evaluation of salary positions with the use of slightly different factors.

America was the birthplace of job evaluation. Large private employers in the United States today typically utilize some type of points rating system; indeed, the system has spread around the world. It might seem that job evaluation has been set since its inception on a path of natural ascendancy in terms of both its acceptability and its sophistication. Such is not really the case. In places there has been considerable union opposition deriving from suspicion of management manipulation, and resistance (especially in the UK by the craft unions which prefer to see their members paid according to the skills they possess rather than exercise). Examples of contemporary resistance can be seen worldwide. It is not particularly popular in Australia or India, and in Japan it is anathema. Even in America certain stimuli to the progress of job evaluation came about almost by accident. This is particularly true on the industrial front. In many ways, the rise of American industrial unions in the 1930s, and later, decisions by the US National War Labor Board gave the impetus necessary to launch job evaluation as a major management technique. It came to Europe about that time; the European explosion of job evaluation is essentially a post-war phenomenon. In the last 40 years it has made rapid advances in all sections of public, commercial and industrial life, in Germany, France, Britain, Sweden, Denmark and the Netherlands. It has also been taken up in the planned economies like the USSR, Poland, Eastern Germany, Czechoslovakia, and recently in Latin American and developing countries in Africa (ILO, 1986).

The European approach, whilst adopting the basic principles, has differed in application from the American, in some cases simply to become broader. In Germany, Sweden, and Denmark it has been fashionable to develop industry-wide job evaluation schemes, and occasionally in the USA (steel) and Britain (coalmining). The culture of industrial relations has influenced the continental trend. In the Netherlands, as is well known, a national scheme was set up after the Second World War and ran successfully for many years. One of the questions which has now come to the fore is whether the results of evaluation are still satisfactory in the event of new forms of work organization (e.g. autonomous work groups, job rotation, etc.). This issue is not exclusively Dutch. Sweden, particularly, has been grappling with this problem. In the United States, little interest has been shown in *national* job evaluation, although in Britain the subject has been aired at least theoretically (Brown, 1973).

Most efforts have been directed at refining the basic principles established in the 1920s, with the use of quantitative methods such as psychological scaling and multiple regression analysis to develop criteria, validation of job factors, and inter-rater reliability (Anderson and Corts, 1973).

Two broad areas can be identified as occupying the interest of current researchers and practitioners. One stems from the search to find a common ingredient in jobs which can be used for a universal pay structure, and the other stems from a desire to incorporate a greater degree of participation.

Elliott Jaques (1964, 1967, 1970) has argued that the main conventional techniques of job evaluation are too subjective, and, in addition, simply reflect the relative bargaining powers of the parties engaged in negotiation. Instead, Jaques has suggested measuring the differences between jobs according to the 'time span of discretion' – that is, the discretionary area of a job as opposed to a job's prescribed duties – and claims that in this way a general and universal pay structure can be established which is both fair and equitable. He has observed that people have ideas about what constitutes fair pay for work and that these unconsciously held norms for various types and levels of work correlate highly with their respective time spans. The theory has attracted a great deal of interest in various parts of the world, but applications have been limited. The idea of a common yardstick applicable to the evaluation of jobs of all types and levels has been taken up by Patterson (1972) who chides economists for their failure adequately to explain differentials and attributes poor industrial relations mainly to the lack of a coherent theory for determining relative differences in pay. Patterson proposes a scheme which uses a single factor, namely, decision-making which he argues is a common criterion for all jobs and has universality. The Patterson scheme of decision-banding is based on this premise.

Participative job evaluation schemes become increasingly popular with the general trend towards a higher level of industrial democracy, and are based on the idea that consensus is at the very root of acceptability. Various means have been harnessed to develop as broad a cross-section of opinion as possible, both in structuring and in applying certain techniques.

Finally, because of the effort and complexity of installing job evaluation in a large-scale organization, and the specialist expertise which may be required, many employers choose to contract the operation out to a firm of management consultants. Some of these firms have developed particular approaches of their own, e.g. Hay–MSL 'Guide-Chart Method' concentrating on know-how, acceptability and problem-solving, and linking the scheme with market rates, the Direct Consensus Method of AIC/Incubon, and 'profiling' schemes. (For a fuller discussion of consultancy schemes, see Livy, 1975.)

For the past fifteen years or so, job evaluation in Britain has been increasingly widely practised. Several surveys have been conducted on the extent of its application, reasons for its adoption, and attitudes towards it. These surveys and analyses have at various times been undertaken by government bodies (the National Board for Prices and Incomes, Office of Manpower Economics, the Pay Board) and by professional bodies (the Institute of Personnel Management and the British Institute of Management).

In 1974 the Pay Board reported on problems of pay relativities in Britain and noted 'evidence of a substantial increase in the number of employees covered by job evaluation schemes'. The Report further went on to highlight a move towards introducing job evaluation in a 'participative' manner, especially where the employees affected were formerly represented by trade unions. 'It is now more usual for workers' representatives to be fully involved in the detailed workings of a scheme and the operation for it – and possibly even in the choice of the scheme to be introduced. Management consultants with experience in introducing job evaluation often state a preference for active union involvement and they even prescribe it as a condition for success for groups with substantial union membership.' The Board reported that job evaluation had become an accepted part of collective bargaining in many sectors of the economy, mainly through the adoption of job evaluation by previously existing bargaining groups but also, to a lesser extent, as part of a major restructuring of the payment system. In schemes for manual workers, the job population covered is normally within the boundaries of a negotiating unit although the Board drew attention to the fact that these boundaries have sometimes been changed by the introduction of 'plant-wide bargaining'. Although in such schemes practice seems to devolve on paying a single rate of basic pay for each job grade, flexibility was observed, in that it was found to be comparatively rare for actual earnings to reflect only the basic rate for the job; other elements were often included which reflected individual performance, overtime, length of service, etc. Similar flexibility was noted in respect of job evaluation schemes for managerial employees who although often covered by the common scheme for management in all establishments, had a 'range' of pay attached to a grade, so that rather than a single 'rate for the job' an individual manager's salary could be adjusted to reflect his performance and the local circumstances.

In 1976 the Institute of Personnel Management published a survey of job evaluation practice in 213 organizations in Britain. 78.8 per cent of respondents were using job evaluation, and 4.6 per cent were about to use it. Only 2.3 per cent had abandoned a scheme (for reasons of conflict or opposition). The reasons most commonly expressed for introducing job evaluation were: to achieve a fair pay structure (94.3 per cent quoted this), to establish a system of job hierarchy (55 per cent of respondents quoted this) – a response particularly prevalent amongst firms employing 500–1000 people. There was an approximately equal frequency of responses (39 per cent each) in respect of three other factors: to attempt to resolve industrial relations problems (especially in engineering); to introduce change in a systematic way; to assist openness in remuneration matters. The overall picture indicated that points rating was the most popular scheme, followed by classification. The Hay–MSL Guide Chart Profile had assumed significant popularity, more than any other consultancy-designed scheme to date. More white collar employees were covered by job evaluation than manual (e.g. 84.3 per cent of clerks, 70.2 per cent of managers, 42.1 per cent of skilled operators); and that many companies had more than one type of scheme in operation.

There was a discernible move towards a participative approach. In 37 per cent of cases responsibility for carrying out the job evaluation exercise was conducted by a joint management and union committee; as compared with 31.4 per cent by the personnel department alone, and 26.9 per cent by personnel and line management jointly. The move towards participation was pronounced in firms with more than 1000 employees. On the whole, satisfaction was expressed with job evaluation, 71.9 per cent did not intend to make any changes. Related difficulties were seen to be the problem of divorcing jobs from job holders, and the maintenance of differentials during a period of inflation. 32 per cent thought it increased the pay bill. 35 per cent thought it would decrease industrial relations problems.

In 1979 the British Institute of Management reported on a similar survey of 236 companies with similar findings. 64 per cent of companies operated one or more schemes; 49 per cent of them had been introduced in the previous five years.

The reasons for increased interest in job evaluation are various. People are constantly looking for new ways of dealing with an old problem – fair pay. Technological change creates new jobs and the demise of others; new and appropriate pay scales have therefore to be found (Grayson, 1982). The size of organizations is a key factor. Jobs which are organizationally related must be interrelated in other ways too – a system of equitable payment is seen as desirable and an aid to job mobility and career structure, and the lack of it as a cause for concern.

Incomes Data Services (1979) noted several reasons for establishing job evaluation as:

1 demands for a rational grading structure
2 union recognition
3 greater participation
4 single status
5 sex discrimination and equal pay
6 decay of old systems
7 technological change
8 mobility, redeployment and staff transfers.

Equal pay and job evaluation

The 1970s also saw the incorporation (by implication) of job evaluation into government legislation. The Equal Pay Act 1970 came into force in 1975 and laid down that 'employers give equal treatment as regards terms and conditions of employment to men and to women . . . for men and women employed on like work . . . and for men and women employed on work rated as equivalent'. No doubt this Act of Parliament stimulated job evaluation in certain areas, although it was still in contravention of the EEC legislation in so far as it did not stipulate the *requirement* of job evaluation, and in due course by 1984 British legislation was amended (Equal Pay (Amendment) Regulations, 1983).

The new regulations make it possible for equal terms and conditions of employment to be enjoyed by people of both sexes if different jobs can be rated as equal in value under a properly constructed, impartial, valid and accurately conducted job evaluation scheme. There are changes in the 'distribution rules' (Thomason, 1980) affecting pay of the two sexes, in particular: gender does not justify differential remuneration; job evaluation plans and procedures should produce results which are non-discriminatory between the sexes. The implication is that traditional 'women's work' is anomalous and should be re-evaluated on unbiased criteria.

Managements are now charged to eliminate any influence of gender upon pay rates and to introduce appropriate job evaluation plans, factors, weightings and mechanisms to achieve this end, together with trained rating panels of both sexes and suitable appeals machinery.

As yet, the situation is fraught with difficulty, uncertainty, and judicial interpretation in Industrial Tribunals. 'The danger in the shortrun is that pressure groups will succeed in their attempts to make job evaluation carry the whole burden of removing sex discrimination in work. Unfortunately, no official guidance on the form of job evaluation plan which the expert should use in making such assessments, nor on the rigour with which such "expert" judgements have to be made, have so far been made public' (Thomason, 1985), although various recommendations have been put forward (EOC, 1984; Gill and Ungerson, 1984). For further discussion of these issues, see Baroness Seear's comments in Chapters 15 and 17.

Summary and conclusions

In the long run, the extent to which job evaluation will be applied depends on the balance of advantage and disadvantage which it is seen to afford. These differ between organizations, industries and cultures. Job evaluation is logical, and attempts to be an objective method of ranking jobs relative to each other. It aims to remove inequities in existing wage/salary structures and to determine sound and consistent differentials within an organization.

The same aims apply in dealing with the problems posed by the creation of new jobs. Job evaluation provides structure and form into which these jobs may be fitted. It seeks to provide a yardstick against which pay claims and/or work content can be judged. It aims to produce a rational, simplified pay structure. Job evaluation may replace antecedent factors which have arisen in the past and which now serve to distort pay scales and it may replace *ad hoc* arrangements occurring in less systematic procedures.

The approaches may be quantitative or non-quantitative, and the points method is the most common. Job evaluation may facilitate the process of negotiation through its aim to clarify ideas about job content and job worth. It is impersonal, concentrating on the job and not the job holder. It attempts to apply uniform standards and is based on the principle of fairness. In its primary aim to collect information about jobs and in the process of job analysis, it may secondarily reveal information which could be used for the improvement of other areas of personnel management, for example, in selection, training, transfer and promotion procedures on the basis of comparative job requirements, and may open up possibilities for job restructuring and job redesign.

Although there are many ways of applying job evaluation in a flexible manner, rapid changes in technology and in the supply and demand for particular skills raise problems of adjustment which may need further study. However logical and consistent a system may be, account has to be taken of limits to political possibility of changing apparently illogical elements in an existing wage structure. Certainly external rates may have to be paid to 'hiring jobs' whether they are compatible with the job evaluation system or not; traditional relationships, however inconsistent, cannot always be altered.

Job evaluation does not provide a complete answer to the pay problem. It has nothing to say about absolute levels of remuneration and little about the size of differentials appropriate to the evaluated job structure. Such matters must be inferred or negotiated. In practice, the process of job rating is to some extent arbitrary because few of the factors can be measured with great accuracy. The process can certainly not be regarded as 'scientific' and can be considered 'objective' at best in the sense that under ideal conditions it is free from deliberate bias. All that can be expected to emerge from the process is a well-considered and honest, but basically subjective, rank order of jobs.

Job evaluation takes a long time to install, requires specialized technical expertise and may be quite costly. The drawing up of job descriptions tends to formalize job contents which may lead to abuse and restrictive practices. Trade unions often regard job evaluation with suspicion and in some cases with hostility. The reliance of job evaluation on jobs, rather than people, is often regarded as an insufficient ground on which to base pay policy. Allowance needs to be made for personal contributions.

A citation of aims and limitations inevitably produces a mixed box of tricks. All job evaluation schemes require to be monitored, reviewed and updated on a regular basis. It should be apparent that job evaluation can offer a lot of common sense. It is in any case only a constituent element of wage and salary administration.

Discussion questions

1   How far is it true to say that job evaluation is based on logic, equity and justice?
2   Can you really compare the content of unlike jobs?
3   Compare the advantages and disadvantages of the main job evaluation methods.
4   Can job evaluation create rigidity?
5   How important should *job content* be in forming the basis for remuneration? Should the personal qualities of job incumbents be ignored or compensated in a remuneration plan?
6   What improvements would you be looking for in new methods of job evaluation?

References

ANDERSON, C. H. and CORTS, D. B. (1973), 'Development of a framework for a factor-ranking benchmark system of job evaluation', US Civil Service Commission: Personnel Research and Development Center, Project 6B132A.

BRITISH INSTITUTE OF MANAGEMENT (1970), *Job Evaluation*, Management Publications Ltd, London.

BRITISH INSTITUTE OF MANAGEMENT (1979), 'Job evaluation', *Management Survey Report No. 46*, London.

BRITISH INSTITUTE OF MANAGEMENT (1983), *National Management Survey*.

BRITISH STANDARDS INSTITUTION (1979), *Glossary of Terms Used in Work Study and Organisation and Methods*, London.

BROWN, W. (1973), *The Earnings Conflict*, Heinemann, London.

ELIZUR, D. (1980), *Job Evaluation: a Systematic Approach*, Gower, London.

EQUAL OPPORTUNITIES COMMISSION (1984), *Job Evaluation Schemes Free of Sex Bias*, EOC, Manchester.

EQUAL PAY ACT 1970, Section I: 'Requirement of equal treatment for men and women in the same employment', HMSO, London.

EQUAL PAY (AMENDMENT) REGULATIONS 1983 (S.I. 1983 No. 1794), HMSO, London.

GILL, D. and UNGERSON, B. (1984), *Equal Pay: the Challenge of Equal Value*, Institute of Personnel Management, London.

GRAYSON, D. (1982), *Job Evaluation and Changing Technology*, Dept. of Employment Work Research Unit, Occasional Paper 23.

INCOMES DATA SERVICES (1979), *Guide to Job Evaluation*, March 1979.

INTERNATIONAL LABOUR ORGANISATION (1986), *Job Evaluation*, ILO, Geneva.

JAQUES, E. (1964), *Time-Span Handbook*, Heinemann, London.

JAQUES, E. (1967), *Equitable Payment: a General Theory of Work, Differential Payment and Individual Progress* (Pelican Library of Business Management), Penguin Books, Harmondsworth.

JAQUES, E. (1970), *Work, Creativity and Social Justice*, Heinemann, London.

KRESS, A. L. (1939), 'How to rate jobs and men', *Factory Management*, **97**, 60–65.

LANGSNER, A. and ZOLLITSCH, H. G. (1967), *Wage and Salary Administration*, South-Western Publishing Co., Cincinnati, Ohio.

LIVY, B. (1975), *Job Evaluation: a Critical Review*, Allen and Unwin, London.

PATTERSON, T. T. (1972), *Job Evaluation, Vol. 1, A New Method*, Business Books, London.

PAY BOARD (1974), 'Problems of pay relativities', Advisory Report No. 2, Cmnd 5535, HMSO, London.

SMITH, I. (1983), *The Management of Remuneration*, Institute of Personnel Management, London.

THAKUR, M. and GILL, D. (1976), 'Job evaluation in practice', *IPM Information Report No. 21*, Institute of Personnel Management, London.

THOMASON, G. F. (1980), *Job Evaluation: Objectives and Methods*, Institute of Personnel Management, London.

THOMASON, G. F. (1985), *Job Evaluation and Equal Pay: a Supplement*, Institute of Personnel Management, London.

CHAPTER 8

Wage and salary administration

by Bryan Livy

Wages

The term 'wage structure' refers to the rate of remuneration paid for various jobs usually within an individual firm or plant. The wage structure must be 'rational' in so far as it is consistent with managerial and economic objectives, and at the same time, secures and maintains an adequate supply of labour. A wage structure must also be 'equitable' particularly with regard to relevant rates for other jobs prevailing within the same enterprise, and to an extent also with external rates.

The term 'wages' has traditionally been applied to the pay packet of manual, blue-collar workers, and the term 'salary' (derived from the Latin 'salt money') to flat-rate payments made to non-manual white-collar workers. These distinctions today are somewhat blurred, particularly with 'staff status' agreements and monthly payroll budgeting, but the mechanism for determining wages and salaries may often be different.

If one looks at the external aspects of a firm's wage or salary structure, it is clear that rates paid cannot differ unduly from those paid for comparable jobs in certain other firms. If levels of remuneration are low by comparison with other employers, it will be impossible to recruit qualified workers and the low level of wages or salaries might engender low morale, excessive labour turnover and high training and recruiting costs. There is, then, the idea of a 'market rate'. It is also clear that wages or salaries should not be too high compared with other employers competing in the same labour market, for this would be uneconomic, unless the firm in question deliberately sets out to be a 'wage leader' (which might make good sense in a tight labour market or in a highly professional, career-orientated firm).

There are significant relationships between rates paid by an individual firm and its external environment – these relationships tend to set a lower limit below which firms cannot vary greatly in fixing their own pay scales, although they do not dictate the precise rates which the firm should pay for each of its own jobs. A firm has a range of discretion within which it can fix its rates, and this discretion is wider for some jobs than for others, since labour is not homogeneous nor is the demand for it consistent. Relative scarcities and supplies of particular skills may appear on the labour market at different points in time. Since a firm's wage policy aims to recruit and retain suitable personnel, much depends on the mobility of wage earners in response to wage differentials. Such a response varies according to attitudes, loyalties, and affiliations, reluctance to move, pension rights and other personal considerations which cannot always be measured by purely economic criteria. The actual possibility of changing one's employment is often limited. Since most employers fill higher paid jobs by internal promotion rather than by external recruitment, the number of 'hiring' jobs may be both limited and confined to the lower end of the pay scale. These considerations of labour mobility may help to illustrate how relationships between external conditions and the rate that the firm has to pay may vary between different groups of jobs.

Where there is a collective agreement which sets out minimum wage rates for a whole industry, an employer cannot pay less than these rates. Indeed, there may also be understandings or agreements between employers as regards maximum rates. And again, rates fixed by collective agreement may in turn reflect relationships with a wage rate paid in other industries, and so on. In the UK, pay determination is dominated by collective bargaining and over three-quarters of its manual workers are covered by some sort of collective agreement. It should be added that the extensive involvement of shop stewards in the pay-fixing process contributes to a wide variety and fragmentation of bargaining arrangements. (See Paul Roots' chapters – especially Chapter 11.)

Wage earners seem to attach great importance to what they regard as an 'equitable' wage structure, judged largely by comparative job content, qualifications, skills, conditions and so forth. They are strongly inclined to compare their present with their former job and their own wages with those of others in terms of comparative reward and prestige. They often resent wage differentials to the advantage of others if such differences cannot be justified by differences in job content or for other good reason. Wage earners also look for a 'steady' wage.

Wages and salaries are at the same time both a cost and an investment. Their costs are reflected in the cost of the final product or service. They are an investment in that they represent money spent on a factor of production – labour – in an attempt to earn a dividend. The constituents of a remuneration policy must therefore embrace such crucial factors as the objectives of the organization, its finances, cash flow and profitability, the state of the labour market, expected demand and supply of various types of labour, any government regulations on pay, anticipated contraction or expansion of the organization, as well as the personal aspirations and inclinations of the workforce. In so far as the organization wishes to survive, it will normally be expected to balance the books and make a profit. In such circumstances, economic considerations may well assume prime importance.

However, it is not only from the point of view of cost control and auditing that pay administration ought to be concerned. There are not only economic factors but also motivational, organizational and environmental ones. An example of a practical approach to a complex situation has been illustrated by a study (Lupton and Gowler, 1970) which drew attention to the wide range of factors which have to be taken into account in selecting a wage payment system. These include product markets, labour markets, technology, and the attitudes and expectations of trade unions and work people. The basic question is: 'What combination of organization, environment and payment system is best fitted to a given set of objectives?' Pay is theoretically inseparable from other organizational variables.

So practical wage fixing is not simply a matter of mathematics or precision engineering; the objectives may be variable, and the processes of wage or salary administration can be carried out in a very flexible way. Precisely because of this plasticity does it become possible to accommodate both the internal and external requirements of a firm's remuneration structure. Normal practice is to assume that people do work very largely for money. Reward systems are designed to compensate for the level of work done, but in addition, for performance, age, length of service, as a means of motivation, to protect employees against external inflationary pressures, and to pass on to them some of the increases in company profitability. Modern employment markets do not function like stock or commodity exchanges where small changes in supply and demand have immediate effects on price. Wage differences among firms, and industries and groups of occupations are not totally independent of differences in the supply of and demand for their various types of labour, but neither are they determined exclusively by economic factors. On variations of pay between jobs, rather than rates for the same job, it has been observed (Robinson, 1970) that such patterns of differentials are quite unalike even in plants in the same industry. A person with a certain skill can be *relatively* highly paid in one firm and *relatively* poorly paid in another. Absolute pay levels normally depend more on an individual firm's policy than on 'market' conditions external to it. If this is so, is the local labour market a myth? Dual labour market theory (Craig *et al.*, 1982) postulates both a primary and secondary labour market. In primary labour markets, jobs are well paid, and employees highly qualified, skilled, productive, and much sought after. In secondary markets, the reverse situation applies – poor conditions, poorly trained or uneducated workers, employment instability – populated largely by the disadvantaged groups.

A further interesting distinction drawn by the previous Pay Board (1974) is between 'differentials' and 'relativities'. *Differentials* were defined as referring to pay differences within a single negotiating group. *Relativities* were defined as relationships between pay and jobs, etc. in different negotiating units, either external (as between those in different plants, companies, or industries), or internal (as between those in different negotiating units within the same plant, part of plant, company, etc. under a single employer). These distinctions have practical implications. In the case of differentials there is usually some negotiating mechanism for dealing with them. In the case of relativities no such mechanism may exist. The conclusion to which one is inevitably drawn, is that internal consistencies are easier to achieve than external ones.

Management needs to staff the enterprise economically. Employees seek a bargain between their contribution and the reward the employer is prepared to offer – the effort bargain. 'Explicitly or implicitly all employers are in a bargaining situation with regard to payment systems' (Armstrong, 1977). But many payment systems are chaotic. Maybe surprisingly, employers often have no clear idea what on earth various remuneration packages are supposed to represent, nor precisely why they are paying the wages they are.

When it comes to the problem of selecting an appropriate payments system, management is faced with making a reasoned selection from available alternatives, devising the detailed procedures, methods of operation, and implementing the decision. A great variety of wage payment systems are commonly in general use. Individual payment systems can be divided into three main categories: time rates, payment by results, and measured day work. There are also group schemes. Each category includes a number of variants.

TIME-RATE

Time-rate, also known as day-rate, or hourly rate, is the system under which operators are simply paid a predetermined rate per week, day or hour for the actual time they have worked. The basic rate is fixed by negotiation, reference to local rates, or by job evaluation, and it only varies with time, not with output or performance. Time-rates are most appropriate where it is impossible or undesirable to apply a payments by results system, or as an alternative to an unsatisfactory piecework system. The advantages of time-rate to employees is that wages are stable and predictable. Managements may argue that they do not proffer sufficient motivation, but in the UK, time-rates form the most common payment system covering some two-thirds of manual workers. The prime consideration is not so much the time worked as the value to the organization of the job done. Time-rates are administratively simple and facilitate labour cost control. The tendency now is for manual workers to have wage rates expressed more in weekly than in hourly terms. Overtime rates are also in common use, and again are negotiated on a time basis.

FINANCIAL INCENTIVES

The choice between financial incentives and psychological motivation has been the subject of much controversy. One thing is clear: it is dangerous to generalize about motivation (see Chapter 19). We should not forget that the reason for introducing an incentive scheme is to motivate people to work harder and better. But it is not feasible to design a comprehensive scheme to satisfy all situations. Factors which motivate people vary with the type of organization, the type of work and the particular job. No form of motivational device will have the same appeal for all workers. The idea of using money as an inducement is not new. Incentive payment schemes date back as far as the seventeenth century. In the early part of this century a number of famous schemes were adopted, by Taylor, Halsey-Weir, Bedeaux. Many of them became highly complicated. One of the main criteria for a good incentive scheme is that it should be understandable, be easily reckonable, and be seen to have a direct link with effort. Financial incentive schemes reward people through increased payment, so the question of calculation always arises, and along with it, questions of measurement and administration. The best incentive schemes are those which are simple, direct and quick to operate. Incentives have traditionally been offered for extra effort or performance. A priori, any incentive scheme should be self-financing.

Under a 'group' incentive scheme, bonuses are paid to the members working within a particular group. Bonuses may be shared out equally, or on a proportional basis. Such bonuses may be paid either according to output achieved or time saved. Clearly group schemes are most appropriate where people have to work together, where teamwork has to be encouraged, or where individual performance cannot be easily measured.

Payment by results

Payment by results systems relate to the pay in whole or in part received by a worker according to the amount and level of output. *Straight piecework* systems may be applied where work is of a purely individual nature and a uniform price per unit may be paid. Examples are now rare, e.g. casual fruit pickers. Most piecework systems provide a minimum earnings level or fall-back rate – e.g. under a 'time-allowed' system if an employee completes the work in less time than planned, he or she is still paid for the original time and thus able to obtain increased earnings. Normally, standard values are set to form the performance scale of a PBR system (e.g. the BSI scale of 75/100 where normal effort is deemed to exist at 75 and standard effort (with incentive) at 100).

There are also *differential piecework* systems under which the wage/cost per unit is adjusted in relation to output, and gains may be shared between the company and the employee. These schemes operate under various names, such as 'premium bonus schemes'.

In the UK, payment by results schemes contribute to the earnings of some 44 per cent of manual men and 34 per cent of manual women. Individual piecework is tending to give way to group incentive schemes. The variable component of wages is tending to diminish. Normally, of course, PBR systems must be based on work study, although there have been some experiments with incentives based on profits. The use of PBR has increased in the public services (gas, electricity, local authorities, health service) in recent years in an attempt to increase labour productivity, but declined elsewhere – in motor car assembly, transport and shipping.

Schemes which link payment with output are particularly susceptible to 'wage drift' deriving from increased automation, the 'creep' of upward negotiations, and the 'ratchet' effect of successive higher incentive payments with each pay round.

Added value

There are several incentive schemes based on the added value principle, but the two classic schemes are the Rucker Plan and the Scanlon Plan. Under the Rucker Plan a standard of productivity is set in relation to past achievements but with the intention of providing an incentive to improve upon that level. The proportion of earnings to added value over the period in question becomes the norm against which all future performance is measured. Improvements in productivity are held in a fund, payable to employees at various intervals – provided there is a gain on standards. The Scanlon Plan is more of a social process, under which suggestions for the improvement of productivity are considered and a formula is agreed for sharing the proceeds. Apart from these two schemes, there are many variations on this theme.

Measured daywork

By measured daywork an employee's pay is fixed on the understanding that specified levels of performance will be maintained. Pay does not fluctuate with short-term variations in performance. Measured daywork (MDW) is a generic term for pay systems which fall in the middle ground between incentive and high daily rate schemes. Since the pay of an employee is fixed on the understanding that his performance will be maintained, this level of performance is known as the 'incentive level' and is calculated in advance. Measured day work relies on work measurement to define required perform-ance and to monitor actual levels. Management is committed to a pre-determined bonus. If desired targets are not met, the scheme needs to be revised. In short, MDW is an attempt to remove some of the disadvantages of PBR whilst maintaining a high degree of effort. See the section on wage structures in Chapter 10.

Merit-rating schemes

Under merit-rating schemes, bonuses are paid to workers in respect of personal qualities, e.g. timekeeping, reliability, efficiency. Points are awarded by supervisors for any qualities selected as being relevant to the job in question. A bonus is paid above the normal rate according to the number of points scored. Merit rating is therefore based on subjective assessment. But there is renewed interest in performance-based rewards for white-collar staff (see later).

Productivity agreements

Productivity agreements, not now so popular as in the 1960s, are still to be found, under which management and unions agree to changes in working practices, hours, manning levels, etc., leading to economies or higher productivity. Such agreements stem from attempts jointly to resolve manpower deployment and the introduction of technological change. In return the employer agrees to higher levels of pay or other benefits. Normally these agreements are negotiated as a 'package deal'.

Profit sharing

Co-partnership and employee share-owning schemes take many forms, but are all aimed at extending share ownership into the employee population. A company may offer its shares to employees on favourable terms, thereby allowing employees to buy a stake in the company. Traditionally share offers were only offered to senior management, but in recent years a number of schemes have been extended to cover all employees. The motivational value of profit-sharing schemes must be dubious since the rewards are sometimes long delayed (deferred income) and not necessarily related to individual effort. However, many employees obviously value share options as a form of savings or investment. Many schemes are an acclaimed success. The TUC takes a fairly hard line against this policy, seeing it as irrelevant to the real issues of industrial democracy and placing an unfair advantage on workers who happen to be in the private sector.

Under profit-sharing schemes employees may be entitled to receive, usually on an annual basis, a share of the firm's profit as an addition to their normal remuneration. The scale of payment will depend upon the level of profitability. The rate at which bonuses are paid are usually expressed as a percentage of an employee's existing salary or wage.

Cashless pay

Statutory provisions relating to wages are contained in the Truck Acts 1831–1940 as amended by the Payment of Wages Act 1960. The Acts determine how payments should be made and what deductions may be sought and claimed. But the Acts themselves only apply to manual workers except domestic servants and so all other employees' wages and deductions therefrom are governed solely by the contract of employment. In 1983, the Government announced its intention to repeal the Truck Acts and other related legislation and issued a consultative document discussing a move towards cashless pay, and legislation in 1986. (See pages 324–5.)

Salary administration

Salary administration refers to the determination of appropriate levels of remuneration for staff employees according to their grade or job, coupled with a consideration of individual merit and performance and tempered by company profitability – 'the process by which staff pay levels are determined, monitored, progressed and controlled' (Armstrong and Murlis, 1980). It does not refer to the administration of the payroll which is usually a financial or accounting function.

Most salary payment systems are relatively straightforward. The amounts paid are determined on an annual basis and normally divided into twelve equal monthly instalments. Bonuses, commission, fringe benefits, might be superimposed, but are generally regarded as separate items.

With an increasing proportion of employees attaining 'staff status' there is a corresponding enlightenment on the part of salary earners in regard to opportunities, comparabilities in earnings, and higher expectations. As well as being paid for the work carried out on a day to day basis, the salaried employee expects that as a reward for his loyalty and long service to his employer, his salary will show a steady increase over the course of time. These factors bring pressure for more rational and logical systems of salary administration concurrent with pressures for more open management.

Salary costs for the employing organization, already large, are an increasing element of the total payroll budget. Salary policy demands attention. Several techniques and subordinate policies combine to contribute to an overall successful policy for salary administration – including job evaluation, performance appraisal and review systems, career progression policies, salary budgeting and forward costing.

Salary administration itself is not something that can be looked at in isolation. Salary administration is an attempt to achieve the objectives formulated in a salary *policy*, which itself ought ideally to be a plan – not simply to pay fair and equitable salaries, but to relate and reconcile career aspirations of employees in terms of current and potential earnings, and personal commitment to total organizational objectives. A host of variables is involved. The broad aim is subordinate to the generally acceptable principle that a comprehensive manpower policy should be a constituent part of corporate strategy.

Budgeting now occupies an important position in the design of most organizational systems. Salary administration is no exception. Budgets are tools in the management process linked to overall corporate planning. Proper use should be made of salary budgeting as an instrument of control. First, the budgets should be built up on a resource basis – including manpower forecasts – and not simply on the assumption that the salary bill will rise by a given percentage per annum. Secondly, actual expenditure should be checked monthly or quarterly against forecast expenditure, and the reasons for major discrepancies investigated. Manpower is a resource like any piece of capital equipment. Whilst companies normally analyse in detail projected returns from capital expenditure, far less attention seems to be applied to forecasting the development and decay of the workforce. A satisfactory administration of the salary system within the manpower plan, should be able to project forward costs of manpower resources, having taken into account promotion, transfers, redundancies, retirements, recruitments, base salaries and fringe benefits, and performance awards. Particularly in industries where staff costs are a high proportion of total costs, such a system is likely to contribute to the accuracy of forecasts of company performance.

The objectives of a pay policy have been summarized by Angela Bowey (1980):

1   To attract and retain staff of sufficient calibre and number to achieve present and future objectives
2   To reward staff according to their contribution
3   To encourage staff to identify their interests with those of the business
4   To motivate suitable staff to accept greater responsibilities and to improve performance
5   To determine fair differentials between jobs of varying responsibility and complexity
6   To ensure that the company gets value for money
7   To provide a framework for a career structure
8   To ensure that employees' living standards are maintained and that earnings are stable.

Planning a salary structure involves a number of interrelated activities which we will look at in turn:

1   Market rates and salary surveys
2   The determination of a salary policy trend line
3   Job grading
4   Spread of range and overlap
5   Salary progressions
6   Maturity curves
7   Anomalies
8   Control mechanisms
9   Implementation.

MARKET RATES AND SALARY SURVEYS

The necessity for maintaining equitable internal differentials through a job evaluation exercise and an acceptable salary scheme must not obscure the fact that some attention must be paid to the 'going rate' for any particular job. The salary structure chosen must be roughly in line with the market, otherwise high staff turnover or dissatisfaction is likely (conversely, companies could be paying too much for their manpower).

Market rates are ultimately the standards against which a salary policy must be compared. Two sorts of problems may well arise. Firstly, market rates may mean that some jobs must be paid in excess of any job evaluation rating, so that exceptions have to be made. Secondly, market rates may change rapidly. This makes a legitimate claim on flexibility, so schemes should be able to accommodate some changes in these rates without requiring complete overhaul, and only minor modification to either the salary structure or the evaluation scheme.

Before deciding any kind of salary policy, a preliminary survey should be made of comparable rates for similar work paid by other organizations. The purpose of a *salary survey* is to identify analogous jobs in the outside labour market and their 'going' or market rate, in order to achieve *external* consistency (i.e. between the organization's own salary levels and those of other firms with which the organization wishes to be compared). Salary surveys can provide data on current salary ranges. It is important that surveys are sufficiently representative of the companies within the industry, and a range of jobs, functions and locations. The information collected is only meaningful for comparative purposes if the jobs surveyed externally are closely related in content to those for which we wish to find answers in pay terms. A careful study therefore requires detailed job descriptions and well-defined levels of responsibility and other occupational requirements. Salary surveys can be extensive, examining a company's whole pay structure, or they may more narrowly be concerned with the pay and conditions of a particular group or groups of employees.

Arrangements for establishing market rates are often informal. Communication may be made with other companies, particularly those which compete in the same labour market. Salary survey 'clubs' are sometimes formed, making an interchange of comparisons using the club member companies' own job descriptions. In this way maybe a dozen or so organizations exchange salary information on a regular basis.

Press advertisements and salaries quoted by recruitment agencies are other sources of information, as can be such publications as *Incomes Data Services*, *Industrial Relations Review and Report* and the Department of Employment's *Gazette*, indicating trends in earnings. Occasional surveys are conducted by trade unions and professional institutions for their own members.

There are in addition many, more specific, published surveys. General surveys such as the Inbucon/AIC survey of executive salaries and fringe benefits, various national management salary surveys, e.g. BIM/REL *National Management Survey*, the Institute of Administrative Management's *Clerical Salaries Analysis*, and those produced by Management Centre Europe, or Hay–MSL and are based on information collected from a large number of participating organizations. Other sources are Computer Economics Ltd and Reward Regional Surveys Ltd. Information can be obtained from a number of sources, and most employers utilize quite a number of surveys. There is bound to be some conflicting evidence and maybe no clear market mode.

There is no such thing as *the* market rate for a job. All that salary surveys can do is to provide a broad indication. Data on salaries is usually presented in a way which shows median salary and some indication of the dispersion around this figure. The median is the central point of the pay range, and from this fact it follows that 50 per cent of the jobs in the survey will be paid more than the median and 50 per cent of the jobs will be paid less. Further detail may also show figures for the upper and lower quartiles. The upper quartile is the point above which the top 25 per cent are paid and the lower quartile is the point below which 25 per cent of the jobs are paid.

Published survey data are only of valid utility if it is possible to relate job titles in the survey to the jobs in one's own organization. The data need to be accurate and relevant, i.e. drawn from a large and reasonably representative sample. Firms supplying information to the survey's organizers have to relate their jobs to a series of standardized job titles or descriptions. This can often mean that interpretation is hedged with difficulty and comparisons based on approximation. For this reason, companies may wish to conduct their own survey, or commission management consultants to do it for them.

Salary surveys provide guidelines on market rates. Organizations must decide where they wish to fit into the pattern with regard to the salary levels they wish to pay – their own 'market posture'. Organizations wishing to stay ahead of the market will gear their salaries to the upper quartile, others will equate closer to the median. Thus, the salary policy of any individual company will show some relationship, although it may not be closely tied, between market rates and the midpoint of their own salary ranges.

THE SALARY POLICY TREND LINE

Let us assume that jobs have been evaluated by a points rating system (as described in Chapter 7). Having performed our own job evaluation exercise and obtained notional ideas about market rates from external salary surveys, the initial stages for the design of a salary structure can be described as follows.

The first step involves plotting a scattergraph of jobs with known salaries (either existing salaries or market rate salaries for benchmark jobs) on the vertical axis and evaluated points ratings on the horizontal axis, as in Fig. 8.1.

We than draw the line of best fit through the scatter either by visual inspection or by the statistical technique of 'least squares' to indicate the salary trend line, as in Fig. 8.2. This trend line should show a positive correlation between job scores and pay rates. However, the *slope* of the curve (i.e. the average rate at which pay increases as jobs increase in evaluated points) can be adjusted as a result of negotiation or organizational policy. Even the position of the schedule itself can be shifted according to desired pay policy. The graph is just a worksheet on which to experiment and come to decisions about pay.

Using selected benchmark jobs for which we know market rates (let us take median and upper quartiles) we can superimpose these data on to our

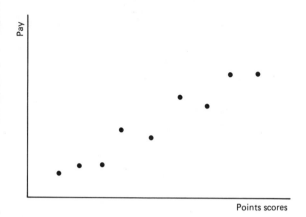

Fig. 8.1   *Scattergraph of points-rated jobs with known salaries*

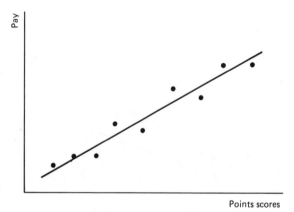

Fig. 8.2   *Trend line through scatter*

existing current trend lines (as in Fig. 8.3) to indicate the relative relationship between internal pay and outside pay.

We must then select and adopt our market posture, as indicated by our intended new salary policy line in Fig. 8.4. We base our design for the salary structure on the proposed salary policy line itself. For simplicity, the salary policy line has been shown as linear. In practice, it is more likely to be exponential, i.e. it will curve upward cumulatively, since grade ranges and salary scales tend to broaden in the higher echelons of the management hierarchy.

JOB GRADING

Any organized salary administration system is dependent on some sort of job grading. Most people have an idea of the way in which increasing status in the organization is associated with pay. The more sophisticated job evaluation schemes aim to put this grading on a rational, explicit basis, by enumerating

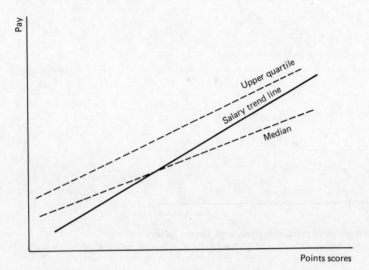

Fig. 8.3   *Salary trend line in relation to upper quartile and median market rates*

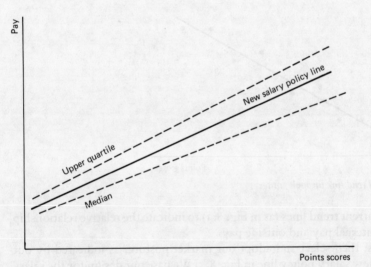

Fig. 8.4   *Selected salary policy line in relation to upper quartile and median market rates*

precisely the criteria by which jobs are to be judged, and scoring each job against these criteria.

The end result of the job evaluation exercise is the classification in some order of every relevant job in the organization. To different levels in this hierarchy, different salary levels will be allocated, in a way depending on the type of salary structure chosen.

When completed, the job evaluation scheme will have ranked or rated every job to be included in the salary scheme. The next operation to be performed with these rated jobs will be that of grading, i.e. subdividing the total range of jobs into groups so that jobs of a similar value will be allocated to a particular grade. The underlying assumption is that all jobs allocated to a particular grade are of broadly equal value.

A decision must be made about the number of grades. Grades must be established according to the proposed organizational structure, or to provide a linear or exponential progression in an individual's projected earnings over time, or to fit market rates.

The number of grades an organization will need will depend on its size and the variations in the levels of jobs involved. Small organizations may need no more than four or five grades, whilst larger ones may have as many as a dozen. Current trends are towards compact grade structures (i.e. fewer grades) to facilitate communications and shorter chains of command.

From the scatterplot, and from our intimate knowledge of the occupational groups represented, various natural grades, or felt-fair divisions may become apparent. If not, they must be determined by more arbitrary means such as splitting up the continuum of points scored into manageable groups or grades according to administrative convenience, or allocating progressive proportions of score ranges to successive grades. Alternatively, taking the shape and slope of our salary policy trend line as the basis, grades can be allocated according to a desired percentage differential between salaries of adjacent grades (see later).

Company practice varies as to the actual number of grades adopted. There should be enough grades to maintain important differentials, but few enough to foster flexibility and permit the rationalization of anomalies.

Although the process of grade demarcation is not scientific and may appear to have arbitrary cut-off points, in practice the translatable effects on an individual's actual salary are modified by the subsequent process of adjusting differentials via variable salary bands for each grade and the use of overlap between them.

For illustration, taking our salary policy trend line in relation to points scores (which are indications of job values), we can divide the structure into grades as in Fig. 8.5. Various trial solutions to the allocation of grades can then be superimposed on the plot and tested.

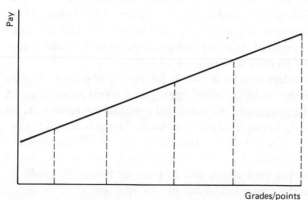

Fig. 8.5 *Structure divided into possible grades*

Finally, a graded salary structure will consist of a sequence of salary ranges for grades, each of which has defined minimum and maximum salaries.

SPREAD OF RANGE AND OVERLAP

The *spread of range* means the width of salary ranges. Commonly this is expressed as a percentage of the grade minimum.

A recent survey by the BIM (1980) confirmed that general policy is to vary widths of salary paybands according to employee category:

15–20 per cent spread of salaries at clerical levels
25–40 per cent at middle management levels
40–60 per cent at senior levels.

The end result is to produce ever widening salary bands. But even a *constant* spread of range (determined as a percentage of range minimum), through the structure would mean that those in higher brackets would receiver bigger ranges.

Overlap between grades is measured by the proportion of a grade which is covered by the next lower grade. This practice acknowledges that there is likely to be some overlap in the relative value of marginal jobs close to grade demarcation lines. Where broadband structures are used, overlap provides the opportunity to reward long-serving members within a particular grade who perhaps for one reason or another will not be promoted to the next grade. In short, overlap measures the extent to which adjacent ranges have salaries in common.

Conventional methodology is to determine salary bands (or widths) as a percentage of the minimum. This practice has grown up where job grading is subject to collective bargaining, and where practice has been to bargain the minimum rate for the grade. The rest of the pay structure is built up from this base. A key point is that differentials between grades become congruent issues. In practice, several variables – minimum rates, overlap and spread of range – inextricably combine to produce a very diffuse area of communality in pay between grades, and which may be difficult to substantiate rationally.

Another slightly different method is therefore worth considering, which does not usurp bargaining strategies and is probably simpler. This is to start out by determining a spread of range for each grade through the construction of *a pay scale around the proposed median salary for each grade*.

Figure 8.6 shows median salaries drawn in for a series of grades. Median salary corresponds to the midpoint of the appropriate points score range. A spread of range may be negotiated or established around the median level for each grade. For example, lower level jobs may have a 10 per cent range (5 per cent above and 5 per cent below the median). We may gradually increase this range as we move up the hierarchy – so that higher level jobs may have, say, a 40 per cent range (20 per cent above and 20 per cent below the median). Flexibility in pay therefore increases as one moves upwards.

To sum up, we can take the midpoint of the score range for each grade as

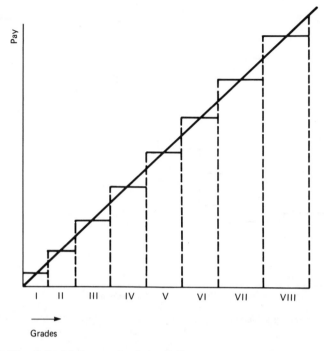

Fig. 8.6 *Median pay levels per grade*

reflecting the median salary which ought to be paid for that grade. Then we must decide on the degree of variance in pay (above and below the median, and to an equal extent in both directions) we wish to see as the basis for forming a salary scale for that particular grade. This also affects the relationship between one grade and another. It simultaneously determines differentials and overlap.

Developing percentage pay scales around median salary levels relating to median points scores means that the operation throughout is more centrally rooted in the job evaluation results than it would be by simply spreading the range upwards as a percentage of minimum for the grade.

Figure 8.7 shows how 'grade boxes' can be established around median pay

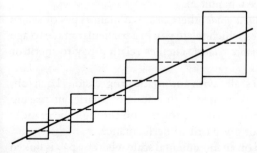

Fig. 8.7 *Grade boxes constructed around median pay levels*

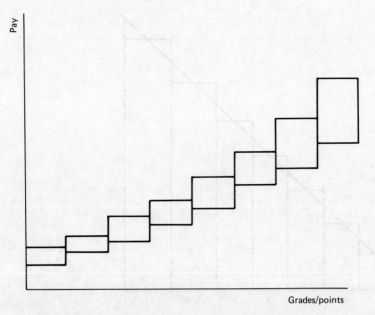

Fig. 8.8   *Segmented series of grade boxes*

levels, and how the spread of range within a grade, and therefore the degree of overlap between grades, may be construed to increase throughout the range.

Finally, a sequential series of grade boxes for the organization as a whole will result as in Fig. 8.8. Each grade box encompasses a range of scores and a corresponding scale of pay. However, a differential series of grade boxes can still be established using minimum rates as the base and the end result may not *seem* so very different.

SALARY PROGRESSIONS

Whatever the salary structure adopted, people will move through a succession of grades over a period of time, in the same way as manpower flows throughout an organization (see Chapter 2).

Looking at movements *within a grade*, there are two main types of salary progression. *Incremental* schemes which relate pay in a particular grade to age or length of service, or *performance related* schemes relating pay to merit or assessment of performance.

Incremental schemes have fixed scales with automatic progression. Each job, or group of jobs in a grade, is associated with a scale of salaries increasing either with age or length of service. Salary progression through the grade is automatic with no allowance for good or bad performance.

A rate for age system is based on an incremental scale whereby pay is linked to the age of individual staff members. Such scales are usually reserved for young employees (normally under 21 years) undergoing training or doing junior clerical, secretarial or other routine work. Pay rises coincide with birthdays, and can cause some administrative problems from an employer's point of view since there is no single annual payround. Although basically inflexible, in some cases they might have merit awards built on to them rather than the criterion of age alone.

Another incremental system is one based on length of service. Once maximum and minimum values are established (i.e. spread of range) the range is then divided into a progression of levels or increments. As in any fixed incremental system, individuals move through the salary range by predetermined stages with increments normally occurring annually. The date selected will normally be an annual review date for all staff simultaneously. Because of its uniformity this kind of system eliminates any kind of bias on the part of management and is preferred by most unions. Salary budgeting is also completely under control (assuming no variation in numbers of staff employed). Incentive, however, is lacking.

Performance-related system

Performance-related systems provide for progression in accordance with an assessment of the merit of the individual and his or her present and future value to the organization.

Such a scheme must contain guidelines as to the appropriate salary levels for particular performance standards, otherwise it becomes difficult to control. Most merit schemes contain certain rules governing individual salary progression.

Merit increments usually vary between 3–10 per cent. In any merit-based system, there will be a position in each range corresponding to a level of acceptable performance. Most firms make this the norm for the job, which all satisfactory employees are expected to reach.

For example, there may be a 'norm' which is a salary level to be reached by, say, average performers after a specified period of time. Progression above this norm would only be on the grounds of above average performance. Those with consistently below average performance ratings would not reach the norm. Many firms use this basic scheme although details vary. The norm *may* be taken as the midpoint of the range. All staff reach this, unless their performance is inadequate. Progression above the norm takes place purely on merit. Alternatively, a norm may be taken lower in the range (often at one-third of the range) and may be guaranteed to be reached in a shorter period. Some firms vary the period of norm attainment according to performance; good performers being able to reach the norm in a shorter period. When there is no norm, control and consistency become hard to achieve.

In performance related schemes, annual increments are triggered by overall assessments of performance. Consecutive increments over time control the rate of progression through a salary range. It might well be that a firm decides to reward performance on a percentage basis (a rate of increase expressed as a percentage of current salary) according to the level of assessment an individual receives. For example:

A = 10%
B = 7%
C = 5%
D = 3% (if any)
E = 0

Staff who continually maintain consistent levels of performance will follow very different salary maturity curves (see later). To prevent an ever-increasing exponential growth in earnings of a salaried employee (and costs to an employer), limits are usually imposed on progression. When an individual reaches the grade maximum, there is an automatic termination of increases until he or she may be promoted into the next grade. Alternatively, there might be a time constraint – the system may be geared to allow progression from minimum to maximum no faster than, say, five years.

Performance-related schemes are fairly strictly controlled by appraisal and restrict flexibility in accommodating other influences on salary levels. The process places heavy demands on the performance appraisal system and accentuates the need for accuracy and consistency. All the problems of superiors' judgement and the need for uniform standards (as discussed in Chapter 6) come home to roost here. The deterministic effects of appraisal on salary can produce variable salary overheads from an employer's point of view and lack of budgetary control, if not managed carefully in accordance with some framework as described.

Neither incremental schemes nor performance-related schemes are often found in their pure form. Incremental schemes usually have some provision for merit, and merit schemes often include an element of automatic salary progression. Nevertheless, the two types reflect different ways in which management may think about pay. The Civil Service, for instance, relates pay very strictly to length of service in many grades, whereas the private sector, for the most part, uses merit schemes. The advantages typically claimed for merit schemes are their high motivational and incentive value and their flexibility. Proponents of incremental schemes stress fairness, administrative simplicity, tight cost control and their proven acceptability to staff. The choice between the two types will probably be influenced by factors other than simply management philosophy, e.g. the nature of the work done, the extent of staff unionization, the need to retain 'high-fliers' and offer competitive incentives, etc. Trade unions favour formalized procedures which counter the arbitrary whims of management.

Hybrid schemes

In between the extremes of pure incremental and pure merit systems lies a whole spectrum of systems having various degrees of flexibility. A few of these will be described. There is of course scope for mixing some features of one scheme with another.

We may have *fixed scales with limited flexibility*, whereby some provision is made for withholding increments or accelerating them, i.e. giving two at a time. Withholding increments is usually rare. Accelerating increments would need to be based on some form of merit assessment. We may also have automatic progression to a specified point in the range, or variable progression.

There is no administrative reason why different schemes cannot be used at different levels in the same organization (at the risk of sacrificing some equity). Typically, supervisory, clerical and lower technical staff will be on a relatively fixed system – since such work may involve little possible performance variation.

Higher up the hierarchy managers may be on 'variable' schemes with salary ranges guaranteeing them a minimum salary but with plenty of scope for merit awards. At the very top of the organization, it is often claimed that 'the job is what the manager makes of it' and that formal job definitions and grading are impossible, making any limits on salaries inappropriate. Pay at these levels is sometimes profit-related.

Banded salary scales

A common way of supplying guidelines for salary progression is to split the range into several bands (*a banded salary scale*). A banded salary structure simply indicates a possible dispersion of performance levels and related pay. Quite commonly, an organization might apply a forced distribution to the bands, i.e. 10 per cent in A, 20 per cent in B, 40 per cent in C, 20 per cent in D, 10 per cent in E (or some other predetermined distribution). A banded salary structure is more mechanistic and inflexible than a scheme which simply operates around a norm for each grade.

Maturity curves

Another way of looking at salary progression is by plotting maturity curves. Such curves form the basis for career progression models for management trainees and/or executives in companies which take an interest in the planned development of their employees. Some firms find it useful to plot graphs of individual salaries against age or length of service or expected rates of career advancement.

Maturity curves, showing planned earnings growth over time, are often relevant for professional, scientific or other highly qualified staff whose work contribution is almost entirely related to their professional capacity, such as research workers in industry. Their starting point is linked to the market rate for their degree or professional qualifications. Salary surveys indicate salaries that people carrying out professional scientific work can expect to reach at certain ages. More than one rate of progression may be provided where it is felt that there should be some scope to reward and encourage individuals. Figure 8.9 illustrates three different starting rates which might be related to

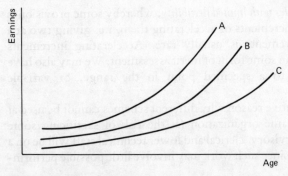

Fig. 8.9   *Maturity curves*

level of qualification (i.e. postgraduate qualifications, first degree, etc.). An individual's progress is not necessarily pre-ordained. The curves illustrate average expected long-term salary trends.

ANOMALIES

Some occupational groups are likely to have market rates clearly above the average for other, similarly evaluated work. Some groups of workers with scarce skills, e.g. computer specialists or medical officers, will *have* to be paid the market rate, irrespective of job evaluation or grading, if their services are to be secured and retained. Although salary ranges with no maximum provide a theoretical capability of accommodating these anomalies, too many will jeopardize the norm and threaten the structure. It is therefore normal for these exceptions to be explicitly recognized as special cases. Various solutions are possible. Separate, temporary norms may be developed, or different factors may be given different weightings in the job evaluation scheme so that anomalies are accounted for at an early stage. The latter solution is more suited to permanent anomalies, although it may give the unions and negotiators the impression that the evaluation scheme is ultimately a manipulative device designed to justify the status quo in pseudo-rational terms. Nevertheless, where large occupational groups of staff are involved, whose position in the evaluated structure is clearly out of alignment (as observed from the scatterplot), varying the weighting may be a workable solution. In this way exceptions need not be actually *created* in the structure.

In some cases, 'personal' rates may be assigned to people who are clearly outside the scope of the salary structure. These should be explicitly recognized as exceptions.

A salary structure of any sort which is superimposed onto the present pattern of salaries will show some people or jobs to be out of line with policies. These are so-called 'red circle' jobs (where payment is above par) and 'blue-circle' jobs (where payment is below par). Any formalized salary system is bound to have to cope with anomalies. There is no overriding reason why actual salary payment should have to correspond to some rational linear or log-linear graphical plot of salaries against job evaluation ratings. Therefore, the presence of anomalies does not mean that excessive amounts of flexibility should be incorporated into the structure; their inevitable presence should have little effect on the *choice* of basic schemes, as such.

With job evaluated schemes anomalies may arise from two causes, (i) their job evaluation rating places them in a grade with a salary range excluding their present salary. Theoretically, a salary structure consisting of the minima only could cope with this situation, since most salaries will be compatible with unlimited ranges, (ii) merit rating which would be used to position people within their grade who cannot justify their present salary, e.g. an individual may be receiving a salary well above the norm for only average work. In this case, as the new structure is introduced, general salary increases are given to people who are at or below the norm and whose position above the norm is justified through good performance. Those people whose salaries are above their proper level, and which are to be reduced, do not receive this general increase. This approach leads to some increase in salary bill. Some reaction from those not receiving the increase is inevitable. Alternatives are for the increase to be held over until a general increase is due anyway, or the introduction of the new salary system can be timed to coincide with such a general increase. As a *laissez-faire* solution, no direct action need be taken at all, allowing promotion flows, retirement and staff turnover eventually to solve the problems.

CONTROL MECHANISMS

Control should be exercised to ensure that every aspect of salary administration conforms to policy. Four aspects of salary control can be distinguished:

(i) *Overall cash limits.* Firstly, an overall limit on the permissible increase in salary bill over the following year needs to be stipulated. Organizations may treat this as a global budget, or the sums may be distributed in a specified way allocated to various departments. Separately from this, or together with it (according to policy), there may be completely general increases granted to cover increases in the cost of living. These increases are more likely to be awarded to departments on a percentage basis, as a given proportion of total salary bill. With general increases, all employees will receive this percentage on their present salary, and all scales and ranges will rise by a similar percentage.

On the strength of a forecast of routine salary increases, wastage and manpower flows between grades, an organization can estimate how much money will be left over for pure merit increases. These are then allocated via salary review procedures and a budget is produced for salary costs in the forthcoming year. Departmental allocations may be monitored in order to ensure they follow policy guidelines on merit increments. Finally, at the end of the year, the budgeted salary cost is compared with the real cost and corrective action may be taken in the next year's awards or in the light of changes in the firm's financial position.

(ii) *Performance*. Performance must be adequately rewarded. This control must operate through the performance appraisal scheme. Central personnel departments must ensure that all merit increments are genuine reflections of ability. This requires considerable liaison with the line managers. Computer printouts of the distribution of assessments by various departments can reveal those which may be making stricter or more lenient assessments than the average, and these departments may be invited to review their standards.

(iii) *Grade control*. Control over general salary levels and costs effectively depends on control over salaries on a grade basis. In a graded structure, it is likely that there will be some sort of norm. The first criterion of effective control, then, must be that this norm is being maintained (a consideration likely to be of interest to staff unions), and this can be calculated by taking average salary in the grade and comparing it with the norm. This index is called a compa-ratio (an abbreviation for 'comparative ratio'). It tells at a glance whether the average salary is above or below the norm and by how much. A compa-ratio figure can be obtained for each grade and a graphical plot shows up immediately those grades where salaries are tending to rise.

Frequently, the compa-ratio is used as a method for midpoint control, particularly where midpoint control is used as the target salary. The index can be used to show to what extent average salaries in a grade deviate from this level. If target salary is the midpoint of the salary range, compa-ratio can be calculated as:

$$\frac{\text{Average of all salaries in the grade}}{\text{Midpoint of the salary range}} \times 100$$

A compa-ratio of 100 would indicate that the average salary is on target. However, if a grade average salary of, for example, £8320 compared with a midpoint salary of £10 400 it would reveal a compa-ratio of 80, cause for investigation and possible remedial action since overall salary levels are too low compared to target. Similarly, a compa-ratio of 120 arising, for example, in a situation where average salaries were £21 000 in a grade with a £17 000 midpoint, would suggest that staff were being overpaid. Remedial action might take the form of modifying future increases.

(iv) *Attrition of salary costs*. Attrition means that, in general, the total salary bill will rise less quickly than would be expected by simply considering general and merit increases, since changes in the number of staff employed also affect the grand total cost. The problem is to determine the amount of attrition and the changes in the salary bill due to changes in staff numbers, so that accurate forecasting and budgeting is possible. Attrition effectively means that more money is available for salary merit increments than might be supposed at first sight. Forecasting the actual amount of attrition is extremely difficult. It requires analysis and forecasting of manpower flows – staff turnover, promotion, recruitment, average salaries of those leaving or joining, and so on. If a firm had an overall level of attrition of 5 per cent, then a merit increase of 5 per cent could be eroded during the year, leaving the total salary bill at the end of the year the same as it was at the beginning.

On a *total* salary cost basis, some idea of the likely erosion of the salary bill over the year is always useful, in that it could be allowed and compensated for in the overall salary budget and a more accurate assessment of the impact of a given increase on year-end salary bill could be made. Cynics might argue that expected attrition can help to finance next year's payround.

Attrition over the whole salary system is analytically equal to the discrepancy between year-end average salary, and the predicted year-end average salary found by taking average salary at the beginning of the year and adding it to the merit, general, promotional and any other increases given during that year.

IMPLEMENTATION

As a general principle, any successful organizational change, such as the introduction of a new salary system, relies on a cooperative attitude on the part of the people it involves. If it also has support and commitment from top management, and is introduced in an open, participative way, then the problems of implementation should be minimized.

Some firms promulgate specific statements of company policy to guide salary administration decisions. Such policies should as far as possible cover all the main aspects.

In companies where trade unions are involved, a joint management and union policy on salary systems needs therefore to be formulated. Items which require agreement may well include, for example:

1   that there should be a fixed number of grades, and the overall shape of the structure
2   that each grade should have an agreed minimum and contain a grade norm to be reached by average performers in a specified time
3   that once at the norm, very good performers should be eligible for merit increases at management's discretion. Average performers would remain there, benefiting only from general cost of living increases
4   that below average performers would take longer to progress to the norm; those who were very unsatisfactory would never get there and may be transferred.

Inflation impacts directly on salary structure, both in an overall sense, and in the way that it sometimes stimulates internal pressures from special groups demanding more pay. Internal differentials can then be upset. There may be a temptation for managements to upgrade staff without adequate increases in responsibility, thus leading to 'grade drift'. Externally, movements in market rates inevitably erode relativities. Negotiated pay increases for certain groups put pressure on a company's own system and make it respond to that pressure. Minimum rates in many occupations are fixed by collective bargaining, so the bargaining power of the respective parties may be the critical factor. Jobs change over time, and job evaluation schemes on which salary structures may be based, inevitably deteriorate. A salary system can only be a relatively temporary device – never permanent.

Indeed, certain aspects may be counter-productive. One critic, James Brennan (1980), has argued that salary ranges inhibit fundamental pay objectives: to attract, retain, and motivate. Personnel managers seek consistency, whilst line managers seek flexibility. Non-bargaining unit jobs have pay scales constructed around a single figure reflecting the competitive market value which becomes the midpoint. Ranges are set by imposing equidistant percentage intervals above and below it, but unlike competitive midpoints these ranges are completely arbitrary. 'Standard percentage intervals just do not reflect reality. The conventional 20 per cent variation around midpoints, for example, assume that all jobs have values that vary 20 per cent above and below the range midpoint.' New recruits are expected to start in the lower part of the range, merit increases are modified by compa-ratio, promotions take the form of movement from grade to grade and the amount of promotion increase depends on the distance between grade midpoints and the resulting range positions in the new job. The salary structure may become a strait-jacket. Eventually cracks appear in the system. Exceptions are made. Before many years have passed, pressure mounts to revise the structure – and the cycle begins again.

PERFORMANCE AWARDS

To provide incentive, flexibility in payment systems, and link reward more directly to individual performance, schemes now attracting attention are those under which managers have discretion in awarding periodic increases in pay to high-performing employees. Such increases may take the form of either percentages of basic pay or cash increments. In a recent survey (IDS/IPM, 1985) of 125 organizations, 42 per cent had changed their policy on merit payments since 1982, and 5 companies had introduced merit pay for the first time. It would seem that they have gained in popularity, although maybe not yet extensively, since the termination of government incomes policies in 1979 (Murlis and Wright, 1985).

Aggressive 'sunrise' or high-tech firms are more likely to be flexible, and open to individual bargaining, than big firms with established salary structures. Where remuneration can be performance-related a simple statistical basis can be set – e.g. 30–40 per cent tied to achievement of goals. Two-tier bonus systems may be linked to both company results and personal targets. It is not so easy in service functions, and in the public sector, highly contentious. But automatic annual pay rises are under attack.

Clearly, in the administration of these schemes there could be problems of equity, since performance cannot always be objectively quantified, resting ultimately on someone's opinion – and different managers may set different standards. The argument in favour is that they restore more power and autonomy to line managers in motivating and rewarding their own staff. The trend is also compatible with discernible devolution of managerial responsibility to operational levels (see Chapter 21).

Fringe benefits

If wages and salaries are defined as the direct reward for productive services, then fringe benefits are indirect and could be regarded as 'non-wages', perks or privileges. If fringe benefits include all indirect rewards, then they must also encompass a wide range of employee services – quite an extensive catalogue.

Strictly speaking, fringe benefits are those forms of compensation which are provided other than basic pay, salaries and wages. They represent some value to the employee at some cost to the employer. In the USA, 'economic supplements' or 'supplementary benefits' are the phrases used. The Germans call them 'invisible wages' and the French 'social wages'. Once restricted to only the largest companies, fringe benefits have now become practically universal. Since the 1960s changes in attitudes towards welfare services have been considerable. The enormous volume of social legislation has led many to believe that all employing organizations are morally responsible for the welfare of their employees, a view held once by the Quakers. It is now suggested that the employer has two obligations: firstly, to compensate workers adequately for actual services rendered, and, secondly, to assume certain obligations of a social nature essentially unrelated to production but existing because of the employment relationship.

Morality apart, fringe benefits may be a response to either a felt need or to what other firms have. They may be instituted from a desire to buy company loyalty, provide a labour market attraction, or be part of a public relations exercise. At times they have helped to reduce inflationary pressures on remuneration packages, and often escaped the higher direct taxation of money wages.

The provision of employee services may imply a voluntary gesture, but employers' voluntary incursion of additional labour costs have often been in response to union demands. Welfare services often fall within the scope of substantive agreements negotiated between unions and employers. A long-standing misinterpretation of fringe benefits was the so-called 'deferred wage theory' (or fallacy). Benefits which workers received were considered to include a right to back-pay for services performed. The spread of fringe benefits using the deferred wages concept has led to confusion to over what was therefore the workers' entitlement or an employer's social obligation. This may all come down to the distinction to what is legally due and what can be achieved by voluntary agreement. Just as wage differentials exist, so too do differentials between fringe benefits.

A modern mix of fringe benefits may include some which are effective immediately (company cars, clothing allowances), and others which constitute deferred income (pensions, insurance schemes). Some benefits may be conditional in the sense that they are not necessarily taken up by every employee (private medical schemes, sabbaticals). In terms of motivation and the effort/reward bargain, a case can be made out for what the Americans call the 'cafeteria' approach from which the employee has freedom to select parts of the compensation package. Tailoring the reward to suit the individual widens his freedom of choice. Administratively, the approach could be cumbersome, and may not be feasible for an entire range of staff.

Fringe benefits artificially (and sometimes substantially) raise manpower costs. The 1982 Survey of Employee Benefits in the UK by Hay Management Consultants found that the average cost of a total benefits package equalled 27 per cent of the cost of salaries. So often, fringe benefits have been introduced piecemeal on an *ad hoc* basis. Benefits should be viewed in relation to a company's other methods of reward. There is a need for a balanced and integrated analysis of benefit costs and values. The first task is to create an integrated package. Consideration should be given to the impact which benefits may have on other pay items. Do, in fact, fringe benefits motivate anyone? Are they just another overhead? Are they just hygiene factors (in Herzberg terminology) which may well lead to dissatisfaction? Spending on benefits and an interpretation of their effects on employee behaviour and performance should regularly be monitored. Employees need to recognize what is available. Equally, employers need some measure of employees' attitudes to benefits. It is all too easy to take things for granted.

The wide range of fringe benefits available to UK staff remains unchanged despite the hardhitting effects of the recession. Although there are some instances where companies are trading down their benefits, for many white-collar workers fringe benefits are even on the increase. For example, 97 per cent of directors and 61 per cent of supporting managers have company cars (BIM National Management Survey, 1983), and 80 per cent of directors and 68 per cent of their managers are entitled to five or more weeks' holiday. Most directors receive free private mileage. Most executives are entitled to first-class rail travel. Interest free loans for season tickets are common. Many company-based schemes for health cover are also extended to families.

The Inland Revenue has made its position clear on the provision of perks. It prefers employers not to give benefits in kind, but rather to pay their employees a proper level of remuneration. This has been reflected in Government moves to tighten tax regulations on, for example, company cars and tax payable on homes let to directors at nominal rents, etc. But there seems to be no stopping the upward trend in fringe benefits. In manufacturing industry alone, fringe benefits rose from 11.1 per cent average pre-tax remuneration in 1964, to 19.4 per cent in 1981 (Green *et al.*, 1985).

INFORMAL REWARDS AND THE HIDDEN ECONOMY

Operating alongside the conventional means of remuneration, one frequently finds work people responding to various unofficial incentives – i.e.

fiddles – which may take the form of cheating the employer of time, goods, or money. Such fiddles may be perpetrated by individuals acting alone, or by groups acting collectively. The term 'fiddles' is often synonymous with 'perks' or 'fringe benefits' or such esoteric terms as 'knock-offs', 'cabbage' in the rag trade, 'weed' amongst fairground workers, 'skimming' or 'creaming' of cash profits, and 'pilferage' and 'moonlighting'. Unfortunately this multiplicity of terms encourages different people to take different perceptions of the same thing according to where they stand in the system, whether they bleed it or are being bled, and whether these informal rewards are recognized or unrecognized. People therefore assume different attitudes, and this sometimes leads to differential and contradictory treatment of offenders. One man's perk is another man's fiddle.

In many places, fiddles are an established part of total earnings. They form a regular part of take-home pay. In many trades and occupations fiddles are institutionalized with management collusion. A blind eye may be turned and frank, open discussion of the problem avoided. Elsewhere, stiff penalties may be meted out. Managements tend to take a moral stance when they lack control over fiddles, and particularly where their own company bears the cost. If someone else bears the cost, it may not seem to matter so much. Managements tend to be tolerant where, for example, driver deliverers 'short change' or 'drop short' to customers. But stealing merchandise from the employer direct is good old-fashioned theft and treated as such. An ambivalent attitude seems to pervade the whole subject. Managers in small companies, for example, are not unknown to collude with employees to avoid tax on tips or overtime working, or even on basic earnings, by unrecorded payments in cash.

Fiddles have hidden, unlawful implications. They are not always below the surface. They are sometimes quite open and visible. Apart from financial gain, it may be that the opportunity to fiddle provides some psychological job satisfaction, in the sense that workers are able to buck the system, gain personal pleasure from winning, and free themselves from formal constraints. Fiddles may often help an organization to function better – they may encourage the establishment of personal relationships. Unofficial incentives may help to lubricate the bottlenecks. Conversely, large-scale fiddling may be seriously damaging. Control of fiddles therefore needs to be taken seriously. One would not wish to impede the smoothness with which transactions are actually carried out. One would wish to plug financial drains, loss of merchandise or misuse of equipment or time. However, to the extent that fiddles may have become an accepted way of life, any attack on them constitutes an attack on an employee's total earnings and may be resisted or invite repercussions. The whole area is extremely tricky. Unfortunately, it is a subject which does not feature prominently in most conventional research in industrial relations. This is a pity, since the value of the black economy seems to be rising, although estimates vary widely.

One of the more serious attempts to study the hidden economy has been made by Gerald Mars (1983). He asks the question whether differences in personality and psychological make-up account for variations in fiddle behaviour, and although he does not answer the question totally, comes to the conclusion that most fiddling can be analysed and accounted for in terms of work structures. He tries to 'link the type of fiddle to the type of job'. To classify fiddles, Mars borrows a model from anthropology which looks at (i) degree of autonomy of action, (ii) degree of group cohesiveness versus individuality. Mars argues that these dimensions conveniently measure the essential character of any work environment, and provide a typology of fiddle practices which can give the personnel manager clues as to the type of fiddle to look for in any situation, and, by implication, possible hints on remedial action or warnings as to when to tread warily.

Summary

Wages and salaries constitute basic forms of financial compensation. There are various methods of wage payments and the choice of an appropriate method should depend on a diagnosis of the work and environmental situation. Wage rates must be related to general market rates for similar types of work. The main wage payment systems are time rates, payment by results schemes, measured daywork, and merit rating schemes.

Salary administration is a systematic process. Most salary systems are based on job evaluation and grading. An organization must establish its own salary policy trend line representing salary progressions through a series of grades. The determination of salary ranges is linked with the spread of range for the grade, differentials between grades and overlap. Individual progress is through salary ranges either by incremental or performance/merit based schemes. There are many variations. Maturity curves can be drawn to plot individual career progressions. Control mechanisms must be adopted to ensure that individual and gross payment levels are in line with policy. This involves salary budgeting and monitoring via compa-ratio and levels of attrition. Salary policies need to be agreed and promulgated. Salary policies are unlikely to be based on static criteria. They therefore need to be revised periodically.

Fringe benefits are supplements to official earnings, which may be either immediate or deferred. Certain basic benefits may sometimes be regarded as a right, e.g. catering and welfare services. The provision of fringe benefits is often selective. More substantial benefits are reserved for higher paid executives, and may represent certain tax advantages. They also help to bind the loyalty of the individual to the firm. On the whole, the incentive power of fringe benefits are difficult to determine – since the rewards may be delayed and not directly related to individual effort. However, the size and scope of fringe benefits seems to be increasing.

Apart from legitimate fringe benefits, various fiddles operate in the so-called hidden economy. These unofficial forms of compensation have attracted considerable interest in recent years.

Discussion questions

1 What factors would you consider in devising a wage payment system?
2 What factors would you consider to be most important in formulating a policy for salary administration?
3 What are the arguments for applying a systematic approach to the determination of salaries?
4 Are there any arguments for paying individual's 'personal' salaries, as opposed to a planned structure?
5 Is it ever possible perfectly to reconcile internal differentials with external relativities?
6 What is a 'rational' payment system?
7 How highly do you regard fringe benefits?
8 In your opinion, would most employees prefer higher wages or salaries to the provision of various goods or facilities in kind?

References

ARMSTRONG, M. (1977), *Handbook of Personnel Management Practice*, Kogan Page, London.
ARMSTRONG, M. and MURLIS, H. (1980), *Handbook of Salary Administration*, Kogan Page, London.
BIM (1980), 'Salary administration – a survey of 216 companies', Management Survey Report, No. 16.
BOWEY, A. (1980), *Handbook of Salary and Wage Systems*, Gower, London.
BOWEY, A. and LUPTON, T. (1972), *Job and Pay Comparisons*, Gower, London.
BRENNAN, E. J. (1980), 'The problem with salary ranges (and a realistic solution)', *Personnel Journal*, March.
CRAIG, C., RUBERY, J., TARLING, R. and WILKINSON, F. (1982), *Labour Market Structures, Industrial Organisation and Low Pay*, Cambridge University Press, London.
GREEN, F., HADJIMATHEOU, G. and SMALL, R. (1985) 'Fringe benefit distribution in Britain', *British Journal of Industrial Relations*, **23** 2 July.
HAY MANAGEMENT CONSULTANTS (1982), *Survey of Employee Benefits*, London.
IDS TOP PAY UNIT (1985), *The Merit Factor: Rewarding Individual Performance*, Incomes Data Services/Institute of Personnel Management, London.
LUPTON, T. and GOWLER, D. (1970), *Selecting a Wage Payment System*, Kogan Page, London.
MARS, G. (1983), *Cheats at Work*, Allen and Unwin, London.
MURLIS, H. and WRIGHT, A. (1985), 'Rewarding the performance of the eager beaver', *Personnel Management*, June.
PAY BOARD (1974), 'Problems of pay relativities', Advisory Report No. 2, Cmnd 5535, HMSO, London.
ROBINSON, D. (1970), *Local Labour Markets and Wage Structures*, Gower, London.

Industrial Relations

Industrial Relations

CHAPTER 9

The context of industrial relations

by Paul Roots
Formerly Director of Industrial Relations, Ford Motor Company

The student and practitioner in industrial relations quickly realizes that the subject involves attitude as a significant factor and that, therefore, what people believe can be as important as what is. In no other field of management is generalized assertion accepted so readily as a substitute for fact. Even experienced managers who will insist on test results before committing materials to the production process or extensive trials before accepting a new machine, and study each element of cost in a capital project proposal, will make important and potentially costly decisions on labour matters based on personal judgements without any substantive data to support them. This chapter, therefore, on the context of industrial relations, deals not only with the institutions and machinery, but with the beliefs that interweave the fabric.

Trade unions

Although associations of craftsmen had existed before, British trade unions as we now know them were formed to give employees the collective strength to protect and further their interests in the conditions created by the industrial revolution. The major general workers unions catering for unskilled or semi-skilled workers did not emerge as a major force in the union movement until the latter part of the last century.

While the early struggles of the unions for recognition and legal status described by the Webbs and others make interesting reading, it is doubtful if one needs to go back beyond the last eighty years to understand union attitudes and behaviour.

Trade union membership has grown, albeit in a spasmodic fashion, from a little more than a million and a half members or twenty per cent of the working population in 1892, to over ten and a half million at the end of 1986. Although this represents a drop of over 2 million from the 1979 peak, Britain still has one of the highest densities of union membership amongst Western democratic societies. Levels of membership, especially in the unions catering for non-craft workers, tend to reflect levels of employment – going down as unemployment increases and vice versa. The overall increase, however, especially in the years since the Second World War conceals changes in the distribution of members from manual or 'blue-collar' unions to salaried or 'white-collar' unions due in part to the increase in the numbers in government, including local government, employment.

Other factors leading to this growth in membership in salaried unions include changes in the nature of office work, e.g. mechanization and the trend to larger offices, which have eroded the close working relationships which often existed between salaried staff and their employers, the rationalization of industries creating job insecurity in types of employment previously seen as secure and the view that union membership was now socially acceptable. This change in the public's perception of unions, which probably started when union cooperation was harnessed for the war effort and Labour leaders such as Ernest Bevin achieved prominent government posts, has become self-perpetuating as social groups with middle class status such as teachers and airline pilots are seen pursuing joint action. The salaried classes have also been quick to recognize the value of organized group pressure, whether it is used in industry to protect their differentials over manual workers or in the community at large to resist the extension of an airport in a rural area.

Classifying unions into tidy categories is becoming increasingly difficult. While the National Union of Railwaymen (and the National Union of Mineworkers until the breakaway UDM) can be truly described as single-industry unions recruiting all or nearly all their members from one industry, only the smaller craft unions now restrict membership to apprenticeship-served craftsmen. The dilution of skill agreements concluded in wartime to meet the needs of a rapidly expanded engineering industry, and the pressures to protect their influence in the workplace against the growing general workers unions have caused the Amalgamated Engineering Union (AEU) to open its membership to the non-skilled. Without this change, in industries such as vehicle manufacture which employ relatively few skilled men, they would not now be Britain's second biggest union.

Pressures to amalgamate, including the need to combat rising administrative costs, have also clouded the old distinctions between craft and non-craft unions. The National Union of Vehicle Builders which once organized the skilled coach building trades was amalgamated into the giant Transport and General Workers Union (TGWU). The Boilermakers whose main power base has traditionally been shipbuilding craftsmen merged with the General and Municipal Workers strong in the public utilities sector. Small craft unions have amalgamated with others as membership has dwindled due to technological change. An illustration of the latter is the coming together of Sheetmetal Workers, Coppersmiths and Heating and Domestic Engineers.

In the white-collar area the unions are still competing for members in a growth market. The Technical Administrative and Supervisory Section of the AUEW (TASS) is expanding from its base membership of draughtsmen and engineers and recruiting in competition with the Association of Professional, Executive, Clerical and Computer Staff (APEX), and the Association of Scientific, Technical and Managerial Staffs (ASTMS) among supervisors, managers and other grades in industrial and commercial undertakings. ASTMS is still the predominant union for foremen in industry, and the Association of Clerical Technical and Supervisory Staffs (ACTS) the white-collar wing of the TGWU despite its title appears to have most of its membership in clerical jobs.

In addition to the factors referred to earlier in this chapter, the increase in salaried union membership, particularly among supervisors and middle management, was stimulated in the 1970s by the effects of inflation, and the fiscal policies of socialist governments which were seen as attacks on middle class conditions. Although the opportunities for further recruitment appear greater in the white-collar sector, the same pressures to streamline administration and services and reduce costs should eventually create the trend towards fewer and bigger unions clearly discernible in the blue-collar sector. The number of unions in Britain, manual and salaried, has fallen from 543 in 1970 to 405 in 1983 mainly through amalgamations, and approximately 80 per cent of the total membership is contained within 25 unions.

The large majority of unions are organized on a three-tier basis, a local district or branch, a larger region or division and a national level. They may also be organized on a trade or industry basis. They are normally governed by full-time officers who are elected or appointed and most unions have processes for electing, if not some or all of the full-time officers, a power-sharing or policy-making group. In other words, the constitutions of unions are designed to give some degree of democracy. Most unions have a chief executive officer who usually has the title of general secretary and, again depending on the union, he may be elected periodically or have a permanent appointment.

Union policy is normally determined at an annual conference of lay delegates, and the majority of large unions are affiliated to the TUC, which also meets annually to discuss and agree policies for the whole trade union movement. TUC membership is not compulsory, and unions are not bound by TUC policy unless it is subsequently adopted by the individual unions by the processes laid down in their own constitutions. Although the moral pressures on unions to conform to TUC policy are strong, the only real sanction is expulsion. As the TUC is the main avenue of access to the Government, government departments and other national and international organizations, the strength of this sanction would appear to be dependent on the degree to which the Government in power is amenable to influence. In practice the unions also influence views and decisions through a whole substructure of committees and bodies whose union members are nominated by the TUC. Examples of such bodies are NEDO, ACAS, and the Health and Safety Commission.

Most unions include in their constitution and rule book a statement of

objectives which invariably embraces social and political aims. The following extracts illustrate this:

> 'To improve the wages and conditions of members and to provide legal means
> to support legislative action to improve members' financial and social condi-
> tions especially by supporting policies which will ultimately give the workers
> ownership and control of industry.'

> Rule 2 – Principal Objects
> Electrical Electronic Telecommunications and Plumbing Union.

> 'enable the Association to take a full part in the political and industrial work of
> the Trade Union, Cooperative and Labour Movements . . . and to promote
> labour representation in Parliament and on all elective governing bodies.'

> Rule 1 – Name, Office, Objects and Constitution
> Association of Patternmakers and Allied Craftsmen.

> 'The furtherance of political objects of any kind.'

> Rule 2(e)
> Transport and General Workers Union.

These are not new developments and the unions have always seen a need to
improve the conditions of their members by pursuing changes in society
through the political processes, as well as seeking changes in wages, benefits
and conditions at the workplace through negotiation with employers. As
organizations which collectively and directly represent a quarter of the adult
population, and indirectly at least a half, they clearly have a right to express
views on any subject which affects or could affect their members. While it is
reasonable and understandable to question the means by which they collect
and project the views of those they represent, it demonstrates a lack of
understanding of the origins and nature of unions to suggest they only have
the limited role of negotiating wages and conditions with employers. Their
political activity can be viewed as an extension of their negotiating role to
extend to all employees, unionized or not, basic conditions of hours,
holidays, safety standards, etc., and to achieve benefits for their members
which are outside the individual employers' control, such as State sick pay
and pensions.

The extent to which unions in Britain have sought improvements in
benefits through political pressure can be contrasted to the situation in the
United States, where the negotiating room has been seen by the unions as the
main arena for gaining unemployment benefit, pensions, medical insurance,
etc. British unions' objectives in their relationships with employers also
extend well beyond the discussion of pay, hours and holidays that some
believe is their legitimate role. Almost equal with what might be termed
these economic objectives, union officials and representatives see their job as
the protection of their members by limiting management authority in
matters which affect employees. Examples of this type of activity are controls

on the amount of work performed, that is the effort side of the wage/effort equation, and this will be more pronounced where their ability to influence the wage side of the equation is limited, e.g. by long-term agreements or measured daywork, insistence on consultation prior to men being transferred to other work or new equipment being introduced and involvement in disciplinary matters.

White collar unions have also quickly extended their role beyond the salary negotiation line. The majority of agreements on the introduction of new technology have been negotiated in the salaried sector, and as is to be expected they show more interest in systems of performance appraisal and promotion opportunities than do unions representing manual workers.

Apart from the tendency to believe, or wish, that unions had a more limited role, one of the more common misconceptions about unions held by managers and others is the belief that they operate by a chain of command similar to that which operates within companies and other large organizations. They wrongly equate the authority of a national union official with that of a senior company executive, a district official with that of middle management and a convenor or senior shop steward with that of a supervisor. The media exposure of senior union officials also encourages managers to believe they have that type of authority, i.e. similar to a senior company executive. Grievance procedures which tend to follow a management chain of command interfacing with shop stewards and upwards to district and other officials reinforces the belief. The reality is far removed from that perception. Because unions were created for the benefit of the membership (companies do not exist for the benefit of employees) the constitutions of unions normally put very strict limits on the authority of their officers. These limits might be very precise, such as the need to get agreement by the members in defined circumstances or, less precise but equally restrictive, by requiring the officer to conform at all times to the policy set by a lay delegate conference. Many union officials whose faces are familiar to the public through television appearances are answerable to councils of manual workers. Unless these realities are appreciated the debate about union power and the effects of legal sanctions cannot be fully understood and, more importantly, unrealistic expectations may be raised when negotiating with union officers.

Failure to understand and accept this limited authority of union officers is a constant source of frustration to managers trying to secure agreement to some necessary change, and it heightens their view of unions as organizations which obstruct the fulfilment of management's legitimate objectives. The extended debates to obtain majority concurrence which are a vital part of the union decision-making process are alien to a manager's normal way of getting results.

Employers' associations

The Trade Union and Labour Relations Act 1974 defined an employers association as an organization of employers whose principal purposes include the regulation of relations between employers and workers or trade unions. Although employers who had banded together for 'commercial' reasons, for example to regulate trade, did sometimes join to negotiate wages with trade unions in the eighteenth and early nineteenth centuries, it was not until the 1850s that they started to form primarily for that purpose.

The growth in numbers and size of unions from that period including the emergence of the new non-craft unions is generally regarded as the reason for the development of employers' associations. Typical of such trends was that in the engineering industry, where an association of engineering employers was formed to combat the Amalgamated Society of Engineers, which had been created by the joining together of most of the craft unions in the industry. The present Engineering Employers Federation (EEF) was formed in 1896 by bringing together a number of smaller and regional bodies.

The influence of employers' associations on the system of industrial relations in Britain is often overlooked. Industry-wide bargaining and the resolution of disputes through established procedures with local and national levels came about primarily from initiatives taken by the associations. Their weaknesses stem from the problems of obtaining consensus views from the member companies. Associations which embrace large companies with professional managements and small owner-managed companies often have to try and reconcile diametrically opposed opinions when for example submitting proposals to the Government on labour legislation. Joint action to resist union claims is seldom successful for any long period, as an individual company's need for cash and profit soon leads the weaker ones to want to make concessions. The large variety of wage systems in some industries also makes it easy for employers to breach the association's pay norms in concealed ways, and few companies are prepared to damage their relations with their own employees or sacrifice profitability for the common good.

An example of the problem of holding member companies together on a given course was the strike in the engineering industry over pay and hours in 1979. Companies with excess production capacity and falling order books were willing to concede extra holidays and shorter working hours when put under pressure, and ignore the concerns of other companies who believed that protecting capacity was necessary for future profitability.

The services provided for member companies, in addition to the advice and assistance in collective bargaining and resolving disputes already referred to, usually include specialist advice on personnel matters such as manpower planning, health and safety and training, legal advice, information on commercial developments in the industry, and representing the industry's views to the Government and other national and international bodies.

The membership of employers' associations like membership of trade unions suffers, although to a lesser extent, from economic recessions. Companies scrutinizing costs may drop their subscription and others go out of business. As the levels of subscriptions in some associations are based on wage and salary bills, companies reducing their labour force may also be reducing their association's income. Precise figures of the number of employers' associations in Britain are difficult to arrive at because of the problems of definition, but the 1984 Report of the Certification Officer suggested there were over 300 separate associations with a membership of over 338 000. And, of course, the Confederation of British Industry (CBI) represents the interests of employers and employers' associations.

VOLUNTARISM AND AGREEMENTS

The system of industrial relations in Britain has been characterized by its voluntary nature. Unlike the United States and other industrialized countries, the law plays a lesser part in the process by which employers and unions come together to bargain over wages and conditions and resolve disputes. Although there is a whole series of statutes affecting industry and employment which employers and unions must recognize and understand, they have played little part in collective bargaining or resolving disputes, although this may change in future.

In those areas where employees are represented by trade unions, agreements exist which give the unions the right to negotiate pay and conditions such as hours of work and holidays (less frequently pensions and other fringe benefits), and the right to represent their members, employees, who have a grievance arising out of something the management has done or has failed to do.

The results of the negotiations on pay and conditions are normally recorded in an agreement which may be a detailed formal document signed by both parties, an exchange of correspondence, minutes of the meeting at which negotiations were concluded, a works notice or some other form. In increasingly few cases there is no written agreement and the employer merely introduces the agreed changes to wages, holidays, etc.

Agreements establishing the union's right to negotiate and represent are often referred to as non-substantive or procedural agreements, and agreements setting out the results of collective bargaining, pay, hours, holidays, etc., as substantive agreements. Although the same people and bodies may be involved in both processes, the collective bargaining and disputes provisions should be separate and distinct. Employees or their representatives should not have the right to dispute the result of the collective bargain through the disputes procedure, although they may use it to challenge an interpretation, e.g. they cannot claim a higher rate of pay than that negotiated, but they could dispute their entitlement to shift premium or overtime pay where they believed a management error had occurred.

Within any one organization any number of unions may claim negotiating and representation rights. To minimize potential problems, employers try to limit the numbers of unions by giving preferred unions exclusive bargaining rights. Unless only one category of worker is employed it is seldom possible to confine it to one union. Some companies have, for example, in addition to unskilled employees who might all be members or potential members of one union, mechanical and electrical maintenance men (usually members of the AEU and Electrical Electronic Telecommunications and Plumbing Union (EETPU) respectively) as well as supervisory and clerical and administrative staff who might or might not be unionized, and might or might not be included in the union rights agreement. Closed shop agreements (see Chapter 13), which might also give check-off facilities, i.e. deduction of union dues from wages at source by the employer, are often devices to enable unions and management to control the number of unions in an establishment, and limit the problems which can be caused by employees not adhering to negotiated conditions. The multi-union situation in Britain, the result of the way in which unionization developed, creates pressures not experienced in all countries, and managements have constructed ways to contain these pressures.

Agreements giving union negotiating rights should specify the categories of workers covered, the 'area' of negotiation, i.e. wages, holidays, hours, etc., the frequency with which negotiations will take place, and preferably detail the mechanics, i.e. the constitution of the negotiating body and how the results of negotiations will be ratified by employees and unions.

Shop stewards and the role they play are features unique to the British industrial relations scene and, like multi-unionism, a result of historical developments. The lack of a legal framework including the special courts which exist elsewhere to determine the rights of employees and unions has led to the workplace battle for rights and the devolution of power to where it can be most effectively used – by union members at the workplace.

Disputes procedures

Disputes or grievance procedures or, more accurately, procedures for the avoidance of disputes, are a central part of the industrial relations system. They exist in varying degrees of sophistication in all industries where unions have representation rights. Their primary purpose is to resolve problems arising between employers and employees in a way that allows the company or organization to function without interruption to its normal business. They are based on three principles:

1 That problems are usually best resolved at source
2 That representatives of management and unions with wider responsibility and experience are involved at successive stages if necessary to resolve the problem.
3 That it is in the interest of employer and employees for normal working and, therefore, wage earning to continue while the problem is discussed.

Strikes to support wage claims, or what in the United States is termed end of contract strikes, are not peculiar to Britain. In fact international comparisons of manhours lost through such strikes put Britain well down the league table. What does appear to be a more serious problem here, however, is the dispute which is in breach of procedure, that is stoppages of work which occur in contravention of the clause contained in practically all procedural agreements which state that there will be no strikes or other industrial action until procedure has been exhausted – in other words until the problem has been discussed at every stage. Unconstitutional action is the term applied to such disputes as distinct from unofficial action, which is action not supported by the union. The latter may, or may not, be unconstitutional.

The reasons put forward for the prevalence of unconstitutional action in the UK are many and varied, and as with all industrial relations problems it is dangerous to generalize or seek simple solutions. Managers regard breaches of procedure as serious failures by unions and look to them to ensure that employees adhere to the agreed method of resolving issues. Trade union officers and stewards on the other hand, although they may share the view that their members would be better carrying on work while they argue their case, do not normally see it in such stark terms, as the following excerpt from the TGWU's pamphlet titled *Plant Level Bargaining* illustrates:

> 'Many disputes procedures in British Industry seem to have been designed so as to put workers in the wrong whenever they disagree with management, and to give employers the opportunity to use the procedure in order to coerce employees into accepting conditions against their will.
>
> It is essential that the union is not morally bound (and of course not legally bound) to act against its members' interests by any procedural arrangements . . .'

Those who see industrial disputes in class warfare terms regard procedures as management devices for channelling conflict and will encourage others to ignore them and substitute direct action. More frequently, however, unions will claim that failures to observe procedures are due to weaknesses in the procedure itself, for example that it is too slow, too lengthy or unfair in that it does not restrict management's freedom to act sufficiently to counterbalance the restriction on their members freedom to act – by taking strike action. It was in response to this last criticism that status quo clauses began to feature in procedure agreements in the 1970s.

Although many procedure agreements contain discussion, including the final stage, within the company, others such as that between the EEF and the Confederation of Shipbuilding and Engineering unions involve stages where the dialogue is progressed between the employers' association and union or unions. This can help to defuse a situation by taking the control of the debate away from those personally involved or responsible for the decisions in the original issue. Others introduce this relatively independent view or a third party by having arbitration or mediation as a last resort.

Views on the value of third-party intervention differ widely, and distinctions are often made between economic and non-economic disputes. Private employers who are prepared to let a third party decide a question of agreement interpretation or act as a final court of appeal against a disciplinary penalty, may not allow an arbitrator to determine their labour costs, something they would regard as a commercial decision and, therefore, a fundamental part of their responsibility towards their shareholders. Such arbitration is not a guaranteed way of resolving problems. Antipathy towards arbitration is sometimes shared by unions including the AEU who would rather rely on their own efforts to bring matters to a conclusion.

Some form of arbitration and conciliation service has been provided by successive governments since the eighteenth century when this role was performed by justices of the peace. Emergency legislation in both world wars provided special bodies to replace the right to strike which was suspended to avoid damaging the national interest. There are now a number of third-party interventions provided by statute.

The main body providing third-party services such as conciliation, arbitration and enquiry is ACAS. The Employment Protection Act 1975 also provided the facility of the Central Arbitration Committee, and the Government has retained the power to set up courts of inquiry. The functions of these bodies and others with the power to arbitrate in more specific areas can be found in the *Industrial Relations Handbook* published by HMSO.

Some industries and companies prefer to arrange private arbitration, and ACAS maintains a list of suitably qualified people who perform the role for a fee.

The wider use of arbitration in the United States is usually explained by the detailed and precise nature of company trade union contracts which make them more susceptible to definitive judgements, the American tradition of resolving a wide range of issues by legal and quasi legal processes and the plentiful supply of legally trained academics and others to act as arbitrators.

Government's role in industrial relations

Although they might wish to maintain and even declare a non-interventionist policy, governments of any party cannot stand aside from industrial relations in Britain. As the country's biggest employer, their policies on wages and conditions for employees in central and local government, the health service and the state-run industries must have an effect on private companies. All political parties recognize that wages are a significant factor in managing the economy. The approach of the two main parties is, however, diametrically opposed. The Labour Party aims to achieve trade union cooperation in return for legislation and policies which unions want, whereas the Conservative Party aims to reduce the unions' influence on wages and productivity. The following quotation from the opening paragraphs of the Green Paper on Trade Union Immunities 1981 illustrates this philosophy:

'For at least a generation now our industrial relations have failed us because they have inhibited improvements in productivity, acted as a disincentive to investment and discouraged innovation. The results are apparent in our poor industrial performance and lower standard of living compared with our major competitors overseas.'

The student of industrial relations, when assessing the arguments for and against more State intervention, particularly those which are part of the debate on the need or otherwise for tighter laws on strikes, should understand that Britain is almost unique in having a system of industrial relations law based on immunities and not positive rights for trade unions. Failure to recognize that in the UK union power is used to obtain and defend what in most other industrialized countries is provided by law can lead to a distorted perception of the industrial relations situation in Britain when compared, for example, with that in West Germany. Managements in Britain tend to see only the advantages of other systems and generally do not appreciate that restrictions on trade union power are balanced by restrictions on employers.

In the field of employee protection, health and safety, rights to appeal against wrongful dismissal, etc., there is more of a consensus among politicians of all parties and, therefore, less danger of laws being reversed once passed. It would appear, however, that the deep divisions in our society, the result of irreversible history, will continue to prevent the bi-partisan approach to the economy essential for long-term planning. In such a situation it is unlikely that changes to industrial relations law will be developed which have the commitment of employers and unions.

Discussion questions

1 Compare and contrast the processes by which policy decisions are made in a trade union (of which you may or may not be a member) and a commercial organization (of which you may or may not be an employee).
2 What are the main factors which you think will affect trade union membership and trade union density in the years to come?
3 What are the functions of Employers' Associations? How do they operate?
4 What do you understand by the principle of 'voluntarism' in British industrial relations? Is this principle becoming weaker?
5 Distinguish between substantive and procedural agreements. Give examples which may be known to you.
6 What are the merits and demerits of exclusive bargaining rights?
7 What do you see as the proper role of Government in industrial relations?

CHAPTER 10

Practical industrial relations at the workplace

by Paul Roots
Formerly Director of Industrial Relations, Ford Motor Company

The previous chapter dealt briefly with the legal, economic and cultural framework of British industrial relations, and the philosophies and attitudes which the participants bring to bear on their relationships within that framework. In this chapter I shall examine the problems which arise at the workplace, and consider ways in which I believe they can be prevented and overcome.

The employer's or management's industrial relations objective is to achieve a state of equilibrium between the company's, employees' and unions' aspirations so that the organization functions effectively and achieves its aim. That aim is to create a surplus or profit from the resources used, people, materials and equipment, to provide goods or services to others. This creation of a surplus from resources used is what enables societies to progress and is not peculiar to capitalist countries. The achievement of good relations, therefore, is not altruistic but a vital element of running an effective organization. This appears a narrow materialistic approach for Personnel people to take unless they appreciate that industrial relations is about people, and that good relations will not exist where the human needs for security, recognition and fulfilment are ignored, and that conversely these needs cannot be met, except in the short term, by the inefficient employer.

Industrial relations problems arise at the workplace when employees' needs as human beings are ignored and when the manager's objectives, or his methods of achieving them, conflict with the employees' objectives. Most conflict occurs over attempts by management, employees or unions to influence either side of the wage/effort bargain. In fact, virtually all industrial relations problems are about earnings, i.e. determination of pay and pay structures, allocation to job or wage category, piece work, bonuses, overtime or effort, e.g. time spent on the job, amount produced, quality, work measurement systems, flexibility between jobs, or resistance to management efforts to influence these factors which result in disciplinary issues.

To minimize conflict, management should aim to produce understood and felt-fair policies which will have the acceptance if not the commitment of the unions and the majority of the workforce. These should include policies for resolving grievances and handling indiscipline. In summary a company's personnel policies should enable it to hire, retain and motivate all employees, and at the workplace be applied by a management which understands the spirit and the intent of each aspect of policy and is trained to handle problems arising. In other words, to minimize problems, the management needs policies which recognize the human needs of individuals and which give it maximum control of those factors in the working environment that are most likely to create conflict between it and employees or between employees and employees.

Wage structures

Although other conditions of employment are regarded as important by employees, with very few exceptions people go to work to earn money to provide for themselves and their families. In considering earnings, and employees usually regard earnings as more important than wage rates, they will compare what they get with earnings for similar work in other companies and what they earn compared with other employees in their own place of work. Pay policies, therefore, have to be designed with both these in mind. The level of pay *vis-à-vis* other employers in the region will influence a company's ability to hire and retain people, and will normally be determined by annual negotiations. Internal differentials however, will be a feature of the company's wage structure, and can cause more problems than wage levels if not well designed and controlled (see Chapter 8). There is no one best way of paying people, and each organization needs to analyse its own needs and plan its wage structure accordingly. Different views are held about the relative merits of payment by results (PBR) systems and measured daywork and other ways of paying for time on the job.

One of the advantages of payment by results is that it reduces the need for supervision and the employer, at least in theory, is only paying for work performed. The most effective PBR systems are those where employees have total control over their work rates and can see a clear and easily recognizable link between their efforts and their earnings. Most systems fail on this latter point because provisions normally have to be made for circumstances where employees are prevented from working at their optimum level, or where output is affected significantly by management actions. This leads to the adoption of complicated formulas for calculating earnings. As the clear relationship between effort and earnings is obscured the incentive effect is reduced.

There is also a potential industrial relations disadvantage in such systems. Because the conditions which govern the earnings centre round the job, the negotiation of the formula and factors affecting the formula are normally at the workplace, i.e. at a point where management's negotiating skills are probably weakest. In an industry where the product or process is subject to frequent changes such negotiations can occur just as frequently, with the potential for disruption that goes with all pay negotiations. This gives shop stewards a power to influence earnings which in other circumstances would be exercised only at the annual negotiations by the full-time officer or senior shop stewards. Apart from the conflict risk inherent in such situations, or perhaps because of it, PBR systems are more prone to wage drift, i.e. wage costs are not so controllable.

Other disadvantages of PBR systems are that they can restrict mobility because of the different earnings potential in different jobs, and can lead to inverse differentials between direct unskilled workers and indirect skilled workers. Efforts to overcome the latter by lieu bonuses etc., lead to complicated wage structures. These factors partly explain the decline in the popularity of PBR systems in recent years, although the decline was arrested as unemployment grew and with it management confidence to resist union pressures and maintain or improve production standards.

The most common system of payment is still payment by the hour, week or month for time spent at work. Although normally described this way, it is important for managers to assert the principle that pay is for time *worked* and not for time spent at the place of work or time clocked. Failure to adopt and maintain such a philosophy can lead to paying employees who have deliberately stopped work due to a dispute, or who are absent without permission from their workplace, albeit still on company premises. Because employees' effort is not geared to earnings, such systems require closer supervision of employees, and conflict tends to be about the supervisors' control of time on the job and work effort.

Whatever system is in operation at the workplace, some method of deciding relativities has to be devised. In the absence of management or union pressures to introduce other methods, the employer can use the simple divisions of skilled (those jobs which require an apprenticeship), semi-skilled and unskilled to determine the rates of manual workers. This has the advantages of being simple and, therefore, easily understood and generally acceptable as it is based on the traditional rules of relating pay to different levels of skill. Three categories are seldom sufficient, however, to reflect the different levels of skill, responsibilities, and conditions that are involved in most companies. More often one will find more than one skilled rate, and indirect workers such as storemen and forklift truck drivers receiving a different rate from direct production workers.

Although many quasi-scientific methods exist for measuring relative job values, the most important factor in determining internal relativities is the custom or tradition in that particular plant locality or industry. Changing an established pattern of differentials is so fraught with problems that there is a saying in personnel circles that the best wage structure is the one you have. Where circumstances arise which make it necessary to change the structure it is worth going to considerable lengths in consulting with unions and employees to get maximum acceptance. 'Felt fairness' is a vital ingredient if conflict over internal relativities is to be avoided, and many a job evaluation system which takes account of skill, training, physical effort, working conditions, etc., fails to get employee commitment because it ignores this point (see Chapter 7). In designing wage structures based on job content it is also important to avoid job descriptions which subsequently become an inflexible basis for job or wage grade demarcations.

Shifts and overtime

In capital intensive industries profitability is closely related to the utilization of installed capacity and although demand will dictate the level of output, theoretically the aim should be to run expensive equipment such as presses or computers as close to twenty-four hours a day as possible. This requires some form of shift working which, because it is generally unpopular with employees, involves premium payments. These too, if conflict is to be avoided, need to be related to custom and practice, be felt fair and closely controlled to avoid wide disparities of earnings developing between shift and day workers. Too wide a gap creates problems when workers have to be moved off of shift rotas due to technological or other changes.

Many types of shift rotas exist and the two factors which determine choice are the needs of the operation and cost. Hidden costs which need careful scrutiny are payments to employees when covering for absenteeism, holiday working, overtime outside normal shift hours and 'call-in' and 'standby' pay. Time spent in studying the options can pay off in much reduced labour costs.

Other considerations include legal restrictions on hours of work of juveniles and females, management cover of the system, integration of activities with non-shift working departments, and employees travel and eating arrangements. Where continuous cover of a process or operation is essential, it is useful to have a clause in shift workers' conditions requiring them to stay on the job until such time as their relief turns up or management makes alternative arrangements for covering the duties.

There are industrial relations advantages in creating and maintaining separate shift identities, for example by each shift having its own representative, so that problems do not automatically spill over from one shift to the next.

To management overtime is a costly necessary evil; to the unions it is something which they believe helps to keep down basic wage rates and which if eliminated would result in more employment. To the average employee overtime is attractive as a means of supplementing income. Because of this dichotomy between the official union view and that of the members, shop stewards often try to argue grievances about reduced overtime opportunities on other grounds.

Although overtime is necessary at times and in some circumstances can provide a cheaper and more flexible alternative to shift working as a means of improving capacity utilization, there are very good reasons for keeping it under strict control. First and foremost is the real risk that pressure on managers, supervisors and employees to produce to full capacity in basic hours tends to relax with the easy availability of extra time. It also encourages employees to 'create' overtime by restricting output or in other ways. Where supervisors are also paid for overtime, their incentive to eliminate such practices is reduced. Regular overtime gives an artificial earnings level which leads to employee discontent when it falls off, and encourages them and their unions to press for overtime sharing arrangements inconsistent with management's needs. Two common examples of this are 'one in all in' arrangements, i.e. the whole department or section working when the job only requires a smaller number, and overtime rotas which involve the overtime being performed by 'the next one on the list' and not necessarily the one best suited to the work. While overtime rotas are obviously a fair way of allocating popular (or unpopular) overtime, where agreed they should include a provision giving management the ultimate right to choose the employees required to work. The union will argue all workers are equal, but if a speedy repair to a complicated piece of machinery is required there is little point in allocating someone with no experience on that particular equipment.

Management control of overtime working can be applied by blanket bans on specific areas or all the plant, or by ensuring that overtime is only paid for if authorized at a senior level, or by giving heads of departments tight overtime budgets. The use of overtime bans as a sanction, although not now so common, is still used by unions and employees. Management's best response is to live with the ban for as long as possible, having previously taken whatever contingency action, e.g. building stocks, is possible in the circumstances. Sometimes the first experience of an overtime ban, by demonstrating what is and what is not essential overtime work, leads to management reducing subsequent overtime levels and planning avoiding action such as putting essential work out to contract. The prudent employer will also take steps to prevent employees minimizing their own loss while causing him maximum inconvenience. He would not, for example, allow a selective ban which still permitted Sunday (maximum overtime premium) working – he would insist the ban was total!

Managers also need to realize that although overtime in most organizations is voluntary, once an employee has agreed to work overtime he or she has the same contractual obligations to attend on time and obey the normal rules of effort, adhering to specified break times, etc. It is surprising how often even experienced supervisors and managers let the voluntary nature of overtime mislead them into allowing lower standards of conduct in overtime hours.

To the extent that salaried workers work shifts and are paid for overtime, all of the above principles apply equally to them.

Work effort

Whether payment by results systems are in operation or not, there are advantages in using appropriate work measurement techniques to set standards against which individual or group effort can be judged. Conventional time and motion study for direct workers, activity sampling for maintenance and other indirect workers, objectives set and agreed between subordinates and seniors linked with performance appraisal forms for middle management are an example of a pattern of measurement that could be applied in most organizations. Once standards are set it is the task of management at all levels to see they are met. At the level of the manual worker, the job of getting the required effort is that of the *supervisor* or *foreman*. Put simply, foremen get paid to make other people work and they do this by making sure that employees have the materials, tools and training, clear instructions as to what is required of them, and the degree of overseeing necessary to overcome problems, including employees' problems. They thus ensure that consistent effort is applied to the work in hand.

It is impossible to overemphasize the importance of the foreman in creating and maintaining good relations at the workplace. As he is often the only member of management the employee meets daily on a face to face basis, to the employee the foreman is the management. The exception to this is in situations where the foreman is identified with the work group and not with the company as happens, for example, with weak foremen who avoid the responsibilities of their position and pass on management instructions 'disowning' them in the process.

Because of the key role foremen play in the industrial relations system, time, effort and money spent on improving their selection and training is one of the best personnel investments that can be made. Skill in handling subordinates and dealing with their problems can prevent issues becoming inflated and substantially reduce the business handled by shop stewards.

The foreman's job is also critical, because he is the one charged with ensuring management's policies are translated into action. It is he who has to see employees are on the job for all the time for which they are paid, obeying the rules regarding safety etc., and applying themselves to producing a minimum standard of work both in quantity and quality terms. He allocates work to employees, and employees to different tasks. His experience teaches him that he must treat people as individuals, and be scrupulously fair if he is to get their cooperation. Often he will use techniques to motivate employees which are not necessarily supported by his superiors, e.g. if his superiors believe in a management style which he knows to be unworkable in practice.

To assist the foreman there need to be recognized policies and procedures covering time spent on and off the job. In a large company, written passes permitting employees to visit the time office, personnel department or medical station during working hours are a useful control. The times of entering and leaving can be recorded on them, thus enabling such periods to be booked separately from job hours and protect the employee against unfair accusations of wasting time. A system of prior appointments arranged by the foreman with the specialist department will also reduce the time spent on such visits. Provision of efficient catering services both for meals and tea breaks, and cloakroom facilities and time clocks close to the working area will also help the foreman to maintain control of the work effort.

The practice sometimes adopted in industry of having the clocking station patrolled at end of shift by supervision to prevent employees leaving the job early to queue at the clock is an admission that foremen are not doing their job of controlling employees at the workplace. Where employees are caught on the clock before time, however, they should be immediately clocked out to provide accurate evidence of the time they were there to support any disciplinary action that may be taken.

'Go slows'

'Go slows' or 'working to rule' are sanctions sometimes applied in support of employees' claims or grievances, and unless tackled promptly by management can prove costly and become a regular form of action. The rule which must be applied is that employees get paid to work normally, defined as the way and at the pace generally obtaining, and anything less than that standard of effort does not attract payment. Faced with a go slow or work to rule the appropriate foreman or manager might first tell the shop steward and then all employees involved that unless normal working is resumed in, say, ten minutes they will not be paid. If normal working is not resumed, the foreman might then identify each individual taking part, making sure not to include people willing to work but prevented from doing so by the others' actions. At the conclusion of the action this list should be passed to the time office with the appropriate instructions.

Lateness and absence

Apart from the obvious costs of lost production due to lateness and absence, the steps taken to cover the job of men absent may create quality problems and grievances among employees who may be moved to unfamiliar work. For all these reasons, adequate policies for minimizing absence and its effects are essential (see Chapter 19).

The key role in any absence control procedure is again played by the foreman. He should have a personal knowledge of each of his subordinates, such as where they live, method of travel to work, state of health and whether there are any domestic circumstances (such as an invalid wife) which have to be taken into account when considering attendance records. The foreman's job is to encourage good attendance and timekeeping in all employees to the point where each accepts it is his own personal responsibility to get to work on time, to give prior warning if some foreseen absence is necessary, and to inform the company as soon as possible when unforeseen absence occurs. A personal interest in employees' health and welfare supported by friendly letters and visits to sick employees have more effect on discouraging lateness and absence than disciplinary sanctions.

Shop stewards will often cooperate in persuading employees to improve their attendance to avoid the problems which absenteeism can cause on a section, and to prevent it becoming a disciplinary issue. Where such an approach fails, however, and disciplinary measures are necessary these should be progressive, i.e. verbal warning, followed by written warning(s), suspension and, in the last resort, dismissal. The objectives of such a policy are to get the employee to be a good timekeeper and attender. Comprehensive and accurate records of each employee's attendance designed to show at a glance significant patterns such as Monday and Friday absence or absence attached to a particular shift or holidays are essential to good absence control. These summary records, as distinct from the clock card which covers a week, need to cover at least a year's attendance and absence so that trends can be recognized. Although kept by the time office or a personnel records section they should be readily available to the foreman who should be required to check them at least monthly. Periodic follow-ups by personnel officers or line managers will quickly show whether poor attendance is being dealt with by the foreman.

Absence and lateness has to be dealt with on an individual basis so that all the circumstances can be taken into account, and it is not advisable to adopt a mechanistic approach, such as two absences in a month warrant a warning and two more a suspension, etc. Such norms quickly become common knowledge and offenders schedule their absence to avoid the penalties.

Discipline

Because most people have an inherent sense of fairness, and because disciplinary actions strike at the roots of job security, discipline can quickly become a highly emotive matter. To avoid such problems most organizations have well-publicized, and often agreed, procedures for handling cases of indiscipline. These are usually designed to ensure that there is a thorough investigation with the right of representation, that someone not immediately involved in the incident passes judgement, and that there is a right of appeal to someone else in the organization.

Some companies' arrangements also include a provision for referring cases to independent arbitration. The Code of Practice on Disciplinary Practice and Procedures issued by ACAS sets down standards for the guidance of employers. Since the establishment of Industrial Tribunals to hear claims of unfair dismissal, most companies have introduced or revised their internal procedures to comply with the Code which is used by tribunals as a standard.

It is normally the function of the personnel officer to see that the disciplinary policy and procedure is correctly applied in each case. It will be necessary first to advise line management on the distinction between the day to day criticisms and cautions, which are part of routine exchanges between supervisors and subordinates, and those matters which call for formal action. It will also be necessary to distinguish between cases of indiscipline, normally a breach of a specific rule or agreement, and poor work performance due to inadequacy which should be handled by counselling, training, transfers to alternative work, etc.

An important part of the personnel officer's function in the disciplinary procedure is to bring a detached judgement to bear which may be more difficult for the line managers more directly involved. It is not uncommon, for example, for a line manager to believe so strongly in demonstrating support for foremen that he finds difficulty in being completely objective if this involves criticism of the way a foreman has behaved in an incident under examination. The personnel officer who feels it necessary to associate himself completely with the line management view of the case will not be capable of fulfilling his proper role in the process, including making sure that all the facts, especially those which may not show the management in the best light, are brought out. Failure to bring out all the relevant facts at an early stage can result in the management as a whole taking up fixed positions on incomplete evidence, a situation which can lead to confrontations with the workforce and an eventual climb down by management.

It will also be part of the personnel officer's job to prepare a comprehensive record of the case and the hearing(s), advise management on appropriate penalties, bearing in mind all the circumstances including precedent and the offender's previous work record. He may subsequently have to represent the company at a tribunal, so he needs to understand the law relating to dismissal (see Chapters 12 and 14).

Associated with its disciplinary policy, the management will also need a policy on whether or not employees are prosecuted for some offences such as stealing or damaging company property. It is important for management to understand that although some offences which are disciplinary matters can also lead to court proceedings, the disciplinary procedure can, and should, be kept entirely separate. The disciplinary procedure is to determine whether an employee is guilty of a breach of company rules, whereas a court will decide whether the actions in question broke any laws. It can be quite proper, for example, to discharge an employee even though a court finds him or her innocent. Neither is there any need to await a court decision before taking such steps, and if an employee refuses to make any defensive statement on the grounds that it may prejudice a court hearing then the company is entitled to come to a decision without such a statement. Managers who find these concepts difficult to grasp should be referred to the tribunal and EAT decisions on such issues which are quite clear. (See Chapter 14.)

Failure to separate out discipline and criminal prosecutions in this way will inevitably lead to long delays while the judicial processes are applied, which can take months, and claims that the employee concerned should be kept in employment or on paid suspension. More serious perhaps than the cost involved is the risk that due to some legal technicality the employee is found innocent of the criminal charge and management comes under strong pressure to reinstate an employee it knows is guilty of serious indiscipline.

In administering its disciplinary policy, management's prime aim should be consistency. As stated earlier, a large part of the risk of conflict associated with discipline stems from employees' sense of fairness and security which has to be satisfied. Nothing strikes employees as more unfair than inconsistency. Consistency of approach by management and employees' feelings of security are linked because people in any society need to know how they stand in relation to their peers and those in authority over them. In the armed services this is evident in the higher morale in well-disciplined units.

Inconsistency in discipline in the workplace may be due to one foreman taking action for behaviour which other foremen ignore or, more usually, foremen forced to take action due to higher management insistence over matters which they have previously tolerated. Indeed consistency is so vital an element of fairness as seen by employees that they will accept much tighter disciplinary standards consistently applied than lower standards inconsistently applied. The personnel officer needs to keep this well in mind when asked to support some sudden management drive on, for example, people queuing at the canteen before the break bell goes. He can then advise his colleagues that such moves may cause a reaction out of all proportion to that anticipated, and that preliminary steps such as individual communications on the problem before disciplinary action is taken will yield better results.

Because increasingly people will only accept what they can understand as necessary and reasonable, companies need to examine their rules to ensure they can all be rationalized. Works rules, unlike most agreements, are not subject to periodic review and often contain outdated requirements. Managers and supervisors who have to enforce the rules, as well as those subjected to them, need to understand and accept the reasons for their existence. The common practice of allowing outdated rules to fall into disuse is not a satisfactory alternative to conscious management decision.

Disciplinary sanctions in general use are formal warnings, suspensions and dismissal. Although less serious offences normally result in these being applied in this sequence, clearly circumstances can occur which justify suspension being applied without prior warnings, or dismissal without prior suspension or warnings. The case law developed by industrial tribunals is a good guide to the offences considered serious enough to warrant instant dismissal, and similarly also demonstrates the circumstances in which a chain of incidents, in themselves minor, can be regarded as sufficient grounds for dismissal. In this latter case, however, recorded progressive action is important.

All forms of disciplinary action should be clearly recorded and communicated to the employee. In the case of dismissal, the employer should confine himself to the simplest form of words, such as gross misconduct, so as not to limit any subsequent arguments he may want to put to an industrial tribunal.

Trade union relations

If, as stated at the beginning of this chapter, management's industrial relations objective is to avoid problems by getting maximum control over those factors in the workplace environment likely to cause conflict, then clearly its policy on the role of unions must be carefully thought through and understood by management, unions, and employees. Where the company recognizes a union or unions, the basis of such policy should be contained in agreements setting out the union's collective bargaining and other representative rights, and preferably also detailing the machinery and facilities given to representatives to carry out their agreed functions. If the company does not recognize trade unions then it is equally important that management and employees know why not, and what alternative methods exist for the establishment of pay and conditions and for registering and resolving grievances. In most big companies a mixture of the two apply in that unions are recognized to represent some categories of employees and other employees are subject to separate conditions. The quickest way to drive all employees into union membership is to treat unrepresented employees less favourably than those whose conditions are negotiated and defended by trade unions.

Avoiding problems due to misunderstanding the role of trade unions requires policy or agreement on the following:

1 The categories of employees represented
2 Whether such representation involves collective bargaining of pay and conditions, representation in grievance situations, or both
3 What conditions are included in the bargaining rights, e.g. does it include all fringe benefits such as pensions and canteen prices?
4 The frequency and method of bargaining, e.g. separate arrangements for each union or category of workers, joint body, full-time union officials, lay representatives, or both and how many.
5 A procedure for discussing and resolving grievances.
6 The number of representative constituencies.
7 How representatives are elected or appointed and results notified.
8 What facilities such representatives have – i.e. time off the job, for what, and whether paid or not, how do they communicate with members, each other and full time officers?
9 How, when and where union dues are to be collected.
10 Rights of non-union employees.

A clear understanding on the above by management, unions and employees will help to make sure that problems arising at the workplace are substantial ones and not based on misunderstanding about relative roles.

First and foremost, workplace representatives are employees with the same obligations as others to attend on time and do the job for which they are hired. They are, therefore, subject to the same disciplinary policy if they breach the rules. Unlike other employees, however, they have duties to perform on behalf of their members and the union which require them to spend time away from their normal job. As representatives are employees paid by the company, they should be made to account for their time, and be required to obtain their supervisor's permission before leaving their job. The freedom given to representatives for their duties will also depend on the degree of responsibility they demonstrate and, therefore, the degree of trust felt by their immediate supervisors. A representative who is known to waste time away from the job is more likely to have his freedom to move around curtailed than one who handles matters expeditiously.

It is important to make a clear distinction between indiscipline as an employee, for which the normal procedure and sanctions should apply, and unacceptable behaviour in the role of representative. The prime purpose for which an employer recognizes and pays representatives is to operate the agreed grievance procedure, including the observing of the 'no strikes' clause. He is entitled to expect that the representative will at all times observe agreements and encourage others to do so, and conduct himself properly, i.e. with courtesy, in his relationships with management. The majority will do so and play a constructive role in resolving problems, but occasionally a representative will use his representative status to avoid work and create problems which would not otherwise exist. Managers should handle such situations in a similar way to improper behaviour by other employees but with the following distinctions.

The representative concerned should first be warned and the convenor or senior representative informed. If the behaviour complained of continues then a more formal warning, confirmed in writing should be given and the district official informed that if there is no improvement the company will have to consider withdrawing the man's representative facilities. The latter is a step with potentially serious consequences and needs to be properly understood and handled.

It is not uncommon to hear supervisors and managers talking about taking away a shop steward's credentials. This management cannot do, as a representative's authority to represent union members is given by the union following its due processes, normally an election confirmed by the branch or district. Only the union, therefore, has the power to reverse that process and remove his representative status, 'his credentials'. To operate as a representative, however, he requires that the management should recognize him as such and give the facilities to consult with his members, contact other representatives and his full-time official and meet with appropriate management. Clearly the management can refuse to grant him such facilities, but without the cooperation of the union this could lead to serious conflict. Naturally, full-time officials are concerned to maintain a mutually beneficial working relationship with employers and will not normally condone behaviour which reflects badly on the reputation of the union. If the official is convinced that the behaviour complained of is not acceptable then he will counsel the representative, or himself arrange for another employee to be appointed as the representative for that area.

Less rare than such cases are those where management becomes aware that an unsuitable employee, e.g. one with a bad timekeeping or disciplinary record is standing in an election for a steward's job. They then quickly tip off the convenor or official that the candidate would be unacceptable because of the difficulties which could occur if further disciplinary action were taken against him, or if he had to defend people on charges he had previously faced himself. Contrary to the impression given by some parts of the media, this degree of cooperation between the parties in industrial relations is not uncommon.

Management's primary aim in all industrial relations problems is to resolve them by discussion within the agreed procedure. Sometimes, however, this proves impossible, and before the procedure is exhausted employees try to influence the decision by stopping work or applying the sanctions referred to earlier in this chapter. Faced with an unconstitutional work stoppage the manager needs to act quickly to contain it. If the employees are still on the premises he needs to explain, either through the shop steward or directly, that the issue is being discussed and can be resolved that way. This dialogue can be valuable in bringing out aspects of the problem not previously seen as significant. Some stoppages are ended merely by arranging or expediting meetings at a more senior level or with the full-time official, i.e. by satisfying employees that their grievance is going to receive adequate and speedy attention. Because the strike is in breach of an agreement, managers will make every effort to get the shop stewards and official to get the issue back within procedure. As stated in an earlier chapter, however, unions do not generally regard 'no strike' clauses as sacrosanct, and will argue that the situation now requires a pragmatic approach to resolve it.

Ending a stoppage where the employees have actually gone home is more difficult, as the initiative to call them together again usually rests with the union representatives. Unless it is a one shift stoppage, or arrangements have already been made for a further meeting, they will not normally exercise this initiative until satisfied that they have a concession from management which will enable them to get a return to work. Management can influence the outcome of any mass meeting by communicating directly to employees, and the letter to employees' homes has become a common device. However, there are few, if any, cases where such direct communications have resulted in a return to work without a meeting addressed by the union first taking place.

Management's leverage in a strike rests almost entirely on the fact that employees are losing earnings, and their aims must be to create sufficient change in the situation, without completely conceding, and to communicate that change to employees in a way that persuades them that further loss of earnings is unjustified.

Constitutional strikes, i.e. those which take place after the procedural steps to resolve the problem have been exhausted, do not generally call for a very different approach except in two obvious ways. Discussions are more likely to be in the control of national union officials who may decide to declare it official, and the management cannot use the argument that an agreement has been breached. If the strike is declared official then the union will pay strike pay (this, however, is usually insufficient to affect the duration of a strike significantly), and picketing will probably be more effective.

Personnel officers should make themselves familiar with the law on picketing (see Chapter 13), but more importantly decide with their colleagues the practicalities of operating in a picketed plant. The Department of Employment has published a Code of Practice on the subject, and the Institute of Personnel Management has a handy checklist which includes such steps as making sure the local police are aware, establishing contact between management and the pickets and advising employees still working of the situation. Sensible precautions will reduce the risk of the dispute being exacerbated by incidents on the picket line. Contact with the pickets on such practical matters as whether or not they can use the company's toilet facilities can provide a channel of communication usually missing in a strike situation.

All strikes are resolved in the end by discussion and compromise whether constitutional or unconstitutional, and whether official or unofficial.

Surveys of industrial action suggest that it is concentrated in a few industries, and much more common in large units, e.g. works or sites employing large numbers, than in smaller ones. To the personnel officer in the average company, therefore, a strike will be an unusual occurrence, indicating, unless it is a strike in support of the annual wage bargaining, that some aspect of personnel policy has slipped out of gear. Every strike, therefore, should be subject to a *post mortem* by management when it is over and after emotions have evaporated but before the facts are forgotten. The following questions are appropriate to such an examination:

If it was unconstitutional why did employees not use the agreed procedure?

Does the procedure need improving, e.g. by agreeing time limits on each stage, by more employee involvement or communication?

Have supervisors and junior management got sufficient skill/authority to deal with employees' grievances quickly?

Did management handle the grievance properly, i.e. with the appropriate urgency and sensitivity?

Were the personnel department involved early enough?

Were management attitudes a significant factor, e.g. did they adopt an open problem-solving approach to the grievance, or an authoritarian win/lose attitude?

What did the dispute cost?

Could it have been avoided, how, at what cost?

Such enquiries might demonstrate a need to improve the procedure or to train supervisors and managers in handling grievances or, and this is more serious, they might show that employees lack confidence in the procedure as a way of resolving problems – more serious because this suggests a breakdown in trust between employees and management which can take a long time to re-establish.

Although strikes caused by politically motivated employees are not unknown, the personnel officer who always assumes they are the cause in his company could miss other factors on which he can take remedial action. Management's objective must always be to create the conditions which reduce conflict, and an atmosphere which encourages all employees and their union representatives to believe that problems can be best resolved by discussion.

Consultation and communications

By establishing some machinery for regular consultation between management and employee representatives, such as a joint committee meeting monthly, exchanges can take place separate from the adversarial atmosphere of the grievance procedure. Companies which take consultation seriously ensure that such committees are kept alive and healthy by using them as a forum for debating all plans and policies affecting the plant and its employees, and by supplying all committee members with the facts and statistics for informed debate. Such committees also ensure that management is aware of employee views and potential problems and can modify its plans to avoid or minimize employee and union resistance. Allowed to develop a proper role in the consultative and communications process, employee representatives acquire a broader understanding of the company's problems and can act as a stabilizing influence in workplace industrial relations.

If workplace problems are to be avoided by policies which address the needs of people, their need for recognition as individuals with intelligence and an interest in their job, company and product must be met. A policy of open communication to all employees meets this need, as well as the more obvious one of avoiding problems caused by misunderstanding. Companies that do not communicate should not be surprised if their employees interpret this as a sign that management does not see them as people with an interest in, and the intelligence to understand, what is going on around them. Where there is no communication from management the information vacuum will be filled by rumour, and employees will turn to their union representatives for information.

Deficiencies in communication can occur at all levels, and policies which do not embrace middle management and supervision will not be successful. To be effective, open communication must become part of management style, reflecting a willingness to involve all employees in the company's plans, problems and successes.

Although this chapter is headed industrial relations at the workplace, it will, I hope, now be obvious to the reader that what is termed industrial relations is inseparable from personnel management. It is all about people, and good industrial relations flow from policies which address employees' needs as human beings and try to reconcile these with the aims of the organization.

Discussion questions

1 Identify and categorize the main sources of conflict which can arise between the interests of management and employees at work.
2 Discuss the advantages and disadvantages of payment-by-results schemes.
3 Why should overtime working sometimes be regarded as 'a necessary evil'?
4 What are the main difficulties in a typical foreman's job? Why is it sometimes said that the foreman 'stands victim not monarch of all he surveys'?
5 What criteria would you adopt for the selection and training of first-line supervisors or foremen?
6 What are the main factors to be borne in mind in drawing up a disciplinary procedure?
7 What are the normal roles and duties of a shop steward?

CHAPTER 11

Collective bargaining

by Paul Roots
Formerly Director of Industrial Relations, Ford Motor Company

Bargaining between employers and employees over pay and conditions has probably existed since the first time that men were paid to work for others. Collective bargaining, that is representatives bargaining on behalf of groups, must be nearly as old. The phrase is generally used today to describe the process by which trade unions negotiate on behalf of their members with employers or their representatives. In this chapter we shall take a brief look at the different types of collective bargaining machinery in Britain, the matters involved, the parties' objectives, and then, in more detail, at the way in which bargaining is planned and conducted, the results implemented and how the process is influenced by external factors.

The advantages of orderly collective bargaining in our industrial society have been widely accepted. From the Royal Commission on Labour in 1891 to the Royal Commission on Trade Unions and Employers Associations in 1968 (The Donovan Commission) the benefits of a formal system of conducting negotiations through representative machinery have been supported. The Whitley Committee of 1917 went further and advocated industry-wide bargaining and recommended a model constitution for such bodies, suggesting the title Joint Industrial Councils.

Collective bargaining can take place at almost any level within industry. At the time of the Donovan Commission the then Ministry of Labour estimated that, including statutory wage fixing bodies and the smallest industries, there were approximately five hundred industries which were covered by industry-wide agreements on pay. Industry-wide bargaining is normally carried out by all the unions and employers associations in the industry meeting in an organized way, and normally with a permanent chairman and secretary. Wage Councils, established under the provisions of the Wages Council Act 1945, like the Trade Boards that preceded them, were introduced to set minimum wages in industries which lacked effective voluntary collective bargaining machinery. There were twenty-six Wages Councils in being at the beginning of 1983, but at the time of writing their future is in doubt. Whether or not covered by such agreements, however, bargaining can take place on a regional level, at individual company level which may embrace one or many plants, at plant level, at department level and, particularly in some types of payment by results situations, at the level of a small group of workers within a department. The level at which negotiations take place will be the result of many factors current and historical. The number and relationship of employers or unions, geographical dispersal of companies, wage structures, technology, the existence of one or more dominant companies and management style are some of the factors which may have led to the focus of collective bargaining being industry, company or plant based.

Even where bargaining is carried out at an industry level, for example in engineering, it does not preclude further bargaining at another level. In most manufacturing industry, this is the norm. In the engineering industry negotiations are carried out between the Engineering Employers Federation (EEF) and the Confederation of Shipbuilding or Engineering Workers, colloquially known as the Confed. They agree minimum rates for specific skilled and unskilled categories, leaving negotiations on each related job classification for individual employers and their union representatives. Basic weekly hours of work are negotiated at EEF Confed level, but the way they are spread, e.g. number and length of shifts, are left for local level discussion. Other matters covered in this industry wide agreement include guaranteed week provisions, overtime, holidays and shift work.

Because the organization of salaried workers into unions is a comparatively recent development, most of the industry-wide collective bargaining arrangements, which are long established, apply to manual workers only. Similarly most bargaining arrangements at company and plant level do not cover all employees. The term bargaining unit is used to define a specific group of employees covered by an agreement on pay or on pay and conditions. A bargaining unit may include different categories of workers and involve one or more unions, and there may be a number of bargaining units within one company or plant.

The most common arrangements at plant level are those involving one bargaining unit covering all manual workers, two where salaried unions are also recognized, or three in those organizations where craft and general workers unions negotiate separately. There is no limit, however, to the number of bargaining units there might be except as prescribed by agreement. Unions tend to group together for bargaining purposes to gain collective strength. Employers in strongly unionized companies generally prefer to deal with as few bargaining units as practicable to preserve a stable pattern of wage relationships by avoiding leap-frogging claims, and to reduce the amount of management time spent on negotiations. Conversely they will try to keep separate bargaining units where it will prevent the spillover of pay and benefits from one group to another.

Employers will often try to avoid recognizing a union's right to negotiate on behalf of a group or all employees, or insist on a minimum level of membership before doing so. Sometimes, however, they will use the union's desire to get recognition to gain the exclusion of other unions, and to gain the most advantageous representation arrangements. They might, for example, seek an agreement which excludes personnel department staff or those with supervisory responsibilities, or those who have access to wage cost and other confidential information. Because the unions' prime reason for existence, what most members pay their contributions for, is to negotiate wage increases they are keen to achieve that right. At the point where they want it but have not the strength to coerce the employer to concede it, the employer is in a 'buyer's market', and the able one uses that to his advantage.

Bargaining units then may embrace all or just some of the employees in an industry, company or component part of a company. It is rare in private industry for the unit to cover employees above supervisory level, although this is not uncommon in the public sector.

Although there are wide variations in the levels at which bargaining takes place, and in the categories of employees covered in bargaining units, this wide variation is not evident in the matters which are negotiated. Until the 1960s the area of collective bargaining was confined almost exclusively to wages, hours of work and holidays, a pattern which had seen little change in the previous eighty years. Pensions, sick pay, accident benefit and unemployment pay had been pursued by the trade unions through legislative action rather than at the negotiating table. A combination of circumstances extended bargaining into the area of fringe benefits during the 1960s:

1   The thirty-five years following the Second World War was the longest period of full employment experienced the UK, and enabled the unions to consolidate their position throughout industry.

2   The prime political objectives of union leaders and other socialists, the nationalization of basic industries coal, steel, transport, educational opportunities for all and the welfare state had been introduced by the post-war Labour Government.

3   Successive phases of voluntary and statutory incomes policies prevented the unions from using their new won strength to boost their members' wage packets.

4   Employers who suffered the disadvantages of restrictive practices and unconstitutional strikes found this compensated for by weak sterling, which in international trade terms gave them cheap labour. Few employers were concerned about or even knew the fringe benefit element of their labour costs.

In looking for loopholes in incomes policies, unions and employers, who were equally concerned to improve their conditions so they could compete for labour, found their attention directed to three areas at different times: to non-wage economic elements such as lay-off pay, pensions and holidays, to wage structure changes and productivity bargaining and to non-economic areas of management prerogatives.

In the different economic conditions of the 1980s there has been an extension of communications and consultation. This development is in turn the result of a number of factors, the belief that employees' attitudes could be changed and harnessed to higher productivity by explaining the cost-competitive problems facing industry and the British economy, the desire to demonstrate that EEC legislation on employee involvement was not needed in the British voluntary system, and the visibility given to the problems of inflation and industry by the media. In general a heightened awareness by unions, employees and the public of the whole area of labour costs, conditions and comparability with Continental practice. The result of these changes is a considerable extension of the matters now discussed by the parties to collective bargaining at all levels. Collective bargaining in Britain then is not simply a coming together at one level of organized labour and employers to argue the sharing of the economic fruits of their joint effort, but a complex dialogue by many groups at many levels on a wide range of economic and non-economic issues.

The objectives of the parties in collective bargaining

The objective of an American trade union was once summed up by its leader in one word, MORE! As the previous paragraphs have shown, however, a union's aims in collective bargaining are likely to be more complex. In any set of negotiations the union will be trying to achieve a mixture of its own and employees' aspirations. The use of the word 'employees' as distinct from members is deliberate, as a union only gets its bargaining rights because of members employed in a particular organization, and the bargaining unit may include employees who are not members. Even if it does not, the union cannot assume that all concerned are committed to union policies. In deciding strategy, therefore, the wise union official will make a careful assessment of the employees' priorities and match union objectives carefully to them. A proper use of the unions' democratic processes will help to keep the two in step, but union officials, like the officials of all representative bodies, have to cope with membership apathy and judge whether the non-apathetic who become the spokesmen are reflecting their own or majority opinion.

The union will also be faced with the task of balancing the competing objectives of different groups within its own membership. It may have to deal with the conflicting views about differentials, piece workers and the rest, day workers and shift workers, male and female employees, the old and young with their different views about pensions, and a whole spectrum of opinion on a range of issues.

In order of importance a union's negotiating objectives will normally be a wage increase for all, improvements in conditions for the majority in the bargaining unit, and some feature which has become union policy such as reduced hours (basic and/or overtime) which may or may not have strong employee support. These items may be repetitive and feature in the claim year after year. Non-economic objectives, such as more involvement in management's decision-making are less likely to feature as part of the collective bargaining dialogue than to appear as the result of a disputed decision either within the avoidance of disputes procedure or following a strike or other collective action.

Employers' collective bargaining objectives similarly may appear simple, to keep down labour costs and resist the erosion of management's rights, but are in reality more complex. The need to keep down costs has to be balanced against the need to hire and retain good calibre employees and to avoid damaging disputes. In times of economic recession or competitive pressures, difficult judgements have to be made about the damage to customer and employee relations that can be caused by a strike or paying for increased wages by pricing action or putting off necessary investment. As in the union, there will also be different views within management of the priorities in a given situation.

The collective bargaining process can be viewed as falling into three separate stages, the mandating and planning stage, the negotiating stage and the ratification and implementation stage.

Mandating and planning

The consideration of all the objectives described above will feature in the planning of collective bargaining. The employer with access to specialist services either in his own personnel department or an employers' association will base his plan on a detailed assessment of the union's claim. In some organizations the process will start even before the claim is made. Newspaper reports will be collected and searched to understand the union's policy, comments from officials and shop stewards will be examined for hints on the union's priorities. Management will assess the strength of employee feeling on different issues which will feature in the negotiations in an effort to judge their willingness to strike. In parallel with these efforts the employer or his association will be conducting surveys of other companies wages and conditions so as to present competitive justification for their position, and to decide what changes they might need to make to compete for recruits in the labour market.

Following this evaluation, or often before it has been completed, the competent employer will cost his possible settlement. He will look particularly closely at elements which will pyramid, that is involve inevitable cost increases in related areas. For example, an increase in hourly base rates will cause increases to overtime and shift premiums where these are expressed as a percentage or fraction of base rates. The cost of holiday pay may also be increased in this way and nearly all wage increases raise pension costs.

It is during the planning and costing stage that the employer will consider whether he should try to offset some of the cost of negotiated increases. He may seek to do this in a number of ways, by increasing productivity, e.g. eliminating inefficient work practices or by amending his wage structure to reduce wage drift. He might even want to 'claw back' some benefit already conceded. Whatever route he decides to follow he will recognize that this increases his negotiating difficulties and plan accordingly.

The degree of sophistication with which this planning and costing takes place will vary considerably from organization to organization, and generally reflect the level of management professionalism in the undertaking.

Where the negotiations are being carried out by anyone other than the owner of the business, the employer's negotiators will be given a mandate so that they know the limits of their authority to commit the owner or owners. This is vital for successful negotiations, and in the more professional organizations this mandate will be detailed, covering each aspect of the claim and precisely formulating the negotiators' authority not only in economic terms but in the degree of strike risk the employer is able to take.

The union's planning will normally be far less structured. Overworked officials, often short of adequate back-up resources, will have one or two meetings with their shop stewards and list their main objectives. Some will use their Branches for this purpose, especially those general workers unions that have company or factory based Branches. Few unions have formal standard procedures for collecting members' views prior to negotiations.

Big unions have their own research officers to assist in the preparation of arguments, and have been known to use the facilities of Ruskin College to prepare claims data. The skilled use of research facilities by unions for collective bargaining purposes, however, tends to be the exception rather than the rule.

The negotiations

Negotiations will either take place on the employer's premises, in facilities provided by an employers' association, or in hired accommodation, e.g. a convenient hotel. A minimum of three but preferably four rooms are required, one for joint meetings, two separate adjournment rooms, and a fourth for secretarial services of typing and duplicating. A number of accessible and private telephones (but not in the joint meeting room) are also valuable. At negotiations which attract the media's attention, such as those in the nationalized industries or big companies regarded as pace setters, it is also advantageous and courteous to have a room where reporters and cameramen can wait. The room where the joint discussions take place should be large enough to accommodate all the known participants, including any note-takers introduced by either side, well ventilated and warm enough in winter, but above all private and quiet. Clattering china disturbing concentration is one of the many drawbacks of negotiating in hotels.

Meetings are agreed well in advance because trade union officials always have very full diaries. Tradition will usually determine whether it is a one meeting negotiation or a series of meetings spread over days or weeks. Despite the pre-arranged starting time it is not uncommon for the union side to seek a delay for last minute consultations. Unlike the management side which can easily arrange a pre-meeting and, in fact, may see each other every day, the officials on the union side may only come together as a group for negotiating purposes with a particular employer or employers' association. If the union negotiating body consists of full-time officers and lay representatives, this is even more likely.

Much has been written about the ritual of negotiations. The term is normally used to describe the formal presentation of arguments in support of a claim which neither side expects to be met, the rebuttal of these arguments and the making of an offer which equally neither side expects to be accepted, and finally, with or without the interspersing of threats, a settlement. Experience has taught most negotiators that traditional patterns of behaviour do have their value. Just as a skilled interviewer eases the tension in a job applicant by starting with easily answered questions, so the tension in the negotiating room, which can be considerable, is eased by the participants initially conforming to expected behaviour patterns. It is during this process that the careful listening and observing of the other side takes place. This pattern continues and gradually, as the debate proceeds and more provocative exchanges take place, the assessment of each other's position is developed.

Ritual or tradition will determine who speaks in the negotiations. There is normally one principal spokesman on either side of the table who may carry the whole argument for his side or encourage others to join in on particular aspects. Experienced negotiators know the importance of disciplined argument and will have agreed with their team beforehand how the debate is going to be conducted. It is often a source of surprise to observers of British negotiations that up to twenty shop stewards and officials may sit for hours in a meeting with only one of their number talking.

The method of recording negotiations varies considerably. Some bodies just make a brief note of the main points and at the other extreme one large company's negotiations are tape-recorded and verbatim reports produced. The most common practice, however, is for both sides to take their own notes of the proceedings but agreed minutes of the more important discussions are a feature of some industry-wide negotiations.

The discussions usually open with a presentation of the union's claim, although on rare occasions employers have tried to set the groundwork by explaining the economic circumstances facing them. Rare because it is breaking the pattern, the ritual, it usually creates resentment among the union side which may feel that its claim is being pre-judged. Arguing for wage increases is the paid union official's primary role, and the employer who attempts to restrict the way he plays that role could pay a penalty in estranged relationships which harm the early negotiating stages and could influence the final outcome.

The degree of sophistication with which the claim is presented will depend on a number of factors, custom and practice, the way the employer customarily argues his case, the views of the union side as to the value of sophisticated arguments, and the time and resources available to the unions for preparing their case. Experienced union negotiators will judge whether the susceptibility of an employer's side to reasoned argument overrides the power factor which is usually the vital element in determining the outcome of negotiations – usually, not always, because sometimes negotiations are conducted in circumstances where both sides are anxious to avoid conflict. The employer's need to stay competitive in the labour market may make him willing to make an offer acceptable to unions and employees.

The employers may make an opening offer at the same meeting the claim is presented. Alternatively they will take away the claim for study and costing and arrange a further meeting to respond. There are no hard and fast rules, but the larger the organization and the more detailed the claim the more likelihood of a delay between the claim and first offer.

A number of considerations will be weighed by the employer in framing an opening offer. It must be pitched high enough to ensure a continuing dialogue, i.e. not provoke a walk-out but it must not be at a level which limits manoeuvrability or raises unrealistic expectations about the finishing point. If there are areas of the claim where the employer does not intend to respond he will try to get that established at this stage and restrict the discussion to issues on which he is prepared to negotiate.

From this point both sides will be trying to persuade the other that they have to move from their position using whatever arguments they believe will have most influence. Their success will depend on the extent to which they have correctly judged the other's priorities and strengths. At what he judges the critical point the employer will make his final offer, and at that stage the unions will have to decide whether to accept or try to achieve more by strike action. If the employer has judged the situation correctly, the employees will not support a strike.

This typical sequence of claim, offer, argument, offer, argument and final offer is considerably more complicated where a range of items is being negotiated, e.g. pay, hours, pensions and vacation, or where the employer is also seeking something in return. In the latter case, for example where productivity bargaining is taking place, the employer would have previously made a judgement about the ability of the union side to deliver whatever is agreed. Productivity bargaining is likely to be more successful if carried out between those who are giving the money and those who are involved in the changes required in return. Full-time union officers cannot make employees adopt more flexible working patterns or give up cherished time off the job or valuable overtime. This type of negotiation also requires a detailed knowledge of workplace practices. Therefore, modifications to the normal negotiating process may have to be made to accommodate different levels of union and management representatives.

Ratification and implementation

As negotiated agreements are not usually legally binding in Britain their 'enforcement' will depend on the commitment of employers, unions and employees. If the union negotiating team did a good job in reflecting its members' aims at the negotiating table then it should be able to sell the results of its efforts and get a majority vote. This is an important part of the process and it is in the interest of both sides to ensure that the terms of the offer including those that might be unpopular are properly understood by all. The represented employees need to understand what they are being asked to accept, and all of management and supervision need to understand the offer so they can deal with questions and help sell the deal.

Like the mandating process, ratification takes different forms. Mass meetings and a show of hands on a straight proposal to accept or reject, votes by each union Branch, or in some unions a formal ballot.

The results of their members' ratification should be formally reported to the employer by the unions and arrangements made to record an agreement. This can be by appending signatures to a written document as is the custom in most large organizations, or by an exchange of letters of offer and acceptance. Only after this stage will the new terms be implemented by the employer. In a simple deal which just increases wages, little is needed except instructions to the firm's wages office to make the necessary adjustments. More complex negotiations, such as those involving productivity bargaining, present different problems. Not only is the communication and ratification aspect vital, but arrangements have to be made to introduce and monitor the changes. The employer will probably train his supervision in handling the changes before the agreement is signed, so that there is no delay in their introduction, and the new pay and practices become linked in employees' minds.

Where an agreement embraces many changes the wise employer will ensure that all the managers and supervisors understand not only the terms but the rationale behind the negotiations. This will enable them to counter criticism from employees and their representatives which might otherwise undermine commitment.

Government influence

The influence of the Government on collective bargaining stems from two sources, their actions as the country's largest employer and the actions they take to control the economy. Experience of different governments since 1960 proves that whether their stated policies are for a planned economy or non-interventionist they try to influence the level of wage settlements. The effects (or lack of) of successive stages of incomes policy on the level of settlements in the period 1965–1981 are illustrated in the Department of Employment's Research Paper No. 36.

The effects of government policy, however, are felt not only in the level of pay settlement but in the type of settlement reached. Incomes policy which allows increases above a norm where linked to increases in productivity, i.e. where they can be shown to be self-financing or non-inflationary, led to the popularity of productivity bargaining in the 1960s and production-linked bonus schemes in the 1970s.

In labour cost terms, a more damaging effect for employers was that created by incomes policies which restricted wage settlements but left fringe benefits unfettered. Many companies found themselves negotiating pensions and lay-off pay for the first time and facing increased union pressure on holiday arrangements and other inflation proof benefits as a result of government policy. In the 1982/83 wage round, sick pay costs were pushed up for most companies as a direct result of the Government's decision to transfer the responsibility for paying state sickness benefit to the employers and thereby putting it on the negotiating table, in many cases for the first time (see Chapter 12).

It is argued that trade unions' monopoly power prevents market forces deciding the level of wages. It is to be assumed, however, that the almost continuous shortage of labour between the end of the Second World War and the economic recession which started with the world oil crisis of 1979 had some influence on wage settlements. Trade union monopoly powers or supply and demand are both over simplifications, however, as employers are not interested in wages but labour costs which are determined by wages, fringes and productivity. In international terms they are also affected by the rate of exchange so that in the post-war 'labour shortage' years there would have been more pressure to keep down wage rates if sterling had been stronger. Conversely, the stronger oil-based pound which made British labour costs uncompetitive would have acted to keep wage settlements down even without high unemployment. The employer, however, has no option but to look at his own circumstances and do whatever he has to to keep his own business viable while observing whatever laws are in effect at the time.

Discussion questions

1 Upon what criteria could a 'bargaining unit' be established?
2 Is there any theoretical limit to the content of collective bargaining?
3 Why should employers be more concerned with labour costs than wages? What factors constitute labour costs?
4 To what extent can collective bargaining be regarded as a process for regulating labour management as well as labour markets?
5 To what extent could collective bargaining be regarded by trade unions as the main means of influencing management decisions and protecting the interests of their members?
6 What are the main assessments and preparations which need to be made by both sides prior to meeting at the negotiating table?

7   Assess the influence of external factors – e.g. economic, market, technological, social, government and legal – which impinge on the content of collective bargaining and relationships between the bargaining parties.

8   How far, and how viable, is it for collective bargaining to be seen as a process of joint regulation rooted in relationships, ritual and mutual understandings and obligations? Is the traditional system still of relevance to the current age?

9   How do you account for an unwillingness to accord legally binding status to collective bargains? What are the pros and cons of this attitude?

PART SIX

Legal Aspects of Employment

CHAPTER 12

Individual rights at work

by Greville Janner, QC, MP

Chairman of the All-Party Parliamentary Safety Group and a member of the House of Commons Select Committee on Employment

Introduction

An employee's rights depend primarily upon his or her contract of service; subject to minimum rights, ensured by statute – the Employment Protection (Consolidation) Act, 1978 (EPCA) as amended by the Employment Acts, 1980 and 1982, and by Regulations. The balance between the protection of employees and the powers of management changes according to the philosophy of the Government; and their interpretation, by binding precedent created by courts ('common law').

The 'common law' (sometimes called judge-made law) is one of the two principal sources of English law – the other is 'statute law'. As the principles of common law were interpreted by the judges in cases before them and written down in the form of case or law reports, the doctrine of binding precedent developed. A decision of the House of Lords binds all other courts. A Court of Appeal or High Court decision binds all courts except those at a higher level. Tribunals are also bound by the decisions of the courts (including the Employment Appeal Tribunal) but not by each other. In all cases it is only the rules of law laid down that are fully binding – not their application to the facts of individual cases.

This system of precedent helps to provide consistency and certainty in our law, but it also results in a lack of flexibility. Statute law is the will of Parliament expressed in Acts and Regulations. Codes of Practice do not have the force of law, but they may be used in evidence in civil or criminal cases. In this chapter, we shall survey this vital area of law, as it relates to personnel managers.

The separation between individual rights ensured by their agreement, with their employers and the effects of *collective* rights on an individual (e.g. the right to join or not to join a trade union) is a narrow one. Collective rights at work are surveyed in Chapter 13.

Contracts of employment

A contract is a legally binding agreement between two or more parties; and a contract of employment is simply a contract between employer and employee. In general, it is for them to agree on its terms. There are some constraints, for instance as outlined below:

1   *Wages Council Regulations* attempt to raise standards for the worst paid and most disadvantaged, e.g. in retail trades and catering. Whether they in fact succeed is highly doubtful. If a trade or industry is affected by Wages Council Orders, those concerned should be checked for details and for change. Since the Wages Act 1986 took effect on 25 September 1986, Wages Councils can only regulate the pay of adults over 21; and they may only lay down a single minimum hourly rate of pay for all workers in the industry, plus overtime rates, rates of permitted deductions for accommodation and special rules for pieceworkers.

2   Every personnel manager '*discriminates*' – but must not do so unlawfully. The law only tries to prevent discrimination on an anti-social basis. Men and women are entitled to equal pay for like work and for work of equal value. One must not pay a woman less than a man for work which is either the same or assessed on the same basis (Equal Pay Act 1970 – as amended). Sex discrimination (on the grounds that a person is male or female or married) *is banned* by the Sex Discrimination Act 1975; and race discrimination (on grounds of colour, race, nationality or national or ethnic origin) by the Race Relations Act 1976. Consider also: Monitoring and positive action (see later).

    Unlawful discrimination may be direct (e.g. 'no blacks', 'no whites' or 'men only') or 'indirect' (e.g. in an immigrant area: 'all applicants must have resided in the locality for at least fifteen years'). It is permitted in limited circumstances (e.g. where sex/race is a 'Genuine Occupational Qualification for the job' – a 'GOQ' – like female attendants in the 'Ladies'; or a Chinese waiter or waitress in a Chinese restaurant. Unlike chefs, waiting staff are part of the decor!).

    Discrimination is also unlawful on the grounds of trade union membership. The rules contained in the EPCA apply to appointment, training, promotion and dismissal.

    Remember: while there are minimum qualifying periods for unfair dismissal protection (broadly: two years – see later), there is no minimum where the employee is sacked on grounds of unlawful discrimination.

3   EPCA requires the provision of *written particulars* of the employee's main terms of service (see later) – but does not specify what those conditions must be.

4   The Health and Safety at Work Act 1974 (see later) creates criminal offences for employers who do not (in broad terms) take such steps as

are reasonably practicable to protect the *health and safety* of employees at work.

Still: employees' main protection comes under their own terms of service. In theory, they and their employer may work out their own destiny. In practice (and especially in times of high recession and massive unemployment), the job applicant generally is in a weak negotiating position. But (as we shall see in Chapter 14) personnel managers should take care to see that terms are (i) agreed; (ii) understood; and (iii) clear and comprehensive. The object of the legal exercise is to keep as far away from disputes, courts and lawyers as intelligent preparation can ensure.

The terms of a contract of employment may be 'express' – written or verbal – and/or 'implied' – that is, implied by statute or custom or by the actions of the parties to the agreement. Many contracts are a mixture of all of these.

The *individual* contract of employment, then, is the agreement between the individual employee and his or her employer.

A *collective* bargain is one made by a recognized trade union or other workers' organization (e.g. staff association) with the employer. It is made collectively on behalf of individuals – but where that bargain deals with the rights of the individual it is generally, and to that extent, enforceable by that individual.

Employers who recruit, take on or appoint employees, make contracts of employment with them. A contract is binding from the moment of agreement and not (unless so provided) when the employee starts work. So if an employer takes on employees and then tells them that they are not wanted, before they have started work, he has broken the contract with the employees who may claim damages in the county court (or High Court for claims over £5000). Conversely, if employees do not turn up on the due date, they are in breach of their contract – but the employer's rights are usually theoretical only (as they are if the employee leaves without giving proper notice – see later).

REQUIRED WRITTEN PARTICULARS OF MAIN TERMS

Employees (thanks to EPCA) are entitled to written particulars of their main terms of service within thirteen weeks of the start of their employment or four weeks from any change. These particulars may be contained in one document or several; and if (for instance) an employer puts up an employee's pay, there is no need to serve new particulars. The change will be recorded in the wage slip or salary statement. If the terms are not set out in a document given to the employee, they must be reasonably available for his or her inspection – on a notice-board or in the personnel office.

Here are the main terms which EPCA requires to be put into writing – together with their effect:

1   The *parties* must be identified – which is especially important if the company is part of a group.

2   The terms must state when the employment began and whether or not it is continuous with any other previous employment. (Among the rights which depend upon *continuity of employment* are: statutory minimum periods of notice and of redundancy pay; qualification for maternity and for unfair dismissal protection; and (generally) pension, Occupational Sick Pay (OSP) and holiday rights).

3   'The scale or rate of *remuneration*, or the method of calculating remuneration and the intervals at which payment is to be made.' Remember to include fringe benefits – there are too many disputes over e.g. company car entitlement – most of which are avoidable if these particulars are carefully provided.

4   An employee is entitled to work – and may be required to work – such *hours* as are agreed and stated. Obviously, here (as in mobility clauses – see later) maximum flexibility is in the employer's interests, minimum in those of the employee. For instance: too many managers are required to work 'such hours as may be required for the proper performance of their duties', while hourly paid employees get overtime – hence too many supervisors and managers are paid less than some of the people for whom they are responsible. Overtime, incidentally, may not be compulsory unless you specifically agree – and record – that it is.

5   Subject to Wages Council Regulations (now only for employees in post before September 1986) and to the rights of women and young persons (only) working in factories, the law guarantees no *holiday rights* whatever to any employee. However, such holiday entitlement *if any* as the employee is entitled to receive under his or her contract of employment should be recorded. Take special care with entitlement when the employment terminates (e.g. Pro rata? And/or what if the employee does not give proper notice or is dismissed for misconduct?).

6   Similarly, the law gives no employee any right to Occupational *Sick Pay*. His OSP entitlement *if any* must be set out in the written particulars. These should now include agreed 'Qualifying Days' (QD) for Statutory Sick Pay (SSP) purposes.

7   Again: An employer is not bound to provide his employees with *pensions*. Occupational pension scheme rights *if any* must be recorded. Employers must state whether or not they have 'contracted out' of the State pension scheme.

8   An employee is entitled to agreed *notice*: in the absence of agreement, to such period as is reasonable; and in any event, to not less than the statutory minimum (see later). Notice must be stated. Equally: particulars should set out the notice which employees are required to give, if they wish to 'terminate their contracts of employment'.

9   The particulars must state an employee's '*job title*' (as opposed to the much more detailed 'job description'). This is especially important for a woman, who is entitled to return to 'her job' after her maternity leave (see later). As always, the more flexible the job title, the greater the employer's freedom to change the employee's work – and to avoid problems of demarcation. Conversely: the worse off the employee.

10   Finally: details must be included of *grievance* and *disciplinary procedures*, regulating (respectively) what an employee should do if he or she has a complaint against the employers, and what the employers may do if they have one against the employee. Alternatively, employers may state where a document containing these rules is 'reasonably accessible'. The ACAS Code of Practice No. 1 'Disciplinary practice and procedures in employment' gives valuable guidance.

ADDITIONAL PARTICULARS

In addition to the particulars required by law, employers *should* also consider the following:

1   The employee's '*place of work*'. If the employee may be required to move, then a 'mobility clause' should be included – otherwise he or she may properly refuse to do so. Once again: flexibility is best for others; the wise manager will aim for certainty for himself or herself.

2   The right to *search*. Employers may only search employees or their property with consent, which should be contained in the terms of service and in any event obtained again at the time. Failure to include the term in the contract will make it more difficult to show that refusal to submit to search is a breach of that contract; failure to do so at the time will make the forcible search a 'trespass to the person' (or assault) or trespass to property (as the case may be).

3   Is there a set of *works rules* or a staff handbook? Or a union agreement? These should be specifically incorporated into the terms of service or they may form no part of them.

4   The ACAS Disciplinary Code recommends inclusion in contracts of particular details of those *offences* which may or which will lead to '*summary dismissal*'. Dismissal is 'summary' where the employee is dismissed without notice or pay in lieu of notice. Take care over 'may' or 'will' – and mind which offences are included and excluded.

5   Any employee who leaves may normally compete against the company, for others or on their own account. Exception: where there is a reasonable (and hence valid) *restraint clause* in the contract. If the company has one, is

it likely to be upheld? If not, is one needed? Drafting restraint clauses requires expert help.

6   Every employment contract has an implied term that the employee will not give away *confidential information* – but if the employer suffers from 'leakage' it may be as well to make the term 'express'. Similarly: an employee should not remove property from the employer's premises without permission (express or implied) – but employers who suffer from 'borrowing' (particularly if it has become an accepted 'perk'), should consider inserting an express term, for the avoidance of doubt.

7   Basic *maternity rights* ('pay' and 'leave') are in EPCA (see later). But should the employees' terms refer to these rights and/or to the employers' own required procedure?

8   Does the employer have special arrangements regarding *retirement*? Or for required union membership (closed shop/Union Membership Agreement (UMA)?) Or for medical examination? Or specific requirements (e.g. holder of driving licence)? They should draw up or obtain a check list suitable to their own needs.[1]

Deductions from Pay

Until the Wages Act 1986, the law here was ancient, obscure and rarely observed. The Wages Act removed the first label; there is no excuse for the second or third.

The new rules – operative since 1 January 1987 – apply to all employees; also to individuals you engage as self-employed contractors. As will be explained, there are extra rules to protect employees in 'retail employment'. This is not just shop assistants – it can cover any employees handling cash transactions with customers: bank tellers, booking office clerks, milk roundsmen, bus conductors, and others.

The basic rule is: you must not *deduct* money from the pay due to the employee; and you must not make the employee *pay back* any money to you. If you do, the employee's remedy is to make a complaint to an industrial tribunal, which can order you to pay over the money – even if you would have had a valid claim to it in the first place.

The exceptions are important: some are obvious, some less straightforward.

1   *Statutory deductions.* You must deduct income tax under PAYE, and National Insurance. These deductions remain lawful.

1 Detailed drafts, precedents and rules are contained in *Janner's Employment Letters* and *Janner's Employment Forms and Procedures*, Business and Legal Publications Ltd, 25 Victoria Street, London, S.W.1.

2   *Payments to third parties.* You can be ordered to pay some of an employee's earnings to courts – to pay off a fine, for instance: this is known as an Attachment of Earnings Order. The DHSS can exceptionally serve deduction orders on you to recover social security payments they have made. These deductions are lawful.

3   *Payments requested by the employee.* The employee can ask you to pay some of his pay to a third party. Most common example: his union subscription. But consider also: payments to the sports club; or to a pension fund he has opted to join instead of belonging to the company pension scheme. Requests of these kinds must be in writing, and must be made *before* the deduction. Otherwise not only can you ignore the request – you can be sued for making the deduction.

4   The employee may agree to deductions, for instance for lateness or poor work. His agreement must either be in writing (beforehand, again), or be included as a term in the contract of employment. In that case there is an extra condition: the contract must be in writing, or the employee must have been given a written note of the clause. Remember, if challenged, you will have trouble proving that point unless you get the employee's signature on a receipt.

5   You can also make good accidental over-payments of wages or expenses by deducting them from a later pay packet.

For retail employees (see above) there is an extra restriction on deductions for cash or stock shortages. This applies where the wages due are calculated by reference to cash shortages as well as where a formal deduction is made. The deduction must not be more than 10 per cent of gross wages in any pay period. Shortages can be deducted in instalments, but never more than a year in arrears. If the employee leaves, the limit does not apply to the final payment to be made – so arrears can, in law at last, absorb the whole of the employee's last pay packet.

This rule was introduced to deal with abuses that had become notorious in some filling stations where employees were simply stopped the difference between sales and takings. The rule is additional to the general restrictions – so deductions will still have to be agreed in writing or in a written term of the contract. Otherwise the Wages Act does not, as many critics argued it should, limit deductions from pay to what is reaonable, but ambiguous terms will be interpreted to cover only reasonable deductions, and plainly unreasonable terms may not be valid at all.

MATERNITY RIGHTS

Apart from rights on dismissal (see later) the law provides some minimal rights for existing employees – in particular: *maternity rights*. These rights have recently been extended by the introduction of Statutory Maternity Pay (SMP) from April 1987. Briefly the rights are:

1 *Maternity leave* – a woman is entitled to return to work provided she has completed two years' continuous employment with you (measured from eleven weeks before the start of the week in which her baby is due) and provided she fulfils a number of detailed formal requirements – most important giving notice before she leaves that she intends to return – see below for further details. The period of leave is up to 29 weeks after the baby is born, plus four weeks if the mother is unable to return then because of illness, or the employer postones her return to make room for her.

2 *Time off for ante-natal care* – this applies to all women – and a reasonable amount of time off with pay must be given. After the first absence the woman must produce evidence of her appointments if required.

3 *Statutory Maternity Pay* – all employees are now entitled to Statutory Maternity Pay provided they have worked the qualifying period and earn at least enough to be liable for National Insurance (£39.00 a week in 1987/8). Confusingly there are two qualifying periods and two rates of pay, but the good news is that employers can – as with Statutory Sick Pay (SSP) recover what they pay (plus a contribution to National Insurance overheads) by deduction from each month's payment of National insurance to the DHSS.

Note: These rights apply to cases of pregnancy or confinement whether or not the employee is married and/or whether or not the woman suffers a miscarriage or has an abortion. Part-timers (less than 16 hours per week or 8 hours after 5 years' continuous service) do not qualify for maternity leave. They are, though, entitled to paid time off work for ante-natal care.

The Employment Act 1980 made a number of changes to the notification which a woman must give if she wants to return to *her* job after having a baby. The right to return to *her* job was also modified. The current position is as follows:

To qualify for maternity leave, the employee must (where reasonably practicable) give notice of her intended absence at least 21 days before it begins – in writing, and also state that she intends to return. As the employee may need her job back (e.g. if the baby is stillborn) and as she loses nothing if she says she intended to return but then decides not to do so, all wise women do state an intention to return.

Not less than 49 days after the week or date of confinement, the employer may serve a written notice on the mother, asking whether she still intends to return. She has 14 days to reply affirmatively and in writing or she will lose her rights. And she must also give written notice at least 21 days before exercising her right to return, setting out the date of her proposed return.

Kindly employers include an appropriate form with s.a.e., when sending their 49 days' notice.

Employers who find that they cannot conveniently replace the employee in her old job, may offer her reasonably suitable alternative employment. If she either accepts or unreasonably refuses this offer, she will lose her right to return. She will also lose that right if her employers employed five or less employees immediately prior to her departure and it is not reasonably practicable for them to take her back in her old job or to offer her suitable alternative work.

SMP applies to all employees who have six months' continuous employment; this is calculated as at 14 weeks before the week the baby is due. Payments are at a flat rate – £32.85 a week in 1987/8 (and taxed like any other pay) and run for up to 18 weeks, starting 11 weeks before the expected week of confinement. *Note*: if the mother-to-be carries on working beyond that date the SMP is postponed until she stops, but if she continues beyond 6 weeks before expected confinement the total period of her SMP is reduced accordingly; likewise if she returns to work before 18 weeks have elapsed.

Women who have completed *two years'* continuous employment qualify for the higher rate of benefit – nine-tenths of normal gross earnings. But this higher rate only applies for the first six weeks that SMP is paid.

SMP is a new and complex subject: if you need to know more, the DHSS produces helpful guidance pamphlets to lead you through the intricacies.

So much for appointment and the creation of the contract of employment. Now for the miseries of termination and dismissal.

ENDING THE CONTRACT

A contract of employment may be ended by:
1   Mutual agreement;
2   Dismissal;
3   Frustration.

Dismissal may be with or without prior notice. If the employer dismisses without notice, then unless the employee has 'repudiated' the contract or it is 'frustrated' (see later), the dismissal may be *wrongful*. *Additionally*, it may be fair or *unfair*.

Mutual agreement

The best way to put an end to a contract of employment is, of course, by genuine mutual agreement.

If an employee is forced into resigning, that is a 'constructive dismissal' (see later). If employees leave voluntarily, then they terminate the contract; if the employers sack or discharge or fire or dismiss by any other name, then they do so and the employees have a series of potential rights:

to claim damages for *wrongful dismissal*, if they do not get their proper notice or pay in lieu;

unfair dismissal remedies, if they are protected, and sacked unfairly; and

redundancy rights if (broadly) their jobs go when they do.

After termination come other legal problems, in particular concerning restraints and references.

Dismissal with notice

An employee is normally entitled to proper notice or pay in lieu. As always, the basic right is that provided by agreement; but if the contract is silent, then he or she is entitled to such period as is 'reasonable'. Again, as always, 'reasonableness' depends upon all the circumstances of the case – including (in this one) the employee's seniority, responsibilities and the sort of notice normally given to people in his or her position.

Dismissal without notice

If the employee 'repudiates' the contract – either by one single but very serious act or by persistent and more minor misconduct – then the employer may dismiss 'summarily'. He is accepting the position that the employee has created. If in doubt, employers should pay money in lieu of notice, but tell the employee in writing and specifically that they are doing so 'without prejudice' to their contention that they could have dismissed summarily. That will prevent use of the payment against the employer, in an unfair dismissal claim.

Frustration

Summary dismissal apart, employers do not have to give notice or pay in lieu if the contract is 'frustrated' – if the bottom has dropped out of the arrangement, usually because the employee is so ill that he or she is never likely to get back to normal work. 'Frustration' for illness is an unpleasant excuse for non-payment of money in lieu of notice, rarely used by decent employers.

Wrongful dismissal

If an employee does not get proper notice or pay in lieu, then the employer has broken the contract and the employee may sue, claiming damages for breach of that contract – for '*wrongful* dismissal'. These will normally be: the remuneration which would have been received during the period of notice, minus anything that had actually been earned during that period, because (again) as in all contract cases, the sufferer must 'mitigate' the loss – that is, keep it to a reasonable minimum.

The same rules apply in reverse and in theory to employees. They must give agreed notice; in the absence of agreement, reasonable notice; and in any event not less than the statutory one week minimum. If they fail to do so, then the employers could in theory sue, claiming damages for breach of contract. But as in practice no employers can ever prove in terms of hard cash what they have lost, any victory is pyrrhic and no employee who leaves without notice is worth suing on that ground.

Fair and unfair dismissal

The Industrial Relations Act 1971 first introduced the rules on unfair dismissal, which have since been strengthened by the Trade Union and Labour Relations Act 1974 and by the Employment Protection Act 1975; consolidated in EPCA; altered and a little reduced by the Employment Acts of 1980 and 1982; and greatly reduced in their impact by Regulations which have:

1   Increased the 'qualifying period' for unfair dismissal protection; and

2   Introduced the 'pre-hearing assessment' into industrial tribunal procedures, combined with a power (seldom and carefully exercised) to award costs against an unsuccessful claimant who behaves 'unreasonably', and not merely (as previously) 'frivolously' or 'vexatiously'.

An employee must be continuously employed by the same or by an associated employer for at least two years before he or she is protected against unfair dismissal.

As we have seen, there is no minimum qualifying period in cases of sex, race or trade union 'discrimination'.

Apart from people not employed for the minimum period, the following are the other main categories excluded from unfair dismissal protection:

1   *Part-timers* – that is, people who 'normally work' less than 16 hours a week, reduced to 8 hours after 5 years' continuous service;

2   *Pensioners* – that is, people above their employers' normal retirement age (if there is no 'normal' age, 65 is the cut-off – after November 1987 for men as well as women, for whom it was previously 60), and

3   Employees who 'normally work' *outside the UK* – which courts have interpreted as meaning: those who are 'based' outside the UK, according to their contracts of employment.

Finally: Please remember that only 'employees' are entitled to protection against unfair dismissal. An employee works under a contract of employment or of service – as opposed to one merely for the provision of services.

Normally, PAYE is deducted at source and the employer effectively controls the work. Employers who are in doubt about the status of a particular person who performs work for them should get their accountants and/or lawyers on the trail.

When is a dismissal fair?

Now suppose that employees qualified for unfair dismissal wish to bring a claim. They must prove that they were dismissed, 'actually' or 'constructively'. The employer will then be required to show the 'statutory reason' for the dismissal. These are:

1   That the employee lacked the 'capability' or 'qualifications' for the job – generally due to age or sickness or change of technical requirements (respectively);

2   Misconduct;

3   Redundancy;

4   Illegality (e.g. a foreigner whose work permit has expired);

5   Some other 'substantial reason'.

An employee who has been with the employer for not less than six months (*Note*: that period has remained unchanged) is entitled to written reasons for the dismissal, within two weeks of the request. Otherwise the claim may be two weeks' pay, from an industrial tribunal.

If unfair dismissal proceedings are in the offing, employers should take special care with the 'reasons' provided. They will probably be tied to them if it comes to a hearing. And information obtained after the dismissal, about an employee's other misbehaviour, cannot (the House of Lords has held) be relevant to the reason for the dismissal itself, although it may affect compensation.

Once the employee has proved qualification and dismissal and the employer has stated the reasons, the tribunal (*Note*: *not* as in the case of 'wrongful' dismissal, a court) will consider 'fairness'. It will look at all the circumstances of the case, including the size and resources of the employer's 'undertaking' and decide whether the decision to dismiss was 'reasonable' in all the circumstances – on procedural grounds and on the merits of the case.

If the dismissal was 'unfair', then the tribunal may award the following remedies:

1   A 'compensatory award' – designed to compensate the employee for his loss. Current maximum: £8500. But the employee's 'contributory conduct' will be taken into account;

2   A 'basic award' – equal to the employee's lost redundancy entitlement. Maximum: £4740;

3   An 'additional award' – where the employers have unreasonably refused
    to comply with a tribunal ruling that they *reinstate* or *re-engage* the unfairly
    dismissed employee. In practice, these awards are extremely rare. An
    order for reinstatement requires the employers to treat the employee as if
    he or she had never been dismissed. Re-engagement will be on such terms
    as are specified by the tribunal. The making of either of these orders is
    entirely at the tribunal's discretion.

Finally, tribunals have additional powers (rarely exercised) where an
employee is sacked for refusing to belong to a union where there is a Union
Membership Agreement (i.e. a closed shop).

In practice, the reality of unfair dismissal cases is far removed from the
theory. Details of the reality and how personnel managers should cope with it
are in Chapter 14, along with a brisk review of tribunal procedures and how
to keep away from them if possible or to cope with them if essential.

Redundancy

Unfortunately, redundancy has long been a major area of tribunal activity.
So consider: what are an employee's rights and how do employers avoid
redundancy problems – in practice as well as in law?

An employee is 'redundant' where he or she is dismissed (broadly) because
the employers no longer carry on business for the purposes for which or in
the place where the employee was employed; or where 'the requirements of
that business for employees to carry out work of a particular kind . . . where
they were so employed, have ceased or diminished or are expected to cease or
diminish'. So where the job goes along with the employee, he or she is
'redundant', and is then entitled:

1   To proper notice or pay in lieu;

2   Not to be made redundant 'unfairly';

3   To such redundancy payment as is agreed – that being not less than the
    applicable statutory minimum.

To avoid 'unfair redundancies', employers must consider carefully the four
possible methods:

1   *Voluntary* redundancy – with likely loss of those employees who are most
    likely to find other work and hence are most willing to move on, in return
    for their tax-free agreed payments;

2   'Last In First Out' (*LIFO*) – a rule of thumb method which keeps
    redundancy payments to the minimum and avoids unfair dismissal
    claims, but which means that the employers will lose their new and
    probably young employees;

3   Selection by *merit* – the employer's views on the demerit of particular employees being unlikely to be shared by them – and hence opening the door to unfair dismissal claims; and/or

4   *Closing* all or part of the business.

If there is a collective agreement which includes provisions for dealing with redundancies, paying compensation or for finding alternative work for redundant workers, the Employment Secretary may, on a joint application from all the parties, make an Order exempting the employees from the statutory provisions, provided certain conditions are satisfied.

An employee becomes entitled to a minimum statutory redundancy payment after two years' continuous service after reaching the age of 18, i.e. minimum age for required redundancy pay: 20. Employers with less than ten employees may recover 35 per cent of required redundancy payments from the Redundancy Fund – any payment over that minimum, and *all* payments by larger employers, have to be met 100 per cent from the employer's own resources.

The employee reaches maximum statutory minimum after twenty years at the appropriate age and remuneration, at present (as in the case of the 'basic award' for unfair dismissal) – £4740. The entitlement is on a sliding scale – details if necessary from local offices of the Department of Employment.

Finally, if an employee is a member of a recognized trade union or is affected by its bargaining, the employer must give the appropriate trade union required notice of the proposed redundancy, or the union may apply for a 'protective award' on the employee's behalf (see Chapter 13).

If the employer becomes insolvent, then EPCA, together with the Employment Act 1982, gives the employee helpful protection. In particular, claims for up to eight weeks' pay or six weeks' holiday pay (together with other rights) get preference in the winding up or the bankruptcy and if there is insufficient money in the employer's kitty to meet them, they are paid out of the Redundancy Fund. *Note*: This protection does not extend to expenses, which an employee advances on the employer's behalf and at his or her own risk. (See Chapter 21.)

Health and safety at work

What are an employee's rights under the Health and Safety at Work Act, 1974?

Section 2 requires an employer to take such steps as are 'reasonably practicable' to protect the employee at work. That duty includes (for instance) a duty to provide and to maintain safe 'plant and systems of work'; to take proper precautions in connection with 'the use, handling, storage and transport of articles and substances'; to provide 'such information, instruction, training and supervision' as is necessary to ensure 'in so far as is reasonably practicable', the health and safety at work of employees; to provide a 'safe place of work', together with a 'working environment . . . that is, so far as is reasonably practicable, safe, without risk to health, and adequate as regards facilities and arrangements for their welfare at work'.

Breach of s. 2 is a criminal offence and the employer – or any 'director, manager or (company) secretary' responsible for the breach, may be prosecuted. Maximum penalty in a magistrates' court: £2000 fine; in a Crown Court ('on indictment'): unlimited fine and/or up to two years' imprisonment (as yet, no one has been imprisoned for causing disaster at work – as opposed to doing so on the road).

Other and more common methods of enforcement of the Act's provisions include the issuing of 'prohibition' and 'improvement' notices by an inspector. The inspector will make a prohibition notice where there is an imminent risk of serious personal injury. It generally operates at once. An improvement notice is not so urgent and normally requires the remedying of some fault within a specified time.

An employee who is injured at work does not have to wait for a prosecution before seeking a remedy. But with one exception, the plaintiff will only get damages if injury, loss or damage, due to the 'negligence' or 'breach of statutory duty' of the employers or some other person employed by them, can be proved.

In practice, unless the injured employees can either get legal aid or the help of a union, they will be deterred from suing by the costs of justice – which is generally available to those who are either poor enough to get legal aid or rich enough not to need it, and middle income people (including personnel managers) commonly come into neither category. Proving positively that the employer failed to take such care as was 'reasonable' in the circumstances often presents major problems.

One case in which our law provides for 'strict', 'no fault' or 'absolute' liability comes under the Employer's Liability (Defective Equipment) Act 1969. If an employee suffers death or personal injury (as opposed to mere pecuniary loss) due to a defect in plant or equipment supplied at work, then the employers are 'deemed' to have been negligent. If the employers can then pass the responsibility back to (for instance) a supplier or to the manufacturer of the defective equipment, that is a matter for them. It is precisely this sort of 'strict liability' which exists in the USA, France and West Germany (but not in the UK) where there is 'strict liability' for death or personal injury caused by defective products, and which will soon be introduced into the UK under the Consumer Protection Act 1987.

Guarantee payments

Additional individual employment rights include 'guarantee payments', the purpose of which is to guarantee to most non-salaried employees a little of the security which their salaried colleagues enjoy. Guarantee pay was first introduced by the Employment Protection Act 1975 and is now in the EPCA 1978 (as amended).

Briefly, every employee who has completed one month's employment with the same employer and is not a part-timer is entitled to a guarantee payment in respect of each complete working day lost because of a diminution in the need for work normally done by him or her. The main exception to this rule is where the 'workless day' is the result of a trade dispute involving the employee's employer or an associated employer.

The right to guarantee pay is also lost where the employee refuses any suitable alternative work offered or where he or she does not comply with the reasonable request to remain available for work.

The amount of guarantee payment for any day is calculated by multiplying the number of normal working hours for the day in question by the guaranteed hourly rate, subject to the overall statutory maximum. This is currently fixed at a maximum of £10.90 per day and guarantee payments are restricted to five days in any three-month period (instead of five days in a fixed calendar quarter, which was the position before the Employment Act 1980). So an employee who has a five-day batch of payments will have to wait another three months before becoming eligible for further payments.

Time off work

There are five main areas where the individual employee may be entitled to time off work. These are now briefly described.

I   TRADE UNION DUTIES

Any employee who is an official of an independent trade union, recognized for the purposes of collective bargaining, is entitled to time off work during working hours and at the normal rate of pay for the purposes of (a) carrying out official duties concerned with industrial relations between the employer and any associated employer and their employees; or (b) undergoing training in aspects of industrial relations relevant to the carrying out of those duties.

Members of trade unions may also take reasonable time off during working hours for the purpose of taking part in specified union activities.

The amount of time off will be that which is reasonable in all the circumstances – and in considering reasonableness, regard will be had to the Code of Practice issued by ACAS.

2   PUBLIC DUTIES

Certain categories of employees holding public positions must be allowed reasonable time off to perform their associated duties. These include Justices of the Peace; members of local authorities; or of statutory tribunals, or of regional health authorities, or of the managing or governing body of an educational institution maintained by local education authorities or of water authorities. Again, the amount of time off allowed is that which is reasonable in all the circumstances. There is no obligation on the employer to pay the employee during time off, unless an agreement to do so has been made with the individual or his or her trade union.

3 REDUNDANCY – JOB HUNTING OR ARRANGING TRAINING FOR FUTURE EMPLOYMENT

Employees given notice of dismissal by reason of redundancy are entitled during their notice periods to reasonable time off during working hours in order to look for new employment or to make arrangements for training for future employment. This right is given to employees of two years' standing who would qualify for redundancy pay.

Time off must (again) be reasonable, with employees paid the appropriate hourly rate for the period of absence from work.

4 SAFETY REPRESENTATIVES

In order to carry out their duties under the Health and Safety at Work Act and the Safety Representatives and Safety Committees Regulations 1977, employees who are union appointed safety representatives are entitled to such time off work with pay as is necessary for the carrying out of their duties. As always, time off should be 'reasonable'. Safety representatives may also have time off to undergo training to enable them to perform their duties better.

5 ANTE–NATAL CARE

The Employment Act 1980 provided pregnant employees, regardless of length of continuous employment, a right not to be unreasonably refused paid time off work to obtain ante-natal care. Other than for her first appointment, the pregnant employee must, on request, produce a certificate of pregnancy from her doctor, midwife or other expert, plus an appointment card.

Monitoring and positive action

Two important codes of practice have introduced concepts of 'monitoring' and of 'positive action'. The Code of the Commission for Racial Equality came into force on 1 April 1984 and the sister Code of the Equal Opportunities Commission on 30 April 1985.

Monitoring means the keeping of careful records of the 'ethnic origins' and of the sex of applicants for jobs as well as for current employees. In general, people should state their own 'ethnic origins'. The CRE provides guidance and suggestions. Methods of monitoring will vary according to the size, nature and needs of the particular business or organization.

'Positive action' means taking positive steps to remedy what would appear to be unlawful discriminatory practices or their results. Applicants for jobs or promotion should be helped to come up to the starting line on an equal basis.

Note: 'Positive discrimination' at the point of selection was, is, and will remain, unlawful. Employers must not discriminate in favour of people because of their sex or marital status or their race or ethnic origin, any more than they are permitted to discriminate against them for that reason. Baroness Seear discusses these matters further in Chapter 18.

SEX DISCRIMINATION AND TIMES OF WORK

Two important cases have shown the dangers of 'indirect' sex discrimination. Both concerned hours of work.

A mother called Holmes took maternity leave and notified the Home Office of her intention to return. She asked for work on a part-time basis. The Department refused, saying that no part-time positions were available within the employee's grade and that under existing contractual terms she only had the right to return to her own job, which meant: full time. Ms Holmes accepted the situation, kept her job, but lost many days' work because she had to look after her child.

When Ms Holmes had a second baby, she again took maternity leave, and again asked to return part-time and was again refused. She claimed that the refusal was due to sex discrimination, and an industrial tribunal and (on appeal) the Employment Appeal Tribunal agreed.

The requirement to work full time indirectly discriminated against women and the Home Office had failed to justify the requirement imposed on Ms Holmes. Whether a requirement to work full time is or is not justified is a matter for the industrial tribunal to decide on the facts of each particular case. Anyway: if a returning mother asks for part-time instead of full time, her employers should be careful before they refuse.

In *Wright* v. *Rugby Borough Council*, a woman asked to change her hours slightly so that she could cope with delivering and collecting her child from nursery school. The Council refused, saying that they did not operate flexitime. An industrial tribunal held that the Council's refusal was discriminatory. It operated unreasonably and unfairly, and mainly against women. Had the employers bothered, they could have fitted in with the mother's requirements. Their failure to do so was in breach of the Sex Discrimination Act.

Sick pay

Sick employees have two possible sources of payment – their employers and the State. With the advent of Statutory Sick Pay (SSP) from 6 April 1983, employers took over (in general and subject to important exceptions – and to due repayment) the State's responsibilities for the first eight weeks of sickness – increased to the first 28 weeks as from April 1986.

Occupational Sick Pay (OSP) was, is, and will remain, entirely a matter for arrangement between employer and employee. With the sole exception of agricultural workers who are assured at least a minimum of payment during illness by their Wages Council Regulations, no other UK employee has any non-contractual rights to his employer's money – subject once again to SSP.

So it is for the employers to negotiate, agree and pay OSP. Because it will be paid out of the employer's money, the public has no concern in the arrangements for documentation, notification or certification of illness or absenteeism control.

Employers should make their OSP arrangements 'express'. (The 1978 Act requires them to set out the main written terms in an employee's statement within 13 weeks of the start of the employment or 4 weeks of any change— see above.) Among those terms which must be recorded is: the employee's right to sick pay *if any*.

Sick pay terms should be agreed and stated. These should nowadays include the SSP Qualifying Days (QDs), which should normally be the days the employee would have worked if well.

If there is no express agreement as to whether or not OSP shall be paid, then the law may imply a term. Latest cases suggest that a requirement to pay will only be implied by past practice or the custom of the trade or occupation and then for such periods as is usual – and hence not (as previously thought) potentially until the employment terminates.

Anyway, wise personnel managers ensure that OSP is agreed – and that the arrangements (including especially notification and certification) dovetail into those for SSP and differ as little as possible from them.

Sick employees who are dismissed may sue for damages for wrongful dismissal if they have not received their proper notice or pay in lieu; and/or they may claim compensation for *unfair* dismissal if they are sacked unreasonably – in each case, as if they were well.

The employee may also qualify for state Sickness Benefit (SB), payable by the DHSS on its own terms. The State decides on its required certification; an employee who has received state Sickness Benefit or any other state incapacity benefit remains 'linked' to it for up to eight weeks after the last day in respect of which he or she received such benefit – and during that eight week period he or she cannot qualify for SSP. In practice, since 1986 the vast majority of employees never qualify for SB, because it is mutually exclusive with SSP; the long-term sick receive instead Invalidity Benefit (which is for most employees a little higher than SB). But the self-employed still depend on SB when ill.

State Sickness Benefit, then, remains in the background. It is available to those who are excluded from SSP. And employers must provide employees who are excluded with one of the only two *required* SSP forms. These are:

1   SSP 1 (E) (affectionately known as 'S.P.I.E.') the exclusion form, to be given to any excluded employee; and
2   SSP 1 (T) (or 'S.P.I.T.') the transfer form, which an employee should receive at the start of his or her twenty-seventh week of a spell of sickness.

Armed with S.P.I.E. or S.P.I.T., the employee will go to the DHSS for his or her money.

No employer or employee can contract out of SSP, nor can any employee be required to pay or contribute towards the cost of its administration. The rules (contained in the Social Security and Housing Benefits Act, 1982) provide that the employer *shall* pay SSP to all employees qualified to receive it. They *shall* set off SSP against OSP (very helpful, this, especially when the employee is sick on holiday) and (conversely) OSP against SSP.

How, then, does SSP operate? First: when is an employee entitled to SSP? For that, he or she must satisfy three 'Qualifying Conditions' (QCs). The first QC: There must be a 'Period of Incapacity for Work' (PIW).

A 'day of incapacity for work' is a day when the employee is sick, physically or mentally, so that he or she is unable to work *whether or not he or she would have been required to work had he or she been well*.

A 'Period of Incapacity for Work' (PIW) is any four or more consecutive days of incapacity. Note carefully:

1   SSP requires the period to be (i) not less than four days; (ii) each of which is a day of sickness; and (iii) which are consecutive.

2   Two or more PIWs may be 'linked' by a period not exceeding eight weeks. When two or more PIWs are linked, the employee only endures 'Waiting Days' (WDs) during the first and not in later PIWs (as we shall see).

The second Qualifying Condition: There must be a 'Period of Entitlement' (POE) – a term which, as usual with SSP jargon, is misleading. A POE is *not* a period when the employee will necessarily be entitled to SSP – but he or she can get no SSP if his or her illness falls outside a POE.

So once a sick employee has a PIW, the employer should then check his POE. This begins with the sickness and ends:

1   When the employee gets better – SSP is only payable to sick people;

2   When the employment ends – SSP is only payable to employees;

3   When a pregnant employee reaches the beginning of the eleventh week before the date of her expected confinement (known as the 'Period of Disqualification'); or

4   When the employee has had his or her full twenty-eight weeks' SSP in one spell of sickness or two or more spells 'linked' as explained above.

A POE cannot arise where the employee is a pensioner (a woman over 60 or a man over 65); or if he or she earns less than the current Lower Earnings Limit; (note that part-timers *do* get SSP, provided that their earnings reach the Lower Earnings Limit); or if employees are linked to a previous spell of illness for which they received state Incapacity Benefit (as explained above – the link ceases after 57 days); or if employees go outside the EEC. (Remember: if inside the EEC, they get SSP – even if they are on holiday); or if an employee is 'in legal custody'.

Now assume that a sick employee has a PIW – or a linked series of PIWs; and that the sickness comes within a POE. The third Qualifying Condition is that SSP is only payable for a 'Qualifying Day'.

Although the Act first says that a Qualifying Day is one which (in broad terms) matches the employee's normal working day, it goes on to state that a Qualifying Day (QD) *shall be* such day as is agreed between an employer and employee or in the absence of agreement, which is fixed according to the Regulations. So employers can fix QDs that suit them, and to which the employees or their unions are prepared to agree.

By carefully agreeing the maximum appropriate QDs, employers maximize the SSP that the employees can get – and which employers can then deduct in full. But from the employers' viewpoint, SSP should generally be payable where it can be set off against remuneration which the employees would normally receive on those days.

From the employees' point of view, the more SSP they get, the better; from the employers' angle, they can deduct the SSP paid; but where the deduction cannot be set off against remuneration which the employees did receive – or would have received had they been well – then the employers lose the chance to set off the SSP.

It is easier to explain how to handle this complex arrangement than to understand it. Briefly: if employees are hourly or weekly paid – or if they are paid monthly or even on an annual salary, but their pay is worked out on the basis of a 260-day working year – then their QDs should match their normal working week.

Conversely: if employees are paid on a genuine annual basis – so that (for instance) if they take a day's unpaid leave, 1/365th of the annual income of each will be deducted (as opposed to 1/260th), then they should be paid on a seven Qualifying Day week – even if they only work five. There must be at least one in every week.

Next: the first three QDs in each PIW are 'Waiting Days' (WDs) during which the employee gets no SSP. But there are no WDs in subsequent PIWs which are linked – hence the importance of linkage.

Once employees are sick on a QD in a PIW which is in a POE and is not a WD, they get their SSP! For each day they will get the appropriate proportion of their current week's fixed scale. Scales are revised for each tax year; since April 1987 there have been only two rates – higher and lower.

Employers should decide on what form of certification they require. Many excellent employers reckon that they are quite as likely to get the truth if the employees certify for themselves and if medical certification is reserved for long-term sickness or doubtful cases. The decision is theirs.

In practice, good absenteeism control depends far more on management attitudes and control than upon forms of notification or certification (see Chapter 19).

Employers should work out, evolve and use the best documentation and record keeping to suit the purposes and the nature of their undertaking. They can computerize everything other than the production of the S.P.I.E. and S.P.I.T. forms – but a computer is only as successful as those who programme it.

Data protection

Every modern personnel department keeps details of employees 'by automatic means' – if not by computer then at least on word processor. So the Data Protection Act 1984 must be complied with. Here is the personnel executive's practical guide to the essentials to data protection, as created by that Act, which is now almost completely in force – the final provision came into effect in November 1987.

The Act is designed to protect living, identifiable individuals – 'data subjects'. Both individuals and companies which 'hold' personal data about 'data subjects' must comply. But only individuals have new rights and protection. It follows that no company will be entitled to access to information on employers' computers. That privilege is restricted to individuals.

Again: the Act applies to automatically processed personal information. So any that is held on traditional files is no more accessible than it was. Remember, though, that however personal the information or however it may be held, it may have to be revealed if it is 'material' (or relevant) to court or tribunal proceedings. 'Discovery' lifts the shroud of secrecy from any documents which may throw light on the matters in legal dispute.

Employers are 'data users' if they 'hold' data. People 'hold data' if (in brief) it forms part of a collection of data processed or intended to be processed by them or on their behalf and they (alone or jointly) control the contents and use of the data.

'Processing' means 'amending, augmenting, deleting or rearranging the data or extracting the information constituting the data'. This definition is so wide that it includes records held on microfiche, where automatic means are used for its retrieval.

People carry on the business of a 'computer bureau' if they provide others with services in respect of personal data. Anyone does that if 'as agent for other persons he causes data to be held by them to be processed . . . or allows other persons the use of equipment in his possession for processing'. The test is: control.

If, then, your company allows its computers to be used by clients or others for the processing of personal data, it operates a 'computer bureau'. Conversely, if a bank or other organization provides computer services for your outfit, that organization is the 'bureau' and, because your company has control over the information, it is the 'data user'.

'Data users' must comply with the basic 'data protection principles', set out in the first Schedule of the Act. In summary, these are:

1   The computerized personal data must be 'obtained and . . . processed, fairly and lawfully';

2   It must be held 'only for one or more specified and lawful purposes'. When your organization registers as a data user, it must specify each of the purposes for which the data will be held or used and it will be unlawful to hold or to use them for any other purpose. Thus:

3   Personal data held for any specified purpose or purposes must not be 'used or disclosed in any manner incompatible with that purpose or those purposes'.

4   Personal data held by automatic means must be 'adequate, relevant and not excessive in relation to that purpose or purposes'. Conversely: if it is inadequate, irrelevant or excessive, there will be a breach of the fourth principle.

5   Personal data shall be 'accurate and, where necessary, kept up to date'. As we shall see, if your company allows data to be inaccurate or to become outdated, the data subject will have new remedies.

6   Personal data shall not be kept for longer than is necessary for the purpose or purposes registered. Out-of-date personal data must be expunged.

7   The most important principle is that: 'An individual shall be entitled

(a)   at all reasonable intervals and without undue delay or expense

   i to be informed by any data user whether he holds personal data of which that individual is the subject; and

   ii to access to any such data held by a data user; and

(b)   where appropriate, to have such data corrected or erased.'

Suppose that disgruntled former employees want to know what your company holds on computer about them. Each may ask: 'have you any computerized personal information about me?'

Provided that there has been a reasonable interval since any such previous request, the company must answer. Section 21 says that it must inform the data user whether it has data about the enquirer and must supply a copy – normally, a print-out. If the company uses code, then it must make the information intelligible by giving such information of 'terms used' as may be necessary.

The data user may, if it wishes require the request to be made in writing and may charge a fee up to ten pounds. And it may require the data subject to provide such information as may be reasonable to establish his or her identity. If the data user cannot comply with the request without revealing information about someone else, then it may refuse to do so. Otherwise, 40 days is the maximum allowed for the reply.

Nor can the data user cunningly update the information after receipt of the request. Apart from amendments or deletions made between the time of the request which 'would have been made regardless of the receipt of request', the print-out must be unamended, errors and all.

If the data subject considers that the information is inaccurate, he or she may require the data user to correct it. If it fails to do so, then application may be made to the Registrar or to the court for an Order that the company do so. The data subject may take the same road if he or she considers that the information is outdated or irrelevant or no longer necessary for you to retain.

Data subjects who can show that they have suffered loss as a result of inaccuracy or of some unauthorized disclosure – that is: disclosure to people other than those registered as intended to receive the personal data – may claim compensation. They have the same rights if the personal data has been wrongfully destroyed.

So apart from access, the data subject is given rights to claim rectification, erasure and compensation. But if the data user fails to comply with the rules, then he or she may also commit a criminal offence.

Prosecutions will be brought by the Registrar or with the consent of the Director of Public Prosecutions, so that in practice there will be no private prosecutions. But here (as under the Health and Safety at Work Act) individuals (who include partners) may be held liable – as well as 'any director, manager, secretary or similar officer' of a company, or anyone 'purporting to act in any such capacity'. A company's officer as well as the company may be convicted if it is proved that the offence has been committed with his or her 'consent' or 'connivance' or to be 'attributable to any neglect' on his or her part.

So this law is not one to be flouted. A simple error by a personnel manager or a member of staff can be corrected or (at worst) may lead to civil proceedings. But failure to provide the protection required by the Act or to comply with an enforcement notice served under its rules may lead to individual or to corporate prosecution – or to both.

Finally: the eighth principle – which applies not only to data users but also to computer bureaux:

> 'Appropriate security measures shall be taken against unauthorized access to, or alteration, disclosure or destruction of, personal data and against accidental loss or destruction of personal data.'

Security is crucial.

All data users and computer bureaux must register, and follow the general rules. There are exceptions – one of which is far less useful to employers than many realize. It is designed to exclude the tiny employer, using (probably) a microcomputer, to tot up the payroll or for basic accounts.

In general: 'personal data held by a data user *only* for . . . calculating amounts payable by way of remuneration or pensions in respect of service in any employment or office or making payments of, or sums deducted from, such remuneration or pensions' are excluded. So are those used only 'for keeping accounts relating to any business or activity . . . or records of purchases, sales or other transactions for the purpose of ensuring that the requisite payments are made by or to him in respect of these transactions or for the purpose of making financial or management forecasts to assist in the conduct of any such business or activity'.

Personal data held 'for payroll and accountancy' purposes *only* are totally exempted. So are those held for 'domestic or other limited purposes'; in general, by members' clubs; and personal data held for purposes of national security. Data will not have to be revealed if they are held for the prevention or detection of crime, the apprehension or prosecution of offenders; or (please note) 'the assessment or collection of any tax or duty'. Other exemptions include data held for statistical or research purposes or held *and controlled* outside the UK.

Now suppose that personal data held for 'payroll and accountancy purposes' is excluded. Section 32 says that even so it 'may be disclosed' (among other reasons) 'to any person, other than the data user, by whom the remuneration or pensions in question are payable' – that is (e.g.) to the employer or pension fund; or 'for the purpose of obtaining actuarial advice'.

The Act is highly complex. It contains 43 Sections and 4 detailed Schedules. Most of it is now in force – including registration and all that goes with it – and the remainder becomes fully operative on 11 November 1987. Meanwhile, wise employers have already prepared for the new scene. For instance they will have asked themselves the following questions:

● Has your company considered in the light of the new rules what personal data – whether concerning employees, customers, clients, suppliers or others – should in future be held on computer, and which should be retained on traditional files?

● Has your department trained its own staff, regarding the Act and its effects?

● Has your company made a careful audit of the various machines – from massive data banks to word processors with memories – on which personal data are held? If a data subject requires access, will your department be able to retrieve the information without undue or expensive effort?

● Has a review been carried out of security measures, to ensure that there is no improper leakage or disclosure?

● Should a member of staff be appointed to take charge of data protection procedures, audits or training?

Finally, the timetable:

The Act received the Royal Assent on 12 July 1984. From 12 September 1984, a data subject could seek compensation through the courts for any damage or associated distress suffered on or after that date by reason of:

(a) The loss of personal data relating to him or her; or

(b) Access being obtained to the data, or its destruction or disclosure, without the authority of the data user or computer bureau.

Registration began on 11 November 1985, when data users and computer bureaux could submit applications to the Registrar. Existing data users and computer bureaux were required to apply for registration before 11 May 1986, when the holding of personal data by an unregistered person became a criminal offence.

From 11 May 1986, a criminal offence is committed by any person who 'knowingly or recklessly provides bureau services without being registered as a computer bureau'. Registered data users became bound to operate within the terms of their registered entries and liable to pay compensation 'in respect of damage or associated distress suffered on or after this date by reason of inaccuracy of personal data'. The court also gained power to order rectification or erasure of inaccurate personal data.

On 11 November 1987, the 'subject access' provisions came into force, giving individuals the right to details of their data. The Registrar's powers of supervision are fully in operation and any notices served before that date now take effect.

If personnel managers act carefully and swiftly, however, the new data protection rules are unlikely to cause problems for them or for their companies. Any failure to do so is an invitation to trouble.

Discussion questions

1   Draw up a hypothetical contract of employment for a new employee.
2   Enumerate an employee's rights under the Health and Safety at Work Act. Where do the statutory responsibilities for upholding this Act lie?
3   As a personnel manager, what particular procedures would you need to consider in formulating a policy for sickness absence and control?
4   On what grounds is a dismissal from employment regarded as fair? When is it unfair? When is it wrongful?
5   Consider the precautions you should take in setting up a computerized personnel information system.

CHAPTER 13

Collective rights at work

by Greville Janner, QC, MP

Chairman of the All-Party Parliamentary Safety Group and a member of the House of Commons Select Committee on Employment

A union is an organization of workers. Its prime purpose is to look after the interests of its members. Individually, an employee is seldom strong when pitted against his management. Collectively, unions have at least a chance of bargaining from strength.

The essential and obvious difference between a free and totalitarian society lies in the right of the individual worker to withdraw his labour if he is dissatisfied with his lot. But while a one man strike has little impact, no employer can ignore collective industrial action. But industrial action inevitably means that the employees concerned are in breach of their own contracts of employment and cause or induce breaches by the company of its contractual obligations. So the law has long accorded protection to unions and their officials and members against many forms of civil and criminal action, when they act (in accordance with the so-called 'golden formula') 'in contemplation of furtherance of a trade dispute'.

As the political pendulum swings, so has union power and protection waxed and waned. In this chapter, we shall survey laws within which our unions operate – including recognition and closed shops; worker participation through collective bargaining, disclosure of information, redundancy consultation and safety committees; the rights of union officials to time off work; and changes in the balance between powers and unions and management, in times of political and economic stress.

Independent and recognized trade unions

The law starts by guaranteeing to employees the right to belong or (now) not to belong either to independent or to non-independent trade unions. The power lies with the independents – which means those not under the control of management and which are certified as independent by the *Certification Officer*.

The Certification Officer (CO) decides 'independence' on the basis of control and domination – not because a union is or is not a TUC affiliate. An appeal from the decision of the CO lies to the EAT. Under the 1980

Employment Act, the CO is also responsible for administering the scheme to provide payments out of public funds towards the expense of secret ballots conducted by independent trade unions.

Most rights, though, go only to those independent trade unions which are 'recognized' – that is (courts have held) those unions recognized by particular employers 'to any substantial extent for the purposes of collective bargaining'.

Suppose that a union applies for recognition and (for whatever reason) the employers wish to refuse it. They may call in ACAS (Advisory, Conciliation and Arbitration Service) who will conciliate and mediate. But ACAS' power to require a ballot and to recommend recognition irrespective of the wishes of the parties was removed by the 1980 Act. Today, recognition disputes join the ranks of other disagreements, to be fought out through normal shop floor pressures and/or negotiating procedures.

We shall now discuss the legal advantages of independent, recognized unions ('IRUs').

Redundancy consultation and notification

Employers are required to consult IRUs if they intend to make redundant any member or other person 'affected by' IRU bargaining. They must do so as early as possible, however few the numbers; if they propose to make 100 or more redundant at one establishment within a period of 90 days, then they must give 90 days' advance warning; if 10 or more at one establishment within 30 days, then 30 days' warning.

Exception: where there are 'special circumstances' which make notification 'not reasonably practicable'. Otherwise, failure to consult gives the union the right to apply to an industrial tribunal for a 'protective award' on behalf of the employees concerned. This will normally be: The amount of payment which the employees would have received during the period of notification, had it been given. It is intended as compensation, not a penalty.

Employers must also notify the Department of Employment in respect of any major redundancies (ten or more, as above). Failure to do so renders the employer liable (in theory, but not in practice) to be fined up to £2000.

Disclosure of information

'For the purposes of all stages of . . . collective bargaining between an employer and representatives of an IRU it shall be the duty of an employer . . . to disclose to those representatives on request all such information relating to his undertaking as is in his possession or that of any associated employer, and is both:

(a)   information without which the trade union representatives would be to a material extent impeded in carrying on with such collective bargaining; and

(b) information which it would be in accordance with good industrial relations practice that he should disclose to them for the purposes of collective bargaining.'

Exceptions include: information which should not be disclosed for reasons of national security or which would involve contravening a statute or which 'has been communicated to the employer in confidence' or which 'relates specifically to an individual, unless he has consented to its being disclosed' or (most important): 'any information the disclosure of which would be seriously prejudicial to the interests of the employer's undertaking, for reasons other than its effect on collective bargaining'. If an employer fails to disclose, a union has a right to bring a case before the Central Arbitration Committee.

In practice, employers tend to be all too ready to provide information when business is bad and unwilling to do so when it is good. Conversely: unions prefer not to know when times are bad, but are inclined to demand disclosure when they suspect that profits are being salted away. A sad commentary on modern industrial relations.

Safety representatives and committees

The Health and Safety at Work Act was followed by Regulations,[1] requiring employers to recognize safety representatives appointed by IRUs; and for setting up of safety committees. Further rules and background advice were provided by the Code[1] and by Guidance Notes[1] respectively.

It is estimated that there are now about 120 000 safety representatives, of whom about half are shop stewards or their equivalent. Their influence varies along with their energy and with the cooperation and encouragement which they receive from management. But they represent a sensible and hopeful form of participation in about the only area of industrial relations practice in which the interests of management and workers are (or certainly should be) largely the same.

Employee involvement

Section 1 of the 1982 Act is, certainly in the long run, one of its most important. Introduced at the last minute and almost as an afterthought, it is potentially powerful.

Any company with more than 250 employees must include in any directors' report a statement describing action taken to maintain or increase

---

1 The Regulations on Safety Representatives and Safety Committees (SI 1977 No. 500) and accompanying Code of Practice and Guidance Notes.

employee involvement during that year. In the words of the Act, this statement must describe 'the action that has been taken during the financial year to introduce, maintain or develop arrangements aimed at

(i) providing employees systematically with information on matters of concern to them as employees;

(ii) consulting employees or their representatives on a regular basis, so that the views of employees can be taken into account in making decisions which are likely to affect their interests;

(iii) encouraging the involvement of employees in the company's perform-ance through an employees' share scheme or by some other means;

(iv) achieving a common awareness on the part of all employees of the financial and economic factors affecting the performance of the company.'

These rules do not, of course, require companies to take any of the steps concerned, but only to report on what they have or have not done. But by forcing auditors and accountants to consult their colleagues in Personnel . . . by propelling personnel people into considering what they have done or should be doing in the area of personnel involvement in industrial relations . . . by pushing directors into considering profit sharing and other financial involvement . . . and especially by showing on paper and for shareholders and (in the case of public companies) the world to see what has not been done – it is intended and likely that voluntary involvement will be increased. As an American judge once said: 'Sunlight is the finest disinfectant!'

With or without the requirements of European example, precedent and requirement, worker involvement (by whatever name) is certain to increase. The Government believes (rightly or wrongly) that the advance should be on a voluntary basis. Section 1 of the 1982 Act is designed to promote that process.

Collective bargaining

Collective bargaining fulfils two main purposes. It regulates arrangements between the parties – sometimes known as *procedural* agreements; and it regulates individual contracts of employment by means of *substantive* agree-ments. Often both procedural and substantive provisions are to be found in a single collective agreement.

Collective bargaining remains the major source of normal, day-to-day union participation in the affairs of business organizations. In a well-regulated company or authority with trade union involvement, unions are brought into the decision-making process if only because changes in systems, methods or organization will eventually require union consent through the bargaining process. But collective bargaining depends upon the recognition of one or more independent trade unions – which is where this analysis began.

Essentially, the whole of this area of law was first structured in the Industrial Relations Act 1971. It was not acceptable to the unions and in 1974 was repealed by the Trade Union and Labour Relations Act, which re-enacted only the unfair dismissal provisions, in slightly strengthened form.

In 1975, the Employment Protection Act increased union strength and powers, introducing rules on redundancy consultation, disclosure of information and time off work for trade union officials to undertake union activities – as well as those insolvency and maternity rights considered in the last chapter.

The then Labour Government had also undertaken to introduce worker participation into the industrial decision-making process. It set up the Bullock Commission, but its recommendations were never accepted. The EEC Fifth Directive, which would introduce compulsory works committees and other forms of participation, remains in draft. Meanwhile, worker participation continues to enter the UK system through the side door.

Now suppose that employers do recognize a trade union. Its officials will bargain with the employers on behalf of their members. In most cases, the outcome of that bargaining will affect not only the members, but also all other employees doing the same or similar work. If only some of the members in (for instance) a job or a unit are unionized, the rest will almost certainly get the same remuneration and other terms as those achieved by the union for its members – indeed a recent case in the Court of Appeal shows that it would be illegal for employers to discriminate between members and non-members over pay rates.

Closed shops

At this stage, the members are likely to say: 'Why should we pay our dues and make our sacrifices while the others get the benefits without making any contribution? Why should we endure "free riders"?' If the membership is sufficiently substantial, it may well seek to make a closed shop agreement (or, to use the proper legal term, a Union Membership Agreement – or UMA) with the management.

If that agreement provides that all employees must be members of the union before they are taken on, then it is a 'pre-entry' UMA; if they must be *or become* members, then it is 'post-entry'. Either way, non-members may say: 'Why should we join a union, if we do not wish to? It's a free country . . .'

There is then a classic conflict of two freedoms. On the one hand, advocates of the closed shop say: 'If they want the benefits but do not wish to belong, then they have the freedom to get a job somewhere else'.

Labour governments traditionally and ideologically support the closed shop; Conservative governments oppose it – hence the curbs introduced by the 1980 and 1982 Employment Acts. In brief, they are as follows:

THE EMPLOYMENT ACT 1980

1 If in a closed shop situation a union 'unreasonably' (a) excludes or (b) expels a person from membership, that employee may go to an industrial tribunal and claim compensation;

2 Any employee may opt out of an UMA, if 'he genuinely objects on grounds of conscience or deeply held personal conviction to being a member of any trade union whatsoever or of a particular trade union'. Until 1980 only a 'religious' objection was enough;

3 It is unfair to dismiss an employee who opts out on any of the above grounds;

4 Irrespective of the above, it is unfair to dismiss an employee for opting out of an UMA formed after 15 August 1980 unless in a secret ballot at least 80 per cent of those eligible to vote have in fact voted in its favour.

In practice, these rules had little effect. Hence the next round.

THE EMPLOYMENT ACT 1982

Recognizing that in reality closed shops remain almost entirely unaffected by the 1980 Act provisions, the Government tried again. Here is a summary of the main changes:

1 Since 1 November 1984, anyone who is sacked for non-union membership in a closed shop situation will automatically be dismissed 'unfairly' – unless the UMA has been 'approved' in a secret ballot within the previous five years. This requires support either by 80 per cent of those eligible to vote or 85 per cent of those actually voting. In other words, a ballot needs to be held for existing closed shops as well as for new ones. (In fact, very few ballots have been held, because of union opposition; ACAS estimates only 1 per cent of workers in closed shops have been balloted. For the rest, any dismissal for non-membership will be unfair.)

2 It becomes automatically unfair to dismiss an employee for non-membership of *any union* – including those which are not 'independent' – outside an 'approved' closed shop.

3 If an employee is fired for refusing to make payments in lieu of union membership subscriptions, then the dismissal is 'deemed' to be on the grounds of non-membership, both outside and inside the closed shop.

4 If an employee has made a complaint that he has been unreasonably excluded or expelled from a union in a UMA situation and is either

successful or if his proceedings are still pending, then it is 'unfair' to dismiss him for non-membership.

5 An employee who opts out of trade union membership so as to avoid a conflict between his code of professional conduct and taking part in ·industrial action is protected against UMA dismissal.

These rules all date from 1 December 1982, except for the five-year ballots which became effective as from 1 November 1984.

Next: actions 'short of dismissal' are covered by the new rules. So if (for instance) an employer keeps the non-joiner on his workforce but disciplines or penalizes him or her in some other way, that too will be unlawful.

This rule applies also to action short of dismissal taken to enforce payments in lieu of union membership. And deducting payments in lieu from an employee's wages is deemed to be 'action short of dismissal'. In a closed shop situation, such action is unlawful if dismissal in the same situation would have been unfair.

Next: suppose that an employer gives way to union pressure and sacks an employee in a closed shop situation. If the employee claimed compensation, the employer could join the union in the action, claiming an indemnity. No employer has yet been so daft as to do so.

Now the complainant as well as the employer may bring the union into this sort of proceeding and the tribunal may award compensation wholly or partly against the union.

COMPENSATION

There is now a *minimum* basic award of £2300 for union membership dismissals, plus a new 'special award', where the complainant requests re-employment. If reinstatement is not ordered, then he or she will get a minimum of £11 500 and a maximum of £23 000. If the tribunal makes a reinstatement order which is complied with, then compensation will (as before) be confined to loss incurred. But if a reinstatement order is not complied with, then the employee will normally get a special award of £17 250 minimum. Both basic and special awards may be reduced when the tribunal thinks it is 'just and equitable' having regard to the conduct of the complainant before the dismissal (what is generally called his 'contributory conduct').

TUC policy is not to hold ballots. Some employers have terminated closed shop agreements. Unions have turned a blind eye in some cases to non-membership.

Recognizing that the rules on closed shop dismissals were almost totally ineffective, the Government hopes to breathe life into all of them by making applications financially lucrative. So employers have to look to their tactics.

Meanwhile: note that guidance on the handling of closed shop situations is contained in the Government's Code – operative since May 1983. Unlike

ACAS Codes (disciplinary, disclosure, time off work), this Code – like its sister on picketing – has been made by the Government, under powers in the 1980 Act.

Industrial Disputes

What, then, of industrial disputes and their solution? How can industrial action be avoided – and what are the current limits on the protection given to strikers?

As always, the object of the exercise should be to avoid disputes. That means:

1 The operation of agreed and intelligent procedures; and
2 Where necessary, the early and helpful intervention of the Advisory, Conciliation and Arbitration Service (ACAS).

As with the individual contract of service, so with collective bargains – you make your own arrangements, as you and the other contracting parties see fit. But, of course, the bargaining strength of a trade union is normally far higher than that of the individual employee. Items to be hammered out in negotiation include procedures for the sorting out of disputes.

Procedures differ according to circumstances – not least the structure of the business and the views and strength of the management and unions concerned. But once the collective bargain is struck, its force depends upon the parties and not upon the law.

In the days of the Industrial Relations Act, a collective bargain was taken to be intended to have legally binding effect – that is, to be enforceable through the courts – unless it provided to the contrary, which it always did. Today, the opposite applies, and a collective bargain will be taken *not* to be intended to be enforceable through legal action unless the contrary is stated – which it almost never is. Still: if commercial contracts were only regarded by the parties to them as having the same binding importance as collective bargains in the world of industrial relations, the courts would have far less business than they do.

Anyway, if management and union come into conflict, the procedures previously agreed between them to deal with such disputes should and nearly always do come into operation. Only when they are exhausted will industrial action normally descend upon the business. And before that happens, ACAS should be called in.

Advisory, Conciliation and Arbitration Service (ACAS)

ACAS is an independent body, neither the pawn of the union, nor in the pocket of management, but available to either for advice and, if both agree, for conciliation, mediation or arbitration. Remember: since the repeal of the old recognition rules and their replacement with nothing other than shop-floor strength and bargaining, ACAS can only operate with the consent of the parties.

The 1975 Act gives ACAS power to advise in almost every industrial situation, ranging from the individual unfair dismissal claim to the most major industrial dispute; from problems of alleged discrimination or arguments over equal pay to wage structures and union procedures. Unlike lawyers, whose advice is chargeable, right or wrong, ACAS advice is free.

If the advice brings no peace, ACAS may conciliate – seek to find a solution by counselling each side. Or it may mediate – a similar process in which, again by consent, it stands in the middle and helps the parties to come to terms.

Arbitration has a more precise and vigorous legal effect. It means the submission of the dispute to the judgement and decision of an independent arbitrator, the parties agreeing in advance to accept his decision as binding. ACAS maintains a panel of arbitrators for this purpose.

ACAS conciliators are generally excellent, vary in their experience, their skill and their judgement. You should get to know your officers before you need them; when asking for help, tell your local office what you need; and if you are dissatisfied with the help you get, then – tactfully but strongly – complain and ask for someone else.

Now suppose that your efforts and those of ACAS fail. You have a dispute on your hands. How can the law then help you?

The best tactic as in all areas but especially this one – is to keep as far away from courts and tribunals as sense and guile can keep you.

The legal process of defending the strength of management while reducing that of unions was begun with the 1980 Employment Act; continued with the 1982 Act and with the 1984 Trade Union Act.

In practice, precisely because most managements well recognize the dangers of legal action in this field, the diminution in union power has come mainly through the recession. Union members have been made redundant, along with the rest; and remaining members are hesitant in following their leaders into battle, fearing that there may be no job for them on their return.

The 1982 Act has increased the danger in two directions – individual and corporate. If an employee goes on strike, he or she is almost inevitably in breach of his or her contract of employment. But the reinstatement of all strikers, without victimization, is an almost invariable term of any agreement for return to work.

Before 1982 employers could with impunity dismiss all those taking part in a strike; but it was 'unfair' to select some for the sack – even if they remained on strike while others had already gone back to their jobs. Thanks to the 1982 Act, employers may now fairly discharge remaining strikers; leaving the returnees in position.

As we have already seen, trade union officials and members are only protected when they act in accordance with 'the golden formula' – that is: 'in contemplation or furtherance of a trade dispute'. By reducing the effect of that definition, the 1980 and later the 1982 Acts have (in theory at least) curbed the strength of industrial action, along with the protection of those who procure or who take it. Other changes (below) have had a more practical impact on employers' freedom – and readiness – to use the law.

Picketing

Primary action is aimed at one's own employer; secondary or further action against other employers not directly involved in the dispute. The 1980 and 1982 Acts and the Code of Practice which followed the first are designed to curb virtually all but primary action – whether picketing, blacking or other 'sympathetic' industrial action. However, secondary industrial action may be permissible against a first supplier or first customer of the employer in dispute.

The wording of the 1980 Act was so convoluted that even Lord Denning proclaimed his inability to understand it. It was also seldom used and largely ineffective. So the 1982 Act tried again.

In brief, unions and their officers and members are protected against most civil and criminal actions 'in contemplation or furtherance of a trade dispute'. This protection does not extend, of course, to thuggery, by whatever name – from blackmail to assault. But it has long enabled collective industrial action to be planned and carried out without the participants being sued for (e.g.) inducing breaches of contract or conspiring to do so. The Government has sought to curb secondary action largely by reducing the protection of those taking part in it.

First: there is no legal protection for those who organize or take part in secondary picketing, whether or not it comes under 'the golden formula'. Only if the person pickets at or near his or her own place of work and the purpose is 'peacefully to obtain or communicate information, or peacefully to persuade a person to work or not to work' will there normally be legal protection.

Exceptions: a trade union official may accompany a member picketing his or her own place of work; mobile and other workers may (in general) picket where they are currently employed; and workers sacked in connection with the dispute may picket at their former place of work.

A trade dispute must be one between workers and their own employers and wholly or mainly about matters such as their terms of work. And the 1982 Act *excludes* (among others and broadly speaking) the following categories from the definition of a 'lawful trade dispute':

Demarcation and other disputes between workers or trade unions;

Disputes between workers and employers other than their own or between a trade union and an employer, when none of that employer's workforce are in dispute with him;

Disputes which are not wholly or mainly concerned with pay and conditions, but only have some connection with them;

Or disputes which relate to matters occurring overseas (e.g. in support of workers' rights in, say, Poland or South Africa), unless the workers taking action in the UK are likely to be affected by its outcome.

Secret ballots

The 1980 Act gave trade unions the right to apply for the cost of a wide variety of important postal ballots to be paid from public funds.

An employer with more than twenty workers can be requested by an independent, recognized trade union, to provide a place on his or her premises where the members may vote in a secret ballot. Refusal could lead to a complaint to an industrial tribunal and to the award of compensation.

No employer has been known to refuse to provide such facilities, nor have we any record of tribunal proceedings under this section.

Both the 1980 and the 1982 Acts introduced secret ballot provisions for the creation of 'approved' union membership agreements. Details follow.

Trade union labour only contracts

Any term or condition of a contract for the supply of goods and services (says the 1982 Act) is void, in so far as it requires all or part of the work to be done by those who are – or who are not – members of trade unions or of a particular union. Trade union labour contracts are (in theory) banned – from tender stage onwards. This prohibition applies to companies as well as to local authorities; and where unions apply pressure to impose or to enforce such requirements, their legal immunities are removed.

So if trade union labour only requirements are included in a contract, the contractor is not obliged to observe them, nor can he be sued for breach of contract if he fails to do so. The contract itself remains valid but those who suffer loss as a result of a breach of this statutory duty may claim declaration, injunctions and/or damages from the court.

As usual with such provisions, they are generally honoured more in the breach than in the performance. As with restrictions on closed shops, employers and unions are in general simply ignoring these new rules and carrying on as before. The trouble which could be created, probably through a maverick action, is obvious.

The Trade Union Act 1984

The Trade Union Act 1984 deals with the election of trade union leaders, secret ballots for industrial action and trade union expenditure on party political matters.

Part I requires that every trade union must elect every voting member of its governing body at least every five years by secret ballot of union members. It must also keep an accurate register of its members' names and addresses.

The Act lays down minimum requirements for the conduct of elections. These concern frequency and balloting arrangements and who is entitled to vote and to stand as a candidate. If a union fails to comply with the Act's requirements on elections or on keeping a register of members, then a member may make a complaint to the Certification Officer or to the courts.

The requirement to compile a membership register came into force in July and the rules on elections on 1 October 1985.

Part II makes it a condition of a trade union's legal immunity for organizing industrial action that it first hold a secret ballot in which all those due to take part in the action are entitled to vote and the majority of those voting take part in the action. The Act lays down minimum requirements for these ballots on: who can vote; arrangements for voting; the ballot question; and the counting and announcement of the results. These rules came into force in September 1984 and apply to any industrial action after that date. A number of employers have already taken out injunctions where unions have not held such ballots, and unions are increasingly holding such ballots.

Part III makes changes to the law relating to trade union political funds. It requires trade unions with political funds to ballot their members at regular intervals on whether they wish their union to continue to spend money on party political matters. Any trade union which has a political fund must pass a new resolution by secret ballot of its members at intervals of not more than ten years if it wishes to continue to spend money on political objects.

The Act also places a duty on employers who deduct trade union subscriptions from their employees' pay through 'check-off' arrangements not to continue to deduct political contributions from any employee who certifies that he or she is exempt from or has applied to contract out of paying such contributions. These provisions came into force in March 1985.

Discussion questions

1   What is meant by a 'recognized' trade union?
2   What are the main functions of ACAS?
3   What are the main functions of a Conciliation Officer?
4   What are the advantages and disadvantages of a Union Management Agreement – from the point of view of (a) management, (b) unions, (c) individual employees?

5 What is the current legal situation regarding picketing – both primary action and secondary action?

6 Consider the implications of the use of the ballot in the conduct of industrial relations.

7 Would you regard the law as central or peripheral to the conduct of good industrial relations and personnel management?

8 Is there a logical (apart from a legal or administrative) distinction between individual and collective rights at work?

9 Some have claimed that in employment relations 'legalism seems to have developed an unstoppable momentum'. Is this true? Is it desirable? Is it avoidable?

CHAPTER 14

Dealing with industrial tribunals

by Greville Janner, QC, MP

Chairman of the All-Party Parliamentary Safety Group and a member of the House of
Commons Select Committee on Employment

Until the Industrial Relations Act 1971, Britain had no legal structure for
industrial relations, Since then, legislation – statutes, regulations and codes –
proliferate; litigation – from industrial tribunals to the House of Lords –
multiplies; and personnel management grew into a vital and specialized
branch in every major industrial and commercial undertaking.

Legislation and litigation are as vital to personnel managers as crimes and
criminals to the police. Practitioners must create and adapt their methods to
suit the times and the circumstances. For personnel managers, these include
the following:

1   In the area of the employee's individual rights, recession and redundancy
    dismissals to some extent made up for the fall (of about 26 per cent) in
    applications to industrial tribunals, resulting from the 1980 doubling (in
    most cases) of the qualifying period for protection, a further drop was
    anticipated when the qualifying period was doubled again after 1985, but
    it seems there is little sign of it so far.

2   The success rate of applications in industrial tribunal hearings – now only
    about 30 per cent – and the cost to employers of *winning* has burgeoned;

3   There are far less jobs available than there were; labour turnover has
    fallen; people are less ready to move; and there has been a comparative lull
    in new employment law (other than in the fields of sick pay, discrimi-
    nation, and restraints on unions).

4   From 1971 until about 1980, the trend was towards specialization in
    personnel and industrial relations management; since then, it has been
    towards spinning off personnel functions, including appointment and
    dismissal, back into general management;

5   For the sake of their own jobs, personnel managers must now concentrate

on tailoring their planning to both the law and the circumstances. This chapter is designed to promote that crucial art.

Industrial tribunals

ITs started in 1965 under the Industrial Training Act 1964, hearing appeals against industrial training levies. Since then they have acquired jurisdiction over disputes involving (among other miseries) redundancy rights, unfair dismissal (remember: *wrongful* dismissal claims go to civil *courts*); equal pay; sex and race discrimination; appeals against prohibition and improvement notices (under the Health and Safety at Work Act); as well as claims by employees (almost always backed by a union) for declarations or interpretations concerning the written particulars of their terms of service. Still: unfair dismissal claims are in the vast majority. So what is their reality?

A steady 60 per cent of unfair dismissal claims are settled with the help of Conciliation Officers; some are simply withdrawn while others (no one knows how many or what percentage) are bought off by employers at a price. Of those that reach a hearing, about 70 per cent *fail*, and even those which succeed result in the claimant getting on average only about £1400.

More important for the employer – or, indeed, for the personnel manager in his or her personal capacity: as an unfair dismissal claim is almost always a passport to permanent unemployment, most unfairly sacked employees prefer not to bring any action for unfair dismissal. In times of recession when jobs are scarce, the higher the employee in the scale, the less likely that he or she will bring a claim. Exception: those areas of the UK in which dismissed employees reckon that they will never get other jobs anyway, in which case they might as well go to the tribunal – and also those very difficult cases where ex-employees are determined regardless of cost to 'clear their name'.

Still: in a company or firm which operates a fair system and follows the rules which follow shortly, its chances of losing the claim are small – but its prospects of losing money as a result of that claim are almost certain.

To cost out an unfair dismissal claim, *you must* tot up not only the legal expenses but (more especially) the cost of management time and that of other employees, in preparing the case and attending at the tribunal, along with the cost of preparing and copying the documentation. Personnel managers who have done this exercise generally find that the cost of *winning* a tribunal case runs somewhere between £1000 and £15 000 depending on its length and complexity and the number of issues and witnesses involved.

Thanks to Regulations introduced in 1980, an employer/respondent may ask for a 'pre-hearing assessment'. This procedure was intended as a sieve, to get rid of hopeless cases. Its success varies in different parts of the UK. If it fails, the employer/respondent has incurred extra costs and the price of a settlement is likely to move up sharply.

The same Regulations gave tribunals power to award costs against an unsuccessful claimant where he or she has behaved 'unreasonably'. This power is seldom exercised and when a respondent is ordered to pay costs, they are generally very low – a tiny proportion only of the expense inevitably incurred by the employer.

So obviously, it is tactically sensible for the personnel manager to settle unfair dismissal cases where possible and reasonable – unless they have to be fought in order to show other potential claimants that the company is not a 'soft touch'. Anyway, the best way to avoid claims or to settle them cheaply is to follow sensible and fair procedures. Here is a checklist of the most important:

1   Has the employee been given at least one warning, preferably in writing, of intended dismissal? Mere complaint of misconduct or poor performance is not enough.

2   Has time been allowed to cool off? Was the employee suspended on full pay while investigation proceeded?

3   Did management follow a fair procedure, and in particular

(a)   Give the employee the opportunity to explain his or her case, however improbable or 'thin' it may be?

(b)   Give the employee (if reasonably practicable) the right to appeal to a higher level of authority?

(c)   Maintain proper documentation and records, including file in which the employee's record is preserved?

(d)   Above all: Had the employer behaved 'reasonably' and hence 'fairly' in the particular case?

If the answer to each of these questions is: yes – then the employers should have little to fear from the threat of tribunal proceedings and if they cannot be settled cheaply, they should be won without too much difficulty. But the more negatives in the answers, the more likely it becomes that the employers will be involved in unnecessary expense. If a case has to be fought then at least the employers should maximize their chances of victory.

If personnel managers are considering the same problem from their personal point of view, then of course they apply these principles in reverse. One reason for the heavy failure rate is the number of poor claims. Another is the inability of the claimant to bring supporting or corroborative evidence, oral or written. Thus:

1   Other colleagues or workmates are not likely to be willing to testify on the claimant's behalf because they fear for their own jobs and future – while the employer will normally be able to bring several people into the witness box; and

2 New employees have little documentation to back their case – while if personnel managers have done their job well, their employers will have plenty!

Moral: personnel executives should recognize the difficulty with oral corroboration and prepare their documents, to avoid proceedings where possible but otherwise so as to win them. In particular: anyone who receives any written complaints concerning their own conduct or performance, should *always* reply in writing, keeping one copy on the file and another at home!

Industrial tribunals are independent judicial bodies. Each has a legally qualified chairman, appointed by the Lord Chancellor. The other two members are drawn from two panels appointed by the Secretary of State for Employment, one after consultation with the TUC and the other in consultation with the CBI. ITs now have a very wide jurisdiction.

If personnel managers cannot avoid industrial tribunal proceedings, then, how can they make the best of them?

Statistics show that employers who are legally represented are only marginally more likely to win their cases than if an articulate personnel manager does the advocacy. Tribunals are more inclined to help litigants in person (which includes those represented by non-lawyers) than they are the professional. In courts, the general rule is: 'He who is his own lawyer has a fool for a client'. In tribunals: 'Do your own representation or your company's, where reasonably practicable'. But remember two points. It is difficult for anyone to be both an advocate and the principal witness. And seek advice beforehand – especially in cases involving such complex issues as discrimination – on any hidden legal pitfalls that may emerge in the case.

Suppose, then, that personnel executives appear in a tribunal – or, for that matter, in a court – whether as a witness of or as an advocate. They should:

1 Do their homework; know the facts; find their way around the documents; and be prepared to explain their case;

2 Prepare their documents and make them into a bundle, in date order; and in a tribunal, prepare six copies – one for each of the members; one for the witness; one for the other side; and one for themselves;

3 Make a 'date chart' – setting out the facts in date order and cross-referencing the documents;

4 Get to know the tribunal or court, so that they feel at home when they arrive with the case; if possible, sit in on other cases before theirs; and watch the procedures and the way in which the tribunal reacts to the witnesses;

5 In a tribunal, people sit both to give evidence and when acting as advocates; in court, they stand. They should address the chairman of the

tribunal or one of the members or a magistrate or JP as 'Sir' or 'Madam' (as the case may be); a Circuit Judge as 'Your Honour'; a High Court Judge as 'My Lord';

6   Watch their demeanour not only when they are giving evidence but also as and when they are sitting in the back of the tribunal or court room – that is when most people give themselves away, as every experienced tribunal member, etc. well knows;

7   Answer the questions asked – as briefly as possible. If they wish to add to their answers, they can say so – but answer first;

8   Make sure that these are heard – keep voices up;

9   If cross-examined, they should not take offence; questioners are doing their job, as the witnesses are their own;

10   Check out the procedures – which are far more informal in a tribunal than in a court. Tribunal proceedings are generally 'opened' by the employer, whose representative will summarize the case and call each witness in turn. Advocates should not ask their own witnesses 'leading questions' – that is, those that suggest the answers. Instead of saying: 'You resigned, didn't you?' they should ask: 'What happened next?' Or 'What did you say?' Leading questions may, of course, be asked of witnesses on the other side;

11   It is important to discover whether the particular tribunal chairman or other adjudicator has his or her idiosyncrasies. The best person to ask about this and other matters is usually the usher or clerk;

12   When giving evidence, a witness may take into the witness box any 'contemporaneous document' – any diary, record book, file or document made at the time of the happening referred to. Not only police officers are entitled to 'refresh their memories' from their notebooks. . . .

13   Finally: no one should hesitate to ask for guidance; and if a question is not understood, ask that it be repeated.

If personnel executives are presenting cases on behalf of employers, they can still let lawyers sort out the law and the tactics and advise on presentation.

INDUSTRIAL TRIBUNAL PROCEDURE (BEFORE THE HEARING)

Almost all claims before an industrial tribunal are commenced on a form IT1 which is available from any local employment office, job centre, employment benefit office or Citizen's Advice Bureau. This 'originating application' must give the employee's name and address, the name and address of the respondent company and particulars of the grounds on which the employee is seeking a decision. The completed form is returned to the Central Office of Tribunals at the address stated on the form. After receiving the form, the Secretary of the Tribunal will send a copy of it to the respondent employer, provided that on the face of it, the applicant is qualified to bring a case – e.g. is within the time limit for commencing the action and has a sufficient period of continuous employment.

Employer respondents have 14 days in which to 'enter an appearance' – that is, to issue or reply to the application on form IT3, which will have been received from the Tribunal Office. Before the hearing of the case in full, a 'pre-hearing assessment' may take place on the application of either parties or on the initiative of the tribunal. This was introduced under the Industrial Tribunals Regulations 1980. The parties may submit oral and written evidence at the pre-hearing assessment. If, contrary to the advice of the tribunal, either party insists on continuing the case of pursuing a particular line of argument, then the party at fault may have an order for costs made against them.

In most cases, copies of all relevant documents are sent to a Conciliation Officer at ACAS, who will try to help the parties to reach an amicable settlement. Any information given to the Conciliation Officer will be treated as confidential and will not be admissible in evidence at the tribunal hearing without the consent of the party who gave the information. The Conciliation Officer may be brought in either before or after an originating application has been filed. If the case is destined for a full hearing, then the parties will be given at least 14 days' notice and if either party is unable to attend an early application for adjournment of the hearing should be made.

THE PERSONNEL MANAGER'S CHECKLIST

Anyway, the first stage in the development of a corporate policy for individual employees is to check through documentation and procedures, and in particular, the following:

1 Are written particulars up to date and do they contain the terms set out in Chapter 12 – properly worded to achieve fairness and so as to reflect the intention of both parties (where appropriate) duly agreed with any union concerned?

2 Is sick pay documentation in order?

3 When were (a) grievance; (b) disciplinary; and (c) dismissal procedures last reviewed? Are they adequately documented?

4 Is the company's health and safety documentation in order? Is there a

'policy statement' (in accordance with s. 2 of the Act) which not only sets out 'policy' and 'organization' but also the 'arrangements' for putting it into effect – and hence identifying the main hazards in each job and how these may be avoided?

5 Are any necessary redundancy procedures properly worked out?

6 Is any union (a) recognition and/or (b) Union Membership Agreement fully documented?

7 Is there a need to negotiate – or to renegotiate any union agreements – procedural or otherwise?

8 Are the personnel executives satisfied with their own written terms of service – or should they attempt to put them into better order, while they still have the power and the influence to do so?

The next area of corporate policy worth careful thought concerns supervisors and management colleagues from the line upwards. The status and morale of supervisors is steadily declining, for reasons of combined law and circumstances. Thus:

1 With the advent of unfair dismissal protection, most supervisors lost their right to dismiss. They are responsible for their team or department or unit, but the ultimate power to decide on who may stay and who should move has been taken from them;

2 Far too many managers and supervisors earn less than at least some of those for whom they are responsible; and money apart, they sometimes even have less holiday rights than their subordinates;

3 Inevitably, the Health and Safety at Work Act and subsequent Regulations have heaped extra responsibility on to supervisors and junior managers, for the health and safety of others – criminal as well as civil liability; above all

4 Union participation – direct or indirect – has led to excellent communication between most managements and their unions, including immediate access on first name terms between convenor and managing director. Supervisors and line or junior managers – and some of their seniors, including personnel executives – often find it easier to get necessary information from union officials, rather than from managerial sources. This arrangement is vastly resented.

So sensible corporate policy should aim at raising the level of confidence of line and junior management; providing training for them, not least in basics of law on appointment, dismissal and health and safety; and should recognize that the growth of managerial and supervisory unions is no coincidence.

It follows that if employers wish to avoid recognition of a particular or any trade union, they must satisfy potential members that they are better off without one. If faced with an inescapable demand for a Union Membership Agreement (UMA) – law or no law – then if employers wish to or must cave in, they should do so while the union is still prepared to agree that the UMA will apply only to future employees and not to existing ones. If employers operate in a closed shop situation, they should recognize the potential dangers to good industrial relations created by recent anti-UMA legislation.

How, then, should employers plan to deal with a non-union employee, in a closed shop situation?

First, they must attend to their recruitment and appointment practices. Just as management must recognize that discrimination on grounds of sex or race is both unlawful and immoral, so it will no doubt decline to appoint non-union people, in breach of a UMA – even if terms of that UMA are no longer enforceable in legal theory.

Difficulties are much more likely to arise when a member tears up his union card. There are three basic ways in which personnel managers deal with this type of maverick:

1   They seek to induce him to return to union membership; if that fails, then

2   They try to get the union to agree to turn a blind eye – perhaps in return for some other favour; or as a last resort

3   They move or promote the individual to some other position in the business, not covered by the UMA.

Avoid dismissal – or 'action short of dismissal' – in closed shop situations, by good management or by cunning. The penalties – in cash and in miseries of battles with unions – are far too great.

Obviously, this sort of argument is worth avoiding for its own sake. But it also interferes with intelligent effort to achieve good relations with unions. To make the best of the rights which the law still provides for unions, check the following:

1   Is your company making as full disclosure of relevant information as it reasonably can? Remember: tell the truth – a union only has to discover an untruth once, and a structure built on trust can no longer exist. The more information offered to the union, the less likely it is to demand information which the employers would prefer not to provide.

Also: managerial and supervisory colleagues should be fully briefed, and information not merely given to unions.

Most 'leakages' of information come from dissatisfied managers – or their sacked secretaries – and not through confidences entrusted to unions.

2   Job insecurity is a menace to effort and to good relations. So if redundancies are inevitable, good employers make them as painless as possible. They do their best to see that the remaining workforce is viable, so that those employees feel that they have a future in the business: and that the company is as generous as possible when dealing with those consigned to the scrap heap;

3   The same generosity should be extended to employees sacked for most other reasons – or who are unable to work through illness. There is nothing like meanness to one employee to sour relations with the rest;

4   While the law only requires employers to 'consult' about intended redundancies and employers are not required to follow the wishes of a union so consulted, good managers always consider whether they may not in fact be able to do so. When jobs are at stake and unions are consulted by personnel managers whom they trust, they may well come up with ideas which save jobs – including sometimes those of the personnel executives themselves;

5   Safety committees are not extensions of management. The Commission's Guidance Notes specifically say that there is no reason why there should be a management majority. There should not. Employees and workforce should choose as chairman the best person for the job – who may well be an experienced union official. Employers and unions should not sit on opposite sides of the table. Both should work on the basis that they have common problems and that their policy aims at health and safety for every level of employee. If they cannot get people to work together in this field, what hope can there be in any other?

6   Wise personnel managers respect union sensibilities, even if they sometimes deplore them. Unions believe (not always wrongly) that courts, judges, lawyers, tribunals and all the rest of the panoply of the law work to their disadvantage. Employers and their representatives should plan to deal with disagreements promptly and by the best, most acceptable and swiftest methods available in their outfit. They should understand that just as their job is to look after the interests of their company, that of the union and of its officials is to care for its membership.

With all these suggestions in mind, are there ways in which personnel managers can helpfully involve union people in their corporate planning? How can they develop feeling among their workforce that employers have some worthwhile participation in the decision-making processes? Does your board declare that 'employees should feel part of the business' – but then resent any attempt they make to take any active part in the management of their own working lives? And in any event, is your company complying constructive rule s. 1 of the 1982 Act, and giving in its director's reports full particulars of 'worker involvement'?

THE MANAGER'S PERSONAL LIABILITY

Finally: a word about the personnel manager's own legal responsibilities. The only place in the whole of our law or its periphery in which the words 'personnel manager' appear is in the Guidance Notes on Health and Safety Representatives and Committees. Guidance Notes (but not Regulations or Code) suggest that 'management representatives should not only include those from line management but such others as works engineers and personnel managers'.

Still: as executives and as management representatives, personnel people do have their own responsibility in law, criminal and civil.

1   The Health and Safety at Work Act imposes a duty on all 'directors, managers and (company) secretaries' to take such steps as are reasonably practicable to protect employees at work. If an unnecessary hazard is caused through failure by a personnel manager to take such steps, then he or she has a personal responsibility.

2   If personnel are involved in criminal activities – theft or corruption, fraud or forgery, for instance – then the personnel managers in charge will only themselves have a criminal liability if they participated in some way in the criminal offence. If they collaborated, conspired, induced or otherwise played a role in the breach of the law, then they will be liable in its penalties, along with the villainous rest. But they are not criminally liable merely because someone under their supervision misbehaved.

3   Equally, the individual personnel managers bear no personal civil liability for contractual or other wrongs, committed in their departments, even if they were personally at fault. They were acting as their principal's 'agents' – and just as principals take the benefit of that which employees do right, so they must accept the responsibility for that which goes wrong. Similarly:

4   If personnel executives' negligence or breach of statutory duty at work causes death or personal injury or financial loss, provided that the mishap occurred 'in the course of your employment', their employers (or their insurers) will have to foot the bill. It has even been held that an individual employee in those circumstances cannot be made personally liable, otherwise (said the Appeal Court) employees would have to be paid more, so that they could take out their own insurance against such risks.

In practice, the personnel manager at fault is far more likely to lose his or her job than to end up in court. If your superiors believe that you are not doing your job properly, then you are as greatly at risk as any employee who comes under your sway – and on precisely the same basis. Indeed, you may well be worse off. Unless you are a civil servant, you are unlikely to be a member of a union which could protect you; for reasons already discussed, you are very unlikely to be able to risk going to an industrial tribunal, for who then would employ you?

Discussion questions

1 What is the function of a 'pre-hearing'?
2 How would you calculate, and what items would you include, in the costing of an unfair dismissal case?
3 What detailed preparations would you make before appearing at an industrial tribunal in any given case?
4 Why do you think that employers who are legally represented in an industrial tribunal are only marginally more likely to win their cases than when a personnel manager does the advocacy?
5 As a personnel manager, what policies would you seek to achieve in order to minimize the possibilities of legal proceedings being taken against your company?

PART SEVEN

Non-Discrimination in Employment

The Baroness Seear would like to express her gratitude to the late John Brock of Charta Mede Ltd for his assistance in compiling this section.

CHAPTER 15

Women in employment

by The Baroness Seear, PC

Liberal Leader in the House of Lords

Distribution of women in the labour force

In June 1984 there were approximately 20.7 million employees in employment in Great Britain of whom 11.6 million were men and 9.1 million or just
under 44 per cent were women. Of these 9.1 million women, 4.2 million, or
slightly over 46 per cent, were working part-time.[1] Over 40 per cent of all
women in employment were in professional and scientific services, which
include teaching and nursing, or in retail distribution and repairs. In only 7 of
the 31 categories of the industrial classification used by the New Earnings
Survey, 1984, did women comprise 44 per cent or over of those employed.
These categories were the textile industry, footwear, clothing and leather,
hotel and catering, retail distribution and repairs, professional and scientific
services, and miscellaneous services. In hotel and catering, retail distribution
and repairs, professional and scientific services and miscellaneous services
over 25 per cent of the women employed were working part-time.[2]

The 1984 New Earnings Survey also shows that for women working full-
time 41.5 per cent were in clerical and related occupations and 19 per cent in
professional and related occupations in education, health and welfare.

Growth in female employment

Women have always contributed directly to the national product. In
medieval times they were economically active on the land and in the home. It
was the farmer's wife who developed the dairy industry from the milking of
the cow to the sale of dairy products in local markets. In the days of the
domestic system women contributed to family income and to the economy
as spinners in the home-based textile industry, and with industrialization
women in this industry moved with their work from home to factory.

In the nineteenth century, whatever other forces may have been at work,

1 *Employment Gazette* **93**(4) April 1985. Historical Supplement No. 1. Table 1.1 and Table 1.4.
   Quoted in Equal Opportunities Commission Ninth Annual Report 1984.
2 New Earnings Survey, 1984. Part E. Table 138. Quoted in Equal Opportunities Commission Ninth Annual Report 1984.

demographic facts made the paid employment of women a virtual necessity. According to the 1851 Census, between the ages of 20 and 40 there were 133 654 more women than men in Great Britain. Of every 100 women in Great Britain of the age of 20 to 40, forty-two were spinsters. By 1861 there were 2 482 028 spinsters of all ages of the age of 15 upwards.

At this time working-class women earned their living as domestic servants or in factories – predominantly textile factories where hours were long and conditions notoriously bad. Others attempted to maintain themselves or to add to the family income by taking outwork in their own homes. The low pay of outworkers and in many small sweat shops led ultimately to the passing of the Trade Boards Act 1909, with the introduction of legally enforceable minimum wages in a limited number of conspicuously badly paid trades.

Single middle-class women were often in dire straits. To become a governess was the one 'socially respectable' solution. Not surprisingly, the supply greatly exceeded the demand. The figure of 21 373 governesses recorded in the Census of 1851 had risen to 55 246 by 1871. For the highly talented and the lucky there were good jobs to be had, but, as in any overcrowded, unorganized and unregulated occupation, life could be wretched for those at the bottom end of the profession. In 1859 a group of educated and determined women established The Society for Promoting the Employment of Women, pressing vigorously for the entry of women into traditional male professional strongholds.[3]

Fortunately for the large numbers of women needing and wanting paid employment, the 1850s saw a rapid expansion in British trade and commerce and with it a rapidly growing demand for clerks. At first, these jobs were held almost exclusively by men: the 1851 Census recorded 11 755 male clerks compared with 15 women, though by 1881 the numbers of female clerks had risen to 5989. The Civil Service took the lead in the employment of women, braving criticism and protest. The dangers thought to arise from men and women working together were met initially by locking the women into a room for their protection. But by 1872, a Mr Scudamore writing in the Post Office Telegraph Report commented: 'The mixture of the sexes involves no risk but is highly beneficial. It raises the tone of the male staff by confining them during many hours of the day to a decency of conversation and demeanour which is not always to be found where men alone are employed'. Male Post Office clerks, fearing the competition of cheap female labour, held protest meetings, but women's advance into office work was not halted, though the pay differential remained.

It was, however, undoubtedly the introduction of the typewriter, the development of shorthand, and the invention of telephone and light office machines which led to women's real breakthrough into office work. With the great expansion in the number of office jobs, many of a new type, women

---

[3]   The facts and quotations in the section on the development of women in office work are based on an article by Dr Rosalie Silverstone: *Office Work for Women: an historical review*. Business History, Volume XVIII, No. 1, Jan. 1976.

were seen less as a threat to the existing labour force than as a much needed additional resource. Throughout the twentieth century the growth in their number continued unabated, until by 1971 there were 2 485 340 women clerical workers, 70 per cent of the total clerical labour force. Of all the jobs done by women 27 per cent were in offices.

Both World Wars influenced the employment position of women. The First World War saw the entry of very large numbers of women into the munitions industry. For the duration they worked in jobs previously held exclusively by men, but after the War they reverted to traditional areas of employment. In the Second World War women again were recruited and trained for many jobs for which they would not have been considered in peacetime and a number of women held very senior positions in administration and in the armed forces.

As Table 15.1 shows, the rate of change in the position of women has been slow.

In professional employment, apart from teaching, nursing and social

Table 15.1   *Women workers in major occupational groups, 1911–1971*[4]

Female workers as a percentage of all workers in each of the major occupational groups identified by Bain and Price.

Occupational groups	1911	1921	1931	1951	1961	1971
Employers and proprietors	18.8	20.5	19.8	20.0	20.4	24.9
White-collar workers	29.8	37.6	35.8	42.3	44.5	47.9
(a) managers and administrators	19.8	17.0	13.0	15.2	15.5	21.6
(b) higher professionals	6.0	5.1	7.5	8.3	9.7	9.9
(c) lower professionals and technicians	62.9	59.4	58.8	53.5	50.8	52.1
(d) foremen and inspectors	4.2	6.5	8.7	13.4	10.3	13.1
(e) clerks	21.4	44.6	46.0	60.2	65.2	73.2
(f) salesmen and shop assistants	35.2	43.6	37.2	51.6	54.9	59.8
All manual workers	30.5	27.9	28.8	26.1	26.0	29.4
(a) skilled	24.0	21.0	21.3	15.7	13.8	13.5
(b) semi-skilled	40.4	40.3	42.9	38.1	39.3	46.5
(c) unskilled	15.5	16.8	15.0	20.3	22.4	37.2
Total occupied population	29.6	29.5	29.8	30.8	32.4	36.5

Source: Table 3 in G. S. Bain and R. Price 'Union growth and employment trends in the United Kingdom 1964–1970'. *British Journal of Industrial Relations*, 10 November 1972, pp. 366–381. The authors' analysis of census data 1911–1961 was repeated with 1971 census data for Great Britain to update their time series.

4   Hakim, C., *Occupational Segregation*, Department of Employment, Research Paper No. 9, November 1979, p. 28.

Table 15.2 *Female membership of selected professional institutes/associations 1984*

Professional institute	Total no. of members [1]	No. of women members [1]	Percentage of women [1]
Hotel Catering and Institutional Management Association 2	22 310	10 766	48.3
Institute of Personnel Management	24 116	9 125	37.8
Institute of Health Service Administrators	5 567	2 082	37.4
British Medical Association	68 577	16 992	24.8
Institute of Bankers 3	118 547	19 525	16.5
Royal Town Planning Institute	9 529	1 286	13.5
The Chartered Insurance Institute	60 753	7 664	12.6
The Law Society (Solicitors) 2	42 984	5 235	12.2
The Rating and Valuation Association 5	4 953	356	7.1
Association of Certified Accountants	80 263	5 203	6.5
Institute of Chartered Accountants of England and Wales	80 263	5 203	6.5
Institute of Marketing	20 925	1 045	5.0
Institution of Chemical Engineers 2	15 916	681	4.3
Royal Institute of Chartered Surveyors	75 919	2 500	3.3
British Institute of Management 4	74 498	1 872	2.51
Institution of Mechanical Engineers	76 391	562	0.7
Institution of Production Engineers	19 484	134	0.7
Chartered Institute of Building	27 033	157	0.6

Notes:
1 Latest available figures as at January 1985 unless otherwise stated
2 As at December 1984
3 As at August 1984
4 As at March 1984
5 As at October 1983
Source: Information supplied by individual institutes.

work, in 1984 women were heavily outnumbered by men as Table 15.2 shows.[5]

It is interesting to note the rate of change in some professions between the years 1971 and 1984. In this period the percentage has risen, for example in the British Medical Association from 17.8 to 24.8; in the Law Society from 4.2 to 12.2; in the Institute of Bankers from 1.2 to 16.5; in the Insurance Institute from 3.7 to 12.6; in the Institute of Mechanical Engineers from 0.1 to 0.7. (It should be noted that the figures are not strictly comparable as a somewhat different system of classification has been used in this table.)[6]

The restricted range of jobs held by women is one reason, though by no means the sole reason, for the marked difference between the earnings of men and of women. In 1984 the average gross hourly earnings of women full-time workers over 18 were 73.5 per cent[7] of men's gross hourly earnings. The difference in average gross weekly earnings for full-time workers over 18 was much greater, with women receiving only 65.8 per cent of men's earnings. The difference is partly accounted for by the difference in hours worked. Women were much less likely to work overtime and to receive overtime premiums. The persistence of marked differences in men's and women's pay is discussed in greater detail in the section dealing with the Equal Pay Act 1970.

Sex segregation and the reasons for it

Employment statistics underline the extent of sex segregation in employment. It may be that such segregation has always existed, but it is certain that since the beginning of modern industrial society it has been taken for granted that there are 'men's jobs' and 'women's jobs', with only a few exceptions where it has been acceptable for work to be done by either a man or a woman. It has been so much a part of the culture that only in recent decades has the position been at all widely challenged. The reasons for this discrimination are both social and economic. As long as women had no control over fertility and most of their adult life was spent childbearing and child rearing, they were plainly at a great disadvantage with men in the labour market, though many women, especially in the textile industry, did manage to combine family responsibilities and paid employment. Employers in the main assumed that women's paid work would be short-term or sporadic, and that it was not worth while to train them. Society saw the man as the responsible head of the family and the breadwinner, the person with the lifetime commitment to paid work. In addition, much of the manual work of industrialized Britain, in mines, railways and engineering was physically heavy, and legal restrictions were placed on women's employment, as in 1842 when it was forbidden to

5 Equal Opportunities Commission. Ninth Annual Report 1984, p. 88.
6 Department of Employment. Manpower Paper No. 11.
7 Equal Opportunities Commission. Ninth Annual Report 1984, p. 82.

employ women in mines, and in the series of Factories Acts which limited the hours women might work, with a prohibition on night work unless special permission was obtained from the Factory Inspectorate.

Limited to a narrow range of low-level jobs with, in many cases, only a temporary commitment to employment, women, with a few outstanding exceptions, tended to accept the position as they found it, and took little action to bring about change. In 1948 in white-collar occupations 33.6 per cent of the male, but only 22.8 per cent of the female employees, were in trade unions and the corresponding figures for manual workers were 63.9 per cent for males and 25.3 per cent for females. By 1980 only 38.6 per cent of potential women members were organized compared with 64.2 per cent of men.[8]

In these circumstances women were in a weak position to defend themselves in the labour market. They were for employers a source of cheap labour, taking jobs at a rate men would not accept. Their cheapness reinforces their segregation, and their segregation made it hard for them to escape from low-paid segregated jobs. Seen as low paid and inadequately organized, women were both a challenge to trade unions and a threat. Until the second half of the twentieth century there is little evidence of trade union action to get rid of job segregation by sex. It is important, however, to note that in some industries, for example in textiles, women were very strongly organized.[9] In the mid-sixties 83 per cent of women in the National Union of Tailors and Garment Workers and 78 per cent of the women in the National Union of Hosiery Workers were unionized. Unionization among women developed rapidly in the 1970s and by 1980 women comprised 29.3 per cent of all union members.[10]

Features of the employment structure which handicap women

A changed attitude towards women and widespread acceptance of the irrationality of sex segregation in employment would not be sufficient to alter substantially the position of women in employment. The disadvantages from which women suffer in competition start in the home and are often perpetuated at school. Different acceptable patterns of behaviour encouraged at home are reinforced when girls at school are not encouraged to study for the mathematical and scientific subjects increasingly required for responsible posts in industry. In 1970 females as a percentage of A-level passes were only 0.5 per cent in technical drawing, 16.7 per cent in physics, 17.6 per cent in mathematics. The corresponding figures in 1983 were 2.9, 21.0 and 29.9 per cent. In the same year 19.6 per cent passed in computer science, a subject not

8   Equal Opportunities Commission. Sixth Annual Report 1981, p. 70.
9   Royal Commission on Trade Unions and Employers' Associations Research Paper, and *Trade Union Growth and Recognition* by G. S. Bain, p. 19, HMSO 1967.
10   Equal Opportunities Commission. Sixth Annual Report 1981, p. 70.

listed in 1970. Women studying engineering and technology as full-time university undergraduates rose from 4.0 per cent in 1975 to 9.1 per cent in 1983.[11]

To have the right educational preparation is important, but so is the opportunity to get the right start in employment. There are career ladders in most industries and professions and it is always an advantage and sometimes essential to start in the right place, even if it is on the lowest rung of the right ladder. The woman graduate who starts as a secretary is far less likely to advance than the man graduate who starts as a management trainee, sometimes quite soon to become personal assistant to the director to whom the woman graduate has for many years been secretary. Staff and research jobs, similarly, are often short ladders, and only rarely have bridges been constructed to enable those who start on short ladders to move to the ladders which lead to the top.

At a lower level it has often in the past been essential to begin working life in an apprenticeship, as it is still in many cases today. Yet, as recent figures show, only 7 per cent of apprenticeships were held by girls.

Women are, therefore, often at a disadvantage as they enter employment. This disadvantage is compounded by the way in which organizations are run. In some industries, for example banking, personnel policies have in the past been based on the assumption of a lifetime career with one employer. Company training is geared to the needs and expectations of such a career and, until recently, it has been assumed that girls are not interested in a lifetime career. Similarly the requirement that staff should give a commitment to be mobile has been a requirement that many women have not felt they could satisfy, if only because they were in no position to know what the future might hold.

These policies have been under review in some organizations in the middle 1980s. Steps have been taken actively to encourage women to return to work after a period of absence to establish a family and it is increasingly being accepted that mobility rules rigidly applied are not always necessary and can be inappropriate for men as well as women.

Childbearing and family responsibilities are widely seen as the main reasons for women's failure to advance to senior positions. Until recently, the wish of some, perhaps of many, women to return to employment after childbearing has not in the main been seriously considered. The availability of part-time work has enabled a large number of women to combine home responsibilities and paid employment. But part-time work has been confined almost entirely to women and the jobs available have been almost entirely unskilled and poorly paid, with little, if any, prospect for promotion. Company selection and promotion policies, and the hours of work, have handicapped the many women whose childbearing responsibilities have made it extremely difficult to conform to traditional employment patterns. For a variety of reasons, including the level of unemployment in the early

1980s, these traditions are being re-examined. Job sharing, and other forms of flexible working, re-entry schemes, maternity leave, and more extensive and appropriate child care provision are being considered. Adjustments in these areas could open up opportunities for women from which they have in the past been virtually excluded.[12]

The issue of equal pay

Given the extent to which women have been confined to a limited range of jobs, and the expectation, not confined to employers, that women had only a short-term commitment to employment, it is not surprising that as has already been shown women's average hourly earnings have always compared unfavourably with men's hourly earnings. This discrepancy did not, however, lead to widespread public protest. Though a minority of mainly middle-class women campaigned against unequal pay from the early years of the twentieth century, as late as 1946 a Royal Commission on Equal Pay did not endorse the principle.

The Trades Union Congress passed a resolution supporting the principle of equal pay in 1882, but action from trade unions was mainly restricted to the insistence that any woman employed on a customary man's job should be paid the male rate. Until the passing of the Equal Pay Act 1970, most collective agreements included a separate rate of pay negotiated for women, lower than the men's rate. Slowly the position began to change. In 1951, the principle of equal pay was supported by the ILO in the Equal Remuneration Convention and Recommendation, a Convention the British government did not at that time sign. The Treaty of Rome in 1957 laid down in Article 119 that 'each Member State shall . . . maintain the application of the principle that men and women shall receive equal pay for equal work'. In 1950 the Civil Service decided to introduce equal pay over a seven-year period.[13] In the sixties European opinion was further influenced by vigorous campaigning and strong anti-discrimination legislation in the United States.

In 1970, when Barbara Castle was Secretary of State for Employment in the Labour Government, the Equal Pay Act was passed: 'to prevent discrimination, as regards terms and conditions of employment between men and women'. This legislation and its impact are examined in Chapter 17, and technical aspects of job evaluation in Chapter 7.

12 For examples of organizations applying new policies in this area see *Incomes Data Services Ltd*, Study No. 340, June 1985. Equal Opportunities.
13 Miss D. E. K. Jones, Civil Service Clerical Association, Trades Union Congress 1950, on Equal Pay in the Public Sector.

Discussion questions

1 What do you consider, at the present time, to be the main economic barriers to growth in the employment of women?
2 What can be done to break down the educational and attitudinal barriers perpetuating the segregation of 'men's jobs' and 'women's jobs'?
3 How do you think employed women will fare in the future?

CHAPTER 16

Ethnic minorities in employment

by The Baroness Seear, PC
Liberal Leader in the House of Lords

There is nothing new about immigration into Britain; neither is there anything new about the anxiety it sometimes causes. At the turn of the century, for example, there was growing public concern about the numbers of European immigrants and particularly Polish and Russian Jews entering the country, which gave rise to a series of dramatic articles in the press. Typical headlines read, 'Invasion of destitute aliens' and 'Foreign undesirables' (1901). There was nothing novel, even, in the reaction of the Government: a Select Committee was set up and, reporting on the issue in 1889, concluded that the numbers involved 'were not large enough to cause alarm'. However, alarm continued to grow. And finally a Royal Commission was appointed on the aliens question to look into the problems created by and confronting European refugees. It reported in 1903 and flatly contradicted most of the arguments which had been used against the new arrivals. Numbers, for example, were very small: only 0.69 per cent of the British population were aliens compared with 1.38 per cent in Germany or 2.66 per cent in France. Aliens were not taking the jobs wanted by the indigenous working man but were filling gaps in the workforce and, surprisingly, a much lower proportion of aliens than indigenous workers were living on poor relief. It reported that aliens were not more lazy, diseased or criminal than the rest of the population and, in short, the alarm which became widespread amongst the public was shown to be founded on myths.

The 1950s and 1960s saw an influx of immigrants into Great Britain. There were acute shortages of labour and low level, unattractive jobs were hard to fill. There were no restrictions on the entry of Commonwealth citizens who came looking for work and by 1966 they numbered about 900 000. In 1962 the first Commonwealth Immigration Act was passed to be followed by further legislation in 1968 and 1971. The rate of immigration declined and by 1974 the New Commonwealth immigrant population, plus those born in Britain, was about one and a half million. By 1981, according to the Census of that year,[1] there were 2.2 million people in Great Britain of New

1 Black and White Britain. The Third PSI Survey. Colin Brown. Policy Studies Institute, 1984.

Commonwealth and Pakistan origin. Of these about 40 per cent (0.9 million) were born in the country and the rest immigrated here.[2]

Table 16.1 shows the numbers of persons resident in private households, whether born inside or outside the United Kingdom, by birthplace of head of household. Those classified as New Commonwealth and Pakistan represent just over 4 per cent of the total and of these no less than 40.5 per cent were born in the United Kingdom.

Table 16.2 gives the breakdown of persons resident in private households with head of household born in the New Commonwealth and Pakistan, by country of origin. This table illustrates the predominance of people of Asian origin among the ethnic minority population, though according to the OPCS these figures include an overcount of about 80 000 for Asians and a possible undercount of 26 000 for Afro-Caribbeans.

For practical purposes the total numbers and percentages of members of ethnic minorities are of less importance than their distribution throughout the country, which is markedly uneven. Table 16.3 gives this distribution throughout the country for the different ethnic groups.

This table shows the concentration of members of ethnic minorities, with 56 per cent in London and the South East, 23 per cent in the Midlands, and 16 per cent in the North and North West. There are relatively few in Scotland. It also shows the uneven distribution of the different groups. 65 per cent of the Afro-Caribbean population is to be found in the South East, with 56 per cent in Greater London, while nearly two-thirds of those of Pakistani origin are in the West Midlands, Yorkshire and Humberside and the North West.

As would be expected since many members of ethnic minorities have come to Britain in the last thirty years, the age distribution among the minorities is different from the age distribution of the population as a whole. Table 16.4 compares this distribution for both males and females. The table shows that the ethnic minority population is much younger than the population as a whole. For males in each age group up to and including the age group 20–29, the percentage is higher among the ethnic minorities than among the total population, and for females it is higher up to and including the age group 30–44.

Full employment passed and with it the opportunities for work which had first attracted immigrants from the New Commonwealth and Pakistan. Figure 16.1 taken from the Home Office Research Unit Study No. 68: 'Ethnic Minorities in Britain' shows the moving average of the registered unemployed rate between 1963 and 1981.

2 Ethnic Minorities in Britain: statistical information on the pattern of settlement. Commission for Racial Equality, 1985. These figures and the accompanying tables must be treated with some caution as no question on ethnic origin was included in the 1981 Census. The Office of Population Censuses and Surveys, using their Labour Force Survey 1981 as a check on the Census figures concluded: 'the information on head of household's birthplace available from the 1981 Census, although it needs careful handling, should provide for most areas of the country – especially those where there are larger numbers of the NCWP population – a fairly robust measure of the settlement pattern, as well as the characteristics, of the main minority populations'.

Table 16.1 *All persons resident in private households, whether born inside or outside the United Kingdom, by birthplace of head of household.*

	All birthplaces	United Kingdom	New Commonwealth and Pakistan (NCWP)
			(figures in brackets=Great Britain %)
All persons			
born inside UK	49 500 141 (93.8)	47 568 059 (98.5)	895 592 (40.5)
born outside UK	3 260 185 (6.2)	722 527 (1.5)	1 311 653 (59.5)
Total persons	52 760 331 (100)	48 290 586 (100)	2 207 245 (100)

Source: Office of Population Censuses and Surveys (OPCS), Registrar General Scotland, *Census 1981: Country of Birth, Great Britain*, Table 3, HMSO, 1983.

Table 16.2 Persons resident in private households with head of household born in the New Commonwealth and Pakistan (NCWP), by country of origin.

(figures in brackets=Great Britain %)

	Caribbean	India	Pakistan	Bangladesh	East Africa	Far East	Mediterranean	Remainder	Total NCWP
All persons									
born inside UK	273 558	261 206	118 252	16 939	48 673	39 742	79 315	57 907	895 592
born outside UK	272 186	412 498	177 209	47 622	132 648	80 381	90 763	98 346	1 311 653
Total persons	545 744	673 704	295 461	64 561	181 321	120 123	170 078	156 253	2 207 245
	(24.7)	(30.5)	(13.4)	(2.9)	(8.2)	(5.4)	(7.7)	(7.2)	(100)

Source: OPCS, Census 1981 *op. cit.*

Table 16.3 Persons resident in private households with head of household born in the New Commonwealth and Pakistan (NCWP), by country of origin

(figures in brackets=GB regions in %)

Region	Total NCWP	Caribbean	India	Pakistan	Bangladesh	East Africa	Remainder
Scotland	46 188 (2.1)	1 508 (0.3)	16 141 (2.4)	9 903 (3.4)	827 (1.3)	3 203 (1.8)	14 606(3.3)
Central Clydeside	21 595 (1.0)	374 (0.1)	8 230 (1.2)	6 772 (2.3)	327 (0.5)	774 (0.4)	5 118(1.1)
Remainder of Scotland	24 593 (1.1)	1 134 (0.2)	7 911 (1.2)	3 131 (1.1)	500 (0.8)	2 429 (1.3)	9 488(2.1)
England	2 136 590 (96.8)	540 770 (99.1)	650 929 (96.6)	282 329 (95.6)	62 382 (96.6)	176 485 (97.3)	423 695(94.9)
Wales	24 467 (1.1)	3 466 (0.6)	6 634 (1.0)	3 229 (1.1)	1 352 (2.1)	1 633 (0.9)	8 153(1.8)
North	26 247 (1.2)	1 177 (0.2)	8 805 (1.3)	6 343 (2.1)	1 025 (1.6)	1 297 (0.7)	7 600(1.7)
Tyne & Wear Met. County	11 367 (0.5)	427 (0.1)	4 130 (0.6)	2 132 (0.7)	675 (1.0)	520 (0.3)	3 483(0.8)
Remainder of North	14 880 (0.7)	750 (0.1)	4 675 (0.7)	4 211 (1.4)	350 (0.5)	777 (0.4)	4 117(0.9)
Yorkshire & Humberside	154 344 (7.0)	26 767 (4.9)	42 676 (6.3)	60 215 (20.4)	4 542 (7.0)	5 089 (2.8)	15 055(3.4)
South Yorks. Met. County	24 606 (1.1)	7 274 (1.3)	4 058 (0.6)	8 947 (3.0)	628 (1.0)	613 (0.3)	3 086(0.7)
West Yorks. Met. County	118 372 (5.4)	18 720 (3.4)	34 715 (5.2)	50 556 (17.1)	3 187 (4.9)	3 673 (2.0)	7 521(1.7)
Remainder of Yorks./H.	11 366 (0.5)	773 (0.1)	3 903 (0.6)	712 (0.2)	727 (1.1)	803 (0.4)	4 448(1.0)

East Midlands	140 991	(6.4)	28 442	(5.2)	62 069	(9.2)	11 906	(4.0)	2 144	(3.3)	22 366	(12.3)	14 064	(3.2)
East Anglia	28 429	(1.3)	5 484	(1.0)	7 683	(1.1)	3 856	(1.3)	723	(1.1)	2 890	(1.6)	7 793	(1.7)
South East	1 227 754	(55.6)	353 120	(64.7)	318 650	(47.3)	88 811	(30.1)	36 500	(56.5)	116 124	(64.0)	314 549	(70.6)
Greater London	945 148	(42.8)	306 792	(56.2)	223 664	(33.2)	52 192	(17.7)	28 888	(44.7)	90 690	(50.0)	242 922	(54.4)
Outer Metropolitan Area	186 459	(8.4)	32 099	(5.9)	63 038	(9.4)	28 987	(9.8)	4 906	(7.6)	17 612	(9.7)	39 817	(7.2)
Outer South East	96 47	(4.4)	14 229	(2.6)	31 948	(4.7)	7 632	(2.6)	2 706	(4.2)	7 822	(4.3)	31 810	(7.2)
South West	63 607	(2.9)	14 795	(2.7)	19 929	(3.0)	4 446	(1.5)	880	(1.4)	4 395	(2.4)	19 162	(4.3)
West Midlands	326 523	(14.8)	84 846	(15.5)	136 773	(20.3)	61 931	(21.0)	9 179	(14.2)	14 566	(8.0)	19 228	(4.3)
West Midlands Met. County	285 350	(12.9)	77 393	(14.2)	120 577	(17.9)	54 819	(18.6)	8 248	(12.8)	11 616	(6.4)	12 697	(2.8)
Remainder of West Midlands	41 173	(1.9)	7 453	(1.4)	16 196	(2.4)	7 112	(2.4)	931	(1.4)	2 950	(1.6)	6 531	(1.5)
North West	168 695	(7.6)	26 139	(4.8)	54 344	(8.1)	44 821	(15.2)	7 389	(11.4)	9 758	(5.4)	26 244	(5.9)
Greater Manchester MC	100 045	(4.5)	20 288	(3.7)	29 612	(4.4)	25 572	(8.7)	5 431	(8.4)	5 939	(3.3)	13 203	(3.0)
Merseyside Met. County	14 823	(0.7)	2 582	(0.5)	3 392	(0.5)	727	(0.2)	445	(0.7)	546	(0.3)	7 131	(1.6)
Remainder of North West	53 827	(2.4)	3 269	(0.6)	21 340	(3.2)	18 522	(6.3)	1 513	(2.3)	3 273	(1.8)	5 910	(1.3)
Total	2 207 245	(100)	545 744	(100)	673 704	(100)	295 461	(100)	64 561	(100)	181 321	(100)	446 454	(100)

Source: Registrar General, Scotland and OPCS Census 1981: *National Report, Great Britain, part 1,* Table II, HMSO, 1983.

Table 16.4 Persons resident in private households, total male and female population and males and females with head of household born in the New Commonwealth and Pakistan (NCWP), age distribution, by country of origin

Males age	Total male population		Total NCWP males		Females age	Total female population		Total NCWP females	
0– 4	1 646 866	(6.4)	121 107	(10.7)	0– 4	1 564 277	(5.8)	115 813	(10.7)
5–15	4 450 302	(17.3)	258 110	(22.9)	5–15	4 231 300	(15.6)	242 977	(22.5)
16–19	1 768 867	(6.9)	95 852	(8.5)	16–19	1 718 776	(6.4)	92 183	(8.6)
20–29	3 735 081	(14.5)	212 517	(18.8)	20–29	3 689 750	(13.6)	215 828	(20.0)
30–44	5 209 181	(20.3)	220 936	(19.5)	30–44	5 187 626	(19.2)	225 844	(20.9)
45–64	5 797 328	(22.6)	189 475	(16.8)	45–59	4 627 979	(17.0)	129 846	(12.1)
65+	3 073 799	(12.0)	30 718	(2.8)	60+	6 059 199	(22.4)	56 039	(5.2)
All ages	25 681 424	(100)	1 128 715	(100)	All ages	27 078 907	(100)	1 078 530	(100)

Source: OPCS, Census 1981: Country of Birth, Great Britain, Table 3, HMSO, 1983.

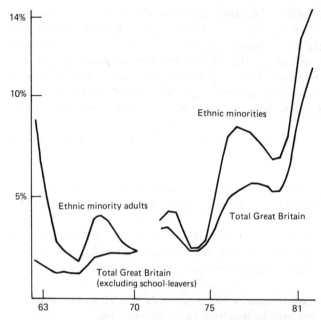

Fig. 16.1   *Registered unemployment rate among population and ethnic minorities. Moving average, males and females 1963–1981. (This figure is based on Figure 9 in* Ethnic Minorities in Britain: a study of trends in their position since 1961 *by S. Field et al.,* Home Office Research Study No. 68, 1981, HMSO, *with additional information for 1981 supplied by the Home Office.*

The break in the middle is explained by a change in the method of calculation. It indicates that the rate of unemployment for the minority groups is much more volatile than that for whites. For example, it falls at a much faster rate in 1963/4 than the rate for whites. This is partly explained by the high rate of immigration at that initial period. However the rate also rose much more rapidly than the average between 1975 and 1977. Rates also varied amongst minority groups themselves. For men, it was most volatile with the West Indians and least with the Indians. Amongst women, the reverse was true. 'On the basis of the estimates, unemployment among West Indian women seems to have followed the national pattern quite closely. But for Indian, Pakistani and Bangladeshi women, unemployment rates rose much more rapidly than the average between 1975 and 1977.' Taking another basis for comparison, the Runnymede Trust in 'Employment, Unemployment and the Black Population', pointed out that between 1972 and 1981 total unemployment increased by 138 per cent but black unemployment increased by 325 per cent. For young people generally, unemployment increased between these two dates by 74 per cent for all unemployed under 25, and by 81 per cent for the black under 25s. Both these figures and the graph from Fig. 16.1 suggest that in times of rapidly rising unemployment, black people are more vulnerable. The main trends have persisted as the 1984 Annual Report of the Commission for Racial Equality confirms when it states:[3] 'According to the Department of Employment Labour Force Survey, which was published in 1984, the level of unemployment for black people is nearly twice as high as it is for white people. This is not because black people lack qualifications. For example, while the unemployment rate for white men with O-levels is 9 per cent, the figure for equally qualified Asian men at 18 per cent is twice as high and the figure for West Indian men at 25 per cent is nearly three times as high.'

The Home Office Research Unit lists four causes of high minority unemployment:

(a) Minorities are concentrated in the younger age groups and all young people find it particularly hard to get jobs when vacancies are few;

(b) by virtue of their recent arrival in Britain minority workers may lack occupational skills and qualifications, and in the case of Asians may have poor English, which could reduce their chances of finding a job;

(c) direct racial discrimination: at times when there is an ample supply of white labour, this may be preferred by employers; and

(d) ethnic minorities are concentrated in certain industrial sectors, types of firm and occupations. In particular they are over-represented in manufacturing industry which is contracting generally, and in insecure, low-status jobs, and such over-representation may, of course, itself be the result of racial discrimination.

It concludes that the first two factors will clearly diminish with time, leaving the latter two. Thus, the importance of eliminating racial discrimination in the workplace is underlined. In addition, minorities still show a disproportionate reliance on manual work and on manufacturing industry, two sectors likely to be particularly badly affected by the current recession, and in the longer term will probably continue to contract.

Members of ethnic minorities who are in employment are distributed throughout industry differently from the distribution of white employees. There are also marked differences between different ethnic groups as Tables 16.5 and 16.6 taken from the Policy Studies Institute's Third Survey show.

Perhaps the most outstanding characteristic of the employment of ethnic minorities is the extent to which they are rarely found in higher levels of work. Table 16.7 which analyses job level by ethnic minority group shows that 69 per cent of Bangladeshi employees and 47 per cent of Muslim employees in the PSI survey were in semi-skilled or unskilled manual jobs compared with 16 per cent of white employees. It is interesting to note, however, that no less than 22 per cent of African Asians and 20 per cent of

3   Commission for Racial Equality, 1984. Annual Report.

Table 16.5 Industry sector by ethnic group: men

Column percentages

	White	West Indian	Asian	Indian	Pakistani	Bangladeshi	African Asian
Mining, Chemicals and Metal Manufacture	9	4	7	7	8	2	6
Engineering and Metals	15	9	13	14	13	8	14
Vehicles and Shipbuilding	5	12	11	13	10	9	7
Textiles, Clothing and Leather	2	3	13	8	20	32	7
All other Manufacturing	10	14	14	13	19	7	10
All Manufacturing and mining industries	41	41	57	55	70	59	45
Construction	8	7	3	3	2	—	4
Transport and communication	10	24	12	16	9	4	12
Distributive Trades	8	6	6	4	3	2	13
All other service industries	23	14	17	16	13	31	18
All service industries	41	45	35	36	25	37	43
Public Administration and Defence	7	3	2	2	—	2	3
Base: All employees (weighted)	1490	972	2167	847	611	177	495
(unweighted)	591	467	1041	401	298	96	227

Table 16.6   *Industry sector by ethnic group: women*

Column percentages

	White	West Indian	Asian	Indian	African Asian
Textiles, Clothing and Leather	4	4	21	24	14
All Manufacturing and Mining Industries	21	20	44	52	35
Transport and Communication	4	6	2	2	2
Distributive Trades	17	8	14	9	23
Professional and Scientific	25	41	16	19	7
All Service Industries	70	72	41	36	43
Public Administration and Defence	6	6	8	7	12
Base: All Employees					
(weighted)	1050	1020	760	431	237
(unweighted)	495	502	340	195	102

Hindus were ranked as Professional, Employer, Management compared with 19 per cent of whites.

In view of the predominantly low level of job held by members of ethnic minorities the PSI findings on earnings given in Table 16.8 is hardly surprising.

The unions

The first sign of official interest at the TUC level was when the General Council brought out the EUC Equal Opportunity clause in March 1975. This read as follows:

> 'The parties to this agreement are committed to the development of positive policies to promote equal opportunity in employment regardless of workers' sex, marital status, creed, colour, race or ethnic origins. This principle will apply in respect of all conditions of work including pay, hours of work, holiday entitlement, overtime and shiftwork, work allocation, guaranteed earnings, sick pay, pensions, recruitment, training, promotion and redundancy (nothing in this clause is designed to undermine the protections for women workers in the Factories Act).

Table 16.7 *Job levels of men: all employees by ethnic group*

Column percentages

Job level	White	West Indian	Asian	Indian	Pakistani	Bangladeshi	African Asian	Muslim	Hindu	Sikh
Professional, Employer, Management	19	5	13	11	10	10	22	11	20	4
Other non-manual	23	10	13	13	8	7	21	8	26	8
Skilled Manual and Foreman	42	48	33	34	39	13	31	33	20	48
Semi-skilled Manual	13	26	34	36	35	57	22	39	28	33
Unskilled Manual	3	9	6	5	8	12	3	8	3	6
Base: Male employees										
(weighted)	1490	972	2167	847	611	177	495	998	571	452
(unweighted)	591	467	1041	401	298	96	227	507	258	213

Table 16.8   *Gross earnings of full-time employees by region*

£ median weekly earnings

	England and Wales	North West	Yorks/ Humberside	West Midlands	East Midlands	South West	South East (excl. London)	London
White men	128.90	141.50	116.20	130.20	135.40	129.20	126.90	129.90
Asian and West Indian men	110.20	98.60	103.70	105.90	96.00	107.50	115.20	118.70

Note: Because of small base sizes, the North, East Anglia and Wales regions have been omitted from this table. In each of these regions, the Asian and West Indian earnings were lower than those of the whites.

The Management undertake to draw opportunities for training and promotion to the attention of all eligible employees, and to inform all employees of this agreement on equal opportunity.

The parties agree that they will review from time to time, through their joint machinery, the operation of this equal opportunity policy.

If any employee considers that he or she is suffering from unequal treatment on the grounds of sex, marital status, creed, colour, race or ethnic origins, he or she may make a complaint which will be dealt with through the agreed procedures for dealing with grievances.'

The General Council endorsed this to the unions with the recommendation that they would negotiate it with the employers as part of their general agreements. It is not known how many such clauses have been negotiated, but in the words of the TUC, 'there is a small nucleus of unions who have developed a coherent strategy in this area and have negotiated the clause with employers'. Some of these unions have gone further and initiated training in race relations for their shop stewards. In addition to this, the TUC train some 20 000 shop stewards each year and part of the ten-day course includes references to race relations woven into the structure of the course itself rather than forming a separate part. There is also a stream of local activity at plant level where local initiatives have been taken by both unions and management to train shop stewards and foremen. It is not known how widespread this activity has become.

Unfortunately, the word has proved mightier than the deed. Although a number of unions have passed resolutions at their annual conferences, sometimes year after year, it has not been often that activity has followed. There have been many good intentions expressed, but relatively little action.

However, in 1984, following the publication of the Code of Practice the TUC passed a resolution which went beyond general condemnation of racism and gave approval to practical steps including support for positive action; the encouragement of monitoring; the need to make rule changes to ensure that racist activity and deliberate acts of unlawful discrimination were disciplinary matters; the need to take particular measures to recruit more black members on training courses and the establishment of appropriate structures, e.g. race equality committees and black member groups to coordinate women's work and racism.

Discussion questions

1 Notwithstanding a number of well-publicized and progressive intentions by official bodies, why do so many problems of ethnic minority employment still persist in practice?
2 Think of what initiatives you would like to take in your own organization. What support or resistance would you expect, and why?
3 Do you, or do you not, think the onus of effective integration of ethnic

minorities into the workplace has been placed too much on the ethnic population itself, whilst the white population tends to pay lip-service to minimum statutory requirements?

4   To what extent might the white population be in need of education with regard to the customs and mores of ethnic groups? How could this be achieved in practice?

CHAPTER 17

Non-discrimination: the legal framework

The Baroness Seear, PC
Liberal Leader in the House of Lords

The Equal Pay Act 1970 is an Act: 'to prevent discrimination as regards terms and conditions of employment between men and women'. It covers all terms and conditions except those concerned with retirement and pensions, with special treatment allowed in connection with childbearing, or where law requires differentiation. Where it is not expressly included in a woman's contract of employment that she shall be given equal treatment, such equal treatment is an implied term.

The Act approaches the removal of inequality in three different ways. (1) Where there is any element of sex discrimination in a collective agreement, the agreement may be referred to the Central Arbitration Committee which has powers to require it to be amended to remove the element of discrimination. (2) Where a job evaluation scheme is in operation, a woman can claim equal pay with a man whose job has been given a similar value in the job evaluation rating, and the same system of evaluation must be used for both jobs. There is, however, in the Act no obligation on an employer to introduce job evaluation. (3) Where job evaluation is not used, a woman has to establish that she is employed in work that is: 'the same or broadly similar' as the work of the man in the establishment with whom she wishes to be compared. Since, to a very large extent, men and women are not employed in the same jobs, the inclusion of the phrase 'or broadly similar' was essential if the majority of women were to benefit from the Act. It does, however, raise difficult questions of interpretation. In deciding whether a man's and a woman's job are in fact 'broadly similar' regard must be had to differences of 'practical importance' in the two jobs, judged by the nature, extent and frequency of the differing element. For example, in the case of *Mrs A. Dugdale and others* v. *Kraft Foods Ltd*, Mrs Dugdale worked in the Quality Control Department of Kraft Foods. The women performed the same work as the men but did not work night shifts or on Sunday mornings – if they had it would have been in contravention of the Factories Act, 1961, from which the company had not applied for exemption. The company maintained this constituted a 'practical difference'. The industrial tribunal agreed with the employer. Mrs Dugdale appealed to the Employment Appeals Tribunal and won her case, the Appeals Tribunal holding that in relation to basic wages the hours worked were irrelevant.

The argument that a woman is entitled to equal pay can also be contested on the grounds of a material difference between the two jobs, a difference which the employer has to establish. In *E. Coombes (Holdings) Ltd* v. *Miss S. Shields*, Miss Shields and the man with whom she sought to be compared worked on the counter in a London shop. The work was identical, but the man was paid more on the ground that he had obligations in relation to security and that this constituted a material difference. The industrial tribunal found for Miss Shields; the Employment Appeal Tribunal reversed the decision; but the Court of Appeal decided in favour of Miss Shields.

It was originally assumed that to establish a claim a woman had to compare her job with the job of a man employed when she was employed. But in the case of *Macarthys Ltd* v. *Mrs W. Smith* in 1980 the European Court of Justice held that the principle of equal pay for equal work applied where a woman receives less pay than a man employed *prior* to the woman being employed and who had done equal work for the employer.

As these cases have illustrated, an issue under this Act can be referred to an industrial tribunal, with a right of appeal on points of law to the Employment Appeals Tribunal, with a further right of appeal, where appropriate, to the Court of Appeal. Cases can be referred to a tribunal either by the person making the claim or by the person against whom the claim is made. In certain instances a case may be referred by the Secretary of State. The tribunal may award payment by way of arrears of remuneration or damages for a period of not more than two years before proceedings were initiated.

A most important development in relation to equal pay arose when in 1982 the European Court of Justice found against the United Kingdom Government in a case brought by the European Commission. The European Commission argued successfully that the United Kingdom was in breach of its treaty obligation under Article 119 of the Treaty of Rome and of the Equal Pay Directive of 1975 because there was no provision for a woman to claim equal pay for work of equal value if a job evaluation scheme had not been carried out, and no obligation on an employer to introduce such a scheme.

In response to this judgment the Equal Pay (Amendment) Regulations, 1983, were drawn up and became law in January 1984. The Regulations established the right to equal pay for work of equal value so that a woman would no longer have to compare her work with that of a man in the same or broadly similar work. Instead she has to establish the equal value of the work she does to that of a man in the same establishment. The workings of the Regulations are complicated and their precise meaning will only be clarified as cases are handled in tribunals and the courts or referred to the European Court of Justice. There have been very few cases brought under the Regulations, but in October 1984 the applicant was successful in the case of *Hayward* v. *Cammell Laird Shipbuilders Ltd*. The applicant, a trained cook working in the company canteen, claimed that her work was of equal value to that of male tradesmen employed as painter, thermal installation engineer and joiner respectively, and the industrial tribunal found in her favour. Since then the employers appealed to the Employment Appeals Tribunal and in June 1986 the EAT ruled that the employers did not have to pay the cook the same pay and overtime rates as the painter, joiner and insulation engineer since the whole of her terms and conditions of employment, and not only pay and overtime rates, had to be considered. The EAT held that when the additional factors were taken into account her terms and conditions of employment were not less favourable than theirs. The Equal Opportunities Commission has issued two booklets for guidance on the Regulations: 'Equal Pay for Work of Equal Value' and 'Judging Equal Value'.

The Equal Pay Act covered terms and conditions of employment but conferred no right to equal access to jobs – to equal opportunity. Since, as has been shown, the labour market is to a high degree segregated by sex, the right to equal pay without an accompanying right to equal opportunity did not tackle fundamental issues affecting the employment position of women.

For members of ethnic minorities, the issue of unequal pay did not arise, in the sense that there was no separate rate of pay for blacks. But the question of unequal opportunity, of the *de facto* restriction of members of ethnic minorities to a limited range of low level jobs was for them, as for women, of great importance. To create legal rights to equal opportunity two Acts were passed: The Sex Discrimination Act 1975, and the Race Relations Act 1976. The Race Relations Act replaced earlier legislation which had attempted on a more limited basis to deal with this issue. In 1976 the EEC issued a directive – Equal Treatment for Men and Women.

The two British Acts are similar in principle and to a large extent in detail. They render unlawful certain kinds of discrimination on grounds of sex or marriage, or in the case of ethnic minorities, on grounds of colour, race, nationality, or ethnic or national origin.

In both Acts the obligation not to discriminate applies to all aspects of employment; to advertisements, to the recruitment and selection procedure, to access to training, to promotion and to disciplinary procedures, redundancy, and dismissal.

In both Acts, some exceptions to the rule are permitted. For women the most important are those listed in s. 7, as genuine occupational qualifications. These include: reasons of physiology – not to be confused with arguments based on physical strength; reasons of decency or privacy, fairly tightly defined; certain residential jobs; special welfare considerations; the provision of personal services promoting welfare or education; jobs where there remain legal restrictions regulating the employment of women; jobs likely to involve work outside the United Kingdom in countries where 'laws or customs are such that the duties could not, or could not effectively, be performed by a woman'; where the job is one of two to be held by a married couple. In relation to members of ethnic minorities the exceptions are: dramatic performances where a part needs to be played by a person of a particular racial group; artists or photographic models, for reasons of authenticity where certain kinds of food or drink are sold to the public; where personal services are rendered for the welfare of the particular group. There are also limitations relating to the size of the undertaking.

Individual cases under both Acts can be taken to industrial tribunals. Tribunals can award damages to be paid if it is established that discrimination has occurred. Damages may include compensation for injury to feelings. The Acts also established the Equal Opportunities Commission and the Commission for Racial Equality to work towards the elimination of discrimination, to promote equality; to keep the working of the legislation under review, and to make recommendations to Government. The Commission of Racial Equality has some responsibility, shared with local authorities, for the work of Community Relations Officers at local level. The Commissions have powers, subject to certain safeguards, to conduct formal investigations when they have reason to believe that unlawful discriminatory acts are being carried out. The Commissions have the right to require relevant information to be provided by the organization or person being investigated. Where the Commission decides that an organization investigated is in breach of the Act it may serve a 'non-discrimination notice', laying down that the organization must not continue to discriminate and must inform the Commission of the changes made to comply with the requirements of the non-discrimination order and of the steps taken to inform persons concerned. The Commission has powers to follow up the investigation to be satisfied that the undertakings given have been carried out.[1]

Legal actions taken under the Equal Pay Act and under the equal opportunity legislation are civil actions and do not involve criminal proceedings, except where they might lead to cases for contempt of court.

It is important to emphasize that the legislation does not, with one exception, permit actions which give a preference to a woman or a member of an ethnic minority regardless of genuine suitability for a job. The law does not permit the introduction of 'quotas', if by a quota is meant the establishment of a fixed number or percentage of jobs which must be filled by, for example, women, without regard to other considerations. A distinction has to be made between a quota, and a target or goal. A target can be set which states that the *aim* is to fill a given percentage of jobs by members of ethnic minorities or women by a given date, but only if sufficient numbers of such persons with the necessary qualifications can be recruited. This implies that management needs to make the effort to seek out suitable candidates and where necessary to provide appropriate training.

It is in relation to training that an exception is made to the rule that no preference is given to any particular group. Under ss. 37 and 38 of the Race Relations Act and ss. 47 and 48 of the Sex Discrimination Act training for a job can be given exclusively for one sex or members of an ethnic minority where in the preceding twelve months the group in question is substantially under-represented. Under-represented groups may also be encouraged to

---

1 Women's rights to equal treatment were reinforced by the EEC Directive of February 1976 on the implementation of the principle of equal treatment for men and women as regards access to employment, vocational training and promotion, and working conditions.

apply for such jobs. Where the training is to be carried out by an employer or other body not covered in s. 37, in the Race Relations Act, and S. 47 in the Sex Discrimination Act, the would-be training body has to be designated for the purpose. Designation can be obtained by application to the Secretary of State for Employment. It is also permissible to encourage such persons to make application for jobs in which they are substantially under-represented. The Engineering Industry Training Board introduced such a training scheme for women technicians in 1976.

One of the most important and least understood sections of both Acts is s. 1(1) (b) which prohibits what has come to be known as 'indirect discrimination'. Direct discrimination is easily understood. It occurs when an employer lays down that only men, or only white women or black women, will be considered for a job – unless the job in question is exempt. Only in exceptional circumstances could a prospective employer be unaware that he is in fact proposing to discriminate. Indirect discrimination, on the other hand, often occurs where the employer is quite unaware of the discriminatory nature of what he is doing. If he lays down a requirement or condition for a job with which a substantial proportion of women or members of ethnic minorities can not in fact comply and they can establish that this is to their detriment, the employer can be challenged to show that the requirement or condition is justifiable in terms of the needs of the job. If it can not be shown to be justifiable, the employer is indirectly discriminating.[2] In 1982 in the CRE Report of a Formal Investigation into Massey Ferguson Perkins Ltd para. 3 it is stated: 'The main reason for the under-representation of blacks, we found, was not direct discrimination, but the company's method of recruitment for hourly paid jobs. They did not advertise or use Job Centres. They did not need to, since jobs with them were so popular. They simply relied on letters of application.' The Commission served a non-discrimination notice on the company requiring them not to discriminate in hourly-paid recruitment and not to apply discriminatory practices by requiring applicants for hourly-paid recruitment to submit a letter of application.

A well-known example of indirect discrimination occurred in the case of *Ms B. M. Price* v. *Civil Service Commission and Another* in 1977. Ms Price applied for a post of Executive Officer in the Civil Service. She was informed that as she was over the age limit of 28 years she could not be considered. Ms Price contended that this was indirectly discriminatory to women as fewer women could comply with such a requirement than men, since many women in their twenties were at home bringing up children. It was ultimately decided that this constituted indirect discrimination and the Civil Service Commission was required to raise the age limit.[3]

Further important cases have extended the rights in relation to redundancy of part-time workers. In the case of *Dick* v. *University of Dundee*, the

2   Commission for Racial Equality. Massey Ferguson Perkins Ltd. Report of a Formal Investigation, 1982.
3   Equal Opportunities Commission. Towards Equality. A Casebook of decisions on Sex Discrimination and Equal Pay 1976–1981.

University decided to review the contracts of part-time workers with a view to making them redundant. Mrs Dick worked part-time in a professional post on a permanent basis. Most of the part-time workers were women. The Industrial Tribunal held that the decision to review part-time workers first was unjustifiable discrimination.[4]

The position of part-time workers has been further strengthened by the decision of the Employment Appeal Tribunal in the case of *Holmes* v. *The Home Office*, 1984. Miss Holmes, a single parent with two children, asked to be allowed to return to work part-time rather than full-time and the Tribunal upheld her claim, though it stated that it was not to be assumed that all such claims would be supported as much would depend on the facts of the case as to whether the requirement to work full-time was justifiable.

Decisions of the European Court of Justice are also tending to bring the rights of part-time workers into line with the rights of full-time workers in a number of ways.

It is worth noting in relation to indirect discrimination, but not only in relation to indirect discrimination, that good personnel management would in many cases ensure against breaches of the Acts. A good person specification should not after all include requirements that can not be justified. When such items are included, potentially valuable recruits may be excluded.

If organizations want official guidance on the employment of ethnic minorities they should study the Code of Practice issued by the Commission for Racial Equality which sets out the legal requirements with suggestions for implementation.[5] A similar Code in relation to equal opportunity employment practices in relation to women has also been issued by the Equal Opportunities Commission.[6]

The Codes, like other codes, do not have the force of law, but can be taken into account in the decisions of industrial tribunals.

Discussion questions

1 Have the Sex Discrimination and Race Relations Acts worked? To what extent may or may not further progress depend on legislative action?
2 What is the difference between equal pay and equal opportunity? Why may it be easier to achieve the former rather than the latter?
3 What can be done to reduce direct discrimination against women and ethnic minorities?
4 What can be done to reduce indirect discrimination against women and ethnic minorities?

4 Equal Opportunities Commission, Seventh Annual Report, pp. 5 and 6.
5 Code of Practice, 1983, publishing by Commission for Racial Equality, 10 Allington Street, SW1. See also 'A Guide to the CRE Code of Practice on Equal Opportunities in Employment' by Anthony Fenley, University of Oxford, 1984.
6 Code of Practice. Equal Opportunities Commission, 1985.

CHAPTER 18

Developing positive policies

by The Baroness Seear, PC
Liberal Leader in the House of Lords

The preceding chapter has outlined the law governing the employment of ethnic minorities and of women. This chapter examines the implications for management of these legal obligations and suggests steps that can be taken to translate them into effective practice.[1]

In any organization, for action to take place some trigger mechanism is needed to initiate that action. These triggers can be activated externally or internally. For example, a visit by the Chairman of the CRE at Board level may lead the Chairman of the organization to formulate and promulgate an equal opportunities policy. These policies are often framed in terms such as: 'It is the policy of Company X that, irrespective of sex, race, colour, ethnic or national origin, all employees shall be accorded equal opportunity in the terms and conditions of employment, and in particular in selection, place-ment, training and promotion'. Such policies can undoubtedly be of value in setting the scene and in giving the necessary sanction of top management in what is often a controversial area. There is, however, a danger that boards of directors may come to believe that once a policy has been produced and disseminated the organization has become an equal opportunity employer. In reality it is an important first step, but a first step only. Unless such policy statements are followed by a plan of action and that plan is carefully monitored, little change is likely in practice to take place.

It may be that action is triggered not by external intervention, but by some event within the organization. For example in one enterprise a newly recruited Indian in the Inspection Department failed to interpret properly the drawings issued to him and brought the Assembly Department to a full stop. This was through no fault of his, but was due to management's failure to discover in the induction process that one of their new staff spoke inadequate English. Analysis showed that a minor misunderstanding had grave and costly consequences. This led management to modify its induction pro-cedure to suit a new type of recruit. When an incident of this kind happens it is all too easy for management to take reflex action based on traditional

---

1 See also Commission for Racial Equality. 'Implementing Equal Employment Opportunity Policies', 1983.

assumptions and practices which can lead to a misinterpretation of the significance of the occurrence. If this is to be avoided, such events require careful analysis within an accepted framework.[2]

This incident brought home the significance of equal opportunity for the organization as a whole more sharply than is likely to be achieved by any general statement of policy. It made visible the existence of problems associated with the employment of ethnic minorities and the need to modify existing personnel practices to cope with the disadvantage of incomers from another culture and with a different language. It was also a practical lesson in the commercial as well as the legal and the humanitarian reasons for action to create equal opportunities.

There are in fact two different but complementary approaches. The policy approach used in isolation, is generally, though not exclusively associated with a central command structure, Theory X type of organization (see Chapter 19) where it is assumed, rightly or wrongly, that policy once promulgated will be put into effect. The analytical approach, in contrast, is found more often in organizations of the organic, decentralized, Theory Y type.

Once it has been decided that action is needed, a strategy has to be developed. Policy is static; strategy is essentially dynamic. Policy is a statement of the intention of the main board, but is incomplete without a strategy for action.

As a first step it is necessary to examine the available data to identify practical issues and to define the strategy. This should include (1) an analysis of existing jobs by grade and pay according to the sex and ethnic groups of the jobholder,[3] (2) a measure of the rate of flow up the hierarchy from one grade to another, also by sex and ethnic group.

Typically such an analysis will show, for both women and for members of ethnic minorities that they are heavily concentrated in the lower grades and in particular jobs within these lower grades. To rise in an organization it is

2   Such a framework might include an examination of:

(1)   What the minority group bring to the situation, in terms of its power, culture, language, religious beliefs, norms and customs.

(2)   What management, trade unions and indigenous workers bring in terms of expectations, stereotype assumptions and prejudices, and of the responses these groups make as a result of such expectations and assumptions.

(3)   The contribution made by the social and technical systems in which the incident occurs, e.g. the established practice of word of mouth recruitment may, unintentionally, lead to the virtual exclusion of members of ethnic minorities; continuous production processes may inhibit the system of prayer demanded by Islam during Ramadan.

(4)   The social and economic environment, e.g. the effect of high unemployment on recruitment standards for example may well have led to often unintended discrimination against those whose English is not good, though it may in fact be good enough for the job in question.

3   The extent to which this can be effectively and accurately undertaken will depend on the existence of a monitoring system to enable the basic figures to be collected.

usually a great advantage, even essential, to start in a position, however low in grade, which provides the training and experience accepted as essential for promotion up the ladder. If it is found that whole categories of employees are virtually excluded from such jobs, then one explanation for their non-appearance in higher grades may already have been identified. The question immediately arises as to why such people do not appear in these key jobs. A building brick in the strategy has been identified.

A second building brick is created when analysis reveals that at a certain level, usually not very high in the organization, there is a virtual disappearance of women and of members of ethnic minorities. This needs to be illuminated by the figure for the rate of flow from one level to another. If it is found that there is little difference in rate of flow from grade 1 to grade 2, but that from grade 4 to grade 5 the percentage upward flow rate for white males is five times the flow rate of women or ethnic minorities, yet another indicator has been provided which suggests, though it does not prove, the existence of inequality of opportunity. Such analysis focuses attention on potential danger spots in terms of equal opportunity: it also provides a framework for the development of strategy.

Such information may well convince top management that action is necessary, partly because it suggests the organization may well be in breach of its legal obligations, but also because when large sections of the labour force fail to gain promotion, it is at least plausible that valuable talent is being ignored and efficiency reduced.

Top management may be convinced of the need to bring about change. But if change is to be real and enduring those who are involved in it must be convinced of the need, and prepared to bring it about. The ability of unions, middle management and supervisors to sabotage change, often very subtly, is well understood by practical managers. To win consent to change is especially important in an area such as equal opportunities. The changes needed may run counter to strongly held beliefs and prejudices, often not fully understood by those who hold them, which have deep psychological and sociological roots. Equal opportunity for men and women at work is an aspect of relations between men and women, which is part of a culture developed over centuries. Such attitudes do not change easily and for some people genuine change of attitude may be impossible, though change of behaviour may none the less be induced.

It is therefore essential that both employees and managers should come to see that change is needed, even though, as individuals they may be reluctant to accept it.

Given the TUC backing for equal opportunity, and its published equal opportunity clause for inclusion in industrial agreements, in theory the introduction of an equal opportunity scheme should not create industrial relations problems. It involves no basic management/union conflict of interest. However, just as managers have varying attitudes towards equal opportunity, so in the same way, unions are not in practice homogeneous in their approach to the question. It is clear that equal opportunity policies will achieve only minimal results unless they are accepted by employees and in unionized concerns by positive union support and re-enforcement. This may take a number of forms, varying from a formal joint agreement to an informal sanction from union representatives with a strong personal commitment to equal opportunity but conscious of only limited support from sections of union membership.

The support of management and supervisors has also to be gained. The knowledge that there is a consensus in favour of change at top management level is clearly important. In a command structure type of organization it is essential and may very well be decisive. In a more decentralized organization, it is valuable, provided top management determination to implement the policy is not seen by local management to conflict with their established right to take decisions at local level. In all types it is important that all levels of management should genuinely accept the policy and generate the will to implement the strategy. In decentralized organizations it is this attitude which is crucial.

For management to be convinced, it must come to recognize that a problem exists. A presentation of data from the initial analysis can be an important step in creating this conviction. It might not be easily done. By far the most common initial management reaction to a discussion of equal opportunity is an assertion that other people undoubtedly have a problem, but they do not. The case from figures may be reinforced by evidence from tribunal cases or from traumatic and costly events such as the incident described earlier. The practical management advantages of equal opportunity, enabling the better use of talent to overcome operational problems, will for some managers be the clinching argument.

Recognition of the existence of a genuine problem is the first step, without which no progress is possible. Managers need also to be convinced that there is something they can in fact do to resolve the problem. At this stage it has been found that what carries conviction is evidence of what has in practice been achieved by people of their own kind, facing similar issues. At the Equal Opportunity Conference for Bankers organized by the EEC in Knokke in 1982, it was unquestionably the down-to-earth account by fellow bankers of what they had done in their banks and why they had done it, that made a real impression on those who had not so far embarked on any such programme.

The support of employees and managers is clearly essential, but since change needs to be brought about with people rather than for them, those most directly affected should also in some way be involved. In one instance a group of younger women with high potential were brought together in a two-day workshop and asked to report on the changes they believed should be introduced. Where ethnic minorities are involved opinion formers in the community should similarly be involved.

Once these key steps have been taken a number of other important decisions can be made. Where should the change take place? What should be done?

Where should the change take place?

At first sight it might appear appropriate to introduce a change programme simultaneously and in a uniform manner throughout the organization as a whole. This has the advantage of consistency in the application of policy and may appear to many people as the only fair way to operate. It has, however, a number of limitations in a large organization with a high degree of diversity and decentralization. Problems and therefore situations differ in different sections, and where management decisions are decentralized local managers will assume that in this matter as in others they have a high degree of discretion in the application of general company policy. The varying approaches adopted by local managements may appear to lack consistency, but the possibility of progressing in different ways in different sections has compensating advantages.

In any change programme, the selection of priorities is crucial. In one area it may be recruitment and selection of staff which calls for immediate attention; in another it may be the methods of appraisal and promotion which are creating difficulty; in a third the emphasis may be on the need to train to minimize the disadvantages suffered by both women and ethnic minorities. Technical, market, or industrial relations considerations may well dictate priorities. For example, where no recruitment is taking place it would be foolish to focus on selection issues. Analysis of the local position will therefore determine priorities with the inevitable result that action will vary in scope, type and intensity throughout the organization, and progress will be made at differing speeds in different parts of the concern. The advantages of this approach include the ability to concentrate effort on issues analysis has shown to be urgent and to learn from the differing methods applied and experience gained.

The implementation of any company policy calls for a plan of action. Objectives need to be defined, a programme devised, and a time-table set for the completion of the programme. This implies a system of monitoring so that progress can be assessed at regular intervals, and remedial action taken if the programme is not on course. For the implementation of marketing or financial policies the need for such a system would for most managers be self-evident. There is no logical reason why the approach should be different for an equal opportunity policy.

When objectives are being set, it is important that those most closely concerned in their achievement should be as closely concerned in their definition. They should be neither too easy to achieve nor too ambitious. An increase of 5 per cent over a two-year period in the number of women in a section in which analysis has shown that the ratio of women to men begins noticeably to decline might well be a realistic amount. The managers concerned should not only be involved, they should be effectively motivated. Experience in the United States suggests that it is important for it to be clearly understood that the achievement of a manager's equal opportunity objectives is taken into account in his annual performance appraisal in line with achievements in relation to production or costs.

To a number of managements the question of monitoring rouses a good deal of anxiety. Monitoring changes in ratios of men and women presents no difficulty. The information is readily available and the subject is not, in this respect, a sensitive one. But the monitoring in relation to ethnic minorities has been widely resisted, and there is no doubt that progress in the development of equal opportunities has been hampered over a number of years by a widespread resistance to monitoring. It has, for example, frequently been alleged that the collection of information about the ethnic origin of employees – information obviously necessary for any monitoring process – was itself discriminatory. The CRE Code of Practice, issued in 1983, makes clear that monitoring is not only acceptable, but is in fact essential. 'Employers', the Code states, 'should regularly monitor the effects of selection decisions and personnel practices and procedures in order to assess whether equal opportunity is being achieved'. It accepts that the information needed for effective monitoring may be obtained in a number of ways. 'It will best be provided by records showing the ethnic origins of existing employees and job applicants. It is recognized that the need for detailed information and the methods of collecting it will vary according to the circumstances of individual establishments. For example, in small firms or in firms with little or no racial minority settlement it will often be adequate to assess the distribution of employees from personal knowledge and visual identification'.[4] To assist in the monitoring process the Commission has issued a further publication 'Monitoring on Equal Opportunity Policy'. The TUC resolution referred to in Chapter 16, also makes it clear that, from the union point of view, monitoring is a necessary and accepted practice.

With objectives set and the monitoring system established, the individual managers need to prepare and implement their own plans. They will begin where they are: there is, after all, nowhere else to start. This requires a review of the personnel in their own areas of responsibility.

They may find, as occurred in one shunting yard, that all the drivers in the cabs were white, all the shunters were black. This kind of 'clustering' is relatively common and is often brought about by word-of-mouth recruitment. Such clustering can create unanticipated difficulties. For example, once this pattern is set, a number of problems are likely to arise: the work groups become exclusive, transfers are difficult, and both recruitment and promotion sources are likely to be limited by the unofficial 'ownership' of the job by the particular ethnic group. Such ethnically homogeneous groups tend to use their own cultural norms of behaviour which may be radically different from norms elsewhere in the organization. This can disrupt the normal procedures for conflict resolution. In one case, a group of Indians from a village in the Punjab were accustomed to solving differences by discussing them as a group. This they proceeded to do on the shop floor, delegating one of their

4   Commission for Racial Equality. Code of Practice, p. 18.

number to tell management what the group had decided. The departmental manager responded by bringing out a chalkboard and discussing their problems in their order of priority. For each issue he produced a solution which was agreed with the group. However, the following day, the chief convenor, who was white, and his deputy, also white, appeared in the manager's office protesting that the manager had not kept to the standard ritual for dealing with conflict: he had not kept to the negotiating procedures. This raised the issue of how far to adapt the organization and its established policies to meet the needs of minorities.

If this incident is examined in terms of the framework suggested on page 402 the following points emerge:

1   The minority group's normal approach for the resolution of a grievance was a form of group discussion, with the findings from the discussion being entrusted to a chosen representative who was expected to convey the group's point of view to management, after which the issues would be thrashed out by all concerned.

2   The management and trade union's assumptions were that such a matter would be put into the hands of the shop steward who would then carry out the discussions with management. This system has the crucial advantage that the shop steward represents all the employees: the Indian traditional system represents very effectively their own group, but their own group alone.

3   The behaviour of the minority group cut across the established social system of the undertaking, though it was an effective way of dealing with the minority group's problems.

In this instance pressures from the external environment did not impinge on the issue.

The steps to be taken to achieve objectives will clearly depend on the outcome of the analysis of the existing position within the area under discussion. But whether changes are to be made within a limited area or for the organization as a whole, point (3) of the system of analysis calls for a systematic examination of the social and technical systems and these clearly cover the main personnel practices and procedures. Major points to be considered include recruitment, selection procedure, training, and promotion.

Recruitment

Advertisements which suggest that only women or only whites will be considered are clearly illegal, unless the job is covered by one of the narrow range of reasons which permit such a limitation (see Chapter 4). It is not only the wording which is important: illustrations can create a strong impression of a preference, even if nothing is stated in words.

The more blatantly discriminatory advertisements which are an established form of direct discrimination have become rare, even if they have not been entirely eliminated, but there are a number of less obvious ways in which discrimination occurs in recruitment. If information about vacancies never reaches large numbers of women and members of ethnic minorities, the whole recruitment system is in fact, however unintentionally, discriminatory. To ensure this does not happen, information should be sent, for example, to single-sex schools as well as to mixed schools and advertisements should be placed in journals widely read by members of ethnic minorities. If personnel are to an overwhelming extent white and male, to rely exclusively on internal advertising or on word of mouth recruitment is to make it most unlikely that women and blacks will be adequately informed of opportunities.

Selection procedure

Selection is the final stage of a process that begins with job description and analysis, job and person specification. It is essential to be certain that the requirements of the person specification are 'justifiable'. It can easily happen that a qualification or requirement which was once essential has ceased to be necessary because of gradual, perhaps unnoticed, changes in the nature of the job. As pointed out in Chapter 17, if such a requirement can not in practice be met by a substantial proportion of either sex or by members of an ethnic minority group, and they are at a disadvantage for this reason, then it is indirect discrimination to insist on this requirement, job specifications need careful vetting with this in mind.

There have been a number of cases where a casual enquirer has been turned away because a gatekeeper or receptionist, inadequately trained, has assumed that because there are in fact no blacks or women in jobs for which there are known to be vacancies, none will be considered. Training in the implementation of non-discriminatory procedures should be given to everyone who has any contact with potential applicants, not merely to those who carry the main responsibility for selection.[5]

The application form can also contain pitfalls. The British Steel Corporation was found to have discriminated because it used competence in completing the application form as an element in selection for a job for which, it was held, such a level of competence was not required. Questions can appear on application forms, about for example a woman's domestic arrangements, which may be held to be discriminatory.

Where tests are used, the need for 'culture free' tests is recognized. This issue is discussed in detail in 'Discriminating Fairly'.[6]

5 'Towards Fairer Selection – A Code for Non-discrimination', IPM Joint Standing Committee on Discrimination, 1978.
6 'Discriminating Fairly' by Runnymede Trust & British Psychological Society, 1980.

Until the implications in anti-discrimination legislation were realized discriminatory practices were not infrequently openly adopted. Some banks, for example, recruited girls for 'jobs' and boys for 'careers', with different O-level requirements. It was argued that since banks offered a lifetime career, and girls did not want a lifetime career, they were suitable candidates for dead-end jobs: a few years and they would be gone. Such a practice is clearly discriminatory.

Training

A major reason why few blacks or women are found in higher level jobs is that few of them have received the requisite training or acquired the necessary experience. It is therefore important to monitor the proportions of members of different sexes and ethnic groups which are included in the organization's internal training schemes or sent on external training courses. Where analysis has shown that there is a disproportionately slow rate of flow up the ladder for any one group, the use of 'designated' training should be considered.

An equally important aspect of training concerns supervisors and managers who need to understand the full implications of equal opportunity policy and to adapt to meet its requirements. For example, where in decentralized organizations, as in multiple retail stores, recruitment and selection is handled by local branch managers they need careful training if discrimination, especially indirect discrimination, is to be avoided.

Promotion

Promotion is clearly a key issue, since it is the main means by which people obtain access to improved pay, status and positions of power. Unless women and members of ethnic minorities are seen to be advancing up the hierarchy, equal opportunities will not be seen to exist in reality. This calls for a careful check on the differential flow rate for the different groups. This flow rate, by identifying discrepancies, alerts management to the need to examine the way in which the promotion system is working. For example, in one large organization in a division of several thousand employees nearly 50 per cent of the operators but only 7 per cent of the supervision were members of ethnic minorities. Systematic attention to flow rates could have prevented the development of this situation at an early stage.

The promotion system includes not only the decision making process but also the key judgemental and appraisal process. Appraisals can easily be discriminatory, often unintentionally, unless those making them are trained to recognize prejudice and stereotyping. In fact the presence of women and ethnic minorities can highlight existing weaknesses in appraisal and promotion systems. Too frequently, there is little if any feedback to establish the validity of the promotion system, even when white males only are affected.

While recruitment, selection, training and promotion are central to equal opportunities, such a scrutiny should be applied to all personnel practices, including disciplinary procedures, hours of work, and holiday provision. Underlying such a scrutiny is the challenge to traditional practices. Most organizations have grown up on assumptions that they depended primarily, if not exclusively, on white males. Practices such as a requirement of mobility or promotion by seniority may still be essential for the success of the concern. But this is not self-evident and can be questioned. If women and ethnic minorities are to be given the opportunity to play the part of which they are capable no established procedures or structures can be sacrosanct. All must be open to challenge.

Discussion questions

1 What steps would you take to ensure that your recruitment and selection procedures were fair and non-discriminatory?
2 Attempt to identify some of the 'building bricks' which may be revealed by analysis, and which may contribute towards positive policies for non-discrimination.
3 What are the practical problems posed by 'monitoring'?
4 Identify key areas in your own organization where changes should be initiated – then define objectives, devise a programme, and set a time-table for the completion of the programme.

PART EIGHT

The Working Environment

CHAPTER 19

Job satisfaction and dissatisfaction

by Bryan Livy

For many people work is a drudge, a daily grind. For others, it is a stimulant. Much depends on the nature of the work itself – whether it excites, challenges and inspires or whether it is confined to routine monotony or heavy, manual effort. In the work-orientated society to which for many years we have become accustomed, it might seem that we have been taught to cherish our right to toil. Why do we work? What makes us do anything?

Motivation is the basis of all human activity. It is a force which impels human beings to behave in a variety of ways. Without motivation, we would be inactive. The activity which results from a motivated state is fuelled by a drive to satisfy certain 'needs' – these needs may be biological or social psychological (expectations, needs for affiliation, creativity and achievement). Motivational force depends upon a basic drive, the strength of various needs at different points in time and the perceived value and expectation of the rewards to be obtained as satisfying agents. Understanding motivation is complex, and the theories presented often eclectic.

It may be asserted that people work for money. But this simple link between work and money is deceptive. There is little evidence to suggest that paying people more will automatically make them work harder. Nor can it be implied that the *only* satisfactions derived from work are monetary.

The role which money, as a reward for work, plays as a motivator of human behaviour and performance, has been the subject of considerable research, debate and theorizing. Over the last century views have changed as to its *relative* importance. Consistently, however, money has remained a sensitive and crucial element in the total reward–compensation package. Issues affecting payment for work, the rate for the job, the grade or scale of payment, questions of differentials, bonuses, incentives, and the like are all capable of evoking very powerful emotions. One may notice the number of industrial disputes expressed largely in terms of pay. One may notice the continual round of negotiations, the constant battle against inflation, professed concern for the less well-paid, anxiety about job security, and endless discussion about a host of factors which might affect the stability of a regular, adequate income. There can be no doubt that in a market economy, work and payment are inseparable. Without money, people are unable to buy the goods and services necessary for survival; they cannot advance in status in the eyes of their fellow men; nor can they make material improvements in their standards of living.

Behavioural scientists have produced a number of models which seek to explain the relationship between pay and work. Because of the intricacies and complexities involved, models have been simplistic in their explanations. They do not provide complete answers, nor do they have universal validity. The twin aims of a concise and acceptable model of behaviour commensurate with a complete appreciation of the interactive drives, attitudes and responses of mankind as a whole are mutually exclusive. The corollary is that a theoretical model albeit based on empirical research cannot always be used as a predictor of behaviour in other situations. Further, the models which have been produced are products of their time; they are often controversial and sometimes conflicting. Unfortunately, some of the research evidence is open to criticism, either on grounds of methodology or upon doubts about conclusions which have been reached.

The progenitor of modern capitalism was a medieval system, in which a man plied his craft, and in which to all intents and purposes, capital was the servant of the man. Man exercised a high degree of control over the means of production – his individual decisions were critical – and the cycle from raw material to finished product and end use were well within the limits of his comprehension. What later has been termed the 'Zeigarnik' effect – that is the ability to see and influence the complete operational cycle, and from which considerable job satisfaction is thought to derive – is well illustrated at this level of technology.

Technology subsequently developed faster than man's individual capacity to influence it or even to comprehend its full ramifications. With it came all the advantages of economies of scale, mass markets, and monolithic impersonal bureaucracies. Man as an individual became isolated and estranged from his own invention. Employment became an instrument in the service of the great machine. Not surprisingly, signs of maladjustment became evident in manifestations of neurotic anxiety and insecurity resulting from alienation and lack of control – but more blatantly in the degree of instrumentality, in the calculated exchanges, existing between employer and employee.

The antecedents of a culture cannot be ignored. Industrialization has had a conditioning influence under which mankind has learned to accept certain values imposed upon him by the system. It was not until the work of an American, Frederick Winslow Taylor (1911) that some of these ideas became crystallized into a managerial theory of motivation.

Taylor's observation was that the main obstacle to efficiency was the failure of managers to coordinate and control industrial operations. He advocated a systematic study of work methods, isolating various elements of work, and by measuring them on a cost and time basis, sought to eliminate waste and decay. His approach was that of an engineer, with emphasis on the physical aspects, and related management structure on functional lines. Planning and organizing were seen as key management roles.

Taylor epitomized the 'Protestant Ethic' – the master–servant relationship in which both parties are predominantly economically motivated, competitive and self-interested. Taylor's success was limited and many of his 'principles of scientific measurement' – particularly with regard to motivation – do not work when applied to group or team activities in modern organizations. They are founded on primitive assumptions about the nature of human needs and behaviour. These assumptions are that people only try to satisfy economic needs at work – the only reward they seek is money; behaviour is always *rational* in the pursuit of maximum financial rewards. Emotional or social needs do not enter the picture. The well-being of the individual is measured purely in economic terms. The employee is obliged to accept or defect. It is a carrot and stick philosophy.

Douglas McGregor (1960) summed up the tenets of this philosophy in what he called Theory X. Management has sole responsibility for organizing men, money, materials and machines in the pursuit of profit. The activities, aspirations and attitudes of people working in the organization must therefore be modified to fit the organizational goals. People are basically lazy, have an inherent dislike of work or responsibility, and must if necessary be coerced or punished. People are resistant to change, insecure (not surprisingly) and prefer to be led. All powers of direction and control are vested in management, who autocratically shall decide what is to be done, how it is to be done, and what is good for the employee.

Many years ago, an Australian, Elton Mayo, working as a management consultant in America, revealed some important considerations almost by accident. The famous 'Hawthorne' experiments were an important landmark in the development of behavioural theory, if for no other reason than the fact that they looked beyond the individual working in isolation, and considered the total group and sub-group in interaction with the physical and social environment and with supervision.

During the first phase of the experiments, 1924–7, designed to find a causal relationship between changes in physical aspects of work and resultant changes in output and satisfaction, alterations were made in levels of illumination afforded to a group of female workers. No direct link was found. Output rose irrespective of the level of lighting; and no positive results were recorded from changes in rest pauses.

The investigators began to look at the organization as a 'social system' and not as an aggregate of individuals. They came to the conclusion that all factors in a work situation are closely related and interactive, a conclusion borne out by the second phase of the experiments, 1927–32. The illumination studies were really the harbinger of the main body of the research which consisted of four main experiments in relay assembly and mica-splitting test rooms and in the bank wiring observation room. Although the findings were equivocal (controlled and rigorous experimental methodology was lacking), one of the implications to emerge was that any group or individual selected as an object of interest will acquire kudos or ego-satisfaction which may well have a positive effect on performance – the so-called 'Hawthorne effect'. Other conditions were that work is not an insular, but a *group* activity; work is not just doing things, but a pattern of social and interpersonal relationships. The need for recognition, security and sense of belonging is more important in determining morale and productivity than physical conditions. Informal groups emerge in work situations and exercise strong social controls. Group norms set limits on any individual's behaviour within the group, and group collaboration and cohesion can be facilitated. Mayo's experiments were significant in starting the so-called 'human relations' school, although they provided insufficient evidence to refute the money incentive.

However, if Taylorism can be criticized, for attributing to man a paramount drive of universal economism, the Human Relations school can be criticized for attributing to him universal sociability (Rose, 1978). Both approaches ignore an employee's out-of-work experiences and attachments. No form of organizational behaviour can really be accounted for without paying some attention to external factors, whether these are of social or cultural origin or community affiliation. When man goes to work, he does not leave part of himself at home. It may indeed be wrong to segregate the study of man at work from his total life environment.

One of the revered conceptual models which focuses on the satisfaction of human needs is that of Abraham Maslow (1968) postulating that man is basically a 'wanting animal' whose lifestyle is predominantly directed towards satisfying various wants. As each want becomes sated, so a new one arises. From the moment of birth an unending chain-reaction is set in motion. There is a general development from the seeking of satisfaction of needs basic to the existence of life itself, through a series of levels, to the pursuit of satisfactions on higher intellectual, cultural and social planes. Maslow's hierarchy is well known, ranging from basic physiological and safety needs, via love and esteem needs to *self-actualization* – needs to develop one's skills, capacities and aptitudes to the full, to search for knowledge, beauty and opportunities for creativity, to develop into a 'whole' man or woman.

Two ideas are inherent in his hierarchy. The first is prepotency; the idea that higher level needs do not become operative until the respective lower level needs have been satisfied. Secondly, a satisfied need cannot be a motivator. A satisfied need cannot incite new goal-directed behaviour. A man cannot be motivated to do something by offering him what he already has. A need which has *not* been satisfied is much more likely to stimulate and call forth new behaviour patterns.

This kind of exposition about human needs and motives, and the opportunities (or lack of them) for their expression in organizational life led to the formulation of McGregor's Theory Y (1960). Theories X and Y were presented as extreme polarizations of management thought. The main tenets of Theory Y are that man has a natural capacity for creativity, imagination and intellectual development. He seeks scope to deploy his talents, and will expand considerable energy in the pursuit of goals to *which he is committed*. He needs to be motivated, therefore, on a higher level than simple carrot and stick philosophy. This is very much in the tradition of the 'Human Relations School' which blossomed after Hawthorne. Treating people in a Theory Y manner will evoke Theory Y responses, and vice versa.

Motivation means more than money. Research which has become classic in this connection is that of Frederick Herzberg and his colleagues. Herzberg *et al.* (1959) published the results of an investigation into the origins of job satisfaction and job dissatisfaction of some 200 engineers and accountants employed in nine separate companies. The investigation was based on individual interviews in which respondents were asked to identify and to report what they felt to be the critical incidents in their jobs which had given rise to exceptionally good feelings and to exceptionally bad feelings. An attempt was made to highlight objective and tangible experiences. Some 5000 statements were classified, and the data broken down to specific events. From the study, two distinct sets of variables and related attitudes emerged. Aspects of work which appeared to be closely associated with high levels of job satisfaction (called by Herzberg 'satisfiers') differed from those associated with low job satisfaction ('dissatisfiers'). The nub is that Herzberg identified an apparent natural dichotomy in the influences at work which gave rise to satisfaction and dissatisfaction. There appeared to be at least an associational relationship, and maybe a causal one, between the elements of work concerned with the *content* of the job (i.e. the work itself, responsibility, advancement, recognition and achievement) – which contained the seeds of personal satisfaction – and the elements of work concerned with the *context* or environment in which it operates (i.e. company policy, styles of super-vision, salary levels, interpersonal relationships, and working conditions) which *could* contain the seeds of personal dissatisfaction, though not satisfaction.

Work experiences related to the job context or environment can cause dissatisfaction because of the need to avoid unpleasantness. It is therefore vital that they are maintained at adequate levels, and such aspects of work have been variously labelled 'maintenance factors', 'hygiene factors' or 'dis-satisfiers'. Although hygiene factors can be a potential source of dissatisfac-tion for hedonistic reasons, because they do not provide *at work* outlets for man's aspirations for growth, they cannot be primary sources of job satisfaction.

The sources of satisfaction, or outlets for self-actualization, derive from those factors which relate to the content of the job and work itself; they have been variously labelled 'motivators', or 'satisfiers'. Herzberg's two sets of factors are quite separate and distinct. They are both uni-polar.

Interpretation of the Herzberg thesis and ways in which it can be translated into practice are probably just as important as the content of the theory itself. The two-factor theory hinges partly on the link between a factor and its durability or potency as a source of satisfaction or dissatisfaction over time. The survey showed that as far as monetary rewards are concerned, their powers of satisfaction were short-lived, and in the long run became impotent. One pay rise soon loses its attraction and gives rise to desires for another.

Yet another psychologist, Schein (1980), developed a more embracing theory of 'complex man'. His basic tenet is that no single theory is by itself adequate. For him, man is driven to fulfil a variety of needs on a variety of planes, and these needs vary, not only from person to person, but within the same person over time.

Individuals have a range of preferences among the outcomes they seek. Explanation of what actually happens is not therefore purely a psychological theory but incorporates ideas about decision theory borrowed from economics. One of the fundamental assumptions is that an individual can assign a utility (value, or valence) to a particular goal (outcome, or incentive). Embryonically these ideas form the basis of expectancy theory.

Victor Vroom (1964, 1968) first posited the ideas of expectancy theory in the form of a truly cognitive model. The cognitive approach views people as purposeful, proactive and adaptably rational. Various outcomes acquire a *valence* (a degree of importance, affective orientation or preference) according to the way in which an individual sees it as having power to attain certain satisfactions. Individuals also have some subjective assessment of the *expectancy* (probability, belief) that given outcomes are feasible and can be achieved. Degrees of elasticity exist in the minds of individuals as to the strength of either valence or expectancy. These ideas, although using different terminology, were taken up by Lawler and Porter (see Fig. 19.1). Essentially, two ratios exist in the minds of individuals – on the one hand, effort and reward; and on the other, effort and performance. Accordingly, an individual will move into a state of equilibrium in balancing the two sets of ratios.

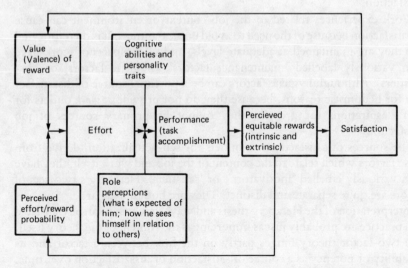

Fig. 19.1 *Adaptation of the theoretical model presented by Lawler and Porter (1967) and Lawler (1971)*

Expectancies, valencies, choices, outcomes and instrumentalities provide a map for the individual (subjectively and sometimes unconsciously) to plan how he or she will go about fulfilling needs and achieving goals.

The theories we have outlined are important not only academically but have positive utility with regard to job satisfaction, performance and the design of work.

Job satisfaction

What is 'job satisfaction'? It is a feeling which individuals may have that their important needs are satisfied by the work they are doing. As a result, they will express a favourable attitude to their jobs. Underlying these sentiments will be a feeling that they will not be better or more easily satisfied in comparable jobs.

The commonest way of measuring people's job satisfaction is to ask them to express an overall view and to itemize particular work aspects which please or displease them. Basically, this is the way employee attitude surveys are constructed. Management may decide to launch an attitude survey in order to identify possible sources of dissatisfaction so that remedial action can be taken. Remedial action may take the form of making improvements in such things as pay, quality of supervision, workmates, the way work is structured. Management's inspiration might be to improve productivity, to improve the quality of working life or to overcome some of the more overt manifestations of dissatisfaction or poor morale, such as absenteeism or labour turnover (see later). Job satisfaction is a complex orientation to work – it has affective, cognitive and behavioural components.

However laudable job satisfaction may be, it does not guarantee high performance. Most studies which had attempted to show a relationship between job satisfaction and performance have failed. A satisfied worker is not necessarily a good worker. There is a difference between the willingness and motivation to perform and acceptable levels of job satisfaction. 'Satisfaction is need fulfilment, while motivation is a term covering the instigation and direction of behaviour aimed at satisfying the need' (Cameron, 1973). Motivation embodies not only fulfilment of personal needs, but also suitable rewards and a mechanism by which various needs or wants may be attained. Rewards which are 'extrinsic' to the job – i.e. an external adjunct to the work itself – such as wages and other monetary inducements constitute part of the 'exchange' between individual and employer, a compensatory aspect of the effort/reward bargain. Valuable and essential as such a trade-off may be, it does not make the worker love his work. He may still be satisfied with his pay but not with his job. There is something missing.

Certain aspects of work are 'intrinsic'. They emanate from the work itself whether the application of skills or craft, a feeling of commitment and responsibility, or pride in high standards.

Recent attempts at improving job satisfaction at work have focused on *job redesign*. A well-established principle of personnel management is 'fitting the job to the person'. This implies that jobs should be shaped to fit human capacities and inclinations and provide opportunities to harness the energies of people performing them. Whilst there can still be no guarantee that higher performance will ensue, badly designed jobs will almost certainly have adverse effects.

Most causes of dissatisfaction at work stem from the restriction of skill required, the repetitiveness of so many jobs, the relentless nature of paced work, lack of freedom to make decisions, and the impersonality of organizations. Work which is monotonous and meaningless is dissatisfying. Satisfying work must provide some degree of challenge, discretion and responsibility, opportunities to use skills and abilities, social contact and variety.

There are a number of sources – theoretical, behavioural and political – from which approaches to job redesign and satisfaction can be seen to have evolved:

1 Limitations of 'scientific management'
2 Herzberg's two-factor theory and the job enrichment approach
3 Expectancy theory and ideas about valency, instrumentality and reward
4 Socio-technical systems
5 Ergonomics
6 Worker participation and industrial democracy.

All these approaches are in fact a reaction to Taylorism and the scientific management school which saw man as a servant to the machine. The principles of scientific management are generally inappropriate to an educated, sophisticated workforce operating in an increasingly complex environment requiring a high degree of flexibility. Most approaches to job redesign embody changes in job content or the relationship between jobs. They involve reshaping jobs physically and socially.

For Herzberg *job enrichment* means building extra responsibilities into a job. John Child (1984) encapsulates three elements of job enrichment:

1 Enlargement of the work cycle
2 Incorporation of indirect elements, e.g. maintenance and inspection
3 Delegation of more decision-making to employees.

Job enrichment is a form of 'vertical' expansion. It is the incorporation of additional levels of skill, autonomy and responsibility. It adds depth to the job. Jobs with higher skill content are of course the ones more conducive to job enrichment, but where there is less need. Administrative and supervisory jobs inherently offer more scope for initiatives.

There is a distinction to be drawn between job enrichment and job enlargement. *Job enlargement* is 'horizontal' expansion. Job enlargement simply means adding additional tasks, increasing job content, without tapping extra reserves of hidden talent, and is not really in the Herzberg tradition. It adds breadth to the job.

We may also think of *job rotation* which means the interchangeability of people between jobs or parts of a job.

The terminology is quite clear and so are attempts to follow any particular line. In short, they are all concerned with job 'improvement', a generic term to cover various processes of 'work restructuring' for either individuals or groups. They break away from the constraints of the pure scientific management school. They are a modern version of human relations management.

From Expectancy Theory comes the idea that an individual maximizes the outcomes he values highly. Expectancy Theory draws out the links between effort and reward, and effort and performance. The theory *can* identify certain points for job redesign (by building in opportunities for 'intrinsic' rewards), although it *cannot* resolve relationships between groups and individual autonomy, nor does it offer much for people seeking purely monetary outcomes. Developing the essential tenets of this theory Hackman and Oldham (1980) signal what they see as important *core dimensions*, relevant to the need for achievement and personal development, taking these as the most desired intrinsic rewards, which are:

1 Feedback
2 Autonomy
3 Task identity
4 Variety.

We will return to these core dimensions in a moment. There are other threads in the story. Originating in the late 1940s, the Tavistock Institute of Human Relations in the UK, sowed the seeds of what became known as 'socio-technical systems' arising from studies in the Durham coalfields (Trist and Bamforth, 1951). Without going into detail, the upshot was that the introduction of the new 'long-wall method of coal-getting', a mechanized method of coalmining, with enormous engineering advantages, jarred in practice with the social system of working which had grown up over decades amongst the miners themselves. The old hand-got, pair-based work group was abolished. New teams were devised. The engineering 'model' was put to the test and failed. Production targets were not met. Antagonism was rife. The interaction between workers modified the purely technical criteria.

Any work organization is an open system incorporating a number of patterned activities. The organization engages in two types of process (i) performing tasks, converting input into output and (ii) maintenance (with regard to plant, staff, equipment, etc.). There is always an interaction between the methods of work, technology, and social relationships. Any change in one part of the system will have repercussions on the others. There are a range of technological, economic, social and political influences bearing on any organizational system and its subsystems. The Tavistock studies brought into fuller realization the interaction between a work group and the technical aspects of the task it has to perform. They took us a step further than the Hawthorne *éclaircissement* of social interactions *per se*. The lesson was that the design of work methods should embrace the technical system together with the social system – hence 'socio-technical systems'. Earlier approaches had concentrated on *either* technical aspects (cf scientific management) *or* social aspects (cf. Human relations school).

At the same time, but separately, the study of ergonomics, which considered on a narrower footing the best fit between operator and machine in the design of machine operations (elaborated in Chapter 20), was gaining ground.

The job design studies undertaken by Trist and his colleagues at the Tavistock Institute in London, and other researches in America and Scandinavia, really proffered an *alternative* to the job enrichment theory advanced by Herzberg. The Tavistock adopted a 'task-centred' approach to participation. New technology was bringing in new social systems of working and new organizational values. With machines taking over much of the drudgery of work, people were being needed and would be needed, for 'non-programmable' activities. New jobs, in other words, would require skills and organizational structures quite different from the ones known at present.

The socio-technical system sees an organization as consisting of independent, technological and social systems operating together. Joint optimization is central to the approach. The assertion is that it is impossible to achieve maximum performance without trying to optimize these connected systems jointly.

There is no doubt that the changes implied in this approach are more radical than simply job enrichment. Socio-technical systems represent a devout wish, sometimes relatively easy and sometimes extremely difficult to fulfil. Technology is important. It is more of a fixed than a variable component in the work situation, although it is rarely a total invariant. Social systems may be adapted. The main problem is the disruptive impact of sudden change. Solutions lie in planning joint changes. 'While over the last decade interest in job design and work organization has come largely from management's concern to improve performance and employee involvement, in the 1980s new technology and its potential for improving productivity and reducing costs has become an increasing force for change. In fact, undoubtedly we have entered the phase of 'technology push' in which new technology is one of the main driving forces for change and is a major factor affecting job design and work organisation' (Bailey, 1983).

There can so easily be maladjustment between human, machine, work process and inter and intra group interaction. Current attempts at job redesign tackle this set of problems. The central focus is on the 'intrinsic' content of a job. Appeal is made to those things which are intrinsically satisfying to the worker. The aim is to enhance achievement and accomplishment.

Where a job is designed in such a way that intrinsic rewards are possible and personal needs are satisfied, then effort to perform is likely to be expended, but these ingredients are interactive and not necessarily causal phenomena. The challenge in job redesign is to identify job characteristics which maximize intrinsic motivation.

From the work of many researchers and commentators (e.g. Cooper, 1974; Emery and Thorsund, 1976; Carby, 1976; Hackman and Oldham, 1980) and the efforts of the Department of Employment's Work Research Unit set up in 1974, the main criteria for the improvement of jobs by design can be distilled:

1 An optimum variety of tasks of reasonably demanding content within a job
2 A meaningful pattern of related tasks within the job cycle
3 The inclusion of auxiliary, preparatory jobs or 'boundary tasks'
4 An optimum length of the work cycle – without too many interruptions, allowing natural rhythms to build up
5 Control over the pace of work
6 Scope for setting standards of quality and quantity
7 Delegated powers of inspection and supervision
8 Feedback of results
9 Job rotation between interdependent or interlocking tasks
10 Physical and social proximity between interdependent jobs
11 Opportunities to learn on the job
12 An optimal area of decision-making – areas of responsibility which individuals can call their own
13 A maximum degree of social support and recognition in the workplace
14 Participation in 'goal setting' and in the clarification of goals
15 Wider knowledge of the work process.

The core dimensions we spoke of earlier – feedback, autonomy, task identity, variety – form the backbone of the above list of attributes. A few comments need to be made. The core dimensions apply to all jobs, whether performed by individuals or groups; they are basic criteria. Where group activities are concerned, consideration must also be given to interlocking tasks, job rotation, and geographical proximity of members and operations.

Emphasis is heavily placed on *variety*. Job variety may be 'spatial' (changed operations or places of work) or 'temporal' (such as job rotation or cycle times) (Cooper, 1974). But variety on its own may not be a true motivator – it may simply reduce boredom. 'Absence of repetitive work does not mean absence of boredom' (Guest *et al.*, 1978).

A second emphasis is on *participation* – in setting localized targets, in monitoring and in the delegation of authority downwards. Job redesign programmes are as much about industrial democracy and bending the rigidities of autocracy, as about economic, psychological or sociological well-being. There is a general move towards creating 'whole' jobs and generating a sense of ownership of a job.

If employees are to adapt successfully to change and acquire new skills they need to perform jobs which will help them to broaden these skills and their knowledge. Employee participation and involvement is enhanced by extending job related decision-making, providing opportunity to learn a new skill, performing a wide range of tasks, and creating a renewed commitment to the job and the organization.

Strategies for job design tend to vary according to the theoretical approach adopted. The main difference in practice is whether increased responsibility is given to an individual or to a group.

AUTONOMOUS WORKING GROUPS

Group working is sometimes introduced by management in response to poor productivity and morale. It attempts to include some semblance of the overall task, to clarify the significance of individual tasks when seen in a wider perspective, and to encourage group autonomy. Such an approach may include the formulation of goals, when and where to work, the distribution of tasks. Indeed, a group may select its own membership and leadership. More generally, however, broad work goals are either specified by management or negotiated. Thereafter, the group may be left to decide how tasks are shared.

Group working is most easily seen in 'batch' production where there are pockets of self-contained responsibility. Within a pocket, or 'cell', workers are trained to be versatile and may operate more than one type of machine or process. This is sometimes known as 'cellular manufacture' or 'group technology'. Groups normally assume responsibility for the day-to-day operations on their part of the production process, including inspection, the allocation of work and supply of materials. In effect, they constitute 'functional' groups. There are wide variations on this theme.

SCANDINAVIAN EXPERIMENTS

It is not in Britain, despite pioneer work in socio-technical systems, that autonomous working groups are associated, but with Scandinavia. Although in Britain certain experiments have become well known, notably in the Esso Oil Refinery at Fawley (Flanders, 1964) and at British Nylon Spinners (Cotgrove et al., 1971), Swedish experiments at Saab and Volvo have received much publicity. The arguments put forward were that in the manufacture of motor vehicles, economies of scale have subtle limits. Whilst machines may eliminate physical stress, a technology which chains people to machines can produce psychological stress and other health and behaviour problems. The idea was to replace an inanimate assembly line by a human work group.

According to the report of Norstedt and Anguren (1973) in 1969 Saab–Scania in Trollhättan were suffering recruitment problems, high labour turnover and absenteeism. The work force had been expressing interest in participation. Management and unions took a joint initiative.

In the chassis plant at Södertälje a conventional assembly line turned out car chassis. As with all assembly lines, the pace of work was controlled, jobs were repetitive, and the line itself susceptible to disturbances, such as disruption in supplies and components. Two trial groups were set up (a total of 40 selected men) in engine finishing and small bore piping operations. Each group began to generate ideas for changing the method of work and they decided to form Production Groups and Development Groups. The Production Groups were small groups with all-round know-how. They decided to limit the tasks as naturally as possible and took on responsibility for quality. Alterations to the way the group worked were allowed to develop gradually and spontaneously. The Development Groups were there to coordinate consultation and reporting between supervisors, workers and specialists. They met regularly to discuss progress. The normal pattern was for one Development Group to service two Production Groups. From this initiative, the idea snowballed. From two groups in 1969 the entire chassis works later became involved (1500 people in 130 Production Groups). Advantages claimed were that the time lost (from unplanned production stoppages) was halved, costs averaged 5 per cent below budget, quality improved and absenteeism was reduced. Experience gained at the chassis factory was later incorporated in the construction of a brand new Saab 99 engine factory, where paced assembly lines were replaced by group assembly.

Volvo, another car company of medium size by international standards, but large for Sweden, took up the call. They thought they would get a better job done if the product stood still so that people could work on it. So at their new Kalmar plant, work stations were stationary. Tasks were varied within the groups. 90 per cent of workers rotated jobs. Materials and work in progress were brought to the work group by an automated 'carrier' (i.e. line comprising a system of computer-controlled mechanical trolleys which replaced the traditional assembly track and ran round the factory at variable speeds on a prescribed circuit set by an electromagnetic strip in the floor). The flow was arranged to 'feed' the semi-finished product into a series of working bays manned by a small group of people responsible for a given range of operations. Workers themselves controlled the speed at which the trolleys moved forward, and they could build up stock by working quickly to cover time-off for rests or the sauna, although the overall pace was negotiated by unions based on work study times. Production at Kalmar began in 1974. There were about 30 work groups (of 15–20 people). A consultative system linked the union's work council with management and employees.

Both at Kalmar and Volvo's own new engine plant at Skövde, the assembly process was split up into areas of group working. Within these groups there was considerable freedom for workers to rotate jobs, design and change the layout of their working area, vary the pace of their work and rest pauses. The Kalmar plant abandoned the usual ground plan for motor vehicle assembly, making it easier to create small workshop areas (but Volvo later went back to traditional rectangular shapes in a series of small buildings).

The experiments were a major innovation in modern work design. In the words of Gyllenhammar (1977) President of Volvo: 'The finest form of organizational development occurs when planning can be entrusted to a group of people, ideally those who do the work'.

But we should not fall into the common trap of thinking that an entire automobile was constructed and assembled by one small group of workers. We are talking about certain operations only.

Prior to the experiments, both Saab and Volvo had been suffering high labour turnover and absenteeism, thought partly to be due to disenchantment with work and to generous social security benefits outside. There were also societal pressures for job reform and improvements in the working environment. Pressures to change were as much economic as political. Volvo reported, for example, an extra 10 per cent investment costs from abandoning the traditional assembly line, hoping for this outlay to be offset by savings, higher product quality, and a tighter retention of the labour force. (Peugeot, however, claims the system adds 30 per cent to both investment and manufacturing costs.)

Was it successful? Saab reported a fall in labour turnover until 1977 (Karlsson, 1978) and Volvo reported lower absenteeism at its Kalmar plant than at its main traditional factory at Torslanda, but not as low as the company had hoped for (Elliott, 1976). Nor has quality met expectations, and unplanned rectification work has been necessary. Some money has been saved by reducing supervisory and back-up staff. Cassandras abound, but with confidence, Volvo have extended the philosophy to their new Vara and Tuve plants (Tynan, 1984).

These new forms of working have not revolutionized the world car making giants, although they have been watching carefully. Peugeot, Fiat and Rover have made minor experiments. On the whole, the giants are not so interested, probably due to the sheer scale of operations and maybe apprehensions about quality. In any case, the concern for involvement and elimination of boredom on the shopfloor has now been overtaken by fears of robotics and redundancies.

A diagnosis is required first of all as to whether a programme for work design is potentially appropriate. Industrial engineers concentrate on production. It may mean that people are under-utilized and unchallenged at work, but they are surprisingly adaptive, and maybe new channels should be sought to syphon their abilities rather than tamper with their existing basic jobs. Technology is inexorably advancing, taking the chore out of work which has been man's dream since the invention of the wheelbarrow. Attempts to humanize inhuman jobs may be a temporary phase.

In the harsh world of reality, employers do not primarily employ people to aid their self-fulfilment. But leaving technological and work design initiatives to management, leaves the workforce exposed and vulnerable. Work redesign raises 'fundamental conflicts of interest inherent in the employment relationship' (Kelly, 1980). There may be mutual benefits to be had, but there are also costs. Indeed 'workers' needs and interests in job redesign are not confined to psychological aspects such as self-actualization or job satisfaction but . . . extend into economic issues such as labour intensity, job security and wage levels' (Kelly). Ironically, job redesign often eliminates labour, and hence jobs.

Any significant change programme must be adequately funded. Wage forms may have to be changed. Harmonization of manual and white-collar terms and conditions might be necessary.

Attitudes to work vary. What do employees want or expect? Job redesign may mean that certain managerial functions are absorbed into the new work methods. Will managers' and supervisors' adrenalin run high from a perceived threat to their authority? Job redesign implies restructuring traditional hierarchies. 'Complete self-government is a myth' (Barritt, 1975). Every worker and group still have a chief. Work groups cannot develop towards self-determination and autonomy without help. The role of supervisor may become crucial (White, 1983). Training needs come to the forefront. Job design can be a learning experience shared by managers, supervisors and workforce.

What are the attitudes of trade unions? Changes which do not involve unions in joint planning and implementation will hardly be appreciated. Certainly a 'high trust' relationship is called for. Ray Wild (Wild and Burchell, 1973) sums up the basic prerequisites:

1 a positive and cooperative attitude between workers and management
2 a desire for a participative approach
3 an absence of instrumental (monetary) attitudes to work
4 'appropriate' industrial relations procedures for negotiation and consultation.

Improvement in the quality of working life is an avowed aim of both the CBI, TUC and government (DE, 1982).

Achievement of these goals requires effort. Apart from attitudes, the logistics of moving from one state to another are formidable. A jungle of committees, working parties, and self-steering project groups can cloud the central issues. Autonomy cannot flourish without a controlling network. It may be tempting to take on too much at once. Most successful experiments have begun on a *small scale*.

QUALITY CIRCLES

Quality Circles are a Japanese import involving direct participation from the shopfloor in analysing and solving work related problems. They require skill and expertise on the part of participants and strong encouragement from top management which must be prepared to delegate some of its traditional powers. Successful Circles seem to work well in bridging the gap between management and workforce, in overcoming management's remoteness and in tapping the reservoir of workplace knowledge. Elsewhere they have failed due to lack of commitment. Insufficient research evidence has been forthcoming to make any categoric assessment. Such is the acclaim where they work well, that they certainly deserve serious consideration.

As is well known, the Japanese from the 1950s onwards, shook off their image as producers of low-priced, shoddy goods. They made a hard-nosed attack on quality built into the product rather than inspected for and amended afterwards. They aimed for zero defects. They wished to cut out the expensive warranty returns that so bedevil much of Western industrial output. They further believed that quality was everyone's business. All employees, not just managers or technical experts, were capable of improving quality and efficiency. 'Quality Circles' were born.

1962 is the year usually cited for the first Quality Circle in Japan. Cleverly, the Japanese had adopted mainly American ideas and adapted them to their own needs (Russell, 1983). But for some 15 years previously the idea had been quietly evolving, an idea nestling snugly into the Japanese ethos. Already the Japanese had developed a participative and consensus style of management. There was a strong emphasis on group effort and collective responsibility – 'Nemawashi'. High trust, mutual obligation, lifelong careers – 'welfare corporatism' (Dore, 1973) – set the tone. In Japan, 'the entire hierarchical strata ranging from the President down to the operator on the floor, or all employees, are subjected to Quality Circle education and training' (Hutchins, 1983); in Japanese – 'ringi seido' – bottom-up management. Mutuality of interests is the dominant theme.

Quality Circles form part of a management philosophy which goes far beyond the Circles themselves. If they are not consistent with the prevailing management style, the best plan is to forget them. The approach is Theory Y. Positive attitudes and commitment on the shopfloor are not bought by extra doses of 'hygiene', but by stimulating intrinsic rewards – for no extra payment. Employee involvement and responsibility bearing directly on product quality can also boost motivation, performance and job satisfaction. The development of Quality Circles is a 'carefully considered business strategy incorporating the principles of behavioural science with the need to improve product quality and utilise the capabilities of a more highly educated workforce' (IPM, 1982).

Voluntary participation is pivotal. Quality Circles give everyone the chance to join in, without putting pressure on them. It is the voluntary nature of Circles which sustain membership and momentum.

Quality Circles may be started on a pilot basis in say three or four different departments. Each Circle may comprise a group of four to ten volunteers who are normally working for the same supervisor.

Circles meet for an hour or so a week, away from the bustle and noise of factory floors or the shrill ring of telephones. Meetings are regular. Circles decide their own agenda. They must have a leader who is familiar with work-related problems and they must also have someone who will facilitate the operation of the group. The choice of the existing supervisor is usually favoured for the leadership role. To this extent, Quality Circles may strengthen the foreman's contribution.

Facilitators are Circle 'helpers' who must be keen and enthusiastic. Again, facilitators are volunteers. Their first job is to stimulate local interest in Quality Circles. Within the Circle they provide administrative support to the leader and foster group processes by providing feedback to the group. The facilitator is not a technical resource, more an enabler. He or she acts as a link between voluntary Circle members and other operatives, and may set up contacts with other groups.

A facilitator may also fulfil the role of coordinator (although sometimes this is separated). The coordinator's job is to administer the programme and to present the core principles of the approach.

In short, the problem chosen for analysis comes from the Circle itself. A problem is identified and solutions considered. The feasibility and costing of these solutions need to be worked out – *by the group*. Finally, the solution is presented to management – and if agreed – implemented and the results monitored. 'If Quality Circles are going to have a permanent value then they must monitor the measurement of changes which they have helped to introduce' (Collard, 1981).

Top management commitment is vital. Does management already encourage delegation? Is it willing to accept devolution? If the answers are negative, Circles will fail. The point is that management at *all levels* need to *listen, consider,* and *act upon* Quality Circle suggestions. Management may feel this undermines traditional prerogatives, for management itself does not participate in actual Circle meetings (IDS, 1985).

Rejection is common (Dale and Hayward, 1984) – by both management and unions. In a climate of recession and redundancy, moods for change are not opportune. Lack of cooperation and inadequate facilitation can kill anything. 'Probably around 50 per cent of companies who have attempted to introduce Circles in the UK have failed' (Hutchins, 1983).

Unfortunately, in much British experience there has been 'the prevalence of a low-trust principle in the management of the workplace . . . Such principles are unlikely to foster either a sense of shared interests or employee commitment to a firm. Indeed, they have played a significant part in the development of systems of industrial relations based on adversarial principles' (Bradley and Hill, 1983). The CBI (1981) in 'The Will to Win' encourages companies to follow successful examples, since the Japanese attribute 16 per cent of profits to Quality Circles.

The natural home of Quality Circles was in electronics, in which 'quality control circles' as they were originally called formed part of a quality control programme. Now we find them in banking, insurance and hospital services, in chemicals, clothing and the retail trade, from Wedgewood china to shipbuilding, from Rolls Royce to British Leyland. Ford, ICI, ICL, Marks & Spencer, Lockheed (in the USA), IBM, ITT, Philips, STC (in electronics) are in the forefront of current practice. Across the globe – Belgium, Brazil, Canada, Denmark, France, Korea, Malaysia, Mexico, Netherlands, Sweden, Taiwan, Thailand, UK, USA – Quality Circles have found a niche far from their native home (Robson, 1982).

Symptoms of job dissatisfaction

Withdrawal from work can take many forms – labour turnover, absenteeism, loss of interest, engagement in reveries, bad timekeeping, extended rest pauses, and possibly even accidents. Nearly all are symptomatic of malaise and reflect negative job attitudes on the part of employees.

In the literature on labour turnover, continual theoretical interest is shown in the relationship between labour turnover and job satisfaction and with absence from work. Quite a lot of research has found positive links between labour turnover and absenteeism. The assumption is frequently made that both measures are strongly correlated because of their common roots, i.e. they both tend to show a negative relationship with overall job satisfaction. But the inconsistency of the relationship has led some investigators to suggest that these forms of withdrawal from work are brought about by different underlying causes. More systematic research is needed to clarify the nature of these differences. Both absenteeism and labour turnover can be triggered by lack of satisfaction, but the actual response may vary according to circumstances. Labour turnover, or 'quit' behaviour, the actual act of leaving, is the response adopted when there are alternative job opportunities available, but absence may occur instead when there is difficulty in finding alternative employment. In any event, both labour turnover and absenteeism can be taken by personnel managers as indications of job dissatisfaction inviting investigation, and possibly remedial action.

LABOUR TURNOVER

Labour turnover refers to the severance of employees from employers, and ways of measuring it were discussed in detail in Chapter 2. Labour turnover is a costly, complex and interactive phenomenon. For years researchers have investigated its pathology and causation, particularly those factors which influence the decisions of individuals to leave their work permanently. Most explanations (Williams et al., 1979) suggest three broad causal areas from which stay or quit decisions originate: (i) general economic factors (e.g. prevailing levels of employment, alternative job opportunities, comparative pay); (ii) organizational factors (e.g. overall job satisfaction, size of work unit); (iii) personal or individual factors (e.g. age, length of service). Whilst research studies often indicate a clear pattern of causation in one particular situation, it does not mean to say that these findings are generalizable or predictive in other situations. Research evidence is in any case often conflicting.

On the *economic* front, a significant factor is the prevailing level of economic activity; the consequent demand for manpower opens up more or fewer alternative jobs. Generally, labour turnover decreases in recession and increases in boom conditions. Such an inverse relationship between turnover and the level of unemployment has been confirmed by numerous studies –

although this may not be universally true for all occupations nationally. If specific alternative job opportunities are at variance with the overall trends in employment, what matters most, where turnover is concerned, is the local labour market, or market for specific skills, rather than the overall national situation, since labour on the whole tends to be geographically immobile. What often happens where there is local competition for labour is that employers react by offering higher pay rates, thereby easing their own recruitment problems, but inducing turnover elsewhere. However, it seems that economic factors alone do not provide a complete explanation of labour turnover, because within the same economic setting and within the same occupation there may be differences in labour turnover rates. True, economic factors may account for the overall rise or fall in turnover rates over a period of years, but they are not enough to explain *persistent* differences between one organization and another, nor one department and another.

A host of *organizational* factors have been studied in relation to labour turnover. In a major review (Porter and Steers, 1973) employee satisfaction with the following are quoted as having a consistent and inverse relationship with turnover: overall job satisfaction, promotion prospects, pay levels, supervisory relations, work group size, peer group interaction, job content, autonomy and responsibility.

With regard to *personal* factors, the two variables which persistently have a strong negative relationship with turnover are age and length of service.

A number of other factors have been researched (Rothwell, 1980), but the evidence linking them with turnover is more equivocal – they include sex, marital status, number of dependants, educational and skill level, and various personality traits as measured by psychological tests.

Another major review of research (Pettman, 1979) identified two main factors affecting labour turnover: (i) the perceived desirability of movement on the part of the employees, and (ii) the perceived ease of movement.

Angela Bowey (1974) identified processes which lead to labour turnover as being either 'pull' or 'push' in nature. 'Pull' processes attract the employee from the organization, and 'push' processes help to propel him on his way.

ABSENTEEISM

The Tavistock researchers argued that absenteeism and turnover were alternatives to each other. Others (Gupta and Jenkins, 1982), suggest there is a progression of withdrawal tendencies from absenteeism to turnover. Both forms of behaviour may be related to dissatisfaction. Obviously it is less of a risk to go absent than to resign. Temporary respite may be all that is required, especially in times of recession.

In a progressive welfare state, one would expect sickness absence to fall. People are getting healthier. Although generally there is an inverse relationship between absence and the level of unemployment, recorded sickness absence overall has tended to rise over the long post-war period.

By 1982, 370m working days were lost every year through certificated

absence. Doctors were issuing 20m national insurance certificates per year
with about 3m covering illness which lasted less than a week (General
Household Survey, HMSO, 1982). Uncertificated absence was without
doubt even greater, but many firms did not record such absences. Sickness or
accident is by far the most common reason given for absence, and represents
five times the amount of time lost in the worst year of strikes.

Since 1982 employees have been able to self-certify absence of seven days
or less, and details of the procedures and legal requirements are explained in
Greville Janner's Chapter 12. The arrival of Statutory Sick Pay has stimulated
a new interest in procedures for recording employees' absence from work
(Howard, 1982).

One bugbear in the problem is the distinction between legitimate absence
(genuine sickness, holidays) and feigned, illegitimate absence (voluntary
withdrawal). 'Absenteeism' combines avoidable and unavoidable absence
rolled into one. Another bugbear is the confusing array of measurements of
absence, less standardized than measures of labour turnover, which make
comparison difficult.

Measures of absenteeism

One weakness in any discussion of the size and extent of absenteeism is the
lack of comprehensive statistics. There are over a dozen different ways of
measuring absenteeism (with variations). The most useful ones are given
below:

1   *Gross numbers of days lost*   One could simply tot up the total number of
days lost in a year by all employees, say 300, but this is not a meaningful
figure unless we relate it to the total number of people employed.

2   *Total absence or lost time rate*   This shows the percentage of available time
which has been lost and can be calculated for a work group, department or
whole organization:

$$\frac{\text{No. of working days lost}}{\text{Total no. of working days available}} \times 100 = \text{lost time rate}$$

The formula reveals a lost time percentage and is akin to the crude labour
turnover index. Of all the measures of absenteeism, the lost time rate is
the one most commonly used.

3   *Frequency or inception rate*   However, we might wish to have a finer
analysis which shows up the average number of episodes or periods of
absence for all employees. This is known as the frequency or inception
rate:

$$\frac{\text{No. of particular episodes of absence in a year}}{\text{Average no. of employees during the year}} \times 100 = \text{frequency rate}$$

The formula relates the number of episodes to the average population at risk. It tells us the number of spells of absence, but not how long they were. It tells us the average propensity with which people took time off, but some periods of absence may have been longer than others (therefore more severe), and so we might wish to look at the duration of absences.

4 *Severity and duration rate*

$$\frac{\text{Total no. of days lost per year}}{\text{Average number of employees during the year}} \times 100 = \text{severity rate}$$

This formula relates the total length of absences to the average population at risk. It shows the average length of time lost per employee.

5 *Point prevalence rate*

$$\frac{\text{No. of persons absent on a given day}}{\text{No. of people employed on that day}} \times 100 = \text{point prevalence rate}$$

This formula is a variation of a frequency rate. We may wish to compare the propensity for people to go absent on a given day (e.g. on a Monday or after a Bank Holiday) and find that it may be higher than on other days.

6 *Individual measures*   The measures described above are helpful, but only give us averages and allow us to look at trends. For the personnel manager who may be concerned at the absence record of an individual employee, with a view to investigating the problem or taking disciplinary action, a more specific measure is needed, and over a period either shorter or longer than a standard year. Three individual measures may be useful:

(a)   The average number of days absent per month.
     Calculated by dividing the total number of days of absence for each employee by the number of months each person had been employed, e.g. if a person had been employed for 18 months and during that time had been absent for a total of 14 days, his or her average monthly absence rate would be $\frac{14}{18}=0.78$ days.

(b)   The average number of episodes of absence per month (individual frequency).
     Calculated by dividing the total number of episodes of absence for each employee by the number of months each person had been employed, e.g. if a person had been employed for 22 months and during that time had been absent on 6 separate occasions, his or her average number of episodes of absence would be $\frac{6}{22}=0.27$ episodes per month.

(c) The average length of episodes of absence in days (individual duration).
Calculated by dividing for each person the total number of days of absence by the number of episodes of absence, e.g. if a person had been absent for 20 days and had been away from work on 2 different occasions, the average length of his or her episodes of absence would be $\frac{20}{2} = 10$ days.

Reasons for absenteeism

Mostly, organizational factors are to blame, and these we can conveniently divide into those which are intrinsic aspects of the job (the work itself) and those which are extrinsic (or hygiene factors leading to dissatisfaction). Additionally, there may be a number of individual factors which have nothing to do with either.

Intrinsic aspects of the job:
Boredom with repetitive work
Frustration of abilities
Poorly defined responsibilities (or lack of them).

Extrinsic aspects of the job:
Dissatisfaction with supervision
Badly organized work flow
Dissatisfaction with pay (either too high or too low)
The sick pay scheme is too good
Poor working conditions
Inconvenient working hours
Poor morale
Lack of integration in the work team
Employee response to grievances – as a sanction
Managerial attitudes (tolerances) of absenteeism

Individual aspects:
Journey to work
Domestic circumstances
Time off to look for another job and attend interviews
Moonlighting

Valencies operating both outside and inside the work situation (after Vroom) akin to Bowey's pull–push analysis of labour turnover may mean that the motivation to go absent may well be two-sided. Morale is strongly asserted to be a key factor affecting absenteeism (with of course a few conflicting refutations). High absenteeism begets high absenteeism.

Sometimes management may create an incentive value of 'absenteeism tolerance', especially in times of high labour turnover and recruitment difficulties. It helps to make a job more attractive, especially if wages are tied. However, when economic conditions change, or unemployment rises, previous levels of absenteeism may persist, since informal absenteeism norms have developed and dissatisfied workers, unable to find alternative jobs, are more readily influenced by the absenteeism norm so long as it is consistent with tenure and income.

In the present economic climate, firms are realizing that absenteeism is a major contributor to costs. High absence levels mean excessive overheads. Short-term absences are likely to be more disruptive and costly than long-term sickness absences. Some costs are fixed costs, such as administration needed for wage adjustments, organizing replacements and redeploying staff, and maybe the levels of stocks held, e.g. of supplies and components in a manufacturing firm to cover contingencies. More variable costs are resultant fluctuations in overtime and perhaps the maintenance of unnecessary high manning levels setting up 'slack' in the system to compensate for an absence norm, the redeployment of labour which is usually less efficient, and maybe the loss of productivity, profitability, and goodwill.

The aim of company policy should be to minimize the disruption caused by absenteeism and seek to alleviate it. Treating employees fairly and compassionately is an obvious fundamental ethic. Overall, management should ensure good, safe, working conditions; renew working systems to see if small working groups are more appropriate; review job design, training, development, communications, and welfare provisions; review supervisory training; establish disciplinary procedures; introduce flexible working hours if possible, and special leave to cover emergencies; and establish absence notification procedures. A jointly determined absence policy is likely to be more effective. Guidelines are shown in the ACAS advisory booklet (No. 5, *Absenteeism* 1981).

Suitable administration and monitoring systems are a matter for the individual firm (Fell, 1983). Individual absence records should give the cause, length and date of absence. If the subsequent analysis of absence records identifies above average absence rates, and if these factors are under management control, some action may be possible. The cost of corrective actions should never outweigh the benefits of increased attendance.

Methods of absence control range from the carrot of attendance bonuses to the stick of disciplinary action. Above all, management's concern must be blatant and visible. Management should first make it clear that records are being kept and that unscheduled absence will not go unnoticed, and will need to be explained. Secondly, management should collate and disseminate summaries of absenteeism figures, maybe with the rider that in certain areas better performance will be expected.

Some companies make additional payments (the carrot) on top of normal pay in order to encourage good attendance. These may work. But amongst a number of problems, in the long term, payment may be taken as part of normal remuneration.

Disciplinary action requires written warnings within defined time limits, and the requirement that individuals concerned be given time to make representation. A referral may be made to the company medical officer, or to the employee's own doctor, as part of the usual procedure for dealing with irregular attenders.

Dealing effectively with absence offenders calls for continuous and coordinated efforts by personnel, line managers and first-line supervisors. Employees and their representatives will want to see managers showing understanding to those who genuinely need to be absent, and a firm hand against those who abuse the system. Fair and consistent policies coupled with disciplinary procedures, good monitoring and constant vigilance are the normally prescribed managerial actions. But to the extent that absenteeism springs from job dissatisfaction, root causes must be identified and appropriate prophylactic measures taken. (See the section on Lateness and Absence in Chapter 10.)

Summary

Job satisfaction is a feeling on the part of an individual that inner intrinsic needs are met at work. Jobs may be deliberately designed to this end. The theoretical bases of job redesign stem from Herzberg's analysis of satisfying and dissatisfying features of work, from expectancy theory, and socio-technical systems which emphasize the interdependence of task, technology and social relationships. Ergonomics and ideas about worker participation are also relevant. The core dimensions which a job should possess are feedback, autonomy, task identity and variety. These may be applied to individual or group jobs. Autonomous working groups have been developed in various places, especially Scandinavia. The success of these experiments must be measured from two points of view – those of employees and employers. Benefits must be weighed against costs. Much of the evidence is equivocal – and rarely in these experiments have there been control groups against which to make comparison. However, there is a distinct move away from the design of jobs on strict economic or engineering criteria. Amongst contemporary attempts to harness the energies and motivation of work-people, Quality Circles (from Japan) are in vogue.

Voluntary labour turnover is a form of withdrawal from work and is usually symptomatic of some underlying dissatisfaction. Quit decisions are usually due to economic, organizational or personal reasons. Both pull and push influences operate in the process. Decisions to stay away are less adventurous than decisions to quit. High absenteeism reflects low morale. Measures of absenteeism are numerous and lack standardization. Patterns of absenteeism vary geographically and seasonally, and according to age and skill level. Management must decide its own tolerances of absenteeism and set up monitoring and control procedures.

Discussion questions

1 Consider what you think to be the main reasons why people work, and list them in order of priority.
2 If managers want to stimulate the motivation of their employees, how do you think they should go about it?
3 Will paying people more money make them work harder?
4 Has Herzberg oversimplified things?
5 Do you think that ideas and theories about motivation are concealed ways to manipulate the workforce?
6 What personal needs do you yourself hope to satisfy from work? How do you compensate for those needs which cannot be satisfied in your job?
7 How would you redesign your own job?
8 How would you redesign your boss's job?
9 What factors, if any, would you *exclude* from a job redesign programme?
10 Can technology and people ever be perfectly compatible?
11 Would you prefer your private life or your business life to be enriched?
12 What should be the role of personnel managers in job redesign programmes?
13 If you are at this moment studying personnel management in a class with others with a tutor in preparation for an examination (i.e. an assessment of quality), would it be possible to turn the group into a Quality Circle? If so, how? If not, why not?
14 Categorize the advantages and disadvantages which may accrue from Quality Circles.
15 Should labour turnover be discouraged?
16 What are the main organizational problems which result from higher than average or rising labour turnover?
17 How would you determine what were normative levels of absenteeism in your own organization?
18 Are there any advantages to be claimed for absenteeism?
19 Why does management tolerance of certain levels of absenteeism seem to exist?
20 What disciplinary and monitoring procedures would you set up to control absenteeism?

References

ACAS (1981), *Absenteeism*, Advisory Booklet No. 5.
AGNEW, B. (1983), 'Quality Circles: an expression of change at the grass roots', *Industrial and Commercial Training*, March.
BAILEY, J. (1983), 'New Technology and its influence on job design', *Industrial and Commercial Training*, April.

BARRITT, R. R. (1975), 'New forms of work organisation', Work Research Unit, Occasional Paper No. 3.

BOWEY, A. (1974), *A Guide to Manpower Planning*, Macmillan, London.

BRADLEY, K. and HILL, S. (1983), 'After Japan: the Quality Circles transplant and productive efficiency', *British Journal of Industrial Relations*, Vol. XXI, Nov. 1983, No. 3.

CAMERON, S. (1973), 'Job Satisfaction: the concept and its measurement', Work Research Unit, Occasional Paper, No. 4.

CARBY, K. (1976), *Job Redesign in Practice*, Institute of Personnel Management, London.

CHILD, J. (1984), *Organisation: a Guide to Problems and Practices*, 2nd edn, Harper and Row, London.

COLLARD, R. (1981), 'The Quality Circle in context', *Personnel Management*, Vol. 13, No. 9.

CONFEDERATION OF BRITISH INDUSTRY (1981), *The Will to Win*, CBI.

COOPER, C. (1974), *Job Design and Job Motivation*, Institute of Personnel Management, London.

COTGROVE, S., DUNHAM, J. and VAMPLESS, C. (1971), *The British Nylon Spinners*, Allen and Unwin, London.

DALE, B. G. and HAYWARD, S. G. (1984), 'A Study of Quality Circles failures', University of Manchester Institute of Science and Technology, Manchester.

DEPARTMENT OF EMPLOYMENT (1982), 'Meeting the challenge of change', Work Research Unit.

DORE, R. P. (1973), *British Factory – Japanese Factory*, Allen and Unwin, London.

ELLIOTT, J. (1976), 'Qualified success for Volvo assembly', *Financial Times*, Nov. 23, 1976.

EMERY, F. and THORSUND, E. (1976), 'Democracy at Work: the Report of the Norwegian Industrial Democracy Program', Martinus Nijhoff Social Services Division, Leiden.

FELL, A. (1983), 'Putting a price on lost time', *Personnel Management*, April.

FLANDERS, A. (1964), *The Fawley Productivity Agreements*, Faber, London.

GUEST, D., WILLIAMS, R. and DELVE, P. (1978), 'Job design and the psychology of boredom', Work Research Unit, Occasional Paper No. 13.

GUPTA, N. and JENKINS, G. D. (1982), 'Absenteeism and turnover: is there a progression?', *Journal of Management Studies*, 19, 41.

GYLLENHAMMAR, P. P. (1977), *People at Work*, Addison-Wesley, Reading, Mass.

HACKMAN, J. R. and LAWLER, E. E. (1971), 'Employer reactions to job characteristics', *Journal of Applied Psychology*, 5, 3.

HACKMAN, J. R. and OLDHAM, G. R. (1980), *Work Redesign*, Addison-Wesley, Reading, Mass.

HERZBERG, F. (1968), *Work and the Nature of Man*, Staples Press, London.

HERZBERG, F., MAUSNER, C., PETERSON, P. O. and CAPWELL, D. F. (1957), *Job Attitudes: Review of Research and Opinion*, Psychological Services of Pittsburgh, Pittsburgh.

HERZBERG, F., MAUSNER, C. and SNYDERMAN, B. (1959), *The Motivation to Work*, Wiley, New York.

HOWARD, G. (1982), *A Guide to Self-Certification*, The Industrial Society, London.

HUTCHINS, D. (1983), 'Quality Circles in context', *Industrial and Commercial Training*, March.

INCOMES DATA SERVICES (1985), *Quality Circles*, Study 352, December.

INSTITUTE OF PERSONNEL MANAGEMENT (1982), *Practical Participation and Involvement III*, 'The individual and the job', IPM, London.

KARLSSON, U. (1978), 'Evaluation of alternative to the traditional assembly line at the body shop of Saab-Scania in Trollhättan, Sweden', Chalmers Institute of Technology, Sweden.

KELLY, J. (1980), 'The Costs of Job Redesign: a Preliminary Analysis', *Industrial Relations Journal*, 11, 3.

LAWLER, E. E. (1971), *Pay and Organizational Effectiveness*, McGraw-Hill, New York.

LAWLER, E. E. and PORTER, L. W. (1967), 'The effect of performance on job satisfaction', *Industrial Relations*, 7.

MASLOW, A. H. (1968), *Towards a Psychology of Being*, 2nd edn, Van Nostrand, Princeton, NJ.

McGREGOR, D. (1960), *The Human Side of Enterprise*, McGraw-Hill, New York.

NORSTEDT, J. P. and ANGUREN, S. (1973), 'Saab-Scania Report', Svenska Arbetsgivareföreningen, Stockholm.

PETTMAN, B. O. (1979), *Some Factors Influencing Labour Turnover; a Review of some Research*, Gower, London.

PORTER, L. W. and STEERS, R. M. (1973), *Labour Turnover and Retention*, Gower, London.

RICE, A. K., HILL, J. M. M. and TRIST, E. L. (1950), 'The representation of labour turnover as a social process', *Human Relations*, **3**.

ROBSON, M. (1982), *Quality Circles – a Practical Guide*, Gower, London.

ROSE, M. (1978), *Industrial Behaviour: Theoretical Development since Taylor*, Penguin, London.

ROTHWELL, S. (1980), *Labour Turnover*, Henley Centre for Employment Policy Studies, Gower, London.

RUSSELL, S. (1983), 'Quality Circles in perspective', Department of the Environment: Work Research Unit, Occasional Paper No. 24, Feb. 1983.

SCHEIN, E. (1980), *Organizational Psychology*, 3rd edn, Prentice Hall, Englewood Cliffs, NJ.

TAYLOR, F. W. (1911, 1947), *Scientific Management*, Harper and Row, New York.

TRADES UNION CONGRESS (1981), *Quality Circles*, TUC.

TRIST, E. L. and BAMFORTH, K. W. (1951), 'Some social and psychological consequences of the longwall method of coal-getting', *Human Relations*, **4**.

TYNAN, O. (1984), Volvo revisited', Information System Abstracts No. 68, Department of the Environment: Work Research Unit.

VROOM, V. H. (1964), *Work and Motivation*, Wiley, Chichester.

VROOM, V. H. (1968), 'Industrial social psychology', in Lindzey, G. and Aronson, C. (eds) *The Handbook of Social Psychology*, Vol. 5, 2nd edn, Addison-Wesley, London.

WHITE, G. (1983), 'Redesign of work organisation – its impact on supervisors', Work Research Unit, Occasional Paper No. 26.

WILD, R. and BIRCHELL, D. (1973). 'Means and ends in job restructuring', *Personnel Review*, Vol. 2, No. 4.

WILLIAMS, A. P. O., LIVY, B. L., SILVERSTONE, R. and ADAMS, P. (1979), 'Factors associated with labour turnover among ancilliary staff workers in two London hospitals, *Journal of Occupational Psychology*, **52**.

CHAPTER 20

The physical working environment: ergonomics, accidents and safety

by Bryan Livy

Ergonomics

Planners and designers who seek to structure man's environment and whose job may be to streamline work situations are constrained by the competing claims of economics, engineering, aesthetics, and ergonomics. Ergonomics has been with us for over half a century. Few people are fully aware of its objectives and methods; many may never have heard of it.

Ergonomics (the British term), human factors engineering (the American term), are concerned with ways of designing machines, operations and working environments so that they match human capacities and limitations. Such matters are the prerogative of no one discipline; ergonomics is a multi-disciplinary affair.

Tiffin and McCormick (1968) have defined its objectives as the search for an 'optimal combination of man, method and machine'. Its aims are to improve human comfort and safety, the quality and quantity of output, whilst simultaneously reducing fatigue, scrap, wastage and time taken.

The accredited father of ergonomics, K. F. H. Murrell, propagated his ideas in the late 1940s. Although it is true that the impetus in ideation and research came from the war effort, the origins of ergonomics study can be traced back earlier than this. In Britain, in 1915 The Health and Munition Workers' Committee, and in 1917 the Industrial Fatigue Research Board (an offshoot of the Medical Research Council) brought together for the first time doctors, engineers, and social scientists, with the prime task of investigating health, productivity and efficiency at work. Later, and more recently, innovations have been made in various branches of the Armed Services and in industry.

From advances in military technology in bringing together the practical engineering approach with the academic physiological/psychological approach in the design of tanks, guns, and aircraft, the simple but inescapable conclusion to be drawn is that whilst men *can* operate poorly designed equipment in bad working environments, such a sub-optimal arrangement is not conducive to a maximization of performance or job satisfaction. The implications are obvious. In the factory, office or home, physical or perceptual operations which have to be executed under bad working conditions can be a major cause of accidents, frustration and contempt for the designers.

Wherever man interacts with his physical environment there is scope for maladjustment. This can be minimized if the software – the human element – is not obliged to mould itself like plasticine around the hardware. We would not want the typist at her desk to inherit bad posture from sitting on an elegant but inappropriate stool, nor the housewife to cover unnecessary mileage in her kitchen which does not conform to any logical, sequential layout. We would not want the driver at the wheel of his car to confuse the flashers with the wipers, squint to see the dials, or grope for the pedals. Everyday examples are well known.

The interaction between man, his workspace and environment can be represented as a system. The concentric circles in Fig. 20.1 denote the integuments which make up the whole complex, based on Chapanis' (1965) model, who regards this system as a 'group of components, some of which are pieces of equipment – designed to work together for some common purpose'. The best fit between human and working environment requires an analysis of each of several levels of interaction:

1 *The people*: characteristics of the relevant populations. Design should cater for at least 90 per cent of expected users.
2 *The task*: what is the nature of the operation? What is required of the operator?

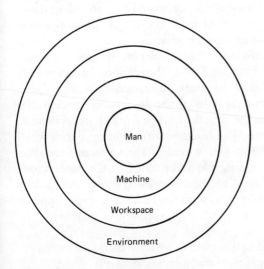

Fig. 20.1 *Integuments of the complex*

3   *Work station*: in what ways do displays provide sensory inputs to the operator? Are they easily interpreted? Are they the best ways? What do controls call for from the operator in the form of psychomotor outputs? Are controls easily and accurately operated? Is there compatibility (in style and sequence) between displays and controls?

4   *The workspace*: what is the effect of chairs/desks/benches on position, posture and reach? What is the interaction with other pieces of equipment? What is the influence of adjacent machines, structures and materials?

5   *The wider environment*: what is the influence of physical conditions (noise, hazards, pollution, etc.)? What about socio-psychological factors (the work team, styles of supervision, pay systems, shift work, welfare, the culture and traditions)?

Ergonomics means starting with the man or woman as an integral part of the system and not just an adjunct to it. It derives its precepts from other established disciplines, from the biological sciences of anatomy, physiology, and anthropometrics (body measurements), from the physical sciences, particularly engineering, and from the social sciences, psychology and anthropology. Primarily it derives from engineering and occupational psychology – hence 'human factors engineering'.

Logistically, man is at the centre. A caveat, however, is called for. We are not concerned with any man, nor the average man, but with the expected user population. Design for 'standard man' can be misleading. Policemen's boots are made in a range of sizes related to the propensity of their users to have big feet. A celebrated gaffe revealed by researchers at Cranfield Institute of Technology into the type of people required to operate a commonly available range of capstan lathes found that the man most suited to operate them with any degree of functional efficiency would be a four foot dwarf with a twelve foot armspan. 'Cranfield man' became an anthropological landmark in the development of ergonomic science.

Design must be related to man's capacities, abilities and attitudes. Information must be obtained about the expected user. The ergonomist can provide the designer with a range of data on human dimensions, power, speed, efficiency and sociological criteria. His multi-disciplinary background enables him to communicate in a technical language from an understanding of the engineer's design problems. The designer can then better decide which functions to allocate to the hardware, which to the software, and how optimally to arrange them. The principle is illustrated by Chapanis' (1965) model of a man–machine system. A modified version is shown in Fig. 20.2.

Failure to analyse and deal adequately with the allocation of functions can lead to error and confusion. Errors which most commonly recur are:

1   Substitution errors (confusing one control with another).
2   Adjustment errors (operating too slowly or too quickly).
3   Forgetting errors (failing to check, etc.).

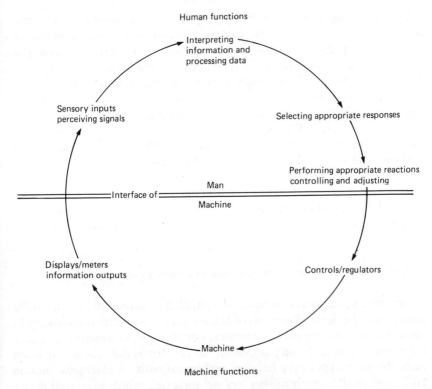

Fig. 20.2 *Man/machine system*

4 Unintentional activation (accidental operation).
5 Perceptual errors (misinterpreting information or not being able to assimilate it all at once).
6 Inability to reach.

Human error may cost lives, time and money. So too it may be argued does machine error. Why then concentrate on human error when machine error itself may be costly and dangerous? Apart from ethical reasons, although machine error tends to peak at a higher degree of seriousness, human error is more susceptible over a wide range of activities and its compound effects may be no less. It is clearly illogical to favour either dimension. In any case, costs in terms of error of any sort are increasing almost logarithmically with growth in the capacity of technology. Consequences of error under automated systems are usually greater and costlier than under conventional operations. Automation has simplified some jobs, but conversely has made others more difficult. Physical demands may be less, but more rapid and accurate perceptual abilities, more precise psychomotor skills and a considerable amount of learning may be called for. People are being used less as sources of energy and more as instruments of judgement and decision.

Although people are surprisingly adaptive in compensating for ineffi-
ciencies in equipment design, the price of compromise is that in moments of
stress or anxiety, the learned habits may break down. A general rule would be
never to make an operator perform an unnatural movement. More specifically, conformity should be sought between mechanical manipulations and
'universal expectancies', or as they are sometimes called 'population
stereotypes'. There are sets of behaviour patterns which are normative.
People are creatures of habit. They expect things to happen from certain
actions and react automatically to certain signals. When controls and displays
conform with universal expectations, we find that:

1   Reaction time (and therefore decision time) is shorter.
2   The first control movement an operator makes is likely to be correct.
3   The operator can use the control faster and make adjustments with finer
    precision.
4   Learning time is reduced.
5   Lower degrees of error are recorded in times of panic.

Controversy exists as to whether the population stereotypes are culturally
determined (i.e. learned patterns of behaviour) or instinctive (unlearned). In
some cases the answer may be obvious. For example, in America or Greece
light switches are in the up position for 'on'. In Britain down is 'on'. In other
cases the stereotypes may have an anatomical basis. A clockwise motion
fairly universally anticipates an 'on' or 'increase', which may well derive
from its being easier to twist the right wrist clockwise from the neutral rest
position than vice versa. The importance of the debate between learned and
unlearned stereotypes poses problems to the extent to which they may be in
conflict with each other. In a stress situation an individual will tend to act
according to natural inclination, possibly in contradiction to the appropriate
'correct' response. Some simple rules commonly applied in industrial settings can help. In instrumentation, speed and accuracy are usually necessary
in transmitting information. Analogue indicators (Fig. 20.3) can give quick
check readings and indicate clearly the rate and direction of change. They can
of course be read accurately but are more prone to erroneous readings than
digital indicators (Fig. 20.4) which conversely convey no sense of proportional representation. Scales of measurement should conform to universal
expectancies or 'motion stereotypes' in perception. The pointers in Fig. 20.5,
which may be mounted on circular, vertical or horizontal scales, suggest
increases according to the direction of the arrows. Negative or reducing
movements are suggested by reverse arrows. Simplicity is the keynote.
Multi-pointer dials (Fig. 20.6) should be avoided. Misreading of multi-
pointer altimeters for example has been the cause of too many aviation
accidents.
Comprehension can be enhanced by differences in size, shape and the use of
colour. The clarity of the London Underground map, for instance, is due
very much to colour-coding, representational fixed sequence tracking, a few

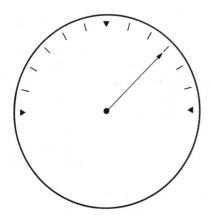

Fig. 20.3   *Analogue indicator*

Fig. 20.4   *Digital indicator*

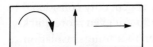

Fig. 20.5   *Pointers*

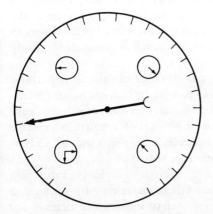

Fig. 20.6   *Multi-pointer dials*

standardized symbols (e.g. BR interchanges) and universal expectations (e.g. north at the top).

Controls, likewise, should be unambiguous. If the operation follows a fixed sequence, controls should be laid out in corresponding order (e.g. machine starting systems). If the sequence is not fixed, controls should be grouped according to their functions (e.g. church organ consoles and radio broadcasting consoles).

The cycle of perceiving, interpreting and controlling is facilitated by sensible groupings, easily readable instruments and accessibility. The usual methods of obtaining information about the interaction of humans with other elements are by film analysis, eye movement recordings, observation, interviews, and questionnaires. Where a counterpart situation exists, it can be used as a take-off. Where not, judgements must be inferred from task and skills analyses. 'Links' are looked for in the connections between component variables to identify, for example, degrees of visual acuity or manual dexterity required. Planning or work layouts can be further facilitated by the use of graphic models, laboratory simulations and mock-ups.

So much for the interface. One needs to look beyond the human/machine module to the surrounding workface and the wider physical and social environment. The physical influences are the easier to quantify. It is well known that noise, vibration, humidity, lighting and temperature can each adversely affect performance. Although there is no systematic evidence which proves that noise universally impairs performance, there is evidence to suggest that it does so on jobs which are not intrinsically satisfying. Moreover, continuous exposure to noise levels above 80 to 90 decibels, depending upon differences between individuals, is generally considered to contribute to hearing loss, and impact noise can induce it even more quickly. Noise control – through machine design, rubber mountings, isolation of noise sources, acoustical treatment, etc. – is clearly desirable.

The effects of vibration depend upon its frequency and intensity. It certainly causes discomfort, but more seriously can inflict physiological damage due to the different resonant frequencies of various organs of the body. Basically vibration is an engineering design problem, but the degree to which it is transmitted to the body can be accentuated or attenuated by body posture (e.g. standing or sitting).

Humidity and temperature outside a critical range can also have harmful effects. The influence of environmental factors on the heat-exchange processes of the body are highly complicated. Subjective feelings of comfort vary according to an individual's age, clothing and level of activity. Acceptable temperatures for work seem to range between 10° Celsius and 26° Celsius according to whether the work is strenuous or sedentary.

Atmospheric control should need no additional emphasis. Protecting people from the impurities which surround them by tackling the problem at source, by providing protective clothing, safety devices, ventilation and exhaust removal systems and so on have the forceful backing of a legal framework.

Illumination, another variable, is one for which precise quantification of its effects on worker behaviour is elusive. International standards vary. In Britain, the intensity of most artificial lighting is about 200 lumen/ft^2 (compared to daylight at about 1000 lumen/ft^2), but it is known that over a certain illumination level further lighting is wasted. Generally speaking, the lighting required for maximum task performance depends on the size of the object being worked on, contrasts in the immediate vicinity, the reflectivity of the surround, glare ratings and the time allowed for seeing. Various formulae incorporating these factors are available for the design of lighting systems, and industrial designers will already be acquainted with them. Similarly, they will be familiar with the use of coloured lights to enhance contrasts, or coloured paints which indicate danger areas in workshops and to give such aesthetic effects as may be considered desirable (height, warmth, width).

Ergonomics, from its theoretical concepts and from empirical data has potential for predicting performance in novel situations. This claim is particularly true at the centre of the system where ergonomics offers tools for both diagnosis and prognosis. However, the claim is not so valid at the periphery of the system. This is not to say that compatibility between human characteristics and the wider environment is an unattainable criterion, rather that scope for the application of ergonomics *per se* is limited and its utility diminishes as we move away from the nucleus into more nebulous areas. Ergonomics may eventually be extended to provide a basis for fitting the technical systems at work to the social organization, but that is a distant goal, for the social environment is much more intractable. Yet even in the outer integuments of the system we have adopted as a ground plan for our discussion, the tentacles of ergonomics can be felt. Social relationships can be confounded by bad configuration of work stations. Conversations with one's fellow men may be impossible. Not only may the verbal transmission of orders and instructions be impeded, but space and sound may also inhibit man's natural social inclinations, thus adding further to feelings of alienation. Similarly, replanning office layouts can evoke conflicts between the desire of management for optimal use of space, efficient communications and work flow, and that of employees for privacy, small group identification, and a 'personalized' setting.

Technical progress and social progress do not necessarily move in harmony. Inevitably there must be some trade-off in the design of any system. Losses in one direction may have to be off-set against gains in another. Perfection on all counts is probably impossible. However, the functions which people are required to perform at work should aim at providing opportunities for intrinsic satisfaction and should be compatible with cultural values and human abilities and attitudes as far as possible.

Ergonomics itself tends to lay stress on performance, comfort and safety. It could also be criticized for its tendency to regard a human being as a black box, as an automaton. It offers a useful, albeit partial, contribution to the study of socio-technical systems and the mutual interaction of man with the physical working environment. 'Productivity, efficiency, superiority and other systems criteria depend not on the man alone nor on the machine alone, but on both and also the effectiveness of their interaction' (Singleton, 1978).

Accidents and safety

A vast number of studies have been undertaken in the area of accident research and most are based either on the personal, individual causes of accidents or on environmental factors. Surprisingly, many researchers have focused on one particular factor and neglected the fact that many accidents clearly have multiple causation. Several researchers have attempted to provide classifications of accident activators, whether mechanical, physical or psychological. Research literature abounds with accident theories, including (i) *pure chance* (all people exposed to the same risk have equal liability to accidents); (ii) *accident-proneness* (accidents are related to innate personal characteristics and some people are more liable to accidents than others), and (contrarily); (iii) *biased liability* (accident liability may be reduced by previous mishaps); (iv) *adjustment to stress* (people not adjusted to work stresses will have higher accident rates. Many accidents are due to inadequate or incorrect motor responses in conditions of emotional stress); (v) *reverie and alienation* (a lack of job involvement will reduce alertness and increase accident rates); (vi) *unconscious motivation* (Freudian self-destructive unconscious wishes underlying some accidents can cause self-punitive acts); (vii) *withdrawal* (accidents provide a socially acceptable reason for avoiding work. Indeed Tavistock studies (Hill and Trist, 1953) in the iron and steel industries showed a positive correlation between accidents and absenteeism – people with the highest accident rate tended to be those prone to other kinds of absenteeism); (viii) *industrial conflict* (the assertion of a positive correlation between accidents and absenteeism can be placed in a broader context – whereas absenteeism and accidents are unorganized manifestations of industrial conflict, organized collective manifestations of conflict such as strikes and industrial disputes may also be in some way related to the root problem. Studies by both Revans (1956) and Beaumont (1979a, b) have positively related industrial accident rates to strikes, and the latter study has also shown that high-accident persons are also the high discipline offenders); (ix) *anxiety* (low skill and training levels, poor supervision, and unsafe working practices).

In a major review of accident research (Hale and Hale, 1972), most accidents seemed to be due to personal or individual factors. But clearly accidents do not happen in isolation; they are triggered by a sequential series of events, and occur within the context of some sort of environment. Apart from the 'individual' theories listed above, there are some broader approaches.

A *domino theory of accidents* suggests that an accident is made up of five independent stages: environment, individual fault, unsafe act, accident, injury. A *situational theory* suggests that accidents are caused by the breakdown of normal working systems.

Most of our knowledge on accident causation still centres on the personal and physical characteristics of 'accident causes' and 'injury sufferers'. Positive correlations with accident rates have been found to exist in the following individual areas:

1 *Age* accident rates peak among young workers (due to inexperience or irresponsibility) and older workers (with a slowing of physical and mental capacities);

2 *Experience* accident rates are higher in the first 3–5 months of employment; after this initial 'breaking-in', age has a greater influence on accident rates;

3 *Health and physical characteristics* – a person's state of health and physical dimensions play a part in some accidents, but overall generalization is difficult since these influences tend to be job-specific.

Contradictory evidence is available regarding positive correlations between the accident rates and sex, fatigue, alcohol, intelligence. Many studies would suggest, however, that these factors do in some cases have an influence.

The convenient theory that certain members of the workforce are accident-prone was – for many years – accepted as the major explanation of industrial, and other, forms of accident. The theory exploded after the classic Greenwood study (1919) of munition workers. It brought with it the assumption that by removing certain people from a work group, the relative frequency of accidents within the group would be reduced. However, when put to the test, it has often been found that while accident-proneness does exist, it may be a significant factor in only a minority of cases. Renewed interest has now been awakened in the concept (Boyle, 1980; McKenna, 1983), and the debate continues to revolve around statistical niceties.

The study of accidents over the last 30 years suggests that certain personality and emotional variables (e.g. aggression, neuroticism and extroversion), age and poor group relations may result in higher accident rates. Nevertheless, no one theory and no single set of factors can explain the causes of all industrial accidents, which are many and varied. It seems evident that an accident may not be the result of a single factor but of a number of interrelated contributory causes. Many of these causal factors are 'job-specific' – for example, physical dimensions are likely to play a part in some accidents because tools amd machinery often place definite limits on the sort of person who can operate them successfully. A conventional definition of an accident is an 'unexpected happening', a disruptive force revealing a weakness in the devised system, but this convenient definition refers to 'situational theory' and does not of itself provide sufficient analysis. Also, accidents are often described in terms of their *severity*, but this provides no clue as to their *causation*. An accident is the result of a preceding malfunction in the system. 'Accidents are defined by their outcomes rather than their antecedent behaviour' (Shaoul, 1976); they are 'the result of an action, usually the *unexpected* result' (Kay, 1978). The causation of accidents is often hidden. Measures to prevent accidents must probe far deeper than superficial appearances. For example, if X drops a brick on Y, injuring Y, Y has an accident. But it was the behaviour of X which incurred it.

ACCIDENTS IN THE UNITED KINGDOM

According to the Pearson Commission (Report of the Royal Commission on Civil Liability, 1978) every year in the United Kingdom about 3 050 000 people are injured and of these about 720 000 (23.6 per cent) occur at work. In 1982, the Health and Safety Commission recorded 624 deaths within its remit. Currently figures issued by the Department of Employment show that the number of fatal accidents occurring at work averages something between 500–600 per year and there are something like over 300 000 other forms of reportable accident, with clear and obvious differences between occupations, although the overall trend is downwards. Interestingly, when comparing the number of days lost through industrial accidents (including diseases) and those lost through industrial disputes, the ratio over recent years has been something like 2:1.

Accident trends have to be judged against the backdrop of changes in industrial structure. Generally, capital has been substituted for labour, service industry has grown while manual work has declined, and more women have entered the labour market. Whilst on the face of it this should be a recipe for fewer accidents, post-war accident rates show differently. Certainly from the late 1950s the overall accident figures rose alarmingly, with a particularly sharp jump from 1963 to 1964, reaching an all-time high in 1969. After 1969 there was an unsteady decline but not to the depths of the 1950s. The trend of reported fatal accidents is more encouraging with a slow fall from the 1950s levels, peaking in 1969, with a steady decline from 1973 until the 1980s.

Intuitively it is not difficult to relate the level of industrial activity to accident rates (if not fatalities; the boom of the 1960s bringing a boom in accidents, the decline of the 1970s bringing a decline in accidents).

The cost of industrial accidents is difficult to quantify because of the problem of identifying all the costs involved and insufficient statistics. Particularly contentious are the costs sustained by the individuals involved and their families with regard to misery and mental anguish, but clearly in aggregate there are gigantic costs to employers, to the State, and to the economy, running into many millions of pounds.

ACCIDENT PREVENTION

Accidents are costly, painful and disruptive. Since the causes of accidents are complex, and cannot be explained by single factor theories, prophylactic measures must themselves be multiple. A start is to collect as much information as possible concerning all accidents. One way of preventing accidents is to attack those things which seem to be related to accident frequency (the actuarial method). This requires a study of accident statistics, based on actual data, to determine those things which seem to be significant to both accidents and 'near-misses'. It calls for detailed records to be compiled of the work environment, the operations carried out, the arrangement of the work, the

physical environment, quality of supervision, training and special characteristics. It may demand a higher level of accuracy in record keeping. Nevertheless, it permits a more thorough investigation and a more informative
account of an accident and might indicate lines of action.

Another means of preventing accidents is via safety education. Surprisingly, achieving success is doubtful. In spite of the fact that safety is clearly in
one's own self-interest, communicating the message is difficult. Many safety
campaigns misfire and there is no one method that is certain. One of the
reasons is that they lack direct reinforcement. Those reading a safety poster
have probably not suffered the kind of accident to which it relates. They do
not therefore apply its message to themselves and when they do they rarely
attribute their safety to its effect. They are more likely to attribute it to their
own skill. When considering safety training, it is important that the safety
aspects of skills training are incorporated at the time the training programme
is being designed rather than as an afterthought. The aim is to train
individuals so that their concept of skill includes safe practices as an integral
part of their work. Training must emphasize that skill does not lie in reducing
the margin of safety, but in maintaining it as widely as possible.

Another approach to accident prevention is via tighter personnel selection.
If it can be shown, from past records, that certain people with previous
biographical background and experiences have had a higher propensity to
have had accidents, then they can be screened out in the recruitment process.

Training, obviously, is a key element in any safety campaign. But skills
training is only one aspect of training which can play a part in reducing
accidents; there is also a need to ensure that managers and supervisors are
encouraged to participate. Safety is after all a joint responsibility.

Some pay systems have an adverse effect on accidents, particularly piecework and payment by results systems. Depending on the importance which
one places on safety, one might seek to redesign job variables so as to reduce
the risks. Clearly, however, there must be some pay-off between the costs of
accident prevention and actual risk reduction. But some simple things can be
borne in mind. Equipment design, the man–machine interface, and the
physical environment can often be improved with a little thought and
minimum cost. The social environment is also important – there is some
evidence to suggest that a cohesive group with high morale is likely to have
higher performance, including less accidents. New technology creates new
hazards, and as yet many of these may be unknown.

SAFETY LEGISLATION

The outlines of the law relating to safety is given by Greville Janner in
Chapter 12. The employer is required to provide evidence to show that there
is a specific policy regarding health and safety in operation throughout the
entire organization. Management has a responsibility to implement company
policy but also has a general responsibility under the Health and Safety at
Work Act that plant and equipment is operating safely and in accordance with

all the requirements of the Act whether specified in the policy document or not. Many organizations have appointed a safety officer, but this officer does not automatically relieve other managers of responsibility in the safety areas. The involvement of the workforce is encouraged by the Act, in the form of safety representatives. These may be elected by fellow employees or by trade unions. Representatives have the right to paid time-off for training purposes and for carrying out their functions. Representatives may consult with employers and inspectors; they may investigate workplaces, hazards, accidents, documents, notify defects, and channel complaints made by their constituents. In reality, however, safety representatives have little power, they simply have extra responsibilities. Real powers lie with the Health and Safety Executive (H.S.E.), the operational arm of the Health and Safety at Work Commission, and the Executive, in collaboration with local authorities, is there to enforce the rules. It provides a unified inspectorate.

Employees are required to notify accidents, and have legal obligations to do so. Since 1980 they have been required to report immediately (normally by telephone) to the relevant enforcement authority any fatality, major injury, or any prescribed dangerous occurrence, under the *Notification of Accidents and Dangerous Occurrences Regulations* (NADO). These reports must be confirmed in writing within seven working days. They are also required to keep records of all accidents resulting in incapacity for more than three days and finally, they are required to complete the forms for industrial disablement or sickness payment when invited to do so by the Department of Health and Social Security.

New regulations, the *Reporting of Injuries, Diseases and Dangerous Occurrences Regulations* (RIDDO) unify all previous reporting arrangements for injuries causing more than three days' absence, certain industrial diseases, and immediate notification of fatalities, etc., as before. New regulations are to be added for finger, thumb and toe amputations, wrist and ankle fractures and certain eye injuries.

Summary

Ergonomics studies the interaction between persons and their immediate working environment. Optional adjustment, job satisfaction and performance are fostered by careful planning of the interplay between technical and human abilities. Ergonomic design also contributes to accident prevention. Accident causation is complex. Safety legislation alone is not enough to ensure safe working conditions. Legislation can stipulate recommendations, precautions, reporting systems and operate an inspectorate, but it does not directly control people's behaviour at work.

Discussion questions

1   How does ergonomics contribute to job satisfaction and performance?
2   What recommendations would you make for the training programme for an ergonomist?
3   Design (a) a facia panel for a motor car
              (b) the controls and layout of an electric cooker.
4   What are the main principles of ergonomics which need to be considered in designing control panels for process industries, e.g. a steel mill or oil refinery?
5   What are the main principles of ergonomics which need to be considered in designing workstations for (a) computer operators, (b) users of visual display units (VDUs)?
6   To what extent can personnel management techniques such as selection and training compensate for inadequate machine design?
7   What are the main determinants of safety at work?
8   Devise safety training programmes for (a) fork-lift truck drivers, (b) hospital porters, (c) refuse collectors, (d) grave diggers.
9   How valuable is the Health and Safety at Work Act?

References

BEAUMONT, P. B. (1979a), 'An analysis of the problem of industrial accidents in Great Britain', *International Journal of Manpower*, **1**, 1.
BEAUMONT, P. B. (1979b), Research Note: 'The relationship between industrial accidents and absenteeism', *Industrial Relations Journal*, **10**, 3.
BOYLE, A. J. (1980), ' "Found experiments" in accident research', *Journal of Occupational Psychology*, **52**.
CHAPANIS, A. (1965), *Man-Machine Engineering*, Tavistock, London.
GREENWOOD, M. and WOODS, H. M. (1919), 'Report on the incidence of industrial accidents', reproduced in Haddow, W. (1964), *Accident Research*, Harper and Row, New York.
HALE, A. R. and HALE, M. (1972), *A Review of Industrial Accident Literature*, HMSO, London.
HILL, J. M. M. and TRIST, E. L. (1953), 'A consideration of industrial accidents as a means of withdrawal from the work situation', *Human Relations*, **6**, 4.
KAY, H. (1978), 'Accidents: Some facts and theories', in: Warr, P. B., *Psychology at Work*, Penguin, London.
McKENNA, F. P. (1983), 'Accident proneness: a conceptual analysis', *Accident Analysis and Prevention*, Vol. 15, 1.
PEARSON REPORT (1978), *Report of the Royal Commission on Civil Liability*, HMSO, London.
REVANS, R. W. (1956), 'Industrial morale and size of unit', *Political Quarterly*, **27**, 3.
SHAUOL, J. E. (1976), 'The use of intermediate criteria for evaluating the effectiveness of accident countermeasures', *Human Factors*, **19**.
SINGLETON, T. (1978), 'Ergonomics and man–machine systems', in: Warr, P. B., *Psychology at Work*, Penguin, London.
TIFFIN, J. and McCORMICK, E. (1968), *Industrial Psychology*, Allen and Unwin, London.

CHAPTER 21

Personnel in change

by Bryan Livy

Management must now actively plan for change and the effects of change. New technology, trends in design, new consumer services, fashions in products, changes in labour markets, competition, mergers and takeovers all strike at organizational success and survival. Len Peach referred to the forces of change in Chapter 1 and showed how they impinge on corporate strategy. Sadly and myopically, elsewhere in management literature in general, there are few examples of serious human resource planning linked to strategic management. Mr Peach emphasized some crucial factors – *inter alia*, anticipating the future need of the organization and gearing mechanisms to propel it forward, developing positive attitudes amongst employees, focusing sharply on the needs of the customer.

From the complacency of the 1960s, the retrenchment of the 1970s, we reach now a new climacteric – an intensely competitive and technological period in the 1980s – with a similar vision into the 1990s. Exhortations are for adaptation, renewal, cost effectiveness, excellence. Timely books *In Search of Excellence* (Peters and Waterman, 1982) and *The Winning Streak* (Goldsmith and Clutterbuck, 1985) gave voice to corporate 'culture' and how better to compete. The search was on to discover the secrets, dubbed a kind of 'holy grail' (Holman, 1985; Thomas, 1985). Companies contemplated their corporate navels afresh. The success motif became the clarion call.

Apart from economic and structural changes in society at large, organizations internally reoriented – for example, in the personnel field, decentralization; smaller work groups with more autonomy; single status; freedom of information; involvement in decision-making; employee ownership.

There have also been notable legislative changes – for example, the pursuit of deregulation, restriction of trade union immunities and confirmation of positive rights for the individual.

In the final chapter of this book, let us review some of the key issues:

- Decentralization
- Industrial relations and the law
- Communications and participation
- The impact of technology
- Handling redundancies
- New modes of work and employee flexibility
- Human resource accounting

Decentralization

A general trend can be detected towards the devolution of management responsibility. The move is designed to make management decisions more immediate at the local level, whilst maintaining tight control over finance and strategic planning. The mood of the moment is to reduce bureaucratic inertia, through flatter organizational structures, shorter lines of command and communication, and reward systems linked to results achieved. The effect is to delineate a clearer distinction between 'strategic' and 'operational' management. Head office staffs are becoming smaller and leaner. In Personnel Management the trend noted in a pilot study (Purcell, 1985) was for personnel decision-making to be pushed back to operational managers in divisions, profit centres, subsidiaries, etc. (see Purcell, J. and Gray, A., 1986). But a Warwick study (Sisson and Scullion, 1985) of the largest 100 UK private sector employers found the trend by no means universal:

> 'Just because there is no corporate personnel department or it is very small does not necessarily mean that strategic personnel matters are being ignored.'

Where it occurs, of course, it may be prejudicial to personnel specialists. Conventional career ladders are becoming shorter and fewer, exacerbated by a possible increase in the use of outside consultants (Torrington, 1986). Some may deprecate this state of affairs, but if kept in balance it may enhance the effectiveness of the function. In places there have been renewed attempts to return the personnel function to line management. One wonders if the wheel has turned full circle. Writing in 1947, Pigors and Myers, fathers of the study of personnel management:

> 'Personnel administration is a *line management responsibility* but a staff function.' (my italics)

But there are dangers in devolution.

> 'In many organizations, top management has given middle managers, who in turn have given first-line supervisors, so many technical responsibilities that they have little time for their personnel responsibilities' (Pigors and Myers).

Indeed, in Britain, it was partly the abdication of line managers of their personnel role which gave rise to the growth of a specialist personnel function.

Debate about relative merits of centralization/decentralization, line and staff functions goes back to the early classical management theorists and beyond. Many of these issues remain diffuse. Prescriptive formulae are lacking.

> 'Like the snark, the principles have proved an elusive quarry, although the hunt is still on 60 years later' (Mant, 1977).

Industrial relations and the law

Trade union membership in the UK stood at some 8 million at the termination of military hostilities in 1945. Thereafter it increased to a peak of 13.3 m in 1979, expanding rapidly during the final decade. But during the four years 1979–83, membership slumped by some 2 m (a fall of 15 per cent compared with a fall in employment of 8 per cent). By the end of 1983, there were 393 unions with a membership of 11.3 m. The number of people in employment in December of that year was 21.3 m (with 3.1 m registered unemployed) (Bain, 1983). If the unemployed are included in the denominator, union density in 1983 fell to under 50 per cent. (If the unemployed are excluded, density remained over 50 per cent.)

Clearly, a number of factors may account for the reversal of fortunes. One is economic – contraction, closures and bankruptcies, another is a hostile political wind from Westminster, yet another is the difficulty trade unions have faced in pursuing their members' interests at a time of upheaval, with a resultant loss of popularity. In many places, trade unions have fought a losing battle for job protection. Where was the support from fellow trade unionists in the 1979 steel strike and the 1984–5 miners' strike? Traditional values of collectivism and solidarity were subjugated to a new pragmatism. Internal dissent was also evident. Individual trade unionists were more ready to challenge their union in the courts.

Legislation brought in during the period 1980–4 tried to control abuses of trade union power, but in so doing knocked badly the traditional system of joint regulation at the workplace, and substituted for it control by legal sanction. Sir John Wood (1985) has remarked: 'legalism seems to have developed an unstoppable momentum . . . the law does not work well as a detailed regulator of continuing relationships'.

The coal miners' strike provided an opportunity to invoke the 1980 and 1982 Employment Acts which removed legal immunity from much industrial action and provided access to union funds once again (as during 1971–4 under the old Industrial Relations Act 1971). With the 1982 Act too came the civil liability of unions for their actions. Courts had powers to fine unions for contempt, and to sequester union assets. There was no limit to the fine a court could impose for contempt (but a legal maximum on damages).

The National Coal Board took up the gauntlet in an attempt to prevent unlawful picketing. To this effect it obtained an injunction, but did not enforce it. As a 'trade dispute' the miners' strike, protected by immunity provisions of the 1974 Trade Union Act, could still be held in breach of the rules – such as no proper ballots. Injunctions were therefore obtained against calling the strike official and paying out strike pay. 'At times it may have seemed as if the entire legal system was involved in unravelling the legal knots created by the miners' strike' (Atkin, 1985).

One recent development in I.R. deserves attention – namely, the no-strike agreements and pendulum arbitration which have been concluded by the EETPU particularly, (and a number of other unions) often in new enterprises. Sole bargaining rights, single status and a consultative framework are granted in return for a no-strike agreement and flexible working arrangements. Industrial action is not entirely precluded (unofficial stoppages can occur), but the aim is consensus. When disputes do occur, pendulum arbitration is binding. Under conventional arbitration, most commonly matters are settled by splitting the difference between the parties. Pendulum arbitration removes the option of a compromise – the arbitrator must find in favour of one or other. The rationale is that a possible win/lose outcome obliges the parties to negotiate as closely to a convergence as possible before resorting to arbitration.

There is no doubt that the style of UK legislation can give rise to many doubts and complexities. Most employment legislation seeks to encompass a whole range of issues within a single provision, and may net some peripheral ones as well. On top of this may come various regulations and case laws. The legal jungle is itself a veritable minefield.

Nevertheless, employment legislation is here to stay. Individual rights at work have remained protected. This means that managers' freedom to act is circumscribed. Uninformed managers may well be troubled and bewildered by laws and codes of practice which have made their jobs more difficult, but in some senses managerial courses of action have become less ambiguous. It seems improbable that any future government would go back on individual rights. However, the whole arena of collective industrial relations legislation is ground for political football. Certainly the current laws have bite, and trade unions are on the defensive. Will the downward trend in trade union membership continue? Will trade unions be able to contribute constructively? Will they be able to develop participative activities and widen their scope beyond the field of wage bargaining?

Communications and participation

Communication pervades everything employers and employees do. Its purpose is to achieve coordinated results. Constant changes call for renewed communications, a flow – which conveys ideas, instructions and reactions.

A communication network is a set of individual or organizational units linked together by patterned information flows. There may be several networks. Formal communication networks are established as part of the overall design of an organization in order to prescribe and limit the flow of information between the organization's members and departments. These are often presented as organization charts. Three major formal networks can be distinguished: downward, upward and horizontal.

Downward communication is the transfer of information from a higher level in the organization to a lower one. Instructions or other job-related information to employees, policy statements, procedures, newsletters, are all examples of downward communications. Some will be verbal, face-to-face; others will be in written format, and seemingly more remote.

Upward communication originates at a lower organization level and permeates upwards. Feedback from subordinates, attitude surveys, consultative committees, suggestion schemes, ballots, are various means by which messages, feelings and opinions can be transmitted.

Horizontal communications occur between individuals and departments at similar levels, crossing functional boundaries, through specialist advisory and monitoring services, inter-functional membership of steering committees, feasibility studies, etc.

Communication networks form a complicated spider's web of many strands branching in many directions, but the hub or centre of activity is the top management decision-making body.

In principle, formal networks should be sufficient to carry the transmission of all communications. In practice, this is not so. In any organization, informal communications networks spring up spontaneously – the grapevine, the old boy network – bypassing officialdom. The aims are speed and simplicity. Such networks or contacts may be transitory, serving particular short-term ends, and then changing as alliances shift – or they may be permanent. Informal networks rarely coincide with formal channels (if they did, they would be unnecessary). They cut across formal links of communication and may complicate matters. Leaking information systems and misrepresentations undermine control, the credibility of authority, and respect for established procedures. (See the section on Consultation and Communications in Chapter 10.)

Business information is not homogeneous. Different kinds of information must be treated differently and channelled differently. It therefore becomes necessary to organize logical systems for handling data. Some data will require *action*, some will not. Some information will be *recurring* and some *non-recurring*. Some information is *formal* in that it passes through formal channels of communication in some standardized documentary format (letters, memos, reports, punched cards, computer tapes). This is the continuous communication of facts, opinions, recommendations, and orders, expressed in some mutually understandable language, such as words, figures and symbols, and which in its execution constitutes a system of control throughout the organization.

Conversely, some information is *informal*, in that it is not reduced to documentary evidence, and in that it is passed by word of mouth, often spontaneously, sometimes unsolicited and rarely recorded. Communications of this type, transmitted in face-to-face conversation between individuals and in groups, or through the medium of the telephone, bridge gaps, delays and remoteness imposed by formal channels – and hence become more personalized. In many cases they may well run counter to the classical principles of good organization.

Indeed, the inherent paradox of the bureaucratic system is that control is vested in the hands of individuals, groups and committees, at various levels in the hierarchy. This network is designed to ensure that the decision-making process does not fall into the hands of the irresponsible or ill-advised, but conversely makes ultimate authority remote from the working situation on the shopfloor or in the office, and renders it difficult for individual employees to identify themselves with the long-term objectives of the organization, or to bring any influence to bear on the making of policy.

Informal communications may offer a palliative, if not a solution, to this dilemma. Engineered attempts to bridge communication gaps – through joint consultation, or widening the scope of collective bargaining, are now being followed by further pressures for greater industrial democracy, disclosure of information, and calls for 'participation'.

To talk of 'employers' and 'employees' as experiencing gaps in communication flows and feedback is to simplify the matter. While there is a continuum from the managing director down to the newest unskilled worker, going through several managerial levels, in addition there are increasing numbers of functional specialists, e.g. technical and advisory staff in limbo at various levels in the hierarchy. By no means are all the problems of communications those between managers and workers. Some of the most acutely felt problems are concerned with communications *within* the management groups, and with communications *within* the workers' groups.

People most commonly complain that they are inadequately informed. This is again ironic in an age when there is often too much information. Most organizations are swamped by over abundance of information on masses of tapes, paper and printouts – containing a lot of pseudo-information – enough to suffocate almost any initiative or effective action. The whole paraphernalia of cybernetics begins and ends with information.

The questions then are what *type* and *quality* of information is useful, and who should have *access* to it.

Access to power sharing is a contemporary demand. Without it, the organization is bound to appear overpowering and impenetrable. People feel alienated from the central purpose and it is not surprising that either resistance or apathy will result.

The Institute of Personnel Management (1981) offer guidelines and suggest a role for the personnel function:

1 Identifying communication needs.
2 Advising management on how to improve the flow of required information.
3 Devising systems for upflow of employee views and opinions.
4 Developing new initiatives.
5 Improving expertise in communications among management personnel.
6 Improving awareness of the benefits of improved communications.
7 Facilitating the flow of information from external sources.
8 Designing appropriate systems in terms of structure and message.

9 Assessing the division of responsibility for communications between management and employee representatives.
10 Assessing what employees want to know.

Ideas of democratic participation are of Greek origin. Western society has employed the principle more in political life than industrial life. Inevitably, this has been challenged.

Participation may be *direct*. Individuals may at their place of work directly influence the content, conduct and environment of their job. Job enrichment, autonomous work methods and similar developments are moves in this direction.

Participation may also be *indirect*, through representatives acting on behalf of groups, and taking more of a long-term view. (Trade unions, works councils, supervisory boards and similar institutions operate in this area.) Indirect participation, so-called, is indirect (or representational) simply because of larger numbers of people involved in some kind of collective group – it is not *intended* to be more remote.

The difference in scope is more critical than the principle of involvement. Direct participation is limited. Indirect participation is power-based, exercised either through more collective bargaining or more representative machinery.

The crux of current debate is the extent to which it may be desirable or feasible to extend the participative process into decision-making. Employee participation has often been linked with organizational and managerial communications. In fact, communication has even been considered as one of the many forms of employee participation. For example, in the Bullock Report (Report of the Bullock Committee of Inquiry on Industrial Democracy, 1977), it was said 'Employee participation may take many forms from improved communication to joint responsibility for decisions, to experiments in job enrichment and participative management'. Communication and participation are often treated as different points along the same continuum. Participation implies a higher degree of employee involvement in decision-making, and effective two-way communication is a prerequisite.

Like many ideas and intentions, the term 'worker participation' means different things to different people. According to one definition, it is 'any set of social or institutional devices by which subordinate employees either individually or collectively become involved in one or more aspects of organizational decision-making within the enterprises in which they work' (Farnham and Pimlott, 1979). Further it 'involves any personal or institutional process by which subordinate employees exert a countervailing and upward pressure on ultimate managerial control within organisations'.

Indirect participation exclusively aims at affecting higher management level decisions and is essentially redistributive in intent. Somewhere between 'employee *participation*' and 'workers *control*' lies the vague area of 'industrial democracy'. The terms are not precise and there is overlap between them. Participation may be loose or positive, direct or indirect.

In the UK interest in participation – as a general movement – gained ground in the 1960s and 1970s. Some of the reasons for this (Guest and Knight, 1979), were:

1 A possible way out of industrial and economic problems.
2 Rising expectations of the workforce.
3 Concern about the concentration of power in industry.
4 An interest in the concept of industrial democracy as an extension of political democracy.
5 Membership of the EEC and particularly the need to consider the implications for company law of the draft Fifth Directive which envisaged some kind of worker representation at board level.

During this time also there had been a change of attitude amongst influential members of the trade union movement. Trade union views were not uniform. Some unions saw participation as a lever for shopfloor control. Others rejected it, claiming their right to protect their members' interests and asserting that democracy required strong opposition (drawing the distinction between participation and negotiation).

The CBI favoured collective bargaining as the main means for improving participation and that 'employee representation at board level will not usually be a suitable form of participation' (CBI, 1977).

On the whole, the individual manager's interest in participation has similarly been equivocal. Decision and control are traditional prerogatives. Would participation lead to anarchy? More constructive managers argued that openness does not necessarily lead to loss of control if it is managed properly, and that participation might well be a suitable vehicle for facilitating change, providing opportunities for job satisfaction, and harnessing the energies of people. An aspirant workforce and liberalizing attitudes of the time gave encouragement to a number of initiatives to be taken. (Indeed, in the public sector, worker directors had already been set up in British Steel and the Post Office.)

But the shelving of the Bullock Report (to which we shall return) and the controversy which surrounded it, plus the onset of recession brought a pause. 'It may, however, be wiser to regard the period round 1980 as a temporary lull rather than a permanent loss of interest in the subject' (Guest, 1983). David Guest cites the stated commitment of the present Conservative government to worker participation (although on a voluntary and flexible basis) and the expected outcome of European legislation (to which again we shall return).

From an operational point of view, Enid Mumford (1981) highlights three crucial issues which need to be considered in any discussion:

1 The structure of participation
2 The content of participation
3 The process of participation.

We may elaborate on these points. The *structure* is a key question. Whilst we may consider participation morally desirable, there is far less agreement about what form it should take. The *content* needs also to be defined. What is the precise jurisdiction of a participative group? Where do decision boundaries lie? Whereas in direct participation, worker decisions are personal and localized, indirect participation can only be achieved through some kind of representational system. Which groups or representatives will participate? Do we need democratically elected representatives? Do we use trade union channels, or do we need a second system of employee representation? Would dual systems become unwieldy? Would reliance on trade union representation be acceptable?

The *content* of participation can vary widely. It might focus narrowly on terms and conditions of work – or broaden into executive decisions and real power-sharing. In the latter case, the time-scale needed for implementation is almost infinite. The training and development needs of people who are to be representatives are of magnitude – magnified further if we are to consider a series of democratically elected representatives (and assuming that they have the basic capacities and a willingness to perform managerial functions). We cannot duck the possibility of real resistance and retrenchment of the managerial elite. The climate of industrial relations must be appropriately receptive if the winds of change are to be any more than a breeze.

So much of the debate is a question of degree. There is also confusion over the various definitions used. Implicit in participation is the need to establish effective systems of consultation and joint decision-making. The development of an effective structure can and should only be seen against a long-term perspective. It will take time for new approaches and initiatives to be modified in the light of experience. Careful consideration needs to be given to the precise role of the consultative mechanism within the organization and the relationship of that mechanism to the management process. Objectives are long-term and may include:

1   A mechanism for employees' contributions to decisions that affect them closely.
2   A forum for joint problem-solving in relation to issues that affect the efficient operation of the organization.

European experience is more advanced in this field. Participative machinery in which worker representatives play a full part is well established. West Germany is well known for its *supervisory boards* (which represent labour but do not necessarily include union members) and *works councils* (which have responsibility for collective bargaining). As a member of the EEC, Britain will at some stage have to comply with certain European requirements, with consequent changes in British company law, although there is such a wrangle going on in Brussels that the outcome is not yet definite. The 1980 Companies Act in the UK made loose provision for the interests of workers as well as shareholders, and the 1982 Employment Act stimulated employee involvement. (See Chapter 13.)

A draft of the Euro-company Statute had been published by the European Commission in 1970. Amongst its provisions, it required a two-tier board structure, works councils for European companies with establishments in more than one member state, and group works councils for European companies with subsidiary companies. More important, however, was the Fifth Directive on Company Structure to coordinate the laws of member states within the EEC regarding the structures of public limited liability companies. It provided for a two-tier board structure with employee representation on the supervisory or top level board, but made no provision relating to works councils, although the Commission considered that the dualist board system and employee participation in the supervisory board remained valuable and realistic objectives. At the time of writing, the Commission is still trying to reformulate the fifth directive on industrial democracy and the European companies statute with its inbuilt requirements to disclose information. The fifth directive aims at harmonization of institutions for achieving industrial democracy. The so-called Vredeling Directive concerns communications, or the flow of information from management to employees in companies operating within the EEC. In November 1983, the British government published a consultative document jointly by the Departments of Employment and of Trade and Industry, noting some discord. Opposition to the directive is widespread in the UK, USA and Japan where multinational companies with European subsidiaries feel threatened by legislation which they believe will lead them to divulge commercial secrets.

The Committee of Inquiry on Industrial Democracy (Bullock Report) in the UK came out in 1977, immediately followed by a White Paper the following year. Briefly, the Committee had been asked to consider methods of employee representation at board level in the private sector in the UK, following TUC proposals to give trade unionists seats on company boards, and impending EEC requirements. 'The TUC moved to support the idea of worker directors, provided that: (a) they represented trade unionists and did not introduce a new, second channel of employee representation; (b) that they exercise real power, having parity with shareholders in the allocation of seats' (on the board) (Palmer, 1983). The Committee recommended that there should be equal representation of employer and shareholder representatives on reconstituted company boards, plus a third group of independent directors – the famous $2x+y$ formula. Employee directors were to have been elected through Joint Representative Committees: shareholders' representatives were to have been elected in the existing manner. All directors should have the same legal duties and responsibilities. Antagonism to the proposals was rife and nothing happened – at that stage. Trade Unionist Lief Mills: 'It was a pity then and it is a pity now that so much of the debate on participation has centralized round the concept of board membership, when really that by itself is meaningless unless there is an effective system of participation throughout the company' (Mills, 1985).

'Despite the controversial nature of industrial democracy, there is widespread agreement from government and both sides of industry that progress in this field can and must be made' (Hanson and Rathkey, 1984). Some form of legislation on participation/democracy will undoubtedly come in the fullness of time. At the moment there is freedom for companies to develop whatever participative procedures seem appropriate. The present government is placing some emphasis on profit-sharing and share ownership as a means of gaining employee commitment.

This is what the debate on communications and participation is all about; how does one achieve the involvement of people and in what ways does one achieve it?

The impact of technology

Technological advance is an historical process, but its accelerating pace is now the dominant feature. Transformation of office and shopfloor work methods may spell efficiency. It also bodes dislocation of established ideas about work, skills, careers, security and management control. Just as people hope for stability and to reap the rewards of success, so do they become jittery about impending change, uncertainty, and possible insecurity. Such changes today may incite resistance or collective action. They certainly open doors for fresh approaches to consultation, participation and planning. New problems are the hardest to handle.

Modern technologies include capital intensive welding techniques, robotics, fibre optics, microprocessors, biochemical engineering. This new technology has been described as the second industrial revolution. Electronics already underpins much of our economic activity. Microelectronics is the technology of putting much electronic capability on a single chip. Few spheres of human activity will remain unscathed. It is possible in the factory of the future for every activity from receipt of customer's order to the finished product to be electronically stored, analysed and controlled – including estimating, design, production planning, quality control, purchasing, component manufacture, assembly, and dispatch, via word processors, office automation, measuring and weighing instruments, traffic control, robotic or 'man-following' systems, information retrieval.

Potential applications are attractive to employers where there is a need for:

1 Reliability
2 Cheapness
3 Speed
4 Where actions are repetitive
5 Where the work environment is hostile or boring to human beings
6 Where quick information retrieval is required
7 Where monitoring, comparison or reaction to situations is required.

Multinationals dominate the world economy, investing in the most profitable products and places. But Britain has fallen behind Japan, USA and West Germany in the technological race. Britain, faced with low investment, less efficiency, declining profitability, and lack of competitiveness is under some pressure to catch up. However, a recent Policy Studies Institute report (1982) indicated some reluctance in the manufacturing sector to adopt new techniques. According to the report, only 50 per cent of manufacturing companies surveyed had applied or even considered the application of microelectronics technology. Capital costs may be one reason, but another is a shortage of suitably skilled staff.

The current economic climate is not conducive to an embracing acceptance of new technology. Recession, high unemployment and declining industrial activity do not stimulate enthusiasm. Whilst employment levels in manufacturing continue to contract (particularly in unskilled areas) and while the number of young people coming on to the labour market continues to increase, for the rest of the 1980s, social attitudes can be expected to be ambivalent.

Moreover, technical feasibility does not necessarily equate with economic viability. The speed of introduction of technology is likely to be modified by a number of economic, social and organizational resistances – or 'moderators' (Rajan, 1985).

The precise impact on employment levels of new technology is difficult to predict. A lot depends on its rate of introduction and expansion or contraction of the economy as a whole. Many pundits have made their predictions but there is a general consensus that some 4–5 million people in the UK will be unemployed by 1990. Whereas, in the 1970s the main area of the employment growth had been in clerical jobs in the service sectors, in the future the number of jobs available in clerical work will sharply decline. It is probably not possible to prove or disprove the general proposition that changing technology may cause unemployment. Alternative employment opportunities should be opened up. In any case, technological unemployment is difficult to measure because it has no common denominator. As a result of technological change, a worker may be underemployed but retained on the payroll, or underemployed because of a transfer to a job not suited to his or her ability and skills, or be laid off temporarily, or he or she may become permanently redundant.

Technological progress does certainly aggravate 'structural' unemployment even if it does not cause it. It creates new products and new industries, modifies skill and worker requirements, shifts the geographical distribution of industry, and accentuates differentials in productivity. Quicker manpower responses are made more difficult.

The more rapid the pace of technological change, the more frequent and drastic are the consequent shifts in manpower requirements. New skills are called for as old ones become obsolete. New industrial communities are built up and old ones abandoned as firms tend to move away from centres of labour supply and nearer to markets and sources of energy. From an industrial relations point of view, however, the potential for disputes is multiplied by rapid changes in job requirements, breeding resentment, fear of redundancy, loss of status or earnings, revised methods of wage payment, and restrictive practices to delay the impact of technological change. Such disputes may be protracted by irrelevant traditional attitudes and accentuated by the urgency of the issues at stake. Long-term solutions to problems of automation need to be negotiated at a high level. Unions want a gradual approach to soften the impact, plus continuous and flexible training arrangements. But it is the fear of redundancy most of all that motivates worker (and trade union) resistance to technological progress, plus resentment over changes in traditional job demarcations. The urge for job security lies deep.

On the credit side, generally speaking, there has been a steady rise in real earnings (for those employed) wherever technological progress has occurred. Many jobs have become more interesting. In spite of concerns for safety, the physical environs in the workshop should be safer (mechanized conveyances, fewer workers in a given space, better hygiene, remote control, TV supervision). Machines have taken over the less pleasant, more strenuous tasks. Ergonomic design is steadily reducing physical effort, nervous strain and fatigue. Job enrichment allows more transferability between jobs and a grasp of several related processes, and hopefully increased satisfaction and responsibility.

Feelings about technology are mixed. It is generally accepted that the impact of technology on jobs will be to increase some and to eliminate others, although it is by no means sure how these effects will balance out. And new technology creates its own new jobs, occupational structures and career opportunities. 'Technology based organizations have key people whose career is based more on the technology than their particular company and who are thus much more mobile. Furthermore, they are likely to value wide experience, to look at challenges more in terms of particular projects than in terms of lifetime careers and be more concerned about getting out of date than about change' (Cowan, 1985).

Those who remain in employment (still the substantial majority of those eligible for work) are likely to experience considerable changes in their patterns of work. 'Deskilling is a real probability for operatives. Elites may emerge with a knowledge of the computerized system while the mass of workers become machine minders. Basic jobs such as those of machine tool operators and word processor operators, whose work remains machine based, can face boring, deskilled occupations. Machines do not need to rest – they can work 24 hours a day. At whatever production level they are set, operators and service mechanics could become their slaves' (TUC).

'*Flexible*' working hours are likely to evolve around the new technologies. There will be new shift work systems. Computerized time recording systems will be able to check 'productive' and 'wasted' time. Individual performance can be monitored. Work measurement becomes tighter. Computer based equipment such as point of sale terminals and computer controlled machine tools will enable workers' performance to be measured more accurately than the old work study techniques. '*Distance supervision*' becomes possible. There will also be the emergence of 'high-tech' home workers plugged in from the sitting room. It may not be necessary to commute to the office at all.

Management control is tightened. New technology poses some big questions for the role of supervisors and middle management. Answers are contradictory. A recent NEDO study (Webb, 1983) concludes that new technology will *erode* central controls. 'User' autonomy will force managers to take important decisions in conjunction with other specialists. Key jobs will be increasingly 'project' rather than 'task' oriented.

New Technology Agreements

Trade unions hope for better living standards and employment prospects. After all, the gains from technology should be shared. Anything else is not human progress. Trade unions have not been hostile, but they have been anxious. Their concerns are the terms on which technology is introduced and the purposes to which it is applied. In the words of Len Murray, 'It is not just a question of accepting the new technology or fighting it. The issue is how we maximize its benefits and minimize its costs' (1980). The range of issues includes trade union organization, negotiating procedures, job security, work organization, hours of work, health and safety, information disclosure, training and retraining.

In the past, many unions have largely concentrated on wages, on maintaining manning levels, and have demarcated where a job is to be done, the tools and materials used. These were attempts to protect jobs and skills. Problems now arise in that computer-based machines and equipment *cut across these demarcation lines*. Machines can be programmed to manufacture, weld, spray, etc., with little human intervention on the shopfloor, and machine pacing can be controlled automatically. Unions are now reviewing traditional approaches to demarcation and are taking positive steps to negotiate training schemes which will give all workers a general understanding of computer-based systems.

Unions are pressing for negotiation and consultation on all aspects of new technology, from initial feasibility studies through to the final solution. To this end trade unions have formulated the concept of 'New Technology Agreements' (NTAs) – to establish procedures whereby employers and unions jointly consider, negotiate and agree major technological advances.

The CBI in its discussion document 'Facing the Future' (1981) rejected the need for formal agreements before introducing new technology. Nor did it wish for security guarantees as a quid pro quo for employee cooperation.

From the debate of the early 1980s concerning new technology agreements, the advantages and disadvantages which seem most to have been articulated are as follows:

Advantages of New Technology Agreements
1   They provide a clear procedural framework.

2 They may help to reduce uncertainty over acceptance.
3 They may help to involve unions at the planning stage.
4 They could help to broaden the range of bargaining issues to include job design, training, etc.
5 They may help to build inter-union cooperation where more than one union is involved.
6 They can provide unions with the possibility of taking the initiative in pressing for technological change.

Disadvantages of New Technology Agreements

1 They confer upon new technology a special status (when it could perhaps be dealt with under existing procedures). It is not a 'separate' negotiating issue.
2 They may slow down the implementation of new technology while negotiations take place.
3 They may involve management in concessions relating to joint regulation.
4 They may impose restrictions on operating freedom.
5 New technology may also include some 'old' problems better resolved by renegotiating existing arguments.
6 There is the constant need to update new technology agreements as technological advances continue to be made.

The message from the TUC (1981): 'Probably the best solution to bargaining about change is for unions to go for a combination of negotiating current agreements alongside agreeing new ones – which may or may not be called new technology agreements'.

Despite differences at national level between employers and trade unions, by 1983 over 200 technology agreements had been signed in the immediate preceding 3–4 years (Webb, 1983). Of these, a high proportion have been concluded in the private sector and most of them embraced white-collar employees.

From the new technology agreements which have been concluded, and from opinions publicly expressed, there would seem to be a dozen or so areas which are of prime concern and interest to work people and which managements can ignore only at their peril.

1 Consultation
2 Job security
3 Management information and disclosure
4 Products and services
5 Job skills
6 Job design
7 Training and retraining
8 Grading and pay
9 Health and safety

10 Work performance control
11 Women and ethnic minorities
12 Shorter working time

Let us look at each of these in turn.

Consultation

Work people (white-collar and blue-collar) want to know what is happening, and, if possible, to be involved. Technological innovations may lead to changes in job content, promotion avenues, and loss of income. People are looking for consultation and co-determination of the effects of technological change at the planning stage. Consultation stops short of negotiation. One third of the NTAs included in the IPM Survey (1983) incorporate an undertaking to 'consult' rather than 'negotiate'. The underlying implication is that it would not be necessary for management to reach a binding agreement before proceeding to introduce change.

Job security

A common feature of most agreements is some form of job security clause, including undertakings to avoid compulsory redundancy and to redeploy staff in return for acceptance and other job changes. Negotiated job security, which ensures no *compulsory* redundancy, must be underpinned by joint regulation of manpower planning, recruitment, training, work loads, career progressions, etc.

Management information and disclosure

Microtechnology can enormously increase the collection and analysis of information relating to product performance, customers, sales, finance, personnel. These inputs contribute to corporate forward planning. Companies may (not unnaturally) be reluctant to disclose their forward plans – but work people are more concerned about the implications for their own jobs. Trade unions themselves may like certain kinds of information to be collected, e.g. work rates, discipline records, accidents, etc.

Products and services

Lack of new technology may be worse than having it. Companies which fail to adapt may go into decline. The TUC put it this way: 'Negotiators must be willing to take the lead in pressing for a joint assessment of the opportunities for using new technological processes and introducing new products on the basis of agreed plans. Unions will often need to take the initiative in pressing for change so as to avoid a belated or inadequate management decision which will have more damaging effect on the workforce'.

Job skills

Deskilling must be seen alongside the creation of new skills. Long established ideas about skills, apprenticeships, and demarcations are being questioned. Changed job skills open up opportunities for job redesign and retraining.

Job design

Many NTAs feature job design/job satisfaction clauses and/or job rotation. New technology can allow for the humanization of work. With imagination there is scope for improving job content so that:

1   Activities involve decision-making and application of knowledge
2   Information about plans and results can be provided
3   Freedom is given in ways of performing job operations
4   Activities can be varied
5   Equipment is ergonomically designed
6   Excessive and humiliating control can be avoided.

Training and retraining

Nobody seems to dispute training and retraining to equip people for new jobs. Women might usefully use the opportunity for negotiating equal opportunities in training, and to use the provision of the Sex Discrimination Act which allows special courses to be put on to enable females to enter traditionally male areas of employment.

Grading and pay

The introduction of new technology is concerned with cutting costs and increasing productivity. Existing work methods, grading and pay are likely to be reviewed. NTAs typically refer to existing procedures such as job evaluation machinery. But job evaluation cannot measure output or productivity, so it cannot be used to tackle all the negotiating issues. For salaried earners, changing job structures *will* call for revised job evaluation. There is a general call for no downgrading or salary loss. As against this, skill shortages in specialist areas have provoked supplementary payments, skewing job evaluation relativities.

Piece-rate schemes will also have to change. Already, where machines rather than people control the speed of production there has been a move to measured daywork. Through measured daywork management attempts to achieve consistent output at the level required. Many continuous process or production lines based on new technology take all control over the pace of work away from the person and place it within the programmed machine. This makes PBR schemes obsolete. In other areas, new technology may leave the worker in control, e.g. key punching tasks. Computer-based machinery can often be programmed to measure the performance of individuals and groups of individuals. There is some union fear that this might reduce bargaining opportunities. Bonus schemes will also need to be re-examined. Technological change is bound to affect types of payment systems and methods used to measure workers' performance.

Health and safety

Most NTAs refer to Health and Safety aspects. Some include limitation clauses such as the need for eye tests for VDU operators as safeguards over the use of VDU screens, or special provisions for epileptics or migraine sufferers. However, with new technology there are many 'unknown quantities' in the workplace. Anyone working near robots could be injured by materials flying off or by the 'thing' itself. Stress is a potential problem. Deskilled, monotonous, socially isolated jobs can cause depression, neuralgia, etc. Shift work means disrupted body rhythms, an intermittent social life, and possible digestive complaints and accidents.

Work performance control

Automated control of work performance is found objectionable. Quite a few NTAs preclude management use of computer-based equipment to monitor or measure the volume of work processed.

Women and ethnic minorities

Women's traditional areas of employment have been hardest hit. Women continue to work in a limited range of occupations (see Chapter 15) in jobs, which despite legislation, are low paid. Ethnic minorities have also taken the brunt. There is a demand for retraining, renewed efforts for equal pay, flexitime and child-care facilities for women.

Shorter working time

Since its inception in 1868, the TUC has pressed for reductions in working time. Surely automation and technology, if it does not create more jobs, will create more time? The question is how the time can be apportioned. The TUC aims for a 35-hour week and retirement at 60. Opportunities might arise for negotiating a reduction in hours, and a reduction in overtime. Ironically, the people who *are* in paid employment are currently (enjoying?) high levels of overtime – at the expense perhaps of a more rational way of work sharing.

Handling redundancies

Dismissing employees as 'surplus to requirements' is a distressing part of personnel management. The causes of redundancy might lie outside anyone's direct control, e.g. recession, loss of orders. Alternatively, they might be the desserts of inefficiency or technological progress. In any event, both the organization and the personnel management function have moral, legal and social responsibilities.

Greville Janner has outlined the basic legal requirements in Chapter 12. Such is the current impact of redundancy, that further comment is needed.

To uphold their responsibilities over the last decade or so many employers have formulated 'redundancy policies'. Where a redundancy policy exists in a firm, it is usually aimed at promoting job security, avoiding redundancies and easing the transition. Good industrial relations practice advocates formulating redundancy policy in advance of crisis situations, in consultation with employees and unions. Criteria for selection of persons to be made redundant, if the need arises, are important. If the procedure is unfairly carried out, an employer may find that he has to meet the cost of awards for unfair dismissal as well as the redundancy payments due.

If a union exists which is recognized for collective bargaining purposes, prior consultation should take place with that union. If some 'customary arrangement or agreed procedure' for selection for redundancy exists, it should be applied. If no such customs exist, then employers should take into account the following criteria:

> length of service
> age
> vacancies elsewhere in the organization
> capability
> attendance record
> conduct
> qualification and experience
> whether there are any volunteers for redundancy
> the views of the employees

At all stages of the redundancy process an employer should expect that he may – particularly in the absence of a customary arrangement or an agreed procedure – have the reasonableness of his actions challenged in an industrial tribunal.

The Employment (Consolidation) Act 1978 brought together in one Act the provision on individual rights previously contained elsewhere (Redundancy Payments Act 1965; Contracts of Employment Act 1972; Trade Union and Labour Relations Act 1974; Employment Protection Act 1975).

Part VI of the 1978 Act (Redundancy Payments) defines dismissal for the purposes of redundancy as: 'an employee who is dismissed will have been dismissed for redundancy if the dismissal is attributable wholly or mainly to the fact that:

(i)   the employer has ceased or intends to cease –
   (a)   to carry on the business for the purposes of which the employee was employed by him; or
   (b)   to carry on the business in the place where the employee was so employed; or
(ii) the requirements of the business for employees –
   (a)   to carry out work of a particular kind; or
   (b)   to carry out work of a particular kind in the place where the employee was employed; or
   (c)   have ceased or diminished, or are expected to cease or diminish.'

In practice, redundancy means dismissing employees if the reasons fall under any of the above headings. An employee who resigns before his employer's notice of dismissal expires may lose his right to a redundancy payment. Redundantees are entitled to minimum lump sum payments as declared by statute (see Chapter 12). Employers can claim rebates from the redundancy fund. Some employers may make compensations in excess of the statutory minima, but *ex gratia* payments are not subject to rebate.

Case law over time has refined some of the ambiguities in the legislation. It is worth citing a few of them, such as an employer's right in certain circumstances to *change the duties* or even the *place of work*. If the contract of employment confines an employee to a very narrow range of duties, and the business no longer needs them, redundancy may occur. However, if the contract covers a wide range of duties, the position may be quite different. If one part of the work increases, and another diminishes, and the contract covers both kinds of work, the employee may be required to switch to the expanding area and dismissal on grounds of redundancy becomes unnecessary.

An employer is also entitled to *reorganize* in the interests of efficiency. To that end he can propose changes in the terms and conditions of service, or dismiss employees if they do not agree. Similarly, *changes in working hours* do not automatically give entitlement to redundancy payment if the employee rejects the proposed change. Also, for the purposes of the statutory definition, the place where the employee 'was employed' means the place at 'which under his contract of employment he could be required to work'. This emphasizes the need for employers to make sure that the contractual position of each employee in terms of his mobility is unambiguously set out.

Legal quibbles and quillets can be complicated, but a broad fact is this: no one is entitled to a redundancy payment unless dismissed for reasons of cessation of work at the workplace. Where an employee accepts an offer of alternative employment (subject to certain provisions of comparability) with the same employer, redundancy is not applicable. Redundancies can be avoided (together with redundancy payments) if the employer offers suitable alternative work. Suitability embraces such issues as:

1 the training, qualifications and skills needed
2 commensurate levels of earnings
3 commensurate status
4 the location or place of work.

To be entitled to a redundancy payment an individual must have been 'continuously employed for a period of two years'. Certain events *do not break* this continuity of employment for redundancy payments purpose:

1 change of job with the same employer
2 change in ownership of the business
3 engagement by an associated employer
4 absence (for sickness, injury, pregnancy – subject to certain provisions)
5 participation in a strike
6 dismissal followed by reinstatement or re-engagement.

An 'Industrial Relations Code of Practice' (1972) was introduced after the 1971 Industrial Relations Act, but when that particular Act was repealed, most of the Code was preserved. The Code imposes no legal obligations but failure to observe its provisions may be taken into account in proceedings before an industrial tribunal. Throughout, the Code emphasizes the need for planned employment policies. Some of the cannons of good behaviour with regard to redundancy are:

1 Responsibility for deciding the size of the workforce rests with management, but before making reductions management should consult employees or their representatives.
2 Any policy for dealing with manpower reduction should be worked out in advance so far as practicable and should form part of an organization's employment policies.
3 In consultation with employee representatives, management should try to avoid redundancies by:
   – restrictions on recruitment
   – retirement of employees who are beyond normal retiring age
   – reduction in overtime
   – short-term working to cover fluctuations in manpower needs
   – retraining or transfer to other work.
4 Where redundancy is unavoidable, management should in consultation with their employees or their representatives:
   – give as much warning as possible
   – consider increasing schemes for voluntary redundancy, retirement, transfers and a phased rundown of the business
   – establish which employees are to be made redundant and the order in which they are to be asked to leave

– offer help to employees in finding other work in cooperation with the Department of Employment and allow reasonable time off for this purpose
– decide how and when to make the facts public.

Under the 1975 Act, employers should *consult* with recognized trade unions at the earliest practical opportunity before redundancies are to take effect. An employer proposing to dismiss as redundant 100 or more employees at one establishment within a period of 90 days – or if more than 10 employees (but less than 100) within 30 days – must undertake such consultations and must also *notify* the Secretary of State for Employment in writing of the proposal within 90 or 30 days respectively in addition to giving 14 days' notice of a claim for rebate.

An employee who has been continuously employed for two years and is under notice of redundancy is entitled to reasonable *time-off* during working hours to look for a new job or make arrangements for training. An employer must also *disclose in writing* the following information at the beginning of the consultation period:

– the reasons for the proposed redundancies
– the number and category of employees who are likely to be affected
– the total numbers in each category
– the proposed criteria to be used for selecting redundancies
– the proposed method for carrying out the redundancies with due regard for any procedure which might exist, including the period over which the redundancies are to take effect.

Under the Code, the employer is required to offer help to other employees in finding alternative employment, including transfers within the organization. If alternative employment can be offered, the employee is entitled to work a *trial period of four weeks*. This period may be extended if *retraining* is involved. During this time the employee must decide on the suitability of the alternative work.

There are certain administrative procedures for paying redundancy sums and for claiming rebates. Employers should contact their local Department of Employment office to obtain redundancy payment *forms*. It is on these forms that employers give notice of their intention to claim rebate, and on which employees are notified of the calculation of their redundancy payment.

In the 1980s, redundancies reached unbearable proportions. Job losses were reported daily. Professor Hunt's remark (1984) that the ejecting role of personnel managers 'excluding, exiting, retiring' has assumed prominence was true but unpalatable. Trade unions have persistently fought redundancies. No one likes them. The trade unions, the Industrial Society, and other bodies have at various times presented 'model redundancy agreements', 'criteria for redundancy' and ideas about good practice.

In 1984, the Institute of Personnel Management, after wide discussion, presented its own proposal in the 'IPM Redundancy Code'. Much of its wisdom incorporates the ideas of others, but the IPM emphasizes the manpower planning function: 'only if organizations recognize the importance of adequate planning and the development of appropriate personnel policies equipping their staff with the skills necessary to meet anticipated changes will they be able to minimize the instance of redundancy'. Central to the IPM proposals are *plans to avoid compulsory redundancies*. Advanced planning is advocated. 'Manpower planning enables management to make better decisions about the training, retraining and development of employees in order to redeploy or promote them . . . manpower planning also provides organizations with opportunities for increased flexibility in their manpower strategies as well as giving advanced warning of likely manpower surpluses and shortages (see Chapter 2).

Emphasis is placed on a *procedural agreement*, which should specify *minimum consultation periods, information to be disclosed, criteria for redundancy*, and management's obligation to consider trade union representation. Information should be delivered to trade union representatives and any comments made by them should be heard. If management rejects any of the representations made, it should state its reasons. The IPM recognizes that the circumstances surrounding redundancies in firms are highly variable. Firms' facilities for dealing with contraction vary widely.

New modes of work and employee flexibility

Employment confers ownership of a valuable possession, but everywhere questions of the tenure of a job are coming under scrutiny. Attempts are made to circumscribe the total fixed personnel costs by new modes of working and more variable contracts of employment. Temporary contracts (i.e. for a fixed duration only) are gaining popularity particularly where employers' visions of long-term trading prospects are blurred, or where employers wish to minimize their liabilities for employment protection. Many such contracts are made for twelve months or less. Part-time employment has grown rapidly in the UK over the last ten years. Strictly, part-time employment is defined as working for less than 30 hours per week (as a maximum) but some of these engagements might be quite minimal; and anyone working less than eight hours has no employment protection rights at all. Part-time work offers more people the opportunity to participate in paid work. Mostly it is to be found in the service sector, featuring mostly women in the more junior jobs. The use of outworkers or homeworkers is also increasing, as are other forms of subcontracting such as franchising. Homeworkers have always formed part of the labour market, but now advances in telecommunications extends the frontiers. Both ICI and Rank-Xerox have reported 'networking' systems. Work-sharing has obvious social attractions, but in some jobs can create problems of continuity. However, there is now an emphasis on 'employee flexibility', arranging working time to suit operational requirements. The question to be addressed is: how can fixed costs be varied? Planned use of temporary staff, part-timers and judicial use of shift or overtime working can increase flexibility in costs, even allowing for the statutory extras.

At least two types of flexibility are apparent – *numerical* flexibility and *occupational* flexibility. To achieve numerical flexibility, headcount is usually reduced to a bare basic minimum – a hard 'core' element of permanent employees. To cope with short-term fluctuations in manning requirements, a buffer stock of 'peripheral' employees – on part-time or temporary contracts – is grafted on to the manpower establishment. There is nothing inherently new in this idea. For example, many seasonal trades (hotels, tourism) have operated in this way. Even large conglomerates such as oil companies contract out certain exploration activities which only occur periodically. It is just that the practice now is extending into other areas of employment. Human resources which are not fully or permanently utilized are no longer being supported during periods of slack in manpower demand, and temporary staff carry the brunt of any future manpower reductions. A quiet revolution seems to be taking place. Perhaps in a prevailing atmosphere of threats of redundancy and closure, employee attitudes have been mollified to accept changes which offer a degree of stability and permanency – at least for the core. Flexible working has often been agreed for a reduction in the average standard working week. Occupational or task flexibility is also a sought-after aim by employers, via lowering demarcation barriers between crafts and grades. Skill versatility is courted. Inevitably, these developments impinge on other manpower policies – such as the need for broad, flexible job evaluated salary grades, and maybe a break from the traditional annual wage bargaining cycle, with pay deals more related to planning periods.

The European Association of Personnel Management (Cosijin, 1985) has noted a reduction in working hours in response to pressures for productivity. Reduced working time may come from investment in new machinery (raising productivity per employee) or by running operations at different times according to demand. The EAPM survey reveals that on average working hours for full-time employees in industry in the UK amount to 39 hours per week (with an average 24 days' holiday entitlement and 8 days' public holiday). Working hours per year amount to 1786 (by comparison: France, 1783; W. Germany, 1760; Netherlands, 1808; Sweden, 1808).

It is the question of total 'annual hours' which is now being raised. The concept of working annual hours (i.e., an agreement between employers and employees of yearly hours to be worked) originated in the Scandinavian pulp and paper mills in 1975–77, and is now introduced in Britain (Lynch, 1985). Essentially the scheme extends flexitime to a full calendar year. A detailed feasibility study is first needed since the whole basis of manpower deployment is changed, and a 'voluntary enabling agreement' is needed to set it in motion. Such schemes offer labour versatility in exchange for stable earnings, and possibly salaried status. It has been noted that motivation can be higher and absenteeism lower (McEwan Young, 1980), and annualization offers greater adaptability in accommodating future technology. Succinctly, annual hours 'put a premium on achieving a workforce which can respond quickly, easily and cheaply to unforeseen changes, which may contract as easily as it expands, in which worked time precisely matches job requirements and in which unit labour costs can be held down' (Atkinson, 1984).

Human resource accounting

Human resource accounting can be approached from two angles: (i) the worth of employees to the organization; (ii) the cost of employees to the organization.

These ideas are not new; they essentially embrace earlier ideas of 'human asset accounting'.

Traditionally, labour as an economic factor of production, has not been regarded as an asset in the accounting sense. It does not appear on the balance sheet. Social scientists have for some years now argued that business activity which ignores the human factor is likely to lead to non-optimal decisions (Likert, 1976). The ideas of Paton (1932), the first accountant to recognize publicly the value of human assets, were disregarded, largely due to inherent difficulties in quantification. Hekimian and Jones (1967) in a celebrated article resuscitated the issue, and suggested capitalization of salary as a possible solution. Other ideas quickly followed (Gilbert, 1970), such as replacement costs and acquisition costs. The accountancy profession gradually, in theory at least, accepted the idea of recording both physical and human assets. But in practice dissent still persisted. A joint study by the Institute of Personnel Management and the Institute of Cost and Management Accountants (Giles and Robinson, 1972) formulated a theory of human asset accounting based on the concept of multiplying salaries and wages by factors (human asset multipliers). The factors concerned were those which would normally form part of a job evaluation exercise – e.g. qualifications and technical expertise, experience of the job requirements – or form part of an appraisal system, e.g. personal qualities, promotion capability, replacement scarcity. The results provide an index of asset value which it is claimed can be checked against the goodwill element of an enterprise valued as a going concern. There are certain easily quantifiable aspects such as recruitment costs and training costs, but some of the assessments are necessarily subjective such as the value of skills exercised or the potential development value of individuals.

But from the point of view of cost control and auditing these issues are important. Although it may be difficult to standardize a system of employment costs, there are some obvious key elements. Recently an approach was published by the Institute of Chartered Accountants (Whiting, 1984), comprising:

1 Initial cost of employment (the capital cost)

2   The wastage rate/expected survival in a job (i.e. the 'life' of the asset represented by initial cost)

3   Continuing cost or maintenance (i.e. the revenue cost or periodic expense).

Initial costs comprise outlays on recruitment, selection and training and time taken to reach experienced worker standard. Continuing costs comprise wages and salaries, fringe benefits and welfare, employers' National Insurance contributions, pensions and other costs such as days not worked, personnel administration and provisions for the possibility of redundancies (which *can* happen and should be provided for as a continuing cost in management accounts).

Other commentators (Tyson, 1985) suggest that not only costs are important, but that personnel objectives should be stated in the language of key business ratios; e.g. sales value per employee, profit per employee, added value per employee. Perhaps the accounting aspect needs rethinking.

Conclusion

People are now seeing not one or two, but numerous changes, in their own lifetime. The rate of change quickens. From natural fears of the unknown spring fears about the future. Who knows what will happen?

As people become more accustomed to the rapidity of change they cope better. They learn to expect it. Their response is in no small way a reflection of the successes or failures they have personally experienced in the past. To some extent the rate of change is controlled by people's acceptance of it.

Man has been adjusting to change since time immemorial. Always, forces of the past resist change – creating a conflict between stability and challenge. Change breaks up old institutions, assumptions and attitudes. New ones are created.

Accelerating change can bewilder. Retrospectively, the past seems satisfying and may be longed for. A golden age seems always to be behind us. The present is perplexing. There are clearly human problems of adaptation in the change process. Tensions are evident. Concern for the present may be preoccupying, drawing our attention away from the future. The critical problem is whether the future comes before we have adjusted to the present.

We now see before us the application of scientific and other original knowledge to practical tasks, an explosion of information, new specialisms and alongside these, obsolescences, decaying chimneystack industries, unemployment. The turbulence brings into intellectual focus the need to reconcile social, economic and political objectives. In a society which remains democratic, consensus is called for. In the workplace, some responsibility for winning consent for the change process rests with personnel management.

Continued application of advanced technology poses a number of problems. Commensurate with ever greater capital accumulation will come an increased need for a range of specialist manpower and a need for better coordination and planning of resources. The role of Personnel will be to develop organizations and manpower, to regulate human/machine relations, to help improve the quality of life.

There is, of course, some incompatibility between the rate of technological change and the degree of change in economic and social expectations. Change is uneven. Technology bestows benefits and costs. The social costs are unemployment, skills obsolescence, personal upheaval. Status, reward, bargaining power, skills and knowledge alter rapidly. Employment opportunities will be reduced in industries where automatic devices have greater comparative advantages. However, there will need to be more preventive and maintenance staff and professionals in the design and planning stages. People will still be needed for adaptive responses where exceptions tend to be the rule. Managers as thinkers will have to respond more quickly.

A Personnel role is to regulate fluctuations in the labour market. Automation forces human adaptation to new jobs. This creates opportunities. The inevitable long-term trend will be towards upgrading the workforce. The impact of technology will be on mental as well as physical labour. Professionals, executives and operatives will all need to renew or replace their skills as the life expectancy of occupational skills decreases. Retraining will be a permanent feature. In many other ways also the integration of the workforce will continue with common staff policies for all grades, a decline in the number of unskilled and a growing trend away from manual labour.

Within the Personnel function itself, technology will take over the chores. Much administration work can be computerized. Freed from pedestrian tasks, Personnel can concern itself more with human relations at work. Lupton's mentorial view of personnel management as 'the technology of the social sciences' takes on meaning. For instance, emphasis will be on conflict management, better manpower planning to reduce unsocial redundancies, improving areas of job satisfaction. The innovative approach of Personnel will become more important.

As cultural changes ensue, we may well expect leisure to become more highly valued than work. Already, the working year becomes progressively shorter as holidays are extended. Fewer people work at all. Maybe 'work' itself is in demise (Handy, 1984).

The abolition of work seems a long way off. In the meantime, work may increasingly come to look more like leisure. Job enrichment, for example, often incorporates elements of leisure into work. As intrinsic rewards become dominant, work becomes fun. If the personnel management function is concerned with people at work, then the personnel specialist must be alive to changes in attitudes to work itself. The Protestant ethic extolling the virtues of hard work has been turned on its head now that technology bears the brunt for us. Paradoxically, the commitment to full employment (and the allied stigma of unemployment) lingers on.

Amongst the workforce one may detect a loss of optimism, a lack of confidence in regard to employment prospects, and particularly security. No one's job is safe. In certain areas – shipbuilding, textiles, motor cycle manufacturing, coal mining – employment contraction has decimated local communities. For the unemployed, bleakness prevails. If large-scale *unemployment* is to be a permanent mode, ways must be found both to fund it and to fill the vacuum. Lord Young, Secretary of State for Employment may claim that governments cannot create jobs, and the recipe for revival lies in the private sector. In fact, the permanency of unemployment as a phenomenon is one of the hottest political potatoes ever. The stark realism is that the unemployed have to be financially supported, for which in the end the wealth can only come from gross national product. Meanwhile, we have a third 'dependent' population (as children and senior citizens are dependent populations). The long-term implications are often shirked. Equally important – what do the unemployed do with their time? Maybe one day the pursuit of leisure, play, learning and pleasure will become the cultural norm. The lucky ones may be the ones who do not have to work. But crystal balls do not cast a distinct image.

Increasing standards of education spur higher individual expectations. Participation and meaningful work are vocalized issues. People demand rights – to be protected and consulted – and for the management of society to be responsible to the producer as well as the consumer. Consultative machinery already exists for this to occur. But as the issue intensifies, new methods are likely to be devised.

In the past personnel management often assumed the mantle of 'social conscience'. Industrial democracy will create the mechanism for the workforce to monitor and protect their own interests. An area of Personnel responsibility may be removed. Conversely, the axis is likely to shift away from palliative medicine to constructive diplomacy in lubricating the machinery for negotiation and bargaining. Already, advanced welfare is giving way to an increasingly utilitarian approach to human resource management, but not an inhumanitarian one. Social attitudes are in flux – and are now certainly more liberal than they were only a couple of decades ago. This is reflected at the workplace. People at work are no longer cogs, they are positive determinants of corporate success or failure. Personnel policy becomes a corporate responsibility.

As trade and industry grow, as larger organizations expand overseas operations, new personnel problems arise. Multinationals exploiting economies of scale operate across boundaries of culture, labour law, currency regulation, wage and salary levels. Each country has its own unique perspectives. Coordinating group personnel policy means personnel staff must broaden their own horizons. Personnel policy again assumes corporate magnitude.

Personnel management performs in a dynamic arena. The portents are that at least in the foreseeable future it has a prime role to play. It both influences and is affected by change. Work patterns are shifting. Lifelong careers may be a thing of the past. No one can predict precisely the speed or direction of change. Increased flexibility and adaptation are going to be called for in *all* work roles. There is a tendency, particularly in larger firms, to maintain highly trained central services but to hand back considerable line management personnel responsibility to where it belongs. Presently, the Personnel profession is itself re-evaluating its own contribution. This reflects its awareness of a changing scene.

There is rarely a perfect fit between man and work. Challenges must now be faced more quickly and more effectively than in the past. The environment is turbulent. The passive responses of old-fashioned personnel management must be pushed aside as the dynamo speeds up. This will call for enormous ingenuity, perseverance and patience on the part of personnel practitioners.

Personnel management is not a science. Its methodology is inexact. Rigorous theory and universal prescription are lacking. However, the approach can be systematic. Sometimes the effectiveness of personnel policies can be quantified, sometimes only judged subjectively. Policies and practice may be constrained by conflicting priorities. Power, politics and profits play their parts.

In many ways, personnel management is not a 'subject' in the conventional sense of the word. It is essentially practical rather than academic. And in spite of quasi-quantification, judgement must be exercised at many points. Critics and cynics may scorn the influence of people's minds, machinations and considered opinions. For them there is no room for human variation nor unscientific deliberation. Were it not for the fact that elements of work may be intangible, were it not for the fact that man's perceptive powers preclude complete rationality and objectivity, then we could live in a mathematical nicety, predestined, predictive and boring. There would be no problem. Happily, we live in reality.

Summary

Personnel decision-making is being pushed back to operational levels, in some cases to line management. A personnel responsibility still remains, but it is tending to become more decentralized.

Trade unions are on the defensive. To some extent this inhibits their ability to contribute constructively. Changes in government will no doubt see changes in collective law.

Communications are of vital importance in holding together any organization. Communications may be downward, upward or horizontal – operating through formal and informal channels. There may be natural or structural barriers to communication flows. All communications are concerned with the transmission of information. Information may be of factual content, or be concerned with feelings, attitudes and opinions. There are qualitative differences in information. Information must be defined, collected, processed, communicated and interpreted. Communication networks need to be coordinated.

There are growing demands for increased consultation. This requires better two-way communication. Joint consultation has been in existence for many years, but is now being superseded by more stringent demands for fuller participation in decision-making. Various forms of industrial democracy are under consideration. The Bullock report in the UK which considered these issues has been shelved. But from the EEC new directives on participatory structures will in due course be forthcoming.

Fears and anxieties are commonly expressed by employees confronted with technological innovation. Their natural resistance to change should be approached via their concern for negotiation, consultation and co-determination of the effects of technological change at the planning stage in regard to (i) job security, (ii) manpower planning, recruitment and training, (iii) work loads, work sharing and working hours, (iv) retraining, (v) planned job changes and the ramifications of new products or services, (vi) health and safety, especially the effects of stress and shift work, (vii) the effects on wage rates and salary scales of changing job structures and the need for revised payment systems, (viii) trade union participation in system design, (ix) qualitative factors, e.g. job redesign and opportunities for job enrichment, (x) financial compensation for work changes, e.g. loss of promotion prospects, changed skill requirements and productivity agreements, (xi) redundancy and the preferred solution by natural wastage, (xii) trade union demands for more than 'presentations' by management of impending changes and a greater desire for participation in the making of decisions which affect management and employees jointly.

New technology has added a new dimension to collective bargaining which has cut across traditional negotiating areas. There is pressure on management not only to consult and disclose information but also to negotiate implications of technological change on employment practices.

Current regulations for redundancy are embodied in the 1978 Employment Protection (Consolidation) Act and in decided cases, although the basic provisions (mainly financial compensation) had existed earlier. Redundancy payments have been adjusted with inflation over time. Consultation, notification, procedural agreements and the disclosure of information are essential requisites. Companies are exhorted to avoid compulsory redundancy wherever possible. Redundancy is but one reaction to contraction (although the only one in the face of bankruptcy).

New modes of work are emerging, as a form of work-sharing and to provide greater flexibility in manpower deployment, e.g. part-time employment, short-term contracts and annualized hours.

Personnel functions are exhorted to appraise their contributions to business objectives. Emphasis is placed on cost-cutting. There is renewed interest in quantification of human inputs and outputs. Ideas about human resource accounting have been regenerated.

We witness now the wholesale application of scientific and technological knowledge to all practical tasks at the workplace – new techniques, and explosion of information, new specialisms. Concurrently, we witness decay, uncertainty, unemployment. The turbulence brings into intellectual focus the need to reconcile social, economic and political objectives. In the workplace, heavy responsibility for winning consent for the change process rests with personnel management.

Discussion questions

1   What are the main obstacles to efficient communications?
2   What is the difference between a 'job property right' and 'the right to a job for life'?
3   Is LIFO (last in, first out) a good criterion for redundancy selection? What other criteria would you suggest?
4   Is repeated redundancy an inevitable prospect for an individual seeking to earn a living in times of rapid change? If so, what effects do you think this will have on (a) attitudes to work? (b) lifestyles?
5   What do you think is the best way to improve employee participation at work?
6   What disadvantages, if any, do you see emanating from increased employee involvement?
7   With reference to your own work organization, where is new technology likely to make its greatest impact? What problems do you foresee? How would you recommend that new technology be introduced?
8   What are the main factors which need to be considered in negotiating a New Technology Agreement?
9   In what ways do you think your own personnel department needs to adjust in the future?
10 Whither personnel management?

References

AIKEN, O. (1985), 'Legal aftermath of the miners' strike', Personnel Management, August.
ATKINSON, J. (1984), 'Manpower strategies for flexible organisations', Personnel Management, August.
BAIN, G. S. (ed.) (1983), Industrial Relations in Britain, Blackwell, Oxford.
BULLOCK REPORT (1977), Report of the Bullock Committee of Inquiry on Industrial Democracy, Cmnd 6706, HMSO, London.
CONFEDERATION OF BRITISH INDUSTRY (1977), In Place of Bullock, CBI.
CONFEDERATION OF BRITISH INDUSTRY (1981), Jobs – Facing the Future, CBI.
COSIJIN, E. (1985), 'European patterns in working time', Personnel Management, July.
COWAN, L. D. (1985), 'The impact of technology in banking', in Livy, B. (ed.), Management and People in Banking, 2nd edn, Institute of Bankers.
DEPARTMENT OF EMPLOYMENT (1972), Industrial Relations Code of Practice, HMSO, London.
FARNHAM, D. and PIMLOTT, J. (1979), Understanding Industrial Relations, Cassell, London.
GILES, W. J. and ROBINSON, D. F. (1972), Human Asset Accounting, Institute of Personnel Management and Institute of Cost and Management Accountants, London.
GOLDSMITH, W. and CLUTTERBUCK, D. (1985), The Winning Streak, Penguin, London.
GUEST, D. (1983), 'Participation', in Williams, A. P. O. (ed.), Using Personnel Research, Gower, London.

GUEST, D. and KNIGHT, K. (1979), *Putting Participation into Practice*, Gower.

HANDY, C. (1984), *The Future of Work*, Blackwell, Oxford.

HANSON, E. and RATHKEY, P. (1984), 'Industrial democracy: a post-Bullock shopfloor view', *British Journal of Industrial Relations* **22**:2, July.

HEKIMIAN, J. S. and JONES, C. H. (1967), 'Put people on your balance sheet', *Harvard Business Review*, Jan/Feb 1967, 105–113.

HOLMAN, G. (1985), 'In search of excellence in personnel management', *Personnel Management*, November.

HUNT, J. (1984), 'The shifting focus of the personnel function', *Personnel Management*, February.

INSTITUTE OF PERSONNEL MANAGEMENT (1981), *Practical Participation and Involvement*, Vol. I, *Communications in Practice*, Institute of Personnel Management, London.

INSTITUTE OF PERSONNEL MANAGEMENT (1981), *Practical Participation and Involvement*, Vol. II, *Representative Structures*, Institute of Personnel Management, London.

INSTITUTE OF PERSONNEL MANAGEMENT (1983), *How to Introduce New Technology: a Practical Guide for Managers*, Institute of Personnel Management, London.

INSTITUTE OF PERSONNEL MANAGEMENT (1984), *Redundancy Code*, Institute of Personnel Management, London.

LIKERT, R. (1976), *New Ways of Managing Conflict*, McGraw-Hill, New York.

LUPTON, T. (1966), *Management and the Social Sciences*, Lyon, Grant & Gleen, London.

LYNCH, P. (1985), 'Annual hours – an idea whose time has come', *Personnel Management*, November.

MANT, A. (1977), *The Rise and Fall of the British Manager*, Macmillan, London.

MAUDE, B. (1977), *Communications at Work*, Business Books.

McEWAN YOUNG, S. (1980), 'Shift work and flexible schedules: are they compatible?', *International Labour Review*, ILO, Jan/Feb.

MILLS, L. (1985), 'Communications and Participation', in Livy, B. (ed.), *Management and People in Banking*, 2nd edn, Institute of Bankers.

MUMFORD, W. (1981), 'Participation – what does it mean and how can it be achieved?', *Manchester Business School Review*, **5**, 3, Summer.

NATIONAL ECONOMIC DEVELOPMENT OFFICE (1983), *Policy for the UK Information Technology Industry*, NEDO.

PALMER, G. (1983), *British Industrial Relations*, Allen and Unwin, London.

PATON, W. A. (1932), *The Accountant's Handbook*, Ronald Press, New York.

PETERS, T. J. and WATERMAN, R. H. (1982), *In Search of Excellence*, Harper and Row, New York.

PIGORS, P. and MYERS, C. (1947), *Personnel Administration: A point of view and Method*, McGraw-Hill, New York.

POLICY STUDIES INSTITUTE (1982), *Microelectronics in Industry*, PSI.

PURCELL, J. (1985), 'Is anybody listening to the corporate personnel department?', *Personnel Management*, September.

PURCELL, J. and GRAY, A. (1986), 'Corporate personnel departments and the management of industrial relations', *Journal of Management Studies*.

RAJAN, A. (1985), 'New technology and jobs', *Personnel Management*, July.

SISSON, K. and SCULLION, H. (1985), 'Putting the corporate personnel department in its place', *Personnel Management*, December.

THOMAS, M. (1985), 'In search of culture: holy grail or gravy train!', *Personnel Management*, September.

TORRINGTON, D. (1986), 'Will consultants take over the personnel function?', *Personnel Management*, February.

TRADES UNION CONGRESS (1980), *New Technology*, TUC.

TRADES UNION CONGRESS (1981), *New Technology and Collective Bargaining*, TUC.

TYSON, S. and FELL, A. (1986), *Evaluating the Personnel Function*, Hutchinson, London.

WEBB, T. (1983), 'Union tactics for the high-tech age', *Personnel Management*, May.

WHITING, E. (1984), *How to get Employment Costs Right*, The Institute of Chartered Accountants, London.

WOOD, SIR J. (1985), 'Is Donovan dead?', *Personnel Management*, August.

Index